THE BLACKWELL HANDBOOK OF PRINCIPLES OF ORGANIZATIONAL BEHAVIOR

Handbooks in Management

Published

Donald L. Sexton and Hans Landström
The Blackwell Handbook of Entrepreneurship

Edwin A. Locke
The Blackwell Handbook of Principles of Organizational Behavior

Forthcoming

Martin Gannon and Karen Newman
The Blackwell Handbook of Cross-cultural Management

Michael Hitt, Edward Freeman and Jeffrey Harrison
The Blackwell Handbook of Strategy

Robert E. Cole, Barrie G. Dale and Noriako Kano
The Blackwell Handbook of Total Quality Management

Randall S. Schuler and Paul Sparrow
*The Blackwell Handbook of International and Comparative
Human Resource Management*

THE BLACKWELL HANDBOOK OF PRINCIPLES OF ORGANIZATIONAL BEHAVIOR

Edited by

EDWIN A. LOCKE
University of Maryland

Copyright © Blackwell Publishers Ltd 2000

Editorial apparatus and arrangement copyright © Edwin A. Locke 2000

First published 2000

2 4 6 8 10 9 7 5 3 1

Blackwell Publishers Ltd
108 Cowley Road
Oxford OX4 1JF
UK

Blackwell Publishers Inc.
350 Main Street
Malden, MA 02148
USA

British Library Cataloguing in Publication Data

A CIP catalogue record for this book is available from the British Library.

Library of Congress Cataloging-in-Publication Data has been applied for

ISBN 0-631-21505-0 (hbk)

Typeset in 10 on 12 pt Baskerville by Ace Filmsetting Ltd, Frome, Somerset
Printed in Great Britain by MPG Books, Bodmin, Cornwall

This book is printed on acid-free paper.

Contents

List of Figures ix

List of Tables x

Contributors and Editor xi

Editor's Introduction xvi

PART I SELECTION 1

1 Select on Intelligence 3
   FRANK L. SCHMIDT AND JOHN E. HUNTER

2 Select on Conscientiousness and Emotional Stability 15
   MURRAY R. BARRICK AND MICHAEL K. MOUNT

3 Structure Interviews to Hire the Best People 29
   CYNTHIA KAY STEVENS

PART II TRAINING AND PERFORMANCE APPRAISAL 41

4 Design Training Systematically 43
   EDUARDO SALAS AND JANIS A. CANNON-BOWERS

5 Design Performance Appraisal Systems to Improve Performance 60
   ANGELO S. DENISI AND JORGE A. GONZALEZ

PART III TURNOVER AND SATISFACTION   73

6 Promote Job Satisfaction through Mental Challenge   75
   TIMOTHY A. JUDGE

7 Control Turnover by Understanding its Causes   90
   THOMAS W. LEE AND TERENCE R. MITCHELL

PART IV MOTIVATION   105

8 Motivate Employee Performance through Goal-setting   107
   GARY P. LATHAM

9 Cultivate Self-efficacy for Personal and Organizational Effectiveness   120
   ALBERT BANDURA

10 Motivate Performance through Empowerment   137
   JAY A. CONGER

11 Pay for Performance   150
   CATHY C. DURHAM AND KATHRYN M. BARTOL

12 Provide Recognition for Performance Improvement   166
   FRED LUTHANS AND ALEXANDER D. STAJKOVIC

13 Promote Procedural Justice to Enhance Acceptance of Work Outcomes   181
   JERALD GREENBERG

PART V TEAM DYNAMICS   197

14 Compose Teams to Assure Successful Boundary Activity   199
   DEBORAH ANCONA AND DAVID CALDWELL

15 Excel through Group Process   211
   GERARDO A. OKHUYSEN AND KATHLEEN M. EISENHARDT

16 Manage Intra-team Conflict through Collaboration   226
   LAURIE WEINGART AND KAREN A. JEHN

Part VI Leadership   239

17 Use Power Effectively   241
    Gary Yukl

18 Lead through Vision and Values   257
    Markus Hauser and Robert J. House

19 Foster Trust through Competence, Honesty, and Integrity   274
    Sabrina Salam

Part VII Organizational Processes   289

20 Design Structure to Fit Strategy   291
    Lex Donaldson

21 Use Participation to Share Information and Distribute Knowledge   304
    John A. Wagner III

22 Make Good Decisions by Effectively Managing the Decision-making Process   316
    Glen Whyte

23 Stimulate Creativity by Fueling Passion   331
    Teresa M. Amabile

24 Manage Stress at Work through Preventive and Proactive Coping   342
    Ralf Schwarzer

25 Manage Conflict through Negotiation and Mediation   356
    M. Susan Taylor

26 Lead Organizational Change by Creating Dissatisfaction and Realigning
    the Organization with New Competitive Realities   370
    Michael Beer

Part VIII Work, Family, Technology, and Culture   387

27 Promote Equal Opportunity by Recognizing Gender Differences in the
    Experience of Work and Family   389
    Nancy P. Rothbard and Jeanne M. Brett

28 Use Information Technology as a Catalyst for Organizational Change   404

MARYAM ALAVI AND JONATHAN PALMER

29 Make Management Practice Fit the National Culture   418

MIRIAM EREZ

Index   435

Figures

6.1 Studies of the relationship between instrinsic job characteristics and job
satisfaction 80
6.2 Job characteristics profiles for job of customer service representative and
manager 81
6.3 Studies of the correlation between intrinsic job characteristics and job
satisfaction for individuals with high and low Growth Need Strength
(GNS) 84
6.4 Job satisfaction levels of elementary and secondary public school teachers
according to perceived influence over school policy, perceived control in
the classroom, and salary 87
9.1 Paths of influence through which perceived self-efficacy and other key
social cognitive factors regulate motivation and performance
accomplishments 121
10.1 Stages of the empowerment process 139
14.1 Critical processes for team performance 204
24.1 A process model of stress and coping 344
24.2 Four coping perspectives 347
26.1 Organizational alignment model 373
27.1 Model of opportunity structure and gender differences in the experience
of work and family roles 391
29.1 The cultural value of collectivism in eight different countries 420
29.2 The cultural value of power distance in eight different countries 421
29.3 The model of cultural self-representation 423
29.4 Management practices according to cultural dimensions of group versus
individual focus, and power distance 425

Tables

4.1 Summary of training phases, principles, and guidelines   44

6.1 Measurement of intrinsic job characteristics: the Job Diagnostic Survey   78

9.1 The distinctive sets of factors within each of the four modes of influence that can affect the construction of efficacy beliefs   125

10.1 Context factors leading to potential lowering of self-efficacy belief   141

25.1 Differences in managers' attempts to influence the behavior of bosses, peers, and employees   357

25.2 Managers' third-party conflict resolution modes   361

Contributors and Editor

Maryam Alavi
Goizueta Business School, Emory University
Maryam_Alavi@bus.emory.edu

Teresa M. Amabile
Harvard Business School
tamabile@hbs.edu

Deborah Ancona
Sloan School of Management
ancona@MIT.EDU

Albert Bandura
Stanford University
Bandura@psych.stanford.edu

Murray R. Barrick
College of Business Administration, Michigan State University
Barrick@MSU.edu

Kathryn M. Bartol
Robert H. Smith School of Business, University of Maryland
kbartol@rhsmith.umd.edu

Michael Beer
Harvard Business School
mbeer@hbs.harvard.edu

Jeanne M. Brett
Kellogg Graduate School – Management, Northwestern University
jmbrett@nwu.edu

David Caldwell
School of Business, University of Santa Clara
dcaldwell@scu.edu

Janis A. Cannon-Bowers
Naval Air Warfare Center
Cannon-bowja@navair.navy.mil

Jay A. Conger
Marshall School of Business, University of Southern California
jconger@sba.usc.edu

Angelo S. DeNisi
Texas A&M University
adenisi@cgsb.tamu.edu

Lex Donaldson
Aus Graduate School of Management – Sydney, University of New South Wales
lexd@agsm.unsw.edu.au

Cathy C. Durham
Department of Management, College of Business Administration and Economics, California State University, Northridge
cathy.durham@csun.edu

Kathleen M. Eisenhardt
Stanford University
KME@leland.Stanford.EDU

Miriam Erez
Faculty of Industrial Engineering and Management, Technion
merez@ie.technion.ac.il

Jorge A. Gonzalez
Texas A&M University
jorge@tamu.edu

Jerald Greenberg
Fisher College of Business, The Ohio State University
greenberg.1@osu.edu

Markus Hauser
Wharton School, University of Pennsylvania
markushauser@hotmail.com

Robert J. House
Wharton School, University of Pennsylvania
House@WmgtFac.Wharton.upenn.edu

John E. Hunter
Michigan State University
hunter@msu.edu

Karen A. Jehn
The Wharton School, University of Pennsylvania
jehnk@wharton.upenn.edu

Timothy A. Judge
University of Iowa
tim-judge@uiowa.edu

Gary P. Latham
Faculty of Management, University of Toronto
latham@fmgmt.mgmt.utoronto.ca

Thomas W. Lee
School of Business Administration, University of Washington
orcas@u.washington.edu

Fred Luthans
College of Business Administration, Department of Management, University of Nebraska
fluthans1@unl.edu

Terence R. Mitchell
Business School, University of Washington
trm@u.washington.edu

Michael K. Mount
College of Business Administration, University of Iowa
michael-mount@uiowa.edu

Gerardo A. Okhuysen
School of Management, University of Texas at Dallas
gerardo@utdallas.edu

Jonathan Palmer
Robert H. Smith School of Business, University of Maryland
jpalmer@rhsmith.umd.edu

Nancy P. Rothbard
Kellogg Graduate School – Management, Northwestern University
rothbard@nwu.edu

Sabrina Salam
Bad Homburg, Germany
Sabrina.Salam@gemcon.com

Eduardo Salas
University of Central Florida
esalas@pegasus.cc.ucf.edu

Frank L. Schmidt
College of Business, University of Iowa
fschmidt@blue.weeg.uiowa.edu

Ralf Schwarzer
Freie Universität Berlin
health@zedat.fu-berlin.de

Alexander D. Stajkovic
University of Wisconsin-Madison
astajkovic@bus.wisc.edu

Cynthia Kay Stevens
Robert H. Smith School of Business, University of Maryland
cstevens@rhsmith.umd.edu

M. Susan Taylor
Robert H. Smith School of Business, University of Maryland
staylor@rhsmith.umd.edu

John A. Wagner III
Michigan State University
wagner@pilot.msu.edu

Laurie Weingart
Carnegie-Mellon University
weingart@cyrus.andrew.cmu.edu

Glen Whyte
Faculty of Management, University of Toronto
whyte@mgmt.utoronto.ca

Gary Yukl
SUNY-Albany
g.yukl@albany.edu

About the Editor

Edwin A. Locke is Dean's Professor of Motivation and Leadership at the Robert H. Smith School of Business at the University of Maryland and is also affiliated with the Department of Psychology. He received his undergraduate degree in psychology from Harvard (1960) and his MA (1962) and Ph.D. (1964) degrees from Cornell. He has published over 200 articles, chapters, and books, including (with G. Latham) *A Theory of Goal Setting and Task Performance*, and (with others) *The Essence of Leadership* and *Prime Movers: The Traits of the Great Wealth Creators* (2000).

Dr Locke is a Fellow of the American Psychological Association (Division of Industrial and Organizational Psychology), the American Psychological Society and the Academy of Management. He has received the Distinguished Scientific Contribution Award from the Society for Industrial Organizational Psychology and the H. Heneman Career Contribution Award from the Academy of Management (Human Resource Division). He has also received the Outstanding Teacher-Scholar Award from the University of Maryland and numerous teaching awards. He serves on the editorial board of *Organizational Behavioral and Human Performance* and has served on the board of the *Journal of Applied Psychology*.

Dr Locke's e-mail address is elocke@rhsmith.umd.edu

Editor's Introduction

I formulated the basic idea for this handbook as an exercise in epistemology. Let me explain.

Over the past 30 years Organizational Behavior (OB) has become a very large field due to an explosion of findings and the subsequent expansion of its sub-fields. It is regrettable that more progress has been made in fragmenting the field rather than in integrating it. Textbooks, for example, typically list dozens of theories about each sub-topic but do little to integrate the "pieces" into an intelligible whole. The students who read these books (typically undergraduates) therefore come away from the course with a half-memorized jumble of disconnected and often contradictory ideas which are soon forgotten. MBAs who are assigned textbook readings no doubt wonder how they could possibly use such material to run a successful business.

The antidote to studying lists of disconnected theories is not to memorize lists of disconnected concrete examples – a process which the case method may (but does not have to) encourage. If a case is analyzed solely on its own terms, it is useless, because every concrete situation is different from every other; thus no generalization is possible. Generalization is only possible using principles. I used the case method for the first time in the fall of 1999 (after 25 years of experimenting with other methods). To make sure the students did not focus just on the events of the cases, I made them formulate useful OB principles by induction from the case material (and a small number of assigned readings) at the end of each class and then made them formulate meta-principles at the end of the course. This seemed to work well. (I am sure that many people who use the case method do the same or the equivalent.)

Let me address now the issue of what principles are and why man needs them.

PRINCIPLES

A principle is a general truth; it is arrived at inductively by observing specific instances of some phenomenon and integrating the common elements while ignoring the differences. This is the same basic procedure that is followed when forming a concept. Consider the concept of triangle. One observes that a sub-set of geometric figures is similar to each other (3–sided) and different from others (e.g., 4-, 5-, and 6-sided, round, oblong, etc.). One focuses on the common element while abstracting out the differences (e.g., size, color, angles) and forms a new mental unit, triangle.

Man's need for concepts and principles stems from the fact that he cannot hold in conscious awareness more than about seven separate objects or entities at the same time. Concepts reduce complexity by tying together an unlimited number of concretes of a particular kind and making them into a single mental unit (e.g. the concept "house" subsumes an unlimited number of structures of a certain type). To quote Ayn Rand, whose epistemology was the inspiration for this volume, the function of concepts is to attain "unit economy," that is, "to reduce a vast amount of information to a minimal number of units."[1] Without a method of integrating one's percepts into concepts, one would be unable to function at a level any different from, and no higher than, the lower animals. One would be limited to responding to what could be observed directly with the senses at a given moment (plus whatever sensory experiences could be retained in memory). One could see the moon and the stars but would never be able to develop the science of astronomy.

Similarly, to extend one's knowledge one combines conceptual abstractions into propositions or principles. A principle is a generalization based on observing numerous specific instances of a phenomenon, e.g., "eating fruits and vegetables leads to better health," or "rewarding people fairly in relation to their performance promotes job satisfaction."

OB PRINCIPLES

It can be asked why no one has thought to write a book focused around OB principles before. There are several possible answers. The most likely is the belief (due to modern philosophy – which is dominated by skepticism) that there aren't any valid principles about anything. Many hold it as an axiom that "everything is contingent" – an obvious self-contradiction. A second reason could be fear or self-doubt; many people do not want to go out on a limb and make any general claims of truth – which would require choosing among completing claims. A third reason could be mental laziness; why attempt to integrate when it is easier just to list everyone's theory and let the students decide?

I believe that OB is now developed enough that it is possible to formulate general principles. (OB and HRM overlap considerably so both fields are actually represented.) I picked 31 topics (of which 29 actually got done) that I believed were amenable to the identification of principles and picked outstanding subject-matter experts to write on each. I asked that each chapter follow a common format:

- identification of the principle and any needed sub-principles;
- justification of the principle(s);
- specification of implementation and/or contingency factors;
- illustrations of the principles through the use of some positive and negative case examples.

I asked that the style not be too academic so that the chapters would make interesting reading for practicing managers and MBAs as well as academics. Most of the authors did what I asked, and I am very grateful to them for that. I make no claim that these are the only important principles in the field. There are plenty of OB topics that are not covered here. Another whole OB or OB-HRM volume could easily be written using the same approach. But I believe that this is a good start. I think we know something and that this knowledge can be promulgated in the form of principles that are accurate, understandable, and retainable.

Because I wanted the chapters to follow a common format and style, I was much more assertive about editing than editors normally are. Some chapters were sent back as many as three times for reworking. I was especially concerned that the chapters not be too academic in tone so that they would be easily understood by managers. Some of the chapter writers had considerable difficulty writing in a non-academic style. Usually, however, they were quite willing to rewrite. In some cases, the authors and I simply could not come to agreement on certain matters. For example, I strongly disagreed with Bob House and Markus Hauser that the motive of self-sacrifice (including the example of Mother Teresa) was of any relevance to business leadership – which I believe is motivated by egoistic passion.[2] Obviously this will be an issue of continuing debate between us.

NOTES

1 From L. Peikoff, *Objectivism: The Philosophy of Ayn Rand*. New York: Dutton, 1991, p. 106.
2 E. A. Locke, *The Prime Movers: Traits of the Great Wealth Creators*. New York: AMACOM Books, 2000.

Part I

SELECTION

1   Select on Intelligence
    FRANK L. SCHMIDT AND JOHN E. HUNTER

2   Select on Conscientiousness and Emotional Stability
    MURRAY R. BARRICK AND MICHAEL K. MOUNT

3   Structure Interviews to Hire the Best People
    CYNTHIA KAY STEVENS

1

Select on Intelligence

FRANK L. SCHMIDT AND JOHN E. HUNTER

Other things equal, higher intelligence leads to better job performance on all jobs. Intelligence is the major determinant of job performance, and therefore hiring people based on intelligence leads to marked improvements in job performance – improvements that have high economic value to the firm. This principle is the subject of this chapter.

This principle is very broad: it applies to all types of jobs at all job levels. Until a couple of decades ago, most people believed that general principles of this sort were impossible in personnel selection and other social science areas. It was believed that each organization, work setting, and job was unique and that it was not possible to know which selection methods would work on any job without conducting a study on that job in that organization. This belief, called the theory of situational specificity, was based on the fact that different validity studies in different organizations appeared to give different results. However, we now know that these "conflicting findings" were mostly due to statistical and measurement artifacts and that some selection procedures have high validity for predicting performance on all jobs (e.g. intelligence) and others do a poor job of predicting performance on *any* job (e.g. graphology) (Schmidt and Hunter, 1998). This discovery was made possible by new methods, called meta-analysis or validity generalization methods, that allow researchers to statistically combine results across many studies.

Meta-analysis has also made possible the development of general principles in many other areas beyond personnel selection (Schmidt, 1992). For example, it has been used to calibrate the relationship between job satisfaction and job performance with precision (Judge, Thorensen, Bono, and Patton, 1999).

What is intelligence? Intelligence is not the ability to adapt to one's environment; insects, mosses, and bacteria are well adapted to their environments, but they are not intelligent. (There are many ways in which organisms can adapt well to their environments; use of intelligence is only one possible way.) Intelligence is the ability to grasp and reason correctly with abstractions (concepts) and solve problems. However, perhaps a more useful definition is that intelligence is the ability to learn. Higher intelligence leads to more rapid learning, and the more complex the material to be learned, the more this is true. Intelligence is often referred to as general mental ability (GMA) and general cognitive ability, and we use all these terms interchangeably in this chapter.

Intelligence is the broadest of all human mental abilities. Narrower abilities include verbal ability, quantitative ability, and spatial ability. These narrower abilities are often referred to as special aptitudes. These special aptitudes do predict job performance (although less well than GMA), but only because special aptitude tests measure general intelligence as well as specific aptitudes (Schmidt, Ones, and Hunter, 1992). It is the GMA component in these specific aptitude tests that predicts job performance. For example, when a test of verbal ability predicts job performance, it is the GMA part of that test – not the specifically verbal part – that does the predicting.

Intelligence predicts many important life outcomes in addition to job performance: performance in school, amount of education obtained, rate of promotion on the job, ultimate job level attained, income, and many other things (Brody, 1992; Herrnstein and Murray, 1994; Gottfredson, 1996; Jensen, 1998). It is even involved in everyday activities such as shopping, driving, and paying bills (Gottfredson, 1996). No other trait – not even conscientiousness – predicts so many important real-world outcomes so well. In this sense, intelligence is the most important trait or construct in all of psychology, and the most "successful" trait in *applied* psychology.

The thousands of studies showing the link between intelligence (GMA) and job performance have been combined into many different meta-analyses. Ree and co-workers have shown this for military jobs (Olea and Ree, 1994; Ree and Earles, 1991, 1992; Ree, Earles, and Teachout, 1994), as have McHenry, Hough, Toquam, Hanson, and Ashworth (1990) in the famous Project A military study. Hunter and Hunter (1984) have shown it for a wide variety of civilian jobs, using the US Employment Service database of studies. Schmidt, Hunter, and Pearlman (1980) have shown it for both civilian and military jobs. Other large meta-analytic studies are described in Hunter and Schmidt (1996). The amount of empirical evidence supporting this principle is today so massive that it is hard to find anyone who questions the principle.

When performance is measured objectively using carefully constructed work sample tests (samples of actual job tasks), the correlation (validity) with intelligence measures is about .70 (Hunter, 1986) – 70 percent as large as the maximum possible value of 1.00, which represents *perfect* prediction. When performance is measured using ratings of job performance by supervisors, the correlation with intelligence measures is .52 for the medium-complexity jobs (over 60 percent of all jobs). For more complex jobs, this value is larger (e.g. .58 for professional and managerial jobs), and for simpler jobs this value is not as high (e.g., .45 for semi-skilled jobs). Another performance measure that is important is amount learned in job training programs. Regardless of job level, intelligence measures predict amount learned in training with validity of about .56 (Hunter and Hunter, 1984).

It is one thing to have overwhelming empirical evidence showing a principle is true and quite another to explain *why* the principle is true. *Why* does GMA predict job performance? The primary reason is that people who are more intelligent learn more job knowledge and learn it faster. The major direct determinant of job performance is not GMA but job knowledge. People who do not know how to do a job cannot perform that job well. Research has shown that considerable job knowledge is required to perform even jobs most college students would think of as "simple jobs," such as truck driver or machine operator. More complex jobs require even more job knowledge. The simplest model of job performance is this: GMA causes job knowledge, which in turn causes job performance. But this model is a little too simple: there is also a causal path directly from GMA to job performance, independent of job knowledge. That is, even when workers have equal job knowledge, the more intelligent workers have higher job performance. This is because there are problems that come up on the job that are not covered by previous job knowledge, and GMA is used directly on the job to solve these problems. Many studies have tested and supported this causal model (Hunter, 1986; Ree, Earles, and Teachout, 1994; Schmidt, Hunter, Outerbridge, and Trattner, 1986). This research is reviewed by Schmidt and Hunter (1992) and Hunter and Schmidt (1996). It has also been shown that over their careers people gradually move into jobs that are consistent with their level of GMA (Wilk, Desmariais, and Sackett, 1995; Wilk and Sackett, 1996). That is, there is process of sorting of people on GMA that takes place gradually over time in everyday life.

There is a broader theory that explains these research results: the traditional psychological theory of human learning (Hunter and Schmidt, 1996). This theory correctly predicted that the effect of GMA would be on the learning of job knowledge. The false theory of situational specificity became widely accepted earlier in the twentieth century because personnel psychologists mistakenly ignored the research on human learning.

Many lay people find it hard to believe that GMA is the dominant determinant of job performance. Often they have known people who were very intelligent but who were dismal failures on the job because of "bad behaviors" such as repeated absences from work, carelessness at work, hostility toward the supervisor, unwillingness to work over-time to meet a deadline, etc. These are examples of bad organizational citizenship behaviors (Organ, 1990). Good citizenship behaviors include willingness to help train new employees, willingness to work late in an emergency or on a holiday, etc. Citizenship behaviors (good and bad) are different from job performance but are often confused with job performance by lay observers. Citizenship behaviors are predicted by tests of conscientiousness (a personality trait) and by integrity tests (which measure a combination of personality traits – conscientiousness, agreeableness, and emotional stability). Low ability leads to an inability to perform well; low conscientiousness leads, not primarily to low performance, but to organizationally disruptive behaviors. These disruptive behaviors are more visible to lay observers (and to many supervisors) than differences between employees in actual performance, probably because they appear so willful. On the other hand, a low-ability employee has difficulty learning how to perform the job, but if he/she has a "good attitude," this employee seems like less of a problem than one showing bad citizenship behaviors. This makes it difficult for some to clearly see the GMA–performance link in the real world (Hunter and Schmidt, 1996).

Of course, low conscientiousness can lead to less effective performance if it results in reduced effort. For objective measures of job performance, empirical evidence indicates that on typical jobs this effect is limited, probably because most jobs are fairly structured, reducing the scope for individual differences in effort to operate (Hunter, Schmidt, and Rauschenberger, in press; Hunter and Schmidt, 1996). However, when supervisors rate job performance, they incorporate into their ratings citizenship behaviors as well as actual job performance (Orr, Sackett, and Mercer, 1989). Hence supervisory ratings reflect a combination of actual job performance and citizenship behaviors. In the case of ratings, low conscientiousness leads to poorer citizenship behaviors, which leads to lower ratings of overall performance. For the typical job, the weight on conscientiousness in predicting objectively measured job performance is only 20 percent as large as the weight on GMA. In predicting supervisory ratings, it is 60 percent as large.

What Is Required to Make this Principle Work?

There are three conditions that are required to make this principle work. That is, there are three conditions that are required for companies to improve job performance levels by using GMA in hiring and to reap the resulting economic benefits.

First, the company must be able to be selective in who it hires. For example, if the labor market is so tight that all who apply for jobs must be hired, then there can be no selection and hence no gain. The gain in job performance per person hired is greatest with low selection ratios. For example, if one company can afford to hire only the top-scoring 10 percent, while another must hire the top-scoring 90 percent of all applicants, then with other things equal the first company will have a much larger gain in job performance.

There is another way to look at this: companies must provide conditions of employment that are good enough to attract more applicants than they have jobs to fill. It is even better when they can go beyond that and attract not only a lot of applicants, but the higher ability ones that are in that applicant pool. In addition, to realize *maximum* value from GMA-based selection, employers must be able to *retain* the high-performing employees they hire.

Second, the company must have some way of measuring GMA. The usual and best procedure is a standardized employment test of general intelligence, such as the Wonderlic Personnel Test. Such tests are readily available at modest cost. Less valid are proxy measures such as grade point average (GPA) or class rank. Such proxy measures are partial measures of intelligence. Also, intelligence can be assessed to some extent during the employment interview (Huffcutt, Roth, and McDaniel, 1996), although this is a much less valid measure of GMA than a written test.

Third, the variability in job performance must be greater than zero. That is, if all applicants after being hired would have the same level of job performance anyway, then nothing can be gained by hiring "the best." This condition is always met. That is, on all jobs studied there have been large differences between different workers in quality and quantity of output. Hunter, Schmidt, and Judiesch (1990) meta-analyzed all available studies and found large differences between employees. In unskilled and semi-skilled jobs, they found workers in the top 1 percent of performance produced over three times as much output as those in the bottom 1 percent. In skilled jobs, top workers produced 15 times as much as bottom workers. In professional and managerial jobs, the differences were even larger. These are very large differences, and they are the reason it pays off so handsomely to hire the best workers.

There is another advantage to hiring the best workers: the pool of talent available for future promotion is greatly increased. This is of great value to employers, because it helps ensure high performance all the way up through the ranks of managers. When the right people are promoted, their value to the firm in their new jobs is even greater than in their original jobs. Thus selection of high-ability people has implications not only for the job they are hired onto, but for other jobs in the organization, too.

ARE THERE EXCEPTIONS TO THIS PRINCIPLE?

As long as the three conditions described above are met, there are no known exceptions to this principle. That is, there are no known cases or situations in which it is inadvisable to select employees for general intelligence.

However, there are some people, particularly labor leaders, who believe there is an exception. These people believe that companies should not select on mental ability if they can select on job experience instead. That is, they believe that job experience is a better predictor of job performance than general intelligence. What does research show? For applicants with job experience of between none and five years, experience *is* a good predictor of job performance. But in the range of higher levels of experience, say from five to 30 years of job experience, job experience does not predict performance very well (Schmidt, Hunter, Outerbridge, and Goff, 1988; Hunter and Schmidt, 1996). On most jobs, once people have about five years of experience, further experience does not contribute much to higher performance. This is probably because experience beyond five years does not lead to further increases in job knowledge. This, in turn, may be due to the fact that after five years of on-the-job learning, people in the typical job are forgetting job knowledge about as fast as they are learning new job knowledge.

Another important fact is this: even for new hires in the one- to five-year range of job experience, where experience is a valid predictor of job performance, the validity declines over time. That is, experience predicts performance quite well for the first three years or so on the job and then starts to decline. By 12 years on the job, experience has low validity. But GMA continues to predict job performance quite well even after people have been on the job 12 years or more.

What this means is that job experience is *not* a *substitute* for GMA. In the long run, hiring on intelligence pays off much more than hiring on job experience (Hunter and Schmidt, 1996). So if you had to choose, you should choose GMA. However, typically you do not have to choose; more than one procedure can be used. It may be desirable to use *both* experience and GMA in hiring; as discussed later, it is usually best to use multiple hiring methods. But in this case, the *weighting* given to GMA should be higher than the weighting given to job experience.

ISSUES IN IMPLEMENTING AN ABILITY-BASED HIRING SYSTEM

One issue is whether an applicant can have too much intelligence for a job. Recently, an applicant was rejected for a job as a police officer in a New Jersey city on grounds that his intelligence test score was too high! This city believed something that many people believe: that intelligence leads to better job performance *but only up to a point*. After that, more intelligence leads to *lower* job performance. Hundreds of studies have shown that this is false. Higher intelligence leads to better job performance up to the highest levels of intelligence (Coward and Sackett, 1990). There is a straight-line (linear) relationship between intelligence and job performance. Why do so many people believe otherwise? Probably because they imagine a university professor or a medical doctor working as a janitor, and they think "This person would be so bored with this job that he would do a poor job." They forget that the university professor or doctor would never apply for the janitor's job to begin with. Among people who actually apply to get real jobs, there is a straight-line relationship between intelligence and performance; the higher the intelligence, the better the job performance. Hence we do not have to worry about hiring people who are too intelligent for the job.

A second issue is the one alluded to earlier: Although intelligence is the best predictor of job performance, it does not follow that use of intelligence *alone* in hiring is the best way to select people. In fact, it is well known that other predictors can be used along with intelligence to produce better predictions of job performance than intelligence alone. For example, for most jobs an intelligence test combined with an integrity test is 27 percent more valid than an intelligence test alone. Adding a structured employment interview to an intelligence test increases validity by 24 percent. Other examples of this sort are given in Schmidt and Hunter (1998). It is almost always possible to add supplementary measures that increase validity. Some of these measures are discussed in chapters 2, 3, and 4.

A third issue is the potential for legal risks. Members of some minority groups, particularly blacks and Hispanics, typically have lower average scores on GMA tests, leading to lower hiring rates. Government agencies such as the Equal Employment Opportunity Commission refer to these lower hiring rates as "adverse impact." The term adverse impact is deceptive, because it implies that the GMA tests *create* the difference in test scores, when in fact the tests only measure real pre-existing differences in mental skills. This is shown by the fact that minorities and non-minorities with the same test scores have the same level of later job performance. That is, the test scores predict equally accurately for all groups; they are predictively fair or unbiased (Schmidt, 1988; Wigdor and Garner, 1982).

Despite this fact, a lower hiring rate for minorities does sometimes lead to lawsuits. Employers can win these suits by demonstrating that the tests are valid predictors of job performance. Today such demonstrations rely increasingly on summaries of kinds of research findings discussed in this chapter, rather than on studies conducted by the employer. (This is part of the move away from the theory of situational specificity, discussed earlier.) Since around the mid-1980s, employers have been winning more and more such suits, and today they prevail in about 80 percent of such suits. And research shows that the value of the increases in job performance from good selection overshadow any potential legal costs stemming from defending against such suits.

However, this does not mean that all employers are willing to use intelligence tests in hiring. Although the percentage of employers using GMA tests has been increasing, some firms view even the possibility of a lawsuit as a public relations disaster. They feel that even if they win, they still lose on the public relations front. And they believe that public relations problems can reduce sales and profits. These firms – mostly larger companies – are willing to tolerate lower levels of job performance to avoid even the possibility of such a problem. Unfortunately for such firms, not using GMA tests does not remove the possibility of lawsuits. Other selection procedures also produce "adverse impact." Employers have tried to reduce adverse impact by introducing various forms of minority preferences in hiring, but courts have recently begun to strike down many forms of minority preferences. For example, under the 1991 Civil Rights Act, it is illegal to adjust test scores or other scores to equalize minority and non-minority hiring rates. This issue is one that will probably remain unsettled for some time.

A fourth issue is whether the use of mental ability tests turns off applicants. Some have argued that applicants do not like to take ability tests. However, surveys of applicant attitudes reveal that they view mental ability as generally relevant to job performance (more so than they do personality, for example), and that they do not have a negative attitude toward such tests. It also appears to be the case that when GMA or other ability tests are used, applicants view the selection requirements as being higher and this increases the status of the job and hence its attractiveness. That is, something that is harder to attain is viewed as being more valuable.

A final issue is whether the economic value of the job performance gains from GMA-based hiring is cancelled out by higher wages and salaries. The argument is that if a firm hires more intelligent people, they will have to pay them more and this will cancel out the gains from the increased job performance. However, in most cases it appears that there is no increase in compensation costs, at least initially. This is especially likely to be the case when few of the firms' competitors use GMA measures in their hiring. Typically there is a pool of available applicants in the area for a particular type of job, and the higher GMA applicants have no immediate effective way to command higher initial wages.

However, after some time on the job, when higher GMA employees have developed high levels of performance, the employer can afford to share some of these gains with such employees in the form of higher wages or salaries. In some cases, this might be necessary to retain high-performing employees. In any event, the payoff to the employer in terms of enhanced job performance is much greater than any increase in compensation cost.

Although most employers, for most jobs, do not pay different people in the same job at different rates, they do typically promote the top workers to higher-level jobs, and this does result in higher pay. But at promotion the value of the worker's performance to the firm increases much more than the worker's pay, creating another large net benefit to the firm of good selection. On the other hand, employers that hire only mediocre or poor workers at entry level find that their higher-level jobs also become filled with mediocre or poor performers. Again, as noted earlier, selection based on GMA improves performance not only in the job in question, but also later in higher-level jobs in the firm.

REAL-WORLD EXAMPLES

We will first look at two negative examples and then examine two positive examples of real-world applications of GMA-based hiring.

US Steel plant at Fairless Hills, PA

Up until 1978, the US Steel plant at Fairless Hills, PA, selected applicants into their skilled trades apprentice programs based on the applicants' total scores on a battery of ability tests. These total scores were a good measure of GMA, and selection was from the top down. The plant maintained apprentice programs in the wide variety of skilled trades needed to run a steel mill: machinists, tool and die makers, electricians, sheet metal workers, etc. The local unit of the United Steelworkers Union, however, did not like this selection method. In negotiations with the union, the company agreed to modify the selection system. In the new system, all applicants who scored above a low cut-off on each test, set at about the seventh-grade level, were considered equally qualified and eligible for hire. Only a few applicants were screened out by this procedure. Applicants in the passing group were selected based on plant seniority only. Hence this plant went from a GMA-based hiring system to one in which GMA played only a very minor role.

The apprentice training center at Fairless Hills was a well-run facility that kept excellent records of apprentice performance from both before and after the change in the selection system. These records showed that after the new selection system was introduced, performance plummeted. Scores on the mastery tests of amount learned in training declined markedly. The flunk-out and drop-out rates increased dramatically. The training time and training costs of those who did make it through the program increased substantially – because many apprentices had to re-take multiple units in the training. And finally, the ratings of later performance on the job out in the plant declined.

This was a well-controlled natural quasi-experiment. The only change made was the lowering of mental ability standards in selection. The training program and the tests given in the program remained the same. The decline in performance was clearly due to the lower intelligence of the new apprentices.

The Washington, DC police force

Up until the mid-1980s the Washington, DC police force was one of the best in the US. Applicants were selected for Police Academy training based on a general intelligence test constructed for the District of Columbia by the US Office of Personnel Management (OPM), as required by then existing Congressional regulations. This test had been challenged legally and the case had gone all the way to the US Supreme Court, where it had been upheld. A background investigation was also part of the selection process. The mayor of Washington, Marion Barry, repeatedly voiced opposition to both the test and the background check on grounds that the failure rate on both was higher for blacks. In 1987, when Congress relinquished control over the selection process to the mayor's office, Barry took responsibility for the selection process out of OPM's hands. He then eliminated both the GMA test and the background test. The replacement selection process was somewhat unclear, but reputedly involved fairly perfunctory interviews.

The first consequence was that the flunk-out rate in the Police Academy soared, with over 80 percent of the new hires being incapable of completing the required training. Failure rates that high were viewed as unacceptable, and so the content of academy training was "dumbed down." When this reduced the failure rate only slightly, the content was further dumbed down, and then dumbed down again. This process of successive adjustments ultimately "solved" the flunk-out problem.

However, the police officers being produced were incompetent. Large numbers of murder indictments had to be dismissed because the reports written by the officers on the scene were unintelligible, due to the low literacy levels. The solution rate for murder cases, formerly one of the highest in the US, declined precipitously to one of the lowest. Firearms accidents soared because officers did not know how to use their sidearms properly. Complaints of police abuse and incompetence from citizens soared. In addition, crime on the police force became quite common. For example, a group of police officers was found to be selling handguns previously confiscated from criminals *back to criminals*! These changes and others are described by Carlson (1993a, 1993b).

In this example, unlike the US Steel example, *two* things are happening. First, people low in intelligence are being hired, resulting in plummeting job performance. Second, criminals are being hired because there was no background investigation to ensure that they were not, and the result was crime on the police force.

Employment in the federal government

We now turn to a more positive example – or at least a less negative one. For many jobs in the federal government, people can either be hired from the outside using a GMA test or they can be promoted from within. When they are promoted from within, GMA tests are usually not used – although they sometimes are. Instead, people are evaluated based on records of their education and training and on appraisals by their supervisors of their performance in their present jobs. These procedures do have some validity but would not be expected to be as valid as GMA-based hiring.

So we can ask the following question: after people have been on the job some time, is the job performance higher for those initially selected using a GMA test? Government researchers at OPM addressed this question in a detailed study of three representative mid-level government jobs: IRS Auditor, Social Security Claims Examiner, and Customs Inspector. In each of these jobs, people hired both ways had been on the job from five to eight years. The measure of job performance was unusually good: it was the sum of a hands-on work sample test, a job knowledge test, and supervisory ratings of job performance.

In all three jobs, those selected years earlier using GMA tests had higher job performance. The average job performance of the non GMA-selected employees was at the fiftieth percentile, while that of the GMA-selected employees was at the seventieth percentile. This is a large difference. If this difference is projected over the federal workforce as a whole, it amounts to *billions* of dollars per year in increased output (Schmidt, Hunter, Outerbridge, and Trattner, 1986).

This was a reasonably controlled quasi-experiment. During the study, the researchers did not know which employees had initially been selected using a GMA measure and which had not. The only relevant difference between the two groups of workers was the method by which they had been hired. This study provides strong evidence that GMA-based hiring pays off in higher job performance.

The Philip Morris plant in Cabarrus County, North Carolina

The US Employment Service began a new nationwide program of employment testing, operated through state employment offices, in the early 1980s. Like its earlier program, it was based on the General Aptitude Test Battery (GATB). One of the three abilities measured in that program was GMA (the other two were general perceptual ability, and general psychomotor ability). This new program was based on the methods of meta-analysis or validity generalization that were mentioned at the beginning of this chapter.

The large Philip Morris plant in Cabarrus County, North Carolina, was one of the first employers to subscribe to this testing program. They signed an agreement under which the state employment service tested and referred the higher-scoring applicants to Philip Morris for possible hire. For the jobs at Philip Morris, most of the weight was placed on GMA in determining who was hired.

The Human Resources Department at Philip Morris decided to conduct a study to compare the performance of GATB-GMA selected workers and workers hired without use of the test. They found that the GMA-selected workers were superior across a variety of performance measures. For example, there was a 35 percent gain in output. The GMA-selected workers learned 8 percent more skills during job training, had 25 percent fewer operator failures and 58 percent fewer disciplinary actions. The incidence of unsafe job behaviors was 35 percent less and the reduction in work days lost to accidents was *82 percent.*

These are large differences. The Philip Morris personnel researchers, Dennis Warmke and William Van Arnam, noted the employment interview used might have contributed somewhat to the performance superiority of these workers. However, they stated that because it was the GMA test that screened out most of the applicants who were not hired, the GMA test was the dominant influence producing the performance improvements. This research is described in McKinney (1984).

CONCLUSION

Higher intelligence leads to better job performance on all jobs, and the increases in job performance resulting from hiring on GMA have high economic value for organizations. Higher intelligence causes higher job performance primarily because it causes people to learn job knowledge faster and to learn more of it. However, intelligence is also used directly on the job to solve performance-related problems, independent of prior job knowledge. The primary requirement that an organization must meet to make GMA-based hiring work well is the ability to attract job applicants and to retain them once they are hired. Despite beliefs to the contrary, hiring on job experience is inferior to hiring on GMA. Although GMA is the most important determinant of job performance, it is not the only determinant. Therefore, firms should use other procedures along with GMA. Finally, we have seen four concrete, graphic, real-world examples of the impact of GMA on job performance.

REFERENCES

Brody, N. (1992). *Intelligence.* New York: Academic Press.
Carlson, T. (1993a). D.C. blues: The rap sheet on the Washington police. *Policy Review*, Winter, 27–33.

Carlson, T. (1993b). Washington's inept police force. *The Wall Street Journal*, November 3.

Coward, W. M., and Sackett, P. R. (1990). Linearity of ability–performance relationships: A re-confirmation. *Journal of Applied Psychology*, 75, 295–300.

Gottfredson, L. S. (1996). Why g matters: The complexity of everyday life. *Intelligence*.

Hartigan, J. A., and Wigdor, A. K. (eds.) (1989). *Fairness in employment testing*. Washington, DC: National Academy of Sciences Press.

Herrnstein, R. J., and Murray, C. (1994). *The bell curve: Intelligence and class structure in American life*. New York: The Free Press.

Huffcutt, A. I., Roth, P. L., and McDaniel, M. A. (1996). A meta-analytic investigation of cognitive ability in employment interview evaluations: Moderating characteristics and implications for incremental validity. *Journal of Applied Psychology*, 81, 459–73.

Hunter, J. E. (1986). Cognitive ability, cognitive aptitudes, job knowledge, and job performance. *Journal of Vocational Behavior*, 29, 340–62.

Hunter, J. E., and Hunter, R. F. (1984). Validity and utility of alternate predictors of job performance. *Psychological Bulletin*, 96, 72–98.

Hunter, J. E., and Schmidt, F. L. (1996). Intelligence and job performance: Economic and social implications. *Psychology, Public Policy, and Law*, 2, 447–72.

Hunter, J. E., Schmidt, F. L., and Judiesch, M. K. (1990). Individual differences in output variability as a function of job complexity. *Journal of Applied Psychology*, 75, 28–42.

Hunter, J. E., Schmidt, F. L., and Rauschenberger, J. M. (in press). Intelligence, motivation, and job performance. Chapter in C. L. Cooper and E. A. Locke (eds.), *I/O psychology: What we know about theory and practice*. Blackwell Publishers.

Jensen, A. R. (1998). *The g factor: The science of mental ability*. Westport, CT: Praeger.

Judge, T. A., Thoresen, C. J., Bono, J. E., and Patton, G. K. (1999). Another look at the relationship between job satisfaction and job performance.

McDaniel, M. A., Whetzel, D. L., Schmidt, F. L., and Maurer, S. (1994). The validity of employment interviews: A comprehensive review and meta-analysis. *Journal of Applied Psychology*, 79, 599–616.

McHenry, J. J., Hough, L. M., Toquam, J. L., Hanson, M. L., and Ashworth, S. (1990). Project A validity results: The relationship between predictor and criterion domains. *Personnel Psychology*, 43, 335–54.

McKinney, M. W. (1984). *Final report: Validity generalization pilot study*. Southern Test Development Field Center, US Employment Service, Raleigh, North Carolina.

Mount, M. K., and Barrick, M. R. (1995). The Big Five personality dimensions: Implications for research and practice in human resources management. In G. Ferris (ed.), *Research in personnel and human resources management* (Vol. 13, pp. 153–200). Greenwich, CT: JAI Press.

Olea, M. M., and Ree, M. J. (1994). Predicting pilot and navigator criteria: Not much more than g. *Journal of Applied Psychology*, 79, 845–51.

Ones, D. S., Viswesvaran, C., and Schmidt, F. L. (1993). Comprehensive meta-analysis of integrity test validities: Findings and implications for personnel selection and theories of job performance. *Journal of Applied Psychology*, 78, 679–703.

Organ, D. W. (1990). *Organizational citizenship behavior: The good soldier syndrome*. Lexington, MA: Lexington Books.

Orr, J. M., Sackett, P. R., and Mercer, M. (1989). The role of prescribed and nonprescribed behaviors in estimating the dollar value of performance. *Journal of Applied Psychology*, 74, 34–40.

Ree, M. J., and Earles, J. A. (1991). Predicting training success: Not much more than g. *Personnel Psychology*, 44, 321–32.

Ree, M. J., and Earles, J. A. (1992). Intelligence is the best predictor of job performance. *Current Directions in Psychological Science*, 1, 86–9.

Ree, M. J., Earles, J. A., and Teachout, M. (1994). Predicting job performance: Not much more than g. *Journal of Applied Psychology*, 79, 518–24.

Schmidt, F. L. (1988). The problem of group differences in ability scores in employment selection. *Journal of Vocational Behavior*, 33, 272–92.

Schmidt, F. L. (1992). What do data really mean? Research findings, meta analysis, and cumulative knowledge in psychology. *American Psychologist*, 47, 1173–81.

Schmidt, F. L., and Hunter, J. E. (1992). Development of causal models of processes determining job performance. *Current Directions in Psychological Science*, 1, 89–92.

Schmidt, F. L., and Hunter, J. E. (1998). The validity and utility of selection methods in personnel psychology: Practical and theoretical implications of 85 years of research findings. *Psychological Bulletin*, 124(2), 262–74.

Schmidt, F. L., Hunter, J. E., McKenzie, R. C., and Muldrow, T. W. (1979). The impact of valid selection procedures on work-force productivity. *Journal of Applied Psychology*, 64, 609–26.

Schmidt, F. L., Hunter, J. E., Outerbridge, A. N., and Goff, S. (1988). The joint relation of experience and ability with job performance: A test of three hypotheses. *Journal of Applied Psychology*, 73, 46–57.

Schmidt, F. L., Hunter, J. E., Outerbridge, A. N., and Trattner, M. H. (1986). The economic impact of job selection methods on the size, productivity, and payroll costs of the Federal work-force: An empirical demonstration. *Personnel Psychology*, 39, 1–29.

Schmidt, F. L., Hunter, J. E., and Pearlman, K. (1980). Task difference and validity of aptitude tests in selection: A red herring. *Journal of Applied Psychology*, 66, 166–85.

Schmidt, F. L., Ones, D. S., and Hunter, J. E. (1992). Personnel selection. *Annual Review of Psychology*, 43, 627–70.

Wigdor, A. K., and Garner W. R. (eds.) (1982). *Ability testing: Uses, consequences, and controversies* (Report of the National Research Council Committee on Ability Testing). Washington, DC: National Academy of Sciences Press.

Wilk, S. L., Desmarais, L. B., and Sackett, P. R. (1995). Gravitation to jobs commensurate with ability: Longitudinal and cross-sectional tests. *Journal of Applied Psychology*, 80, 79–85.

Wilk, S. L., and Sackett, P. R. (1996). Longitudinal analysis of ability-job complexity fit and job change. *Personnel Psychology*, 49, 937–67.

2

Select on Conscientiousness and Emotional Stability

Murray R. Barrick and Michael K. Mount

Behavior in organizations is a function of an individual's ability, his/her motivation, and the constraints inherent in the situation. This chapter focuses on the prediction of workplace behaviors that are influenced by an individual's motivation, particularly as measured by the personality dimensions of conscientiousness and emotional stability. The previous chapter clearly showed that general intelligence predicts job performance. However, many important workplace behaviors are a function of the individual's motivation or willingness to perform them and, consequently, are not predicted well by general intelligence. When asked what employee skills managers consider important for workplace success, they ordinarily list the following attributes as critical for success at work:

- be free from substance abuse
- demonstrate honesty and integrity
- pay attention to the person speaking
- follow directions given verbally
- show respect for others
- show pride
- be punctual in attendance.

The behaviors listed above (and others not listed) are influenced largely by an individual's motivation. Therefore, in order to identify individuals who are likely to exhibit such behaviors, it is necessary to assess relevant personality characteristics rather than general mental ability. The universal principle that we advocate in this chapter is that organizations should routinely select on the personality dimensions of conscientiousness and emotional stability. A sub-principle of the chapter is that organizations should also select on other personality dimensions, but such practices should be dictated by the specific requirements of the job or the particular criterion.

Personality can be defined as an individual's relatively stable and enduring pattern of thoughts, feelings, and actions. Although more than 15,000 trait terms in the English language can be used to describe personality, most researchers agree that the structure of personality consists of five broad dimensions, often called the Big Five or the Five Factor Model (FFM) of personality: conscientiousness (i.e. dependable, industrious, efficient, and achievement oriented), emotional stability (i.e., calm, steady, self-confident, and secure), extraversion (i.e., gregarious, sociable, ambitious, and active), agreeableness (i.e., courteous, helpful, trusting, cooperative, and considerate), and openness to experience (i.e., cultured, intellectual, imaginative, and analytical).

Validity of Conscientiousness and Emotional Stability

Other things being equal, individuals high on conscientiousness perform better on the job. This principle is very broad and, like intelligence, it applies to all job types at all job levels. Conscientious individuals are achievement oriented, hard working, dependable, persistent, responsible, organized, careful, and reliable. Such traits are fundamentally related to motivation at work. They lead to increased effort, they direct effort toward specific goals, and they help sustain effort over time.

Similarly, individuals high on emotional stability perform better on the job. This principle is also quite broad, although the research evidence to date is not as strong as for conscientiousness. Viewed from the negative pole, neurotic individuals are nervous, high-strung, stress prone, moody, lack self-esteem, and are insecure. Such traits tend to inhibit positive motivational tendencies at work. That is, individuals who spend time worrying about their performance, doubt their abilities, require assurance from others, are depressed, and are stress prone are unable to develop adequate coping strategies and cannot focus attention on the tasks at hand. In short, traits associated with the low end of emotional stability (neuroticism) lead to poor performance.

These general principles are derived from the results of several meta-analytic studies that have examined the relationship between personality traits and job performance (e.g. Barrick and Mount, 1991; Barrick, Mount, and Judge, 1999; Hough, 1992; Hurtz and Donovan, 1998; Salgado, 1997, 1998). Collectively, these studies demonstrate that conscientiousness, and to a lesser extent, emotional stability, are valid predictors of job performance in a wide variety of jobs. For example, Barrick et al. (1999) reviewed eight meta-analyses conducted since 1990 and reported that measures of conscientiousness and emotional stability predicted overall job performance with an average true score validity of .24 and .15 respectively. This evidence demonstrates that selecting on conscientiousness and emotional stability will increase overall job performance, just like selecting on intelligence will. Furthermore, because conscientiousness and emotional stability have very small (or zero) correlations with intelligence and with each other, each adds unique information to the prediction of job performance. Thus, deciding to hire applicants with higher intelligence, conscientiousness, and emotional stability in combination will result in an increase in the number of employees who perform assigned job tasks effectively.

Aside from the findings that conscientiousness and emotional stability predict overall work performance, which is an important criterion for all organizations, there are other reasons to select employees on these two broad personality traits. Conscientiousness and emotional stability predict outcomes that are not typically included in an overall job performance criterion. These include regularly coming to work on time, staying with the organization rather than leaving, contributing more positive "citizenship" behaviors, including helping others when needed, training or mentoring newcomers, minimizing or solving conflicts within the work group, and maintaining personal discipline by avoiding negative behaviors such as alcohol and substance abuse, rules infractions, and other counterproductive behaviors. All of these are critical to organizational success, yet are not necessarily assessed through an overall performance criterion. Further, none of these important work outcomes are predicted well by general intelligence.

It is well known that turnover is a major cost to employers. A major goal of many employers is to hire employees who not only perform well but also stay on the job for a long period of time, particularly in tight labor markets. Conscientiousness and emotional stability have been found to consistently (negatively) predict an individual's propensity to withdraw from the job. Barrick and Mount (1996) showed that voluntary turnover was predicted by both personality traits, with true score correlations across two firms ranging from −.21 to −.26. Similarly, DeMatteo, White, Teplitzky, and Sachs (1991) found emotional stability was the best predictor, and conscientiousness was the second-best predictor of turnover in the military. Selecting on conscientiousness and emotional stability will reduce workforce instability such as excessive turnover, absenteeism, and tardiness.

Another important reason to select on conscientiousness and emotional stability is that they are centrally related to the concepts of integrity and customer service, both of which are strongly related to successful job performance. Considering integrity first, employers are very interested in eliminating counterproductive or antisocial behavior at work, including belligerence with customers or co-workers, "badmouthing" the organization, sabotage of equipment or products, theft of goods or money, and excessive alcohol or drug abuse. Research demonstrates integrity tests are valid predictors of these behaviors (Ones, Viswesvaran, and Schmidt, 1993), and also predict supervisory ratings of performance ($\rho = .46$). In addition, Ones (1993) identified more than 100 studies reporting correlations between integrity tests and temperament measures. She found that integrity tests were related primarily to conscientiousness and emotional stability (along with agreeableness).

Turning to the customer service concept, Frei and McDaniel (1998) reported a mean validity of customer service measures for predicting supervisory ratings of performance of .50. Customer service measures were strongly related to conscientiousness and emotional stability (again, along with agreeableness). Ones and Viswesvaran (1996) found that emotional stability emerged as the strongest personality-based predictor of customer service orientation followed by conscientiousness. Thus, a major component of what is measured by integrity tests and customer service tests is conscientiousness and emotional stability.

Selecting on conscientiousness and emotional stability is also important from the viewpoint of conforming to existing laws and legal precedents. A key question is whether a predictor unintentionally discriminates by screening out a disproportionate number of minorities and women. To the extent this happens, the predictor has adverse impact, which may result in legal action. Research consistently demonstrates a large mean difference of approximately one standard deviation between African Americans and Whites on intelligence. In contrast, there are relatively small sub-group differences on conscientiousness and emotional stability. For example, in a meta-analysis reported by Hough (1995), differences between African American and Hispanic sub-groups versus

White sub-groups were very small (d ranges from −.06 to .04; N up to 142,000). Similar non-significant differences have also been found for gender. In a meta-analysis by Feingold (1994), only small gender differences were found on measures of conscientiousness and emotional stability ($d = -.10$ and $-.14$, respectively, where women scored slightly higher; with N larger than 60,000). Thus, from a legal perspective, selecting on conscientiousness and emotional stability (and other personality dimensions) is advantageous because it does not appear to result in adverse impact which could lead to litigation.

In summary, employees selected using conscientiousness and emotional stability are not only better overall performers, but also actively look for more responsibility and challenges, are more service oriented, and exhibit greater integrity and fewer irresponsible behaviors. In addition, deciding whom to hire using conscientiousness and emotional stability is not likely to result in legal challenges.

RELATIONSHIP OF CONSCIENTIOUSNESS AND EMOTIONAL STABILITY TO WORK-RELATED ATTITUDES

Another reason to select on conscientiousness and emotional stability is that they are related to work-related attitudes, which in turn have been shown to affect performance. For example, conscientiousness and emotional stability are positively related to job satisfaction. Judge, Higgins, Thoresen, and Barrick (1999) found that conscientiousness and emotional stability assessed at an early age (12–14) were strong predictors of overall job satisfaction in late adulthood ($r = .40$ and $.34$ respectively), even after controlling for clinicians' ratings of extraversion, openness to experience, and agreeableness. In turn, job satisfaction has been shown to be positively related to performance.

Conscientiousness and emotional stability are also among the strongest personality-based predictors of life satisfaction (DeNeve and Cooper, 1998). It has been argued that conscientiousness plays a major role in both job and life satisfaction because conscientious behavior is instrumental in attaining outcomes such as career success that achievement-oriented people value (McCrae and Costa, 1991). Schmutte and Ryff (1997) concluded that those high in conscientiousness are more satisfied because they achieve a heightened sense of control and competence through their diligent and responsible behavior. Thus conscientiousness is instrumental in attaining desired outcomes and fostering control, which leads to greater satisfaction.

The effects of emotional stability on satisfaction are complex and are best viewed from the negative pole (i.e., neuroticism). People who suffer from low emotional stability experience greater distress and reduced job and life satisfaction because they experience more adverse events, and react negatively and more strongly when such problems occur. Higher levels of emotional stability result in greater satisfaction because stable people have more confidence to approach stressful work, have a more positive view of themselves, others, and the world around them, and do not let negative emotions and dysfunctional thought processes distract them from the task at hand. Overall, these results show that conscientiousness and emotional stability are fundamentally important to success at work, but are also important to satisfaction at work as well as one's overall satisfaction in life. It is not an exaggeration to say that conscientiousness and emotional stability are fundamentally important to overall life success.

How Do Conscientiousness and Emotional Stability Affect Job Performance?

The literature accumulated to date convincingly demonstrates that there are numerous advantages to organizations when applicants are selected on conscientiousness. But how does conscientiousness affect performance? As discussed below it affects job performance both directly and indirectly. It has a direct effect on performance because all other things equal, conscientious individuals are more reliable and dependable, are more careful and thorough, and are highly achievement oriented. All of these traits lead directly to success at work.

Conscientiousness has an indirect effect on task performance through its effects on self-regulatory processes. These self-regulatory processes work primarily through motivational or "will-do" performance factors. An especially important mechanism by which conscientiousness affects performance indirectly is through the amount of effort exerted. Mount and Barrick (1995) found that conscientiousness correlates highly with amount of effort exerted ($\rho = .51$). This strong relationship indicates that conscientiousness affects task performance through increased time on task, which in turn affects performance through its effect on other mediating variables. For example, increased time on task leads to greater quantity of output, all other things equal. It also provides more opportunities to practice and provides more exposure to a wider variety of problems. Both of these increase job knowledge, which in turn increases task performance. (As discussed in the previous chapter, there is a strong correlation between job knowledge and job performance.)

Conscientiousness also affects performance indirectly through its effect on quality. Mount and Barrick (1995) found that conscientiousness is strongly correlated with quality ($\rho = .44$). This makes sense because conscientious people plan and organize their work, and are careful, thorough, and detail oriented. Such individuals are more likely to spot problems and errors in processes and output. This leads to better-quality work, which in turn leads to higher performance. These traits are also likely to lead to fewer accidents and safety violations.

Similarly, conscientious people are dependable, reliable, and abide by rules. They are less likely to engage in counterproductive behaviors such as theft, rules infractions, violence on the job, sabotage, and so forth. In turn, each of these counterproductive behaviors is associated with job performance (negatively). In a related but positive vein these same traits lead to positive citizenship behaviors. Such behaviors include willingness to help in emergency or overload situations, taking on tasks no one else is willing to do, and going beyond prescribed role requirements to get the job done. Conscientiousness has been shown to be a valid predictor of these behaviors, which in turn have been shown to be related to positive supervisory ratings.

Conscientiousness also affects performance through its effect on positive self-efficacy. That is, because conscientious people develop greater job knowledge and produce more and better-quality output, they develop more positive beliefs about their capabilities to accomplish particular tasks. Chen, Casper, and Cortina (1999) have shown that conscientiousness predicts self-efficacy and, in turn, self-efficacy is related to task performance.

Another way conscientiousness indirectly affects job performance is through goal-setting processes. Conscientious people are more likely to set goals which in turn leads to higher performance. (See chapter 8 for a detailed discussion of the positive effects of goal setting.) A study by Barrick, Mount, and Strauss (1993) showed that highly conscientious sales representatives are more likely to set goals autonomously and to be more committed to their goal, which, in turn, led to higher performance. Barrick et al. (1993) found that about half of the total effect of conscientiousness on performance was indirect.

In summary, conscientiousness has both direct and indirect effects on performance, largely through its effects on "will-do" performance factors. Conscientious people exert more effort, which in turn leads to greater job knowledge and greater work output. Conscientiousness leads to better planned and organized work and work that is done more carefully with more attention to detail, which leads to better quality and fewer accidents and safety violations. Increased job knowledge and greater quality work lead to greater confidence that the individual can accomplish a specific task, which in turn leads to higher job performance. In addition conscientious individuals set goals and are more committed to them, which in turn leads to better performance.

Motivation also appears to be the primary mechanism through which emotional stability affects job performance. A recent meta-analysis (Hough, Eaton, Dunnette, Kamp, and McCloy, 1990) reported a correlation of .16 ($\rho = .25$[1]) between emotional stability (Hough et al. use the term adjustment) and effort. Furthermore, the ABLE military study reported a correlation of .17 ($\rho = .27$[1]) between emotional stability (also labeled adjustment) and effort and leadership (Hough et al., 1990). This makes sense as those prone to greater anxiety and insecurity (low on emotional stability) tend to be fearful of novel situations, be more concerned about failure, and are more susceptible to feelings of dependence and helplessness (Judge, Locke, and Durham, 1997). Those who experience greater and more frequent negative emotions may choose to withhold effort rather than risk the potential affective consequences of failure. Researchers label this phenomenon the "self-handicapping" paradox (Rhodewalt, 1994). In addition, the tendency of people to behave in this way, particularly within the context of achievement (i.e., job) settings, is fundamental to the learned helplessness theory of depression (Seligman, 1978). Taken together, these findings suggest that the inability of neurotics to cope with fear of failure substantively impacts job performance through their effects on motivational level.

Research also suggests emotional stability affects the employee's ability and willingness to get along with other employees. Mount, Barrick, and Stewart (1998) demonstrate that emotional stability is correlated with performance in jobs that involve considerable interpersonal interaction, particularly when the interaction involves helping, cooperating with, and nurturing others ($\rho = .18$). These effects were found to be even stronger in work teams ($\rho = .27$). It is logical that employees low on emotional stability are likely to be more anxious, moody, and to express more negative affectivity, which could suppress or even inhibit cooperation. Reduced cooperation and teamwork, in turn, lead to less success at work.

Emotional stability also affects motivation at work through its moderately strong effect ($\rho = .33$) on self-efficacy (Judge, Locke, Durham, and Kluger, 1998). In essence, people who do not see themselves as worthy and able are less confident, and interpret their environment through a negative lens. Thus, they are more likely to view themselves as victims, rate themselves and peers less favorably, and tend to be more dissatisfied with themselves, their jobs, and lives in general (Judge et al., 1997; Hogan and Briggs, 1984; Watson and Clark, 1984). These perceptions are likely to influence one's estimate of one's fundamental capabilities to cope with work's exigencies. Taken together, people who are emotionally stable are more motivated because they feel greater confidence and control at work, are more willing to engage in novel situations, and view life more positively.

Emotional stability is also (negatively) related to counterproductive behavior, which in turn affects job performance. Hough et al. (1990) found a very large correlation of $-.43$ ($\rho = -.68$[1]) between emotional stability and delinquency. In an extension of that meta-analysis, Hough (1992) reported a correlation of .41 ($\rho = .64$[1]) between emotional stability (labeled adjustment) and law-abiding behavior. In essence, emotionally unstable employees commit more theft, more delinquent or even criminal offenses, and have greater incidences of absenteeism, tardiness, disciplinary actions, and fail to follow the rules. Further support for the importance of emotional stability can be found by examining meta-analytic evidence (Hough et al., 1990; Hough, 1992) about its relationship to commendable behavior ($\rho = .24$[1]) and personal discipline ($\rho = .19$[1]). Employees scoring high on emotional stability are likely to be steady, calm, and predictable, which helps them obtain more commendations and recognition at work. In turn, commendations along with fewer disciplinary actions and reprimands have been linked to higher performance ratings (Borman, White, Pulakos, and Oppler, 1991).

In sum, people who are more confident, secure, and unflappable are more motivated at work, which in turn increases performance. They are also more cooperative and more actively participate in teamwork, which leads to higher job performance. Furthermore, emotionally stable people are more committed to work and can more effectively cope with short- and long-term changes at work, which enhances success. Poor "copers" continually find themselves in situations they appraise as exceeding their cognitive resources and level of motivation, while effective "copers" may seek out situations that they find challenging or provide opportunities for personal growth. They are also more likely to abide by the organization's rules and policies, and will exhibit more commendable behaviors, which in turn leads to higher performance. In essence, stable employees are predisposed to view events, themselves, and others in a positive light, can cope better, are more confident, motivated, and committed to work, are willing to help others, and adhere to organizational rules and policies, which enables the employee to be more successful at work.

EXCEPTIONS TO THIS UNIVERSAL PRINCIPLE

The general principle in this chapter is that individuals should be selected on their level of conscientiousness and emotional stability. However, this does not mean that these are the only valid personality dimensions that predict performance. A sub-principle of this chapter is that individuals should be selected on other personality dimensions according to the specific requirements of the job and/or the nature of the criterion. Research has shown that the other three personality dimensions in the FFM model (agreeableness, extroversion, and openness to experience) are relevant in some jobs or for some specific types of criteria. To clearly identify when these relationships are likely to be non-zero, practitioners need to focus more on job requirements, demands, or what now are labeled competencies. This does not imply an extensive, time-consuming, content-specific job analysis. Rather, it suggests the relevance of these personality traits depends on the requirements and competencies generally demanded by the job to achieve successful job performance. For example, if the job requires extensive interpersonal interaction of a cooperative nature, agreeableness would be expected to be an important predictor. In fact, recent research demonstrates that agreeableness is the single best predictor of teamwork and is also related to service orientation (Mount et al., 1998). In contrast, if the nature of the interpersonal interaction is competitive or requires persuasion or negotiating, then one would expect extraversion to be a relevant predictor. Thus, extraversion has been found to be a valid predictor of success in sales and management jobs (Barrick and Mount, 1991). Finally, it would be expected that companies that are seeking employees who are flexible and highly adaptive to the rapid changes frequently encountered at work would select on openness to experience. To date, however, there is very little evidence to support this hypothesis. This is somewhat surprising, particularly when one recognizes that college students tend to be almost a full standard deviation higher on this attribute than non-college students are. However, as one would expect, employees higher on openness to experience tend to have higher training performance than those low in openness (Barrick and Mount, 1991). Thus, to date, the only criterion openness to experience appears relevant for is training success. It should also be noted that trainees scoring higher on extraversion have been found to be more successful during training. This has been attributed to extraverts' increased and more active participation during training.

IMPLEMENTING THESE PRINCIPLES

The general principle that we have discussed is that employers should select applicants who are hardworking, dependable, achievement-striving (i.e., conscientious) as well as not temperamental, not stress prone, not anxious, and not worrisome (i.e., emotionally stable). This is not a particularly surprising statement; however, a necessary first step before a principle can be implemented is that it must be well understood. In this vein, much progress has been made in the past decade in understanding how conscientiousness and emotional stability relate to job performance. Equally important to the implementation of these principles has been the contribution of industrial-organizational psychologists to the development of reliable and valid measures of these concepts.

The use of personality assessment to select applicants requires collecting "personal" data. To make sure that accurate data are collected in a fair manner, attention must be given to the relevance of various personality traits, privacy and confidentiality of the information, and some consideration of the "demands" of the applicant setting. Implementation requires that the organization accurately identifies and measures applicant qualifications relative to job requirements. Thus, before assessing personality traits, a job analysis should be conducted to identify critical competencies and job requirements. By understanding the critical requirements of the job, one will recognize which personality traits are relevant predictors, in addition to conscientiousness and emotional stability. However, some consideration must be given to the "job" itself. Today organizations are moving away from the use of narrow, well-defined jobs and towards broader, less well-defined, more amorphous jobs, with constantly changing content. The changing structure of jobs implies there will be greater emphasis on those traits and qualities that are valid for all jobs (intelligence, conscientiousness, and emotional stability). Nevertheless, it will be desirable to select on the other three personality traits (extraversion, agreeableness, and openness to experience) when those traits are valid predictors of requirements for jobs likely to be encountered by the people being hired.

Once it is known which specific traits will be assessed, consideration must also be given to the best means for assessing personality. Research illustrates that co-workers, customers, and supervisors at work can rate a person's personality, and those assessments have been found to predict job performance better than self-reports of personality. For example, Mount, Barrick, and Strauss (1994) found that the validity of co-worker and customer ratings of conscientiousness was .37 and .42, respectively, in predicting supervisor ratings of performance. The magnitude of these relationships approaches that of general intelligence. The drawback of using observer ratings, however, is that they cannot be used for external hiring.

The most common means of assessing personality is through self-report personality tests. There are several valid measures of the Big Five traits. For example, the *Personal characteristics inventory* (Mount, Barrick, Laffitte, and Callans, 1999) is a self-report measure of the Big Five that asks applicants to report their agreement or disagreement with 150 sentences. The measure takes about 30 minutes to complete and has a fifth- to sixth-grade reading level. Another commonly used measure of the Big Five is the *Hogan personality inventory* (Hogan and Hogan, 1995). Responses to the *HPI* can be scored to yield measures of occupational success as well as employee reliability and service orientation. A third alternative is the *NEO personality inventory*, which is also based on the Big Five typology (Costa and McCrae, 1992). There are several versions of the *NEO* and it has been translated into several languages.

An implementation concern in the use of personality inventories is that testing may be seen as an invasion of privacy and confidentiality. Personality testing is a means to learn about applicants' traditional ways of thinking, feeling, and acting, and critics contend such probing is a violation of privacy rights. Although a general right to privacy is not explicitly stated in the US Constitution, some states, such as California, do incorporate such a right in their state constitutions. However, employers who assess only job-relevant personality traits should be able to prevail in these states. Courts generally seem inclined to accept an argument that the information obtained bears a relationship to some legitimate employer goal, such as higher job performance. Nevertheless, a practitioner should examine the items of the personality test to determine whether there are invasive or offensive test items. To evaluate items, the practitioner must consider the need to balance the employer's right to know versus the employee's right to privacy.

Finally, some consideration of the demands of the applicant setting must be taken. There is some concern that applicants may distort their responses to personality tests. This concern becomes apparent when one considers the nature of some personality items. For example, few applicants would agree with the statement that "others would describe me as lazy or irresponsible at work," if they desperately wanted the job. Given the near impossibility of verifying responses to some of these questions, the possibility that impression management influences responses is quite real. In fact, research suggests applicants do manage impressions, as scores are higher by one-half standard deviation between applicant versus non-applicant settings. Given that a job is on the line when applicants complete a personality test, the tendency to enhance their impression is undeniable. Nevertheless, research clearly shows (Barrick and Mount, 1996) that impression management does not significantly detract from the predictive validity of the tests. Thus, it has yet to be shown that faking undermines the predictive validity of personality tests in selection. However, an important implication from these findings is that practitioners should not rely on norms based on incumbent responses, as they will tend to be one-half standard deviation lower than norms derived from incumbent samples.

In sum, significant progress has been made in understanding the magnitude of the relationship between conscientiousness and emotional stability and job performance and the processes by which these concepts affect performance. Successful implementation of the principles we advocate requires reliable and valid measures of both conscientiousness and emotional stability. Over the past decade several measures of the five-factor taxonomy of personality have been developed. None the less, additional research is needed to further develop and refine these measures to overcome potential problems associated with impression management and socially desirable responding.

REAL-WORLD EXAMPLES

Relationship of conscientiousness and emotional stability to career success

A recent study (Judge et al., 1999) investigated the relationship between traits from the Big Five model of personality to success in careers spanning over 50 years. The ability to predict success 50 years after assessing personality provides a rigorous test of the utility of selecting applicants using conscientiousness and emotional stability. The data for this study were obtained from the Intergenerational Studies Program, administered by the Institute of Human Development, University of California at Berkeley. The sample (average $N = 194$) was derived from children born in Berkeley, California in 1928 and 1929. Many measurements were collected from participants over the 60-year course of the study. For example, there were two studies during later childhood (11–13 and again 16–18), as well as three major follow-up studies conducted when participants were in early adulthood (30–38), middle age (41–50), and in late adulthood (53–62). In addition to collecting personality and intelligence test data, the subject's job satisfaction, income, and occupational status were collected during each of these studies. Thus, the records were rich with personality and career data, and comparisons were made across data collected at five different points in time (ranging from childhood to late adulthood).

Both childhood and early adulthood assessments of personality revealed enduring relationships between personality traits and later career success. For example, childhood assessments of conscientiousness and emotional stability predicted job satisfaction ($r = .40$ and .22 respectively), income (.16 and .26 respectively), and occupational status ($r = .49$ and .26 respectively), even in late adulthood. These results show that knowledge about one's conscientiousness and emotional stability early in life proved to be an effective predictor of satisfaction and success in one's later career, even over a 50-year time span. Results also demonstrated that these two personality traits explained significant incremental variance in these measures of career success, even after controlling for the influence of intelligence. Taken together, these results show that highly conscientious and emotionally stable children earned higher salaries, were more satisfied with their work, and attained higher positions in the social hierarchy later in life. Obviously, organizations will be better off selecting individuals who are conscientious and emotionally adjusted, as they will be rewarded by those decisions with higher performance and more committed employees for years to come.

The generalizability of conscientiousness and emotional stability as predictors

During the 1980s, the army conducted the Selection and Classification Project (Project A). Project A was a seven-year effort that was designed to investigate how the contributions of selection could maximize performance within the constraints of one of the largest operational personnel systems in the world. The army personnel system includes over 276 jobs and hires, almost exclusively, inexperienced and untrained persons to fill them. A major goal of Project A was to develop a battery of predictor measures that would best serve the needs of all the jobs in the entire selection system for entry-level enlisted personnel. Thus, this project examined all of the major domains of individual differences that had potential for generating useful predictor variables. Several versions of the test battery were developed and examined in an iterative sequence, with each round of testing involving thousands of recruits or enlisted personnel. Rather than review the extensive list of predictors examined, interested readers are referred to Peterson, Hough, Dunnette, Rosse, Houston, Toquam, and Wing (1990). Suffice it to say that the range of individual differences was extraordinarily comprehensive, ranging from administrative/ archival records to training achievement tests.

The study also rigorously modeled job performance to better understand what these individual differences were predicting. Project A examined whether a single model of performance would be stable across the large number of jobs available. Multiple methods were used to generate over 200 performance indicators of a sub-sample of jobs. An iterative procedure resulted in the identification of five broad performance dimensions that were found in all jobs. Two of these performance measures focus on specific technical competence called core technical proficiency and general soldiering proficiency. While the former dimension appears to be a basic performance component for any job (core task proficiency), the latter dimension would almost surely be specific to the military. The analysis also identified three non job-specific performance dimensions that are more under motivational control. These are called effort/leadership, maintaining personal discipline, and physical fitness/military bearing. Again, while military bearing is unique to the military, the other two dimensions are quite likely basic performance components of almost any job. Although job performance was found to be multidimensional, an overall decision could scale each performance measure by its relative importance for a particular personnel decision or job.

The findings (McHenry, Hough, Toquam, Hanson, and Ashworth, 1990) from this large-scale project were that intelligence tests provided the best prediction of job-specific and general task proficiency (core technical proficiency and general soldiering proficiency), whereas the personality composites, particularly those traits measuring conscientiousness and emotional stability, were the best predictors of giving extra effort and leadership (multiple $R = .33$, uncorrected), exhibiting personal discipline (multiple $R = .32$, uncorrected), and physical fitness and military bearing (multiple $R = .37$, uncorrected). The study also illustrated the incremental validity contributed by other predictors over intelligence. The greatest amount of incremental validity was generated by the personality measures, especially when predicting effort and leadership ($\Delta R = .11$), personal discipline ($\Delta R = .19$), and physical fitness and military bearing ($\Delta R = .21$). These results show the generalizable value of using conscientiousness and emotional stability for purposes of selection.

CONCLUSION

The general principle in this chapter is that organizations should select employees based on their conscientiousness and emotional stability. A sub-principle is that organizations should also select on agreeableness, extraversion, or openness to experience when they have been shown to be relevant for specific criteria or requirements of the job. Hiring applicants who are more intelligent (as advocated in the first chapter) will result in employees who are capable of acquiring more work-related facts and principles as well as greater procedural knowledge and skill. This contributes to job success, particularly on the core substantive or technical tasks central to the job. But hiring smart people is not enough. Hiring applicants who are more conscientious and emotionally stable will result in employees who are predisposed to exert greater effort at work, who persist at work for a longer period of time, are able to more effectively cope with stress, and are more committed to work. In addition, these employees are likely to be more responsible and helpful to others at work, are more likely to remain on the job, and are less likely to engage in counterproductive behaviors at work. In conclusion, hiring people who work smarter (select on intelligence), and who work harder and cope better (select on conscientiousness and emotional stability), will lead to increased individual productivity which in turn will lead to increased organizational effectiveness.

NOTE

1 These meta-analytic estimates were not corrected for statistical artifacts in the original article, as most meta-analyses are. Thus, to make these meta-analytic estimates more comparable to other results discussed in this article, they were fully corrected for measurement error in the predictor and criterion, as well as for range restriction (Hunter and Schmidt, 1990). To correct these estimates, the values reported by Barrick et al. (1999) were used: where the average sample weighted predictor reliability value across prior meta-analyses was .78; criterion reliability was .55; and range restriction was .93.

REFERENCES

Barrick, M. R., and Mount, M. K. (1991). The Big Five personality dimensions and job performance: A meta-analysis. *Personnel Psychology*, 44, 1–26.
Barrick, M. R., and Mount, M. K. (1996). Effects of impression management and self-deception on

the predictive validity of personality constructs. *Journal of Applied Psychology*, 81, 261–72.

Barrick, M. R., Mount, M. K., and Judge, T. A. (1999). The FFM personality dimensions and job performance: Meta-analysis of meta-analyses. Paper presented at the 15th Annual Conference of the Society of Industrial and Organizational Psychology, Atlanta, GA.

Barrick, M. R., Mount, M. K., and Strauss, J. P. (1993). Conscientiousness and performance of sales representatives: Test of the mediating effects of goal setting. *Journal of Applied Psychology*, 78, 715–22.

Borman, W. C., White, L. A., Pulakos, E. D., and Oppler, S. H. (1991). Models of supervisor job performance ratings. *Journal of Applied Psychology*, 76, 863–72.

Chen, G., Casper, W. J., and Cortina, J. M. (1999). Meta-analytic examination of the relationships among cognitive ability, conscientiousness, self-efficacy, and task performance. Paper presented at the annual meeting of the Society of Industrial-Organizational Psychology, Atlanta.

Costa, P. T. Jr., and McCrae, R. R. (1992). *Revised NEO personality inventory and Five-Factor model inventory professional manual.* Odessa, FL.: Psychological Assessment Resources.

DeMatteo, J. S., White, L. A., Teplitzky, M. L., and Sachs, S. A. (1991). Relationship between temperament constructs and selection for special forces training. Paper presented at the 33rd Annual Conference of the Military Testing Association, October, San Antonio, TX.

DeNeve K. M., and Cooper H. (1998). The happy personality: A meta-analysis of 137 personality traits and subjective well-being. *Psychological Bulletin*, 124, 197–229.

Feingold, A. (1994). Gender differences in personality: A meta-analysis. *Psychological Bulletin*, 116, 429–56.

Frei, R. L., and McDaniel, M. A. (1998). Validity of customer service measures in personnel selection: A review of criterion and construct evidence. *Human Performance*, 11, 1–27.

Hogan, R., and Hogan, J. (1995). *Hogan personality inventory manual.* Tulsa, OK: Hogan Assessment Systems.

Hogan, R. T., and Briggs, S. R. (1984). Noncognitive measures of social intelligence. *Personnel Selection & Training Bulletin*, 5, 184–90.

Hough, L. M. (1992). The "Big-Five" personality variables – Construct confusion: Description versus prediction. *Human Performance*, 5, 139–55.

Hough, L. M. (1995). Applicant self descriptions: Evaluating strategies for reducing distortion. Paper presented at the 10th Annual Convention of the Society of Industrial and Organizational Psychology, Orlando.

Hough, L. M., Eaton, N. K., Dunnette, M. D., Kamp, J. D., and McCloy, R. A. (1990). Criterion-related validities of personality constructs and the effect of response distortion on those validities. *Journal of Applied Psychology Monograph*, 75, 581–95.

Hunter, J. E., and Schmidt, F. L. (1990). *Methods of meta-analysis.* Newbury Park, CA: Sage Publications.

Hurtz, G. M., and Donovan, J. J. (1998). Personality and job performance: Will the real "Big Five" please stand up? Paper presented at the 13th Annual Conference of the Society for Industrial and Organizational Psychology, Dallas, TX.

Judge, T. A., Higgins, C. A., Thoresen, C. J., and Barrick, M. R. (1999). The Big Five personality traits, general mental ability, and career success across the life span. *Personnel Psychology*, 621–52.

Judge, T. A., Locke, E. A., and Durham, C. C. (1997). The dispositional causes of job satisfaction: A core evaluations approach. *Research in Organizational Behavior*, 19, 151–88.

Judge, T. A., Locke, E. A., Durham, C. C., and Kluger, A. N. (1998). Dispositional effects on job and life satisfaction: The role of core evaluations. *Journal of Applied Psychology*, 83, 17–34.

McCrae, R. R., and Costa, P. T. (1991). The NEO Personality-Inventory: Using the 5-Factor Model in Counseling. *Journal of Counseling Development*, 69, 637–72.

McHenry, J. J., Hough, L. M., Toquam, J. L., Hanson, M. A., and Ashworth, S. (1990). Project

A validity results: The relationship between predictor and criterion domains. *Personnel Psychology*, 43, 335–54.

Mount, M. K., and Barrick, M. R. (1995). The Big Five personality dimensions: Implications for research and practice in human resource management. *Research in Personnel and Human Resources Management*, 13, 153–200.

Mount, M. K., Barrick, M. R., Laffitte, L. J., and Callans, M. C. (1999)*Personal Characteristics Inventory user's manual*. Libertyville: Ill.: Wonderlic Consulting.

Mount, M. K., Barrick, M. R., and Stewart, G. L. (1998). Five-factor model of personality and performance in jobs involving interpersonal interactions. *Human Performance*, 11, 145–65.

Mount, M. K., Barrick, M. R., and Strauss, J. P. (1994). Validity of observer ratings of the Big Five personality factors. *Journal of Applied Psychology*, 79, 272–80.

Ones, D. S. (1993). The construct validity of integrity tests. Unpublished doctoral dissertation, University of Iowa.

Ones, D. S., and Viswesvaran, C. (1996). Bandwidth-fidelity dilemma in personality measurement for personnel selection. *Journal of Organizational Behavior*, 17, 609–26.

Ones, D. S., Viswesvaran, C., and Schmidt, F. L. (1993). Meta-analysis of integrity test validities: Findings and implications for personnel selection and theories of job performance. *Journal of Applied Psychology Monograph*, 78, 679–703.

Peterson, N. G., Hough, L. M., Dunnette, M. D., Rosse, R. L., Houston, J. S., Toquam, J. L., and Wing, H. (1990). Project A: Specification of the predictor domain and development of new selection/classification tests. *Personnel Psychology*, 43, 247–76.

Rhodewalt, F. (1994). Conceptions of ability, achievement goals and individual differences in self-handicapping behavior: On the application of implicit theories. *Journal of Personality*, 62, 67–85.

Salgado, J. F. (1997). The five-factor model of personality and job performance in the European Community. *Journal of Applied Psychology*, 82, 30–43.

Salgado, J. F. (1998). Criterion validity of personality measures based and non-based on the five-factor model. Paper presented at the 106th Annual Convention of the American Psychological Association, San Francisco.

Schmutte P. S., and Ryff, C. D. (1997). Personality and well-being: Re-examining methods and meanings. *Journal of Personality & Social Psychology*, 73, 549–59.

Seligman, M. E. P. (1978). Learned helplessness in humans: Critique and reformulation. *Journal of Abnormal Psychology*, 87, 49–74.

Watson, D., and Clark, L. A. (1984). Negative affectivity: The disposition to experience aversive emotional states. *Psychological Bulletin*, 96, 465–90.

3

Structure Interviews to Hire the Best People

CYNTHIA KAY STEVENS

Employment interviews are selection/recruitment devices in which applicants and employers interact (e.g., face-to-face, via telephone) to gather data from each other that will aid in making employment decisions. Because applicants and employers often have multiple job opportunities or applicants, respectively, from which to choose, it is important to gather accurate information quickly and easily. Interviews provide a flexible tool for gathering and disseminating such information. Unlike other selection tools (e.g., tests, biodata inventories), interviews don't require expert help or large samples to develop, implement, or interpret the data collected. Moreover, interviews can be easily adapted to accomplish multiple goals – introducing applicants and employers, attracting applicant interest, screening out unsuitable applicants, becoming comfortable with the chosen option. This flexibility may account for its popularity; interviews (along with reference checks) are the most common selection procedure used across a wide range of jobs and industries (BNA, 1988; see Dipboye, 1992).

Their flexibility also makes interviews a difficult tool to use effectively. Interviews can vary widely in question types and sequences, topics covered, numbers of interviewers and applicants present, and consistency of these elements across applicants, as well as how much training and information interviewers have beforehand and what is done with their evaluations and recommendations afterward. Some interview formats are better than others at accomplishing various selection and recruitment goals; mismatches between the format and interview goal can limit or even interfere with managers' abilities to meet selection and recruitment goals.

Empirical research has concentrated on interview usefulness in making selection decisions, as measured by their criterion-related validity – that is, the correlation between interviewers' ratings and hired applicants' job performances. Although this research has yielded useful information about the interview formats needed to make good hiring decisions, the use of interviews to achieve other organizational goals, such as attracting good applicants, suggests the need for a broader perspective on what features make interviews effective.

At issue is the need to make good *joint* decisions – that is, to offer jobs to and successfully attract applicants with the best performance potential, and to reject or be rejected by applicants with low performance potential. To do this, managers should *structure* interviews to present and collect useful information in ways that help both themselves and applicants evaluate relevant, important issues.

The purpose of this chapter is to review and summarize what we know about decision-making and interviews as it pertains to improving applicant and organizational hiring decisions. A primary theme of this chapter is that, by taking into account how such joint decisions are made, managers can structure interviews to improve decision processes and outcomes. I begin by describing the decision-making literature as it pertains to the task of evaluating applicants and job opportunities. I then consider what we know about interviews and the factors that affect hiring decisions and job choices. Next, I discuss several principles for structuring interviews to facilitate effective decision-making. Finally, I conclude with examples of how ineffective interviews can be restructured to better accomplish both recruitment and selection goals.

DECISION-MAKING RESEARCH

Researchers using different theories have converged on the notion that when decision makers are confronted with multiple options, they often use a two-stage decision process (e.g., Beach, 1990; Payne, Bettman, and Johnson, 1988; Soelberg, 1967; Svenson, 1992). Although their details differ, these theories suggest that decision makers first reduce the total number of options by screening out clearly unsuitable options, often using simple decision rules. For example, a manager might decide that, if applicants don't have at least a GPA of 3.3 or two years of work experience, they should be rejected. During this simple screening process, decision makers often identify a prospective top choice, that is, an option that seems particularly likely to fit the decision criteria. At the second stage, decision makers evaluate the remaining options more thoroughly with the goal of choosing the "best" option. Unless a single option survives the initial screening process (in which case, it is chosen; Beach, 1990), decision makers usually devote more effort to this second-stage evaluation, although they often (but not always) select the prospective top choice from the first stage. This two-stage evaluation process has many parallels with employment interview decisions. Both applicants and interviewers may make initial decisions about whether to interview on the basis of little preliminary information (e.g., presence of grammatical errors in cover letters, company reputation or familiarity), and they often use later information (including that gained from interviews) to evaluate each other more thoroughly.

Within this two-stage evaluation/decision process, researchers have identified a variety of cognitive, motivational, and contextual factors that can influence decision-making. The *cognitive factors* include how decisions are framed (e.g., as the potential gain or potential loss of good candidates; Tversky and Kahneman, 1981), a variety of heuristics or mental shortcuts in evaluating options (e.g., using the similarity of applicants' profiles to those of successful job incumbents to judge suitability; Tversky and Kahneman, 1974), and a propensity to look for information that confirms, rather than disconfirms, one's expectations (Snyder and Swann, 1978). *Motivational factors* include decision makers' goals, which can include the desire to be accurate, the desire to have a good rationale for one's choice, or the desire to minimize the effort needed to reach a decision (Tyszka, 1998), and the desire to reach a particular conclusion or to choose a particular option (Kunda, 1990). Finally, *contextual factors* include the characteristics of the set of available options and whether options are evaluated one at a time or jointly (Hsee, Blount, Loewenstein, and Bazerman, 1999). Decision researchers often find that preferences shift depending on how options are presented – for example, a job candidate of average qualifications might be evaluated differently if interviewed as the only person available for the job rather than as one of several people available to be hired.

DECISION-MAKING IN INTERVIEWS

Interviews represent an applied situation in which employers and applicants collect information to make decisions about each other. As such, it is useful to examine what is known about their effects on interviewers' and applicants' decisions, given what we know about how malleable decision-making is generally.

Interviewers' decisions

With regard to interviewers, studies show that their judgments can be swayed by many of the cognitive, motivational, and contextual factors that affect other types of decisions. Interviewers often rely on stereotypes as mental shortcuts to help them determine applicant suitability, such as race, gender, age, or even weight-related biases (e.g., Gordon, Rozelle, and Baxter, 1988; Hitt and Barr, 1989; Pingitore, Dugoni, Tindale, and Spring, 1994). Perhaps because interviews are frequently used to screen out unsuitable applicants, interviewers give significantly more weight to negative than to positive information when judging applicant suitability (Macan and Dipboye, 1988; Rowe, 1989). Furthermore, interviewers often do not fully understand how they weight information about applicants in forming suitability judgments: they overestimate the importance of minor cues and underestimate the importance of major cues in how they have reached their judgments (Zedeck and Kafry, 1977).

Several features of the interview context and task can shift interviewers' motivation and thus their judgments. Research indicates that when determining applicant suitability, interviewers often consider personal qualities (e.g., interpersonal skills, goal orientation, appearance), how much they like applicants, and how well they think applicants would fit with their organization's culture (Rynes and Gerhart, 1990). This subjectivity leaves room for applicants to present themselves as likable, and thus garner more favorable interviewer evaluations. Further, studies have shown repeatedly that interviewers use résumé and other information about applicants to form preliminary impressions about applicant suitability, and then behave in ways during the interview to gather information that confirms their preliminary impressions (Dougherty, Turban, and Callender, 1994). Contextual factors such as whether applicants are evaluated sequentially (versus all at the same time) and the number of openings also influence suitability judgments, such that applicants are held to higher standards when evaluated as part of a larger pool or when there are fewer openings available (Huber, Northcraft, and Neale, 1990).

Given that interviewers' judgments can be influenced by so many different factors, an important question is whether interviewers in general can do a reasonable job of predicting which applicants will perform well if hired. Research has shown that individual differences exist in how accurate interviewers are at predicting performance – some interviewers consistently do a better job than others (Dougherty, Ebert, and Callender, 1986). Training interviewers does help improve their ability to predict who will perform well (Dougherty et al., 1986), as does having interviewers set goals to form accurate impressions (Neuberg, 1989). However, the biggest gains in predicting which applicants will perform well on the job seem to come from *structuring* interviews. Across interviewers, the use of structured interview formats leads to better prediction of job performance (correlations range from .35 to .62) than does the use of unstructured interviews (correlations range from .14 to .33; see Huffcutt and Arthur, 1994; McDaniel, Whetzel, Schmidt, and Maurer, 1994; Wiesner and Cronshaw, 1988).

Applicants' decisions

Although far less research has examined applicants' decision processes, the existing studies do suggest that many cognitive, motivational, and contextual factors can sway applicants' judgments. As with interviewers, applicants are concerned about finding jobs whose attributes provide a good fit with their interests and needs (Rynes, Bretz, and Gerhart, 1991). Applicants evaluate a job's attributes more positively, however, if their interviewer was personable and friendly during the interview (Turban and Dougherty, 1992). Applicants also show bias in their judgments depending on their view of the decision context: they evaluate jobs more favorably after the interview if they expect to have fewer total job offers than they do if they expect to have many offers (Stevens, 1997).

Researchers have not examined whether applicants' decisions following interviews predict their subsequent job satisfaction or tenure with organizations. None the less, some data indicate that interviews providing structured, realistic job information may help applicants self-select out of jobs in which they might be unhappy, and among those who do accept jobs, exposure to realistic job information leads to longer tenure on the job (see Premack and Wanous, 1985). This effect may be limited to situations in which applicants have other job offers from which to choose, however (Saks, Wiesner, and Summers, 1994).

Structured interviews

Although interview structure does appear to be an important means for improving joint decision-making, it is not always clear what it means to structure an interview. I define *interview structure* as any standardization of the interview format, which can occur across several dimensions. Campion, Palmer, and Campion (1997) identified 15 possible dimensions of interview structure, including their content and process. The *content* dimensions include basing question content on job analysis, asking the same questions of all applicants, asking better questions, limiting applicant questions, reducing the use of prompts or elaboration, ensuring that all interviews are of the same length, and eliminating interviewers' access to background information about applicants received before the interview. The *process* dimensions include scoring each answer with anchored rating scales, taking detailed notes, using multiple interviewers, having the same interviewers rate all applicants, restricting cross-talk among interviewers, using statistical procedures to combine interviewers' ratings, and training all interviewers. The next section uses research findings to derive sub-principles about which of these dimensions to structure to improve organizations' and applicants' decisions.

IMPROVING DECISION-MAKING THROUGH INTERVIEW STRUCTURE

Structuring interviews to improve decision-making necessarily involves trade-offs between the use of standardized practices and interviewer/applicant discretion. That is, highly structured interview formats substantially reduce interviewer and applicant flexibility to adapt interviews to meet their needs. For interviewers, this may lessen job challenge and satisfaction (see chapter 6 below), thereby undermining motivation or performance. Among applicants, reduced discretion may lead them to view the interview procedures as unfair or as signals that the organization does not value employees' independent contributions (Rynes, 1989). For these reasons, the principles below are designed to balance the benefits of structure with the need for some discretion.

Sub-principle 1: train interviewers

Providing training in effective selection and recruitment techniques enables interviewers to adapt interviews to the needs of each situation while improving decision-making by adding some structure. If interviewers need to concentrate on selection during their interviews (i.e., due to large numbers of applicants who cannot be screened with other preliminary devices such as cognitive ability tests; see chapter 1 above), training can focus on how to generate interview questions based on job analysis that differentiate good from poor performers. Research indicates that, without training, interviewers ask fewer open-ended, secondary, and performance-differentiating questions (Stevens, 1998). Screening-oriented interviewers can also be trained to evaluate applicants' answers by making finer discriminations among performance levels. Again, research suggests that untrained interviewers are significantly harsher in their evaluations than are trained interviewers when screening applicants (Stevens, 1998). Thus, training can help ensure that interviewers' evaluations are more consistent across different contexts (e.g., number of openings, interview purpose).

If interviewers must focus on recruitment (e.g., due to labor shortages), they can be trained to volunteer helpful information for use in applicants' decision-making. They should also be trained to listen carefully to applicants' questions and concerns and to respond warmly, as these behaviors predict increased applicant attraction (Turban and Dougherty, 1992). Regardless of the interview's purpose, all interviewers should be trained to control the flow and sequence of topics discussed during interviews. Without training, interviewers do not provide an overview of how the interview time will be spent and often digress into unrelated topics while using less than the allotted time for interviewing purposes (Stevens, 1998). Moreover, applicants perceive untrained interviewers as less professional and less organized than they do trained interviewers. For some applicants, this may result in lowered organizational attraction, due to inferences about how employees are likely to be treated (e.g., Rynes, 1989).

Sub-principle 2: develop standard questions and scoring criteria, based on job analysis, for use with all applicants

In some cases, it may be impractical to provide extensive interviewer training or to ask interviewers to develop their own job-related questions. In these cases, organizations may wish to replace or supplement interviewer training with an organizational initiative to develop standardized questions for particular job categories. Such initiatives would be most relevant when interviews are oriented toward selection. Standardized questions improve decision-making by ensuring that the information obtained is job relevant and comparable across all applicants. Moreover, using a set of standard questions and evaluation criteria prepared in advance may reduce confirmatory bias among interviewers, who look for and behave in ways that prompt applicants to give information consistent with interviewers' preliminary expectations (Dougherty et al., 1994).

Sub-principle 3: request that interviewers take detailed notes on applicants' answers

Taking notes on how applicants respond to each question can ensure accurate recall of the information conveyed. It can also increase learning (Kiewra, DuBois, Christian, McShane, Meyerhoffer, and Roskelley, 1991) and may communicate to applicants that interviewers are interested in what they have to say. Requesting that interviewers record the details of answers, rather than their conclusions about applicants, can reduce task complexity – interviewers can listen to and follow up on applicants' answers without having to simultaneously rate answers *in situ*. This should help them consider more carefully what applicants have to say, and make ratings without the added pressure of maintaining the interview dialog or shielding their evaluations from applicants who are seated nearby.

Sub-principle 4: if pre-interview information about applicants is provided, ensure that it is valid

Research has shown that, when interviewers have access to information about applicants before the interview (e.g., from résumés or test scores), this information leads them to form hypotheses about applicant suitability (Snyder and Swann, 1978). Given that decision makers try to identify their prospective top choices during initial screening, this tendency is not surprising. However, two problems may arise. First, interviewers may behave in ways that prompt applicants to confirm interviewers' expectations. Second, the incremental validity – the added benefit of using interviews along with other selection devices to predict job performance – is reduced.

These problems have led some researchers to recommend that all pre-interview information about applicants be withheld from interviewers (e.g., Dipboye, 1989). Although this would ensure that interviewers are not biased, it may not be practical. For example, this procedure would not enable interviewers to clarify or probe incomplete or ambiguous résumé or application information. It also makes it harder for interviewers to understand the work or educational context of applicants' answers to interview questions; applicants' answers to the same behavioral interview question might be evaluated differently if interviewers knew more about the circumstances in which applicants' behavior occurred. Finally, the downsizing and restructuring initiatives in many organizations have limited the staff available to make hiring decisions. Often the same individuals must both screen résumés to determine whom to interview and then conduct the interviews. Withholding pre-interview information about applicants in such circumstances is not possible.

If interviews are being used to help *recruit* applicants, access to pre-interview information may be helpful in determining how to discuss the job and company. The primary concern here would be to ensure that any pre-interview information provided is valid – for example, cognitive ability test scores or data about prior job performance. If interviewers' pre-interview expectations are based on valid information, behavioral confirmation tendencies during the interview should pose less of a problem.

The concern about incremental validity – what interviews add to selection decisions beyond what is provided by other selection devices – is an issue primarily if organizations require multiple, non-redundant predictors of job performance. This might be the case if the job is one in which excellent performance is needed quickly and performance problems may lead to catastrophic results (e.g., senior management positions, jobs involving handling of hazardous equipment or materials). In these situations, pre-interview information might be usefully withheld. In less extreme situations, however, valid pre-interview information might be released to help managers reach greater confidence in their final selection of applicants. Recall that the second stage in many decisions involves differentiating options to choose the best one; thus, interviews may be less important as predictors of performance than in helping organizational representatives feel comfortable with the applicants selected.

Sub-principle 5: ask applicants about their decision processes and criteria, and share realistic information tailored to those processes and criteria

Just as managers are interested in applicants who fit with their organizations, applicants typically seek organizations that provide a good fit with their interests and needs (Rynes, Bretz, and Gerhart, 1991). Applicants are concerned about many of the same criteria: job type, location, pay level, training opportunities. However, the type of information they want and how these criteria will affect their decision process varies both across applicants and across time among the same applicants. Accordingly, interviewers can structure interviews to help applicants make good decisions by asking about the factors that will be important in applicants' decisions and the context in which their decisions will be made.

There are several benefits to this form of interview structure. First, interviewers can offer realistic information tailored to applicants' interests, rather than providing a standard "speech" about their organizations' positive attributes. To the extent that other firms do not provide such individualized approaches, this practice may help firms gain an advantage in attracting applicants' interest. A second benefit is that such information can help interviewers estimate the probability that an offer would be accepted if extended. Applicants for whom one's organization does not meet important criteria are less likely to accept offers, and firms that identify likely mismatches early may better spend their time and effort pursuing other attractive applicants who are more likely to accept offers.

Interviewers may also find it helpful to inquire about applicants' decision process, particularly the number of offers they expect to receive or have received. This contextual factor has been shown to have dramatic effects on decision-making in other contexts – decision makers may reverse their preference for the same option when it is presented by itself instead of as one of multiple options from which to choose (Hsee et al., 1999). Consistent with this, recruitment research has shown that applicants who expect to receive fewer offers evaluate a given firm more favorably after their interviews with that firm than do applicants who expect to receive multiple job offers (Stevens, 1997). Interviewers thus may gain insight into how their recruitment information will be received by asking about applicants' expectations for success in their job searches.

CASE EXAMPLES

I have suggested that structure helps interviewers gather and disseminate information useful for making decisions. To illustrate this process, I will provide several examples from my own research. The first example comes from the transcript of an untrained interviewer who was screening applicants for a large public accounting firm. My research found that untrained interviewers ask fewer open-ended, follow-up, and performance-differentiating questions. They also tend to ask patterns of such questions in ways that are transparent – that is, phrased to indicate the desired response. This interviewer's questions are typical of this (the numbers represent turns at talk).

211. **INTERVIEWER.** What else have you done that ah, you feel would be helpful to you in public accounting?
212. **APPLICANT.** Oh, gee, as far as extracurricular? Well I was in a lot of service clubs and, you know, I've worked with people, done March of Dimes, things like that. Just dealing with people.
213. **INTERVIEWER.** How would you say your communication skills are?
214. **APPLICANT.** I think they're pretty good. I think I have pretty good communication skills. Listening is part of it, yeah, so –
215. **INTERVIEWER.** Okay.

When screening applicants, this interviewer would obtain more useful information by rephrasing and following up on these questions. For example, the question about what the applicant has done that would be helpful in a career in public accounting would yield more helpful data if the interviewer asked follow-up questions about what roles the applicant had held in various service clubs, and what specific things she had done for the March of Dimes. Asking about specific instances in which the applicant had worked with other people in these roles would provide important clues about how the applicant would interact with clients and co-workers. Likewise, the question about communication skills would prompt most applicants to answer that they had good communication skills – the "right" answer is transparent. Rather than asking the applicant to evaluate her own skills and taking this information at face value, the interviewer might instead ask about instances in which the applicant has had to deal with misunderstandings with other students or co-workers, and what she did to address the problem. Answers to this type of question would provide more concrete data about the applicant's communication skills and would allow fewer opportunities for the applicant to manage the interviewer's impression.

In contrast, the following (edited) segment shows how trained interviewers with standardized questions phrased to follow up on and differentiate applicants' performance potential can gather high-quality information.

103. **INTERVIEWER.** Now I'd like to spend a little bit of time talking about decision-making and problem-solving. Tell me about a particular difficult decision you had to make.

104. **APPLICANT.** Um, well . . . that ah, decision on the design approach, it was very difficult for me. 'Cause I didn't want to − I had the authority to overrule the design team. But I didn't want to use that um, unless I was absolutely sure they were wrong. I didn't want to alienate either the architect-engineer or the design team. And that resulted in a lot of squabbles and a lot of running back and forth negotiating between people to find out what − what was the best way . . .

105. **INTERVIEWER.** Mmm. So what were the things, some things you just considered in your decision?

106. **APPLICANT.** Um, I had to consider the qualifications of the person. Ah, whether they really knew what they were talking about. Um, another factor was there was a definite bias between the design team and the architect-engineer. They all took many years of, of infighting. And I had to try to consider how much of this is just due to the fact that "This person's designing it so I know it's no good," as opposed to, "It's just . . . not going to work in our best interests."

107. **INTERVIEWER.** Okay. And so what do you . . . see then you decided where you ended up going with . . . ?

108. **APPLICANT.** Design team's modifications, even though it was more expensive. In the long run, it proved to be ah, a better, um more cost-effective way of operating.

Recruitment goals can also be met by structuring interviews through training and use of standardized questions. My research has indicated that recruitment-oriented interviewers were less likely than screening-oriented interviewers to receive training. Given that untrained interviewers are perceived as less organized and less professional, this trend is unfortunate. Untrained interviewers tended to talk more and to jump around between asking and answering questions, providing unrequested information, and digressing into non job-related topics. This problem is illustrated in the next example, in which an untrained interviewer attempted to recruit an applicant for an insurance sales position. Although this segment is edited, much of the dialog between this interviewer and applicant followed the same pattern in which the interviewer did most of the talking.

25–31. **INTERVIEWER.** Here are some reasons why you would want to choose a career with [name of firm]. We guarantee your income while you start, develop your own image on being your own boss, getting, ah, getting into management career status, extra benefits, ah, and on the back here, are twelve good reasons . . . why you would want to be an insurance agent. And, um, here is, ah, a brochure that explains ah, the training program in general . . . terms. It's a lifelong training program. Um, we have, we feel, the finest training, uh, in the industry, ahh, as a company . . . And I believe, in my district, we have, ah, the finest training in America simply because we use the company training in the first six–twelve months or so, and after that we go into material, we make available to you material from the Insurance Institute of America. Now when I say make available to you, ah, we recruit and train people from all walks of life. Some people can't handle the material from the Insurance Institute of America because it's college level and/or they don't have the math background or they don't have the interest, study skills . . . to do it. I put on six people in 19[. . .] and to date, ah, none of them have taken advantage of all the material that I could give them. Because, well, it's not all bad either. Some of them, three of them are college students and they're doing so well that they don't have the time, they won't take the time to, to attend the course. Ah, one of 'em has gone through a couple of 'em or attempted to go through a couple of 'em, but, ah, nevertheless I've kept my end of the bargain and I would make it available to her and now in their second or third year, ah, they would take it a little more serious, ah, the more advanced learning of insurance. Okay?

32. **APPLICANT.** Um-hmm.
33. **INTERVIEWER.** So we say we'll make it available to you, if you're good enough to take advantage of it, that's fine.
34. **APPLICANT.** Um-hmm.

This interviewer clearly has a lot of positive information about his company to convey to applicants. Yet, this approach – doing all of the talking, without finding out the applicant's interests or criteria for making decisions – doesn't allow him to tailor his "pitch" to her as an individual. He may or may not cover information about his company that would be of interest to her. A smarter strategy would be to ask her questions about why she was exploring a career in insurance sales, what she is looking for in a job or company, and what other jobs and organizations she has considered. Not only would this approach be more efficient in communicating the information of greatest interest to her, but it would also convey interest and concern in her as an individual. This interviewer might also spend some time talking about the less attractive aspects of being in insurance sales as a way to make the rest of the information he provides appear more balanced and credible.

A better way to approach this issue is provided in the final example, which is too lengthy to reprint here. The opening was for a human resources internship rotation program in a large conglomerate, and the interviewer determined through the résumé and some preliminary questions that the applicant had outstanding qualifications. She then shifted the focus of their discussion to the factors that would be important in the applicant's decision, and discovered that his wife was applying to medical schools across the country. This enabled the interviewer to pinpoint several divisions to which he could be assigned that were located near his wife's preferred schools. Note that, had she relied on a prepared speech about the company's programs and benefits, she would have neglected to provide this critical information about how her company could meet this applicant's needs.

SUMMARY

Interviews are typically used as one in a set of selection/recruitment tools for helping to make organizational entry decisions. Because they are flexible, interviews can be used to accomplish multiple purposes, such as recruitment, introductions, screening out unsuitable candidates, and so on. This flexibility can also be a hindrance, however, as research on decision-making shows that decision processes are susceptible to myriad cognitive, motivational, and contextual influences that may degrade the quality of the final decision.

Increasing interview structure can help managers achieve their recruitment or selection goals by helping to minimize the impact of extraneous influences on interviewers' and applicants' decision processes. Structuring interviews introduces some standardization in procedures to make the judgments that follow less variable. Wisely structuring interviews to balance the need for standardization with the need for interviewer and applicant discretion can ensure that both organizations and applicants get the most out of the process.

REFERENCES

Beach, L. R. (1990). *Image theory: Decision making in personal and organizational contexts.* Chichester, UK: Wiley.

Bureau of National Affairs (1988). *Recruiting and selection procedures.* PPF Survey No. 146, May.

Campion, M. A., Palmer, D. K., and Campion, J. E. (1997). A review of structure in the selection interview. *Personnel Psychology*, 50, 655–702.

Dipboye, R. L. (1989). Threats to the incremental validity of interviewer judgments. In R. W. Eder and G. R. Ferris (eds.), *The employment interview: Theory, research, and practice* (45–60). Newbury Park, CA: Sage.

Dipboye, R. L. (1992). *Selection interviews: Process perspectives.* Cincinnati, OH: South-Western Publishing Co.

Dougherty, T. W., Ebert, R. J., and Callender, J. C. (1986). Policy capturing in the employment interview. *Journal of Applied Psychology*, 71, 9–15.

Dougherty, T. W., Turban, D. B., and Callender, J. C. (1994). Confirming first impressions in the employment interview: A field study of interviewer behavior. *Journal of Applied Psychology*, 79, 659–65.

Gordon, R. A., Rozelle, R. M., and Baxter, J. C. (1988). The effect of applicant age, job level, and accountability on the evaluation of job applicants. *Organizational Behavior and Human Decision Processes*, 41, 20–33.

Hitt, M. A., and Barr, S. H. (1989). Managerial selection decision models: Examination of configural cue processing. *Journal of Applied Psychology*, 74, 53–61.

Hsee, C. K., Blount, S., Loewenstein, G. F., and Bazerman, M. H. (1999). Preference reversals between joint and separate evaluations of options: A review and theoretical analysis. *Psychological Bulletin*, 125, 576–90.

Huber, V. L., Northcraft, G. B., and Neale, M. A. (1990). Effects of decision strategy and number of openings on employment selection decisions. *Organizational Behavior and Human Decision Processes*, 45, 276–84.

Huffcutt, A. I., and Arthur, W. Jr. (1994). Hunter and Hunter (1984) revisited: Interview validity for entry-level jobs. *Journal of Applied Psychology*, 79, 184–90.

Kiewra, K. A., DuBois, N. F., Christain, D., McShane, A., Meyerhoffer, M. Y., and Roskelley, D. (1991). Note-taking functions and techniques. *Journal of Educational Psychology*, 83, 240–5.

Kunda, Z. (1990). The case for motivated reasoning. *Psychological Bulletin*, 108, 480–98.

Macan, T. H., and Dipboye, R. L. (1988). The effects of interviewers' initial impressions on information gathering. *Organizational Behavior and Human Decision Processes*, 42, 364–87.

McDaniel, M. A., Whetzel, D. L., Schmidt, F. L., and Maurer, S. D. (1994). The validity of employment interviews: A comprehensive review and meta-analysis. *Journal of Applied Psychology*, 79, 599–616.

Neuberg, S. L. (1989). The goal of forming accurate impressions during social interaction: Attenuating the impact of negative expectancies. *Journal of Personality and Social Psychology*, 56, 374–86.

Payne, J. W., Bettman, J. R., and Johnson, E. J. (1988). Adaptive strategy selection in decision making. *Journal of Experimental Psychology: Learning, Memory and Cognition*, 14, 534–52.

Pingitore, R., Dugoni, B. L., Tindale, R. S., and Spring, B. (1994). Bias against overweight job applicants in a simulated employment interview. *Journal of Applied Psychology*, 79, 909–17.

Premack, S. L., and Wanous, J. P. (1985). A meta-analysis of realistic job preview experiments. *Journal of Applied Psychology*, 70, 706–19.

Rowe, P. M. (1989). Unfavorable information and interview decisions. In R. W. Eder and G. R. Ferris (eds.), *The employment interview: Theory, research and practice* (pp. 77–89). Newbury Park, CA: Sage.

Rynes, S. L. (1989). The employment interview as a recruitment device. In R. W. Eder and G. R. Ferris (eds.), *The employment interview: Theory, research and practice* (pp. 127–41). Newbury Park, CA: Sage.

Rynes, S. L., Bretz, R. D., and Gerhart, B. (1991). The importance of recruitment in job choice: A different way of looking. *Personnel Psychology*, 44, 487–521.

Rynes, S., and Gerhart, B. (1990). Interviewer assessments of applicant "fit": An exploratory investigation. *Personnel Psychology*, 43, 13–35.

Saks, A. M., Wiesner, W. H., and Summers, R. J. (1994). Effects of job previews on self-selection and job choice. *Journal of Vocational Behavior*, 44, 297–316.

Snyder, M., and Swann, W. B. (1978). Hypothesis-testing processes in social interaction. *Journal of Personality and Social Psychology*, 36, 1202–12.

Soelberg, P. (1967). Unprogrammed decision making. *Industrial Management Review*, 8, 19–29.

Stevens, C. K. (1997). Effects of pre-interview beliefs on applicants' reactions to campus interviews. *Academy of Management Journal*, 40, 947–66.

Stevens, C. K. (1998). Antecedents of interview interactions, interviewers' ratings, and applicants' reactions. *Personnel Psychology*, 51, 55–85.

Svenson, O. (1992). Differentiation and consolidation theory of human decision making: A frame of reference for the study of pre- and post-decision processes. *Acta Psychologica*, 80, 143–68.

Turban, D. B., and Dougherty, T. W. (1992). Influences of campus recruiting on applicant attraction to firms. *Academy of Management Journal*, 35, 739–65.

Tversky, A., and Kahneman, D. (1974). Judgment under uncertainty: Heuristics and biases. *Science*, 185, 1124–30.

Tversky, A., and Kahneman, D. (1981). The framing of decisions and the psychology of choice. *Science*, 211, 453–8.

Tyszka, T. (1998). Two pairs of conflicting motives in decision making. *Organizational Behavior and Human Decision Processes*, 74, 189–211.

Wiesner, W. H., and Cronshaw, S. F. (1988). A meta-analytic investigation of the impact of interview format and degree of structure on the validity of the employment interview. *Journal of Occupational Psychology*, 61, 275–90.

Zedeck, S., and Kafry, D. (1977). Capturing rater policies for processing evaluation data. *Organizational Behavior and Human Performance*, 18, 269–94.

Part II

TRAINING AND PERFORMANCE APPRAISAL

4   Design Training Systematically
    EDUARDO SALAS AND JANIS A. CANNON-BOWERS

5   Design Performance Appraisal Systems to Improve Performance
    ANGELO S. DeNISI AND JORGE A. GONZALEZ

4

Design Training Systematically

EDUARDO SALAS AND JANIS A. CANNON-BOWERS

All employees undertake some form of formal or informal training throughout their professional careers. In fact, learning and training are a way of life in modern organizations, with employees expected to hold up-to-date, job-relevant knowledge, skills, and attitudes (KSAs: traditionally in the literature the "A" refers to ability; for our purpose here we refer to it as attitudes). Organizations also require that these KSAs are applied appropriately to the job as a means to remain competitive and to function effectively and profitably. Given the global economy and explosion of technology in recent years, the market demands these attributes from organizations – higher productivity, better service, higher profits, better performance, and increased quality. So organizations must provide (for the most part) the means for employees to acquire and maintain the needed KSAs. Human capital is the biggest asset organizations possess and they invest heavily in this capital. In fact, we know that organizations invest $55.3 billion in training their workforces (Bassi and Van Buren, 1998), and are responsible for providing workplace learning and performance-improvement interventions. Given this investment, organizations are being more strategic in demanding and supplying workplace learning opportunities. Training is going through a revolution in organizations and is enjoying some interesting times.

This concern for workplace learning and investment in training by industry and government has generated an explosion of training research from many disciplines. Educational, cognitive, social, military, industrial/organizational, and human factors psychologists, in conjunction with management scholars and system designers, have all contributed to a wealth of information about the design and delivery of training. We know more about training effectiveness than ever before. The field is now richer theoretically, methodologically, and empirically (Tannenbaum and Yukl, 1992). The literature on training continues to grow and has a promising future. There is also a concerted effort by scientists and practitioners of training to impact practice, exploit technological advances, manage knowledge, provide continuous learning environments, and make a difference in organizations.

In this chapter, we discuss four general training phases. These phases, if executed systematically, will generate effective training. We have also extracted from the research

Table 4.1 Summary of training phases, principles, and guidelines

Phase of training	Guiding principles	Guidelines
Analyze training needs	Focus on uncovering needed KSAs	◆ Analyze tasks for knowledge (cognitive) requirements as well as skill requirements ◆ Analyze tasks for attitude requirements ◆ Don't rely only on what subject-matter experts (SMEs) say about the tasks ◆ Employ sound principles of job/task analysis ◆ Train competencies, not tasks ◆ Seek to train common competencies that underlie several tasks ◆ Develop specific training objectives
	Prepare the organization for training	◆ Ensure the organization sends positive messages about training ◆ Allow employees to select training when possible ◆ Make mandatory training as painless as possible ◆ Ensure that employees see the value of training (valance)
Design and develop instruction	Rely on sound theories of learning as a basis for training design	◆ Seek guidance from literature
	Set up appropriate pre-practice conditions	◆ Use advance organizers where appropriate ◆ Use pre-practice briefs ◆ Train meta-cognitive strategies
	Apply sound instructional principles	◆ Tailor instructional strategy to match targeted KSAs/training objectives ◆ Provide hands-on practice where feasible (including role-plays) ◆ Provide models/demonstrations of desired behavior ◆ Ensure that underlying knowledge has been trained, before moving to skills ◆ Set difficult but achievable goals in training ◆ Design training to build self- (or collective-) efficacy ◆ Provide feedback in accordance with the guidelines in the literature ◆ To maximize transfer, structure the practice conditions

Seek to diagnose and remedy **KSA** deficiencies	• Measure performance against stated objectives • Develop measures of process as well as outcome • Develop measures at both the team and individual level (if applicable) • Use technology to aid measurement • Tailor subsequent instruction to current achievement level
Implement training Set up the training environment	◆ Train the trainers ◆ Ensure that the training facility is comfortable ◆ Provide adequate equipment/resources
Set a climate for learning	◆ Encourage participation ◆ Provide a non-critical environment ◆ Use feedback constructively ◆ Exploit technology to support the learning process
Prepare the environment to transfer the KSAs to the job	◆ Provide incentives for transfer ◆ Provide opportunities to practice targeted **KSAs** ◆ Ensure supervisory support ◆ Implement relapse prevention procedures ◆ Reinforce desired behavior ◆ Show employees the value of newly acquired KSAs
Evaluate the training Determine training effectiveness	◆ Examine training objectives and build evaluation criteria linked to those objectives ◆ Measure knowledge acquisition to diagnose the effectiveness of training ◆ Measure performance on the job ◆ Measure job-related attitudes
Assess organizational impact	◆ Ensure a link between training objectives and desired organizational outcomes ◆ Measure desired outcomes ◆ Measure outcomes at the appropriate level

generated over the last two decades (and maybe more) several guiding principles and guidelines in support of each phase. These phases, and the associated guiding principles and guidelines, represent what we know works, what needs to be done, and what must be considered when designing and delivering training in organizations. We hope that these will guide those in the practice of delivering and implementing training and provide food for thought for those interested in research.

We start with our most important advice: *Be systematic*. Effective training is accomplished when we approach it in sequential phases. As noted, effective training requires attention to four phases. We discuss these below and under each offer specific principles (i.e., principles to guide the focus and shape the essential elements needed in each phase) and guidelines. These are also summarized in table 4.1.

ANALYZE TRAINING NEEDS

Analyzing training needs is probably the most critical phase in designing training. Decisions made at the onset of training design drive the rest of the process. So analyzing training needs must be accomplished with care. Activities in this phase include determining skill deficiencies, forecasting new skill requirements, and setting an environment in the organization to facilitate learning.

Focus on uncovering needed KSAs

To uncover KSAs one must conduct a task analysis/cognitive task analysis. There are many tools for conducting these analyses (Levine, 1983; Klein and Militello, in press), all yielding a decomposition of the task requirements into the required KSAs to perform each. When conducting a task analysis/cognitive task analysis one needs to pay attention to several issues. For example, given the influence of information technology in most modern jobs, and thereby placing higher demand on cognitive skills, organizations should analyze tasks to uncover the knowledge (cognitive) requirements as well as skill requirements. We tend to focus on the "S" (of KSAs) because it is easier to observe, record, and track observable skills rather than relatively unobservable knowledge. And traditional task job/analysis approaches are good at delineating skills. But organizations (and traditional instructional design models) too often ignore the "K", an important component of many jobs. Knowledge – what one knows or needs to know about the tasks, the people, or the situation – is the basis for decision-making, judgment, problem detection and attention management. Therefore, understanding the knowledge requirements of a job, means identifying the strategies for making decisions, the patterns used to make a judgment, and the cues that are important for performing tasks. All of these are critical for designing, for example, effective decision-making training.

Attention should also be paid to the attitude requirements of a job. Job-related emotions are also an integral part of what people do in their work. Emotions shape how, when, and if people perform a task. What people feel about a task in some cases is as important as what they think or do. Attitudes such as self-efficacy, goal orientation, collective orientation, and mutual trust have been demonstrated to be powerful predictors of individual and group learning (e.g., Ford et al., 1997, 1998; Driskell and Salas,

1992). Despite this, organizations often overlook or underestimate attitude requirements. One way to be thorough in uncovering the needed KSAs is to employ sound principles of job/task analysis and cognitive task analysis (Levine, 1983; Klein and Militello, in press).

When conducting a task/cognitive analysis, designers almost always rely on subject-matter experts (SMEs). SME input and knowledge about the tasks are crucial. However, SME input must be managed. There are two issues here. First, we know that SMEs often have a difficult time articulating what they know. In fact, expertise is not necessarily accessible so that extracting task information is more an art than a science. However, knowledge elicitation techniques that help the process, and these seem to work (see Cooke, 1994), have been developed of late.

Second, SMEs know about the job, but not (necessarily) about designing training. We should rely on SMEs to articulate the task requirements, and rely on training experts for designing and delivering training. In many organizations, the SMEs (task experts) are also considered the training experts and sometimes even the training designers, which may lead to costly and inefficient training. SMEs, like others who are not training professionals, often hold simplistic models of training since they are not familiar with the science of training. In short, we recommend not relying only on SME input for designing training. Organizations should not assume that anyone who has ever attended training is an instructional expert. Instead, SMEs should be consulted for task requirements; training experts for designing training.

Prepare the organization and trainees for training

Recent models of training effectiveness clearly suggest that there are pre-training conditions that facilitate learning (e.g., Tannenbaum, Mathieu, Salas, and Cannon-Bowers, 1991). For example, the climate of an organization plays an integral role in the effectiveness of the training. That is, the perceived amount of support provided by the organization toward training dictates the learning outcome and transfer of what was learned back to the job. There are steps that organizations can take before designing and delivering training that will maximize success. First, we suggest conducting an organizational analysis. That is, determine whether the organization is ready for training. How is training to be used in the organization? What messages does the organization send with training? What are the rules (written or unwritten), policies, and procedures for training in the organization? These issues all affect how the organization communicates its values about training to its employees. We offer several suggestions about how to prepare the organization and trainees for training. For example, we suggest ensuring the organization sends positive messages about training. Ensure that employees see the benefit of training and are rewarded for seeking workplace learning opportunities – use training as a reward, not a punishment. Also, having a choice about attending training makes a difference. When trainees have a choice of attending, they have a higher motivation to learn; therefore, allow employees to select training when possible. In some cases, regulatory mandates dictate that certain training is completed. However, organizations should make mandatory training as painless as possible. When training is mandatory, provide motivational incentives (e.g. time off) where possible. Furthermore, how the organization communicates who goes to training also makes a difference. The manner in which trainees are selected and notified influences the satisfaction, motivation, and the outcome of the training. Finally, an aspect ignored by many organizations is the lack of communication to the trainees about the value of learning. Often employees ask themselves: Why do I have to take this training? Is this training important? How will it help me advance or help me to do a better job? Ensuring that employees see the value of training (valance) will go a long way in ensuring that targeted material is learned and applied to the job.

In sum, determining training needs is essential. Knowing what, why, when, who, and how to train before designing training is an organizational imperative. This is the first and most important step for designing and delivering effective training. A focus on uncovering needed KSAs and preparing the organization and trainees is an essential principle for getting the most out of training.

DESIGN AND DEVELOP INSTRUCTION

The second phase of training development consists of designing and developing the instructional content, objectives, materials, and curricula and preparing all the resources needed for delivering the training (whether on-the-job, within the organization's training department or in a remote facility). A number of very important choices happen during this phase. The instructional developer needs to decide, for example, in what medium the instruction will be delivered; in what sequence it will be delivered; what examples are appropriate for the content; how will trainees practice; what feedback will be delivered (and how); and what the instructor's role will be. These decisions determine the structure and nature of training. And the science of training can provide some guidance.

Rely on sound theories of learning as a basis for training design

Training is a behavioral/cognitive/affective event (Kraiger, Ford, and Salas, 1993). According to Goldstein (1993: 3), training is defined as "the acquisition of skills, concepts, or attitudes which result in improved performance in another environment." Training is about imparting job-relevant KSAs. It is about KSA acquisition and the transfer of these to the job and to novel situations. It is about improving the behavioral repertoire of employees so that they can cope with task demands. Therefore, training is designed to produce, for example, more capable supervisors, safer and more competent pilots, or more effective sales associates. The focus of the training is to ensure the trainees learn, for example, conflict resolution skills, leadership skills, decision-making skills or interpersonal skills. While these may seem like diverse and unrelated knowledge, skills, and attitudes, we know that learning occurs when trainees are presented with information about the task, when they are presented with examples or models of effective (or ineffective) performance; when they are allowed to practice the KSAs; and when feedback is given during and after the task is performed. While this sequence may seem obvious (and it is), current emphasis is often on the technology or the delivery mechanism of training, which detracts from the core of training – learning. A focus on learning then underscores the importance of conducting thorough training need analysis (as discussed above); designing learning environments; choosing relevant instructional strategies; facilitating transfer; and evaluating the training. We discuss these below in more detail.

We must not lose sight when designing training systems that learning is a dynamic process. Learning occurs over time; it is not a one-time event, single program, or isolated lecture. It is a continuous process that evolves and matures over time. Expert performance develops over ten years or more. Further, research shows that expertise develops with exposure to a variety of situations, with consistent and prolonged practice, and with feedback from either the task itself or from a coach/instructor. Research on expertise has provided useful insights about skill acquisition and learning with direct relevance to the design of training. These insights, generated by a science of learning, provide guidance on how to design effective learning environments (e.g., creating conditions for practice), for selecting instructional strategies (e.g., determining how to present and demonstrate job-relevant knowledge), facilitating transfer (e.g., what to reinforce on the job), and for evaluating the efficiency of training (e.g., what behavior, actions or events to measure). So, a focus on learning allows training designers to rely on the science of training.

The importance of theory in training (and for that matter in all applied psychology) cannot be overstated. Without theory, training design and delivery can lead to poor learning outcomes. Without theory, training research (and practice) becomes piecemeal and trivial, and the accumulation of knowledge is retarded. Training must comprise a set of theoretically based instructional strategies, methods, tools and content. In fact, a common misperception in organizations is that practice makes perfect. Organizations just want trainees to practice as much as possible in simulations or on the job. Few would argue that some practice is needed to learn a task. But not all practice is created equal. Practice needs to be guided, feedback has to be given, and it has to be related to the training objectives.

Training is more than just a program or a nice facility in the wilderness. And as already stated, training is more than just technology (e.g., multi-media). Therefore, designers must rely on theories to guide training design, and there are a number of theories that are useful. For example, Anderson's ACT (Anderson, 1983), mental models (Johnson-Laird, 1983), self-regulation (Collins, Brown, and Newman, 1989), metacognition (Cohen, Freeman, and Wolf, 1996), social learning (Bandura, 1986) and individual differences (Ackerman, 1987) just to name a few. There are also a number of frameworks that are relevant as well. For example, frameworks concerning transfer of training (Baldwin and Ford, 1988), training effectiveness (Tannenbaum, et al., 1991; Noe, 1986) and team training (Salas and Cannon-Bowers, 1997) can all inform training design.

Set up appropriate pre-practice conditions

Recently it has been suggested that attention needs to be paid to the pre-practice environment as a means to improve training (Cannon-Bowers, Rhodenizer, Salas, and Bowers, 1998). Specifically, it has been argued that steps can be taken before training begins that will enhance learning. For example, providing trainees with attentional advice – that is, information about which strategies will lead to optimal learning. In addition, training metacognitive (self-regulatory) skills can help trainees better manage their own learning process.

Other pre-practice conditions that can enhance learning include: advance organizers (i.e., providing organization of material ahead of training); goal orientation (i.e., getting trainees to focus on mastery of learning objectives rather than performance outcomes);

and preparatory information (i.e., explanation of psychological or emotional reactions that are likely to occur in stressful or difficult environments). In team training situations, team pre-briefs are also useful as a means to define team member roles and responsibilities and lay out coordination demands.

One of the greatest advantages of exploiting pre-practice conditions as a means to enhance learning is that they are relatively cheap and easy to implement. Certainly, it is worth an organization's while to investigate the applicability of these interventions to their training situations.

Apply sound instructional principles

Training is about applying pedagogically sound principles to the design and delivery of training. And there are many principles in the literature. These include, just to name a few: provide immediate and specific feedback, provide training in context, use cognitive and behavioral modeling, break complex tasks into simple pieces, ensure the active participation of the trainee, and allow for meaningful practice. It is our experience that many instructional designers do not use pedagogical principles to guide their design decisions. The problem is that application of this information may be more an art than a science. At the heart of the issue is the fact that the science of training has not (yet, at least) generated sufficient prescriptive guidance on how, when, and where to apply these principles. There is not one place or source where instructional designers can go to obtain specific, concrete, or clear guidance. The reasons for this are many and go beyond the scope of this chapter. However, there is some good news. Progress has been made and there are some pedagogically sound principles that can be used today. For example, we know that in order to elicit the targeted KSAs, designers should embed opportunities to practice them in exercises or simulations. These opportunities, in the form of events or "triggers," allow the observation (and practice) of the required KSAs so that subsequent feedback can be generated. Similarly, designers should ensure that two additional conditions are created. One is that the exercises, role-plays, or simulations provide hands-on practice (where feasible and affordable) of the targeted KSAs; a second is that the instructional strategy chosen provides models and/or demonstrations of desired behavior. So basically, designers should tailor the instructional strategy to match targeted KSAs and training objectives.

Another important consideration for instructional designers is that in structuring the sequence for training, one needs to ensure that the underlying knowledge has been trained, before moving to skills. Trainees must know what the concepts, rules, definitions, or procedures are before applying them to the task.

In addition, there are pockets of literature that provide specific guidance for designers. The goal-setting literature tells us to set difficult, but achievable goals in training. The feedback literature suggests, for example, that during skill acquisition one should provide accurate, relevant, and timely knowledge of results that are useful (there are many other feedback principles). Social learning theory clearly demonstrates that training should be designed to build self- as well as collective- (in the case of team training) efficacy. And the transfer of training literature shows that to maximize transfer, practice needs to be structured and sequenced in a way consistent with the targeted KSAs on the job. It also stands to reason that training should seek to impart underlying competencies – the KSAs – and not train tasks *per se*. Training tasks is inefficient and, depending on the complexity of the job, may be impossible to achieve. Conversely, training underlying competencies facilitates transfer of skills to many tasks. Also, designers should seek to train common competencies that underlie several tasks. This will also enhance the probabilities of transfer of the trained skills to the job.

So, there are pedagogically sound principles (see table 4.1) that can guide the design process. These must be followed to ensure effective training delivery.

Seek to diagnose and remedy KSA deficiencies

The issue of measurement is of paramount concern to training design and delivery. Measurement is the basis for learning. Measurement creates opportunities to assess what has been learned and what else is needed. Therefore, all training must measure performance against stated objectives. In order to be diagnostic in training, the measurement system must be sensitive to moment-to-moment changes in skill acquisition and must determine the level achieved. Clearly, then, for training one needs to develop measures of process as well as outcome. In addition to developing measures of process and outcome, the level of analysis is also a crucial consideration. Consideration must be given to developing measures at both the team and individual levels (if applicable). Recent technological advances in personal computers afford new opportunities for measurement. Today, hand-held devices (i.e., portable PCs) can be used to measure performance during training unobtrusively. In fact, technology should be exploited to aid measurement where appropriate and affordable.

In sum, designing and developing instruction requires a focus on learning, on applying learning principles, and on seeking to diagnose and remedy KSA deficiencies. Instructional developers need to employ the science of training to inform their decisions on design. This is another imperative.

IMPLEMENT TRAINING

Training cannot be isolated from the organization system of which it is part. The organizational climate matters for training: the policies and procedures in the organization make a difference in how training is perceived; the opportunities to practice the recently acquired KSAs facilitate transfer of training; how trainees were selected for or chose training influences learning; how management communicates the importance (or not) of training to employees has an impact on training effectiveness; the level of congruence between individual and organization goals determines the impact of training (Kozlowski and Salas, 1997); and organizational conditions before and after training affect learning outcomes (Noe, 1986).

Set up the training environment

Where and how the training is conducted is important. Some organizations do not consider this essential and do not spend the time in the "little details." However, ignoring these details may send signals to trainees that the organization does not care about them. The basics of training have to be covered; many of these are simple things. To begin with, organizations should make sure the training facility (or where the training will be conducted) is comfortable and pleasant to the trainees. That is, the room temperature is adequate, the sitting arrangements are organized to support the type of training, there is enough light, and the facility has adequate equipment and instrumentation. While covering these issues will not guarantee learning, they will enable learning. Setting up the training environment is a necessary but not sufficient condition for learning. Another area of concern here is the trainer and his/her preparation. Organizations often ignore or underestimate the importance of preparing the trainers to be effective. Unfortunately, much of the variability in learning can be attributed to the instructor and his/her abilities. Simply stated – train the trainer.

Set a climate for learning

How the training is delivered can also facilitate or hinder learning. Creating a learning environment is not difficult – a few simple suggestions are worth mentioning. First, encourage participation from the trainees. Design training such that interaction and practice is required. Very little is learned when one is passive during the learning process. Next, from the onset the learning environment should be one that is supportive, non-critical, and where errors are allowed. Trainees will be more engaged and willing to exert more effort if they believe that there are no negative consequences for trying the new KSAs during the training. Similarly, ensure that the feedback provided is constructive. It can be critical, but must be presented in a way that gives trainees the sense that it will lead to better acquisition of the skills. Certainly, one way to encourage participation and engage trainees is through the use of technology. Technology (e.g., multimedia systems, games), when carefully inserted in the training to support the learning process, can create wonderful results. Like anything else, however, technology needs to be managed so that it is relevant and supports the training objectives, not just because it "looks good."

Prepare the transfer environment

This is a principle often overlooked by organizations. What happens after the training is delivered is as important as what gets done (and how) before and during training. Many organizations fail to manage and prepare the transfer setting. Even after designing, delivering, and implementing the best training system, the organization must create procedures and mechanisms for post-training support to facilitate transfer of KSAs to the job. Otherwise, the training may end up being a waste of time, money, and effort for all involved.

There are several ways to increase the probability that trainees will apply the newly acquired KSAs on the job. These are simple, relatively cheap, and require good communication as a means to manage the post-training climate. For example, organizations can provide incentives (e.g., time off, monetary rewards) to encourage trainees to use the new KSAs. These incentives can be communicated – clearly, concisely, and precisely – to the trainees as they leave the learning experience. These incentives should be linked to specific behaviors or actions related to the training objectives. In this manner, the trainee knows what to expect and ought to be encouraged to apply what was learned.

The trainee alone cannot be responsible for ensuring transfer – back on the job, a key player is the supervisor. Supervisor and peers must also be prepared to deal with employees who have acquired new KSAs: they can make or break the transfer of KSAs by rewarding appropriate behavior. Too often, trainees return to the job only to be told to forget everything they learned in training and are shown the "real" way to accomplish the job. This situation requires two actions. First, the needs-analysis process must better align the training with actual practices on the job. Second, organizations should ensure that supervisors are encouraged to reinforce employees when behaviors or actions are taken that indicate the application of the learned KSAs.

In addition, organizations need to show employees the value of the newly acquired KSAs to their jobs and their success, and to the success of the organization. That is, it must be understood that application of the new KSAs is a worthwhile activity with tangible payoffs. Therefore, employees will be motivated to exert the required effort. Second, supervisors need to provide or create opportunities for trainees to practice the learned KSAs. In addition, to avoid problems in the long run, relapse prevention procedures should be implemented so that employees do not revert to old behaviors or habits.

Transfer of training is not difficult. But it takes commitment from the organization, management, and supervisors. It takes managing the transfer process by putting in place managerial systems that help – reward systems, managerial support, and opportunities to practice. It demands continuous attention until desired outcomes are achieved.

Evaluate Training

The final phase in training system design involves developing mechanisms to assess whether training was effective, and more importantly, why it was effective (or ineffective) so that required improvements can be made. Unfortunately, many organizations do not evaluate training effectiveness. A primary reason is that training evaluation can be costly and resource intensive. It often requires specialized expertise and a team of people who can collect and interpret performance data. However, organizations fail to consider that ineffective training can be far more costly in the long run (in terms of poor performance, errors, and missed opportunities) than an investment up front in training evaluation. Therefore, it is imperative that organizations assess the effectiveness of training and use the information gathered through such assessments as a means to improve training design.

Determine training effectiveness

An effective training evaluation involves several steps. To begin with, it is important to establish a clear link between the training objectives and what is measured in the evaluation. While this may seem obvious, it is sometimes the case that organizations expect training to accomplish goals that were never intended by the training in the first place. In addition, if training is only one factor in a complex phenomenon, then it alone cannot be expected to effect the desired change. For example, it may not be reasonable to expect that a training system designed to impart knowledge about safety would actually result in fewer accidents if other factors such as fatigue could contribute to accidents as well. Therefore, the first step in any good training evaluation is to carefully examine training objectives and then build evaluation criteria that are linked closely to those objectives.

Once training objectives have been examined, it is necessary to develop measures of learning (i.e., whether trainees actually acquired the targeted knowledge). Recently, training experts have argued that insufficient attention has been paid to measuring the cognitive outcomes of training (Kraiger et al., 1993). This practice of ignoring cognitive components is troublesome for several reasons. First, in some cases the training is designed to impart knowledge; hence the only way to assess training effectiveness is to measure knowledge acquisition. An example here would be training designed to teach employees about a new product line. It should be noted that there are issues associated with measuring knowledge with simple paper-and-pencil tests (see Kraiger et al., 1993). Modern training experts have looked to constructs such as schema and mental models as drivers of the knowledge-measurement process.

A second reason to measure knowledge acquisition is that it is often the case that skilled performance has an underlying knowledge component. Therefore, knowledge measures are essential for diagnosing the effectiveness (or ineffectiveness) of training. For example, if a trainee fails to behave as intended after training, it may be because he/she did not acquire requisite knowledge, or, having acquired knowledge appropriately, did not adequately acquire the skill. This example highlights once again the importance of diagnostic measures of training effectiveness. Without them, training designers are left to wonder why training did or did not work, and are unable to apply the correct remedial strategy.

The next step in a full evaluation of training effectiveness is to measure what Kirkpatrick calls training performance (Kirkpatrick, 1976). By this is meant assessing whether targeted skills were acquired. The actual instruments used to measure training performance will vary as a function of the task. In some cases, requiring the trainee to perform a job sample may be the best way to assess training performance. Where appropriate, role-plays or simulations of the actual task may also be used as a means to assess training performance. In any case, the goal of this phase of evaluation is to determine whether trainees have acquired the targeted behavior before going back to the job.

Another outcome of training that should be measured is job-related attitudes. In particular, it has been found consistently that training should build self-efficacy, and that self-efficacy, in turn, will positively affect performance. Therefore, moderate to high self-efficacy should be evident if training is successful. A number of measures of self-efficacy have been employed in past research and can be tailored to a variety of applications and tasks (Mathieu and Martineau, 1997).

Once it has been determined that training has imparted the desired knowledge, skills, and attitudes, the next phase of the evaluation is to assess performance back on the job. A major complication with this type of assessment is that many factors will affect job performance besides the training. In fact, making a direct link between training and job performance can be quite difficult. However, it is essential to make this link because it is the only way to determine whether the training system has value to the organization. There are a number of ways to assess job performance, including observation, supervisor judgment, peer assessment, self-report, or other, unobtrusive measures. This final category would include collecting outcome data (either manually or by computer), consulting naturally occurring performance records (e.g., sales or safety logs), or using archival data.

Once training evaluation data have been collected they can be used to accomplish several goals. First of all, evaluation data can be used as feedback for the course. If the targeted knowledge and skills have not been acquired, changes to the training are necessary. Moreover, if the evaluation was conducted properly, the nature of these changes should be apparent. For example, if trainees are learning material successfully in training but are not able to transfer that knowledge to the job, it may be that the training is falling short in imparting needed skills. On the other hand, the training may be successful in teaching the targeted knowledge and skills, but trainees are still not performing as desired on the job. In this case, it would seem that an assessment of the training objectives or the job environment itself is in order.

Assess organizational impact

Another aspect of training evaluation involves assessing whether training had the desired impact on organization-level variables (e.g., overall productivity, safety, and quality). As with other aspects of evaluation, it is first necessary to establish that the training objectives are directly linked to the desired organizational outcomes. Obviously, if they are not, then either the training objectives or expectations of the organization regarding what training can accomplish must change. But even when training objectives and desired outcomes are aligned appropriately, training may still not lead to the expected change. This is due to the fact that, as stated previously, many variables will affect the attainment of a particular outcome besides training. Hence, care must be taken to at least consider extraneous factors when assessing the impact of training.

It must also be recognized that in assessing the effect of training on the organization, the level at which the outcome is being measured must also be taken into account (see Kozlowski et al., 2000). For example, if a training program is designed to promote cleanliness among employees, it may be appropriate to "sum" cleanliness behaviors across employees and departments to arrive at an overall index of cleanliness. This index could then be used to assess whether a training program designed to increase cleanliness was successful. On the other hand, if the behavior of one department is dependent on another, then a simple summing of behavior may not be appropriate. Instead, it may be important to measure the desired outcome at the department level, since interactions among organizational units could obscure the true picture.

Overall, it is in the organization's best interest to evaluate training effectiveness. Knowing not only *whether* a training program is successful but also, more specifically, *why* it was (or was not) successful, can provide information crucial to future decision-making. Specifically, decisions about how to change or upgrade the training, whether to revisit the training objectives, or whether to change expectations about training outcomes, all hinge on good training-evaluation data. Moreover, ineffective training is costly and potentially dangerous. It behooves any organization to find out whether the training it provides is effective and how it might be improved.

A SUCCESS: THE AVIATION EXPERIENCE

Teamwork improves performance in some jobs; in others, it is an imperative. For example, teamwork in the cockpit is essential – lives depend on it. We know that 60–80 percent of the accidents or mishaps in aviation are due to human error, and a large percentage of those are caused by coordination problems in the cockpit. Research on team training has developed instructional strategies to enhance teamwork in complex environments such as the cockpit. These strategies are being applied now throughout the aviation industry.

In fact, the military aviation community (and the commercial airlines as well) have been systematically implementing team training (see Weiner, Kanki, and Helmreich, 1993). More specifically, the navy has designed and delivered team training for its aviation platforms for a number of years. And this team training was designed systematically.

Training scientists and learning specialists, in partnership with subject-matter experts (i.e. pilots), developed a methodology that systematically helps instructional developers design and deliver Crew Resource Management (CRM) training in the navy (Salas, Prince, et al., 1999). This methodology illustrates how to apply the four phases outlined in this chapter. It begins with an identification of operational/mission requirements and the required team competencies (i.e., needs analysis). Extensive interviews and observations were conducted in order to ensure the required KSAs for coordination were identified. The literature was reviewed and a theoretical framework developed. In parallel to this process, the scientists, sponsors, users, and industry representatives met on an ongoing basis to discuss organiza-tional procedures and policies that needed to be in place as the methodology evolved. In the end, this proved to be a very valuable dialogue – it prepared the navy for the training. Specifically, it created a learning climate – before the training was implemented, during, and after. Once training objectives were derived and validated by SMEs, the methodology called for designing and creating opportunities for practice and feedback, developing measurement tools for feedback, and implementing the training. The methodology ended with suggestions for ensuring that a multi-component evaluation protocol was built into the training (see Salas, Prince, et al., 1999 for an in-depth discussion).

This methodology has been translated into a detailed set of specifications. These are a set of step-by-step instructions that can be used by instructional designers to develop the curriculum and supporting materials. Evaluation of those communities that have fol-lowed this methodology suggest that crews react better to the instruction, learn more about teamwork, and exhibit more teamwork behaviors in the cockpit when needed (Salas, Fowlkes, et al., 1999) as a result of the training.

In sum, this methodology has been implemented and tested in several communities – and it works (Salas, Fowlkes, et al., 1999). It works because the methodology uncovers the needed KSAs, prepares the organization for the training, relies on theories of learning, and applies sound instructional principles to the design of the team training. It works because the training seeks to diagnose and remedy KSAs deficiencies. It works because the implementation process sets the right climate for learning and transfer and evaluates its impact. It works because the methodology guides the instructional developer through a *systematic process* incorporating all the phases outlined here, and utilizes the best information that the science of training can offer.

A FAILURE: TRAINING THE SALES FORCE

Sales at a large telecommunications company were down for the third quarter. Manage-ment reviewed several strategies to improve sales and concluded that one solution would be to improve training for the large, dispersed sales force. For the sake of expediency, the training department began using a needs analysis they conducted several years before as a basis to develop enhanced training. Their plan was first to update the original needs analysis, and then to develop new training strategies on the basis of what they found. They also began investigating new training technologies as a possible means to reduce training delivery costs. However, management was so intent on doing something quickly that the training department was ultimately pressured into purchasing a generic, off-the-shelf training package by a local vendor. One of the features of the package that appealed to management was that the course could be delivered over the Web, saving the time and expense of having the sales force travel to the main office to receive the training. Hence, even though the package was costly to purchase, the company believed that it was a bargain compared to the expense of developing a new package in-house and delivering it in person to the sales force.

Six months after the training had been delivered, sales were still declining. Management turned to the training department for answers. Because no measures of training performance had been collected, the training department had little information upon which to base its diagnosis. For lack of a better idea, members of the training department began questioning the sales force to see if they could determine why the training was not working. Among other things, the sales people reported that the training was slow and boring, and that it did not teach them any new sales techniques. They also complained that, without an instructor, it was impossible to get clarification on things they did not understand. Moreover, they reported that they believed that sales were off not because they needed training in basic sales techniques, but because so many new products were being introduced that they could not keep up. In fact, several of the sales people requested meetings with design engineers just so they could get updated product information. The training department took these findings back to management and requested that they be allowed to design a new training package, beginning with an updated needs analysis to determine the real training deficiencies.

So how could this company have avoided this costly mistake? Our contention is that, had they engaged in a systematic training design and delivery process, they would have provided effective training and not invested in a useless product. For example, a careful needs analysis would have revealed the specific performance deficiency. In addition, a better assessment of the training delivery – especially as it related to trainee motivation – would have indicated that the Web-based course may not have been the best choice. Unfortunately, cases like this occur all too frequently, but can easily be avoided if a systematic process for training design and delivery is followed.

CONCLUDING REMARKS

We conclude as we started, with this advice – design training systematically. Recent advances in cognition and learning science and findings of training research, coupled with what we know about best training practices and sound instructional design, provide all of the ingredients required for organizations to accomplish their learning needs. We suspect that the recent explosion of training research (see Ford, et al., 1997; Quinones and Ephrenstein, 1997) will generate more guidance to help organizations to design training systematically in the coming years.

References

Ackerman, P. L. (1987). Individual differences in skill learning: An integration of psychometric and information processing perspectives. *Psychological Bulletin*, 102, 3–27.

Anderson, J. R. (1983). *The architecture of cognition*. Cambridge, MA: Harvard University Press.

Baldwin, T. T., and Ford, J. K. (1988). Transfer of training: A review and directions for future research. *Personnel Psychology*, 41, 63–105.

Baldwin, T. T., and Magjuka, R. J. (1997). Training as an organizational episode: Pretraining influences on trainee motivation. In J. K. Ford and Associates (eds.), *Improving training effectiveness in work organizations* (pp. 99–127). Hillsdale, NJ: LEA.

Bandura, A. (1986). *Social foundations of thought and action: A social cognitive theory*. Englewood Cliffs, NJ: Prentice-Hall.

Bassi, L. J., and Van Buren, M. E. (1998). Leading-edge practices, industry facts and figures, and (at last!) evidence that investment in people pays off in better performance. *The 1998 ASTD State of the Industry Report*.

Cannon-Bowers, J. A., Rhodenizer, L., Salas, E., and Bowers, C. A. (1998). A framework for understanding pre-practice conditions and their impact on learning. *Personnel Psychology*, 51, 291–320.

Cohen, M. S., Freeman, J. T., and Wolf, S. (1996). Metarecognition in time-stressed decision making: Recognizing, critiquing, and correcting. *Human Factors*, 38, 206–19.

Collins, A., Brown, J. S., and Newman, S. E. (1989). Cognitive apprenticeship: Teaching the craft of reading, writing, and mathematics. In L. B. Resnick (ed.), *Knowing and learning: Essays in honor of Robert Glaser* (pp. 453–94). Hillsdale, NJ: Erlbaum.

Cooke, N. J. (1994). Varieties of knowledge elicitation techniques. *International Journal of Human-Computer Studies*, 41, 801–49.

Driskell, J. E. and Salas, E. (1992). Collective behavior and team performance. *Human Factors*, 34(3), 277–88.

Ford, J. K., Kozlowski, S. W. J., Kraiger, K., Salas, E., and Teachout, M. S. (eds.) (1997). *Improving training effectiveness in work organizations*. Hillsdale, NJ: LEA.

Ford, J. K., Smith, E. M., Weisshein, D. A., Gully, S. M., and Salas, E. (1998). The influence of goal orientation, metacognitive activity, and practice strategies on learning outcomes and transfer. *Journal of Applied Psychology*, 83, 218–33.

Goldstein, I. L. (1993) *Training in organizations: Needs assessment, development, and evaluation*, 3rd edn. Pacific Grove, CA: Brooks/Cole.

Johnson-Laird, P. N. (1983). *Mental models: Towards a cognitive science of language, inference, and consciousness*. Cambridge, MA: Harvard University Press.

Kirkpatrick, D. L. (1976). Evaluation of training. In R. L. Craig (ed.), *Training and development handbook: A guide to human resource development* (pp.18-1–18-27). New York: McGraw-Hill.

Klein, G., and Militello, L. (in press). Some guidelines for conducting a cognitive task analysis. In E. Salas (ed.), *Human/technology interaction in complex systems*. Greenwich, CT: JAI Press.

Kozlowski, S. W. J., Brown, K., Weisbein, D. A., Cannon-Bowers, J. A. and Salas, E. (2000). A multilevel approach to training effectiveness: Enhancing horizontal and vertical transfer. In K. J. Klein and S. W. J. Kozlowski (eds.), *Multilevel theory, research and methods in organizations* (pp. 157–210). San Francisco, CA: Jossey-Bass.

Kozlowski, S. W. J., and Salas, E. (1997). An organizational system approach for the implementation and transfer of training. In J. K. Ford and Associates (eds.), *Improving training effectiveness in work organizations* (pp. 247–90). Hillsdale, NJ: LEA.

Kraiger, K., Ford, J. K., and Salas, E. (1993). Application of cognitive, skill-based, and affective theories of learning outcomes to new methods of training evaluation [monograph]. *Journal of*

Applied Psychology, 78, 311–28.

Levine, E. L. (1983). *Everything you always wanted to know about job analysis*. Tampa, FL: Mariner.

Mathieu, J. E., and Martineau, J. W. (1997). Individual and situational influences in training motivation. In J. K. Ford and Associates (eds.), *Improving training effectiveness in work organizations* (pp. 193–222). Hillsdale, NJ: LEA.

Noe, R. A. (1986). Trainees' attributes and attitudes: Neglected influences on training effectiveness. *Academy of Management Review*, 11, 736–49.

Noe, R. A., and Schmitt, N. (1986). The influence of trainee attitudes on training effectiveness: Test of a model. *Personnel Psychology*, 39, 497–523.

Quinones, M. A., and Ehrenstein, A. (eds.) (1997). *Training for a rapidly changing workplace: Applications of psychological research*. Washington, DC: APA.

Salas, E., and Cannon-Bowers, J. A. (1997). Methods, tools, and strategies for team training. In M. A. Quinones and A. Ehrenstein (eds.), *Training for a rapidly changing workplace* (pp. 249–79). Washington, DC: APA.

Salas, E., Cannon-Bowers, J. A., and Blickensderfer, E. L. (1997). Enhancing reciprocity between training theory and training practice: Principles, guidelines, and specifications. In J. K. Ford and Associates (eds.), *Improving training effectiveness in work organizations* (pp. 291–322). Hillsdale, NJ: LEA.

Salas, E., Fowlkes, J. E., Stout, R. J., Milanovich, D. M., and Prince, C. (1999). Does CRM training improve teamwork skills in the cockpit? Two evaluation studies. *Human Factors*, 41, 327–43.

Salas, E., Prince, C., Bowers, C. A., Stout, R. J., Oser, R. L., and Cannon-Bowers, J. A. (1999). A methodology for enhancing crew resource management training. *Human Factors*, 41, 161–72.

Tannenbaum, S. I., Mathieu, J. E., Salas, E., and Cannon-Bowers, J. A. (1991). Meeting trainees' expectations: The influence of training fulfillment on the development of commitment, self-efficacy, and motivation. *Journal of Applied Psychology*, 76, 759–69.

Tannenbaum, S. I., and Yukl, G. (1992). Training and development in work organizations. *Annual Review of Psychology*, 43, 399–441.

Weiner, E. L., Kanki, B. G., and Helmreich, R. L. (eds.) (1993). *Cockpit resource management*. San Diego, CA: Academic Press.

5

Design Performance Appraisal Systems to Improve Performance

Angelo S. DeNisi and Jorge A. Gonzalez

Over the years, a number of scholars and practitioners have written about the purposes for which organizations conduct performance appraisals. For the most part, these purposes have been collapsed into broad categories such as administrative decision-making (e.g., allocation of merit pay) and developmental feedback. Some other theorists, though, have included more detailed applications and/or have expanded the list to include things such as providing a standard for evaluating the effectiveness of organizational interventions, a criterion measure for validating selection devices (Cleveland et al., 1989), or a means of communicating expectations (Murphy and Cleveland, 1995).

Although all of these applications are legitimate uses for performance appraisal, the varied nature of the list has led to confusion and to some misguided research efforts. Our basic principle for this chapter is that organizations *should* conduct performance appraisals to improve performance, while recognizing that the targeted performance exists at several levels of analysis, extending from the level of the individual to the level of the firm.

If we consider the basic reasons usually proposed for conducting appraisals – decision-making and developmental feedback – it is easy to see how these can be subsumed under the basic principle of improving performance. First, the appraisal provides the employee (as well as his or her supervisor) with information about his or her strengths and weaknesses. Also, information as to how the employee can go about improving performance in areas of weakness can be provided when the appraisal process is carried out effectively. Thus, this function of appraisals can be viewed as providing the employee with the information needed to improve performance, and enabling any required changes in behavior.

The decision-making aspect of performance appraisal provides a (hopefully) graphic demonstration that performing well on the job is associated with rewards such as more money and/or a promotion. Therefore, this function provides the incentive for improving performance. Once the employee sees that improved performance on the job can lead to valued outcomes, he or she should be more motivated to improve that performance. Viewed in this way, there are not two separate goals for conducting performance appraisal, but only one goal with two paths. The ultimate purpose for conducting performance appraisals is to improve performance.

But what of the fact that, in many organizations, appraisal information is used for applications that are different from performance improvement? For example, performance appraisals are an important source of information concerning training needs, and they can later be used to evaluate training as well. Another common use of performance appraisals is to provide a performance measure to be used in the validation of tests and other selection techniques used for selection purposes. In other words, the process of establishing the criterion-related validity of a test (or any selection technique) typically involves establishing a relationship between test scores and job performance. Such a relationship is important for any test to be of use in practice, but it is also required in defending the use of a test that has been found to have disparate impact.

We will argue that applications other than the improvement of performance represent secondary purposes for conducting appraisals. For these different applications, there are other measures or indices that could also be used, and appraisals are used simply because they are defensible and easy to understand, and because they seem reasonable. Furthermore, we believe that attention to performance appraisal for these secondary purposes (especially as criterion measures) has moved appraisal research and practice in a direction that is contrary to the real purpose of appraisals. We will also give examples of problems that arise when appraisal systems are designed with the wrong goals in mind. Finally, we will discuss some suggestions for designing appraisal systems to maximize their chances of improving performance.

Secondary Purposes for Conducting Appraisals

With the statement of our basic principle, we do not mean to suggest that appraisals are not useful in other applications. We acknowledge that an effective appraisal can point to areas where further development or training is required by identifying areas of weakness. Furthermore, performance appraisals can be used to help evaluate the effectiveness of a training program or any other organizational intervention (e.g., a new pay system). Thus, we surely recognize the importance of using performance appraisals to answer a variety of questions that arise in organizations.

The issue, however, is whether any of these applications represent the primary reason for conducting appraisals in organizations. The answer, it seems to us, is clearly "no." Performance appraisal systems are designed primarily as a means of obtaining information about employee performance with the ultimate goal of improving that performance. Organizations that do not use or validate tests still conduct appraisals to make decisions about salary and promotions, or to provide developmental feedback. On the other hand, organizations that do not conduct appraisals rely upon other means (such as attitude survey data, or measures of actual output) for evaluating the effectiveness of organizational interventions. Thus, there are substitutes available for appraisals for some applications, and appraisals are common even when other applications are not relevant.

The use of performance appraisal for various purposes may seem to be a minor issue since, once an appraisal system is in place, it makes sense for an organization to use appraisal information for any number of applications. However, this is not a minor issue.

Different applications have different appraisal system needs. Thus, if appraisals were meant to be used primarily as criterion measures in validation studies, it would be important for those systems to have certain attributes which would be less critical if those appraisals were meant to be used primarily for improving performance (and vice versa).

Specifically, if appraisals were to be used primarily as criterion measures, having accurate ratings would be more important than having ratings that make sense and are acceptable to the ratee. It wouldn't matter if the ratee believed the ratings or not or if the ratings helped the ratee understand his or her performance problems or not. All that would matter is that the criterion measure used was the most valid and reliable possible. When we think of appraisals as being conducted to improve performance, we cannot afford to sacrifice employee acceptance and understanding for the sake of improved accuracy. Thus, an appraisal system that involves complex calculations and analyses to insure accurate ratings would be unacceptable if those calculations meant that the ratee didn't act upon the feedback received because he or she didn't understand or accept it.

The problem is that much of the research on improving appraisals has been conducted from the perspective of appraisals as criterion measures rather than as methods for improving performance. As a result, much of the research has been somewhat misguided, and there is a perception that this research is not relevant for the needs of practice. Furthermore, when scholars review different appraisal systems, they do so primarily from the perspective of using the ratings as criterion measures, rather than using the ratings as a means of improving performance (although, as we shall note, there are a few exceptions to this statement).

Therefore, we turn now to a discussion of the requirements for using appraisals as criterion measures. Specifically, we will discuss how this focus has led to a preoccupation with rating accuracy which has hindered the development of appraisal systems designed to improve performance.

PERFORMANCE APPRAISALS AS CRITERIA: THE ROLE OF ACCURACY

Perhaps the greatest challenge to the design of more effective appraisal systems has been the concern over the use of appraisals as criterion measures. Most typically, this has involved test validation, where we wish to determine if scores on a test are related to ratings of performance. Evidence that such a relationship exists has been considered evidence of the "job-relatedness" of a test (cf. Griggs v. Duke Power, 1971), which is crucial in defending the use of a test found to have disparate impact. Therefore, it is not surprising that so much attention has been paid to appraisals used in this setting. In fact, it would be reasonable to suggest that this has been the primary focus of industrial/organizational psychologists interested in performance appraisals.

This is not necessarily a problem, except that this focus has, in turn, led to a focus on improving appraisal accuracy at all costs. The impetus for this concern on accuracy goes back quite a few years to the suggestion that one of the problems with finding relationships between test scores and performance ratings was that the performance ratings – i.e., the criteria – were not accurate. Thus, if we could improve rating accuracy, we would better be able to demonstrate the relationships we believed might exist. Interestingly, during a period from the 1950s through the 1970s, the concern in the performance appraisal literature over rating errors was really the result of trying to find ways to improve accuracy. Scholars and practitioners at the time generally believed that if we could eliminate problems such as overly lenient ratings, or highly intercorrelated ratings (i.e., halo), the resulting rating would be more accurate. Scholars even advanced suggestions for training raters to eliminate rating errors. The ultimate goal of all these efforts, however, was to make the final ratings more accurate (e.g., Latham et al., 1975).

Related to the goal of improving accuracy, scholars were also concerned with improving the psychometric properties of the ratings. Although rating accuracy is not the same as rating validity or reliability, the concepts are surely related. The interest in psychometric properties, then, was based on at least two sets of assumptions. First, if ratings were more reliable and valid, they would be easier to predict (i.e., this would maximize any correlations with predictor variables), which would make the process of test validation easier to accomplish. This assumption is clearly a reasonable one. The second set of assumptions was that, if accuracy were related to reliability, then anything we did to make ratings more reliable and valid should also result in their being more valid. Furthermore, since rating accuracy *per se* was difficult to assess while validity and reliability were much easier to assess, it made sense to simply focus on improving reliability and validity. Both sets of assumptions, however, are open to debate.

In any case, this focus led to a concern over the exact nature of the rating scales that should be used in performance appraisals. Specifically, we became concerned with the number of points on the scale, the anchors used on those scales, and whether the scales should include ratings of behaviors, traits or goals (see reviews by DeNisi, 1996; Landy and Farr, 1980). In all cases, identifying the "right" number of scale points, the "best" anchors, or the "optimal" rating format were believed to result in more valid and more accurate ratings. It is interesting to note that the general conclusion from this body of research was that no one rating-scale format was clearly superior to the others on these criteria (cf. Landy and Farr, 1980).

This focus on rating validity and accuracy continued as appraisal research became more process oriented, and we embarked on an era where "cognitive" approaches dominated the literature (cf. DeNisi, 1996). Although much of the work in this area was conceptual, the dependent variable was almost always rating accuracy when empirical studies were conducted. For example, some studies reported that keeping structured performance diaries resulted in more accurate ratings (DeNisi, Robbins, and Cafferty, 1989), while others reported that relying upon previous levels of performance resulted in less accurate ratings of present performance (Murphy et al., 1985).

This stream of research resulted in an even stronger focus on rating accuracy, but this closer attention resulted in questions about some of the assumptions that had guided research in the past. An important paper by Murphy and Balzer (1989) provided strong empirical evidence that indices of rater errors were unrelated to measures of rating accuracy and, as such, we should cease using rater error measures in appraisal research. A later paper by Murphy (1991) was also quite influential in arguing that there were different types of accuracy, and that we needed to first decide which type of accuracy we were interested in maximizing. We will return to some points from this paper later, since the two types of accuracy discussed by Murphy are relevant for the present discussion. Specifically, he distinguished between classification accuracy, which was defined as having the truly best performer receiving the highest ratings (and so on through the group of ratees), and behavioral accuracy, where the ratings received by a given ratee reflected accurately that ratee's strengths and weaknesses.

Other scholars took these arguments in a different direction. They noted that various studies where rating accuracy was used as a dependent variable actually operationalized accuracy differently. These authors therefore generated more precise definitions of rating accuracy which considered different sources of inaccuracy, and which resulted in increasingly complex calculations (e.g., Day and Sulsky, 1995). At this point, then, rating accuracy became a goal for its own sake, regardless of its relevance.

But where did this concern lead us? We had learned that we could design rating scales to improve reliability, validity, and accuracy. We had learned that the nature of the rating instrument, in itself, was not critical for these outcomes. We had learned that, if we focused on "frame of reference" training rather than error training, we could train raters to be more accurate (e.g., Pulakos, 1984). Finally, we had learned that there were many definitions of rating accuracy that we could use, and that our choice of a definition probably affected our results. Yet, at the same time, we began to see indications that, perhaps, these efforts had been misguided to some extent. Murphy and Cleveland (1995) were the most articulate spokespersons for the view that, even if a rater could provide accurate ratings, he or she might choose not to. They also presented some factors that could influence this decision, suggesting that rater motivation might be as important a dependent measure as rating accuracy. But, more critically, others began challenging whether rating accuracy and validity were really the right measures in the first place.

IMPROVING PERFORMANCE AND NEW CRITERION MEASURES

In a chapter on performance appraisal, Ilgen (1993) presented arguments for why rating accuracy might well be the "wrong goal" in appraisals research. He suggested, as we do, that the concerns over accuracy were based on our grounding in test theory and psychometric concerns, but that rating accuracy was probably not as important for applied appraisals as it was for other types of appraisals. Interestingly, in the same volume, Dickinson (1993) presented a model of ratee attitudes towards appraisals which stated that appraisal effectiveness was a function of both feedback attitudes and the motivation to respond to that feedback (i.e., to change behavior). In his model, Dickinson further suggested that feedback attitudes were a function of the perceived accuracy of the appraisals and subsequent feedback.

But, once we shift our focus to concerns over perceived accuracy, it becomes clear that our concerns over rating accuracy *per se* need to change as well. Before discussing this shift, it is important to make clear that we believe that, all other things equal, it is always better to have more accurate ratings. In fact, in an ideal world, the best way to improve perceived accuracy would be to increase the actual accuracy of the ratings and then explain to the ratees exactly how the ratings were derived, but we do not live in this ideal world. Instead, we live in a world where the definition of rating accuracy is unclear, open to discussion, and often results in elaborate and difficult to understand calculations. Also, we typically cannot assess accuracy directly (without incurring enormous financial and non-financial costs), and therefore have to rely upon proxy measures.

Thus, although rating accuracy should always be an important goal, concerns over perceived accuracy could result in some trade-offs. For example, a number of years ago, there was a heated debate over the use of computer monitoring of performance. Advocates pointed out that computer monitoring was more accurate than alternative methods of evaluation, and therefore should be used. These writers acknowledged that computer monitoring might be stressful for some employees, but argued that this would be more than offset by the fact that performance would be measured more accurately and feedback could be immediate (e.g., Chalykoff and Kochan, 1989). Opponents downplayed issues of accuracy and emphasized the stress on employees, arguing that these systems made a modern office into an "electronic sweatshop" (e.g., Nussbaum and duRivage, 1986). Debates over the use of computer monitoring continue, but the nature of the arguments on both sides are a clear illustration of how different views on the importance of rating accuracy lead to different recommendations about the design of appraisal systems.

Therefore, although it would be an exaggeration to suggest that we do not need to be concerned with the accuracy of the ratings at all, it seems that there might be other concerns that would be more pressing than trying to find ways to maximize rating accuracy. It also seems that a focus on perceived accuracy would lead us to different conclusions about what factors are likely to make appraisals more effective.

For example, we noted earlier that several authors had suggested that the relationship between rating "errors" and rating accuracy was not very strong, and therefore, we should cease using error measures as indices of accuracy. But, if we shift our attention to perceived accuracy, does it follow that rating errors should be dropped because they are not related to perceived accuracy either? We think not. We believe that indices of rating error may well be related to perceived accuracy.

It must be clear, however, that these "error" measures are probably not measures of rating errors at all. Unless we know the "true" distribution of a set of ratings, we cannot say that a set of ratings is "too lenient" or "too severe." Likewise, unless we know a person's "true" strengths and weaknesses, we cannot say that a set of highly intercorrelated ratings is less accurate than a set of ratings that is uncorrelated. Therefore, we should abandon terminology relating these measures to rating errors and discuss them in a more neutral manner. DeNisi and Peters (1996) attempted to do this by referring to indices of rating elevation instead of referring to leniency or leniency error. They also referred to indices of variance with ratees and between ratees. That is, none of these measures were assumed to be good or bad. Instead, they simply described certain characteristics of the ratings obtained – some ratings were higher than others, some raters were more likely to give different ratings to different ratees, and some raters were more likely to rate any ratee the same in all areas.

In their study, DeNisi and Peters (1996) used these measures as criterion measures and reported that interventions which affected these indices were also related (in the same direction) to perceptions of the fairness and accuracy of the appraisal process. While this is not the same as establishing a direct link between these characteristics and perceived accuracy, these results are encouraging. Thus, whether or not measures of elevation or dispersion are related to accuracy, they could well be related to perceived accuracy, and so to appraisal effectiveness.

On the other hand, it would seem clear that the more complex indices of accuracy discussed earlier would play little role in this context. That is, ratees are unlikely to understand what "differential stereotype accuracy" is and are therefore not likely to accept this as an indication of whether or not ratings are accurate. But raters might easily believe that a set of ratings that fails to discriminate at all among ratees (i.e., everyone is rated the same) is probably not an accurate reflection of true performance differences. Likewise, a set of ratings that suggest a ratee is strong in every area is less likely to be perceived as accurate when compared to ratings that indicate clear areas of strength and weakness. Of course, these ratings are even more likely to be perceived as accurate if they agree with the ratee's beliefs about his or her strengths and weaknesses.

Note, too, that these different indices parallel the two broader types of accuracy discussed by Murphy (1991). Specifically, within-ratee discrimination would seem to be related to perceptions about "behavioral accuracy," while elevation and between-ratee discrimination would seem to be related to perceptions about "classification accuracy." Therefore, characteristics and distribution of the ratings may be important predictors of perceptions of accuracy and the subsequent effectiveness of an appraisal system. Yet we realize that, even if increasing dispersion in a set of ratings leads to perceptions of greater accuracy, we do not want to advocate that organizations seek to increase dispersion for its own sake, since this could lead to other problems. None the less, it is worth noting that these "error" indices might help us to understand perceptions of accuracy.

RATEES MUST BE ABLE TO UNDERSTAND THE RATING PROCESS

Even though appraisal accuracy is important, as we have discussed, the ratee's perception of appraisal accuracy also has important implications for the effectiveness of appraisal systems. It is therefore essential that we identify factors or variables that are likely to increase perceptions of accuracy without actually sacrificing accuracy. One such factor, we believe, is the ability of the ratees to understand how their ratings were derived. Here, we discuss the sub-principle that ratees must understand the rating process. This, of course, is related to perceptions of procedural justice, which helps determine one's perceptions of fairness. We believe, however, that it relates to perceptions of accuracy as well (see Folger et al., 1992 for a more complete discussion of the role of justice perceptions in determining reactions to appraisals). We will focus on two more specific aspects of ratees' need to understand – the importance of clear standards and simple-to-use rating instruments.

Evaluation standards refer to clear statements about what behaviors or outcomes constitute performance at different levels of effectiveness (cf. Bobko and Colella, 1994). If these standards are stated in clear terms, are understood and accepted by the raters, and are communicated to the ratees, much of the process underlying performance appraisals should become transparent. Frame-of-reference training has been shown to be an effective means of communicating these standards to raters, and this training has been found to result in generally more accurate ratings (e.g., Pulakos, 1984). If an organization expanded this training to make sure that *ratees* understood the standards and how they were applied, this could also lead to perceptions that ratings were accurate, as well as fair.

In addition, it is important that the scales used for appraisal are not too complicated.

When interest in developing new and better appraisal instruments was at its height, there were a number of proposals for rather complex appraisal procedures. For example, some such as the Mixed Standards Rating Scale (Blanz and Ghiselli, 1972) were actually designed to confuse the rater as to what performance dimension was being evaluated in order to force the rater to be more consistent. Other procedures such as Kane's Performance Distribution Assessment (Kane, 1982), involve complex calculations that transform ratings into evaluations. If the underlying goal of an appraisal system were to maximize accuracy, these systems might be reasonable, but they are less acceptable if we want to maximize the perceptions of accuracy. Ratees will question ratings with which they disagree when they do not understand how the ratings were derived.

It is therefore worth noting that Behaviorally Anchored Rating Scales (or BARS, Smith and Kendall, 1963) were designed to make rating scales and the bases for ratings clear and easily understood by all parties. The intent was to make the scales easier for the raters to use, and to make the resultant ratings more acceptable (and helpful) to the ratees. As noted above, comparisons of different types of rating-scale formats failed to find one that was clearly superior to all others. These studies, however, focused on psychometric properties and/or rating accuracy as dependent measures. It may well be that the characteristics of BARS and how they are developed make ratings based on these scales more effective for improving performance, and it may be time to re-evaluate their effectiveness in light of the real goal of appraisal systems.

A general drive towards understanding and relative simplicity should determine other aspects of the rating instrument as well. Systems that include complicated instructions or ambiguous anchors (e.g., asking raters to agree or disagree with an item stated in negative terms) are less likely to be understood by ratees, and so ratings obtained with these systems are less likely to produce improvements in performance.

Finally, documentation to support ratings, and/or ratings that focus on behaviors rather than traits, should also lead to increased perceptions of fairness. Thus, systems that include performance diaries or incident logs, which have also been found to relate to more accurate ratings (e.g., DeNisi, Robbins, and Cafferty, 1989), should increase perceptions of accuracy since the rater will be able to support ratings with specific incidents or examples of behavior. Perhaps one of the reasons why goal-based appraisal instruments have become so popular is that they are easy to understand, focus on behaviors, and usually require specific incidents to support ratings.

AT WHICH LEVEL DO WE DESIRE TO CHANGE PERFORMANCE?

One final but critical issue needs to be addressed before we can conclude the case for our principle. That issue is the level at which we desire the performance change to occur. Many studies of the effectiveness of feedback are conducted at the level of the individual. Those studies would typically examine the effects of performance appraisal-related feedback on changes in the individual's level of performance. Although this is essentially the type of change we have suggested should be the target of performance appraisal, we should consider whether this level of change is enough.

Several years ago, Huselid (1995) demonstrated that there was a relationship between HR practices (such as performance appraisal) and firm-level performance. That is, HR practices were related to such outcomes as profits, return on investment, and even stock prices. Thus it became clearer that the kinds of interventions we design could have an impact beyond the level of the individual employee's performance. This leads us to another important sub-principle: performance appraisal interventions should lead to improvements in performance *at the level of the firm*. Any intervention that has an effect *only* at the level of the individual employee is simply not very effective or useful. If our practices and interventions cannot improve firm performance, they will not continue to be supported. Unfortunately, it has been a general criticism of I/O psychology, OB, and HR that much of what we propose does *not* relate to firm-level performance.

The issue, then, is how do we influence behavior and performance at higher levels of analysis to eventually influence firm performance? Some scholars have suggested models whereby influencing behavior at the individual level does result in interactions that influence collective constructs and behavior at higher levels of analysis. Moreover, they have proposed specific mechanisms through which this impact takes place (e.g., Morgeson and Hofmann, 1999; Kozlowski, et al., 1999). Others have noted that performance appraisals must be aimed at the level of performance of interest at the time. So, for example, individual-level performance should be appraised (primarily) when we are interested in changing individual-level performance, but we should target appraisals at the level of the corporation if we wish to influence performance at that level (DeNisi, 2000).

Regardless of the level at which we actually do target our appraisals, firms must include them in a system that will allow individual-level performance changes to translate into changes in performance at higher levels. Thus, rather than being concerned solely with the accuracy of the ratings, managers and scholars must be more concerned that the ratings are accepted and perceived as fair and accurate. They should also be concerned on whether the appraisals provide feedback that allows the recipient to understand how to improve performance at the organizational level of analysis.

In this way, we can design appraisal systems that lead to changes in performance. These systems may or may not result in the most accurate appraisals possible, but they will result in ratings accurate *enough* for employees to perceive them as accurate, and ratings that are easy to understand and justify, resulting in perceptions that the system is fair. But, exactly, what can we do to improve perceptions of accuracy and acceptance of ratings so that they *do* result in performance improvements? We will discuss a specific case where an organization did some things that we believe helped accomplish this critical goal. We will follow with a second case; a brief discussion of a system that was designed to maximize the *wrong* goals.

A CASE INVOLVING 360-DEGREE APPRAISALS

In recent years, 360-degree appraisals (or multi-source appraisals) have become quite popular. These appraisals combine evaluations obtained from raters who have different relationships with the ratee, such as peers, subordinates, and supervisors. Ideally, only raters who have expertise about a specific area of performance rate the target on that area, so that the ratee receives ratings and feedback only from those in the best position to make those evaluations. These appraisals were supposed to be used for feedback and development only, although they are increasingly being used for decision-making as well, and, in many cases, all raters evaluate a ratee in all areas of performance, regardless of their areas of expertise (London and Smither, 1995). This is especially critical for us since ratings from "unqualified" raters would be less likely to be perceived as accurate, and would reduce ratees' acceptance of the feedback. Both of these conditions would reduce the chances that performance improvements would take place.

But a bank in a large metropolitan area in Texas recently implemented a 360-degree appraisal system for high-level managers, which was designed to maximize the effectiveness of the appraisals. Each ratee evaluated him- or herself in every area on the rating form, and the ratee identified peers, supervisors, and subordinates (3–5 each) who would provide ratings as well. Ratings from each source were combined and reported to the ratee so that each ratee was provided information on his or her self-rating in an area plus the averaged ratings from peers, the averaged ratings from supervisors, and the averaged ratings from subordinates. Then a personal coach was assigned to each ratee, to help the ratee determine which ratings were most relevant for each area of performance, and to develop a performance improvement plan. Thus the coach could help the rater make sense of the ratings and make them more acceptable to the ratee, as well as help insure that desired performance improvements would occur.

Note that raters were not trained in any way to provide better ratings, and there was no real concern over the psychometric properties of the ratings. Yet, the bank reported improvements in individual performance following the implementation of this system, as well as improvements in indices of corporate performance (such as the percentage of bad loans), and attributed these improvements to the new appraisal system.

We would suggest that the success of this system was due to the fact that the bank paid more attention to factors likely to result in acceptance and perceived accuracy of the ratings. Allowing the ratees to choose who will rate them might not result in the most accurate ratings; none the less, it will result in better acceptance of those ratings. Averaging the individual ratings from each source does not take into consideration the validity of individual ratings, but it does provide a simple-to-understand source of feedback that also protects the identity of an individual rater. Finally, the use of a coach allows the ratee to interpret the performance feedback in the way that is most useful and allows him or her to formulate a strategy for performance improvement.

COMPUTERIZED SCORING SCHEMES AND APPRAISALS IN OHIO

There are countless examples we could provide of organizations that designed their appraisals systems to accomplish the wrong goals, or that were designed with no real goals in mind. But, a number of years ago, a city government in Ohio designed and implemented an appraisal system that was intended to be as accurate a system as possible. The jobs involved were all civil service, but there were substantial merit pay increases associated with outstanding performance, and so everyone was concerned with how appraisals decisions were determined. As a result, the city employed a consulting firm who had developed a computer-scored appraisal system that they had used in several other municipalities. The system involved a complex set of ratings for a ratee, derived from different sources (but not 360-degree systems). All the ratings were submit-

ted to the consultant's headquarters (in California) for final scoring. The exact procedures and algorithms used were never explained to us, but the consultant's computer
program weighted the ratings according to how well the rater had been evaluated. The
assumption was that people who were better performers were also better raters (an idea
that had actually been proposed much earlier: cf. Kirchner and Reisberg, 1962), and so
their ratings should be given greater weight in determining an employee's overall
performance evaluation, thereby making those evaluations more accurate.

But, no one understood exactly what happened to the ratings when they were sent to
California, and no one knew how the relative weights were determined. What they did
know, however, was that higher-level managers *seemed* to receive higher merit pay
increases, and everyone seemed to know someone who had had received high ratings
from a supervisor, and yet did not receive a big merit pay increase. As a result, all
attention turned to figuring out the system and how to get someone a merit pay increase.

There is no way of knowing whether the ratings that were derived by this system were
any more accurate than they would have otherwise been, but it didn't matter. What did
matter was that ratees did not perceive the ratings to be accurate, and they were
generally seen as being biased (except by those who received large merit pay increases,
of course). Several hearings by the Civil Service Commission convinced the city that they
should try to develop a new system.

CONCLUSIONS AND RECOMMENDATIONS

Performance appraisals should be conducted in such a way as to maximize the
chances of improving performance. This is ultimately the purpose behind appraisals and, in fact, we should really be interested in performance at the corporate or
firm level. When we accept this basic principle, it has clear implications for the
ways in which we design appraisal systems, and the factors that we attend to in
their design and implementation. The concern over the accuracy of appraisals
stems from the use of appraisals as criterion measures in validation studies.
Although this application is critically important, it is not the primary reason for
conducting appraisals. Therefore, a focus on increasing appraisal accuracy can lead
to misguided efforts that make appraisal instruments more complex and difficult to
understand (as in the case above). Instead, we must focus on ways to increase
perceived accuracy of appraisals. Although true accuracy is (hopefully) not independent of perceived accuracy, the two are clearly not the same thing. Once we
accept this basic principle, it follows that appraisal systems should be designed such
that:

◆ ratee input is allowed, both in terms of self-evaluations of performance and in
terms of the selection of factors that are included in the evaluation
◆ rating instruments are as clear and simple to use as possible
◆ the standards for performance are clear and communicated to all parties
◆ there are clear goals for employee performance improvement
◆ the appraisal system makes sense to all the relevant parties.

If these sub-principles replace the need to maximize appraisal accuracy and psychometric purity, we will be more likely to design and implement appraisal systems that truly are aimed at improving performance. A recent paper by Kluger and DeNisi (1996) discussed factors that are related to the effectiveness of feedback interventions for improving performance. Performance appraisal research would perhaps better serve the ultimate goal of improving firm performance if appraisal systems relied more heavily on research in this area, rather than upon research aimed at improving the psychometric properties of ratings.

REFERENCES

Blanz, F., and Ghiselli, E. E. (1972). The mixed standard scale: A new rating system. *Personnel Psychology*, 25, 185–99.

Bobko, P., and Colella, A. J. (1994). Setting performance standards: A review and research propositions. *Personnel Psychology*, 46, 243–60.

Chalykoff, J., and Kochan, T. A. (1989). Computer-aided monitoring: Its influence on employee job satisfaction and turnover. *Personnel Psychology*, 42, 807–34.

Cleveland, J. N., Murphy, K. R., and Williams, R. E. (1989). Multiple uses of performance appraisal: Prevalence and correlates. *Journal of Applied Psychology*, 74, 130–5.

Day, D. V., and Sulsky, L. M. (1995). Effects of frame of reference training and information configuration on memory organization and rating accuracy. *Journal of Applied Psychology*, 80, 158–67.

DeNisi, A. S. (1996). *A cognitive approach to performance appraisal: A program of research*. London: Routledge.

DeNisi, A. S. (2000). Performance appraisal and performance management: A multiple levels analysis. In K.L. Klein and S. W. J. Kozlowski (eds.), *Multilevel theory, research, and methods in organizations*. (pp. 121–56) San Francisco: Jossey-Bass.

DeNisi, A. S., Cafferty, T. P., and Meglino, B. M. (1984). A cognitive view of the performance appraisal process: A model and research propositions. *Organizational Behavior and Human Performance*, 33, 360–96.

DeNisi, A. S., and Peters, L. H. (1996). The organization of information in memory and the performance appraisal process: Evidence from the field. *Journal of Applied Psychology*, 81, 717–37.

DeNisi, A. S., Robbins, T., and Cafferty, T. P. (1989). The organization of information used for performance appraisals: The role of diary-keeping. *Journal of Applied Psychology*, 74, 124–9.

Dickinson, T. L. (1993). Attitudes about performance appraisal. In H. Schuler, J. L. Farr, and M. Smith (eds.), *Personnel selection and assessment: Individual and organizational perspectives* (pp. 141–62). Hillsdale, NJ: Lawrence Erlbaum Associates.

Folger, R., Konovsky, M. A., and Cropanzano, R. (1992). A due process metaphor for performance appraisal. In L. Cummings and B. Staw (eds.), *Research in organizational behavior* (Vol. 14, pp. 129–77). Greenwich, CT: JAI Press.

Griggs v. Duke Power (1971). 401 US 424.

Huselid, M. A. (1995). The impact of human resources practices on turnover, productivity, and corporate financial performance. *Academy of Management Journal*, 38, 635–72.

Ilgen, D. R. (1993). Performance appraisal accuracy: An illusive or sometimes misguided goal? In H. Schuler, J. L. Farr, and M. Smith (eds.), *Personnel selection and assessment: Individual and organizational perspectives* (pp. 235–52). Hillsdale, NJ: Lawrence Erlbaum Associates.

Kane, J. S. (1982). Rethinking the problem of measuring performance: Some new conclusions and a new appraisal method to fit them. Paper presented at the Fourth Johns Hopkins University National Symposium on Educational Research.

Kirchner, W. K., and Reisberg, D. J. (1962). Differences between better and less effective supervisors in appraisals of subordinates. *Personnel Psychology*, 15, 295–302.

Kluger, A. N., and DeNisi, A. S. (1996). The effects of feedback interventions on performance: A historical review, a meta-analysis, and a preliminary feedback intervention theory. *Psychological Bulletin*, 119, 254–84.

Kozlowski, S. W. J., Gully, S. M., Nason, E. R., and Smith, E. M. (1999). Developing adaptive teams: A theory of compilation and performance across levels and time. In D. R. Ilgen and E. D. Pulakos (eds.), *The changing nature of work and performance: Implications for staffing, personnel actions, and development* (pp. 240–92). San Francisco: Jossey-Bass.

Landy, F. J., and Farr, J. (1980). Performance rating. *Psychological Bulletin*, 87, 72–102.

Latham, G. P., Wexley, K. N., and Pursell, E. D. (1975). Training managers to minimize errors in the observation of behavior. *Journal of Applied Psychology*, 60, 550–5.

London, M. L., and Smither, J. W. (1995). Can multi-source feedback change perceptions of goal accomplishment, self-evaluations, and performance related outcomes? Theory-based applications and directions for research. *Personnel Psychology*, 48, 803–39.

Morgeson, F. P., and Hofmann, D. A. (1999). The structure and function of collective constructs: Implications for multilevel research and theory development. *Academy of Management Review*, 24, 249–65.

Murphy, K. R. (1991). Criterion issues in performance appraisal research: Behavioral accuracy versus classification accuracy. *Organizational Behavior and Human Decision Processes*, 50, 45–50.

Murphy, K. R., and Balzer, W. K. (1989). Rater errors and rating accuracy. *Journal of Applied Psychology*, 74, 619–24.

Murphy, K. R., Balzer, W. K., Lockhart, M. C., and Eisenman, E. J. (1985). Effects of previous performance on evaluations of present performance. *Journal of Applied Psychology*, 70, 72–84.

Murphy, K. R., and Cleveland, J. N. (1995). *Understanding performance appraisal: Social, organizational, and goal-based perspectives.* Thousand Oaks, CA: Sage Publications.

Nussbaum, K., and duRivage, V. (1986). Computer monitoring: Mismanagement by remote control. *Business and Society Review*, 56, 16–20.

Pulakos, E. D. (1984). A comparison of two rater training programs: Error training versus accuracy training. *Journal of Applied Psychology*, 69, 581–8.

Smith, P. C., and Kendall, L. M. (1963). Retranslation of expectations: An approach to the construction of unambiguous anchors for rating scales. *Journal of Applied Psychology*, 47, 149–55.

Part III

TURNOVER AND SATISFACTION

6 Promote Job Satisfaction through Mental Challenge
    TIMOTHY A. JUDGE

7 Control Turnover by Understanding its Causes
    THOMAS W. LEE AND TERENCE R. MITCHELL

6

Promote Job Satisfaction through Mental Challenge

Timothy A. Judge

The most popular definition of job satisfaction was supplied by Locke (1976), who defined it as ". . . a pleasurable or positive emotional state resulting from the appraisal of one's job or job experiences" (p. 1304). There are many possible influences on how favorably one appraises one's job, and numerous theories of job satisfaction have attempted to delineate these influences. Empirical evidence, however, has suggested only one clear aspect of the work environment that consistently influences job satisfaction – the intrinsic challenge present in the work itself. This leads to the general principle that will be the focus of this chapter – that mentally challenging work is the key to job satisfaction. Thus, the most effective way an organization can promote job satisfaction of its employees is to enhance the mental challenge in their jobs, and the most consequential way most individuals can improve their own job satisfaction is to seek out mentally challenging work.

Before discussing this principle in more detail, however, it is important to demonstrate the importance of the principle. Roznowski and Hulin (1992) have commented that just as a job applicant's score on a valid cognitive ability test is the single most important datum an organization can have pre-hire (see chapter 1 above), scores on a valid measure of job satisfaction are the most important pieces of information organizations can have post-hire. Yet many organizations openly question whether they need to be concerned with job satisfaction. One study of how job satisfaction is viewed by managers (Judge and Church, in press) drew the following comments:

- ◆ "Job satisfaction is virtually never discussed in the senior staff meetings I attend within our business unit."
- ◆ "Job satisfaction is not measured. Because this is Wall Street, money talks. If people weren't happy, they could have moved their whole team elsewhere."
- ◆ "Job satisfaction is not measured or considered at all."
- ◆ "There is some questioning of whether job satisfaction is desirable anyway."

Organizations would be well advised to place more importance on job satisfaction. It is related to many outcomes that individuals and organizations find important. Some of the outcomes that job satisfaction have been linked to are:

◆ *Life satisfaction*. Evidence indicates that job satisfaction and life satisfaction correlate moderately to strongly with each other. Our best estimate of the correlation between job and life satisfaction is +.44 (Tait, Padgett, and Baldwin, 1989). Since the job is a significant part of life, the correlation between job and life satisfaction makes sense – one's job experiences spill over onto life. Thus, people who have jobs that they like are more likely to lead happy lives.

◆ *Job performance*. The relationship between job satisfaction and performance has an interesting history. In 1985, a quantitative review of the literature suggested that the true correlation between job satisfaction and performance was .17 (Iaffaldano and Muchinsky, 1985). However, more recent evidence reveals that the relationship is much larger. A comprehensive review of 300 studies determined that when the correlations are corrected for the effects of sampling error and measurement error, the average true score correlation between overall job satisfaction and job perform-ance is .30 (Judge, Thoresen, Bono, and Patton, 1998). Thus, it does appear that a happy worker is more likely to be a productive one. Evidence also exists for a relationship at the work unit level – units whose average employee is satisfied with his or her job are more likely to perform at a higher level than business units whose employees are less satisfied, and to be more profitable as a result (Harter and Creglow, 1998). Of course, the relationship between satisfaction and performance may be reciprocal. Not only may employees who are happy with their jobs be more productive, but performing a job well may lead to satisfaction with the job.

◆ *Withdrawal behaviors*. Job satisfaction displays relatively consistent, negative, and weak correlations with absenteeism and turnover. The average correlation is generally in the −.25 range. Job dissatisfaction appears to display weak, negative – but significant – correlations with other specific withdrawal behaviors, including unioni-zation, lateness, drug abuse, and retirement. Both Fisher and Locke (1992) and Roznowski and Hulin (1992) have shown that when these specific behaviors are aggregated as indicators of a general withdrawal syndrome, job satisfaction is quite predictive.

Thus far, job satisfaction has been defined and it has been shown that job satisfaction matters. Thus, any principle that reveals how to best promote job satisfaction is impor-tant to understand. With this foundation, in the next section of the chapter, the model that best describes the principle – that job satisfaction is best achieved through mentally challenging work – will be reviewed.

JOB CHARACTERISTICS MODEL

The theory that best describes the role of the work environment in providing mentally challenging work is the Job Characteristics Model (JCM). The Job Characteristics Model argues that the intrinsic nature of work is the core underlying factor causing employees to be satisfied with their jobs. The model, in its full explication by Hackman and Oldham (1980), focuses on five core job characteristics that make one's work challenging and fulfilling: (1) *task identity* – degree to which one can see one's work from beginning to end; (2) *task significance* – degree to which one's work is seen as important and significant;

(3) *skill variety* – degree to which job allows employees to do different tasks; (4) *autonomy* – degree to which employee has control and discretion over how to conduct their job; (5) *feedback* – degree to which the work itself provides feedback on how the employee is performing the job. According to the theory, jobs that are enriched to provide these core characteristics are likely to be meet individuals' needs for mental challenge and fulfillment in their work, and thus will be more satisfying and motivating to employees.

Measurement of job characteristics

There are various ways intrinsic job characteristics can be measured. The Job Diagnostic Survey (JDS) measures the extent to which the five core intrinsic job characteristics are present in the job. Items from the JDS appear in table 6.1. When responding to items in the table, individuals circle the number (from 1 to 7) that is the most accurate description of their job. The JDS can be used to rate almost any type of job. Ideally, one would give the JDS to a number of people in an organization within a job type to get a reliable measurement of the job characteristics. The JDS is not copyrighted and thus is free to use. However, care must be taken in administering the JDS. The reader interested in measuring intrinsic job characteristics should consult Hackman and Oldham (1980), who provide all of the JDS items, along with an excellent discussion of administrative issues.

Research support

There are several indirect pieces of evidence supporting Hackman and Oldham's model. First, when individuals are asked to evaluate different facets of their job such as pay, promotion opportunities, co-workers, and so forth, the nature of the work itself generally emerges as the most important job facet (Jurgensen, 1978). Second, of the major job satisfaction facets – pay, promotion opportunities, co-workers, supervision, and the work itself – satisfaction with the work itself, far and away, best predicts overall job satisfaction. Thus, if we are interested in understanding what causes people to be satisfied with their jobs, the nature of the work (intrinsic job characteristics) is the first place to start. Unfortunately, managers often think employees are most desirous of pay to the exclusion of other job attributes such as challenging work. For example, a 1997 survey indicated that, out of ten job attributes, employees ranked interesting work as the most important job attribute (good wages was ranked fifth), whereas when it came to what managers thought employees wanted, good wages ranked first while interesting work ranked fifth (Kovach, 1997).

Research directly testing the relationship between workers' reports of job characteristics and job satisfaction has produced consistently positive results. Figure 6.1 displays correlations (corrected for measurement error) between intrinsic job characteristics and job satisfaction in the 23 studies in the literature that have investigated the direct relationship (Frye, 1996). As the figure shows, all of the correlations are positive, and all are moderate to strong in magnitude. Across the 23 studies, the average correlation is .48. The empirical data suggest that intrinsic job characteristics are the most consistently significant situational predictor of job satisfaction.

TABLE 6.1 Measurement of intrinsic job characteristics: the Job Diagnostic Survey

1 How much *autonomy* is there in your job? That is, to what extent does your job permit you to decide *on your own* how to go about doing the work?

Very little; the job gives me almost no personal "say" about how and when the work is done	Moderate autonomy: many things are standardized and not under my control, but I can make some decisions about work	Very much; the job gives me almost complete responsibility for deciding how and when the work is done

2 To what extent does your job involve doing a *"whole" and identifiable piece of work*? That is, is the job a complete piece of work that has an obvious beginning and end? Or is it only a small part of the overall piece of work, which is finished by other people or by automatic machines?

My job is only a tiny part of the overall piece of work; the results of my activities cannot be seen in the final product or service	My job is a moderate-sized "chunk" of the overall piece of work; my own contributions can be seen in the final outcome	My job involves doing the whole piece of work, from start to finish; the results of my activities are easily seen in the final product or service

3 How much *variety* is there in your job? That is, to what extent does the job require you to do many different things at work, using a variety of your skills and talents?

Very little; the job requires me to do the same routine things over and over again	Moderate variety	Very much; the job requires me to do many different things, using a number of different skills and talents

4 In general, how *significant or important* is your job? That is, are the results of your work likely to significantly affect the lives or well-being of other people?

Not very significant; the outcomes of my work are *not* likely to have important effects on other people	Moderately significant	Highly significant; the outcomes of my work can affect other people in very important ways

(continues)

(Table 6.1 continued)

5 To what extent does *doing the job itself* provide you with information about your work performance? That is, does the actual *work itself* provide clues about how well you are doing – aside from any "feedback" co-workers or supervisors may provide?

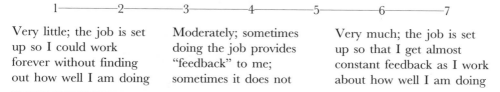

| Very little; the job is set up so I could work forever without finding out how well I am doing | Moderately; sometimes doing the job provides "feedback" to me; sometimes it does not | Very much; the job is set up so that I get almost constant feedback as I work about how well I am doing |

Source: Hackman and Oldham (1980)

How to increase mental challenge in jobs

Ever been in a car accident? If you have, you will remember picking up the phone to call your insurance company and, inevitably, talking to many different people, recounting the details of your accident several times. It may be weeks or even months before your claim is settled and, if you ever happen to call to inquire about the status of your claim, you may discover that your claim is buried somewhere in the system. As a customer in this situation, you probably feel irritated and poorly served, being passed around like a hot potato. But have you ever wondered what the implications of such a system are for employees? When each employee specializes in processing one part of the claim, the mental challenge afforded by the job suffers. Over and over, the same person may answer the phone from customers, take down basic details of the accident, and then pass on the claim to someone else, never to see it again. Even the job of claims adjuster can be broken into segments that are very specialized. When individuals repeatedly perform narrow and specialized tasks, they are unlikely to see their work as very challenging or intrinsically motivating.

As an example of how to diagnose and change a work system in this situation, assume we have administered the JDS to several customer service representatives (CSRs) and managers of a local branch office of an insurance company. Assume the average JDS scores for each job characteristic are as depicted in figure 6.2. From this figure, you can determine where the problems are and, if one is to improve CSR attitudes, where changes need to be made. Specifically, as compared to managers, CSRs report especially low levels of skill variety, task identity, and autonomy. Under such circumstances, you would expect the average CSR to report a low level of job satisfaction. But what can be done about it? How can the profile of a CSR job be made to look more like that of the manager? Before specifically addressing this question, let us consider some general ways of increasing intrinsic job characteristics.

♦ *Job rotation.* Job rotation is when employees perform different jobs; typically, rotation occurs once employees have mastered their present job and are no longer chal-lenged by it. Many companies use job rotation to increase flexibility – i.e. having

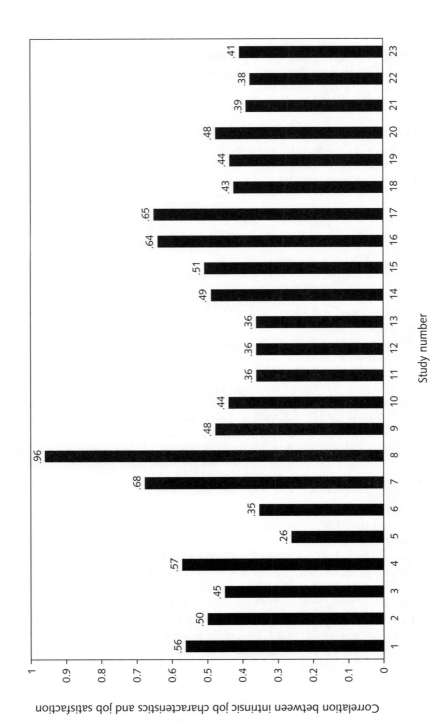

FIGURE 6.1 Studies of the relationship between intrinsic job characteristics and job satisfaction

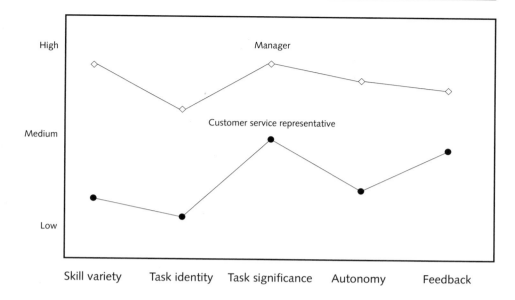

FIGURE 6.2 Job characteristics profiles for job of customer service representative and manager

employees capable of performing a wide variety of jobs allows adjustments to be made due to absenteeism, injury, or changes in product demand. However, there are also substantial satisfaction benefits. America West uses job rotation, according to CEO Mike Conway, to "give the employees a better job, to give them more job variety. It's more challenging, and for those who are interested in upward mobility, it exposes them to about 16 different areas of the company versus one they would be exposed to if we specialized" (Garfield, 1992: 8). Some companies even pay people for successfully rotating into new jobs; such pay systems are referred to as "skill-based pay."

◆ *Job enlargement.* Job enlargement, sometimes called horizontal loading, involves expanding the number of tasks associated with a particular job. The difference between job enlargement and job rotation may seem subtle. The difference is that with job rotation, jobs are not really redesigned. Employees simply systematically move from one job to another, but while they are performing a job, the nature of the work has not changed. Job enlargement is a more fundamental intervention because it involves actually changing the job. For example, an assembly-line worker who formerly performed one discrete operation (bolting the seat to the floor of a car) may instead be part of a team that performs many phases of the assembly operation. Another example would be workers in a grocery store who may work at the checkout counter, stock shelves, or clean, depending on what needs to be done.

◆ *Job enrichment.* Job enrichment, sometimes referred to as vertical loading, involves increasing the *responsibilities* of the job. Compared to job enlargement, the increase in the variety in the work of an enriched job may be no more than of an enlarged job, but the responsibility (and often autonomy) of the job is increased. For example, self-managed work teams may take on responsibilities such as staffing, scheduling, and performance appraisal formerly assigned to the team's supervisor. One example of job enrichment occurred at the Duncan Hines angel food cake factory in Jackson, Tennessee. Workers who combined the ingredients for the cake mix were given letters from customers who had had problems with the cake mix. Employees could call up customers to help them solve their problems and, in the meantime, perhaps learn how to make better mixes or provide clearer instructions (Johns, 1996). A similar job enrichment program was undertaken in a totally different industry. John Deere enriched some of its assembly-line operation jobs so that workers in these jobs also took on sales responsibilities.

Now let us return to our insurance company example. Having learned about the ways in which intrinsic job characteristics can be increased, how could we redesign the CSR job? Rotating CSRs through different specialties could increase skill variety. Providing CSRs with feedback on the resolution of each claim could raise task identity. Giving CSRs more latitude in servicing customers could increase autonomy. Though each of these piecemeal changes may have merit, a deeper approach would be to assign CSRs responsibility for entire claims. Although there are some aspects of the job that a CSR may not be able to accomplish on their own, these could be referred to a claims adjuster, or CSRs could be trained to take on some of the duties of a claims adjuster. By assigning an employee responsibility for the entire claim, both horizontal and vertical loading are increased. Horizontal loading is enhanced because the CSR may need to arrange a rental car for the customer, determine whether a check has been processed, or negotiate with another insurance company representative about payment on a claim. Vertical loading is increased by giving the CSR discretion to make decisions about various aspects of the claim (e.g., whether to provide a loaner car for a particular claim, prioritizing claims, etc.). Aetna Life & Casualty, one of the largest insurance companies in the US, has redesigned its jobs in such a manner (Jacob, 1992). The downside of redesigns such as this comes in the form of training costs, and the recognition that there are some employees who do not welcome challenging work. However, research indicates that the benefits of job redesign generally outweigh these costs (Cascio, 1991).

Criticisms and limitations

The Job Characteristics Model has amassed a great deal of support in the research literature. Despite the support, there have been several criticisms of the model. Two of the most important concerns are reviewed below.

Measurement of job characteristics. The JCM assumes that job characteristics cause job satisfaction. It is important to remember that the measures of intrinsic job characteristics typically are perceptual. According to some researchers, perceptual measures are susceptible to biasing influences such as mood. If employees' mood at the time of rating their job characteristics and job satisfaction affects both ratings, the correlation between perceptions of job characteristics and job satisfaction would be inflated (i.e., the real relationship would be lower than it appears). Furthermore, there are concerns that the relationship is not solely from job characteristics to job satisfaction; job satisfaction may also (or instead) cause perceptions of job characteristics. Although some research has supported these criticisms, other research has shown that when these limitations are remedied (e.g., using objective measures of job characteristics), a relationship between job characteristics and job satisfaction still exists (Glick, Jenkins, and Gupta, 1986). Thus, while these criticisms are important to keep in mind, they do not undermine the model.

Combining the dimensions.   In the original formulation, the five intrinsic job characteristics were combined with what Hackman and Oldham (1980) called a Motivating Potential Score (MPS). According to the authors, the five job characteristics were combined in the following manner:

$$MPS = \left(\frac{\text{Skill variety} + \text{Task identity} + \text{Task significance}}{3} \right) \times \text{Autonomy} \times \text{Feedback}$$

Using this formula, if employees rate each of the five dimensions as "3" on the 1–7 scale (see table 6.1), MPS = 27 ($3 \times 3 \times 3$). On the other hand, if employees rate each of the five dimensions as "5," MPS = 125 ($5 \times 5 \times 5$). This formulaic combination of the five core characteristics has not been supported. Research indicates that simply adding the dimensions works better. Thus, rather than the MPS scores of 27 and 125 in the above examples, simply adding the five characteristics would result in scores of 15 and 25. I do not view this as a serious problem with the theory. How the scores are optimally combined does not go to the heart of the theory. If there is a better method of combining the five core job characteristics than that originally proposed by Hackman and Oldham (1980), wonderful. The support for the original MPS formulation was scant, and thus we have learned that the theory is most useful when the five job characteristic ratings are simply added.

EXCEPTIONS TO THE PRINCIPLE

Employees with low growth need strength

In considering the recommendation that organizations should increase the mental challenge of jobs, one might wonder whether everyone seeks mental challenge in their work. Indeed, the relationship between intrinsic job characteristics and job satisfaction depends on employees' Growth Need Strength (GNS). Growth Need Strength is employees' desire for personal development, especially as it applies to work. High GNS employees want their jobs to contribute to their personal growth, and derive satisfaction from performing challenging and personally rewarding activities. One of the ways GNS is measured is by asking employees, with a survey, to choose between one job that is high on extrinsic rewards (such as pay) and one that is high on intrinsic rewards. For example, one item asks the employee to choose between "A job where the pay is very good" and "A job

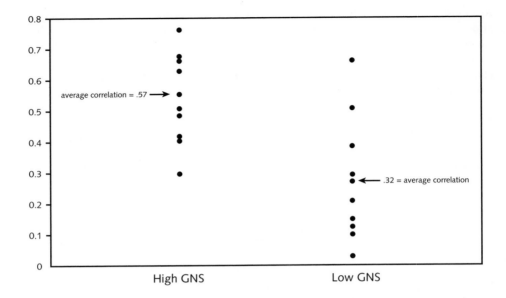

FIGURE 6.3 Studies of the correlation between intrinsic job characteristics and job satisfaction for individuals with high and low Growth Need Strength (GNS)

where there is considerable opportunity to be creative and innovative." Individuals who strongly prefer the latter job are likely to be high on GNS – all else equal, high GNS people prefer jobs that are challenging and interesting, which allow them to work autonomously and use a number of skills, over jobs that are otherwise rewarding (high pay, good supervision, pleasant co-workers, etc.). According to the model, intrinsic job characteristics are especially satisfying for individuals who score high on GNS. In fact, research supports this aspect of the theory. As is shown in figure 6.3, across the ten studies that have investigated the role of GNS in the relationship between intrinsic job characteristics and job satisfaction, the relationship tends to be stronger for employees with high GNS (average $r = .68$) than for those with low GNS (average r = .38). However, as the figure shows, it is important to note that intrinsic job characteristics are related to job satisfaction even for those who score low on GNS (Frye, 1996).

Employees who value other job attributes

Thus far we have established that job satisfaction is best promoted through intrinsically challenging work because most employees value the work itself more than other job attributes. One exception to this principle is that employees who do not care about intrinsic job characteristics (low GNS) will be less satisfied by challenging work. A more generalized means of considering this exception is through values. It may not be that only employees with low GNS will respond less favorably to intrinsic job characteristics; the exception would also apply to employees who value other job or organizational attributes. Following his definition of values as that which one desires or considers important, Locke (1976) argued that individuals' values would determine what satisfied them on the job. Only the unfulfilled job values that were valued by the individual would be dissatisfying. Thus, value-percept theory predicts that discrepancies between what is desired and received are dissatisfying only if the job facet is important to the individual. Because as a general rule individuals value work more than other job attributes, Locke's argument is consistent with the general principle described in this chapter. Thus, if intrinsic job characteristics were the most important job facet to most individuals, then Locke's theory would predict that increasing the level of intrinsic job characteristics (thus reducing the have–want discrepancy with respect to intrinsic characteristics) would be the most effective means of raising employees' job satisfaction. However, it must be recognized that when an employee does not value challenging work, other values must be fulfilled to satisfy the person.

Personality

Implicit in Locke's definition is the importance of both feeling and thinking. People's evaluation of their jobs is a process of rational thought (how is my pay relative to my peers, is my work as challenging as I would like?), but it also is influenced by people's dispositional outlook. Research has shown that unhappy children become dissatisfied workers later in life (Staw, Bell, and Clausen, 1986). There is even evidence that job satisfaction is inherited (see Arvey, Carter, and Buerkley, 1991). Thus, part of the reason we like or dislike our jobs has nothing to do with the jobs. Rather, it is due to our dispositional outlook that derives from our genes and early childhood experiences. Judge, Locke, Durham, and Kluger (1998) have found that the key dispositional factor leading to job satisfaction is core self-evaluations – if we have a positive self-regard, we are likely to see our jobs positively and undertake jobs that are challenging.

Dispositions are important in understanding job satisfaction. To a large extent, they are what cause two people with the same job to be differentially satisfied by it. The main practical implication of the dispositional source of job satisfaction is that if employers wish to raise satisfaction levels of their workforce, they need to select applicants with positive dispositions. However, the dispositional source of job satisfaction does not invalidate the general principle presented in this chapter; it merely explains why the general principle is not perfectly true (as almost no general principle is in seeking to explain something as complex as human behavior).

CASE STUDIES

Job satisfaction of public school teachers

In 1993–4, the US Department of Education surveyed roughly 36,000 of America's public school teachers in an effort to determine the factors influencing teacher satisfaction. The teachers were questioned about a wide variety of issues, and background questions were also included in the study. The public school teachers included in the study were quite diverse in demographics, educational background, experience, community type, school size, class size, and socio-economic status of students in the school. These background characteristics, however, were only weakly related to teacher satisfaction. As the authors of the report concluded, "the analyses show that certain teacher background variables and school characteristics are only weakly related to teacher satisfaction; (they are not) . . . useful in predicting a teacher's satisfaction" (Perie, Baker, and Whitener, 1997: 51). This is consistent with what has been found in the literature on job satisfaction – demographic and background characteristics are not important predictors of job satisfaction.

The study also found that compensation was only "modestly related" to teacher satisfaction. Although the pay of teachers in public schools varies greatly – it is not unusual in a public school to observe $2:1$ or even $3:1$ differences in salary among teachers, even for those teaching the same subject – this variance in pay does not predict differences in satisfaction. So what did influence satisfaction in this study? The authors found that the most important influences on job satisfaction were work characteristics. As is shown in figure 6.4, teachers who felt that they had an influence over school policy and felt they were in control of their classroom were much more likely to be satisfied with their jobs than teachers who felt they did not have influence or control. The figure also shows that pay did little to separate satisfied and dissatisfied teachers.

This analysis shows that what makes the most difference in teacher satisfaction is not how or even what they are compensated, but how much influence they have over their work. As the authors of this study concluded:

> These findings provide information to policy makers interested in increasing the satisfaction levels of teachers. Very few of teacher background or nominal school characteristics that are an inseparable part of any school of community were associated with teacher satisfaction. Instead, this report demonstrated that teacher satisfaction may be shaped in part by workplace conditions that are within the reach of policy at the school and district levels. Focusing on workplace conditions, therefore, is a feasible way to improve teacher satisfaction . . . The results of this study imply that involving teachers in school-wide policy decisions and giving them some degree of control in their classrooms are associated with high levels of career satisfaction . . . If, as the literature suggests, teacher satisfaction related to both teaching quality and turnover rates, focusing on policies related to satisfaction may go a long way towards improving the quality of instruction in our nation's schools. (Perie et al., 1997: 52)

Unfortunately, the largest union representing the interests of teachers – the National Education Association (NEA) – has traditionally focused its efforts on political lobbying (Chapman, 1999), to the exclusion of workplace reform that would result in greater teacher satisfaction. If schools, labor unions, teachers (who must assume some responsibility for the NEA's focus), and parents want to improve public schools, these results suggest that they should consider making the teaching environment more satisfying to teachers by improving teacher's influence over their work. This can effectively be accomplished by increasing intrinsic job characteristics.

Tom Warner

Tom Warner owns a plumbing, heating, and air-conditioning business in the Annapolis, Maryland area. Warner had observed over the past few years that his business had fallen off somewhat in his primary market – commercial property-management firms. In order

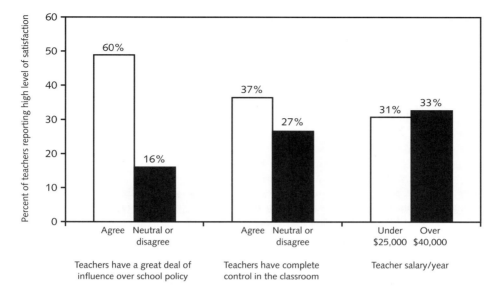

FIGURE 6.4 Job satisfaction levels of elementary and secondary public school teachers according to perceived influence over school policy, perceived control in the classroom, and salary

(*Source*: Perie, Baker, and Whitener, 1997)

to cut costs, these firms were hiring handymen to do work in-house. Thus, Warner decided to pursue the residential market. But how could his business, with more than 250 people, compete against little mom-and-pop operators who built personal relationships with many clients? Warner's answer was to expand the jobs of his plumbers, electricians, and technicians so that each operated like they owned their own business.

Warner divided Annapolis territory into smaller territories of approximately 10,000 households. Each of his non-staff employees was given a territory. The employees were trained in how to run their territory as if it were their own business. They learned sales techniques, budgeting, negotiating, cost estimating, and how to handle customer complaints. Warner's vision was to run his business using a staff of technically superb, friendly, and ambitious mechanics who operate like small-town tradespeople despite the big-city reality.

The redesign of mechanics' jobs has been quite successful. Although initially turnover increased (perhaps because low GNS employees did not like the redesigned jobs), the remaining employees have developed a strong sense of pride and ownership in their territory. The average mechanic puts in 63 hours a week. They not only fix pipes and repair heaters, they generate referrals, schedule their own work, do their own estimates, handle their own equipment, develop their own advertising campaigns, and collect their own receivables. Warner provides training, trucks, tools, phones, pagers, dispatchers, and an all-night answering service. He also performs such chores as payroll and taxes. His mechanics are then free to run their businesses the best way they see fit.

CONCLUSION

Job satisfaction matters. Employees who are satisfied with their jobs tend to perform better, withdraw less, and lead happier and healthier lives. Organizations whose employees are satisfied with their jobs are more likely to be productive and profitable. The single most effective way organizations can achieve a satisfied workforce is to provide their employees with mentally challenging work.

REFERENCES

Arvey, R. D., Carter, G. W., and Buerkley, D. K. (1991). Job satisfaction: Dispositional and situational influences. *International Review of Industrial and Organizational Psychology*, 6, 359–83.

Cascio, W. F. (1991). *Costing human resources: The financial impact of behavior in organizations*. Boston: PWS-Kent.

Chapman, M. (1999). The NEA's political lesson plan. *Investors Business Daily*, Jan. 5.

Fisher, C. D., and Locke, E. A. (1992). The new look in job satisfaction research and theory. In C. J. Cranny, P. C. Smith, and E. F. Stone (eds.), *Job satisfaction* (pp. 165–94). New York: Lexington.

Frye, C. M. (1996). New evidence for the Job Characteristics Model: A meta-analysis of the job characteristics–job satisfaction relationship using composite correlations. Paper presented at the Eleventh Annual Meeting of the Society for Industrial and Organizational Psychology, San Diego, CA.

Garfield, C. (1992). Creating successful partnerships with employees. *At Work*, 8 (May–June).

Glick, W. H., Jenkins, G. D. Jr., and Gupta, N. (1986). Method versus substance: How strong are underlying relationships between job characteristics and attitudinal outcomes? *Academy of Management Journal*, 29, 441–64.

Hackman, J. R., and Oldham, G. R. (1980). *Work redesign*. Reading, MA: Addison-Wesley.

Harter, J. K., and Creglow, A. (1998). *A meta-analysis and utility analysis of the relationship between core GWA employee perceptions and business outcomes*. Working paper 2.0, The Gallup Organization.

Iaffaldano, M. R., and Muchinsky, P. M. (1985). Job satisfaction and job performance: A meta-analysis. *Psychological Bulletin*, 97, 251–73.

Jacob, R. (1992). Thriving in a lame economy. *Fortune*, Oct. 5, 44–54.

Johns, G. (1996). *Organizational behavior*. New York: HarperCollins.

Judge, T. A., and Church, A. H. (in press). Job satisfaction: Research and practice. In C. L. Cooper and E. A. Locke (eds.), *I/O psychology: What we know about theory and practice*. Oxford: Blackwell.

Judge, T. A., Locke, E. A., Durham, C. C., and Kluger, A. N. (1998). Dispositional effects on job and life satisfaction: The role of core evaluations. *Journal of Applied Psychology*, 83, 17–34.

Judge, T. A., Thoresen, C. J., Bono, J. E., and Patton, G. K. (1998). The job satisfaction–job performance relationship: 1939–1998. Paper presented at the Academy of Management National Meeting, San Diego, CA.

Jurgensen, C. E. (1978). Job preferences (What makes a job good or bad?). *Journal of Applied Psychology*, 50, 479–87.

Kovach, K. A. (1997). Do you know your staff? *Industry Trends*, Sept. 26.

Locke, E. A. (1976). The nature and causes of job satisfaction. In M. D. Dunnette (Ed.), *Handbook of industrial and organizational psychology* (pp. 1297–343). Chicago: Rand McNally.

Perie, M., Baker, D. P., and Whitener, S. (1997). *Job satisfaction among America's teachers: Effects of workplace conditions, background characteristics, and teacher compensation.* Washington, DC: US Department of Education.

Roznowski, M., and Hulin, C. (1992). The scientific merit of valid measures of general constructs with special reference to job satisfaction and job withdrawal. In C. J. Cranny, P. C. Smith, and E. F. Stone (eds.), *Job satisfaction* (pp. 123–63). New York: Lexington.

Staw, B. M., Bell, N. E., and Clausen, J. A. (1986). The dispositional approach to job attitudes: A lifetime longitudinal test. *Administrative Science Quarterly*, 31, 437–53.

Tait, M., Padgett, M. Y., and Baldwin, T. T. (1989). Job and life satisfaction: A re-evaluation of the strength of the relationship and gender effects as a function of the data of the study. *Journal of Applied Psychology*, 74, 502–7.

7

Control Turnover by Understanding its Causes

Thomas W. Lee and Terence R. Mitchell

It's no secret, of course, that many people quit their jobs. Whether voluntary employee turnover is a problem, however, "depends." Sometimes, an individual's volitional quitting can be a *major* problem. In certain parts of the food and beverage industry, for example, turnover is routinely well over 100 percent annually, and many managers must often worry about simply having enough employees to keep their operations running. In segments of the software industry, moreover, losing a single key knowledge worker can not only decrease the likelihood of a project's success, but it can also reduce investors' confidence in the firm and thereby dramatically lower that firm's stock price. Sometimes, employee turnover can be far less of a problem, and in some cases it is even desired. If employees can be readily hired, trained, and meshed into the company's operations and culture, quitting might only be a minor nuisance. Relatedly, turnover may even be desirable because it serves as an immediate constraint on labor costs. Thus, employee turnover is not necessarily bad or good. Instead, it is an ongoing organizational issue that needs to be managed, and understanding employees' leaving is essential to its control.

Among academic scholars of organizational behavior, there are three *complementary* approaches to understanding the turnover process. Two of these forms focus on who quits and how they quit. In the first approach, leaving is traditionally described through a process initiated by an individual's feelings and beliefs. More specifically, job dissatisfaction is theorized to initiate a variety of job-search behaviors and corresponding comparative evaluations on the identified employment opportunities that, in turn, set the stage for an employee's quitting. In the second approach, a non-traditional and *social* psychological orientation is applied to an employee's leaving, and this approach is named the "unfolding model of voluntary turnover." In contrast to traditional ideas, the unfolding model (a) describes multiple quitting processes, (b) includes non-cognitive and external-to-the-person factors, and (c) explains how relative *job satisfaction* can prompt an employee's departure. In the third approach, understanding focuses on the company's definition of the circumstances surrounding a person's leaving. Viewed from the manager's perspective, the questions are whether an employee's quitting is functional or dysfunctional, avoidable or unavoidable.

Based on these three approaches, we clarify in this chapter how turnover might best be understood and managed. First, each of these three approaches is described, and their corroborating statistical evidence summarized. Based on this body of evidence, controlling turnover *begins* with monitoring for signs that allow for the anticipation of future employee quitting. Second, we identify *what* signs to monitor. Third, action implications are offered. In other words, we suggest what to do *after* observing the signs for the enhanced likelihood of turnover. Fourth, notable exceptions are explained. That is, we suggest conditions under which our recommended signs and actions may be more or less meaningful.

APPROACH 1. WHAT THE TRADITIONAL IDEAS ABOUT TURNOVER TELL US

Monitor job attitudes and withdrawal cognitions

The theorized linkages

Based on the evidence to date, managers have *good* reason to expect links between job (dis)satisfaction and employee turnover. (See Hom and Griffeth, 1995, for an excellent and a comprehensive academic treatment of the major psychological theories of turnover.) First, the lower the level of an employee's job satisfaction, the lower will be the level of his or her organizational commitment. Second, the lower these job attitudes, the stronger will be the initial thoughts, feelings, and expected positive outcomes of quitting. Next, according to this traditional approach, these thoughts, feelings, and expected positive outcomes lead *most* people to search for another job. The job opportunities found during this job search are then evaluated, though it is uncertain whether a set of multiple job opportunities are simultaneously compared or whether single job opportunities are compared in sequence. Most likely, the specific nature of this comparison process depends on what opportunities are actually discovered during job search and the job seeker's mental abilities (see chapter 1 above). Finally, actual quitting occurs when a "better" job opportunity is found. We hasten to note that "better" has rarely been fully defined. Most often, improved economic outcomes are implied (e.g., compensation and financial opportunities) but seldom explicitly stated.

The statistical evidence

Perhaps equally enlightening as the traditional dissatisfaction-induced leaving processes themselves, the statistical findings provide *compelling* reason for a manager to expect the following stable and consistent relationships. The statistics that are provided in parentheses below are: (a) averaged across multiple studies; (b) weighted by typically very large sample sizes; and (c) statistically significant. Furthermore, these values are taken from reports, which quantitatively summarize the data from numerous empirical studies, by Hom and Griffeth (1995), Mathieu and Zajac (1990), and Spector (1997). Our description of a statistic's size (e.g., large, moderate or small) derives from the common standards in the social sciences.

First, overall job satisfaction strongly correlates with organizational commitment (r = .53), and the intentions to search for another job (r = −.60) and to leave (r = −.46). More specifically, lower scores on job attitude measures are consistently associated with more thoughts of leaving and job-search activities. Second, job satisfaction (r = −.19), organizational commitment (r = −.28), thoughts of quitting (r = .27), and intentions to search (r = .27) and to leave (r = .35) correlate moderately well *but* predictively over time with *actual turnover behavior*. In other words, these variables are consistently associated with employee actions. Third, until people quit, less satisfied employees are absent slightly more often (r's between −.10 and −.15), somewhat less helpful to co-workers (r's between .22 and .26), and perform their jobs more poorly (r = .25). Similarly, less committed employees are also absent slightly more often (r = −.10), less motivated in general (r = .53), even less motivated intrinsically (r = .69), and perform their jobs more poorly (r = .14) as well. Thus, employees with poor job attitudes can be difficult to manage. (For a related discussion, see chapter 6 above.)

What to monitor first: job attitudes

Every traditional theory on employee turnover includes job dissatisfaction as either the primary starting point or as an early stage in the turnover process. Moreover, the statistical evidence indicates *consistent* and *large* correlations (cited above) between job satisfaction and the intermediate variables (e.g., organizational commitment, intention to search or to leave) before actual employee turnover occurs. In turn, the evidence reveals *consistent, moderate-sized, and predictive over time* correlations between the intermediate variables and actual quitting. When considered together − and from the singular interest in controlling turnover − *job satisfaction*, certainly, and *organizational commitment*, probably, should be monitored as clear and compelling indicators of future employees' quitting.

What to monitor second: global withdrawal cognitions

These traditional approaches most often include factors such as thoughts of quitting, expected utility of job search, cost of quitting, intention to search, evaluation of alternative jobs, comparisons between current and alternative jobs, and intention to leave as separate entities. Correspondingly, organizational behavior researchers have sought to measure and study these variables as separate entities. An enduring problem, however, is that these intermediate variables (between job satisfaction and turnover) are difficult to separate accurately (e.g., using various statistical methods). As a result, several turnover scholars have sought to simplify the meaning of these "intermediate steps." More specifically, these numerous factors have been reconceptualized and empirically measured as a global and broader-based variable labeled "withdrawal cognitions." When measured directly, global withdrawal cognitions consistently, moderately in magnitude but predictively over time correlate with actual turnover (r = .30). A manager can certainly monitor each immediate variable separately, but the long-standing bias toward parsimony and simplicity held by social scientists and managers suggests the desirability of monitoring for *signs* of employees' global or general withdrawal cognitions. In short, the "evidence" informs us to monitor job attitudes and global withdrawal cognitions as preliminary signs of employees' leaving.

APPROACH 2. WHAT THE UNFOLDING MODEL OF VOLUNTARY TURNOVER TELLS US

Monitor shocks and paths, as well as job attitudes and global withdrawal cognitions

The overall model

In contrast to traditional turnover ideas, the unfolding model offers a broader perspective. (See Lee and Mitchell, 1994, for a detailed description of this model.) Based on the evolving evidence to date, managers should have confidence that the unfolding model broadly and accurately describes the leaving process. More specifically, the unfolding model informs us about *four* basic patterns of thoughts and actions (or psychological "paths") to leaving organizations. In one particular pattern, which is labeled "path 4," leaving is seen as *quite* similar to the traditional ideas of turnover described above. Job dissatisfaction prompts thoughts of leaving that lead, in turn, to job search, evaluation of alternatives, and eventual departure from the job. Thus, much of the statistical evidence on the traditional ideas about turnover *also* pertains to path 4 leaving as well. From an applied perspective, both traditional and path 4 approaches inform the manager to monitor employees' *negative* or *declining* job attitudes. (Although not major, the primary difference between traditional and path 4 processes is that the former implies substantial job dissatisfaction prompts quitting, whereas the latter implies a slow and gradual onset of dissatisfaction, which in turn initiates the leaving process.)

In paths 1, 2, and 3, a fundamentally different pattern is asserted. In contrast to dissatisfaction-induced quitting, the leaving process begins with a shock that is a jarring and an external-to-the-person precipitating event. Shocks serve to shake people out of their daily, habitual, and ongoing patterns and routines. Although all shocks are mediated by an individual's perceptual processes, of course, their jarring nature renders them easily identifiable, describable, and understandable by the employee and manager. Thus, shocks are a conceptual tool that keeps monitoring and observations firmly grounded on work behaviors and the employee's immediate situation. In our research, for example, people report that shocks can be: (a) positive (e.g., acceptance into graduate school) or negative (e.g., a nurse being forced into a life-threatening emergency surgery for which she was unprepared); (b) expected (e.g., a spouse's retirement) or unexpected (e.g., being denied a six-month leave of absence); and (c) organization-related (e.g., the hospital shifts from individual-based to team-based nursing) or personal (e.g., becoming pregnant with one's third child). As a result, shocks *augment* job attitudes and global withdrawal cognitions as key antecedent signals to subsequent employee turnover and are easily identified.

Monitor for specific paths

Whereas monitoring for job attitudes, global withdrawal cognitions, and shocks is fairly straightforward, determining *which* specific path employees may take can be more complicated; but such monitoring offers the manager greater understanding of turnover. In path 1, a shock triggers a person to use a *pre-existing* action plan (or what social psychologists call a script). Minimal (or virtually no) mental deliberations occur. A person leaves *without* considering his or her current attachment to the organization (e.g., organizational commitment) and *without* considering her or his current job alternatives. Unlike traditional ideas and path 4, moreover, job satisfaction is essentially *irrelevant*. In path 1, a satisfied person can appear to leave abruptly but is in fact following a pre-planned course of action. For example, an interviewee reported the following: "It was very simple; I am going to graduate school . . . It had nothing to do with my job. It had everything to do with my personal situation . . . Very quickly, as soon as I got the letter that I was accepted into graduate school, the decision was made" (Lee, Mitchell, Wise, and Fireman, 1996: 17). Note that path 1 involves a shock (e.g., the acceptance letter), script (e.g., return to graduate school), no job search and no evaluation of alternatives.

In path 2, a shock prompts a person to reconsider his or her basic attachment to the organization (e.g., commitment) because of *violations* to one's basic values, personal or professional goals, and/or plans for goal attainment (which are called "images"). After completing these mental deliberations, a person leaves the organization *without* a search for work alternatives. Unlike traditional ideas and path 4 but like path 1, job satisfaction is also largely *irrelevant*. In path 2, a satisfied person can leave abruptly because she or he is reacting to the shock itself. For example, an academic colleague of the authors recently left his tenured professorship at a major research university. In his words, he told us the following:

> I went into my dean's office to discuss some executive teaching and consulting that I was doing. We got into this huge disagreement over whether this was an appropriate activity for me to spend time on and whether it was good for the university. As the argument got more intense, it was clear that my contributions to the school and the ethical foundation of my professional choices were being questioned. I tendered my resignation within three days.

Note that path 2 involves a shock (e.g., the argument), no script, violations (e.g., images of personal and professional goal attainment), no job search and no evaluation of alternatives.

In path 3, a shock initiates a person to consider whether an attachment could form with another organization because of violations to one's basic values, personal or professional goals, and/or plans for goal attainment. The mental deliberations due to the shock and violations lead an individual to search for another job and to evaluate specific alternatives and one's current job. Unlike traditional ideas and paths 1 and 2, a reasonably job-satisfied person can leave for a *more* satisfying job. In path 3, job dissatisfaction may or may *not* be present. Recently, we reported the following example of path 3 leaving:

> . . . Sammy Lew (a fictitious name) was a forty-five year old former electrical engineer who had worked for a major military-defense company. [Mr. Lew] . . . had worked for the same firm since graduation twenty-three years earlier. For the last ten years, Mr. Lew supervised a group of twelve engineers. When asked why he left his former company to become a real estate developer, Mr. Lew said that . . . it was the departure from the firm of another work group member. That departure left Mr. Lew as the work group's oldest and clearly most out-of-date engineer. [He realized that] he had minimal advancement prospects and that "it was time to move on." As such, he evaluated his interests, aspirations, and available opportunities. Although he had no particular connection to his new profession, real estate development appeared, on balance, his best choice. He quit the defense company upon finding an acceptable job in real estate. (Lee and Maurer, 1997: 249)

Note that path 3 involves a shock (e.g., the co-worker's quitting), no script, violations (e.g., images of professional goal attainment), job search (e.g., finding real-estate work), and evaluation of alternatives (e.g., in comparison to his interests, aspirations, and available alternatives).

The statistical evidence

Accurate classifications.   A fundamental test of the unfolding model is whether its four paths can accurately describe employees' actual leaving (as opposed to intentions to leave). To date, we are aware of two published empirical tests of the unfolding model. In an initial *qualitative* study, Lee et al. (1996) reported that, as hypothesized, 6, 6, 8, and 13 nurses could be accurately classified into paths 1–4, respectively (33 of 44). In a subsequent *quantitative* test of a revised unfolding model, which used a set of revised questions based on suggestions and results from their earlier study, Lee, Mitchell, Holtom, McDaniel, and Hill (1999) reported that, as predicted, 6, 7, 136, and 63 former accountants from Big 6 public accounting firms could be accurately classified into paths 1–4 respectively (212 of 229). When comparing classifications made from the initial versus revised unfolding models, the accuracy of classification among former Big 6 employees improved significantly to 96 percent from 75 percent.

Path speed.   In addition to accurate classifications, a second testable attribute of the unfolding model involves the speed in which the four paths unfold. More specifically, paths vary by their levels of mental deliberation. For example, extensive evaluation of alternatives should take more time than doing no or minimal evaluations. Furthermore, paths differ by whether their basic features are readily available for mental deliberation. If job search is required, for instance, information about alternative employment is less readily available than if no job search is involved. Thus, the path speed should vary systematically. Among nurses, Lee et al. (1996) reported that the median durations of paths 1 and 2 were significantly quicker than that of path 4. Among accountants, Lee et al. (1999) reported shorter durations for paths 1 and 2 than for 3 and 4, and a shorter duration for path 3 than for path 4.

Shock characteristics.   On their small sample of 44 nurses, Lee et al. (1996) reported that: (a) path 1 was significantly associated with expected and personal shocks (e.g., your spouse relocates); (b) path 2 was significantly associated with organizational and negative shocks (e.g., you are passed over for promotion); and (c) path 3 was significantly associated with organizational shocks (e.g., you receive a competitive job offer). With their larger sample of 229 former Big 6 accountants, Lee et al. (1999) replicated two of their earlier findings. In particular, path 1 significantly associated with personal shocks, and path 3 significantly associated with organizational shocks. When taken together, these two significant associations may be robust across industries, occupations, and gender.

In sum, monitoring for shocks is not enough. Managers must also analyze a shock's content and draw inferences about paths. This information can help a manager decide how quickly they need to act (e.g., in paths 1 or 2) and what factors might inhibit leaving. In comparison to the traditional approach (i.e., dissatisfaction-induced quitting), the unfolding model identifies additional considerations and adds richness to our understanding of the turnover process.

APPROACH 3. WHAT THE CIRCUMSTANCES SURROUNDING TURNOVER TELL US

Monitoring for signs of voluntary quitting may not be enough

Is turnover functional and avoidable?

A prevailing belief among many organizational behavior scholars and practicing managers is that employee turnover should be minimized, though not necessarily eliminated. In the 1990s, for example, this view became quite salient because of the very robust US economy and historically low unemployment levels. From the manager's perspective, moreover, turnover can substantially increase the costs of staffing, training, and general administration. More subtly, turnover can also often disrupt a business unit's operations and increase the workloads of remaining employees.

In contrast to this prevailing belief, a small body of empirical research indicates that turnover should be more carefully managed rather than minimized. (See Maertz and Campion, 1998, for a thorough discussion of these issues.) Most compelling, employee turnover can be beneficial to a company if marginal performers voluntarily leave. Whereas "truly bad" performers might likely be fired, for instance, having too many marginal performers (i.e., those persons who are not sufficiently bad to fire) can minimize a firm's productivity. The value accrued by encouraging these people to resign can often offset that individual's overall replacement costs. In a related vein, the new employees can oftentimes be a source of new ideas and mechanisms to shake remaining employees out of their inertia (cf. "getting new blood"). In those situations where labor costs are deemed critical and quite variable relative to others (e.g., fast-food restaurants, community colleges), turnover can result in substantial savings in compensation-related expenses and thereby enhance organizational productivity (e.g., replace higher-wage and long-tenured counter clerks with lower-paid new workers; replace permanent faculty with part-time lecturers). In short, employee turnover should *not* simply be minimized or dismissed as an unmanageable process.

The statistical evidence

Two empirical studies directly address the functionality and avoidability of leaving. Based on the termination records for a seven-month period, Dalton, Krackhardt, and Porter (1981) first identified the volitional quitting of 1,389 former tellers from 190 bank branches. Next, each former teller's immediate supervisor reported judgments about (a) their preference on rehiring that person, (b) the former employee's job performance, and (c) the ease of replacing that leaver. These voluntary leavers represented a 32 percent overall turnover rate. When voluntary leavers were classified into dysfunctional (e.g., good employees quit) versus functional (e.g., marginal employees quit) based on the supervisor's judgments on preference for rehire and job performance, the turnover rate of dysfunctional leavers dropped to 18 percent. When classified by ease of replacement, dysfunctional turnover (e.g., hard to replace) dropped to 9 percent of the overall turnover rate. These data are compelling. More specifically, they indicate that the quitting of *some* people is actually functional or good for the company.

On a sample of nurses, Abelson (1987) compared the "immediate variables" (as defined above for the traditional ideas of turnover) among 136 stayers, 30 avoidable leavers, and 16 unavoidable leavers over a one-year period. Levels of job satisfaction and organizational commitment were significantly *lower* for avoidable than unavoidable leavers and stayers. That is, people who left for unavoidable reasons (e.g., a spouse relocates) had satisfaction and commitment levels comparable to those who stayed. People who left for avoidable reasons (e.g., bad work schedules) had lower attitudes than those who stayed or those who left for unavoidable reasons. In addition, levels of thinking of quitting and intentions to search and to leave were significantly *higher* for avoidable leavers than unavoidable leavers and stayers.

Should turnover be encouraged or discouraged?

When considered together, these data indicate the discernibility, if not the outright desirability, of further classifying voluntary turnover by functionality and avoidability. Nevertheless, it remains the manager's decision as to: (a) whether dysfunctional turnover should be discouraged; (b) whether functional turnover should be encouraged; and (c) whether such turnover is also avoidable or unavoidable. These decisions focus the manager on differentiating between those people he or she wants to keep and those people whose departure is less of a concern.

ACTION IMPLICATIONS

When considered together, these tentative results suggest the value in (a) monitoring for job attitudes, global withdrawal cognitions, shocks, and paths, and (b) deciding the functionality and avoidability of voluntary turnover. Although each firm's and manager's situation will be different, general action implications can be inferred from the three reviewed approaches. Initially, a company needs to decide and perhaps rank-order the "value to the firm" of each employee. That is, managers need to decide – based on a sound definition of job performance – which people's leaving should be seen as functional quits and those that should be seen as dysfunctional quits.

Job performance and the issue of functionality and avoidability

To judge whether a particular employee's quitting would be functional and perhaps avoidable, managers must have some definition of job performance. More specifically, what constitutes job performance? Because of the long-term influence from our colleagues in personnel and industrial psychology, job performance is commonly determined by a job analysis and often operationalized by the content of the firm's employee evaluation form. Historically, a host of traditional variables have been applied, which include, for example, observable work behaviors (e.g., cooperation), measurable employee actions (e.g., number of seconds between the end of one and beginning of another telemarketer's phone call), supervisory judgments (e.g., quality, quantity, and overall performance), tangible work outputs (e.g., number of widgets produced each day) or generated revenues (e.g., total sales dollars, the region's adjusted sales potential).

An emergent issue among organizational behavior scholars is whether job performance has been too narrowly defined and whether our dominant definition is myopic. Underlying these various and traditional performance variables is the standard and prescribed job. More specifically, performance is often tied very closely to the job's formally required tasks. Scholars of organizational behavior have recently asked whether focusing on and measuring performance based on a job's required tasks and behaviors is too restrictive.

Substantial research evidence shows that: whatever it is that gets measured directs employee attention (e.g., dimensions of job performance); setting standards or goals directs employee efforts and behaviors (e.g., good versus bad job performance); and providing feedback allows for corrective actions toward the set standard (e.g., the semi-annual job performance evaluation meeting). We *know* that, by focusing attention toward one's narrowly prescribed job tasks, work effort, behavior, and performance follow accordingly. It is not surprising then that focusing on one's own job can also distract such work effort, behavior, and performance *away* from other beneficial organizational actions. For a lower-level employee, for example, a focus on one's job may decrease the likelihood of helping another employee do his or her job. At the immediate cost of lost opportunity of doing one's own prescribed job, that lower-level employee may impose larger costs on organizational effectiveness by *not* helping another employee perform or learn to perform a job. For a higher-level manager, a focus on one's narrowly defined job may decrease the likelihood of meeting the larger organizational and managerial role of representing the company at recognized industry and community events. At no cost to doing one's own job, for instance, this manager may voluntarily represent the company's commitment to corporate social responsibility, community well-being or individual citizenship. Thus, employees may overly focus on the immediate job and thereby actually hurt larger organizational functioning.

Organizational behavior scholars have labeled our traditional focus on well-defined and prescribed job behaviors as task performance, in-role performance or job performance. In contrast, the broader focus that includes non job-specific effort, behavior, and performance but still benefits the larger firm is labeled role performance, contextual performance or organizational citizenship behavior. In making decisions about an employee's functional versus dysfunctional and avoidable versus unavoidable quitting, managers should *also* decide whether individual and organizational effectiveness can be enhanced by a traditional focus on the narrowly defined job (cf. task, in-role) functions or by a broader focus on task- *and* context-performance. In our judgment, the broader focus is typically better than the narrower view toward individual and organizational effectiveness.

The details of the unfolding model

The unfolding model becomes particularly helpful because (a) of its detail, (b) path 4 captures much of the traditional approach, and (c) shocks capture much of the avoidablility issue. Because the speed of path 1 quitting can be unpredictable and the speed of path 2 quitting can be quite quick, managers may have minimal opportunity to respond to shocks that may initiate leaving. Instead, they may need to have already in place a mechanism that allows for proactive and quick actions aimed at encouraging *or* discouraging an employee's leaving (e.g., pre-existing realistic job previews, quick and informal grievance procedures, open-door policies by the firm's top executives). One technique that we've developed is to gather examples of (or stories about) actual shocks (i.e., specific events that initiate actual quitting) from leavers and other examples of (or stories about) events that prompted stayers to think about quitting. Managers can then simply list these examples and ask current employees (a) whether these events would prompt thoughts of leaving and (b) what scripts they might have in place and follow if the event were to occur. This information can help managers anticipate the events that likely prompt thoughts of quitting and scripted actions. As a result, the informed manager can elect to be proactive (or inactive) in discouraging (or encouraging) leaving.

In contrast, quitting in paths 3 and 4 is more predictable and slower. People search for alternatives and evaluate the located options. Managers may have more opportunity to respond. Thus, they may have more opportunity to craft individualized actions that can encourage or discourage quitting (e.g., matching pay increases from external job offers, dealing with accumulated job dissatisfactions, restructuring one's job responsibilities, reassigning employees to other units within the company, loaning employees to external service organizations like the United Way).

How to monitor job attitudes, global withdrawal cognitions, shocks, and paths

Surveys. Job satisfaction, organizational commitment, and global withdrawal cognitions can be efficiently and validly measured via corporate surveys. In particular, these job attitudes and cognitions can be assessed with standard, professionally developed and well-researched measures (i.e., validated scales). For several of the better-known scales, moreover, they are copyrighted and commercially available. Some of these validated scales measure *global* job satisfaction, organizational commitment, and withdrawal cognitions, whereas others measure *facets* of satisfaction, commitment, and withdrawal cognitions. Although valid, standard scales are often quite long. As a result, questionnaire length can discourage survey completion, and less information is actually (and commonly) obtained. Although less reliable and less valid than the longer standard scales, researchers and managers often must compose and use a smaller number of original questions (e.g., one to five items) to measure overall job satisfaction, organizational commitment, and global withdrawal cognitions. Albeit less desirable, long-standing research practice and enduring empirical evidence indicate an *acceptable* trade-off between shorter questionnaire length and lower (though adequate) strength in predicting voluntary turnover (e.g., Arnold and Feldman, 1982).

Management by wandering around (MBWA).   Although shocks and paths can be measured with surveys, these concepts are relatively new. As a result, there are *no* standard and validated scales for their measurement. In addition to the technique of listing actual and potential shocks and scripts (described above), there are other useful techniques for identifying paths. In their delightful book, *In search of excellence*, Peters and Waterman (1982) initially recommended MBWA. The idea is simple and appealing. Managers should *prioritize* and *allocate* a certain portion of their day to watching, talking, and generally interacting with their employees. If done consistently and sincerely, understanding, empathy, and trust should develop. As a direct result, managers should readily learn: (a) what individuals interpret as shocks; (b) whether scripts exist; (c) the specific content of images and if image violations occur; and (d) whether job search cognitions and behaviors are engaged.

SOME NOTABLE EXCEPTIONS

The research that we've reviewed offers some clear advice on managing (or controlling) employee turnover. First, managers should monitor for signs or predictors of employees' quitting. Based on the substantial amount of statistical evidence, the effective and valid signs of leaving are the employees' levels of job satisfaction, organizational commitment, and global withdrawal cognitions. Albeit based on only two studies, additional signs that move monitoring beyond traditional job attitudes are shocks and paths characteristics (e.g., scripts, search and evaluation). Second, managers should decide whether the voluntary quitting is functional (versus dysfunctional) and avoidable (versus unavoidable). That is, retention should be viewed selectively. Moreover, we strongly recommend that this judgment be based on a broader, non-traditional view of job performance (i.e., both in-role/task- and contextual/citizenship-based performance). Third, managers can readily obtain information for this monitoring by routine, traditional, and periodic employee surveys and/or by "management by wandering around." With that said, however, there are a number of considerations that should strengthen or weaken our recommended actions.

Importance of workforce stability

Selective retention is *less* important in situations where workforce stability is *less* critical; conversely stated, of course, retention is more important in situations where stability is more critical. Three questions immediately arise. First, are replacement employees readily available? If replacement employees are readily available, selective retention should be less important to managers. An immediate indicator of availability is the unemployment rate in the "relevant labor market." Numerous studies indicate, for example, a consistent and very substantial relationship between aggregate turnover and unemployment rates (r's commonly .80 and higher). In general, the higher the unemployment rate, the higher should be the availability of replacement employees.

Second, can the requisite job-specific knowledge, skills, and abilities (as well as broader needs for contextual, citizenship-based performance) be readily taught? If success in training is relatively quick and inexpensive, selective retention should also be less of an issue. Two immediate and related indicators of training success are the job's organizational level and whether advanced education is required. In general, lower-level (e.g., non-exempt) jobs that do not require advanced educational experiences (e.g., bachelor's or master's degrees) should lend themselves to quicker and less expensive training than higher-level (e.g., exempt) positions that require higher education. When considered together, lower-level jobs that are filled primarily with non college-educated persons and that occur in labor markets with high unemployment rates strongly suggest far less attention might be devoted to selective retention. (For a related discussion, see chapter 21 below.)

Third, it is becoming increasingly clear that many employees are valued for their "human capital and intellectual property." More specifically, some employees may have specialized knowledge that is critical to organizational effectiveness – even if a particular employee is a marginal performer or if that knowledge can be readily conveyed through training. With the (incredible) pace of organizational change and the competitive nature of many industries, human capital and intellectual property *should* become increasingly important in a manager's judgment about what is and what is not functional turnover.

Organizational types

Selective retention and workforce stability can be *less* critical in certain organizational types. In particular, turnover is likely *unimportant* in *temporary* organizations whose sole purpose is to create a given project or produce a certain service, and then, by design, disband. Common examples include independent motion picture productions (e.g., shooting a movie), political campaigns (e.g., winning an election) and joint ventures intended to spread risk across the multiple participants (e.g., oil exploration). Similarly, bureaucracies, which are relatively *buffered* from market forces (e.g., state and local governments, public universities), may have *limited concern* with retention and stability because, for example, of sufficient slack resources, adequate time to forecast accurately human resource requirements, or *de facto* monopoly position. Finally, those organizations where creativity and innovation are critical to survival might actually consider *encouraging* departures (e.g., think tanks, innovation centers, and advertising firms).

ADDITIONAL CASE EXAMPLES

As a new century opens, dramatic and non-traditional stories about employees' quitting are becoming *common*. Our speculation is that these stories will become even more so. For example, Nirav Tolia, 27, left Yahoo! as a senior manager of its e-commerce marketing and *$10 million in unvested options*. The reason he left: upon hearing a "really interesting start-up idea from a friend [the shock]," he decided in only *one* day's time to pursue his dream [a script] of a net start-up e-commerce company (a.k.a. path 1; Bronson, 1999). Joining Tolia, Ramanathan Guha, 34, left America Online as one of its senior ranking engineers and *$4 million in unvested options* also to pursue this shared dream. In 1995, Patty Stonesifer said, "I have the very best job in the industry," leading Microsoft's Interactive Media unit. In 1996, she left to spend more time with her husband and two teenagers. The reason she left: she turned 40 years old [a shock] and reassessed what she wanted to do in the next 20 years [fit/compatibility with the shock and her values, goals, and plans for goal attainment] (a.k.a. path 2; Rebello and Hof, 1996). In 1999, she holds a senior leadership role at the Bill and Melissa Gates Foundation. These and other less dramatic stories exemplify the market-driven imperative to understand better and take proactive actions to manage employees' leaving.

"The more things change, the more things stay the same"

Given that people will and do quit firms, how have companies begun to control the leaving of these kinds of extraordinary and other less extraordinary (a.k.a. normal) people? Certainly, there is no single magic bullet that all firms should follow. With increasing frequency, however, many firms have (re)turned to the *old fashion* and in the 1990s followed the now *counter-intuitive* idea of proactively building *loyalty* via mutual company and employee commitment (Bernstein, 1998). In other words, they seek to prevent the seeds of leaving (e.g., shock, image violations, and decline in job attitudes) *before* they get planted.

With these ideas in mind, Booze, Allen & Hamilton implemented *job rotation* to help their consultants balance family and work stresses. During periods of unusual family turmoil, for example, consultants can be reassigned to jobs with stable hours and minimal travel; as a result, it is easier for their employees to deal with the work–family stresses. At International Paper (IP) and Citigroup, for instance, *career development programs* have been implemented. At IP, 13,000 white-collar workers must meet annually (and separately from their performance appraisal meetings) to map their long-term career strategies and their next specific job move. At Citigroup, 10,000 managers are reviewed twice a year to identify their next job placement.

Explaining these proactive efforts to control employee turnover via enhanced loyalty, Raymond V. Gilmartin, CEO of Merck & Co. offered the following: "The company is responsible for providing the environment in which people can achieve their full potential, and employees are responsible for developing their skills . . . That's the key to our ability *to attract and retain talent*, and it defines the *new employment relationship* as I see it today" (italics added; Bernstein, 1998: 68).

In short, labor market imperatives are driving firms to manage the quitting process proactively, and the research in organizational behavior provides strong and compelling managerial tactics.

Conclusion

In our view, this chapter mirrors a larger megapoint that underlies this entire volume. More specifically, the research on organizational behavior offers discernible, interpretable, logically consistent, and most often empirically verifiable foundation principles. With respect to controlling turnover, we *confidently* advise the following. First, decide whether that employee's quitting is functional (versus dysfunctional) and avoidable (versus unavoidable). Second, anticipate an employee's leaving by monitoring job attitudes, global withdrawal cognitions, shocks, and paths. Third, look at the shocks or levels (and reasons) of job dissatisfaction and decide whether there is anything the company can do (i.e., is this turnover avoidable?). Fourth, determine whether that employee is likely to leave more quickly (i.e., paths 1 and 2) or slowly (i.e., paths 3 and 4), which in turn advises a manager to be proactive (for path 1 and path 2 processes) or more reactive (for path 3 and path 4 processes). Fifth, gather most or all of this information by routine employee surveys and/or "management by wandering around" (i.e., talk to people). Finally, consider whether selective retention and workforce security is sufficiently important in your particular firm's situation.

Simply put, our prescriptions say that turnover is a process that requires more active attention and management than it typically receives. Employee surveys are routinely administered, for example, but this information is infrequently used for specific and proactive interventions aimed at controlling turnover. Similarly, many companies designate their "key" employees whose leaving would be clearly dysfunctional but take little action to understand the events that prompt their thoughts of leaving. Also, companies can better anticipate employees' reactions to shocks by managing the information immediately before *and* after the occurrence of a particular jarring event. Job counseling can be made available, for instance, to deflect path 3 and 4 processes. Finally, companies can simply make it harder for employees to leave by "embedding" their key employees in the organization (Mitchell, Holtom, Lee, Erez, and Sablynski, 1999). For example, using teams, having people serve as mentors or having responsibilities for projects maintains attachments (or linkages) to firms. Generous perks and rewards contingent on continued tenure can also render turnover less appealing. In sum, controlling turnover requires substantial understanding of the phenomenon and the willingness to be proactive or reactive in managing the quitting process. Ultimately, appropriate management of turnover can increase organizational effectiveness and the bottom line.

REFERENCES

Abelson, M. (1987). Examination of avoidable and unavoidable turnover. *Journal of Applied Psychology*, 72, 382–6.

Arnold, H. J., and Feldman, D. C. (1982). A multivariate analysis of the determinants of job turnover. *Journal of Applied Psychology*, 67, 350–60.

Bernstein, A. (1998). We want you to stay. Really. *Business Week* (June 22), 67–72.

Bronson, P. (1999). Instant company. *The New York Times Magazine* (July 11), 44–7.

Dalton, D. R., Krackhart, D. M., and Porter, L. W. (1981). Functional turnover: an empirical assessment. *Journal of Applied Psychology*, 66, 716–21.

Hom, P. W., and Griffeth, R. W. (1995). *Employee Turnover*. Cincinnati, OH: South-Western College Publishing.

Lee, T. W., and Maurer, S. D. (1997). The retention of knowledge workers with the unfolding model of voluntary turnover. *Human Resource Management Review*, 7, 247–75.

Lee, T. W., and Mitchell, T. R. (1994). An alternative approach: the unfolding model of voluntary employee turnover. *Academy of Management Review*, 19, 51–89.

Lee, T. W., Mitchell, T. R., Holtom, B. C., McDaniel, L. S., and Hill, J. W. (1999). The unfolding model of turnover: A replication and extension. *Academy of Management Journal*, 42, 450–62.

Lee, T. W., Mitchell, T. R., Wise, L., and Fireman, S. (1996). An unfolding model of voluntary employee turnover. *Academy of Management Journal*, 39, 5–36.

Maetz, C. P. Jr., and Campion, M. A. (1998). 25 years of voluntary turnover research: A review and critique. In C. L. Cooper and I. T. Robertson (eds.), *International review of industrial and organizational psychology* (Vol. 13, pp. 49–81). New York: John Wiley & Sons.

Mathieu, J. E., and Zajac, D. M. (1990). A review and meta-analysis of the antecedents, correlates, and consequences of organizational commitment. *Psychological Bulletin*, 108, 171–94.

Mitchell, T. R., Holtom, B. C., Lee, T. W., Erez, M., and Sablynski, C. J. (1999). The retention of employees: The role of organizational embeddedness. Paper presented at the 59th annual meeting of the Academy of Management, Chicago, IL, Aug.

Peters, T. J., and Waterman, R. H. (1982). *In search of excellence*. New York: Harper & Row.

Rebello, K., and Hof, R. D. (1996). She's smart, she's successful, she's outta here. *Business Week* (11 Nov.), 40.

Spector, P. E. (1997). *Job Satisfaction*. Thousand Oaks, CA: Sage Publications.

Part IV

MOTIVATION

8   Motivate Employee Performance through Goal-setting
      GARY P. LATHAM

9   Cultivate Self-efficacy for Personal and Organizational
    Effectiveness
      ALBERT BANDURA

10 Motivate Performance through Empowerment
      JAY A. CONGER

11 Pay for Performance
      CATHY C. DURHAM AND KATHRYN M. BARTOL

12 Provide Recognition for Performance Improvement
      FRED LUTHANS AND ALEXANDER D. STAJKOVIC

13 Promote Procedural Justice to Enhance Acceptance of Work
    Outcomes
      JERALD GREENBERG

8

Motivate Employee Performance through Goal-setting

Gary P. Latham

Goal-setting (Locke and Latham, 1990a) is among the most valid and practical theories of employee motivation. This conclusion has been reached by multiple authors working independently (e.g., Earley and Lee, 1992 ; Miner, 1984; Pinder, 1984, 1998). The conclusion is based on the fact that the theory has been shown to predict, influence, and explain the behavior of over 40,000 people in numerous countries (e.g., Australia, Canada, the Caribbean, England, Germany, Israel, Japan, and the United States), in both laboratory and field settings, involving at least 88 different tasks in occupations that included logging, word processing, engineering, and teaching in a university. Although developed as a theory of motivation in the workplace, it has been used effectively in sport psychology (Weinberg, 1994). Most recently the theory has been found useful for promoting the motivational processes of brain-injured patients (Gauggel, 1999; Prigatano, Wong, Williams, and Plenge, 1997).

MAIN PRINCIPLE

The theory states that the simplest most direct motivational explanation of why some people perform better than others is because they have different performance goals (Latham and Locke, 1991). The essence of the theory is fourfold. First, difficult specific goals lead to significantly higher performance than easy goals, no goals, or even the setting of an abstract goal such as urging people to do their best. Second, holding ability constant, as this is a theory of motivation, and given that there is goal commitment, the higher the goal the higher the performance. Third, variables such as praise, feedback, or the involvement of people in decision-making only influences behavior to the extent that it leads to the setting of and commitment to a specific difficult goal. Fourth, goal-setting, in addition to affecting the three mechanisms of motivation, namely, choice, effort, and persistence, can also have a cognitive benefit. It can influence choice, effort, and persistence to discover ways to attain the goal.

SUB-PRINCIPLES

There are at least four sub-principles necessary for deriving the motivational benefits of goal-setting. The goal must be challenging and specific, feedback must be provided on progress in relation to goal attainment, ways must be found to maintain goal commitment, and resources must be provided for and obstacles removed to goal attainment.

Set challenging specific goals

The goal must be both challenging and specific. Given adequate ability and commitment to the goal, the higher the goal the higher the performance. This is because people normally adjust their level of effort to the difficulty of the goal. In addition to being targets to attain, goals are the standards by which one judges one's adequacy or success. Challenging goals facilitate pride in accomplishment. People with low goals are minimally satisfied with low performance attainment, and become increasingly satisfied with every level of attainment that exceeds their goal. This is also true for individuals with a high goal. To be minimally satisfied, they must accomplish more than those who have a low goal. Consequently, they set a high goal to attain before they will be satisfied with their accomplishment. In short, to be satisfied, employees with high standards must accomplish more than those with low standards. In addition, an employee's outcome expectancies are typically higher for the attainment of high rather than low goals because the outcome one can expect from attaining a challenging goal usually includes such factors as an increase in feelings of self- efficacy, recognition from peers, a salary increase, a job promotion, etc. As a result people, in most instances, commit to high goals.

Goal specificity facilitates an employee's focus in that it makes explicit what it is the individual has chosen to exert effort to persist in attaining. Specificity also facilitates measurement or feedback on progress toward goal attainment. A drawback of an abstract goal such as "do your best" is that it allows people to give themselves the benefit of the doubt concerning the adequacy of their performance (Kernan and Lord, 1989). Thus maximum effort is not aroused. For feedback to be used intelligently, it must be interpreted in relation to a specific goal. Goal specificity clarifies for the employee what constitutes effective performance.

For goal-setting to be maximally effective, the goal and the measurement of progress toward its attainment must be aligned. Thus, if a logger wants to increase productivity by 15 percent, the performance measure must be the number of trees cut down divided by the hours worked. If a scientist in the organization's R&D division wishes to increase client satisfaction, the goal set can be a specific increase in the frequency of behaviors emitted that have been identified through job analysis as necessary for client satisfaction. Goals and the measures of their attainment that have appeared in the scientific literature include physical effort, quantity and quality measures of production, costs, profits, and job behavior.

Challenging, specific goals affect persistence (Latham and Locke, 1991). When no time limits are imposed, specific high goals induce people to work faster or harder than is the case when low or abstract goals are set. Without time limits, specific high goals induce people to work until the goal is attained. With time limits, difficult specific goals lead to more effort per unit of time. The American Pulpwood Association found that when paper companies impose quotas on the number of days that they will buy wood from pulpwood crews, the crews cut as much wood in the restricted number of days as they do in a normal five-day work week (Latham and Locke, 1975).

In summary, setting specific, challenging goals is important for increasing both job satisfaction and job performance. Job satisfaction is the result of an appraisal of one's performance against one's goals. Job satisfaction is not a result of the person alone or the job alone, but of the person in relation to the job. To the extent that one's job performance is appraised as fulfilling or facilitating the attainment of one's goals, satisfaction is high (Locke and Latham, 1990b).

Provide feedback in relation to goals

A truism attributed to the late Mason Haire is "that which gets measured gets done." This is because the act of measurement conveys cogently what the organization truly values versus what it may state that it values. However, the accuracy of Haire's statement is improved through the insertion of the word goals: that which is measured in relation to goals is done. Both goal-setting theory and empirical research indicate that in the absence of goal-setting, feedback has no effect on performance. This is because feedback is only information; its effect on action depends on how it is appraised and what decisions are made with respect to it.

For example, the Weyerhaeuser Company found that engineers and scientists who were urged to do their best after receiving a performance appraisal performed no better than their counterparts in a control group. A significant increase in performance occurred only among those engineers and scientists who received feedback in relation to specific high goals (Latham, Mitchell, and Dossett, 1978).

Feedback, however, is a moderator of goal-setting. Without feedback, the positive benefit of goal-setting is minimized (Erez, 1977). This is because goals direct effort and persistence. Feedback is a relational concept. It allows people to discern what they should continue doing, stop doing, or start doing to attain the goal.

Gain goal commitment

Once the goal is set, ways must be found to gain commitment to it. Commitment is the *sine qua non* of goal-setting. Without it, goal-setting is a meaningless exercise. Two primary ways to gain commitment are to focus on an individual's outcome expectancies and self-efficacy (see chapter 9 below)

A downside of setting challenging specific goals is that people may obtain tangible evidence that they did not attain them. A teenager has multiple test scores that provide strong evidence of failure in math. An employee in a consulting firm may have hours and hours of wasted effort, non-billable hours, on a potential client who subsequently took the business to a competitor. The result can be feelings of loss of control. People learn on the basis of data (e.g., revenue, client surveys, staff turnover) that they have failed to attain their goal no matter how much they have truly tried to attain it. Through such repeated experiences they learn to give up; they learn helplessness. Thus there are employees who have learned that they cannot increase revenue with existing clients, they have learned that they are poor at bringing in new clients, and there are still others who have learned that they are not able to work effectively with staff. They have tangible evidence to support their conclusions that they should give up attempts to attain the goal.

The solutions for maintaining goal commitment are at least twofold. A first step, as noted above, is to focus on *outcome expectancies*. The role of a coach is to help people see the relationship between what they do and the outcome of their actions; to help people realize the outcomes that they can expect as a result of what they do. An early example of how outcome expectancies affect goal commitment can be found in a study by Lashley (1929) who cited a case of a man who after 900 repetitions was not able to master the alphabet. After the man was bet 100 cigarettes that he could not learn the alphabet in a week, he proceeded to do so in only ten trials.

Because the concept of outcome expectancies is as useful in one's personal life as it is in an organizational setting, allow me to share a personal example. Recently, I arrived home to discover my four children, ages 19–25, on the front step. They greeted me with the warning not to enter the house as Mom was in a horrific mood. As she walked across the kitchen floor, her foot came out of a shoe that had stuck to dried milk. As she fell, her hand braced her from injury as it slipped into an open dishwasher that oozed with leftover breakfast food.

For me to announce that I would solve the problem would not only have been lunacy on my part, it would have fostered dependence: "Let's wait until Dad gets here; he can fix anything." To look for blame would have been equally foolhardy on my part: "So what did you do to get your mother in such a bad mood?" "I don't know." "It wasn't me." "She is always in a bad mood." "I bet you did something, Dad."

The primary job of a coach is to improve performance rather than focus on blame. This is done through increasing the person's sense of control regarding the attainment of their goals. It is done by helping people to realize the outcomes they can expect from engaging in specific actions. Thus, I simply asked each of them "What can you do within the next 30 seconds to improve Mom's mood?" Setting a goal focuses attention on discovering solutions to its attainment.

One son offered to clean the kitchen, another said he would get us both a drink, the third said he would make dinner. My daughter quietly ran off to prepare a bath for my wife. The outcome, as expected, was a dramatic upswing in my wife's affect and behavior.

A second step to maintaining goal commitment is to increase the person's *self-efficacy*. Self-efficacy is the strong belief, the conviction that "I can cause . . . I can bring about . . . I can make happen . . . ". Self-efficacy is different from self-esteem in that the latter refers to affect. How much does Pat like Pat? Self-efficacy is task specific. The two are not necessarily related.

Pat can have low self-esteem and high self-efficacy regarding ability to bring in new clients. Conversely, Pat may love Pat more than anyone else could possibly love Pat. Yet Pat may have low self-efficacy in the ability to make a persuasive presentation to a potential client. Conversely, Pat may have low self-esteem due to a variety of events that have occurred in Pat's past. Pat has said and done things that are deeply regretted. For these reasons no one dislikes Pat today more than Pat does. Nevertheless, Pat believes (high self-efficacy) that there is no one who is as effective in bringing in new business to the firm. Because self-efficacy is task specific, an individual may have high self-efficacy on ability to work effectively with staff, low self-efficacy on working effectively with clients, and moderate self-efficacy on ability to work effectively within the firm.

People who have problems with self-esteem should be referred to clinical psychologists. People who have low self-efficacy can be coached in the workplace.

Bandura (1986, 1997) has shown that it is not just our ability that holds us back or propels us forward, it is also our perception of our ability. People with low self-efficacy look for tangible evidence to abandon a goal. A failure is confirmation that it is useless to persist in goal attainment. Conversely, people with high self-efficacy commit to high goals. They view obstacles and setbacks to goal attainment as challenges to overcome, as sources of excitement to be savored.

A possible indicator of low self-efficacy is denigration. Statements such as "I have no use for computers" should be probed by coaches as it may indicate a fear of lack of ability to do what is required to attain the goal.

High self-efficacy can be induced in the workplace in at least three ways: enactive mastery, modeling, and persuasion from a significant other. Enactive mastery involves sequencing a task in such a way that all but guarantees early successes. For example, to increase confidence in the use of a laptop, the following steps should be followed: (a) open/close, (b) on-off, (c) keyboard skills. Early successes through "small wins" build confidence that "I can do this," and that the goal is indeed attainable.

An effective coach does not abandon an employee during the early stages of learning to attain a goal. To leave the employee to master keyboard skills before teaching the process of "save" is to provide the employee with a reason for abandoning the laptop in favor of pen and paper. All that was typed is lost forever when the laptop is turned off in the absence of knowledge of the necessity to "save."

A way to induce the employee to return to the laptop after all has been lost forever is to focus on potential outcomes that are perceived as desirable by that individual. If the person is one who loses everything that is filed, explain how material can be saved and retrieved easily on a hard drive or a disc. If the person hates the traditional "snail" mail system, show how hitting two keys on the computer will send material any place in the world in seconds. In short, enable the person to see the relationship between mastery of the laptop and the desired outcomes the person can expect.

A second way to increase self-efficacy regarding goal commitment is through the use of models. The job of coach is to find people with whom the goal setter identifies who have either mastered the task, or are in the process of doing so. For example, directing a manager who is struggling in the development of staff to another manager who has the "magic touch" with staff is necessary, but not sufficient for increasing self-efficacy. It can even backfire as a coaching technique if this is all that is done because the person who is struggling may give up on coaching after concluding that "I will never acquire that 'magic touch'. " Directing this manager to visit an additional colleague who has struggled recently in the past, and has subsequently improved the performance of staff, increases the belief that "if she can, so can I."

Visiting a benchmark company can be a demotivating experience. The idea underlying benchmarking is to minimize reinventing the wheel on the part of people in other organizations. Through benchmarking, the acquisition of KSAs is accelerated. But the downside of benchmarking is that visitors can leave full of admiration for what they have witnessed, and demoralized because they are convinced that they do not have the ability to model it. "Their management system is different from ours. Their union contract is nothing like ours. There is no way that we can be like them." To combat low self-efficacy, a coach must find an organization, in addition to the one that will be used as a benchmark, with whom we can identify – an organization that has significantly improved its performance relative to that benchmark, or is in the process of doing so. Finding and visiting this additional organization increases the belief that "if they can, so can we."

The American Pulpwood Association found that supervisory presence is also a key to goal commitment and productivity (Ronan, Latham and Kinne, 1973). When the goal is assigned by a supportive authority figure, goal commitment and performance are high (Latham and Saari, 1979a). These findings are supported by a meta-analysis that showed a 56 percent average gain in productivity when management commitment to an MBO (Management by Objectives) program is high versus a 6 percent increase when their commitment is low (Rodgers and Hunter, 1991). Thus, it is not surprising that Bandura (see chapter 9) found that a third way of increasing self-efficacy is through persuasion from a significant other. People tend to behave in accordance with the expectations of those people who are significant to them. Assigned goals usually lead to high goal commitment because listening to the assignment without objection is in itself a form of consent (Salancik, 1977). Assigning the goal implies that the recipient is capable of attaining it, which in turn increase the person's self-efficacy regarding the task.

Bandura, a past president of the American Psychological Association, and currently the Honorary President of the Canadian Psychological Association, addressed a class-room of executives as follows:

> We know that intelligence is fixed. You either have it or you don't. We are going to put you through a simulation consisting of tasks that you typically confront as CEOs. I know you will find these tasks frustrating and seemingly impossible.

In an adjoining room, he addressed the other half of the class of executives as follows:

> We know that intelligence is not fixed. Intelligence is the ability to apply what you have learned on previous tasks to present ones. We are going to put you through a simulation consisting of tasks that you typically confront as CEOs. I know that you will find these tasks challenging and fun.

Several hours later he pushed back the dividing wall. The people in the second group were laughing among themselves as to how similar the simulation was to their daily work lives, and how much they had learned from their experiences that afternoon. The people in the first group were truly angry and frustrated. They demanded to be allowed to go through the same simulation as the second group before their four weeks of executive education at Stanford came to a close. The simulation that they had gone through they claimed, was not similar to what they encountered on their jobs and hence was a waste of their time.

In short, both groups behaved in accordance with Bandura's expectations of them, despite the fact that the simulation was identical for both groups. These expectations were communicated in only seconds.

A coach may or may not be a significant other for the person who is being coached. Thus a role of a coach is to determine the identity of the person's significant other, and have that individual or individuals communicate, if true, why they believe the person can attain the goal.

The most powerful significant other is one's self. Verbal self-guidance or functional self-talk can increase or debilitate self-confidence in goal attainment. We are often our worst enemy. Millman and Latham (in press) trained displaced managers to systematically monitor their self-talk to exclude negative comments and increase positive ones with respect to job attainment. Within nine months, 48 percent of the people who were trained obtained a job that paid ± $10,000 of their previous job; only one person of eight in the control group was able to do so. The self-efficacy of the participants in the group who were trained in functional self-talk was significantly higher than those in the control group.

The order in which these two steps, outcome expectancies and self-efficacy, should be implemented varies by individual. If outcome expectancies are already high, this step may be skipped in favor of focusing immediately on self-efficacy.

Provide resources needed to attain the goal

Goals are unlikely to be attained if situational constraints blocking their attainment are not removed. Thus the organization needs to ensure that the time, money, people, and equipment necessary for goal attainment exist. Most importantly the measurement system must not only allow accurate tracking of goal progress, it must be aligned with and supportive of goal attainment.

For example, a newly hired professor may set a goal to receive a mean score of 5 or higher on a seven-point scale of teaching effectiveness rated by students. If the measurement system for promotion and tenure focuses primarily on publications in mainstream academic journals, and resources are provided primarily for conducting research, commitment to this teaching goal may quickly wane.

Arguably, the most important resource necessary for accruing the positive benefits of goal-setting is the employee's ability. Organizations must provide the required training to give people the knowledge and skill to attain the goal. This is because the relation of goal difficulty to performance is curvilinear. Performance levels off after the limit of ability has been reached (Locke, Fredrick, Brukner, and Bobko, 1984).

EXCEPTIONS TO PRINCIPLES

Learning versus outcome goals

Consistent with the above findings regarding an individual's ability are studies by Earley, Connolly, and Ekegren (1989) as well as Kanfer and Ackerman (1989). They found that when people lack the requisite knowledge to master a task, because they are in the early stages of learning, urging them to do their best results in higher performance than setting a specific difficult goal. The reasons are at least threefold (Locke and Latham, 1990a). First, such tasks are complex for people. Thus the direct goal mechanisms of effort, persistence, and choice are no longer sufficient to ensure high performance. This is because people have yet to learn the correct strategy for performing effectively. Second, such tasks require primarily learning rather than motivation. People have no problem-solving processes for these tasks to draw upon. Third, people with specific high goals feel pressure to perform well immediately. As a result, they focus more on their desire to get results than on learning the correct way of performing the task. In short, tasks that are straightforward as well as those that are complex for an individual require attentional resources, but the resource demands of the latter tasks are greater than those of the former (Kanfer, 1990). Where tasks fall within the problem-solving abilities of people, as in cases where they have had experience with the task, specific difficult outcome goals lead to the development and execution of task-specific strategies. Truck drivers at Weyerhaeuser found ways to increase truck loads (Latham and Baldes, 1975) and to decrease truck turnaround time (Latham and Saari, 1982) after being assigned a specific difficult goal.

These explanations are consistent with Dweck's (1986) experiments with young children. Children in a learning mode who are given task-mastery goals do not do as well as those who are urged to do their best on tasks where they have had little or no experience.

Winters and Latham (1996) replicated the above results using a complex class-scheduling task developed by Earley (1985). However, they found that the deleterious effect of a specific difficult goal on performance was not due to a fault in goal-setting theory, but rather in the type of goal that was set. Consistent with the previous findings, there was a decrease in performance when a specific high-outcome goal was set regarding the number of schedules to be produced relative to simply urging people to do their best. But, when a high-learning goal was set in terms of discovering a specific number of ways to solve the task, performance was significantly higher in this condition than it was when people were urged to do their best or had set an outcome goal. This is because a learning goal requires people to focus on understanding the task that is required of them and develop a plan for performing it correctly. High performance is not always the result of high effort or persistence, but rather, high cognitive understanding of the task and strategy or plan necessary to complete it (Frese and Zapf, 1994; Hacker, 1987).

Environmental uncertainty

Among the biggest impediments to goal-setting is environmental uncertainty (Locke and Latham, 1990a). This is because the information required to set learning or outcome goals may be unavailable. And even when such information is available, it may become obsolete due to rapid changes in the environment. Thus as uncertainty increases, it becomes increasingly difficult to set and commit to a long-term goal.

In a simulation of such a situation, Latham and Seijts (1999) replicated the findings of Earley et al. (1987) and Kanfer and Ackerman (1989) using a business game where high school students were paid on a piece-rate basis to make toys, and the dollar amounts paid for the toys changed continuously without warning. Setting a specific high-outcome goal resulted in profits that were significantly worse than urging the students to do their best. But when proximal outcome goals were set in addition to the distal goal, profit was significantly higher than in the other two conditions. This is because in highly dynamic situations, it is important to actively search for feedback and react quickly to it (Frese and Zapf, 1994). In addition, Dorner (1991) has found that performance errors on a dynamic task are often due to deficient decomposition of a goal into proximal goals. Proximal goals can increase what Frese and Zapf (1994) call error management. Errors provide information to employees as to whether their picture of reality is congruent with goal attainment. There is an increase in informative feedback when proximal or sub-goals are set relative to setting a distal goal only.

In addition to being informative, the setting of proximal goals can also be motivational relative to a distal goal that is far into the future. Moreover, the attainment of proximal goals can increase commitment, through enactive mastery, to attain the distal goal (Bandura, 1986).

Issues in Implementation

For what should goals be set? As a theory of motivation, a goal refers to a desired outcome in terms of level of performance to be attained on a task. Goal content refers to the object or result that is sought after (Locke and Latham, 1990a). Thus goals should be set for outcomes that are critical or valued by the individual or the organization in which the person is employed. An employee may have a career goal, a job goal, a financial goal, as well as psychological goals including job satisfaction and self-efficacy.

Because a goal is the object or aim of an action, the completion of a task can be a goal. As noted by Locke and Latham (1990a), in most goal-setting studies the term goal refers to attaining a specific standard of proficiency on a given task within a specific time frame. This has resulted in practitioners of goal-setting creating the acronym SMART, namely goals that are *s*pecific, *m*easurable, *a*ttainable, *r*elevant, and have a *t*ime frame (Mealiea and Latham, 1996).

Who should set the goals?

A seminal study at the General Electric Company (Meyer, Kay, and French, 1965) revealed that it is not so important who sets the goal as it is that a specific challenging goal in fact be set. However, subsequent laboratory and field experiments revealed contradictory findings. Erez and her colleagues (e.g., Erez, 1986; Erez and Arad, 1986; Erez, Earley, and Hulin, 1985) found that goal commitment and subsequent perform-ance is higher when employees participate in the setting of the goal than was the case when the goals were assigned. A series of 11 studies by Latham and his colleagues (e.g., Latham and Saari, 1979a, 1979b; Latham and Steele, 1983) found that when goal difficulty is held constant, goal commitment and performance are the same regardless of whether the goal is assigned or set participatively.

In what is rare if not unique in science, the two antagonists, Erez and Latham, did a series of collaborative studies, with Locke as a mediator, to discover the basis for their conflicting findings (Latham, Erez, and Locke, 1988). They found that their methodology was highly similar in the way that goals were set participatively, yet highly different in the way in which the goals were assigned. In what would be expected, based on Greenberg's organizational justice principles (see chapter 13 below), when the assigned goal was given tersely, it had an inferior effect on performance relative to participatively set goals. When an assigned goal from an authority figure included a logic or rationale, it had the same positive effect on goal commitment and performance as did a participatively set goal. Reasons for this null finding for the superior motivational effect of employee participation in decision-making on performance is elaborated upon by Wagner (see chapter 21 below).

Subsequent research by Latham, Winters, and Locke (1994) revealed that Erez had been correct in arguing the benefit of participation in goal-setting; but she was right to do so for the wrong reason. The benefit is primarily cognitive rather than motivational. Employee participation in decision-making has a positive effect on performance to the extent that it increases self-efficacy and the discovery of task-relevant strategies. When this does not occur, when these two variables are partialed out, participation in decision-making has a negligible effect on performance.

Training self-regulation

The management of oneself lies at the core of goal-setting theory. Setting a goal and taking action to attain it is a volitional process. Holding goal difficulty constant, self-set goals are as effective, but not more effective, in increasing performance as are goals that are assigned or set participatively (Locke and Latham, 1990a). This finding is the basis for training people in skills in self-management.

Example: The University of Washington.   The University of Washington trained their maintenance employees (carpenters, mechanics, electricians) in self-regulation to increase their job attendance (Frayne and Latham, 1987). The training took place in a group setting, for one hour a week for eight weeks. In the first session, the principles of goal-setting were explained to the trainees. In session 2, the trainees generated reasons for their low job attendance. The third session focused on the value of setting behavioral and outcome (days present) goals for attendance. In the fourth session, the importance of self-monitoring one's behavior was discussed. Specifically, the trainees were taught to use charts and diaries to record (a) their own attendance, (b) the reasons for missing one or more days of the week, and (c) the steps that were followed to subsequently return to work. The trainees identified rewards and punishers in the fifth session that they would self-administer contingent upon their attendance. In the sixth session the trainees wrote a behavioral contract with themselves. The contract specified in writing the goal(s) to be attained, the time frame for attaining it, the outcomes of attaining or failing to attain the goal(s), and the task strategies necessary for attaining the goal(s). The seventh session emphasized maintenance. That is, discussion focused on issues that might result in a relapse in absenteeism, planning for such situations should they occur, and developing strategies for dealing with such situations. During the final week of training, the trainer reviewed each technique presented in the program, answered questions from the trainees regarding these skills, and clarified expectations for self-management.

Observe that the training took explicit account of goal-setting moderators and sub-principles discussed earlier in this chapter. Goal commitment was the focus of sessions 5 and 6 where rewards and punishers were selected, and a behavioral contract was written. Feedback through self-monitoring was emphasized in session 4. The complexity of the task and the situational constraints were the focus of session 2, where employees specified in writing the behavior that they believed would enable them to get to work, and session 7, where they outlined possibilities for a relapse and what could be done to overcome such issues.

Participatory group discussions occurred throughout the eight weeks of training. The main benefit of participation, as noted earlier, is cognitive; thus the training focused the attention of each person in the group on identifying effective strategies for overcoming obstacles to attaining the goal. In this way self-efficacy was increased. Self-efficacy correlated significantly in the study with subsequent job attendance. Three months later employee attendance was significantly higher in the training than in the control group.

The University of Washington conducted a six-month and a nine-month follow-up study to determine the long-term effects of this training. Employees who had been trained in self-management continued to have higher job attendance than those in the control group. Moreover, when the people in the control group were subsequently given the same training in self-management, but by a different trainer, they too showed the same positive improvement in their self-efficacy with regard to coping with obstacles perceived by them as preventing them from coming to work. Moreover, their job attendance increased to the same level as that which the original training group had achieved three months after it had been trained (Latham and Frayne, 1989).

When are goals ineffective?

The answer to this question is given throughout this chapter. For example, both the American Pulpwood Association and Weyerhaeuser found that when the goal is abstract, such as urging loggers to do their best, productivity is lower than when a specific difficult goal is set (Latham and Kinne, 1974; Latham and Yukl, 1975). They also found that – when goals are set and supervisory supportiveness is lacking – turnover is high, people quit (Ronan, Latham, and Kinne, 1973). When specific challenging outcome goals were set before people had acquired knowledge and skill to perform the task, the performance of airforce cadets dropped (Kanfer and Ackerman, 1989).

SUMMARY

Specific challenging goals are motivational regardless of whether they are self-set, set participatively, or assigned. If the person has the knowledge and skill necessary to perform the task, outcome goals should be set. If the requisite knowledge or skill is lacking, learning goals should be set. If the moderators and sub-principles described in this chapter are taken into account by practitioners of goal-setting, the probability that performance and satisfaction will increase is above .90 (Locke and Latham, 1990a). No other theory of motivation has been found to be as consistently effective in the workplace as goal-setting.

REFERENCES

Bandura, A. (1986). *Social foundations of thought and action: A social cognitive theory*. Englewood-Cliffs, NJ: Prentice-Hall.

Bandura, A. (1997). *Self-efficacy*. New York: W. H. Freeman.

Dorner, D. (1991). The investigation of action regulation in uncertain and complex situations. In J. Rasmussen, G. Brehmer, and J. Leplat (eds.), *Distributed decision making: Cognitive models for cooperative work* (pp. 349–56). New York: Wiley.

Dweck, C. S. (1986). Motivational processes affecting learning. *American Psychologist*, 41, 1040–8.

Earley, P. C. (1985). Influence of information, choice and task complexity upon goal acceptance, performance, and personal goals. *Journal of Applied Psychology*, 70, 481–91.

Earley, P. C., Connolly, T., and Ekegren, G. (1989). Goals, strategy development and task performance: Some limits to the efficacy of goal setting. *Journal of Applied Psychology*, 74, 24–33.

Earley, P. C., and Lee, C. (1992). Comparative peer evaluations of organizational behavior theories. *Organizational Development Journal*, 10(4), 37–42.

Earley, C. P., Wojnaroski, P., and Prest, W. (1987). Task planning and energy expended: Exploration of how goals influence performance. *Journal of Applied Psychology*, 72, 107–14.

Erez, M. (1977). Feedback: A necessary condition for the goal setting–performance relationship. *Journal of Applied Psychology*, 62, 624–7.

Erez, M. (1986). The congruence of goal setting strategies with socio-cultural values, and its effect on performance. *Journal of Management*, 12, 83–90.

Erez, M., and Arad, R. (1986). Participative goal setting: Social, motivational, and cognitive factors. *Journal of Applied Psychology*, 71, 591–7.

Erez, M., Earley, P. C., and Hulin, C. L. (1985). The impact of participation on goal acceptance and performance: A two-step model. *Academy of Management Journal*, 28, 50–66.

Frayne, C. A., and Latham, G. P. (1987). The application of social learning theory to employee self-management of attendance. *Journal of Applied Psychology*, 72, 387–92.

Frese, M., and Zapf, D. (1994). Action as the core of work psychology: A German approach. In H. C. Triandis, M. D. Dunnette, and L. M. Hough (eds.), *Handbook of industrial and organizational psychology*, 2nd edn. (Vol. 4, pp. 271–340). Palo Alto, CA: Consulting Psychologists Press.

Gauggel, S. (1999). Goal-setting and its influence on the performance of brain-damaged patients. Unpublished doctoral dissertation, Philipps University of Marburg, Germany.

Greenberg, J. (1987). A taxonomy of organizational justice theories. *Academy of Management Review*, 12, 9–22.

Hacker, W. (1987). Computerization versus computer aided mental work. In M. Frese, E. Ulich, and W. Dzida (eds.), *Psychological issues of human–computer interaction in the workplace* (pp. 115–30). Amsterdam: North-Holland.

Kanfer, R. (1990). Motivation theory and industrial and organizational theory. In M. D. Dunnette and L. M. Hough (eds.), *Handbook of industrial and organizational psychology*, 2nd edn. (Vol. 1, pp. 75– 170). Palo Alto, CA: Consulting Psychologists Press.

Kanfer, R., and Ackerman, P. L. (1989). Motivation and cognitive abilities: An integrative/aptitude-treatment interaction approach to skill acquisition. *Journal of Applied Psychology*, 74, 657–90.

Kernan, M. C., and Lord, R. G. (1989). Effects of participative versus assigned goals and feedback in a multitrial task. *Motivation and Emotion*, 12, 75–86.

Lashley, K. S. (1929). *Brain mechanisms and intelligence.* Chicago: University of Chicago Press.

Latham, G. P., and Baldes, J. J. (1975). The "practical significance" of Locke's theory of goal setting. *Journal of Applied Psychology*, 60, 122–4.

Latham, G. P. and Frayne, C. (1989). Self-management training for increasing job attendance: A follow-up and a replication. *Journal of Applied Psychology*, 74, 411–16.

Latham, G. P., Erez, M., and Locke, E. A. (1988). Resolving scientific disputes by the joint design of crucial experiments by the antagonists: Application to the Erez–Latham dispute regarding participation in goal setting. *Journal of Applied Psychology*, 73(4), 753–72.

Latham, E. P. and Kinne, S. B. (1974). Improving job performance through training in goal setting. *Journal of Applied Psychology*, 59, 187–91. Reprinted in K. N. Wexley and G. A. Yukl (eds.), *Organizational behavior and industrial psychology*. New York: Oxford, 1975.

Latham, G. P., and Locke, E. A. (1975). Increasing productivity with decreasing time limits: A field replication of Parkinson's law. *Journal of Applied Psychology*, 60, 524–6.

Latham, G. P., and Locke, E. A. (1991). Self regulation through goal setting. *Organizational Behavior and Human Decision Process*, 50, 212–47.

Latham, G. P., Mitchell, T. R., and Dossett, D. L. (1978). The importance of participative goal setting and anticipated rewards on goal difficulty and job performance. *Journal of Applied Psychology*, 63, 170–1.

Latham, G. P., and Saari, L. M. (1979a). The effects of holding goal difficulty constant on assigned and participatively set goals. *Academy of Management Journal*, 22, 163–8.

Latham, G. P., and Saari, L. M. (1979b). The importance of supportive relationships in goal setting. *Journal of Applied Psychology*, 64, 151–6.

Latham, G. P., and Saari, L. M. (1982). The importance of union acceptance for productivity improvement through goal setting. *Personnel Psychology*, 35, 781–7.

Latham, G. P., and Seijts, G. H. (1999). The effects of proximal and distal goals on performance on a moderately complex task. *Journal of Organizational Behavior*, 20, 421–9.

Latham, G. P., and Steele, T. P. (1983). The motivational effects of participation versus goal setting on performance. *Academy of Management Journal*, 26, 406–17.

Latham, G. P., Winters, D. C., and Locke, E. A. (1994). Cognitive and motivational effects of participation: A mediator study. *Journal of Organizational Behavior*, 15, 49–63.

Latham, G. P., and Yukl, G. A. (1975). Assigned versus participative goal setting with educated and uneducated wood workers. *Journal of Applied Psychology*, 60, 299–302.

Locke, E. A., Frederick, E., Buckner, E., and Bobko, P. (1984). Effect of previously assigned goals on self-set goals and performance. *Journal of Applied Psychology*, 69, 694–9.

Locke, E. A., and Latham, G. P. (1990a). *A theory of goal setting and task performance.* Englewood Cliffs, NJ: Prentice Hall.

Locke, E. A., and Latham, G. P. (1990b). Work motivation: The high performance cycle. In U. Kleinbeck and H. Thierry (eds.), *Work motivation*. Hillsdale, NJ: Lawrence Erlbaum.

Mealiea, L. W., and Latham, G. P. (1996). *Skills for managerial success: Theory, experience, and practice.* Toronto, ON: Irwin.

Meyer, H. H., Kay, E., and French, J. R. P. Jr. (1965). Split roles in performance appraisal. *Harvard Business Review*, 43, 123–9.

Millman, Z., and Latham, G. P. (in press). Increasing re-employment through training in verbal self guidance. In M. Erez, U. Kleinbeck, and H. K. Thierry (eds.), *Work motivation in the context of a globalizing economy*. Hillsdale, NJ: Lawrence Erlbaum.

Miner, J. B. (1984). The validity and usefulness of theories in an emerging organizational science. *Academy of Management Review*, 9, 296–306.

Pinder, C. C. (1984). *Work motivation: Theory, issues and applications.* Glenview, IL: Scott, Foresman.

Pinder, C. C. (1998). *Work motivation in organizational behavior.* Toronto, ON: Prentice-Hall.

Prigatano, G. P., Wong, J. L., Williams, C., and Plenge, K. L. (1997). Prescribed versus actual length of stay and impatient neurorehabilitation outcome for brain dysfunctional patients. *Archives of Physical Medicine and Rehabilitation*, 78, 621–9.

Rodgers, R., and Hunter, J. E. (1991). Impact of management by objectives on organizational productivity. *Journal of Applied Psychology*, 76, 322–36.

Ronan, W. W., Latham, G. P., and Kinne, S. B. (1973). The effects of goal setting and supervision on worker behavior in an industrial situation. *Journal of Applied Psychology*, 58, 302–7.

Salancik, G. (1977). Commitment and the control of organizational behavior and belief. In B. M. Staw and G. R. Salancik (eds.), *New direction in organizational behavior*. Chicago: St. Clair Press.

Weinberg, R. S. (1994). Goal setting and performance in sport and exercise settings: A synthesis and critique. *Medicine and Science in Sports and Exercise*, 26, 469–77.

Winters, D., and Latham, G. P. (1996). The effect of learning versus outcome goals on a simple versus a complex task. *Group and Organization Management*, 21, 236–50.

9

Cultivate Self-efficacy for Personal and Organizational Effectiveness

ALBERT BANDURA

Human behavior is extensively motivated and regulated anticipatorily by cognitive self-influence. Among the mechanisms of self-influence, none is more focal or pervading than belief of personal efficacy. Unless people believe that they can produce desired effects and forestall undesired ones by their actions, they have little incentive to act. Whatever other factors may operate as motivators, they are rooted in the core belief that one has the power to produce desired results. That self-efficacy belief is a vital personal resource is amply documented by meta-analyses of findings from diverse spheres of functioning under laboratory and naturalistic conditions (Holden, 1991; Holden, Moncher, Schinke, and Barker, 1990; Multon, Brown, and Lent, 1991; Stajkovic and Luthans, 1998).

Perceived efficacy occupies a pivotal role in causal structures because it affects human functioning not only directly, but through its impact on other important classes of determinants. These determinants include goal aspirations, incentives and disincentives rooted in outcome expectations, and perceived impediments and opportunity structures. Figure 9.1 presents the structure of the causal model.

Efficacy beliefs affect self-motivation through their impact on goals and aspirations. It is partly on the basis of efficacy beliefs that people choose what goal challenges to undertake, how much effort to invest in the endeavor, and how long to persevere in the face of difficulties (Bandura, 1997; Locke and Latham, 1990). When faced with obstacles, setbacks, and failures, those who doubt their capabilities slacken their efforts, give up, or settle for mediocre solutions. Those who have a strong belief in their capabilities redouble their effort to master the challenges.

Perceived efficacy, similarly, plays an influential role in the incentive and disincentive potential of outcome expectations. The outcomes people anticipate depend largely on their beliefs of how well they can perform in given situations. Those of high efficacy expect to gain favorable outcomes through good performance, whereas those who expect poor performances of themselves conjure up negative outcomes.

In theories of motivation founded on the incentives of cognized outcomes, such as expectancy-value theories, motivation is governed by the expectation that a given behavior will produce certain outcomes and the value placed on those outcomes. This

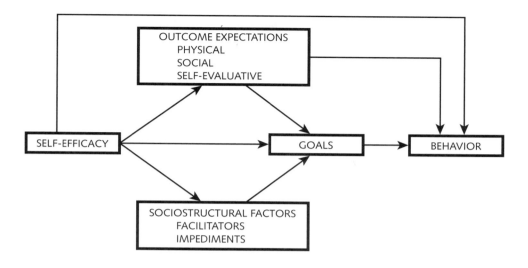

FIGURE 9.1 Paths of influence through which perceived self-efficacy and other key social cognitive factors regulate motivation and performance accomplishments

type of theory includes only one of the two belief systems governing motivation. People act on their beliefs about what they can do, as well as on their beliefs about the likely outcomes of performance. There are countless activities which, if done well, produce valued outcomes, but they are not pursued by people who doubt they can do what it takes to succeed. They exclude entire classes of options rapidly on self-efficacy grounds without bothering to analyze their costs and benefits. Conversely, those of high efficacy expect their efforts to bring success and are not easily dissuaded by negative outcomes.

Rational models of motivation and decision-making that exclude efficacy judgment sacrifice explanatory and predictive power. Perceived self-efficacy not only sets the slate of options for consideration, but also regulates their implementation. Making a decision in no way ensures that individuals will execute the needed course of action successfully, and stick to it in the face of difficulties. A psychology of decision-making requires a psychology of action grounded in enabling and sustaining efficacy beliefs. One must add a performative self to the decisional self, otherwise the decider is left stranded in thought.

Beliefs of personal efficacy shape whether people attend to the opportunities, or to the impediments that their life circumstances present and how formidable the obstacles appear (Krueger and Dickson, 1993, 1994). People of high efficacy focus on the opportunities worth pursuing, and view obstacles as surmountable. Through ingenuity and perseverance they figure out ways of exercising some control even in environments of limited opportunities and many constraints. Those beset with self-doubts dwell on impediments which they view as obstacles over which they can exert little control, and easily convince themselves of the futility of effort. They achieve limited success even in environments that provide many opportunities.

Diverse organizational impact of perceived self-efficacy

The scope of the organizational impact of perceived self-efficacy will be summarized briefly before presenting the strategies for altering efficacy belief systems. To begin with, perceived self-efficacy is an influential determinant of career choice and development. The higher a person's perceived efficacy to fulfill educational requirements and occupational roles the wider the career options they seriously consider pursuing, the greater the interest they have in them, the better they prepare themselves educationally for different occupational careers, and the greater their staying power in challenging career pursuits (Lent, Brown, and Hackett, 1994).

New employees receive training designed to prepare them for the occupational roles they will be performing. Those of low perceived efficacy prefer prescriptive training that tells them how to perform the roles as traditionally structured (Jones, 1986; Saks, 1995). Employees of high perceived efficacy prefer training that enables them to restructure their roles innovatively by adding new elements and functions to the customary duties. Self-efficacious employees take greater initiative in their occupational self-development and generate ideas that help to improve work processes (Speier and Frese, 1997). Organizations that provide their new employees with guided mastery experiences, effective co-workers as models, and enabling performance feedback enhance employees self-efficacy, emotional well-being, satisfaction, and level of productivity (Saks, 1994, 1995). Other organizational practices, such as job enrichment and mutually supportive communication, also build employees' perceived efficacy to take on broader functions and a proactive work role (Parker, 1998). Self-efficacy theory provides a conceptual framework within which to study the determinants in effective work design and the mechanisms through which they enhance organizational functioning.

Work life is increasingly structured on a team-based model in which management and operational functions are assigned to the workers themselves. A self-management work structure changes the model of supervisory managership from hierarchical control to facilitative guidance that provides the necessary resources, instructive guidance, and support that teams need to do their work effectively (Stewart and Manz, 1995). Enabling organizational structures build managers' efficacy to operate as facilitators of productive team work (Laschruger and Shamian, 1994). The perceived collective efficacy of self-managed teams predicts the members' satisfaction and productivity (Lindsley, Mathieu, Heffner, and Brass, 1994; Little and Madigan, 1994).

The development of new business ventures and the renewal of established ones depends heavily on innovativeness and entrepreneurship. With many resourceful competitors around, viability requires continual ingenuity. Entrepreneurs have to be willing to take risks under uncertainty. Those of high efficacy focus on the opportunities worth pursuing, whereas the less self-efficacious dwell on the risks to be avoided (Krueger and Dickson, 1993, 1994). Hence, perceived self-efficacy predicts entrepreneurship and which patent inventors are likely to start new business ventures (Chen, Greene, and Crick, 1998; Markman and Baron, 1999). Venturers who achieve high growth in companies they have founded, or transform those they bought, have a vision of what they wish to achieve, a firm belief in their efficacy to realize it, set challenging growth goals, and come up with innovative production and marketing strategies (Baum, 1994).

Effective leadership and workforces require receptivity to innovators that can improve the quality and productivity of organizations. Managers' perceived technical efficacy influences their readiness to adopt electronic technologies (Jorde-Bloom and Ford, 1988). Efficacy beliefs affect not only managers' receptivity to technological innovations, but also the readiness with which employees adopt them (Hill, Smith, and Mann, 1987; McDonald and Seagall, 1992). Efficacy-fostered adoption of new technologies, in turn, alters the organizational network structure and confers influence on early adopters within an organization over time (Burkardt and Brass, 1990).

Perceived self-efficacy to fulfill occupational demands affects the level of stress and physical health of employees. Those of low efficacy are stressed both emotionally and physiologically by perceived overload in which task demands exceed their perceived coping capabilities, whereas those who hold a high belief in their efficacy and that of their group are unfazed by heavy workloads (Jex and Bliese, 1999). Perceived self-efficacy must be added to the demands-control model of occupational stress to improve its predictability. High job demands with opportunity to exercise control over various facets of the work environment is unperturbing to job-holders of high perceived efficacy, but cardiovascularly stressful to those of low perceived efficacy (Schaubroeck and Merritt, 1997). Efforts to reduce occupational stressfulness by increasing job control without raising efficacy to manage the increased responsibilities will do more harm than good. For the self-efficacious, job underload can be a stressor. Indeed, employees of high efficacy are stressed by perceived underload in which they feel thwarted and frustrated by organizational constraints in developing and using their potentialities (Matsui and Onglatco, 1992). Exposure to chronic occupational stressors and with a low sense of efficacy to manage job demands and to enlist social support in times of difficulty, increases vulnerability to burnout (Brouwers and Tomic, in press a, b; Leiter, 1992). This syndrome is characterized by physical and emotional exhaustion, depersonalization of clients, lack of any sense of personal accomplishment, and occupational disengagement through cynicism about one's work.

A resilient sense of efficacy provides the necessary staying power in the tortuous pursuit of innovation and excellence. Yet the very undaunted self-efficacy that breeds success in tough ventures may perpetuate adherence to courses of action that hold little prospect of eventual success. Thus, for example, managers of high perceived efficacy are more prone than those of low efficacy to escalate commitment to unproductive ventures (Whyte and Saks, 1999; Whyte, Saks, and Hook, 1997), and to remain wedded to previously successful practices despite altered realities that place them at competitive disadvantage (Audia, Locke, and Smith, in press). The corrective for the perils of success is not enfeeblement of personal efficacy. Such a disenabling remedy would undermine aspiration, innovation, and human accomplishments in endeavors presenting tough odds. Individuals who are highly assured in their capabilities and the effectiveness of their strategies are disinclined to seek discordant information that would suggest the need for corrective adjustments. The challenge is to preserve the considerable functional value of resilient self-efficacy, but to institute information monitoring and social feedback systems that can help to identify practices that are beyond the point of utility.

It is easy to achieve veridical judgment. Simply punish optimism. The motivational belief system that fosters accomplishments in difficult endeavors combines realism about tough odds with optimism that through self-development and perseverant effort one can beat those odds. We study intensively the risks of over-confidence, but ignore the prevalent personal and social costs of under-confidence. This bias probably stems from the fact that the costs of lost opportunities and underdeveloped potentialities are deferred and less noticeable than those of venturesome missteps. The heavy selective focus on the risk of over-confidence stands in stark contrast to the entrepreneurial spirit driving the modern workplace in our rapidly changing world.

The functional value of veridical self-appraisal depends on the nature of the venture. In activities where the margins of error are narrow and missteps can produce costly or injurious consequences, one is best served by veridical efficacy appraisal. It is a different matter when difficult accomplishments can produce substantial personal or social benefits and the personal costs involve time, effort, and expendable resources. People have to decide whether to invest their efforts and resources in ventures that are difficult to fulfill, and how much hardship they are willing to endure in formidable pursuits that may have huge payoffs but are strewn with obstacles and uncertainties. Turning visions into realities is an arduous process with uncertain outcomes. Societies enjoy the considerable benefits of the eventual accomplishments in the arts, sciences, and technologies of its persisters and risk-takers. Realists trade on the merchandizable products that flow from the creations of innovative persisters. To paraphrase the astute observation of George Bernard Shaw, since reasonable people adapt to the world and unreasonable ones try to to alter it, human progress depends on the unreasonable ones.

Given the generality and centrality of the self-efficacy mechanism in the causal structures governing diverse aspects of organizational functioning, programs aimed at developing a resilient sense of efficacy can yield significant dividends in performance accomplishments and personal well-being. The strategies for developing and strengthening beliefs of personal efficacy are addressed in the sections that follow. Social cognitive theory lends itself readily to personal and social applications, which are extensively reviewed elsewhere (Bandura, 1986, 1997). The present chapter summarizes the relevant principles of change and provides some examples in the organizational field for purposes of illustration.

Sources of Self-efficacy

Self-efficacy beliefs are constructed from four principal sources of information: they include enactive mastery experiences; vicarious experiences that alter efficacy beliefs through transmission of competencies and comparison with the attainment of others; verbal persuasion and allied types of social influences that one possesses certain capabilities; and physiological and affective states from which people partly judge their capableness, strength, and vulnerability to dysfunction. Any given influence may operate through one or more of these forms of efficacy conveyance.

Information for judging personal efficacy, whether conveyed enactively, vicariously, persuasively, or somatically is not inherently informative. It is only raw data. Experiences become instructive through cognitive processing of efficacy information and reflective thought. One must distinguish between information conveyed by events and information as selected and integrated into self-efficacy judgments.

The cognitive processing of efficacy information involves two separate functions. The first is the types of information people attend to and use as indicators of personal efficacy.

TABLE 9.1 The distinctive sets of factors within each of the four modes of influence that can affect the construction of efficacy beliefs

Enactive efficacy information	*Vicarious efficacy information*
Interpretive biases	Model attribute similarity
Perceived task difficulty and diagnosticity	Model performance similarity
Effort expenditure	Model historical similarity
Amount of external aid received	Multiplicity and diversity of modeling
Situational circumstances of performance	Mastery or coping modeling
Transient affective and physical states	Exemplification of coping strategies
Temporal pattern of successes and failures	Portrayal of task demands
Selective bias in self-monitoring of performance	
Selective bias in memory for performance attainments	
Persuasory efficacy information	*Somatic and affective efficacy information*
Credibility	Degree of attentional focus on somatic states
Expertness	Interpretive biases regarding somatic states
Consensus	Perceived source of affective arousal
Degree of appraisal disparity	Level of arousal
Familiarity with task demands	Situational circumstances of arousal

Social cognitive theory specifies the set of efficacy indicators that are unique to each of the four major modes of influence. These are summarized in table 9.1. For example, judgments of efficacy based on performance attainments may vary depending on people's interpretive biases, the perceived difficulty of the task, how hard they worked at it, how much help they received, the conditions under which they performed, their emotional and physical state at the time, their rate of improvement over time, and biases in how they monitor and recall their attainments.

The indicators people single out provide the information base on which the self-appraisal process operates. The second function in efficacy judgment involves the combination rules or heuristics people use to weight and integrate efficacy information from the diverse sources in forming their efficacy judgments. The informativeness of the various efficacy indicants will vary for different spheres of functioning. The various sources of efficacy information may be integrated additively, multiplicatively, configurally, or heuristically. This judgmental process is not entirely dispassionate. Strong preconceptions and affective proclivities can alter self-efficacy appraisals positively or negatively.

The multiple benefits of a strong sense of personal efficacy do not arise simply from the incantation of capability. Saying something should not be confused with believing it to be so. A sense of personal efficacy is constructed through a complex process of self-persuasion based on constellations of efficacy information conveyed enactively, vicariously, socially, and physiologically.

Enablement through guided mastery

Guided mastery provides one of the most effective ways of cultivating competencies. However, a skill is only as good as its execution, which is heavily governed by self-regulatory and motivational factors. Individuals may, therefore, perform poorly, adequately, or highly with the same set of skills depending on the beliefs they hold about their capabilities in given situations (Bandura, 1997). As previously noted, mastery experiences, especially those gained through perseverant effort and ability to learn from setbacks and mistakes, builds a resilient sense of efficacy.

The method that produces the best gains in both self-efficacy and skill combines three components (Bandura, 1986). First, the appropriate skills are modeled to convey the basic rules and strategies. Second, the learners receive guided practice under simulated conditions to develop proficiency in the skills. Third, they are provided with a graduated transfer program that helps them to apply their newly learned skills in work situations in ways that will bring them success.

Instructive modeling.   Modeling is the first step in developing competencies. Complex skills are broken down into sub-skills, which can be modeled on videotape in easily mastered steps. Subdividing complex skills into sub-skills produces better learning than trying to teach everything at once. After the sub-skills are learned by this means, they can be combined into complex strategies to serve different purposes. Effective modeling teaches general rules and strategies for dealing with different situations rather than only specific responses or scripted routines. Voice-over narration of the rules and strategies as they are being modeled, and brief summaries of the rules enhance development of generic competencies.

The execution of skills must be varied to suit changing circumstances. People who learn rules in the abstract usually do a poor job in applying them in particular situations. Teaching abstract rules with varied brief examples promotes generalizability of the skills being taught by showing how the rules and strategies can be widely applied and adjusted to fit changing conditions. A single lengthy example teaches how to apply the rule in that particular situation but provides no instruction on how to adapt its application to varying situations.

People also fail to apply what they have learned, or do so only half-heartedly, if they distrust their ability to do it successfully. Therefore, modeling influences must be designed to build a sense of personal efficacy as well as to convey knowledge about rules and strategies. The impact of modeling on beliefs about one's capabilities is greatly increased by perceived similarity to the models. Learners adopt modeled ways more readily if they see individuals similar to themselves solve problems successfully with the modeled strategies than if they regard the models as very different from themselves. The characteristics of models, the type of problems with which they cope, and the situations in which they apply their skills should be made to appear similar to the trainees' own circumstances.

Guided skill perfection. Factual and procedural knowledge alone will not beget proficient performance. Knowledge structures are transformed into proficient action through a conception-matching process. The feedback accompanying enactments provides the information needed to detect and correct mismatches between the generic conception of requisite skills and action. This comparative process is repeated until a close match is achieved. Putting into practice what one has learned cognitively can also reveal gaps and flaws in the guiding conception. Recognizing what one does not know contributes to the refinement of cognitive representations by further modeling and verbal instruction regarding the problematic aspects of the representation.

In the transformational phase of competency development, learners test their newly acquired skills in simulated situations where they need not fear making mistakes or appearing inadequate. This is best achieved by role rehearsal in which they practice handling the types of situations they have to manage in their work environment. Mastery of skills can be facilitated by combining cognitive and behavioral rehearsal. In cognitive rehearsal, people rehearse mentally how they will translate strategies into what they say and do to manage given situations.

In perfecting their skills, people need informative feedback about how they are doing. A common problem is that they do not fully observe their own behavior. Informative feedback enables them to make corrective adjustments to get their behavior to fit their idea of how things should be done. Videotape replays are widely used for this purpose. Simply being shown replays of one's own behavior, however, usually has mixed effects (Hung and Rosenthal, 1981). To produce good results, the feedback must direct attention to the corrective changes that need to be made. It should call attention to successes and improvements and correct deficiencies in a supportive and constructive way so as to strengthen perceived efficacy. Some of the gains accompanying informative feedback result from raising people's beliefs in their efficacy rather than solely from further skill development.

The feedback that is most informative and achieves the greatest improvements takes the form of corrective modeling. In this approach, the sub-skills that have not been adequately learned are further modeled and learners rehearse them until they master them.

Effective functioning requires more than learning how to apply rules and strategies for managing organizational demands. The transactions of occupational life are littered with impediments, discordances, and stressors. Many of the problems of occupational functioning reflect failures of self-management rather than deficiencies of knowledge and technical skills. Therefore, an important aspect of competency development includes training in resiliency to difficulties. As we shall see later, this requires skill in cognitive self-guidance, self-motivation, and strategies for counteracting self-debilitating reactions to troublesome situations that can easily unhinge one. Gist, Bavetta, and Stevens (1990) augmented a guided model training in negotiation skills with a self-management component. In the latter phase, trainees were taught how to anticipate potential stressors, devise ways of overcoming them, monitor the adequacy of their coping approach, and use self-incentives to sustain their efforts. Trainees who had the benefit of the supplemental self-management training were better at applying learned negotiation skills in new contractual situations presenting conflictful and intimidating elements and negotiated more favorable outcomes than trainees who did not. The self-managers made flexible use of the wide range of strategies they had been taught, whereas their counterparts were more likely to persevere with only a few of the strategies when they encountered negative reactions.

Transfer training by self-directed success.   Modeling and simulated enactments are well suited for creating competencies. But new skills are unlikely to be used for long unless they prove useful when they are put into practice in work situations. People must experience sufficient success using what they have learned to believe in themselves and the value of the new ways. This is best achieved by a transfer program in which newly acquired skills are first tried on the job in situations likely to produce good results. Learners are assigned selected problems they often encounter in their everyday situations. After they try their hand at it, they discuss their successes and where they ran into difficulties for further instructive training. As learners gain skill and confidence in handling easier situations, they gradually take on more difficult problems. If people have not had sufficient practice to convince themselves of their new effectiveness, they apply the skills they have been taught weakly and inconsistently. They rapidly abandon their skills when they fail to get quick results or experience difficulties.

Mastery modeling is now increasingly used, especially in videotaped form, to develop competencies. But its potential is not fully realized if training programs do not provide sufficient practice to achieve proficiency in the modeled skills or if they lack an adequate transfer program that provides success with the new skills in the natural environment. Such programs rarely include training in resiliency through practice on how to handle setbacks and failure. When instructive modeling is combined with guided role rehearsal and a guided transfer program, this mode of organizational training usually produces excellent results. Because trainees learn and perfect effective ways of managing task demands under lifelike conditions, problems of transferring the new skills to everyday life are markedly reduced.

A mastery modeling program devised by Latham and Saari (1979) to teach supervisors the interpersonal skills they need to work effectively through others is an excellent case in point. Supervisors have an important impact on the morale and productivity of an organization. Yet they are often selected for their technical competencies and job-related knowledge, whereas their success in the supervisory role depends largely on their interpersonal skills to guide, enable, and motivate those they supervise.

Latham and Saari used videotape modeling of prototypic work situations to teach supervisors how to manage the demands of their supervisory role. They were taught how to increase motivation, give recognition, correct poor work habits, discuss potential disciplinary problems, reduce absenteeism, handle employee complaints, and overcome resistance to changes in work practices (Goldstein and Sorcher, 1974). Summary guidelines defining key steps in the rules and strategies being modeled were provided to aid learning and memorability. The group of supervisors discussed and then practiced the skills in role-playing scenarios using incidents they previously had to manage in their work. They received instructive feedback to help them improve and perfect their skills.

To facilitate transfer of supervisory skills to their work environment, they were instructed to use the skills they had learned on the job during the next week. They later reviewed their successes and difficulties in applying the skills. If they encountered problems, the incidents were re-enacted and the supervisors received further training through instructive modeling and role rehearsal on how to manage such situations. Supervisors who had received the guided mastery training performed more skillfully both in role-playing situations and on the job assessed a year later than did supervisors who did not receive the training. Because the skills proved highly functional, the supervisors adhered to them. The effects of weak training programs, relying heavily as they often do, on enthusiastic persuasion, rapidly dissipates as the initial burst of enthusiasm fades through failure to produce good results. Simply explaining to supervisors in the control group the rules and strategies for how to handle problems on the job without modeling and guided role rehearsal did not improve their supervisory skills. Because this approach provides supervisors with the tools for solving the problems they face, they express favorable reactions to it.

Supervisory skills instilled by guided mastery improve the morale and productivity of organizations (Porras and Anderson, 1981; Porras et al., 1982). Compared to the productivity of control plants, the one that received that guided mastery program improved supervisory problem-solving skills, had a significantly lower absentee rate, lower turnover of employees, and a 17 percent increase in the monthly level of productivity over a six-month period. This surpassed the productivity of the control plants. Mastery modeling produces multiple benefits in sales similar to those in production as reflected in enhanced productivity, and a lower rate of turnover in personnel (Meyer and Raich, 1983).

There are no training short-cuts or quick fixes for perceived inefficacy, dysfunctional work habits, and deficient self-regulatory and occupational competencies. As is true in other pursuits, the methods that are least effective are most widely used for ease of delivery, whereas enablement methods of proven value are used less often because they require greater investment of time and effort.

The application of guided mastery for markedly different purposes, such as the elimination of anxiety, stress reactions, and phobic dysfunctions, further illustrates the power and generality of this approach. To overcome distress and phobic avoidance people have to confront their perceived threats and gain mastery over them. When people avoid what they fear, they lose touch with the reality they shun. Guided mastery provides a quick and effective way of restoring reality testing. It provides disconfirming tests of faulty beliefs. But even more important, mastery experiences that are structured to develop coping skills provide persuasive confirmatory tests that one can exercise control over potential threats. However, individuals are not about to do what they dread. Therefore, one must create enabling environmental conditions so that individuals who are beset with profound self-doubt can perform successfully despite themselves. This is achieved by enlisting a variety of performance mastery aids (Bandura, 1997).

Feared activities are first modeled to show people how to cope effectively with threats and to disconfirm their worst fears. Difficult or intimidating tasks are broken down into sub-tasks of readily mastered steps. The change program is conducted in this step-wise fashion until the most taxing or threatening activities are mastered. Joint performance of intimidating activities with the implementor further enables inefficacious individuals to attempt activities they resist doing by themselves. Another method for overcoming resistance is to have individuals perform the feared activity for only a short time. As they become bolder, the length of involvement is extended. With gains in mastery the provisional performance aids are withdrawn to verify that coping attainments stem from the exercise of enhanced personal efficacy rather than from mastery aids. Dysfunctional styles of thinking that arise in the coping transactions are corrected and coping strategies that foster successful performance are suggested. In the final phase, self-directed mastery experiences are arranged that provide the newly emboldened individuals with opportunities to confront their nemeses and succeed entirely on their own to strengthen and generalize their sense of coping efficacy.

This mastery-oriented approach instills a robust sense of coping efficacy, eliminates anxiety arousal, activation of stress-related hormones, perturbing ruminations and nightmares, and wipes out phobic behavior (Bandura, 1997; Williams, 1992). Guided mastery is ideally suited for ridding oneself of other dysfunctional mindsets that create emotional distress and impair interpersonal effectiveness.

Cognitive mastery modeling

A great deal of professional work involves making judgments and finding solutions to problems by drawing on one's knowledge, constructing new knowledge structures, and applying decision rules. Competency in problem-solving requires the development of thinking skills for how to seek reliable information and put it to good use. People can learn thinking skills and how to apply them by observing the decision rules and reasoning strategies models use as they arrive at solutions.

Over the years, organizational training relied almost exclusively on the traditional lecture format despite its limited effectiveness. Mastery modeling works much better than lectures (Burke and Day, 1986). With the advent of the computer, talking heads are being replaced by self-paced instructional diskettes that provide step-by-step instruction, structured drills, and feedback of accuracy.

Comparative tests indicate that cognitive modeling may provide a better approach to the development of higher-order cognitive competencies. In teaching reasoning skills through cognitive modeling, performers verbalize their strategies aloud as they engage in problem-solving activities (Meichenbaum, 1984). The thoughts guiding their decisions and actions are thus made observable. During cognitive modeling, the models verbalize their thoughts as they analyze the problem, seek information relevant to it, generate alternative solutions, judge the likely outcomes associated with each alternative, and select the best way of implementing the chosen solution. They also verbalize their strategies for handling difficulties, how to recover from errors, and how to motivate themselves.

Modeling thinking skills and action strategies together can aid development of reasoning skills in several ways. Watching models verbalize their thoughts as they solve problems commands attention. Hearing the rules verbalized as the action strategies are implemented produces faster learning than only being told the rules or seeing only the actions modeled. Modeling also provides an informative context in which to demonstrate how to go about solving problems. The rules and strategies of reasoning can be repeated in different forms as often as needed to develop generative thinking skills. Varied application of reasoning strategies increases understanding of them.

Observing models verbalize how they use their cognitive skills to solve problems highlights the capacity to exercise control over one's thought processes, which can boost observers' sense of efficacy over and above the strategic information conveyed. Similarity to succeeding models boosts the instructional impact. And finally, modeling how to manage failures and setbacks fosters resilience to difficulties.

Gist (1989) taught managers how to generate ideas to improve the quality of organizational functioning and customer service by providing them with guidelines and practice in innovative problem-solving. Cognitive modeling, in which models verbalized strategies for generating ideas, proved superior to presenting the same guidelines solely in the traditional lecture format. Managers who had the benefit of cognitive modeling expressed a higher sense of efficacy and generated considerably more ideas and ideas of greater variety. Regardless of format of instruction, the higher the instilled efficacy beliefs, the more abundant and varied were the generated ideas.

The advantages of cognitive mastery modeling are even more evident when the effectiveness of alternative instructional methods are examined as a function of trainees' pre-existing level of perceived efficacy. Gist, Rosen, and Schwoerer (1988) taught managers with a computerized tutorial how to operate a spreadsheet program and use it to solve business problems. Cognitive modeling provided the same information and the same opportunities to practice the computer skills but used a videotape of a model demonstrating how to perform the computer task.

Videotaped cognitive modeling instilled a uniformly high sense of efficacy to acquire computer software skills regardless of whether managers began the training self-assured or self-doubting of their computer capabilities. A computerized tutorial exerted weaker effects on efficacy beliefs and was especially ineffective with managers who were insecure in their computer efficacy. Cognitive modeling also promoted a high level of computer skill development. The higher the pre-existing and the instilled efficacy beliefs, the better the skill development. The benefits of mastery modeling extend beyond development of technical skills. Compared to the computer tutorial training, mastery modeling produced a more effective working style, less negative affect during training, and higher satisfaction with the training program. Mastery modeling provides an instructional vehicle that lends itself well for enlisting affective and motivational determinants of competency development.

We are entering a new era in which the construction of knowledge and development of expertise will rely increasingly on electronic inquiry. Much information is currently available only in electronic rather than print form. The electronic network technologies greatly expand opportunities to attain expertise. Skill in electronic search is emerging as an essential competency. Knowledge construction through electronic inquiry is not simply a mechanical application of a set of cognitive operators to an existing knowledge base. Rather, it is a challenging process in which affective, motivational, and self-regulatory factors influence how information is gathered, evaluated, and integrated into knowledge structures.

Information-seekers face an avalanche of information in diverse sources of varying value and reliability. The amount of information on the Internet and the number and types of sites are doubling rapidly. Concepts with interrelated elements must be used to organize and guide efforts to find the most relevant information. Small changes in strategies can lead down radically different information pathways, many of which may be unfruitful. It is hard to know whether one is on the right track, or on an unproductive one. It requires a robust sense of efficacy to find one's way around this mounting volume and complexity of information. People who doubt their efficacy to conduct productive inquiries, and to manage the electronic technology, can quickly become overwhelmed.

In developing the cognitive skills for untangling the Web, individuals were taught how to frame the electronic inquiry be selecting key constructs and finding reliable sources; how to broaden the scope and depth of inquiry by using appropriate connectors; and how to sequence the inquiry optimally (Debouski, Wood, and Bandura, 1999). Compared to a group that received a computer tutorial, those who had benefit of cognitive modeling that conveyed the same search rules gained higher perceived efficacy and satisfaction in knowledge construction. They spent less time in errors and redundancies, used better search and sequencing strategies, learned more, and were more successful in constructing new knowledge. Putting a human face with whom one can identify in electronic instructional systems substantially boosts their power.

Cultivation of self-regulatory competencies

People have the capacity for self-directedness through the exercise of self-influence. The accelerated growth of knowledge and rapid pace of social and technological change are placing a premium on capabilities for self-motivation and self-development. Indeed, to keep up with a world that is rapidly changing, people have to develop, upgrade, and reform their competencies in continual self-renewal. To achieve this, they must develop skills in regulating the cognitive, motivational, affective, and social determinants of their functioning.

Self-management is exercised through a variety of interlinked self-referent processes including self-monitoring, self-efficacy appraisal, personal goal-setting, and enlistment of motivating incentives (Bandura, 1986, 1991; Locke and Latham, 1990). Knowledge of how these various sub-functions of self-regulation operate provides particularized guides on how to develop and implement this capability.

People cannot influence their own motivation and actions very well if they do not keep track of their thought patterns and performances, their situational influences, and the immediate and distal effects they produce. Therefore, success in self-regulation partly depends on the fidelity, consistency, and temporal proximity of self-monitoring. Observing one's pattern of behavior is the first step toward doing something to affect it, but, in itself, such information provides little basis for self-directed reactions.

Goals and aspirations play a pivotal role in the exercise of self-directedness. Goals motivate by enlisting self-evaluative involvement in activities rather than directly. Once people commit themselves to goal challenges two types of affective motivators come into play – people seek *self-satisfaction* from fulfilling valued goals, and are prompted to intensify their efforts by *discontent* with sub-standard performances. Activation of evaluative self-influence operates through a comparitor process in which perceived performance is judged against one's personal standard. Self-motivation through goal challenges, therefore, requires explicit goals and informative feedback on how one is doing. Neither goals without knowing how one is doing, nor knowing how one is doing without any goals is motivating (Bandura, 1991).

Motivational goal effects are mediated by three types of self-influences – perceived self-efficacy for goal attainment, evaluative self-reactions, and adjustment of personal standards in light of one's attainments. The more people bring these self-influences to bear on themselves, the greater the effort they exert and sustain to accomplish what they seek.

Goals do not automatically activate the self-reactive influences that govern level of motivation. Certain properties of goal structures determine how strongly the self-system will become enlisted in any given endeavor. These properties include goal specificity, proximity, and level of challenge.

Goals often have little impact because they are too general and personally noncommiting. To create productive involvement in activities, goals must be explicit so as to indicate the type and amount of effort needed to attain them. The amount of effort enlisted and satisfaction that accompany different goals depends on the level at which they are set. Strong interest and involvement in activities is sparked by challenges. The effectiveness of goals in regulating motivation and performance depends on how far into the future they are projected. Long-range goals provide the vision and give direction to one's activities. But they are too distant to serve as current motivators. There are too many competing activities at hand for distant futures to exert much impact on current behavior. It is too easy to put off serious efforts in the present, to the tomorrows of each day. Self-motivation is best sustained by attainable sub-goal challenges that lead to distant aspirations. Short-term sub-goals motivate and guide effort in the here and now. Challenging sub-goals are a good way of building perceived efficacy and intrinsic interest where they are lacking (Bandura, 1991, 1997). There are several ways they achieve these effects. Sustained effort builds competencies. Sub-goal attainments provide clear markers of increasing mastery. Evidence of progress builds efficacy. Sub-goal attainments also bring self-satisfaction. Satisfying experiences build intrinsic interest in activities.

Goal systems structured along the lines described above function as remarkable robust motivators across diverse activity domains, environmental settings, populations, and time spans (Bandura, 1997; Locke and Latham, 1990). Chapter 8 above provides further guidelines on how to structure and implement goal systems for productive engagement in personal and organizational pursuits.

Effective self-regulation is also central to personal management of emotional states and problem behaviors that have a negative spillover on work performance. Employee absenteeism costs United States industries billions of dollars each year. It is a serious problem that disrupts work schedules, raises costs, and decreases productivity. Frayne and Latham (1987) provide the elements for an effective self-management system to reduce absenteeism. Employees who often missed work were taught in groups how to manage their motivation and behavior more effectively. They kept a record of their work attendance. They analyzed the personal and social problems that prevented them from getting to work, and were taught strategies for overcoming these obstacles. They set themselves short-term goals for work attendance, and rewarded themselves for meeting their goals. Training in self-regulation increased employees' beliefs in their efficacy to overcome the obstacles that led them to miss work. They improved their work attendance and maintained these changes over time (Latham and Frayne, 1989). The stronger they believed in their self-management capabilities, the better was their work attendance. A control group of employees who did not receive the program in self-regulation continued their absentee ways.

The guiding principles and applications reviewed in the preceding sections underscore the centrality of perceived self-efficacy as a personal resource that yields dividends in motivation, performance attainments, and emotional well-being. Social cognitive theory embeds perceived efficacy within a broad network of sociocognitive factors. Because these factors are modifiable and the theory specifies their determinants and modes of operation, it lends itself readily to diverse social applications.

NOTE

Preparation of this chapter and some of cited studies from my program of research were supported by a grant from the Spencer Foundation. Some sections of this chapter contain revised, updated, and expanded material from the book *Self-efficacy: The exercise of control* (New York: Freeman, 1997).

REFERENCES

Audia, G., Locke, E. A., and Smith, K. G. (in press). The paradox of success: An archival and a laboratory study of strategic persistence following a radical environmental change. *Academy of Management Journal*.

Bandura, A. (1986). *Social foundations of thought and action: A social cognitive theory*. Englewood Cliffs, NJ: Prentice-Hall.

Bandura, A. (1991). Self-regulation of motivation through anticipatory and self-regulatory mechanisms. In R. A. Dienstbier (ed.), *Perspectives on motivation: Nebraska symposium on motivation* (Vol. 38, pp. 69–164). Lincoln: University of Nebraska Press.

Bandura, A. (1997). *Self-efficacy: The exercise of control*. New York: Freeman.

Baum, J. R. (1994). The relation of traits, competencies, vision, motivation, and strategy to venture growth. Unpublished doctoral dissertation, University of Maryland.

Brouwers, A., and Tomic, W. (in press, a). Teacher burnout, perceived self-efficacy in classroom management, and student disruptive behavior in secondary education. *Education and Society*.

Brouwers, A., and Tomic, W. (in press, b). A longitudinal study of teacher burnout and perceived self-efficacy in classroom management. *Teaching and Teacher Education*.

Burke, M. J., and Day, R. R. (1986). A cumulative study of the effectiveness of management training. *Journal of Applied Psychology*, 71, 232–45.

Burkhardt, M. E., and Brass, D. J. (1990). Changing patterns or patterns of change: The effects of a change in technology on social network structure and power. *Administrative Science Quarterly*, 35, 104–27.

Chen, C. C., Greene, P. G., and Crick, A. (1998). Does entrepreneurial self-efficacy distinguish entrepreneurs from managers? *Journal of Business Venturing*, 13, 295–316.

Debouski, S., Wood, R. E., and Bandura, A. (1999). Impact of guided mastery and enactive exploration on self-regulatory mechanisms and knowledge construction through electronic inquiry. Submitted for publication.

Frayne, C. A., and Latham, G. P. (1987). Application of social learning theory to employee self-management of attendance. *Journal of Applied Psychology*, 72, 387–92.

Gist, M. E. (1989). The influence of training method on self-efficacy and idea generation among managers. *Personnel Psychology*, 42, 787–805.

Gist, M. E., Bavetta, A. G., and Stevens, C. K. (1990). Transfer training method: Its influence on skill generalization, skill repetition, and performance level. *Personnel Psychology*, 43, 501–23.

Gist, M., Rosen, B., and Schwoerer, C. (1988). The influence of training method and trainee age on the acquisition of computer skills. *Personnel Psychology*, 41, 255–65.

Goldstein, A. P., and Sorcher, M. (1974). *Changing supervisor behavior*. New York: Pergamon.

Hill, T., Smith, N. D., and Mann, M. F. (1987). Role of efficacy expectations in predicting the decision to use advanced technologies: The case of computers. *Journal of Applied Psychology*, 72, 307–13.

Holden, G. (1991). The relationship of self-efficacy appraisals to subsequent health related outcomes: A meta-analysis. *Social Work in Health Care*, 16, 53–93.

Holden, G., Moncher, M. S., Schinke, S. P., and Barker, K. M. (1990). Self-efficacy of children and adolescents: A meta- analysis. *Psychological Reports*, 66, 1044–6.

Hung, J. H., and Rosenthal, T. L. (1981). Therapeutic videotaped playback. In J. L. Fryrear and R. Fleshman (eds.), *Videotherapy in mental health* (pp. 5–46). Springfield, IL: Thomas.

Jex, S. M., and Bliese, P. D. (1999). Efficacy beliefs as a moderator of the impact of work-related stressors: A multilevel study. *Journal of Applied Psychology*, 84, 349–61.

Jones, G. R. (1986). Socialization tactics, self-efficacy, and newcomers' adjustment to organizations. *Academy of Management Journal*, 29, 262–79.

Jorde-Bloom, P., and Ford, M. (1988). Factors influencing early childhood administrators' decisions regarding the adoption of computer technology. *Journal of Educational Computing Research*, 4, 31–47.

Krueger, N. F. Jr., and Dickson, P. R. (1993). Self-efficacy and perceptions of opportunities and threats. *Psychological Reports*, 72, 1235–40.

Krueger, N. Jr., and Dickson, P. R. (1994). How believing in ourselves increases risk taking: Perceived self-efficacy and opportunity recognition. *Decision Sciences*, 25, 385–400.

Laschruger, H. K. S., and Shamian, J. (1994). Staff nurses' and nurse managers' perceptions of job-related empowerment and managerial self-efficacy. *Journal of Nursing Administration*, 24, 38–47.

Latham, G. P., and Frayne, C. A. (1989). Self-management training for increasing job attendance: A follow-up and a replication. *Journal of Applied Psychology*, 74, 411–16.

Latham, G. P., and Saari, L. M. (1979). Application of social learning theory to training supervisors through behavioral modeling. *Journal of Applied Psychology*, 64, 239–46.

Leiter, M. P. (1992). Burnout as a crisis in self-efficacy: Conceptual and practical implications. *Work & Stress*, 6, 107–15.

Lent, R. W., Brown, S. D., and Hackett, G. (1994). Toward a unifying social cognitive theory of career and academic interest, choice, and performance. *Journal of Vocational Behavior*, 45, 79–122.

Lindsley, D. H., Mathieu, J. E., Heffner, T. S., and Brass, D. J. (1994). Team efficacy, potency, and performance: A longitudinal examination of reciprocal processes. Paper presented at the Society of Industrial-Organizational Psychology, Nashville, TN, April.

Little, B. L., and Madigan, R. M. (1994). Motivation in work teams: A test of the construct of collective efficacy. Paper presented at the annual meeting of the Academy of Management, Houston, TX, Aug.

Locke, E. A., and Latham, G. P. (1990). *A theory of goal setting and task performance*. Englewood Cliffs, NJ: Prentice-Hall.

Markman, G. D., and Baron, R. A. (1999). Cognitive mechanisms: Potential differences between entrepreneurs and non-entrepreneurs. Paper presented at the Babson College/Kauffman Foundation Entrepreneurship Conference, May.

Matsui, T., and Onglatco, M. L. (1992). Career self-efficacy as a moderator of the relation between occupational stress and strain. *Journal of Vocational Behavior*, 41, 79–88.

McDonald, T., and Siegall, M. (1992). The effects of technological self-efficacy and job focus on job performance, attitudes, and withdrawal behaviors. *The Journal of Psychology*, 126, 465–75.

Meichenbaum, D. (1984). Teaching thinking: A cognitive-behavioral perspective. In R. Glaser, S. Chipman, and J. Segal (eds.), *Thinking and learning skills*, Vol. 2: *Research and Open Questions* (pp. 407–26). Hillsdale, NJ: Erlbaum.

Meyer, H. H., and Raich, M. S. (1983). An objective evaluation of a behavior modeling training program. *Personnel Psychology*, 36, 755–61.

Multon, K. D., Brown, S. D., and Lent, R. W. (1991). Relation of self-efficacy beliefs to academic outcomes: A meta-analytic investigation. *Journal of Counseling Psychology*, 38, 30–8.

Parker, S. K. (1998). Enhancing role breadth self-efficacy: The roles of job enrichment and other organizational interventions. *Journal of Applied Psychology*, 83, 835–52.

Porras, J. I., and Anderson, B. (1981). Improving managerial effectiveness through modeling-based training. *Organizational Dynamics*, Spring, 60–77.

Porras, J. I., Hargis, K., Patterson, K. J., Maxfield, D. G., Roberts, N., and Bies, R. J. (1982). Modeling-based organizational development: A longitudinal assessment. *Journal of Applied Behavioral Science*, 18, 433–46.

Saks, A. M. (1994). Moderating effects of self-efficacy for the relationship between training method and anxiety and stress reactions of newcomers. *Journal of Organizational Behavior*, 15, 639–54.

Saks, A. M. (1995). Longitudinal field investigation of the moderating and mediating effects of self-efficacy on the relationship between training and newcomer adjustment. *Journal of Applied Psychology*, 80, 211–25.

Schaubroeck, J., and Merritt, D. E. (1997). Divergent effects of job control on coping with work stressors: The key role of self-efficacy. *Academy of Management Journal*, 40, 738–54.

Speirer, C., and Frese, M. (1997). Generalized self-efficacy as a mediator and moderator between control and complexity at work and personal initiative: A longitudinal field study in East Germany. *Human Performance*, 10(2), 171–92.

Stajkovic, A. D., and Luthans, F. (1998). Self-efficacy and work-related performance: A meta-analysis. *Psychological Bulletin*, 124, 240–61.

Stewart, G. L., and Manz, C. C. (1995). Leadership for self-managing work teams: A typology and integrative model. *Human Relations*, 48, 747–70.

Whyte, G., and Saks, A. (1999). Expert decision making in escalation situations: The role of self-efficacy. Submitted for publication.

Whyte, G., Saks, A., and Hook, S. (1997). When success breeds failure: The role of perceived self-efficacy in escalating commitment to a losing course of action. *Journal of Organizational Behavior*, 18, 415–32.

Williams, S. L. (1992). Perceived self-efficacy and phobic disability. In R. Schwarzer (ed.), *Self-efficacy: Thought control of action* (pp. 149–76). Washington, DC: Hemisphere.

10

Motivate Performance through Empowerment

JAY A. CONGER

Empowerment is a motivational concept – meaning to enable. To enable, in this case, implies creating conditions for heightening motivation through the development of an individual's sense of personal power and meaning related to tasks. More specifically, empowerment can be defined as a psychological state where four cognitions of the individual (meaning, competence, choice, impact) act in concert to foster a proactive, positive, and self-confident orientation towards one's work. For the individual, empowerment on a personal level is experienced as both greater work satisfaction and effectiveness in terms of fulfilling work role expectations and in more innovative behavior on the job (Spreitzer, 1995; Spreitzer, Kizilos, and Nason 1994). In terms of empowerment's impact on performance motivation, it affects both the initiation and persistence of an individual's task behavior (Bandura, 1997). As such, these processes allow managers to set higher performance goals for employees and to have these goals accepted. Empowerment processes also allow managers to lessen the emotional impact of demoralizing organizational changes and to mobilize organizational members in the face of difficult challenges. Finally, experiences in team-building within organizations (Beckhard, 1969; Neilsen, 1986) suggest that empowerment techniques can play a crucial role in group development, maintenance, and task performance.

In the management literature, empowerment is commonly associated with a set of managerial techniques or the act of sharing power with others. For example, the idea of delegation and the decentralization of decision-making power has long been equated with the notion of empowerment (Burke, 1986; Kanter, 1983). Burke's (1986) position is representative: "To empower, implies the granting of power – delegation of authority" (p. 51). As a result, we find historically that much of the literature on empowerment deals with participative management techniques such as goal-setting by subordinates, management by objectives, and quality circles as the means of sharing power or delegating authority (Likert, 1961, 1967; McGregor, 1960). This line of reasoning, however, does not adequately address the nature of empowerment as actually experienced by subordinates. For example, it begs the question: does the sharing of authority and resources with subordinates automatically empower them? Reality would suggest otherwise. The empowerment process is far more complex.

To best understand empowerment, it is important to view notions of power and control from a psychological perspective – as motivational and/or expectancy belief-states that are *internal* to individuals. For instance, individuals are assumed to have a need for power (McClelland, 1975) where power connotes an internal urge to influence and control other people. A related but more inclusive disposition to control and cope with life events has been proposed by several psychologists who have dealt with the issues of internal/external locus of control (Rotter, 1966), locus of causality (deCharms 1968), and learned helplessness (Abramson, Garber, and Seligman, 1980). Individuals' power needs are met when they perceive that they have power or when they believe they can adequately cope with events, situations, and/or the people they confront. On the other hand, individuals' power needs are frustrated when they feel powerless or when they believe that they are unable to cope with the task and social demands of their environment.

Power in this motivational sense refers to an intrinsic need for self-determination (Deci, 1975) or a belief in personal self-efficacy (Bandura, 1986). Under this conceptualization, power has its base within an actor's motivational disposition. Any managerial strategy or technique that strengthens this self-determination need or self-efficacy belief of employees will make them feel more powerful. Conversely, any strategy that weakens the self-determination need or self-efficacy belief of employees will increase their feelings of powerlessness.

From the perspective of empowerment, this notion of power as an internal state can be thought of in an even broader fashion. For example, we today conceive of empowerment comprising at least four cognitions: an individual's sense of meaning, competence, choice, and impact (Thomas and Velthouse, 1990). In this case, *meaning* is essentially determined by an individual's assessment of the value of a task in light of their own ideals, values, or standards (Brief and Nord, 1990). *Competence*, or self-efficacy, is the individual's belief that they possess the capability to skillfully perform task activities. *Choice* refers to an individual's belief that they see themselves to be the locus of causality for their behavior (deCharms, 1968). In other words, they perceive their behavior as self-determined (Deci and Ryan, 1985). Finally, *impact* conveys the sense that one has "made a difference" in accomplishing a task – in other words, producing the intended effects (Ashforth, 1989; Thomas and Velthouse, 1990). These dimensions are not so much outcomes or predictors but rather they comprise the essence of empowerment (Spreitzer, Kizilos, and Nason, 1994).

So how does empowerment work to motivate performance? If we think about the four cognitions described above, each makes a specific contribution. *Meaning* provides motivational energy. When individuals feel a high level of meaning concerning a task, they are more likely to show greater levels of commitment, involvement, and concentration of energy because of personal identification with the task (Kanter, 1979; Sjoberg, Olsson, and Salay, 1983; Thomas and Velthouse, 1990). In contrast, low levels of meaningfulness are thought to produce detachment and apathy towards work (May, 1969). Feelings of *competence* or self-efficacy reflect an individual's belief that they possess the capabilities necessary to do a task well. As a result, such feelings have been shown to produce greater initiation, high levels of effort, and persistence in the face of obstacles (Bandura, 1997).

Low self-efficacy feelings, on the other hand, lead individuals to avoid situations that trigger such feelings. As a result, individuals will fail to confront their fears concerning efficacy and in turn avoid opportunities to improve their competence (Bandura, 1997). A strong sense of *choice* creates a sense that the individual is the source of their actions. It therefore produces in individuals greater initiative, resiliency, creativity, and flexibility in task efforts (Deci and Ryan, 1985). Finally, a sense of *impact* determines whether individuals feel that they are making a difference — that their actions are having an influence (Thomas and Velthouse, 1990). In contrast, the lack of a personal sense of impact (or a sense of helplessness) reduces motivation and dampens the ability to recognize opportunities (Abramson et al., 1978). Taken together, these four cognitions complement and reinforce one another to heighten an individual's motivation to perform.

The actual process of empowerment can be viewed along six stages that include the psychological state of an empowering experience, its antecedent conditions, and its behavioral consequences. The six stages are shown in figure 10.1.

The first stage is the diagnosis of conditions within the individual and their organization that are responsible for feelings of powerlessness. This leads to the use of empowerment strategies by managers in stage 2. The employment of these strategies is aimed at not only removing some of the conditions responsible for powerlessness, but also (and more importantly) at providing subordinates with empowerment information in stage 3. As a result of receiving such information, individuals then interpret it in stage 4 according to personal styles of assessment. If these styles assess the information as empowering, then an individual will feel empowered (stage 5) and the behavioral effects of empowerment will be observed in stage 6.

Starting with the first stage (the context), there are specific individual and contextual factors that contribute to the lowering of empowerment feelings among organizational members (Block, 1987; Conger, 1989; Kanter, 1979, 1983; Thomas and Velthouse, 1990). For example, individuals contribute to their own empowerment or disempowerment depending upon their psychological makeup and its impact on how they interpret events.

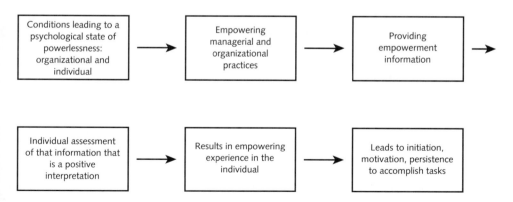

FIGURE 10.1 Stages of the empowerment process
Source: Adapted from Conger and Kanungo (1988)

Depressed individuals are less likely to see successes as indicative of their own competence (Abramson et al., 1978). Others may have standards of perfection that reduce perceptions of personal impact and efficacy (Ellis, 1980). For these very reasons, careful selection is necessary. From the standpoint of organizational factors, table 10.1 identifies some of the principal factors that influence empowerment outcomes. These are organized into four categories: (a) organizational, (b) supervisory style, (c) reward systems, and (d) job design. For instance, *organizations* with high levels of formalization and impersonal control systems can stifle member initiative, meaningfulness, and sense of responsibility. Authoritarian and patriarchal *supervisory styles* can strip control and discretion from organizational members. *Rewards* may not be allocated on the basis of members' competence or innovative behavior, but rather on their blind compliance with formalized control from the top. When organizations do not provide rewards that are valued by members, and when the rewards are not based on member competence, initiative, and innovative job behavior, employees' sense of powerlessness increases (Sims, 1977; Szilagyi, 1980). Finally, when *jobs* provide very little challenge and meaning, and when they involve role ambiguity, role conflict, and role overload, employees can feel a crippling sense of powerlessness.

To address such conditions (stage 2), there are a number of management practices that can restore or heighten a sense of empowerment. For example, at the *organizational level*, company policies and cultures can emphasize self-determination, collaboration over competition, high performance standards, non-discrimination, and meritocracy. In addition, organizations that provide multiple sources of loosely committed resources at decentralized or local levels, that structure open communications systems, and that create extensive network-forming devices are more likely to be empowering (Kanter, 1983).

Leadership and/or supervisory practices which have been identified as empowering include (a) expressing confidence in subordinates accompanied by high performance expectations (Burke, 1986; Conger, 1989; House, 1977; Neilsen, 1986); (b) fostering opportunities for subordinates to participate in decision-making or to create their own jobs (Block, 1987; Burke, 1986; Conger, 1989; House 1977; Kanter, 1979; Neilsen, 1986; Strauss, 1977); (c) providing autonomy from bureaucratic constraint (Block, 1987; Kanter, 1979); and (d) setting inspirational and/or meaningful goals (Bennis and Nanus, 1985; Block, 1987; Conger and Kanungo, 1998; McClelland, 1975; Tichy and Devanna, 1986).

Reward systems that emphasize innovative/unusual performance and high incentive values have a significant probability of fostering a greater sense of self-efficacy (Kanter, 1979; Kanungo, 1987; Lawler, 1971, 1977). Jobs that provide task variety, personal relevance, appropriate autonomy and control, low levels of established routines and rules, and high advancement prospects are more likely to empower subordinates (Block, 1987; Hackman, Oldham, Janson, and Purdy, 1975; Kanter, 1979; Oldham, 1976; Strauss, 1977).

The above practices can be viewed from the different perspectives of either formal/organizational mechanisms or individual/informal techniques. Organizations require both types to effectively instill a context of empowerment. For example, when organizations engage in participation programs, they establish formal systems that empower organizational members through the sharing of formal power and authority. In order for

TABLE 10.1 Context factors leading to potential lowering of self-efficacy belief

Organizational factors
Significant organizational changes/transitions
Start-up ventures
Competitive pressures
Impersonal bureaucratic climate
Poor communications/network-forming systems
Highly centralized organizational resources

Supervisory style
Authoritarian (high control)
Negativism (emphasis on failures)
Lack of reason for actions/consequences

Reward systems
Non-contingency (arbitrary reward allocation)
Low incentive value of rewards
Lack of competence-based rewards
Lack of innovation-based rewards

Job design
Lack of role clarity
Lack of training and technical support
Unrealistic goals
Lack of appropriate authority/discretion
Low task variety
Limited participation in programs, meetings, decisions that have a direct impact
    on job performance
Lack of appropriate/necessary resources
Lack of network-forming opportunities
Highly established work routines
High rule structure
Low advancement opportunities
Lack of meaningful goals/tasks
Limited contact with senior management

Source: Adapted from Conger and Kanungo (1988), 471–82

this sharing of power to be effective at the individual level, however, employees must perceive it as increasing their sense of self-efficacy – which is accomplished largely through the more informal practices of individual managers and in their one-on-one interactions with subordinates and co-workers. Empowerment initiatives which rely on a singular approach such as the delegation of decision-making usually prove to be ineffective. Rather, initiatives must be supported on multiple levels and by multiple interventions. In the ideal case, they would involve a highly supportive organizational culture, training and developmental experiences that heighten one's sense of competence, involvement in goal-setting or in the means to achieve goals, job designs that are highly meaningful to employees, the selection of supervisors open to empowerment approaches and proactive in their use, and the selection and promotion of employees whose interpretative schemes are biased towards constructive and enabling self-assessments (Liden and Arad, 1995; Spreitzer, Kizilos, and Nason, 1994).

In order to be effective, the empowerment practices outlined above must directly provide information to employees about personal efficacy, a sense of choice, meaningfulness of the task, and impact (stage 3). For example, on the dimension of competence or self-efficacy Bandura (1986, 1997) has identified four sources of such information: enactive attainment, vicarious experience, persuasion/feedback, and emotional arousal state. Information in personal efficacy through *enactive attainment* refers to an individual's authentic mastery experience directly related to the job. For example, a manager can allocate or structure tasks that provide an empowering experience for an individual. When subordinates perform complex tasks or are given more responsibility in their jobs, they have the opportunity to test their efficacy and to receive feedback. Initial success experiences (through successively moderate increments in task complexity and responsibility along with training to acquire new skills) provide positive information which may in turn make one feel more capable and, therefore, empowered.

Empowerment information can also come from the *vicarious experiences* of observing similar others (i.e., co-workers) who perform successfully on the job. Very often, a supervisor's exemplary behaviors empower subordinates to believe that they can behave in a like manner or that they can at least achieve some improvement in their performance. Words of encouragement, performance feedback, mentoring advice, and other forms of social *persuasion* are often used by leaders, managers, and group members to provide empowerment information to subordinates and co-workers (Conger, 1989). For instance, leaders may use annual meetings to provide empowering information in the form of praise and encouragement for exceptional performance. Through positive performance evaluations, managers may similarly foster an empowered state.

Finally, personal competence expectations are affected by one's *emotional arousal* state. Individuals are more likely to feel competent when they are not experiencing strong aversive arousal. Emotional arousal states that result from dysfunctional levels of stress, fear, anxiety, depression, and so forth, both on and off the job, can lower self-efficacy expectations. Therefore empowerment strategies that provide information in the form of emotional support for subordinates and that create a supportive and trusting group atmosphere (Neilsen, 1986) can be more effective in strengthening self-efficacy beliefs. For example, employees' stress, anxiety, and tension on the job can be reduced by managers clearly defining employees' roles, reducing information overload, and offering them technical assistance to accomplish job tasks. Similarly, the impact of depression and self-doubt on subordinates as a result of failures on the job could be lessened by their supervisor's attributing such failures to external and unstable factors such as task difficulty, inadequate support systems, and so forth, rather than attributing it to the individual's efforts or abilities (Weiner, 1985).

As a result of receiving the above forms of information, employees will interpret this information according to their individual styles of assessment in stage 4. In other words, subjective interpretations will determine whether the information is seen as empowering or not. In the next section discussing exceptions, we will describe this assessment process in greater depth since it directly affects the success of any empowerment initiative. If the information is indeed interpreted as empowering, then the individual will enter stage 5 – a state of psychological empowerment – and the behavioral effects of empowerment will be noticed in stage 6.

POSSIBLE EXCEPTIONS

Although we have focused on the positive outcomes of the management practices designed to empower, it is conceivable that these practices might also lead to negative outcomes. Specifically, empowerment could produce a state of over-confidence and, in turn, misjudgments on the part of individuals. Because of a sense of false confidence in positive outcomes, employees might persist in efforts that, in actuality, are tactical or strategic errors. Similarly, individuals might over-extend themselves through tasks which are largely impossible to accomplish. As well, leaders might use such practices to garner commitment to tasks which are largely self-serving for the leader. The positive personal effects that are felt by followers during empowering experiences may blind them to the leader's own ego-driven agenda and manipulation.

There may also be situations where managers and organizations have little latitude to increase a sense of empowerment. For example, some jobs are highly mechanistic and routine. No matter what attempts are made at redesign, the jobs remain essentially the same. Serious economic downturns or intense competitive situations may limit an organization's ability to provide inspiring goals or appealing rewards other than simple job security. Trapped in autocratic cultures, managers wishing to empower may find themselves constrained by the larger system – their efforts at empowerment largely negated by the overriding culture or design elements of the organization.

Finally, there is the crucial issue of individual differences. During the process of empowerment, individuals are making subjective assessments about information and specific tasks. One individual may assess the same information quite differently from another. For example, some styles of assessment are self-enhancing and others are self-debilitating (Peale, 1954). As such, what might be an empowering experience for one individual may be a disempowering or non-empowering one for another. In the latter case, an individual may set dysfunctional standards in the form of absolutistic "musts" concerning tasks (Ellis, 1980). They may have the personal standard of "Perfection is my goal on all dimensions of this task." Such standards tend to reduce a person's assessment of their impact since anything short of perfection is seen as failure (Ellis, 1980; Thomas and Velthouse, 1990). Individuals can also get trapped in self-reinforcing cycles. Low personal assessments of their competence can lead to low initiative and inactivity which further reinforces perceptions of low impact and a sense of little competence (Thomas and Velthouse, 1990). An individual's level of confidence in themselves also plays a central role. The motivation to undertake any new activity requires a measure of self-confidence. If an individual has a strong foundation of belief in themselves, they are likely to be more optimistic than others when engaging in activities where information about task assessments are uncertain or cloudy (Thomas and Velthouse, 1990). In addition, individuals vary to the degree in which they invest themselves psychologically in tasks. Termed global meaningfulness, this concept describes an individual's overall level of caring or commitment to tasks. People differ considerably along this dimension (Solomon and Patch, 1970). Individuals with low levels of global meaningfulness tend to experience alienation and are less likely to believe that new tasks will be meaningful (Thomas and Velthouse, 1990).

Given the above psychological dynamics, empowerment interventions must take into careful consideration the individual, their personal assessments, and the task. For some, their psychological outlook may prove a serious barrier to empowerment. Instead it will be their capacity for self-reflection and learning that will determine over the long term whether they can at some point experience empowerment. At the same time, extended and persistent efforts at empowerment on the part of supervisors will be required under such circumstances. With some individuals, there may be little that a manager or co-worker can do to empower them. This is especially true for individuals who are in a psychologically unbalanced or depressed state. Outside professional help – for example, psychotherapy – may be the only possible option. For this very reason, careful selection and placement are critical factors.

REAL-WORLD EXAMPLES

To understand how empowerment works in the real world, we will look first at two positive examples and one negative example. Each will be drawn from case studies of actions undertaken by senior organizational leaders to empower their workforces.

Richard Branson, the Virgin Group

As chief executive officer of the Virgin Group (a diversified British company encompassing entertainment/communications businesses and an airline), Richard Branson employs a variety of means to empower members of the company. At an organizational level, he preserves an entrepreneurial atmosphere through a Japanese-style *keiretsu* structure whereby the 500 companies under the Virgin Group operate quasi-independently but collaboratively in a global network (Kets de Vries and Dick, 1995). Once a company reaches a certain size, it is split into several organizations so that employees retain their sense of identity with their organization and a small-company, entrepreneurial atmosphere is preserved. At the individual level, each unit is led by a managing director who has considerable freedom to lead the business as they see fit and who has an equity position in the company. Decision-making within the company is therefore decentralized. At the same time, senior managers have access to Branson for advice and guidance. In addition to a direct telephone line, there is a fax line to Branson through which they can reach him 24 hours a day (Kets de Vries and Dick, 1995).

To further promote individual entrepreneurship within the company, employees with attractive ideas for new ventures are provided with seed capital and ownership. As a result, many of the Virgin companies are the product of employee ideas. A bridal service division called Virgin Bride, for example, was the idea of a Virgin Airways stewardess to whom Branson provided "venture capital." The company's new ventures allow Branson to stretch and develop employees by creating more opportunities for upward mobility and greater responsibility (Kets de Vries and Dick, 1995).

A central tenet of the company culture is the importance of employees. Branson's maxim is staff first, customers second, and shareholders third. As a result, he has created a culture which is egalitarian, non-bureaucratic, friendly, and family-like in atmosphere. The culture is one where people enjoy their work and have fun. It is also one which emphasizes proactivity. As Branson likes to say, "We can decide on something in the morning and have it in operation by the afternoon" (Kets de Vries and Dick, 1995). Taken together, the corporate culture, the company's organizational design/reward systems, and Branson's leadership style work effectively to create a cadre of empowered managers.

Jack Welch, General Electric

An executive or manager can put in place mechanisms to promote an empowering organizational culture that values free information-sharing through participation and feedback systems, meaningful jobs through enrichment and goal-setting programs, and rewards for competence and initiative. Jack Welch, the chief executive officer of General Electric, implemented such a program entitled Work Out throughout the corporation. Its principal purpose was to undermine layers of bureaucracy and other roadblocks to employee empowerment at lower levels of the organization (Bower and Dial, 1993; Tichy and Sherman, 1993). The program created forums for employees to speak candidly about unnecessary work in their jobs and the management of their business units without fear of retribution from senior managers. Its second objective was to stimulate immediate action on the issues that surfaced. In two- to three-day sessions of 50 to 100 people, these forums openly critiqued the management practices and processes in an operation with a strong focus specifically on identifying bureaucracy and unproductive behaviors that impeded employees' effectiveness or efficacy. In essence, these forums tackled the barriers to empowerment. At the end of each session, the unit's manager received direct feedback from employees on their findings and recommendations for action. In response, the rules stipulated that the manager had to "on the spot" accept or reject recommendations at the meeting or else appoint a team to investigate and provide solutions by an agreed-upon date. As the process has evolved, issues have since moved on to address more complicated and structural barriers such as cross-functional processes and departmental boundaries. At the end of its first two years, some 2,000 Work Out sessions have been conducted with over 90 percent of the suggestions acted upon (Bowers and Dial, 1993; Tichy and Sherman, 1993).

As noted earlier in this chapter, one of the organizational barriers to empowerment centers on supervisors' needs to control. A principal objective behind Work Out was to redefine this relationship of control between a supervisor and their subordinates. Jack Welch explains: "Ultimately, we are talking about redefining the relationship between boss and subordinate. I want to get to the point where people challenge their bosses every day: 'Why do you require me to do these wasteful things? . . . Trust me to do my job, and don't waste all of my time trying to deal with you on the control issue'" (Tichy and Charan, 1989: 118). What is particularly interesting about this example is that it is an empowerment intervention instituted by an individual who demonstrates very directive and demanding leadership. Welch, for example, is known to routinely fire the bottom 5–10 percent of his senior managers for performance below his standards. He also sets well-defined goals for the organization. At the same time, he is a great believer in the ability of front-line individuals to address business problems and opportunities, that unnecessary bureaucracy is a major barrier to empowerment, and that individuals must have the freedom to choose the means necessary to reach set goals. It is therefore possible to have both strong leadership and empowerment.

Frank Borman, Eastern Airlines

After leaving his career at NASA, the former astronaut Frank Borman joined Eastern Airlines and eventually became president of the airline in 1975. Eastern had been losing money for a number of years, and Borman saw his management mission to restore both profitability and discipline to Eastern. Though it is not completely clear whether the airline could ever have been saved given its very high costs and poor route structure, it is clear that Borman is an example of how one leader's actions can intensify a state of disempowerment. He began the first few months of his presidency by firing or demoting 24 vice-presidents. His leadership approach was a command style, and he could often be quite callous and macho in his demeanor. For example, he once asked a female vice-president to fetch him a cup of coffee during a meeting. During the frequent grounding of aircraft due to mechanical problems, he demanded of his managers: "Have you fixed it yet, or are you going to make dinner out of it?" (Petzinger, 1995: 166). His autocratic style stripped decision-making autonomy from junior levels.

His major focus for restoring the company, however, was on employees and their wages. He used a never-ending stream of company crises to persuade employees to give up wages that they were about to receive. He explained to employees that their future depended largely on their willingness to cut their own salaries. He would send out letters highlighting the value of self-sacrifice: "One of the great joys in life is found in subordinating one's personal desires and efforts to the success of the group" (Petzinger, 1995: 168). In return for these sacrifices, Borman offered little other than sheer survival. No compelling and optimistic vision of the future was portrayed for Eastern employees – instead the sacrifices would only be enough to bridge the organization to the next crisis. A poem from one member of the machinist union, Barbara Mungovan, captured employees' sentiments about their CEO and his tactics: "In good faith I took a wage freeze . . . You said you had to have it, to help Eastern survive. I gave up things I needed, I gave up a new car. Then you spent my money on a 'union busting' seminar. I gave up my vacation, and my skiing trip. And all you gave to me was more gloom and doom lip . . . You feel now you don't need us, after we supported you . . . You say you can fly without us, that it's easy to do. Frank, if you really think you can, then God bless you" (Petzinger, 1995: 174–5).

He trivialized employees' sacrifices saying that wage concessions were in one case no more than "the cost of a few six packs of beer." Deeply offended by this and the image that Eastern employees were simple, beer-drinking, blue-collar workers, union members soon were wearing lapel pins stating NO DEPOSIT, NO RETURN (Petzinger, 1995: 174). Borman went further, however, with his tactics. One program transformed his employees essentially into the company's bankers enabling Borman to borrow millions of dollars from them with "loans" that were unsecured, bore no interest, and were repaid only if the money was later available (which over the years proved not to be the case). The plan was called the "variable earnings plan" or VEP. Under VEP, employees tied a portion of their salaries to the company's profitability. If company earnings totaled less than stipulated levels, employees received less than full pay. In later years, when the company saw only losses, the employees saw only reduced wages. The plan came to be nicknamed the "veritable extortion plan" by the employees.

As his tenure as president progressed, the competitive situation worsened. Discount-fare airlines such as People Express and Continental invaded many of the company's principal markets. Competitors were not only stealing passengers but forcing Eastern Airlines to discount its fares. At the same time, Borman had decided to modernize his fleet, purchasing new Boeing 757s whose high debt-servicing demands accelerated the strain on the company's balance sheets. At one point, in a moment of desperation, Borman ceded to union demands for greater voice in decisions in return for additional wage cuts. As a result, employees received shares in the company along with access to Eastern's internal financial reports and three seats on the Eastern board. These changes briefly brought about a more participatory mood within Eastern and were marked by a new program for employees to identify cost-saving initiatives. Privately, however, Borman felt that all union involvement was "crap" (Petzinger, 1995). As a result, participation soon came to an end. By 1985, the competition introduced super discount fares on Eastern's critical route from New York to Florida. Borman now had another crisis on his hands and again sought to wrestle wage concessions out of his employees. In a letter to employees, he described the earlier union concessions as "temporary programs" which were no longer enough. Asking for 20 percent of their wages in return, he said "We must look beyond Band-Aids" – the "Band-Aids" referring to the employee programs (Petzinger, 1995: 250). Such talk further outraged the workforce. The company's unions rallied together to oust Borman. Sensing that his own credibility with the workforce had expired, Borman resorted to threats of selling the airline to Frank Lorenzo, the notorious chief of Texas Air, who was well known for union-busting. This bargaining chip, however, soon grew into a reality. By 1986, the board had decided to sell the airline to Lorenzo. By this point, the damage to the company's marketplace position and balance sheet was already extensive. A highly defensive workforce saw little reason to help out. The extent of their fury was evident when company airline mechanics were placed under investigation by the FAA on suspicion of sabotaging aircraft, and customer service levels plummeted. By 1989, awash in debt and with a trickling stream of revenues, Eastern Airlines entered bankruptcy and vanished into airline history.

From the perspective of a negative example of empowerment, the Borman story illustrates how one senior leader through their personal actions can significantly affect the state of empowerment throughout an entire organization. His authoritarian style, negativism, lack of a compelling organizational vision, low incentive/low innovation-based rewards, poor personal perceptions of his own workforce, and confrontational approach all contributed to a highly disempowered workforce.

References

Abramson, L. Y., Garber, J., and Seligman, M. E. P. (1980). Learned helplessness in humans: An attributional analysis. In J. Garber and M. E. P. Seligman (eds.), *Human helplessness: Theory and applications* (pp. 3–34). New York: Academic Press.

Abramson, L., Seligman, M., and Teasdale, J. (1978). Learned helplessness in humans: Critique and reformulation. *Journal of Abnormal Psychology*, 87, 19–74.

Ashford, B. E. (1989). The experience of powerlessness in organizations. *Organizational Behavior and Human Decision Processes*, 43, 207–42.

Bandura, A. (1986). *Social foundations of thought and action: A social-cognitive view.* Englewood Cliffs, NJ: Prentice-Hall.

Bandura, A. (1997). *Self-efficacy: The exercise of control.* New York: W. H. Freeman.

Beckhard, R. (1969). *Organization development: Strategies and models.* Reading, MA: Addison-Wesley.

Bennis, W., and Nanus, B. (1985). *Leaders.* New York: Harper & Row.

Block, P. (1987). *The Empowered Manager.* San Francisco: Jossey-Bass.

Bower, J. L., and Dial, J. (1993). *Jack Welch: General Electric's revolutionary.* Boston: Harvard Business School.

Brief, A., and Nord, W. R. (1990). *Meaning of Occupational Work.* Lexington, MA: Lexington Books.

Burke, W. (1986). Leadership as empowering others. In S. Srivastra (ed.), *Executive power* (pp. 51–77). San Francisco: Jossey-Bass.

Conger, J. A. (1989). Leadership: The art of empowering others. *Academy of Management Executive*, 33, 17–24.

Conger, J. A., and Kanungo, R. N. (1988). The empowerment process: Integrating theory and practice. *Academy of Management Review*, 31, 471–82.

Conger, J. A., and Kanungo, R. N. (1998). *Charismatic leadership in organizations.* Thousand Oaks, CA: Sage Publications.

deCharms, R. (1968). *Personal causation: The internal affective determinants of behavior.* New York: Academic Press.

Deci, E. L. (1975). *Intrinsic motivation.* New York: Plenum.

Deci, E. L., and Ryan, R. M. (1985). *Intrinsic motivation and self-determination in human behavior.* New York: Plenum.

Ellis, A. (1980). An overview of the clinical theory of rational-emotive therapy. In R. Grieger and J. Boyd (eds.), *Rational-emotive therapy* (pp. 1–31). New York: Van Nostrand Reinhold.

Hackman, J. R., Oldham, G. R., Janson, R., and Purdy, K. (1975). New strategy for job enrichment. *California Management Review*, 17(4), 57–71.

House, R. J. (1977). A 1976 theory of charismatic leadership. In J. G. Hunt and L. L. Larson (eds.), *Leadership: The cutting edge* (pp. 189–207). Carbondale: Southern Illinois University Press.

Kanter, R. M. (1979). Power failure in management circuits. *Harvard Business Review*, 57(4), 65–75.

Kanter, R. M. (1983). *The change masters.* New York: Simon & Schuster.

Kanungo, R. N. (1987). Reward management: A new look. In S. L. Dolan and R. S. Schuler (eds.), *Canadian readings in personnel and human resource management* (pp. 261–75). St. Paul: West.

Kets de Vries, M. F. R. and Dick, R. J. (1995). *Branson's Virgin: The coming of age of a counter-cultural enterprise.* Fontainebleau, France: INSEAD.

Lawler, E. E. (1971). *Pay and organizational effectiveness: A psychological view.* New York: McGraw-Hill.

Lawler, E. E. (1977). Reward systems. In J. R. Hackman and L. J. Suttle (eds.), *Improving life at work: Behavioral science approaches to organizational change* (pp. 163–226). Santa Monica, CA: Goodyear.

Liden, R. C., and Arad, S. (1995). A power perspective of empowerment and work teams: Implications for human resource management research. *Research in Personnel and Human Resources Management*, 14.

Likert, R. (1961). *New patterns of management.* New York: McGraw-Hill.

Likert, R. (1967). *The human organization.* New York: McGraw-Hill.

May, R. (1969). *Love and will.* New York: Dell.

McClelland, D. C. (1975). *Power: The inner experience.* New York: Irvington Press.

McGregor, D. (1960). *The human side of enterprise.* New York: McGraw-Hill.

Neilsen, E. (1986). Empowerment strategies: Balancing authority and responsibility. In S. Srivastra (ed.), *Executive power* (pp. 78–110). San Francisco: Jossey-Bass.

Oldham, G. R. (1976). The motivational strategies used by supervisors' relationships to effectiveness indicators. *Organizational behavior and human performance*, 15, 66–86.

Peale, N. V. (1954). *The power of positive thinking.* New York: Prentice-Hall.

Petzinger, T. (1995). *Hard landing.* New York: Random House.

Rotter, J. B. (1966). Generalized expectancies for internal versus external control of reinforcement. *Psychological Monographs*, 80.

Sims, H. P. (1977). The leader as a manager of reinforcement contingencies. In J. G. Hunt and L. L. Larson (eds.), *Leadership: The cutting edge* (pp. 121–37). Carbondale: Southern Illinois University Press.

Sjoberg, L. G., Olsson, and Salay, F. (1983). Cathectic orientation, goal setting, and mood. *Journal of Personality Assessment*, 47, 307–13.

Solomon, P., and Patch, V. D. (1970). *Handbook of psychiatry*, 2nd edn. Los Angeles: Lange Medical Publications.

Spreitzer, G. M. (1995). Individual empowerment in the workplace: Dimensions, measurement, and validation. *Academy of Management Journal*, 38, 1442–65.

Spreitzer, G. M., Kizilos, M. A., and Nason, S. W. (1994). A dimensional analysis of the relationship between psychological empowerment and effectiveness, satisfaction, and strain. Paper presented at the Western Academy of Management Meetings.

Strauss, G. (1977). Managerial practices. In J. R. Hackman and L. J. Suttle (eds.), *Improving life at work: Behavioral science approaches to organizational change* (pp. 297–363). Santa Monica, CA: Goodyear.

Szilagyi, A. D. (1980). Causal inferences between leader reward behavior and subordinate goal attainment, absenteeism, and work satisfaction. *Journal of Occupational Psychology*, 53, 195–204.

Thomas, K. W., and Velthouse, B. A. (1990). Cognitive elements of empowerment. *Academy of Management Review*, 15, 666–81.

Tichy, N. M., and Charan, R. (1989). Speed, simplicity, and self-confidence: An interview with Jack Welch. *Harvard Business Review*, Sept.–Oct., 112–20.

Tichy, N. M., and Devanna, M. A. (1986). *The transformational leader.* New York: Wiley.

Tichy, N. M., and Sherman, S. (1993). *Control your destiny or someone else will.* New York: Currency Doubleday.

Weiner, B. (1985). An attributional theory of achievement motivation and emotion. *Psychological Review*, 92, 548–73.

11

Pay for Performance

CATHY C. DURHAM AND KATHRYN M. BARTOL

THE PRINCIPLE

Our principle is pay for performance. This principle involves providing monetary rewards through carefully designed compensation systems that base pay on measured performance within the control of participants. It also includes incorporating appropriate concerns for procedural and distributive justice. In most situations, properly designed pay for performance systems will lead to better performance results.

Pay for performance systems make major contributions to performance through two main mechanisms. First, they positively influence the motivation to perform. Second, they impact the attraction and retention patterns of organizations (i.e., who joins and who remains), thereby affecting the caliber of individuals available to perform.

A number of different pay delivery plans qualify as pay for performance systems, although they vary with respect to how closely they tie pay to performance. Pay for performance systems can deliver monetary rewards at the individual, small group, and/ or divisional or organizational level. Evidence suggests that pay for performance at each of these levels can positively impact performance.

Individual level

At the individual level, there are three major types of pay for performance systems: traditional incentive systems, variable pay configurations, and merit pay plans. Traditional incentive plans include piece-rate plans and sales commissions. With piece-rate incentive plans, an employee is paid a specified rate for each unit produced or each service provided. Mitchell, Lewin, and Lawler (1990) estimate that proper use of piece-rate plans leads to performance gains in the 10–15 percent range. Based on their review of the literature, Locke, Feren, McCaleb, Shaw, and Denny (1980) concluded that the median productivity improvement from piece-rate plans is 30 percent. A recent meta-analysis involving mainly piece-rate pay found support for the notion that financial incentives are associated with higher performance in terms of quantity and also found no detrimental impact on quality (Jenkins, Mitra, Gupta, and Shaw, 1998). The other traditional incentive, the commission, is a sales incentive that is typically expressed as a percentage of sales dollars, a percentage of gross profit margins, or some dollar amount for each unit sold (Colletti and Cichelli, 1993). The available research suggests that sales commission schemes can be effective (e.g., Banker, Lee, Potter, and Srinivasan, 1996; Ford, Walker, and Churchhill, 1985; Harrison, Virick, and William, 1996).

The second major type of individual-level pay for performance plan, variable pay, is performance-related compensation that does not permanently increase base pay, and that must be re-earned to be received again. The traditional pay plans just discussed actually constitute forms of variable pay, albeit forms in which a greater proportion of pay is typically tied to performance than is the case with newer emerging forms of variable pay. A popular current variable pay form is a lump-sum bonus for achieving particular goals. Because base pay tends to move up more slowly with variable pay plans, the amount of bonus that can be earned needs to be substantial to make up for the fact that part of the pay is "at risk" (Schuster and Zingheim, 1992). The risk is associated with the possibility that goals might not be met and, therefore, the pay not earned. Evidence suggests that variable pay plans, such as bonus plans, are useful in boosting performance (e.g., Chung and Vickery, 1976; Lee, 1988; Yukl and Latham, 1975).

The third major type of individual-level pay for performance plan, merit pay, rewards individuals for past work behaviors and outcomes by adding dollar amounts to their base pay (Milkovich and Newman, 1999). Merit pay is the most widely used pay system in US organizations (Bretz, Milkovich, and Read, 1992; O'Dell, 1987). Based on a review of 25 studies, Heneman (1992) concludes that merit pay plans appear to be moderately effective in influencing performance. In support of this view, Harris, Gilbreath, and Sunday (1998) argue that the cross-sectional studies which have constituted the bulk of the research on merit pay may significantly understate the impact of merit pay. They provide evidence that the cumulative effects of various types of merit pay adjustments linked to performance, such as those related to promotions, can be substantial.

Team level

In addition to pay for performance at the individual level, there is growing interest in pay for performance plans focused on small groups or teams. Small group pay plans provide monetary rewards based on the measured performance of the group or team. Small work groups or teams are official (designated or recognized by management) multi-person work units composed of individuals who operate interdependently in the performance of tasks that affect others associated within the organization (Guzzo and Dickson, 1996; Hackman, 1987). One survey found that almost 70 percent of Fortune 1000 companies are using some type of work group or team incentives (Lawler, Mohrman, and Ledford, 1995). The impetus for the greater attention to group-level rewards is the increasing use of teams in organizations (Bartol and Hagmann, 1992). Evidence suggests that performance gains can be associated with the use of monetary rewards for groups (Cotton and Cook, 1982; Gomez-Mejia and Balkin, 1989; Wagner, Rubin, and Callahan, 1988; Wageman and Baker, 1997), but that the results are likely to be heavily influenced by situational factors (DeMatteo, Eby, and Sundstrom, 1998).

Organizational level

At the organizational level, three pay systems that potentially link pay and performance are gainsharing, profit-sharing, and stock options. Gainsharing is a compensation plan in which an organization shares with employees a portion of the added earnings obtained through their collective increases in productivity (Henderson, 1997). Such plans usually involve a significant portion of an organization's employees and possibly all. In large organizations, plans may apply to plants, divisions, or other significant subsystems of the organization. In recent years, gainsharing plans have been growing in popularity. The available evidence on gainsharing indicates that such plans have generally led to gains in productivity (US General Accounting Office, 1981; Graham-Moore and Ross, 1990; Kaufman, 1992; Welbourne and Gomez-Mejia, 1988).

The second type of organization-level pay system aimed at performance is profit-sharing. Such plans provide payments to employees based on the profitability of the business. Payments can be made through current distribution plans, deferred plans, or a combination of both, although most companies establish deferred plans because of the associated tax advantages. According to one estimate, more than 60 percent of Fortune 1000 companies have profit-sharing plans (Lawler et al., 1995). Data supporting the performance effects of profit-sharing plans is somewhat unclear. A meta-analysis by Weitzman and Kruse (1990) estimates an average positive productivity effect of 7.4 percent for profit-sharing plans, but their study also considered gainsharing plans in this figure. One possible weakness inherent in profit-sharing plans as a direct means of boosting performance is that it can be somewhat difficult to establish a clear connection (sometimes referred to as "line of sight") between individual actions and impact on profits. This is particularly true because accounting and financial management practices can also impact the "bottom line." In addition, the deferred nature of many of these plans may not provide strong valence with respect to motivating performance.

A third type of organization-level reward system is employee stock ownership. One study of Fortune 1000 companies showed that 71 percent had stock ownership programs of some type (Lawler et al., 1995). The most rapidly growing approach is via stock options. Stock options give employees the right to purchase a specific amount of stock at a designated price over a specified time period. Stock options have been commonly offered to executives, but recently more companies have been providing broad-based stock option plans that extend to middle and sometimes lower levels of the organization (Chingos and Engel, 1998). The basic rationale is that employees will be more concerned about the long-term success of the organization if they can reap the benefits as reflected in the rising price of the organization's stock. Although there are not sufficient data available at this point to conclude that stock options increase employee efforts and thereby positively influence organizational performance, extending ownership may have benefits in terms of positive equity perceptions. One study found that when stock prices have risen above the option price, lower-level employees tend to exercise their options shortly after vesting, a factor that may truncate some of the longer-term motivation potential (Huddart and Lang, 1996).

Overall effects

Aside from the impacts of specific types of pay plans on performance at the level of the organization to which they are directed (e.g., individual, group, and organization), there is also evidence that the presence of pay for performance systems generally has a positive influence on overall organizational performance. In this regard, however, there is some debate regarding whether there are best practices that are applicable to most organizations (Gerhart, Trevor, and Graham, 1996; Huselid, 1995), or whether it is important to match pay systems to particular strategies (Montemayor, 1994; Youndt, Snell, Dean, and Lepak, 1996).

The direct impact of pay plans on performance is not the only effect to consider. Growing evidence suggests that there are indirect pay plan effects stemming from influences on attraction and retention patterns in organizations. For example, several studies support the notion that the level of compensation influences attraction to organizations (e.g., Saks, Wiesner, and Summers, 1996; Schwoerer and Rosen, 1989; Williams and Dreher, 1992). Moreover, research suggests that organization attraction is also related to specific aspects of pay systems. For example, individuals appear to be more attracted to organizations in which the pay system base increases on individual rather than group performance and on job outcomes rather than acquiring new skills (Cable and Judge, 1994; Highhouse, Stierwalt, Bachiochi, Elder, and Fisher, 1999). Individuals may also be more attracted to organizations that offer fixed pay, rather than variable pay, unless there is sufficient upside potential to balance the pay risk (Bartol and Locke, in press).

Other studies suggest that pay for performance can have a positive effect on retention. For example, research indicates positive relationships between employee perceptions of pay for performance and both pay satisfaction (Heneman, Greenberger, and Strasser, 1988; Huber, Seybolt, and Venemon, 1992) and job satisfaction (Kopelman, 1976), factors that are related to intention to leave and turnover (see chapter 7 above). There is some evidence that profit-sharing is an important determinant of organizational commitment (Florkowski and Schuster, 1992), which has been shown to be related to turnover. Based on a meta-analysis, Williams and Livingston (1994) argue that pay for performance systems encourage better performers to remain with the organization while inducing poorer performers to leave.

Interestingly, due to the flexibility and control over labor costs that it provides, variable pay may also reduce turnover. By having more money allocated to bonuses or other forms of variable pay, an organization can shrink its payroll costs during downturns rather than downsize. Gerhart and Trevor (1996) provide evidence that variable pay plans lessen organizational employment variability, allowing for greater employment stability for employees and their organizations.

WHAT IS REQUIRED TO MAKE THE PRINCIPLE WORK?

Define performance

First, it is essential to identify explicitly what performance is desired. Clearly defining performance, however, requires looking beyond individual jobs and thinking strategically about the organization as a whole. It means developing a business model based on what drives the business (e.g., customer satisfaction), after which goals can be set at the various levels of the organization and determinations made about what will be rewarded. Without a business model (or with the wrong one), management risks setting goals and rewarding employees for the wrong things – and finding its employees doing those wrong things very efficiently, to the organization's detriment. Focusing on what drives the business leads to the setting of appropriate performance goals for individual employees at all organizational levels. Then, the act of tying incentives to the achievement of those goals will have not only motivational but also informational value, because people will receive a clear message about what specific behaviors and/or outcomes are expected via communications about the reward system. A temptation to resist is that of defining performance in terms of job aspects that are easily quantifiable, thereby ignoring job dimensions that may be critically important but difficult to measure. This can lead an organization to fall into the trap of "rewarding A while hoping for B" (Kerr, 1995). For pay for performance to be effective, strategically important job dimensions – even hard-to-measure ones – must be identified, communicated, assessed, and rewarded.

Ensure competence

Second, employees must have the appropriate knowledge, skills, and abilities (KSAs) to perform at the desired level. Instituting pay for performance is a futile exercise if employees are unable to perform at the level required to receive the reward. Hiring people who possess (or can readily obtain through training) the relevant KSAs is essential.

Make pay systems commensurate with employees' values

Pay for performance will only work if the rewards being offered are valued and the amount is viewed as sufficient, given what employees are being asked to accomplish. Employers can generally assume that money is a value to their employees, both practically and symbolically. Some employees, however, may not value the incremental gain being offered for high-level performance if the amount is viewed as paltry and thus not worth the additional effort. Further, a pay system can fail if it is perceived as undermining employees' other values. For example, individuals may be uninterested in obtaining even a substantial amount of additional pay if they believe that achieving performance goals means sacrificing greater personal values, such as time to pursue their own interests, a low-stress work environment, or a commitment to high-quality work or to standards of ethical behavior.

Use non-financial motivators too

Most employers assume that money is an effective motivator because it enables employees to buy things that they want or need. Also, money is important from a justice standpoint, giving high performers what is due them for their exceptional contributions to the organization's success. None the less, exclusive reliance on financial incentives would be an unwise policy because it would ignore other important sources of work motivation. Non-monetary motivators include a diverse assortment of activities, such as providing interesting and important work assignments (see chapter 6 above), engendering commitment to the realization of a vision (or to a visionary leader), assigning challenging goals in conjunction with ongoing performance feedback, granting autonomy regarding how a job is accomplished (see chapter 10 above), providing public and/or private recognition for outstanding contributions (see chapter 12 below), or simply enabling one to do work that one loves.

Amabile (1993) argues that it is possible to achieve "motivational synergy" by encouraging both intrinsic and extrinsic motivation. She posits that intrinsic motivation arises from the value of the work itself to the person. It can be fostered through such measures as matching employees to tasks on the basis of their skills and interests, designing work to be optimally challenging, and bringing together diverse individuals in high-performing work teams. Amabile further suggests that, when creativity is particularly important, it may be best to hold off heavily emphasizing extrinsic motivators during the problem presentation and idea generation stages when intrinsic motivation appears to be most important. Extrinsic factors may be particularly helpful during the sometimes difficult validation and implementation stages. Based on a meta-analytic study, Eisenberger and Cameron (1996) also argue that tangible rewards can enhance, rather than undermine, the effects of intrinsic motivation, if the rewards are dependent on performance.

Target the appropriate organizational level

Performance-based pay must be at the appropriate level. Increasingly, firms are rewarding performance at the group and/or organizational levels rather than at the individual level alone, in hopes of boosting organizational performance through enhanced information-sharing, group decision-making, and teamwork (Bartol and Hagmann, 1992). Lawler (1971) argues that the distinction between individual and group pay plans is important because individual and group plans are viewed differently by employees and have different effects. A key decision for management, then, concerns whether incentive pay should be based on individual or group performance. Further, if the organization chooses to reward group performance, decisions must be made about what constitutes a "group" for performance-measurement purposes. For example, will group-based pay be based on the performance of a team, a work unit, a division, or the entire organization?

There has been little actual research to offer guidance regarding the level of performance to which incentives should be tied, although several views have been advanced by compensation experts (e.g., Gomez-Mejia and Balkin, 1992; Mitchell et al., 1990; Montemayor, 1994). Key factors that should be considered when making this important decision include:

- ◆ *Nature of the task.* Pay for performance at the individual level is considered most appropriate when the work is designed for individuals, where the need for integration with others is negligible, where group performance means only the sum of members' individual performances, or where the work is simple, repetitive, and stable. For sequential teams that perform various tasks in a predetermined order, so that group performance cannot exceed that of the lowest individual member, it has been recommended that base pay be skill based, and team incentives be team bonuses with payouts distributed as a percentage of base pay. Alternatively, group-based incentive programs, through which all members receive equal shares of a team bonus, are generally considered appropriate when teams are composed of individuals from the same organizational level, when members have complementary roles and must depend upon each other and interact intensively to accomplish their work, so that group performance is enhanced by cooperation, and when the nature of the technology and workflows allows for the identification of distinct groups that are relatively independent of one another.

- *Ability to measure performance.* Good performance measures are critically important in any pay for performance plan. Pfeffer (1998) argues that performance can often be more reliably assessed at aggregate than at individual levels. He concludes that individual incentive pay should be replaced by collective rewards based on organizational or sub-unit performance that highlight the interdependence among organizational members. Although many are unwilling to go as far as Pfeffer in discounting the potential value of individual incentives, most agree that group incentives are a suitable alternative when the identification of individual contributors is difficult due to the nature of the task. For gainsharing plans in particular, it is not only necessary that there be good performance measures for the unit or plant, but also that there be a reliable performance history in order to develop a gainsharing formula. When group performance is rewarded, however, it is none the less important, particularly in Western cultures, to provide a means for identifying individual contributions to the group effort (e.g., through peer evaluations), so that members keep in mind their accountability at both the individual and team levels.

- *Organizational culture.* Group incentive plans are best suited to situations in which the organizational culture emphasizes group achievements. Group incentives work best when free riding is unlikely (e.g., because members hold each other accountable or because employees are professionals who possess high intrinsic motivation). If a corporate culture is strongly individualistic and competitive, group plans such as team incentives will likely encounter considerable resistance from organizational members accustomed to focusing on individual accomplishments.

- *Management's purpose.* Group incentives are recommended in situations in which there is a need to align the interests of multiple individuals into a common goal, or when management wishes to foster entrepreneurship at the group level. At the organizational level, profit-sharing is often used to communicate the importance of the firm's financial performance to employees, heightening their awareness of the overall financial performance of the organization by making a portion of their pay vary with it. This is thought to be most motivating when employees believe that they can substantially influence the profit measure, such as in smaller organizations and those in which the means by which profits are achieved are well understood.

Some have proposed mixed models, whereby incentive pay is based partially on individual measures of performance and partially on group measures. Based on a survey by Hewitt Associates, Abosch and Reidy (1996) reported that organizations that rated their own teams as effective had a "healthy balance" between individual and team-based systems. There is some evidence that mixed models may be problematic, however. Wageman (1995) found that teams having mixed forms of reward (i.e., rewards based on both individual and group performance), mixed tasks (i.e., some tasks performed solely by individuals and some by interdependent groups), or both, had lower performance than those with task and pay designs that were clearly either individual level or team level. She proposes that mixed tasks and rewards may lead to inferior performance by adding a group element to what is primarily an individual task, thereby undermining attention to the task. Also, with mixed tasks there are limited opportunities to develop team skills and strategies. In addition, teams executing mixed tasks may need more time to adjust because of the greater complexity of tasks that have both individual and group perform-ance components. Another complicating factor is that some workers may prefer indi-vidual pay over team-based pay (Cable and Judge, 1994). Team members at Motorola, for example, wanted annual merit raises to be based on individual rather than team performance (Gedvilas, 1997). The question remains, then, how best (or when) to mix individual and group-based incentive plans.

Make pay commensurate with the level of risk employees are required to bear

Risk refers to uncertainty about outcomes (Sitkin and Pablo, 1992), and, by definition, pay for performance systems involve uncertain outcomes for employees. Individuals tend to be risk averse concerning pay, because they have no way of minimizing their income risk through diversification, as investors are able to do with their stock portfolios.

At least five factors can affect employees' perceptions concerning the riskiness of a pay for performance plan. First is the proportion of employee pay that is performance based. Although the average percentage of variable pay in the US is only 5 percent, the proportion ranges widely, from 0 to 70 percent (and even to 100 percent for salespersons; Gomez-Mejia and Balkin, 1992). The higher the proportion of variable pay, the more risk the employee must bear, in a trade-off between income security and the potential for higher earnings (Gomez-Mejia, Balkin, and Cardy, 1998). At some point the level of risk may be perceived as so great that it would be unacceptable to the majority of employees, regardless of the potential for high pay. The second factor that influences employees' perceptions of risk is their self-efficacy that they can achieve the performance goals on which pay is contingent. Those who are confident of their ability to perform at a high level should perceive contingent pay as less risky than those who are less confident of their ability. Third, to the extent that the performance measure on which pay is based is influenced by factors outside individual employees' control (e.g., technology or macro-economic factors affecting profits or stock prices), perceived risk for the employee is increased. For example, CEOs run the risk of losing income (and even employment) if the companies for which they are responsible are unsuccessful – whatever the cause. A fourth factor affecting employee perceptions of risk is the amount of time between performance and the receipt of rewards. Because the future is uncertain, deferred rewards involve more risk than immediate ones. For employees to accept a pay system offering long-term rewards, they must be willing to delay gratification in the hopes of greater (but uncertain) future returns. Intertemporal choice research (e.g., Shelley, 1993) indicates that managers may expect to be compensated for the loss of immediate compensation by the payment of a premium that is far in excess of the amount the time value of money would imply – a finding that is probably true of non-managerial employees as well. Finally, perceived risk is greater if individuals frame pay for perform-ance in terms of potential losses instead of potential gains. A system that places in doubt an amount of pay that employees are already counting on will be seen as riskier than one that offers an identical amount as a potential increase in pay. Considering these factors will help incentive system designers determine what level of pay is required to offset employees' perceived risk.

POSSIBLE EXCEPTIONS TO THE PRINCIPLE OF PAYING FOR PERFORMANCE

It does not make sense for an employer to offer to pay employees more unless the employer will actually get more in the bargain. When, therefore, might it be unwise (or even counterproductive) to offer incentives?

When employees are learning

In learning situations, when employees are attempting to "get up to speed" on a new task, offering performance-based pay may frustrate more than it motivates. Performance failures that are a natural part of learning may be exaggerated in the learner's mind because of failure not only to perform the task but also to obtain the monetary reward. Thus, it is unwise to pay for performance until employees are able to perform at the desired level.

When the employer can monitor

Agency theory (Jensen and Meckling, 1976) suggests that financial incentives are unnec-essary when employers can easily monitor employees' behavior (e.g., by direct observa-tion or through information systems) and give them ongoing direction and feedback. In such situations, employees' awareness that they are being monitored obviates paying for performance.

When other motivators are sufficient or compensatory

Some people value other aspects of their jobs more than they value pay – factors such as interesting work, autonomy, desirable location, benefits that meet their needs, or having a boss they love working for. Such individuals will often accept lower pay in order to have what is more important to them in their jobs.

When the company is unionized

Union contracts constrain an employer's pay policies, and thus under collective bargain-ing agreements it may be impossible to pay for performance, especially at the individual level. When incentives are included in a union contract, they are usually group incentives, because group pay is viewed as encouraging cohesion rather than competition among members.

EXAMPLES

Paying for individual performance

Woodson (1999) provides an example of the diffusion of pay for performance to a group that has traditionally received fixed salaries with automatic, annual pay increases – physicians employed by healthcare organizations. She presents case studies of two organizations (a large, multispecialty group practice and a medical school affiliated with an academic medical center) that changed their approaches to physician compensation. One of her examples was a 400-physician multispecialty group practice that was experiencing declines in operating margins. Physicians had little incentive to change behavior that was detrimental to the practice as a whole, because salary levels were increased automatically, no matter what level of performance was achieved. Expectations were ill defined, and performance reviews were viewed as meaningless exercises. The group's governing board decided that the practice could no longer afford a pay system that increased its labor costs every year without contributing substantially to bottom-line and quality improvements, and so it developed a new program with 27 broad salary ranges, one for each specialty. Now, advancement through a pay range is no longer automatic but is based on a physician's skills, capabilities, and accomplishments in all domains of physician performance, including clinical quality, use of resources, and patient satisfaction. During the transition to the new system, the board was careful to ensure that no physician's pay was decreased. Over the next few years, bonuses are expected to reach 20 percent of a physician's base salary. Woodson (1999) notes that in both organizations she studied, replacing traditional pay systems with systems that tied pay to performance resulted in both improved physician performance and lower overhead costs.

Sears, Roebuck and Company provides an example of the perils of rewarding employees for the wrong things. The company had to pay out millions of dollars to consumers in a series of lawsuits in 1992 – lawsuits that were directly tied to the company's compensation system. Employees in Sears Auto Centers had been paid straight commission based on the parts and services they sold to customers who brought their cars in for repair. The incentive plan encouraged employees to find and "repair" defects that did not actually exist. Because of the ensuing scandal, Sears abolished commissions and sales goals in its automotive division. Now the company uses several forms of pay for performance, such as straight commission for appliance salespeople, and salary plus commission or other forms of incentive pay (e.g., pay based on customer satisfaction ratings or overall business objectives) for others (Ganzel, 1998).

Paying for team performance

In 1995, Silicon Valley's Solectron Corporation – the only two-time winner of the prestigious Baldridge Award (1991 and 1997) – reorganized production around self-directed work teams that have responsibility for entire portions of the production process. The change to teams necessitated discontinuing a company-wide variable pay plan, which failed to support appropriate team behaviors, in favor of a participatively developed team incentive system. Participation by team members and managers in the design of the pay system heightened their commitment to the plan, which was introduced to the entire workforce through extensive communication and training. Since implementation, regular meetings and ongoing communication ensure that teams know how the plan is working. Specific goals of each team result from negotiations with team managers, and team goals are posted, both to motivate high-level performance and to stimulate recognition by peers and managers when teams' goals are achieved. Bonus payments are made quarterly and shared equally by team members, based on quality of team output and productivity against a team standard (Lawler, 1999). In addition to team bonuses, Selectron employees (including temporary contract workers) receive variable pay based on individual, site, and corporate goal achievement (McClenahen, 1998). Solectron's pay system has led to improvements in quality, productivity, and satisfaction with pay, presumably because individuals feel more in control of how they are paid. It continues to undergo fine-tuning, however, as management extends its reconsideration of compensation to the issues of how merit pay and base pay should be determined in a team environment (Lawler, 1999).

Lawler (1999) provides an example of team-based incentives having unforeseen negative consequences. Motorola had team-based pay for performance plans in many of its manufacturing facilities, which offered potentially large bonuses for teams that met specific performance objectives. The incentive plan often succeeded in motivating the teams to perform well as teams, but it failed to address the interdependencies that existed among the teams and that necessitated their cooperating with each other. Therefore, the incentive system inadvertently caused conflict among teams over access to resources, and teams viewed the system as unfair whenever some teams got large bonuses and others did not. Because of the discord among teams and because organizational units were optimizing their own performance to the detriment of the organization as a whole, Motorola eventually abandoned the team-based plans. Lawler (1999) draws from Motorola's experience the lesson that team incentive plans should only be used where teams operate relatively autonomously. When teams are interdependent, he suggests that using a gainsharing or profit-sharing plan that rewards team members based on the performance of the larger organizational unit can serve to integrate teams into the rest of the organization.

Paying for organizational performance

Lincoln Electric Company, based in Cleveland, Ohio, is world renowned for the high quality of its arc-welding and related products. The company is equally noted for a factory worker compensation system that pays for performance at both the individual and organizational levels. Individual pay is based on a piecework system that has been in place at the company since 1914, and year-end annual bonuses are based on the organization's annual profits. Individual payouts for the year-end bonus are determined by two semi-annual performance ratings on four factors: dependability, quality, output, and ideas and cooperation (Hodgetts, 1997). Hundreds of the workers have earned $70,000 to $80,000 per year, and some have topped $100,000 (Hastings, 1999). The company guarantees at least 30 hours of full-time work per week for employees with three years or more of service. In return, workers must be willing to work at any assignment at the pay rate for the position and also accept overtime when demand conditions warrant (Chilton, 1994). The company also has a generous retirement plan. Interestingly, though, Lincoln Electric ran into severe difficulties when it attempted to apply the piecework and bonus system in Europe, South America, and Japan as part of its international expansion efforts. The company has, however, been successful in transplanting the system to operations in Mexico City (Hastings, 1999).

Miller and Schuster (1995) describe the failure of a gainsharing plan at a federally owned and operated industrial complex whose main mission was the maintenance, repair, and rebuilding of military equipment. The complex employed 4,800 civilian workers, including several levels of management who ultimately reported to military offices. A local branch of the American Federation of Government Employees represented almost 60 percent of the hourly personnel. The gainsharing plan was developed in response to an order from an off-site military commander who wished to increase hourly productivity. The plan was designed by senior managers with no input from line personnel, union leadership, or gainsharing consultants. A total of 460 employees were involved in the gainsharing plan, which was initiated as a 15-month pilot program. The plan base and payout levels differed for various units and, although computed monthly, were distributed quarterly. The formula design apparently was flawed, and it quickly caused feelings of inequity and dissatisfaction across units. The top departments in terms of monetary gain and payout earned did not register actual productivity gains, while several departments that did show productivity gains actually received lower payouts. Middle managers particularly were frustrated by their lack of input into the plan design. Both managers and production employees viewed the fact that the plan was labeled a pilot program as evidence that there was actually little commitment to it by upper management. Consensus also developed among participants that the quarterly period for payout was too long. Ultimately few if any gains in productivity materialized and the plan was eventually discontinued, but not before it seriously damaged an effectively functioning quality program that it partially overlapped.

Global pay

Organizations with international operations are presented with some unique challenges when they attempt to pay for performance at the organizational (and thus global) level. None the less, multinational firms are increasingly instituting global pay in an attempt to attract skilled workers and create organizational cultures in which employees feel part of the same company regardless of their location. Gross and Winterup (1999) describe the global pay practices of Cisco Systems, a maker of Internet equipment with 17,000 employees worldwide. The company sets base pay at the 65th percentile in every labor market and offers variable pay that brings total remuneration to the 75th percentile. Cisco Systems' global strategy includes the use of stock options, but its commitment to doing so has meant that the company has had to work hard to ensure that the pay is understood, accepted, and deployed to the benefit rather than to the detriment of workers worldwide. Problems it has encountered include: regulations in China and Russia that prohibit citizens from holding securities in foreign companies; the up-front taxing of stock options in The Netherlands (as compared to their being taxed when they are exercised in the US); France's punitive taxes levied against employees who sell their options in the first five years; and the need in India to reduce stock option grants for employees by half, so that they would not reap such huge capital gains (in comparison to the country's per capita income) that they would be able to take early retirement in only a few years. These examples illustrate the importance of staying abreast of labor markets and changing laws wherever a company has operations, but Cisco Systems is convinced that doing so is worth the effort because it enables the firm to recruit and retain superior employees worldwide.

CONCLUSION

Paying for performance works. It communicates what factors are most important to the company's success and focuses employees' attention and effort on those factors. It is fair, because it pays more to those who contribute more. In turn, it attracts individuals who can perform at high levels and, by recognizing and rewarding them for doing so, makes them want to remain.

REFERENCES

Amabile, T. M. (1993). Motivational synergy: Toward new conceptualizations of intrinsic and extrinsic motivation in the workplace. *Human Resource Management Review*, 3, 185–201.

Abosch, K. S., and Reidy, D. B. (1996). Supporting teams through rewards systems. *ACA Journal*, Winter, 72–81.

Banker, R. D., Lee, S.-Y., Potter, G., and Srinivasan, S. (1996). Contextual analysis of performance impacts of outcome-based incentive compensation. *Academy of Management Journal*, 39, 920–48.

Bartol, K. M., and Hagmann, L. L. (1992). Team-based pay plans: A key to effective teamwork. *Compensation and Benefits Review*, Nov.–Dec., 24–9.

Bartol, K. M., and Locke, E. A. (in press). Incentives and motivation. In S. Rynes and B. Gerhardt (eds.), *Compensation in organizations: Progress and prospects*. San Francisco, CA: New Lexington Press.

Bretz, R. D., Milkovich, G. T., and Read, W. (1992). The current state of performance appraisal research and practice: Concerns, directions, and implications. *Journal of Management*, 18, 321–52.

Cable, D. M., and Judge, T. A. (1994). Pay preferences and job search decisions: A person–organization fit perspective. *Personnel Psychology*, 47, 317–48.

Chilton, K. W. (1994). Lincoln Electric's incentive system: A reservoir of trust. *Compensation & Benefits Review*, 26 (Nov.–Dec.), 29–34.

Chingos, P. T., and Engel, M. M. (1998). Trends in stock option plans and long-term incentives. *ACA Journal*, 7, 13–18.

Chung, K. H., and Vickery, W. D. (1976). Relative effectiveness and joint effects of three selected reinforcements in a repetitive task situation. *Organizational Behavior and Human Decision Processes*, 16, 114–42.

Colletti, J. A., and Cichelli, D. L. (1993). *Designing sales compensation plans: An approach to developing and implementing incentive plans for salespeople*. Scottsdale: American Compensation Association.

Cotton, M. S., and Cook, J. L. (1982). Meta-analyses and the effects of various reward systems: Some different conclusions from Johnson et al. *Psychological Bulletin*, 92, 176–83.

DeMatteo, J. S., Eby, L. T., and Sundstrom, E. (1998). Team-based rewards: Current empirical evidence and directions for future research. *Research in Organizational Behavior*, 20, 141–83.

Eisenberger, R., and Cameron, J. (1996). Detrimental effects of reward: Reality or myth? *American Psychologist*, 51, 1153–66.

Florkowski, G. W., and Schuster, M. H. (1992). Support for profit sharing and organizational commitment: A path analysis. *Human Relations*, 45, 507–23.

Ford, N. M., Walker, O. C., and Churchhill, G. A. (1985). Differences in the attractiveness of alternative rewards among industrial salespeople: Additional evidence. *Journal of Business Research*, 13, 123–38.

Ganzel, R. (1998). What's wrong with pay for performance? *Training*, 35(12), 34–40.

Gedvilas, C. (1997). Recognizing and rewarding team performance at Motorola. *ACA News*, 40 (Feb.), 6–9.

Gerhart, G., and Trevor, C. O. (1996). Employment variability under different compensation systems. *Academy of Management Journal*, 39, 1692–712.

Gerhart, G., Trevor, C. O., and Graham, M. E. (1996). New directions in compensation research: Synergies, risk, and survival. *Research in Personnel and Human Resources Management*, 14, 143–203.

Gomez-Mejia, L. R., and Balkin, D. B. (1989). Effectiveness of individual and aggregate compensation strategies. *Industrial Relations*, 28, 431–45.

Gomez-Mejia, L. R., and Balkin, D. B. (1992). *Compensation, organizational strategy, and firm performance.* Cincinnati, OH: South-Western.

Gomez-Mejia, L. R., Balkin, D. B., and Cardy, R. L. (1998). *Managing Human Resources*, 2nd edn. Upper Saddle River, NJ: Prentice-Hall.

Graham-Moore, B. E., and Ross, T. L. (1990). *Gainsharing.* Washington, DC: The Bureau of National Affairs.

Gross, S. E., and Winterup, P. L. (1999). Global pay? Maybe not yet! *Compensation and Benefits Review*, 30(4), 25–34.

Guzzo, R. A., and Dickson, M. W. (1996). Teams in organizations: Recent research on performance and effectiveness. *Annual Review of Psychology*, 47, 307–38.

Hackman, J. R. (1987). The design of work teams. In J. W. Lorsch (ed.), *Handbook of organizational behavior* (pp. 315–42). Englewood Cliffs, NJ: Prentice-Hall.

Harris, M. M., Gilbreath, B., and Sunday, J. A. (1998). A longitudinal examination of a merit pay system: Relationships among performance ratings, merit increases, and total pay increases. *Journal of Applied Psychology*, 83, 825–31.

Harrison, D. A., Virick, M., and William, S. (1996). Working without a net: Time, performance, and turnover under maximally contingent rewards. *Journal of Applied Psychology*, 81, 331–45.

Hastings, D. F. (1999). Lincoln Electric's harsh lessons from international expansion. *Harvard Business Review*, 77 (May–June), 163–78.

Henderson, R. I. (1997). *Compensation management in a knowledge-based world*, 7th edn. Upper Saddle River, NJ: Prentice-Hall.

Heneman, R. L. (1992). *Merit pay: Linking pay increases to performance ratings.* Reading, MA: Addison-Wesley.

Heneman, R. L., Greenberger, D. B., and Strasser, S. (1988). The relationship between pay- for-performance perceptions and pay satisfaction. *Academy of Management Journal*, 32, 466–76.

Highhouse, S., Stierwalt, S. L., Bachiochi, P., Elder, A. E., and Fisher, G. (1999). Effects of advertised human resource management practices on attraction of African American applicants. *Personnel Psychology*, 52, 425–42.

Hodgetts, R. M. (1997). Discussing incentive compensation with Donald Hastings of Lincoln Electric. *Compensation & Benefits Review*, 29 (Sept.), 60–6.

Huber, V. L., Seybolt, P. M., and Venemon, K. (1992). The relationship between individual inputs, perceptions, and multidimensional pay satisfaction. *Journal of Applied Social Psychology*, 22, 1356–73.

Huddart, S., and Lang, M. (1996). Employee stock option exercises: An empirical analysis. *Journal of Accounting and Economics*, 21, 5–43.

Huselid, M. (1995). The impact of human resources management practices on turnover, productivity, and corporate financial performance. *Academy of Management Journal*, 38, 635–72.

Jenkins, G. D. Jr., Mitra, A., Gupta, N., and Shaw, J. D. (1998). Are financial incentives related to performance? A meta-analytic review of empirical research. *Journal of Applied Psychology*, 83, 777–87.

Jensen, M., and Meckling, M. (1976). Theory of the firm: Managerial behavior, agency costs and ownership structure. *Journal of Financial Economics*, 3, 305–60.

Kaufman, R. (1992). The effects of Improshare on productivity. *Industrial & Labor Relations Review*, 45, 311–22.

Kerr, S. (1995). On the folly of rewarding A, while hoping for B. *Academy of Management Executive*, 9 (Feb.), 7–14.

Kopelman, R. E. (1976). Organizational control system responsiveness, expectancy theory constructs, and work motivation: Some interrelations and causal connections. *Personnel Psychology*, 29, 205–20.

Lawler, E. E. III. (1971). *Pay and organizational effectiveness: A psychological view*. New York: McGraw-Hill.

Lawler, E. E. III. (1999). Creating effective pay systems for teams. In E. Sundstrom and Associates (eds.), *Supporting work team effectiveness: Best management practices for fostering high performance* (pp. 188–212). San Francisco: Jossey-Bass.

Lawler, E. E. III, Mohrman, S., and Ledford, G. E. Jr. (1995). *Creating high performance organizations*. San Francisco: Jossey-Bass.

Lee, C. (1988). The effects of goal setting and monetary incentives on self-efficacy and performance. *Journal of Business & Psychology*, 2, 366–72.

Locke, E. A., Feren, D. B., McCaleb, V. M., Shaw, K. N., and Denny, A. T. (1980). The relative effectiveness of four methods of motivating employee performance. In K. D. Duncan, M. M. Gruneberg, and D. Wallis (eds.), *Changes in working life* (pp. 363–88). London: Wiley.

McClenahen, J. S. (1998). Solectron Corp., *Industry Week*, 247(19), 68–70.

Milkovich, G. T., and Newman, J. M. (1999). *Compensation*, 6th edn. Burr Ridge, IL: Irwin/McGraw-Hill.

Miller, C., and Schuster, M. H. (1995). The anatomy of a failure: A non-recommended application of gainsharing and its predictable effects on productivity in a public sector setting. *Public Administration Quarterly*, 19, 217–24.

Mitchell, D. J. B., Lewin, D., and Lawler, E. E. III. (1990). Alternative pay systems, firm performance, and productivity. In A. S. Blinder (ed.), *Paying for productivity: A look at the evidence* (pp. 15–94). Washington, DC: The Brookings Institution.

Montemayor, E. F. (1994). A model for aligning teamwork and pay. *ACA Journal*, 3(2), 18–25.

O'Dell, C. (1987). *People, performance and pay*. Houston: American Productivity Center.

Pfeffer, J. (1998). Six dangerous myths about pay. *Harvard Business Review*, 76 (May–June), 108–19.

Saks, A. M., Wiesner, W. H., and Summers, R. J. (1996). Effects of job previews and compensation policy on applicant attraction and job choice. *Journal of Vocational Behavior*, 49, 68–85.

Schuster, J. R., and Zingheim, P. K. (1992). *The new pay: Linking employee and organizational performance*. New York: Lexington Books.

Schwoerer, C., and Rosen, B. (1989). Effects of employment-at-will policies and compensation policies on corporate image and job pursuit intentions. *Journal of Applied Psychology*, 74, 653–6.

Shelley, M. (1993). Outcome signs, question frames, and discount rates. *Management Science*, 39 (7), 806–15.

Sitkin, S. B., and Pablo, A. L. (1992). Reconceptualizing the determinants of risk behavior. *Academy of Management Review*, 17, 9–38.

US General Accounting Office (1981). *Productivity sharing programs: Can they contribute to productivity improvement?* (AFMD Publication No. 81–22). Washington, DC: Author.

Wageman, R. (1995). Interdependence and group effectiveness. *Administrative Science Quarterly*, 40, 145–80.

Wageman, R., and Baker, G. (1997). Incentives and cooperation: The joint effects of task and reward interdependence on group performance. *Journal of Organizational Behavior*, 18, 139–58.

Wagner, J. A. III, Rubin, P. A., and Callahan, T. J. (1988). Incentive payment and nonmanagerial productivity: An interrupted time series analysis of magnitude and trend. *Organizational Behavior and Human Decision Process*, 42, 47–74.

Weitzman, M. L., and Kruse, D. L. (1990). Profit sharing and productivity. In A. S. Blinder (ed.), *Paying for productivity: A look at the evidence* (pp. 95–141). Washington, DC: The Brookings Institution.

Welbourne, T. M., and Gomez-Mejia, L. R. (1988). Gainsharing revisited. *Compensation & Benefits Review*, 20 (July–Aug.), 19–28.

Williams, C. R., and Livingstone, L. P. (1994). Another look at the relationship between performance and voluntary turnover. *Academy of Management Journal*, 37, 269–98.

Williams, M. L., and Dreher, G. F. (1992). Compensation system attributes and applicant pool characterisitics. *Academy of Management Journal*, 35, 571–95.

Woodson, S. B. (1999). Making the connection between physician performance and pay. *Healthcare Financial Management*, 53(2), 39–44.

Youndt, M. A., Snell, S. A., Dean, J. W. Jr., and Lepak, D. P. (1996). Human resource management, manufacturing strategy, and firm performance. *Academy of Management Journal*, 39, 836–66.

Yukl, G. A., and Latham, G. P. (1975). Consequences of reinforcement schedules and incentive magnitude for employee performance: Problems encountered in an industrial setting. *Journal of Applied Psychology*, 60, 294–8.

12

Provide Recognition for Performance Improvement

FRED LUTHANS AND ALEXANDER D. STAJKOVIC

> It is difficult to conceive of a society populated with people who are
> completely unmoved by the respect, approval, and reproof of others.
> (Bandura, 1986: 235)

One of the most agreed upon principles in the field of organizational behavior is that positive reinforcers contingently administered to critical employee behaviors will lead to performance improvement. As Bandura (1986) notes: "human behavior . . . cannot be fully understood without considering the regulatory influence of response consequences" (p. 228). Early on, Vroom (1964) emphatically stated that "without a doubt the law of effect or principle of reinforcement must be included among the most substantiated findings of experimental psychology and is at the same time among the most useful findings for an applied psychology concerned with control of human behavior" (p. 13). The two major types of positive reinforcers or incentive motivators used to improve employee performance are money and recognition. Money was the subject of the preceding chapter. The principle of this chapter is that providing contingent recognition will lead to improved employee performance.

There is a subtle distinction between the term "social recognition" and "recognition" *per se*. In the workplace, we define social recognition as an individual or group providing usually informal acknowledgement, approval, and genuine appreciation for work well done to another individual or group. It should be noted that this definition does not include phony praise, "attaboys," or randomized pats on the back. Recognition *per se* refers more to a formal program such as employee of the month or million dollars in sales round table. Both can be administered on a public basis (e.g., a staff meeting in the case of social recognition or the company newsletter or banquet in the case of a recognition program). Social recognition, however, tends to be informal and is administered more on a one-on-one private level, both verbally or in writing.

The broad appeal of social recognition in the workplace is that it applies to everyone (top to bottom in the organization), no one gets too much of it (no satiation principle here), it is readily available to everyone to use, and it doesn't cost anything. As Tom

Cash, Senior VP of American Express, noted: "Human beings need to be recognized and rewarded for special efforts. You don't even have to give them much. What they want is tangible proof that you really care about the job they do" (Nelson, 1994). To demonstrate these claims, simply ask yourself, are you or anyone you know suffering from too much social recognition? When Bob Hope, well into his eighties was asked, "Why don't you retire?" he quickly answered, "Because the darn fish don't applaud!" Besides this common-sense appeal of social recognition as a powerful incentive motivator, there is also considerable theory and research supporting its effectiveness in the workplace. Most of this chapter refers to social recognition, but will not contain the word "social" when referring to more formal recognition programs.

The Use of Recognition in Classic Behavioral Management

Under classic behavioral management based on reinforcement theory, social recognition is considered to be universally applicable. In particular, if social recognition is provided on a contingent basis in managing employee behavior, it can be a powerful motivator for performance improvement. For example, under the Luthans and Kreitner (1975, 1985) organizational behavior modification (OB Mod.) approach, after the critical employee performance behaviors are identified, measured, and functionally analyzed, social recognition is contingently applied to increase the frequency of the identified functional behaviors, which subsequently results in performance improvement. Examples in both manufacturing and service organizations can help clarify the conceptual premises of recognition in behavioral management.

In a manufacturing setting, an identified desired performance behavior may be something like the productive use of idle time during preventative maintenance. The contingent social recognition would be delivered by a supervisor saying to a worker, "I noticed that you helped out Steve while your equipment was being serviced by the maintenance guys." In this instance, it is important to note that the recognition did not include a "gushy" thank you or phony praise for doing what this worker was supposed to be doing, but instead the worker simply "knew that his supervisor knew" that he had gone out of his way to help out a fellow worker. Because of the received social recognition from the supervisor, the worker will, likely, tend to repeat this helping behavior in the future. In other words, instead of receiving no consequence for this desired behavior (which will lead to extinction), or a punishing outcome of having to work harder (which will lead to a decrease), the supervisor providing contingent social recognition will strengthen the worker's behavior and enhance the productivity of the unit.

In a service setting such as a bank, an identified desired performance behavior, say, of tellers may be providing customers with information about various products that the bank offers. As in the manufacturing example above, upon observing this behavior, the supervisor would provide contingent social recognition by saying something like, "I overheard your explanation to Ms. Smith about how to obtain, use, and the advantages of a debit card. I am sure we will be adding her to our debit card business." The social recognition provided in this case, again, took the form of a positive incentive motivator with an aim of increasing the desired service behavior, which subsequently leads to increased performance.

A large number of studies over the years have verified that social recognition is indeed a powerful incentive motivator for employee behaviors leading to performance improvement in both manufacturing and service organizations. A recent meta-analysis of all studies over the past 20 years that used the OB Mod. approach to behavioral management found an overall average effect of 17 percent improved performance using all types of interventions and about the same when social recognition was the intervention. However, when social recognition was analyzed in combination with performance feedback, an even higher average increase in both manufacturing and service organizations was found (Stajkovic and Luthans, 1997; Luthans and Stajkovic, 1999). Interestingly, the use of money as the intervention had about the same impact as the social recognition in the service organizations, but when the social recognition was combined with performance feedback, it had about the same impact as the money in manufacturing and about twice the impact as the money in service applications.

In addition to this quantitative evidence affirming the power that social recognition can have on performance improvement, the practitioner-oriented, professional literature also contains some empirical support. For example, a recent nationwide survey of US workers found that about seven out of ten report that non-monetary forms of recognition provide the best motivation (*HR Focus*, 1999). A contingency implication was that this same survey found employees favor recognition from managers and supervisors by a margin of almost 2 : 1 over recognition from co-workers or other sources. Another survey conducted by the Council of Communication Management found that recognition for a job well done is the top motivator of employee performance, but in the same survey a third of the managers themselves report that they would rather work in an organization where they could receive better recognition (Nelson, 1994).

Of particular note is a meta-analysis conducted on the Gallup Organization database of 28 studies involving 105,680 employee responses to surveys from a wide variety of organizations. The survey item dealing with recognition ("In the last seven days, I have received recognition or praise for doing good work") was significantly related to 2,528 business units' outcome measures of customer satisfaction/loyalty, profitability, and productivity, but not turnover (Harter and Creglow, 1999). However, conventional "wisdom" and some surveys (Nelson, 1996) do indicate that social recognition (or at least appreciation), along with the other desirable outsomes, also is a major determinant of retention. Such discrepancies are why comprehensive theoretical analysis becomes important for better understanding of social recognition.

A SOCIAL COGNITIVE THEORY ANALYSIS OF SOCIAL RECOGNITION

The use of social recognition in classic behavioral management is based on reinforcement theory, which assumes that the causal agents of employee behaviors are found in the functional relationship between the environmental consequences and the behavior they effect (Komaki, 1986; Luthans and Stajkovic, 1999; Stajkovic and Luthans, 1997). However, the explanatory power of the reinforcement approach to human action has been questioned on the grounds that it falls short of providing the needed conceptual process-oriented analysis as to the nature and operating processes of outcome determinants such as social recognition (Bandura, 1986, 1997; Locke, 1997; Stajkovic and Luthans, 1998a, 1998b).

Social cognitive theory (Bandura, 1986, 1997, 1999) is emerging as a more comprehensive explanation of organizational behavior in general (Stajkovic and Luthans, 1998b), and incentive motivators such as social recognition in particular (Stajkovic and Luthans, 2000). Specifically, based on Bandura's (1999) premise that human agency is mostly grounded in social systems, the social cognitive explanation of the nature of social recognition as an incentive motivator for employee performance would focus on its three major dimensions: (1) outcome utility; (2) informative content; and (3) the mechanisms through which it operates to control employee behavior (Stajkovic and Luthans, 2000). A process-oriented analysis of social recognition along these three factors clearly leads to a more comprehensive, deeper, and, importantly, additive understanding of its underlying mechanisms, than is provided by reinforcement theory alone.

Outcome utility of social recognition

Bandura (1986) argues that social recognition derives its outcome utility from its predictive value and not from the social reactions themselves as reinforcement theory would suggest. Social recognition (personal acknowledgement and approval) precedes and could be perceived to lead to desired employee outcomes such as a promotion, raise, or an assignment to a desired project. In other words, received social recognition may indicate to an employee a potentially upcoming desired outcome utility (and incentive value). In terms of the magnitude of its effectiveness in affecting employee behavior, social recognition given by those who have the power and resources to make desired outcomes a reality for the recipient (e.g., managers, supervisors), will have a stronger effect than the social recognition provided by those who may not have such power or resources (e.g., an outside vendor). However, social recognition provided by those who may not have financial resources and/or promotion power at their disposal, but have considerable social respect and credibility (e.g., an admired peer or mentor) may also be powerful in its effect on employee behavior for it may lead to desirable outcomes such as being included in the "in-group." Thus, the social cognitive approach predicts that employees will engage in behaviors that receive social recognition, especially from those that can provide desired material and/or social outcomes.

Informative content of social recognition

Social recognition, as we define it, has relatively less informative content than, for example, quantitatively based feedback. Yet, since the effective way of providing social recognition focuses on specifics, there may be a different informative content value in what is being expressed. However, it is important to note here that the "scale" for the informative value of social recognition focuses on the content value of what has been delivered and not necessarily on the quantity of praise. In particular, showing employees how much their work is appreciated through social recognition is not achieved by frequently using non-contingent standardized phrases (e.g., "good job!"), but by the acts of social recognition that convey genuine personal involvement, appreciation, and grati-tude for the successful performance. This is because indiscriminate approval that does not eventually result in tangible benefits becomes an "empty reward," thus lacking the potential to control human action. It is the difference between the indiscriminate approval and the genuine appreciation with promising outcomes that portrays the informative continuum of social recognition. For example, instead of a generic phrase such as "good job," the recognition giver would provide specific information such as "I know that you stayed late last night to finish the graphs that I gave you at the last minute. They made my presentation a great success in the meeting this morning." This detailed form of social recognition not only conveys acknowledgement and genuine appreciation, but also information for motivating subsequent desired behavior.

The regulatory mechanism

The third dimension of a social cognitive explanation of social recognition focuses on the regulatory mechanism through which social recognition impacts human action. We have argued (Stajkovic and Luthans, 2000) that the basic human capability of forethought (Bandura, 1986; Stajkovic and Luthans, 1998b) is the means to cognitively operationalize recognition as an incentive motivator. The forethought regulatory mechanism is ex-plained as follows:

> Based on the recognition received and, thus, the perceived prediction of desired conse-quences to come, people will self-regulate their future behaviors by forethought. By using forethought, employees may plan courses of action for the near future, anticipate the likely consequences of their future actions, and set performance goals for themselves. Thus, people first anticipate certain outcomes based on recognition received, and then through fore-thought, they initiate and guide their actions in an anticipatory fashion. (Stajkovic and Luthans, 2000)

Thus, the forethought is the regulatory mechanism that permits perceived future desired outcomes based on the social recognition to be transferred into current employee behaviors that lead to performance improvement. The above explanations of the nature and underlying mechanisms of social recognition represent the social cognitive approach to this incentive motivator, and is how the social recognition principle is defined and explained in this chapter.

MODERATORS OF SOCIAL RECOGNITION

Based on traditional applications of reinforcement theory and behavioral management, it has usually been implied that social recognition has no exceptions or moderators as to its positive impact on performance. Unlike money, social recognition, as used in behavioral management, is portrayed as always being a positive reinforcer (it strengthens and increases the preceding behavior). Even though, as the opening comments of this chapter indicate, recognition is most often thought of as applying to everyone and no one gets tired of it, the social cognitive conceptual analysis as outlined above and the recent meta-analysis of OB Mod. model interventions (Stajkovic and Luthans, 1997) seem to indicate that there may be moderators of the relationship between social recognition and performance.

Type of organization

One clear moderator that emerged from our meta-analysis of OB Mod. was the type of organization. The analysis found that the average effect sizes for all the different interventions varied significantly between manufacturing and service applications (Stajkovic and Luthans, 1997). In particular, all interventions, including social recognition, had a greater impact on performance in manufacturing organizations than in service organizations. A possible explanation of these findings may be that it is simply more difficult to identify performance-related behaviors to provide contingent social recognition in service than in manufacturing organizations, rather than to assume the lesser effect of social recognition in service organizations.

Task complexity

The social cognitive explanation of social recognition points to some additional qualifying refinements and potential moderators. In particular, we believe that the level of task complexity may be another important moderator of the relationship between social recognition and work performance. This is because different levels of task complexity have different effects on the behavioral, information-processing, and cognitive capacities of the task performer (Bandura, 1997; Stajkovic and Luthans, 1998a; Wood, 1986). Specifically, the higher the task complexity, the greater the demands on the employee's (1) knowledge, (2) skill capacity, (3) behavioral facility, (4) information-processing ability, (5) persistence, and (6) self-efficacy (Bandura, 1986, 1997; Stajkovic and Luthans, 1998a). Given these types of demands for highly complex tasks, social recognition from significant others takes on relatively more importance. Those performing complex tasks such as in technical engineering or computer systems work or creative activities such as in advertising or product development may place more value on social recognition from relevant others than on money. On the other hand, there is evidence that those doing routine, low-complexity tasks give relatively more value to money than to social recognition from their supervisors (Stajkovic and Luthans, 2000). In other words, the more complex the task, the more value is placed on the social recognition.

THE ROLE OF SOCIAL RECOGNITION IN BUILDING SELF-EFFICACY

Self-efficacy is an important derivative of social cognitive theory (Bandura, 1997; Stajkovic and Luthans, 1998b) and social recognition may be an input into its development and the resulting performance improvement. Self-efficacy is precisely defined as the belief in one's capabilities to organize cognitive and behavioral facilities and execute the courses of action required to produce desired outcomes in a specific context and on a specific task (Bandura, 1997; Stajkovic and Luthans, 1998a, 1998b), but for the purposes of this chapter can be thought of as the belief or confidence one has to successfully accomplish a specific task. In performing a specific task, an employee's self-efficacy determines whether the necessary behavior will be initiated, how much effort will be expended and sustained, and how much persistence and resilience there will be in the face of obstacles, problems, or even failure (Bandura, 1997, 1999; Stajkovic and Luthans, 1998b). With this profile, it is not surprising that self-efficacy has been shown to be strongly related to work performance (a .38 weighted average correlation in our recent meta-analysis of 114 studies, Stajkovic and Luthans, 1998a).

Unlike personality traits, self-efficacy is generally recognized to be a state variable that can be developed and trained. The most important inputs into the development of self-efficacy are generally acknowledged to be mastery experiences, modeling/vicarious learning, social persuasion, and physiological and/or psychological arousal (Bandura, 1997; Stajkovic and Luthans, 1998b). However, social recognition may also have direct or at least indirect implications for each of these developmental dimensions of self-efficacy. For example: (1) social recognition may be perceived as confirmation of success; (2) seeing others being socially recognized would be vicariously reinforcing; (3) social recognition framed as social persuasion would enhance the receivers' beliefs as to what they can do with what they already have (without requiring new knowledge and skills); and (4) of course, recognition would likely provide support and encouragement for employees to stay on the course of action and persist when meeting performance obstacles and problems. In other words, social recognition may help build self-efficacy, and those with higher self-efficacy will perform better. As Bandura (1997) notes, it is not behavior (and in this case the consequence of recognition) that causes behavior, but what is psychologically made out of it (in this case efficacy development).

FORMAL RECOGNITION PROGRAMS DRAWN FROM PRACTICAL EXPERIENCE

So far the discussion has focused on the conceptual and empirical properties of *social* recognition in terms of its nature and relationship to work performance. However, as the introductory definitions indicated, another way to consider recognition is from the perspective of more formal programs commonly used to recognize employees in real-world organizations. In that vein, largely based on one-shot experiences and anecdotal evidence, Nelson (1994) gives practicing managers *1001 Ways to Reward Employees*. This best-selling little handbook, according to the book jacket, is "A chock-full guide to rewards of every conceivable type for every conceivable situation."

Nelson (1994) provides specific recognition program guidelines on:

- ◆ WHO (outstanding individual employees or teams/groups in terms of productivity, quality, suggestions, customer service, sales, attendance or safety)
- ◆ WHAT (time off, vacations, field trips, special events, educational classes, benefits, gift certificates, cash prizes, merchandise, trophies, pins or plaques)
- ◆ HOW (nomination procedures, representative committees, point systems or contests)
- ◆ WHERE (newsletters, regularly scheduled meetings or specific celebrations/banquets).

There are also specific company examples of recognition programs, such as at Home Depot, where each store picks an Employee of the Month (the criterion being someone who has given time to an area of the store that technically lies outside his or her responsibility). The recipient is given $100, a merit badge (five badges earn an extra $50), a special pin to wear on his or her apron, and the honoree's name engraved on a plaque displayed at the front of the store.

Our discussion of the theory and research point out *why* recognition should be used, and this handbook points out to managers that they no longer have the excuse of not using recognition because they do not know the pragmatics of who, what, how or where. The book also supports the use of both social and more formal recognition programs with highlighted quotes (e.g., Mary Kay Ash – "There are two things people want more than sex and money . . . recognition and praise"); and specific guidelines for administering recognition (e.g., match the reward to the person, match the reward to the achievement, and be timely and specific).

IMPLEMENTATION GUIDELINES FROM THEORY AND RESEARCH

The principle of this chapter is drawn from reinforcement and social cognitive theories and is supported by the findings from the meta-analysis of research studies over the past 20 years (Stajkovic and Luthans, 1997). It says that managers providing social recognition contingent upon individual employees' desired behaviors will lead to performance improvement. Although the recognition that is inherent in formal, non-financial reward systems and programs (giving a plaque) described above are included in the definitional domain of the principle, we suggest theory would predict that *social* recognition based on personal attention and appreciation has a relatively stronger impact on performance than the formal recognition programs. This is because the one-on-one contingently administered social recognition (of the form stated earlier: "the employee knows that his or her supervisor/manager knows") tends to be more valued and have more universal appeal than do formal recognition programs. Too often, some type of recognition award or benefit tends to be valuable to the reward giver but not necessarily to the reward recipient. As noted in our recent article (Luthans and Stajkovic, 1999), monetary rewards do not necessarily reinforce (strengthen, increase the frequency of) employee performance behaviors, and this would also apply to formal recognition programs.

The reason formal recognition programs may not have the desired effects, especially over time, is because they may easily turn into being phony, not valued by the recipient, or go against the cultural norms. For example, a formal recognition award such as the "Golden Banana" at Hewlett-Packard or "Employee of the Month" given at many companies can initially be a reinforcer, but over time may cross the fine line and become an empty reward and be perceived even in a negative light. The first few Employee of the Month recipients may be very deserving instances that everyone would agree with, but over time selections become more and more controversial and subjective, usually resulting in selecting less-qualified or not qualified employees. At this point company politics often come into play and those who truly deserved the recognition feel betrayed. In this case, the program would actually produce negative effects (e.g., "rewarding A while hoping for B"). Also, from a (collectivistic) cultural values and individual differences standpoint, although everyone may like to be recognized for their efforts and achieve-ments, not everyone likes to be singled out in the public way that usually goes along with formal recognition.

The implementation guideline to get around these problems associated with formal recognition would follow from the reinforcement and social cognitive theoretical frame-works. One suggestion would be to use formal recognition awards contingent upon objectively measured performance. The key is that everyone involved must perceive that the formal, public recognition is truly deserved. For example, formal awards based on sales performance (the famous pink Cadillac at Mary Kay Cosmetics or a plaque given for selling five million at a real-estate firm's banquet) would be appropriate and effective, but many outstanding performer of the month awards (or administrator-nominated, and not voted upon by students, teaching awards in academic institutions for that matter) may not be. The latter are subjectively determined and in order to be effective as a reinforcer for performance improvement, they must be as objective as possible and be perceived by the recipient, and even more so by others, as being fairly and objectively selected (i.e., procedural and also distributive justice). This guideline is compatible with both reinforcement (e.g., objective, contingent consequence) and social cognitive (e.g., perceived fairness, justice, and vicarious learning) theories.

Although the theory-based implementation guideline would be to depend on and provide relatively more informal social recognition than formal recognition (as defined at the beginning of the chapter), it does not rule out the importance of the need for some formal recognition. Contingently given informal, private social recognition dominates the reinforcement-based behavioral management approach and has been clearly demonstrated by empirical research to increase performance (Stajkovic and Luthans, 1997). However, the more comprehensive social cognitive theory also suggests the importance of grounding informal, private social recognition in the formal, public recognition domain: the more objective and fair this formal recognition, the better. The following example provided by a practicing consultant is indicative of such a social cognitive application guideline:

> If people receive social reinforcement on the four-to-one ratio (a minimum of four socials to one tangible) and receive reinforcers for behaviors, not only results, they will view the tangible as a symbolic representation of appreciation. Then tangibles become items which serve as reminders of the social reinforcement they have already received. A tangible reinforcer carries the most impact when it symbolizes the recognized behavior or result. (Allen, 1994: 25)

Again, reinforcement theory would say that the social recognition is reinforcing *per se*, but the social cognitive theory would suggest that the formal recognition is at least needed once in a while to provide outcome utility (e.g., a raise, promotion, or special assign-ment), informative content (what does the organization value), and regulatory mechanism (forethought on developing strategies to obtain desired outcomes).

RESEARCH-BASED APPLICATION EXAMPLES

Nelson's (1994) book contains 1,001 real-world examples, a number of which are short cases of mostly formal recognition programs in well-known firms such as Kodak,

Honeywell, American Express, IBM, GTE, Procter and Gamble, and a host of smaller organizations. Most of these are richly described with specific individuals and details of the form of recognition which was used to improve performance. However, only a very few of these provide any, even descriptive, data on the effectiveness of these formal recognition programs, and of course none uses research designs or statistical analysis to test hypotheses or draw causal conclusions. Thus, these examples provide, at best, anecdotal evidence and testimony on the effectiveness of mostly formal recognition programs in improving performance.

By contrast, the following examples are representative of our own empirical studies of manufacturing and service applications using contingent social recognition interventions. Most of these allow causal conclusions to be drawn on the effectiveness of social recognition in improving performance. These studies are summarized and largely drawn from Luthans (1992: 247–56) and generally followed the five step OB Mod. model (identify, measure, functionally analyze, intervene with contingent social recognition, sometimes in combination with feedback, and evaluate) (Luthans and Kreitner, 1975, 1985; Stajkovic and Luthans, 1997; Luthans and Stajkovic, 1999).

Medium-size light manufacturing firm

This field study conducted by Ottemann and Luthans had two matched groups (experimental and control) of nine production supervisors each. The experimental group received training in classic behavioral management by the researchers. The intervention involved supervisors' social recognition contingent upon their workers exhibiting the identified performance-related behaviors. On the charts kept by each trainee (step 2 of the OB Mod. behavioral management approach) it was clearly shown that in all cases they were able to change critical performance-related employee behaviors. Examples of behavioral changes accomplished by the supervisors included decreasing the number of complaints, reducing the group scrap rate, decreasing the number of overlooked defective pieces, and reducing the assembly reject rate. The most important result of the study, however, was the significant impact that the social recognition intervention had on the performance of the supervisors' departments. It was found that the experimental group's departments (those in which the supervisors used the social recognition intervention in their behavioral management) significantly outperformed the control group's departments.

Large-size manufacturing plant (supplier to the telecommunications industry)

This study started off as a replication of the study summarized above, but was disrupted by labor relations conflict and a strike at the national level preventing completion of the full analysis. However, the following summarizes some typical cases of behavioral change that occurred in the production unit of this manufacturing firm through contingent social recognition:

1 *Use of idle time.* One supervisor had a worker with a lot of idle time. Instead of using this time productively by helping others, the worker would pretend to look busy and stretch out the day. The supervisor intervened by giving the worker

social recognition contingent upon the worker's helping out at other jobs during idle time. This approach dramatically increased the worker's productive use of idle time.

2 *Low performer*. A production worker in one of the supervisor's departments was producing below standard (80.3 percent of standard over a six-month period). The low performance was not deemed to be an ability, technical, training, or standards problem. After analyzing the situation, the supervisor used an intervention of social recognition to increase the types of behaviors that would lead to higher output. This intervention resulted in a 93 percent of standard performance level, with no decrease in quality.

3 *Group quality*. One supervisor had a problem with the quality of work in his department. Objective measurement verified this problem. After analyzing the situation, the supervisor used social recognition on the group as a whole. Shortly after the use of this intervention strategy, the group attained the quality standard for the first time in three years.

4 *Group attendance*. Another supervisor felt that he had an attendance problem in his department. Objective measurement revealed 92 percent attendance, which was not as big a problem as he had thought. However, he established the goal of 100 percent. After he used contingent social recognition on the group, 100 percent attendance was attained rapidly. An interesting anecdote told by this supervisor was that one of his workers was riding to work from a small town in a car pool early one morning when they hit a deer. The car was disabled by the accident. Co-workers who worked in other departments in the plant and were also riding in the car pool called relatives and went back home for the day. This worker, however, did not want to ruin the 100 percent attendance record, so she hitchhiked to work by herself and made it on time.

5 *Problem with another department*. One supervisor felt that the performance of his department was being adversely affected by the unrecoverable time of truck-lift operators who were not directly under his supervision. After obtaining objective measurement and conducting an analysis of the situation, the supervisor decided to use social recognition with the informal group leader and the supervisor of the truck-lift operators. The intervention substantially reduced the unrecoverable time affecting the operational performance of his department.

These five examples are only representative of the types of behavior that the supervisors using a social recognition intervention were able to change. Cumulatively, such individual behavioral projects were able to improve the overall performance of these supervisors' departments.

Largest meat-packing plant in the world

This study was conducted by Luthans, Maciag and Rosenkrantz in the very tough, labor intensive meat-packing industry. In the largest packing plant in the world (in terms of employees and output), 135 production supervisors were trained by the researchers in classic behavioral management and used social recognition as the intervention. The recognition was contingently applied by the trained supervisors to identified employee-desired behaviors such as performing a particular operation more efficiently and delivering a certain piece of material in a more timely manner.

This behavioral management with social recognition as the intervention had a positive impact on all product areas in which it was applied. There was wide variation, but utility analysis indicated that although there was only a 2 percent gain in product 2, this still translated to an annualized value of nearly $900,000 in this company, and the 1.4 percent gain in product 6 equated to an annualized value of about $750,000. The projected annual values of the productivity gains in other product areas were estimated for this company as follows: product 1: $259,000; product 3: $510,000; product 4: $371,000; and product 5: an impressive overall $2.276 million gain.

Large comprehensive hospital

This hospital study in the fast-growing, but much less structured than manufacturing, healthcare industry was conducted by Snyder and Luthans. As in the manufacturing applications, 11 supervisors from medical service, business, and operations units were trained by the researchers in behavioral management and used contingent social recognition as the intervention. The results showed that there was improvement in all the performance measures. For example, over the two months of the intervention, emergency room registration errors (per day) decreased by 76 percent; medical records errors (per person per audit) decreased by 97 percent; average output of transcriptionists increased by 2 percent; EKG procedures accomplished increased by 11 percent; drug output (doses) in pharmacy increased by 21 percent and waste decreased by 25 percent; retake rates (percent) in radiology decreased by 11 percent; and in the admitting office time to admit decreased by 69 percent and average cost decreased by 22 percent. In other words, the social recognition was effective in modifying a broad range of performance-related behaviors in a hospital setting. This approach seemed to affect both the quality and the quantity performance measures. Moreover, the data indicate that each of the trained supervisors was successful in applying contingent social recognition, despite the whole range of complex situations encountered.

The teller line in a bank

Unlike the manufacturing and even the hospital applications, which had specific performance outcome measures, this service application conducted by Luthans, Fox, and Davis measured teller–customer quality service interactions as rated by customers. The experimental group in this study was the teller line at a branch of a medium-sized bank and the control group were the tellers at another branch of the same bank. The researchers gathered pre-intervention, intervention, and post-intervention data unobtrusively (around the corner from the teller line) from customers right after the interaction with the tellers in both the experimental and control groups. The customers rated the service they received according to six key dimensions that were identified from the service literature and this bank's management as being most important: greeting, eye contact, speed of service, degree of help offered, personal recognition of the customer, and appreciation for the customers' business. An overall perception of the quality service for the transaction was also obtained. These ratings were gathered randomly over a ten-day period in each phase of the experiment. Since the data were collected out of sight of the tellers, they were unaware this was happening (follow-up checks indicated this was the case).

The intervention consisted of identifying, fully describing in behavioral terms, and emphasizing the importance to customer service of the six dimensions to the tellers and their supervisors in the experimental group. In particular, the supervisors were carefully instructed by the researchers to provide contingent recognition when observing these six dimensions being exhibited by their tellers. This recognition was given throughout the intervention period, but then the recognition was withdrawn in the post-intervention (reversal) period. The researchers were frequently on site to remind the supervisors during both phases of the experiment, and manipulation checks verified the procedures were in effect.

The results indicated that four of the six dimensions (greeting, speed of service, personal recognition, and appreciation) were significantly higher in the experimental group. The overall measure of quality service was not different between the control and experimental groups during pre-intervention, significantly higher for the experimental group during intervention, and then not different during the post-intervention period when the social recognition was deliberately withheld by the supervisors. In other words, like the manufacturing applications, a contingent social recognition intervention seemed to have a causal positive impact on customer service performance in this bank.

Largest credit card processing operation in the world

In this recent study, Stajkovic and Luthans (2000) examined the relative differences in effects among monetary incentives, social recognition, and performance feedback on a routine, low task-complexity job in the largest credit card processing operation in the world (58 million accounts outsourced from banks, retailers, and e-commerce firms). In terms of application procedures, the trained supervisors administered social recognition contingent upon workers performing the specific behaviors identified in step 1 of the OB Mod. model. As we have emphasized throughout the chapter, supervisors were *explicitly* instructed that administering social recognition and attention was not to be "sugary" praise or a "pat on the back." Rather, the intention was to let the worker know that the supervisor "knew" that he/she was doing the behaviors previously communicated to be important to performance. For example, the trained supervisors said things such as, "When I was walking through your area on my way to the front office this morning, I saw you making a sequence check, that's what we're really concentrating on." Follow-up checks indicated this social recognition intervention was indeed taking place.

The results of this study indicated: (a) the monetary incentives had a greater impact on performance improvement (31.7 percent) than the social recognition (24 percent) and performance feedback (20 percent); (b) social recognition produced stronger effects on performance than performance feedback. These findings represent the first time that the most commonly used incentive motivators such as money, social recognition, and performance feedback have been empirically shown to have different effect magnitudes on work performance when all three motivators are applied through the same, conceptually grounded and empirically verified, methods. Although monetary incentives had a bigger impact (and this verifies the earlier discussion of moderators that for low-complexity tasks, social recognition may not be as valued), social recognition still held its own as being an important way to improve performance.

From no recognition PepsiCo to Tricon cheesehead awards

The research-based applications summarized above all showed an increase in perform-ance once social recognition was contingently applied. Another type of example was recently reported in the popular business press.

When Pizza Hut, Taco Bell, and KFC were part of PepsiCo a few years ago, their managers felt they were "poor cousins" in the corporate giant. They complained of never receiving any recognition from corporate management for their efforts and performance suffered. When PepsiCo finally spun off this troubled division, the result was Tricon, which became the world's largest restaurant company in units and second behind McDonald's in sales. The President, David Novak, was determined to "make up for the sins of the past" and tried to revive Tricon with an obsession for recognizing jobs well done. In his own words, "We want to be the Mary Kay of recognition" (Barron, 1999: 153). Novak doesn't give out pink Cadillacs, but he has sent out thousands of handwrit-ten thank-you's, flies successful store managers to headquarters and wines and dines them, and he gives out unusual awards (for example, he gave a Pizza Hut general manager a foam cheesehead for achieving a crew turnover rate of 56 percent in an industry where 200 percent is normal). As the CEO noted, "I wondered why anyone would be moved by getting a cheesehead, but I've seen people cry. People love recogni-tion. If I had to do it over again, I would have done more of this at PepsiCo" (Barron, 1999: 153). Importantly, since this recognition has been implemented, restaurant operat-ing margins have increased from 11 percent under PepsiCo to 16 percent and debt has been cut by $1.7 billion. The recognition seems to be paying off for Tricon.

CONCLUSION

The organizational behavior principle for this chapter is that providing social recognition leads to performance improvement. Social recognition was initially given a theoretical explanation in reinforcement theory for its universal appeal, but in a more comprehensive and additive sense, its more complex nature needs further explanation as provided by social cognitive theory. Recent meta-analytic research reveals that the type of organization moderates the social recognition-performance relationships. Social cognitive analysis also suggests that moderators such as task complexity come into play and the level of self-efficacy may be enhanced by social recognition and support, which in turn helps predict and explain performance improvement.

Because of the broad appeal and popular use of both informal social recognition and more formal recognition programs, there are numerous examples and guide-lines for effective implementation. However, in the academic literature, there are surprisingly few studies that test the impact of social recognition on work perform-ance. The representative studies summarized here indicate that the principle does seem to hold in both manufacturing and service applications. However, this chapter also points out the need to go beyond the reinforcement approach with social cognitive theory explanations and there are moderators that need to be considered in implementing social recognition in effective performance management.

REFERENCES

Allen, J. (1994). In B. Nelson, *1001 ways to reward employees*: 25. New York: Workman.

Bandura, A. (1986). *Social foundations of thought and action*. Englewood Cliffs, NJ: Prentice-Hall.

Bandura, A. (1997). *Self-efficacy: The exercise of control*. New York: Freeman.

Bandura, A. (1999). Social cognitive theory: An agentic perspective. *Asian Journal of Social Psychology*, 2, 21–41.

Barron, K. (1999). Praise and poodles with that order. *Forbes*, Sept. 20, 152–3.

Harter, J. K., and Creglow, A. (1999). A meta-analysis and utility analysis of the relationship between core employee opinions and business outcomes. In M. Buckingham and C. Coffman (eds.), *First, break all the rules* (pp. 255–67). New York: Simon & Schuster.

HR Focus (1999). April, 5.

Komaki, J. (1986). Toward effective supervision: An operant analysis and comparison of managers at work. *Journal of Applied Psychology*, 71, 270–9.

Locke, E. A. (1997). The motivation to work: What we know. *Advances in Motivation and Achievement*, 10, 375–412.

Luthans, F. (1992). *Organizational behavior*, 6th edn. New York: McGraw-Hill.

Luthans, F., and Kreitner, R. (1975). *Organizational behavior modification*. Glenview, IL: Scott, Foresman.

Luthans, F., and Kreitner, R. (1985). *Organizational behavior modification and beyond*. Glenview, IL: Scott, Foresman.

Luthans, F., and Stajkovic, A. D. (1999). Reinforce for performance: The need to go beyond pay and even rewards. *Academy of Management Executive*, 13(2), 49–57.

Nelson, B. (1994). *1001 ways to reward employees*. New York: Workman.

Nelson, B. (1996). Secrets of successful employee recognition. *Quality Digest*, Aug., 26–8.

Stajkovic, A. D., and Luthans, F. (1997). A meta-analysis of the effects of organizational behavior modification on task performance, 1975–95. *Academy of Management Journal*, 40, 1122–49.

Stajkovic, A. D., and Luthans, F. (1998a). Self-efficacy and work-related performance: A meta-analysis. *Psychological Bulletin*, 124, 240–61.

Stajkovic, A. D., and Luthans, F. (1998b). Social cognitive theory and self-efficacy: Going beyond traditional motivational and behavioral approaches. *Organizational Dynamics*, 26(4), 62–74.

Stajkovic, A. D., and Luthans, F. (2000). The differential engagement and relative effects of incentive motivators on work performance. *Academy of Management Journal* (forthcoming).

Vroom, V. H. (1964). *Work motivation*. New York: Wiley.

Wood, R. (1986). Task complexity: Definition of the construct. *Organizational Behavior and Human Decision Processes*, 37, 60–82.

13

Promote Procedural Justice to Enhance Acceptance of Work Outcomes

Jerald Greenberg

The term *procedural justice* refers to the perceived fairness of the procedures used to allocate resources (Greenberg, 1987). This concept was imported to the organizational sciences by Greenberg and Folger (1983) and Folger and Greenberg (1985) from the field of socio-legal studies, where it was used to explain disputants' reactions to the procedures used to determine the resolution of conflicts (Thibaut and Walker, 1975). The conceptual extrapolation was straightforward: when assessing the fairness of organizational decisions (e.g., the allocation of pay and other resources), employees take into account not only what those decisions are (i.e., outcomes, such as pay and performance ratings), but also the manner in which those decisions are made (i.e., procedures).

Although this notion may appear deceptively simple today, in the mid-1980s it represented a completely new approach to understanding people's perceptions of fairness in organizations (Greenberg, 1987). At the time, the concept of procedural justice supplemented the prevailing approach to fairness in the workplace – Adams's equity theory (1965), which focused on the relative distribution of outcomes (i.e., rewards) and inputs (i.e., contributions) between individuals. However, because of its excessively narrow approach, and despite efforts to broaden the theory's scope and applicability to complex social settings (Walster, Walster, and Berscheid, 1978), theorists raised questions about equity theory's capacity to answer fundamental questions about fairness that arise in organizations. Nowhere is this sentiment more clearly expressed than in an especially influential piece by Leventhal (1980) with the provocative title, "What should be done with equity theory?"

Not surprisingly, when Greenberg and Folger (1983) and Folger and Greenberg (1985) introduced the concept of procedural justice to the organizational literature and shared ideas about its potential applicability, they filled a void for a waiting audience of scientists who already embraced the idea that fairness was important in the workplace, but who were dissatisfied with the narrow approach offered by equity theory (for more on the history of organizational justice concepts, see Byrne and Cropanzano, 2000). Since the mid-1980s research and theory on procedural justice has developed rapidly – so much so, in fact, that this topic is now one of the most popularly researched areas in the field of organizational behavior (Colguitt, Conlon, Wesson, Porter, and Ng, in press; Cropanzano and Greenberg, 1997).

From among the many research findings regarding procedural justice reported in recent years has emerged a phenomenon that is sufficiently robust to be considered a principle of organizational behavior: *Fair procedures enhance acceptance of organizational outcomes*. That is to say, people are inclined to accept the results of organizational decisions they believe are made using procedures they believe are fair. For example, in a large-scale survey study Alexander and Ruderman (1987) found that the more employees believed their companies used fair procedures (as defined in various ways), the more positively they evaluated their supervisors, the more they trusted management, and the less inclined they were to leave their jobs (for a review of similar findings, see Lind and Tyler, 1988).

Two questions arise in this connection: (1) How do people define "fair procedures"? and (2) What specific organizational outcomes are affected? Research bearing on this principle addresses the definitional question by distinguishing between the manner – structural or social – in which procedural fairness is promoted. This distinction, introduced by Greenberg (1993a), may be framed as two sub-principles. My discussion of these sub-principles will address the outcome question by highlighting the wide variety of organizational outcomes to which people's reactions are influenced by their perceptions of procedural justice.

STRUCTURAL AND INTERPERSONAL SUB-PRINCIPLES

The first sub-principle is based on structural determinants of fairness – that is, contextual factors affecting how resource allocation decisions are made. The second sub-principle focuses on interpersonal determinants of fairness, which focuses on the way individuals are treated in the course of making allocation decisions.

Structural determinants of procedural justice

Following from Thibaut and Walker's (1975) pioneering socio-legal research, the earliest determinant of procedural justice to be considered in organizations was voice in organizational decisions. Specifically, it has been established that *people better accept organizational decisions to the extent that they have a say in determining them* – even if they cannot control the outcomes directly (Greenberg and Folger, 1983). A second set of structural criteria has been identified by Leventhal, Karuza, and Fry's (1980) procedural preferences model. Specifically, this approach claims that fairness is promoted by procedures that: are applied consistently, suppress bias, are based on accurate information, may be corrected, are representative of the interests of all parties, and follow prevailing ethical standards. In general, we know that *people better accept organizational decisions to the extent that they have been made using these criteria* (Greenberg, 1986a).

Several lines of research illustrate these structural sub-criteria of procedural justice. Among the earliest findings applying procedural justice to organizational settings were those showing that employees responded positively to performance appraisal procedures in which they exercised voice – that is, systems that gave them some say in how their evaluations were determined. For example, studies have found that employees' opinions of their companies' appraisal systems are positively correlated to their beliefs about the opportunities they have to express their own viewpoints (Dipboye and de Pontbraind, 1981; Lissak, 1983) – even when controlling for the outcomes from those systems (Landy, Barnes-Farrell, and Cleveland, 1980). More recent research has shown that voice is just one of several procedural factors – such as adequate notice, fair hearing, and judgment based on evidence – that enhance perceptions of performance appraisal systems and the decisions resulting from them (Folger and Cropanzano, 1998).

Additional research has shown that procedural variables similar to those identified by Thibaut and Walker (1975) and by Leventhal et al. (1980) also account for employees' reactions to other organizational phenomena. For example, Kim and Mauborgne (1993) have noted that employees' acceptance of their companies' strategic plans is enhanced to the extent that they are able to engage in bilateral communication and are given an opportunity to refute ideas. Similarly, personnel policies, such as the procedures used to screen employees for drug use (Konovsky and Cropanzano, 1993) and those used to make personnel selection decisions (Gilliland, 1994) are better accepted to the degree that they incorporate various procedural elements, such as accuracy, allowing for corrections, and providing opportunities for voice.

Two different explanations have been advanced to account for these findings (for an overview, see Cropanzano and Greenberg, 1997). First, the *instrumental (or self-interest) model* asserts that procedures that provide voice and that base decisions on accurate information that is consistently applied are ones that are in all employees' long-term best interest (Tyler, 1987). And, to the extent that employees believe these procedures will benefit them, they are likely to accept them and the decisions resulting from them. A second orientation, the *relational (or group-value) model*, substitutes an interpersonally oriented approach for this rational-economic one. Specifically, this model focuses on the social status and self-esteem that people derive from their interactions with groups. People value long-term relationships with groups, which leads them to value procedures that promote group solidarity. Procedures that incorporate the various structural elements we have discussed are important in this regard insofar as they cultivate the impression that the decision-maker is unbiased, trustworthy, and acting in a way that affirms the individual's standing as a group member (Tyler and Lind, 1992). Research supports both approaches, leading scientists to view them as complementary, rather than competing explanations. As Cropanzano and Greenberg (1997) have concluded, "Both perspectives provide important insight into the underlying reasons why procedural justice has been shown to be so important in organizations" (p. 336).

Interpersonal determinants of procedural justice

Inspired by the work of Bies and his associates (Bies and Moag, 1986; Greenberg, Bies, and Eskew, 1991), scientists have recognized that people perceive fair procedures not only in terms of the structural mechanisms through which decisions are made, but also by the interpersonal treatment they receive in the course of making those decisions. Illustrating this phenomenon, Greenberg (1990a) found that employees who felt underpaid (because of a temporary pay cut) expressed their dissatisfaction by stealing twice as much from their company when officials treated them in a distant and uncaring manner while announcing the pay cut as compared to when officials treated them with dignity and respect. The manner of treatment affected the employees' fairness perceptions and their willingness to act on those perceptions by stealing company property: the same exact pay cuts were better accepted by employees who were given the bad news in a kind and caring manner. This illustrates the second sub-principle of procedural justice: *People better accept organizational outcomes to the extent that they have been treated positively in the course of introducing those outcomes.*

Research has established that two determinants of "positive" interpersonal treatment are responsible for mitigating people's negative reactions to undesirable outcomes: (1) *social sensitivity* – the extent to which people believe they have been treated with dignity and respect, and (2) *informational justification* – the extent to which people believe they have adequate information about the procedures affecting them. For example, in a lab study, Greenberg (1993b) manipulated each of these factors independently after violating participants' expectations by paying them less than expected. The participants then were given an opportunity to retaliate anonymously by taking money back from the researcher. It was found that retaliation was lower when the underpayment was explained in a highly sensitive manner as opposed to an insensitive manner, and when a thorough explanation was given for the unexpected turn of events than when a superficial explanation was offered. In fact, the lowest overall rate of retaliation occurred when levels of both social sensitivity and information were high. This positive interpersonal treatment mitigated participants' beliefs about the unfairness of the same undesirable outcomes, leading them to accept those outcomes and diminishing their motivation to retaliate.

Another study by Greenberg (1994) demonstrated an identical effect in an organization that was about to introduce a smoking ban. This policy change (which is likely to be rejected by smokers) was introduced in a manner that systematically manipulated the amount of information about the need for the smoking ban as well as the level of sensitivity expressed for the difficulty the ban was likely to create for smokers. Employees who smoked expressed greater willingness to go along with the ban when it was thoroughly explained and when it was presented in a socially sensitive manner. However, low levels of each of these variables led smokers to reject the smoking ban – especially when they occurred together. The hardship endured by the smokers as they faced this policy change was mitigated by the use of interpersonally fair procedures.

In yet another setting, Lind, Greenberg, Scott, and Welchans (in press) interviewed almost 1,000 unemployed people about their reactions to being fired or laid off from their jobs. The better the explanations respondents believed they received about the termination decision, and the more dignity and respect they received in the course of being let go, the better they accepted the termination decision. Importantly, these feelings were predictive of a key indicant of acceptance – bringing legal suit on the grounds of wrongful termination. Specifically, individuals who believed they were treated in a dignified manner by company officials in the course of being terminated and who believed that the explanations they received about the termination decision were adequate were significantly less inclined to bring suit against their former employers for wrongful termination than those who received more superficial explanations delivered in a less sensitive manner.

The processes underlying these effects have received attention from several theorists. For example, the relational (or group value) model (Tyler and Lind, 1992) identified earlier is clearly relevant insofar as it explains how positive interpersonal treatment may send a message to employees about their standing in groups that are important to them. It also is possible that people who are harmed by outcomes (pay cuts, smoking bans, and job termination in the above examples) are highly sensitive to information in their environments that sheds light on what is happening to them, leading them to seek and to listen to any available explanations (Schaubroeck, May, and Brown, 1994). When these explanations are presented by an organizational agent in a caring and sensitive manner, the message is sent that the company's intent is not malicious, discouraging employees from taking extreme measures (e.g., stealing and suing) to express their dissatisfaction with procedures. Indeed, research has shown that simply delivering negative outcomes (e.g., pay cuts) is insufficient to trigger most people's tendencies to behave aggressively in organizations. Rather, such extreme reactions tend to occur only when the "insult of insensitive treatment" is added to the "injury of undesirable outcomes" (Greenberg and Alge, 1998). In short, it is clear that people are highly sensitive to the social manner in which organizational decisions are made, and that this is a key element of their perceptions of fairness in the workplace – and their willingness to redress perceived unfairness.

SPECIAL CASES AND EXCEPTIONS

Having described the central principle of procedural justice and its two major sub-principles, the stage now is set to identify several key qualifying conditions under which they are likely to occur.

Outcome valence

Research has established that procedural justice's effects on the acceptance of organizational outcomes are qualified by the valence of the outcomes involved (Brockner and Weisenfeld, 1996). Specifically, fair procedures matter more to people when outcomes are negative than when they are positive. Generally, employees receiving positive outcomes tend to be so pleased with what they got that they are unconcerned with how they got it. However, concerns about procedure become salient when outcomes are negative. After all, people who don't receive what they want are likely to ask "why?" and the answers they seek are likely to be framed in terms of the procedures used to determine those outcomes. As Greenberg (1986b) has explained, people may feel that it is inappropriate to express their dissatisfaction with undesirable outcomes for fear of appearing to be "sore losers," but that it almost always is appropriate to ask questions about "how" outcomes were determined. Indeed, the basis for appealing grades in most universities and the verdicts of court cases is based not on dissatisfaction with the outcomes (although this may be the underlying motive for the appeal), but on the propriety of the procedures used to determine them. And, because procedures hold the key to understanding outcomes, their salience is heightened when outcomes are negative.

Although procedural justice might matter more when outcomes are negative than when positive, this applies to people's acceptance of organizational outcomes, but not to organizations themselves. Indeed, high levels of procedural justice can have beneficial effects on commitment to the organization in question even when outcomes are positive.

For example, Greenberg (1994) found that a smoking ban that was explained fairly had stronger effects on smokers (for whom the impact was negative) than on non-smokers (for whom the impact was positive). However, both smokers and non-smokers expressed high levels of commitment to the organization when it used fair procedures. Apparently, organizations that use fair procedures send strong messages about their underlying commitment to fairness, which enhances employees' commitment to the organization regardless of the outcomes they receive from it.

The limits of voice

If the granting of voice enhances acceptance of outcomes, then it may be assumed that more voice promotes greater acceptance. However, recent research suggests that such an assumption is fallacious. Specifically, two studies have shown that the benefits of the magnitude of voice are non-linear. For example, Hunton, Wall, and Price (1998) conducted a study in which they manipulated the number of supervisory decisions (0, 5, 10, 15, or 20) over which participants were given voice. Participants expressed greater satisfaction with decisions over which they had any degree of voice than decisions over which they had no voice at all. However, increasing levels of voice (from 5 through 20) had no effects whatsoever. These data suggest that the benefits associated with voice appear to be a simple binary matter rather than a matter of degree.

Additional evidence suggests that under some conditions, at least, high levels of voice actually may reduce satisfaction with outcomes. Notably, Peterson (1999) measured laboratory subjects' satisfaction with leaders in situations in which the parties were in conflict with each other over group decision problems. Corroborating other studies, Peterson (1999) found that satisfaction was greater among participants who were given an opportunity to explain their suggestions for solving a group problem (moderate voice condition) than those who were not given any such opportunity (no voice condition). However, he also found that when leaders gave participants surprisingly high levels of voice, participants believed that the leader was behaving inappropriately by relinquishing his or her power, and were less satisfied than they were in the moderate voice condition. In other words, Peterson (1999) found that satisfaction had an inverted-U relationship with magnitude of voice.

Because the findings of Hunton et al. (1998) and Peterson (1999) are new and have not been replicated, it is unclear how generalizable they are to other settings. However, they lead us to be cautious about the limits of the effects of voice that have been described in the literature to date.

Voice and social sensitivity must be sincere

In addition to qualifications regarding the amount of voice given, another qualification of the principle of procedural justice concerns the sincerity of voice. Specifically, granting employees a voice in the making of decisions leads them to believe that their voice will be listened to, which raises their expectations about the outcomes they will receive. Accordingly, employees who believe that the voice they are offered is insincere (such as would be the case if no one is listening to them) will not be satisfied with the resulting outcomes. In fact, insofar as employees' expectations about the outcomes first are raised, but later are dashed when confronted with a less positive reality, they may be more dissatisfied than they would be if their expectations were never raised in the first place – a phenomenon called the "frustration effect" (Greenberg and Folger, 1983). Not surprisingly, the practice of falsely creating the illusion of voice in the workplace is considered unwise insofar as it may backfire, leading employees to reject not only the outcomes, but the organization itself (Greenberg, 1990b).

The negative effects of insincerity also may be seen in the case of explanations for undesirable organizational outcomes. In other words, for perceptions of procedural justice to be enhanced by the issuing of explanations for outcomes, it is necessary for those explanations to be not only accurate and thorough, but also to be perceived as genuine and sincere (Shapiro, Buttner, and Barry, 1994). Should employees suspect that the explanations they are receiving about outcomes are insincere – or worse, manipulative – the benefits of providing explanations are negated. In fact, under such circumstances, the organizational agent's manipulative intent is likely to reflect negatively on impressions of the organization itself, making matters worse (Greenberg, 1990b). In other words, unless employees are convinced that their superiors are "being straight" with them, the use of explanations is likely to backfire.

Issues in Implementation

Having established what can be done to promote procedural justice in the workplace and the benefits of doing so, it is worthwhile to consider matters of implementation. In other words, we may ask if people actually do seek to establish procedural justice in organizations, and if so, how they go about doing so. I now will address these questions.

When do people follow interpersonally fair procedures?

Advising managers to follow interpersonally fair procedures is a curious business. My experience has been that those who don't reject the advice as being too commonsensical to be useful reject it on the grounds that they already treat people with dignity and respect. Although managers may articulate the wisdom of treating their employees in this manner, recent evidence suggest that they do not always do so.

Demonstrating this, Folger and Skarlicki (1998) had students perform an in-basket exercise, part of which required them to explain their decisions to lay off employees under one of two conditions. Either the participants themselves were cited as having made the bad decisions that made the layoff necessary, or the layoffs were explained as being the result of unforeseen economic conditions. Participants who believed that the layoff victims knew that their own mismanagement triggered the layoffs spent significantly less time explaining their layoff decisions than those who were able to attribute the layoffs to external conditions. Folger and Skarlicki explain that these "truncated dismissals" are evidence for "distancing" among people who do not want to face those they have harmed. These results are interesting insofar as it is the very people who are responsible for harming others who stand to benefit most by explaining their actions and apologizing for them. By not doing so, they may be escaping an uncomfortable situation, but they are not taking advantage of an opportunity to promote the image of themselves as being fair. In other words, those who most need to be interpersonally fair may not always be so.

Another recent study suggests that the degree to which people demonstrate interpersonal sensitivity depends on the reactions of the others to whom they are giving negative outcomes. Specifically, Korsgaard, Roberson, and Rymph (1998) conducted a lab experiment in which participants were required to appraise the performance of co-workers with whom they worked on a task. Although participants believed that their co-workers were naïve college students like themselves, they were, in reality, experimental accomplices who responded in one of two different ways that were carefully scripted to systematically manipulate assertiveness. In the high assertive condition the co-worker directly expressed opinions about his or her own performance, cited specific examples to support those opinions, and asked for clarification. Non-verbally, they also maintained high levels of eye contact and maintained a forward body posture. In the low assertive condition the co-worker acted in an obverse fashion. Participants' statements to their co-workers were taped and later coded with respect to the two key dimensions of interpersonal justice described earlier – the degree of sensitivity and consideration shown, and the degree to which he or she offered explanations for the performance ratings given. Korsegaard and her associates found that participants demonstrated significantly higher degrees of interpersonally fair behavior in response to assertive co-workers than to non-assertive co-workers. Apparently, the assertive style was effective in getting others to be more forthcoming with explanations that helped explain the situations they faced.

It is important to note that both the Folger and Skarlicki (1998) study and the Korsgaard et al. (1998) study are recent laboratory investigations whose results have not been tested for generalizability. As such, it may be premature to paint a completely clear picture of the conditions under which managers will behave in an interpersonally fair manner. However, it is apparent that various conditions mitigate the tendency to do so.

Training managers in procedural justice

Acknowledging that it is in their own best interest for managers to follow the principles of procedural justice outlined here, officials from several companies recently have allowed organizational researchers to train supervisory personnel in ways of enhancing procedural justice. The effectiveness of these training efforts has been documented in the literature.

For example, Cole and Latham (1997) trained 71 unionized Canadian supervisors on six key aspects of procedural justice whose relevance to disciplinary settings had been established earlier (Ball, 1991): (1) explanation of the performance problem, (2) the demeanor of the supervisor, (3) subordinates' control over the process, (4) arbitrariness, (5) employee counseling, and (6) privacy. The training consisted of role-playing exercises conducted in small groups held over five half-days. To assess the effectiveness of the training, two groups of expert judges evaluated the behavior of the supervisors who role-played supervisors administering discipline in various test scenarios. Not only did the judges agree that managers who were trained behaved more fairly than those in an untrained, control group, but they also predicted that the trained group would perform better as supervisors than the control group. Although Cole and Latham's (1997) findings do not assess the effectiveness of training on the job, they suggest that managers can be trained to emulate specific behaviors that enhance procedural justice.

However, two additional studies have shown that managers trained in various aspects of procedural justice do, in fact, behave in ways that yield beneficial organizational results. For example, Skarlicki and Latham (1996) trained managers in various aspects of procedural justice in an effort to enhance the level of organizational citizenship behavior (OCB) among a group of union laborers. The managers were trained on various determinants of procedural justice, including ways of providing voice, and techniques for facilitating the fairness of the social interaction between labor and management. Training consisted of lecture, case study, role-playing, and group discussions conducted in four three-hour sessions held over a three-week period. Three months after training, incidents of OCB were found to be higher among employees of the trained managers than the untrained ones, suggesting that OCB can be enhanced directly by training managers to behave fairly toward their employees.

In another study, Greenberg (1999) trained managers of retail stores in ways of enhancing procedural justice after noting that store employees were highly dissatisfied with their jobs and expressed these feelings by stealing merchandise. Not only did employees describe their managers as being disrespectful, uncaring, insensitive, and generally unconcerned with their welfare, but they also reported that supervisory personnel routinely failed to involve them in decisions, keeping them in the dark about the underlying reasons for various company policies. In short, levels of procedural justice were low. Greenberg (1999) designed an intervention to turn this around by systematically training managers in techniques of delegation, supportive communication, and other aspects of procedural justice. The training occurred in one store (randomly selected from several in the chain) for two hours per week over an eight-week period. It consisted of involving the participants in a variety of role-playing exercises, having them read and analyze several cases, and discussing managerial problems at their stores.

Compared to a second store location whose managers received training on an unrelated topic, and a third in which managers received no training at all, Greenberg (1999) found that the training was effective not only at improving employees' job satisfaction, commitment, and turnover intentions, but also at cutting the rate of employee theft in half! Expressing the importance of fair interpersonal treatment in this regard, one employee interviewed in a focus group said, "[my supervisor] used to be a real SOB, and I hated working for him, so I stole every chance I got. Now, he's so kind to me, I'd feel bad about taking anything."

Taken together, these studies reveal that managers may be trained effectively in techniques for enhancing procedural justice and that such training is effective in improving various aspects of organizational functioning. Because these efforts are recent, we cannot determine how long-lasting the benefits may be. Also, because there have been so few investigations in this area, we do not know precisely what forms of training are most effective at improving specific dependent variables. Despite these uncertainties, it appears that the benefits of systematically attempting to promote procedural justice in organizations are very promising.

PROCEDURAL JUSTICE AND INJUSTICE IN ACTION: SOME CASE EXAMPLES

The various principles I have described may be illustrated by several real-life examples reported in the popular press. These examples illustrate both the benefits that result from promoting procedural justice and the problems that result from violating procedural justice.

Promoting procedural justice: making professional football fair

Several recent rule changes by the National Football League (NFL) illustrate the importance of granting voice in organizational decisions, and of the roles of correctability and accuracy in ensuring procedural justice.

The NFL's instant replay rule: the role of correctability.   After a seven-year hiatus, in 1999, the NFL reinstated a rule that gives coaches an opportunity to challenge (with various restrictions) the judgments of field officials they believe were erroneous. Officials are given 90 seconds to watch a replay of the play in question and to decide whether or not to reverse their initial judgment (National Football League, 1999). Pressure on the league to reintroduce this procedure resulted from public outcries of unfairness that followed from several patently erroneous calls by officials that would have changed the outcome of several games during the 1998 season. The appeal of the instant replay rule as a device for maintaining fairness in football follows from the Leventhal et al. (1980) correctability rule: Fair procedures are ones that can be corrected if proven to be in error.

The NFL's modified coin-toss procedure: the quest for accuracy.   On December 6, 1998, the NFL altered the procedure it used to determine which team would determine whether it wanted to begin the game by kicking or receiving the football. According to the old procedure, as the referee threw a coin into the air a designated captain of the visiting team called heads or tails. If the coin landed with the side identified facing up, that player's team would have the option. However, if the captain lost the toss, the opposing team had the option.

Although this procedure had worked well for 22 years, a critical incident occurred on the Thanksgiving Day 1998 game between the Pittsburgh Steelers and the Detroit Lions (National Football League, 1998). Apparently, referee Phil Luckett misunderstood the call made by Pittsburgh's Jerome Bettis, leading the Steelers to lose the coin toss that opened the critical overtime period. Television replays appeared to have Bettis calling tails as the coin was in the air, only to have the referee award the ball to the Lions after the coin landed tails.

To avoid future occurrences of what NFL Commissioner Paul Tabliabue referred to as "an unfortunate incident," league officials changed the coin-toss procedure. According to the new procedure, the heads-or-tails call is made in advance of the coin toss, thereby allowing any uncertainties to be addressed before the outcome is known. As a further safeguard, two additional officials, the back judge and the field judge, will provide a check, if needed, by witnessing the ceremony. Under the old procedure, these officials merely escorted the team captains to mid-field, but did not remain there for the coin toss.

Although these minute procedural details may appear to be trivial to the uninitiated, any football fan will argue otherwise. To the extent that critical outcomes in the big business of professional football may hinge on such decisions, it is crucial to base them on the fairest possible procedures. Indeed, what NFL officials appear to be doing is evoking the Leventhal et al. (1980) accuracy rule. As simple as it may be, it's clear that the NFL sought to tinker with the coin-toss procedure so as to make it as accurate – hence as fair – as possible.

The dangers of violating procedural justice

Several interesting cases illustrate the kinds of problems that may result in organizations whose leaders are insensitive to matters of procedural justice.

New York City taxi drivers strike: the importance of voice.   On May 12, 1998, most of New York City's 44,000 taxi drivers staged a one-day strike that all but paralyzed commuting within the US's largest city (Allen, 1998). The action was in response to Mayor Rudolph W. Giuliani's imposition of new safety rules, which included: requiring drivers to take a defensive driving class, raising the fines for smoking in a cab, and revoking their taxi license for being convicted of too many moving violations. Most drivers did not oppose these rules. However, they were very threatened by the unilateral manner in which the mayor imposed them. In the words of a union official representing several thousand drivers, "We are not questioning the regulations, we are questioning the fashion" (p. C1).

Therein lies the problem. Because Mayor Giuliani failed to give the drivers a voice in policies affecting them, they felt that they were unfairly treated, leading them to protest as they did – and souring relations between cab drivers and city officials. Ironically, insofar as most drivers believed the mayor's plan to be reasonable, the protest could have been avoided by simply giving the drivers a voice in determining the rules governing their operation. Perhaps Mayor Giuliani should have familiarized himself with research on procedural justice!

The firing of a college football coach: the importance of information.   As might be expected on any late fall day in Columbus, Ohio, the talk around town in mid-November, 1987 centered on the Ohio State University's (OSU) impending football game against its arch-rival, the University of Michigan. One week before the big game, however, something happened that transformed that chatter from statistics about the number of yards likely to be gained by the offense to figures about the number of dollars likely to be awarded in an impending legal settlement. The critical incident was the sudden firing of OSU's football coach, Earle Bruce, by University President Edward Jennings.

Naturally, this dramatic incident sparked public curiosity, especially given its timing. However, curiosity turned to moral outrage when President Jennings, citing the need to keep personnel matters private, refused to explain the reasons for his sudden decision. Analyzing this incident, Lewicki (1988) noted that leaders of public organizations with highly visible performance and large constituencies, such as OSU, need to be sensitive to perceptions of the fairness of their actions. By not providing an adequate explanation for his dramatic decision, President Jennings violated the public's consensually perceived "right" of full disclosure, leading him to be labeled as unfair and eroding his public support. This case suggests that it is not only the victims of undesirable outcomes themselves, but also their supporters, for whom fairness demands clear information about the basis for outcome decisions. (By the way, as a show of support for their outgoing coach, and spurred by feelings of outrage, OSU players went on to defeat their rivals!)

The James Dailey case: an extreme reaction to insensitive treatment. Although most people are quietly resigned to losing their battles with government bureaucracies, every once in a while someone feels pushed to the brink of desperation and takes things too far. That was the case with James L. Dailey when, on November 13, 1996, he entered the Columbus office of the Ohio Bureau of Workers' Compensation (BWC) with several guns and cans of gasoline in hand, and took three employees hostage. Curiously, the story Dailey told after being overcome by SWAT officers almost eight hours later led the public to view him as a sympathetic figure rather than a violent madman (Stephens, Cadwallader, and Baird, 1996).

Dailey had injured his neck and back while on the job four years earlier. From then through the time he exploded in rage, Dailey fought constant battles with the BWC for relief. His claims for benefits were granted intermittently, but only after appealing several rejection decisions. Then, after Dailey's benefits had run out, the BWC held two hearings resulting in a final ruling to terminate his compensation permanently. Desperate for money, Dailey was distraught, but this alone didn't trigger his aggressive behavior. What pushed Dailey to the brink was his belief that the government agency that ostensibly existed to help him was being unfair by not showing any interest in him (Doulin, St. Clair, and Baird, 1996). Instead, the BWC came across as cold and unsympathetic, and more concerned with saving money than with offering assistance. This image was prompted by what Dailey saw as giving mere perfunctory attention to his case – "going through the motions" to "make it look good," but planning in advance to discount or not consider the relevant medical evidence.

Although no one condoned Dailey's actions, the public readily understood his frustrations and empathized with the unfair treatment he received. Many sympathetic citizens contributed to a fund to help Dailey's family while he fought eight felony counts. One anonymous citizen even paid the $50,000 bail bond that enabled Dailey to be released from jail so he could spend Christmas with his family (Cadwallader, 1996). What made this accused felon a sympathetic character is that people readily related to how little guys often get beaten by uncaring, heartless government agencies like the BWC. The insult of a denied claim that Dailey faced was added to by the injury of the insensitive treatment he received in the course of this decision being made. Although Dailey's reactions are more extreme than most, the frustration he expressed is in keeping with the negative reactions to insensitive treatment demonstrated in the research reviewed here.

CONCLUSION

There can be no doubt that in less than two decades the concept of procedural justice has advanced with remarkable speed (Colquitt et al., in press), especially given the glacial pace at which most scientific ideas develop. In relatively short time we have moved from extrapolating that the borrowed concept of procedural justice may be relevant to organizations (Greenberg and Folger, 1983), to acknowledging that it does, in fact, explain behavior in organizations (Greenberg and Tyler, 1987), to recognizing its central role in promoting organizational well-being (Greenberg, 1996). Now, by acknowledging its status as a construct around which a guiding principle of organizational behavior may be identified, it is clear that procedural justice has emerged from the awkward intellectual adolescent it was considered to be only a few years ago (Greenberg, 1993c) to mature scientific adulthood.

REFERENCES

Adams, J. S. (1965). Inequity in social exchange. In L. Berkowitz (ed.), *Advances in experimental social psychology* (Vol. 2, pp. 267–99). New York: Academic Press.

Alexander, S., and Ruderman, M. (1987). The role of procedural and distributive justice in organizational behavior. *Social Justice Research*, 1, 177–98.

Allen, M. (1998). Giuliani threatens action if cabbies fail to cancel a protest. *New York Times*, May 15, p. C1.

Ball, G. A. (1991). Outcomes of punishment incidents: The role of subordinate perceptions, individual differences, and leader behavior. Unpublished doctoral dissertation, Pennsylvania State University.

Bies, R. J., and Moag, J. S. (1986). Interactional justice: Communication criteria of fairness. In R. J. Lewicki, B. H. Sheppard, and M. Bazerman (eds.), *Research on negotiation in organizations* (Vol. 1, pp. 43–55). Greenwich, CT: JAI Press.

Brockner, J., and Weisenfeld, B. M. (1996). The interactive impact of procedural and outcome fairness on reactions to a decision: The effects of what you do depend on how you do it. *Psychological Bulletin*, 120, 189–208.

Byrne, Z., and Cropanzano, R. (2000). History of organizational justice: The founders speak. In R. Cropanzano (ed.), *Justice in the workplace*, Vol. 2: *From theory to practice*. Mahwah, NJ: Erlbaum.

Cadwallader, B. (1996). Some afraid after Dailey freed on bail. *Columbus Dispatch*, Dec. 26, pp. 1C–2C.

Cole, N. D., and Latham, G. P. (1997). Effects of training in procedural justice on perceptions of disciplinary fairness by unionized employees and disciplinary subject matter experts. *Journal of Applied Psychology*, 82, 699–705.

Colguitt, J. A., Conlon, D. E., Wesson, M. J., Porter, C. O. L. H., Ng, K. Y. (in press). Justice at the millennium: A meta-analytic review of 25 years of organizational justice research. *Journal of Applied Psychology*.

Cropanzano, R., and Greenberg, J. (1997). Progress in organizational justice: Tunneling through the maze. In C. L. Cooper and I. T. Robertson (eds.), *International review of industrial and organizational psychology* (Vol. 12, pp. 317–72). London: Wiley.

Dipboye, R. L., and de Pontbraind, R. (1981). Correlates of employee reactions to performance appraisals and appraisal systems. *Journal of Applied Psychology*, 66, 248–51.

Doulin, T., St. Clair, D., and Baird, D. (1996). Sides hold court in hostage case. *Columbus Dispatch*, Nov. 15, pp. 1A–2A.

Folger, R., and Cropanzano, R. (1998). *Organizational justice and human resource management.* Thousand Oaks, CA: Sage.

Folger, R., and Greenberg, J. (1985). Procedural justice: An interpretive analysis of personnel systems. In K. Rowland and G. Ferris (eds.), *Research in personnel and human resources management* (Vol. 3, pp. 141–83). Greenwich, CT: JAI Press.

Folger, R., and Skarlicki, D. P. (1998). When tough times make tough bosses: Managerial distancing as a function of layoff blame. *Academy of Management Journal*, 41, 79–87.

Gilliland, S. W. (1994). The perceived fairness of selection systems: An organizational justice perspective. *Academy of Management Review*, 18, 694–734.

Greenberg, J. (1986a). Determinants of perceived fairness of performance evaluations. *Journal of Applied Psychology*, 71, 340–2.

Greenberg, J. (1986b). Organizational performance appraisal procedures: What makes them fair? In R. J. Lewicki, B. H. Sheppard, and M. H. Bazerman (eds.), *Research on negotiation in organizations* (Vol. 1, pp. 25–41). Greenwich, CT: JAI Press.

Greenberg, J. (1987). A taxonomy of organizational justice theories. *Academy of Management Review*, 12, 9–22.

Greenberg, J. (1990a). Employee theft as a reaction to underpayment inequity: The hidden costs of pay cuts. *Journal of Applied Psychology*, 72, 55–61.

Greenberg, J. (1990b). Looking fair vs. being fair: Managing impressions of organizational justice. In. B. M. Staw and L. L. Cummings (eds.), *Research in organizational behavior* (Vol. 12, pp. 111–57). Greenwich, CT: JAI Press.

Greenberg, J. (1993a). The social side of fairness: Interpersonal and informational classes of organizational justice. In R. Cropanzano (ed.), *Justice in the workplace: Approaching fairness in human resource management* (pp. 79–103). Hillsdale, NJ: Erlbaum.

Greenberg, J. (1993b). Stealing in the name of justice: Informational and interpersonal moderators of theft reactions to underpayment inequity. *Organizational Behavior and Human Decision Processes*, 54, 81–103.

Greenberg, J. (1993c). The intellectual adolescence of organizational justice: You've come a long way, maybe. *Social Justice Research*, 6, 135–47.

Greenberg, J. (1994). Using socially fair treatment to promote acceptance of a work site smoking ban. *Journal of Applied Psychology*, 79, 288–97.

Greenberg, J. (1996). *The quest for justice on the job*. Thousand Oaks, CA: Sage.

Greenberg, J. (1999). Interpersonal justice training (IJT) for reducing employee theft: Some preliminary results. Unpublished manuscript. Ohio State University, Columbus, OH.

Greenberg, J., and Alge, B. J. (1998). Aggressive reactions to workplace injustice. In R. W. Griffin, A. O'Leary-Kelly, and J. M. Collins (eds.), *Dysfunctional behavior in organizations: Violent and deviant behavior* (pp. 83–118). Stamford, CT: JAI Press.

Greenberg, J., Bies, R. J., and Eskew, D. E. (1991). Establishing fairness in the eye of the beholder: Managing impressions of organizational justice. In R. Giacalone and P. Rosenfeld (eds.), *Applied impression management: How image making affects managerial decisions* (pp. 111–32). Newbury Park, CA: Sage.

Greenberg, J., and Folger, R. (1983). Procedural justice, participation, and the fair process effect in groups and organizations. In P. B. Paulus (ed.), *Basic group processes* (pp. 235–56). New York: Springer-Verlag.

Greenberg, J., and Tyler, T. R. (1987) Why procedural justice in organizations? *Social Justice Research*, 1, 127–42.

Hunton, J. E., Wall, T. W., and Price, K. H. (1998). The value of voice in participative decision making. *Journal of Applied Psychology*, 83, 788–97.

Kim, W. C., and Mauborgne, R. A. (1993). Procedural justice, attitudes, and subsidiary management compliance with multinationals' corporate strategic decisions. *Academy of Management Journal*, 36, 502–26.

Konovsky, M. A., and Cropanzano, R. (1993). Justice considerations in employee drug testing. In R. Cropanzano (ed.), *Justice in the workplace: Approaching fairness in human resource management* (pp. 171–92). Hillsdale, NJ: Erlbaum.

Korsgaard, M. A., Roberson, L., and Rymph, R. D. (1998). What motivates fairness? The role of subordinate assertive behavior on managers' interactional fairness. *Journal of Applied Psychology*, 83, 731–44.

Landy, F. J., Barnes-Farrell, J., and Cleveland, J. (1980). Correlates of perceived fairness and accuracy of performance evaluation: A follow-up. *Journal of Applied Psychology*, 65, 355–6.

Leventhal, G. S. (1980). What should be done with equity theory? In K. J. Gergen, M. S. Greenberg, and R. H. Willis (eds.), *Social exchanges: Advances in theory and research* (pp. 27–55). New York: Plenum.

Leventhal, G. S., Karuza, J., and Fry, W. R. (1980). Beyond fairness: A theory of allocation preferences. In G. Mikula (ed.), *Justice and social interaction* (pp. 167–218). New York: Springer-Verlag.

Lewicki, R. J. (1988). The public face of justice: Ineffective management of an organizational justice problem. In J. Greenberg and R. J. Bies (chairs), *Communicating fairness in organizations*. Symposium presented at the meeting of the Academy of Management, Anaheim, CA, Aug.

Lind, E. A., Greenberg, J., Scott, K. S., and Welchans, T. D. (in press). The winding road from employee to complainant: Situational and psychological determinants of wrongful termination lawsuits. *Administrative Science Quarterly*.

Lind, E. A., and Tyler, T. R. (1988). *The social psychology of procedural justice*. New York: Plenum.

Lissak, R. I. (1983). Procedural fairness: How employees evaluate procedures. Unpublished doctoral dissertation, University of Illinois, Urbana-Champaign.

National Football League (1998). *NFL modifies coin toss procedures*, Nov. 30. Retrieved January 18, 1999 from the World Wide Web: http://www.nfl.com/news/981130coin.html.

National Football League (1999). *Commissioner's news conference*, Aug. 21. Retrieved August 25, 1999 from the World Wide Web: http://www.nfl.com/news/0123.tagliabue.html.

Peterson, R. S. (1999). Can you have too much of a good thing? The limits of voice for improving satisfaction with leaders. *Personality and Social Psychology Bulletin*, 25, 313–24.

Schaubroeck, J., May, D. R., and Brown, F. W. (1994). Procedural justice explanations and employee reactions to economic hardship: A field experiment. *Journal of Applied Psychology*, 79, 455–60.

Shapiro, D. L., Buttner, H. B., and Barry, B. (1994). Explanations: What factors enhance their perceived adequacy? *Organizational Behavior and Human Decision Processes*, 58, 346–68.

Skarlicki, D. P., and Latham, G. P. (1996). Increasing citizenship behavior within a labor union: A test of organizational justice theory. *Journal of Applied Psychology*, 81, 161–9.

Stephens, S., Cadwallader, B., and Baird, D. (1996). Hostage drama ends: Injury at work leads to despair. *Columbus Dispatch*, Nov. 14, pp. 1A–2A.

Thibaut, J., and Walker, L. (1975). *Procedural justice: A psychological analysis*. Hillsdale, NJ: Erlbaum.

Tyler, T. R. (1987). Conditions leading to value expressive effects in judgments of procedural justice: A test of four models. *Journal of Personality and Social Psychology*, 52, 333–44.

Tyler, T. R., and Lind. E. A. (1992). A relational model of authority in groups. In M. P. Zanna (ed.), *Advances in experimental social psychology* (Vol. 25, pp. 115–91). San Diego: Academic Press.

Walster, E., Walster., G. W., and Berscheid, E. (1978). *Equity: Theory and research*. Boston: Allyn & Bacon.

Part V

TEAM DYNAMICS

14   Compose Teams to Assure Successful Boundary Activity
     DEBORAH ANCONA AND DAVID CALDWELL

15   Excel through Group Process
     GERARDO A. OKHUYSEN AND KATHLEEN M. EISENHARDT

16   Manage Intra-team Conflict through Collaboration
     LAURIE WEINGART AND KAREN A. JEHN

14

Compose Teams to Assure Successful Boundary Activity

Deborah Ancona and David Caldwell

The basic principle we propose here is that teams should be composed of individuals who can effectively carry out external boundary activity. The central argument is that teams need people who can bridge to the outside – people who can get resources, negotiate agreements, and know who to contact for expertise. A number of studies (cf. Ancona and Caldwell, 1992; Gladstein, 1984; Hansen, 1999) have shown that external boundary activity is a key predictor of team performance. Therefore, an important element in deciding on a team's composition should be to ensure that such activity takes place.

This principle is very broad. In our view, it applies most directly to temporary teams or taskforces that are created for a particular purpose and then transfer their work product to others within the organization. Typically, these teams draw on resources and information throughout the organization and often must gain the support of other entities within the organization if they are to be successful.

However, composing a team to deal with external issues is increasingly important for a broad range of teams. As organizations get flatter, more global, and more cross-functional, fewer work groups can remain isolated and focus solely on internal activity and work. The greater the complexity of the work and the higher the interdependence with other organization units, the more the team will need to engage in a complex web of external relationships to manage the coordination, knowledge transfer, and political maneuvering necessary to get its tasks accomplished.

JUSTIFICATION OF THE PRINCIPLE

It is our assertion that the external activities of interdependent organization teams are related to their performance. Although relatively little research has directly addressed this issue – in part because many of our theories of group activities were developed using laboratory groups that do not have external links – the notion that groups require effective interaction with external systems has its roots in the writings of early social psychologists (cf. Homans, 1950; Lewin, 1951). This general idea was expanded throughout the 1970s and early 1980s by open systems theorists (Katz and Kahn, 1978), researchers studying boundary spanning behavior (Roberts and O'Reilly, 1979; Tushman, 1977), and writings on autonomous work groups (cf. Cummings, 1978).

More direct empirical support for this assertion comes from several arenas. Those studying innovation have written extensively about the transfer of technical information across boundaries (Allen, 1971, 1984; Aldrich and Herker, 1977; Katz and Tushman, 1979). In general, those results showed that in R&D teams with uncertain tasks, boundary-spanning activity was related to performance. Those studying manufacturing product and process development projects have found a positive relation between external interactions and manager ratings of performance, as have those studying product development team performance (cf. Scott, 1997).

We also assert that it is not simply the frequency of external communication that is important but rather the content of that communication. Frequent communication with outsiders may be necessary for effective boundary management but it alone is not sufficient. The content and quality of interactions with outsiders will determine whether the team is able to tap into the power structure of the firm, understand and manage how the team's outputs fit into the broader workflow of the organization, and gain the information and the expertise from outside the team's boundaries that are necessary for success. In a study of 45 product development teams, we found that team members engaged in different activities in dealing with outside groups, and it was the extent to which team members engaged in these activities that was related to team performance. We found that effectiveness in product development was most likely when team members engaged in two sets of activities: (1) those that were designed to promote the team and secure resources; and (2) those that led to tighter links with other groups linked through the workflow. The frequency of communication with outsiders as such was unrelated to the performance of the teams. Interestingly, we also found that performance was negatively related to the frequency with which groups engaged in broad scanning of the environment, particularly when these activities were done late in the project (Ancona and Caldwell, 1992). Once the product idea was developed, the more successful teams cut down on broad, general communication and increased the number of exchanges aimed at acquiring specific information or coordinating distinct tasks. Less successful teams continued to seek out general information about markets and technologies.

MECHANISMS FOR MEETING EXTERNAL DEMANDS

How does one compose a team to meet external demands? Three aspects of team composition seem particularly relevant: (1) the background characteristics of individual team members, particularly the functional area to which the individuals are assigned; (2) the connections of team members to relevant networks inside and outside the organization; and (3) the configuration and nature of team members' assignments on the team. Although background characteristics have been studied extensively in prior research, we examine their effects on external linkages as well as internal dynamics. Network connections are the ties members have to individuals outside the group. Such ties represent the potential resources team members can access. The third component, team configuration, represents the level of involvement individual members have with the team.

The first step in designing a team to meet external demands is to develop an understanding of the key resources members must acquire from other groups, learn the expectations others have for the group, and understand how the group's product fits into the broader strategic initiatives of the firm. In part, this means acquiring knowledge about the political "structure" of the organization as well as the location of information and resources that will benefit the group. Clearly, some individuals understand the nature of this network of information and resources better than others, and this understanding is a source of power for individuals who have it (Krackhardt, 1990).

Once the critical links between the team and outside groups have been identified, the team can be formed to meet these critical connections. Three design variables can be used to manage these connections with other groups. We begin by describing the variables and then lay out some of the issues to be considered in applying these variables to team design.

Diversity in function

The first mechanism for designing a team that can effectively manage its boundaries is to select people for the team who can represent and have expertise in the functional areas that will contribute to the group's ultimate product. Based on a thorough review of studies of groups in organizations, Williams and O'Reilly (1998) conclude that teams made up of members from a variety of functional areas perform at a higher level than teams that do not have that diversity.

For example, functionally diverse top management teams are more successful in making administrative innovations (Bantel and Jackson, 1989) and in responding to environmental shocks (Keck and Tushman, 1993) than are less diverse teams. There seems to be both an internal and external rationale for the superior performance of functionally diverse teams. Internally, such teams have a greater collective range of viewpoints and more information exchange within the team (Glick, Miller, and Huber, 1993) than do less diverse teams. This broader range of shared knowledge and experience should allow the group to make more creative decisions than when the group has less information at its disposal. Externally, functionally diverse teams are likely to have greater communication with those outside the group and more links to external resources than less diverse groups (Ancona and Caldwell, 1992).

Members' connections to other groups and individuals

A second tool for managing team boundaries is including individuals on the team who have connections or relationships with others outside the group. The connections between individuals in organizations can vary in terms of their strength. A strong tie describes a relationship that is characterized by closeness, reciprocation, and substantial time spent with the other party. A weak tie is a relationship that does not have this level of closeness and connection (Granovetter, 1973). The nature of the ties within a network leads to predictable outcomes. Strong ties tend to bond similar people to one another and results in mutual attachments among the network members. In contrast, networks characterized by weak ties tend to be more diffuse and have fewer reciprocal connections (Krackhardt, 1992). Surprisingly, it seems that a mix of strong and weak ties is most beneficial.

The distinction between strong and weak ties is important in understanding how groups connect to outsiders. Networks that are characterized by strong ties tend to have a great deal of redundant information. Since team members tend to know the same people, they tend to learn the same things. Generally members in strong networks tend not to go outside their networks, in part because maintaining strong ties requires a certain amount of time and effort. In contrast, networks based on weak ties tend to contain much less redundant information. When weak ties exist, members of a group tend to know different people and therefore the group has access to a greater variety of information and contacts. And because weak ties require less time to maintain than strong ties, group members can potentially have more of them (Burt, 1992).

Weak ties have the potential of providing the group with access to a great many sources of information and may therefore help the team identify relevant resources or knowledge they did not know existed. It is a somewhat different issue when one thinks about how information and resources may be transferred to the team. Sharing information or a new technology often requires a substantial amount of effort by the giver. Individuals (or groups) are likely to be more willing to expend the time and effort to aid someone with whom they have a close, meaningful relationship – in other words, with whom they have a strong tie. Thus, composing a team for external boundary-spanning will require some combination of strong and weak ties.

Team configuration

A third approach to composing a team that effectively manages its boundaries is through configuring the roles of team members. Most models of teams – particularly those based on laboratory research – assume equal involvement and commitment of all team members to the effort. We do not believe this assumption holds true for most teams in organizations. Composing teams with the assumption that individual members will make differential contributions to the team's effort provides an effective option for dealing with boundary management issues.

When teams must deal with a large number of external entities or draw information from many sources there are alternatives in how the team could be composed. The team could contain members who represent all these important groups. Doing so has the potential to eliminate much of the need for boundary activity at the expense of creating a very large team. On the other hand, a smaller team would not have direct representation from all relevant groups and would therefore require greater boundary activity to guarantee success. An effective way of dealing with the need for including representation without expanding the size of the team is through configuring team member roles. That is, team members can be assigned limited roles on a team, yet still provide external information to the team or links to other groups. There are four mechanisms for doing this (Ancona and Caldwell, 1997):

- ◆ First, teams can bring experts into a team for a limited time or for a very specific aspect of the project. This allows the team to make use of the information or expertise of critical outsiders without having to integrate those individuals into the group.
- ◆ Second, teams can shift composition over the life-cycle of the project. That is, individuals who have specific information or external contacts can be assigned to a team for a limited time. Some members of the team could come and go, based on

the boundary activities necessary at a particular time.

♦ Third, some members could be assigned a part-time role on a team. Individuals whose expertise or contacts are needed over the length of the project, but who may have other demands on their time or somewhat limited knowledge of broader project issues, could serve on the team on a part-time basis.

♦ Fourth, the decision-making roles of team members could be differentiated. For teams working on highly complex, interdependent projects, the need for information and coordination with other groups may be too high to be accomplished exclusively through boundary management or the part-time or part-cycle involvement of some members. Such situations may require the expansion of the team. However, as the team grows in size difficulties in decision-making and coordination may arise. One response to this is to develop a two-tiered membership made up of a relatively small number of core members – who play a major role in decision-making – and a larger number of peripheral members – who play a more limited role, but are none the less full-fledged team members.

USING FUNCTIONAL DIVERSITY, TIES, AND TEAM CONFIGURATION FOR TEAM COMPOSITION

Once a group has developed an understanding of important interfaces that must be managed, specific decisions about who should serve on the team can be made. In our view, the team should contain individuals from the range of functions that will be responsible for the product or process under development. For example, if a team is developing a product that will ultimately have to be manufactured and sold, the team should have representation from production and sales.

A second design principle is to include members on the team who have appropriate connections to others in the organization. In our view, this implies a mix of strong and weak ties with other individuals. It is important to have individuals on the team who understand the knowledge and resources that may be spread out through the entire organization and even outside the organization. This implies that the team needs members who are connected to a wide range of different networks both inside and outside the organization. In other words, the team needs an extensive set of weak ties. However, it is at least as important that the team have deep connections with the groups with whom it must directly interface and work with to solve problems. This implies that the team includes members who have strong ties with other individuals who are in positions to provide resources or information to the group. Without a strong tie to a team member, an outsider may not be willing to expend effort in helping the team understand complex information or acquire resources. A recent study (Hansen, 1999) provides support for this general notion that both types of ties may be related to a team's success. He found that weak inter-unit ties help a project team search for useful knowledge in other sub-units but impede the transfer of complex knowledge. Transfer tends to be facilitated by a strong tie. He also found that weak inter-unit ties speed up project completion when knowledge needed from other groups is simple, but slows down completion when the knowledge is complex.

Finally, configuring individuals' roles is a valuable tool for enhancing other decisions.

If a team needs extensive information, but only at a particular time, including individuals on the team, but in a limited way may allow the "external resources" of the team to be expanded without permanently increasing the size of the team. These design variables allow for a great deal of flexibility in meeting external demands.

CONTINGENCIES AND LIMITATIONS

Our central principle is that teams should be composed to maximize external boundary-spanning activity. Is this always the case? In answering this question, we think there are two factors that must be considered. First, groups differ in the extent to which they must work with one another *and* work with outsiders to perform effectively. Second, composition choices made to manage boundary activities have the potential to affect how team members work with one another.

The first contingency factor is the nature of the group's task. Consider four types of team tasks that vary in the complexity of *both* the external or boundary activities and the internal or cooperative activities they must accomplish to be successful (see figure 14.1). Along one axis are internal coordination demands that can be categorized as high or low. High demands require that team members interact frequently to exchange information and coordinate work while low demands do not require such interaction. Along the other axis are external coordination and political demands that can also be high or low. High demands require that teams interact extensively with people external to the team to access information, coordinate work, and acquire resources and support. Low demands do not require this depth or complexity of external interaction.

Increasingly, as organizations become flatter and more flexible, as work becomes more complex, and knowledge workers take on complex tasks in teams, more teams will be

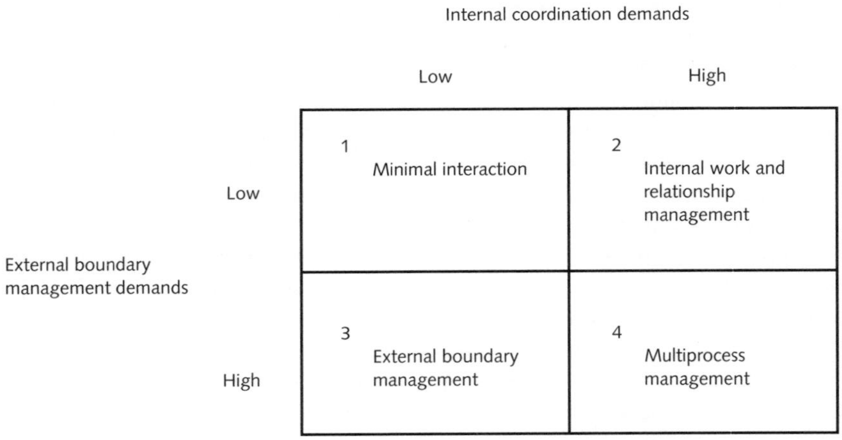

Internal coordination demands

	Low	High
Low	1 Minimal interaction	2 Internal work and relationship management
High	3 External boundary management	4 Multiprocess management

External boundary management demands

FIGURE 14.1 Critical processes for team performance

Source: Based on a model in Ancona and Nadler (1989)

found in cells 3 and 4, where external demands are high, than in the past. It is for these types of teams that our principle holds. Cell 1 is hardly even a team, but rather more of a set of people who have some aggregated output that is divorced from others in the organization. Cell 2 could represent teams that are configured to brainstorm creative ideas or solve a very circumscribed problem. Here all the necessary information resides in the team and there is little need to have others implement the team's ideas. In each of these two cases, external interactions are minimal and our principle would not apply. Instead the team would need to be designed with internal demands being dominant. The focus would be to find the optimal number of people who have appropriate information and skills and the motivation to work together (cf. Campion, Medsker, and Higgs, 1993).

In contrast, cell 3 teams need to focus almost exclusively on external boundary management while cell 4 teams need to carry out multiprocess management – internal work management, relationship management, and external boundary management. Our principle holds for cell 3 while cell 4 requires that both internal and external demands be considered. In our view, more and more teams are moving toward cell 4 because organizations are increasingly using teams to replace formal structures and systems. Because of this, we believe that selecting team members on the basis of their abilities to bridge to outsiders while still being able to share information, handle conflict, and coordinate work with other team members will grow in importance.

While the matrix presented above presents teams as having a single task, most teams have tasks that change over time, so teams may move from one cell to another over their lives. For example, product development teams move from: (a) exploring product ideas to (b) prototyping and exploiting technological achievements to (c) exporting the product to others for manufacturing and marketing. Research has shown that while external boundary management is important throughout this process, it is more important for the exploration and exportation stages and less important during the prototyping and exploiting stage. At a more general level, the task demands at each stage of work need to be assessed and the team composition needs to shift accordingly. It is because of these changing task demands that team configuration is so important. It is through part-cycle membership, the use of experts, and shifting roles that shifting external demands can be met.

Although we argue that staffing a team to deal effectively with external groups is important for team success, it is important that the team be able to develop effective internal processes too. In addition to dealing with outsiders, a team needs to create an identity that affords some separation from the larger organization (Hackman and Morris, 1975; Louis and Yan, 1999). This may be a somewhat delicate balance. As Alderfer points out, teams that have too much boundary activity may find it hard to set and keep that "separateness" and to maintain the cohesion necessary to work as a team. On the other hand, a team with too much cohesion and too strong an identity may be less likely to productively engage external groups than teams without such cohesiveness (Janis, 1982).

Thus, composition needs to be based on external demands while assuring internal communication and cohesion. Designing a team to meet external demands may lead to a very heterogeneous group. In addition, if individuals on the team are spending a great deal of time interacting with outsiders, it may be useful to do things to enhance the ability of the team members to work together. This can be achieved by having some level of homogeneity or similarity among team members (e.g., having people with similar tenure to facilitate communication, ensuring that there is a shared goal among team members, etc.). It may also be facilitated by introducing management practices that create identity and facilitate conflict resolution (Jehn, 1995).

CASE STUDIES

One of us was recently involved in a project with a multinational integrated oil company.* Two of the teams that were observed illustrate the role of composition in managing external activities and in the ultimate success of the projects. Although the teams were addressing different issues, both were formed in response to the problem that the company's traditional exploration areas and strata were becoming depleted and that investigating new areas or different strata would require different techniques than had been used in the past.

In 1995, the alpha project team was created to develop new exploration methods for a specific geographic area. In addition, the team was to identify specific tracts in that area that the company should try to acquire because they showed the promise of large reserves.

The alpha project team consisted of 17 members from three different geographic-based organizations in the company who represented a number of departments based on different geological and geophysical disciplines. Traditionally, these discipline-based departments had worked sequentially on problems rather than as a part of a team, and our interviews indicated that many individuals were skeptical of this team approach. Team members were chosen for their technical expertise and were assigned to the project on a full-time basis. A group of three managers from one of the geographic organizations was created to oversee the team's efforts.

Although there was some initial skepticism from some of the team members, the group quickly developed effective processes for working together. The team held several seminars and went on field excursions together to observe the geological area they were investigating. As is true of many large teams, members often concentrate their efforts on different parts of the task. In the alpha team, project work was done by cross-functional sub-groups within the team and a Lotus Notes database was developed to track the status of the numerous activities. There was a great deal of informal communication between team members and although they had limited experience working in teams, they soon found that combining their knowledge led to solving key problems. Team members developed strong ties with one another.

Other than bi-weekly meetings with the steering committee and informal contacts with other experts in their respective fields, the team had little external contact. In fact, team members spent so much time with one another and so little with their functional departments that others outside the team commented that the team had a tendency to isolate itself from the rest of the company. The team leader took on nearly all the external activities of the team, particularly those with management. Team members primarily confined their external activities to exchanging technical information with others.

How successful was the alpha team? The two goals of the alpha team were to develop new exploration technologies and to apply these technologies to exploration of a new field. As might be expected based on the points we have made previously, the team was very successful in finding new and effective ways to evaluate potential hydrocarbon prospects but was not as successful in getting its ideas accepted and utilized within the organization.

In the oil industry, companies may submit competitive applications to the government to obtain a license to further explore and develop the field. Once a license is obtained there is further exploration, and potentially, the development and the construction of a site. Deciding when to bid on a site and gaining government approval requires careful analysis of the site and accurate projections of the oil that can be extracted from it using various technologies. Once technology decisions were made, the alpha team left it to the steering committee to "transfer" the conclusions of their work to top management and the other groups who were responsible for developing and submitting competitive applications. Unfortunately there was a gap between the findings and their application and it took a very long time for the results of the team to be disseminated within the organization. In fact, the company was never able to obtain licenses for the areas the alpha team studied and for which they developed the technology. There is a somewhat successful end to the story. Once the alpha team was disbanded and members transferred to other teams, some consulted on a similar project. For this project, the alpha team's technology was used to develop successful bids and ultimately successful fields.

At about the same time the alpha team was formed, a second team, the beta team, also came into being. Like the alpha team, the beta team was created to come up with innovative ways to explore new areas. The beta team differed from the alpha team in two important ways. First, it was responsible for both developing a new exploration technology and completing a bid on a specific project. In other words, it took on the next phase of work and had to implement its findings. Second, the beta team included members from two other firms with whom a joint application would be prepared (in the oil industry, companies often partner with one another for competitive advantage or to undertake a large bid).

The team was composed of 15 experts from the company and one from each of the partner companies. The beta team, like the alpha team, contained members with different areas of geological expertise. Like the alpha team, team members also worked full-time on the project and shared common space. The team even used a similar process as the alpha team subdividing the task and working in cross-functional sub-groups. Like alpha, the beta team was able to develop innovative technical solutions to problems in exploration.

Unlike the alpha team, this one added a new member six months after its formation. This new member was a field development expert who would eventually work on the application and developing the site that was chosen. Initially he joined project meetings as an observer but later moved on to be an active contributor. Also unlike the alpha team, this team did not have its external links handled by a manager; rather, the team made numerous presentations to top management about project organization, cross-functional teams, alliances between oil companies, and their results. Despite its co-location, the beta team was not seen by others in the organization as isolated.

The beta team was able to move quickly from technical problems to the application phase. Although the first application bid prepared by the beta team was rejected, the team continued and prepared a new application that was accepted. The beta team was ultimately held up as a role model of collaboration between functions and across company boundaries.

How did composition contribute to outcomes of the alpha and beta teams? In both cases, the teams were composed of individuals from different functional areas. Both teams were co-located and had full-time members. There were substantial differences between the teams, however. The alpha team members were selected strictly on the basis of their technical expertise. Beta team members, especially those from the other companies, were selected both for their technical skills and for their connections to important networks throughout the organizations of which they were members. The beta team also shifted its membership by bringing in a specialized expert midway through its work and assigning this individual a specialized role. Perhaps most important, the beta team did not "delegate" boundary activity to one person as did the alpha team. Successfully completing the types of projects alpha and beta were assigned frequently requires more boundary management activity than can be accomplished by one or a small group of individuals. Finally, the internal processes of the two groups were somewhat different. The members of the alpha group worked extensively with one another, usually to the exclusion of external activities. This was not the case in the beta team.

CONCLUSIONS

Compared to other areas of investigation of small groups, composition has been relatively neglected despite its obvious importance (Moreland, Hogg, and Hains, 1994). Even the research that has been done has not led to systematic conclusions. In a summary of research on composition, Moreland, Levine, and Wingert note that ". . . few researchers study group composition, and no general theory guides their work. Progress toward understanding group composition has thus been slow and sporadic" (1996: 11).

In our view, much of this lack of progress has come about because much of the research has been done with groups that do not have meaningful external connections. Unfortunately, such groups do not reflect the true nature of most organizational groups. For most groups in organizations, links with other groups and the external environment are critical for success. Information and resources must be imported if teams are to make effective decisions and the output of the group must be transferred to others. We propose that selecting group members on their ability to facilitate these boundary activities can be an important element in teams' success.

NOTE

* We would like to acknowledge the contribution of Jon Lippe in acquiring these data.

REFERENCES

Aldrich, H. E., and Herker, D. (1977). Boundary spanning roles and organization structure. *Academy of Management Review*, 2, 217–30.

Allen, T. J. (1971). Communications, technology transfer, and the role of the technical gatekeeper. *R&D Management*, 1, 14–21.

Allen, T. J. (1984). Managing the flow of technology: Technology transfer and the dissemination of technological information within the R&D organization. Cambridge, MA: MIT Press.

Ancona, D. G., and Caldwell, D. F. (1992). Bridging the boundary: External activity and performance in organizational teams. *Administrative Science Quarterly*, 37, 634–65.

Ancona, D. G., and Caldwell, D. F. (1997). Rethinking team composition from the outside in. In M. E. Neale, E. A. Mannix, and D. H. Gruenfeld (eds.), *Research on managing groups and teams* Vol. 1, pp. 21–37. Stamford, CT: JAI Press.

Ancona, D. G., and Nadler, D. A. (1989). Top hats and executive tales: Designing the senior team. *Sloan Management Review*, 31, 19–28.

Bantel, K., and Jackson, S. (1989). Top management and innovations in banking: Does the composition of the team make a difference? *Strategic Management Journal*, 10, 107–24.

Burt, R. (1992). *Structural holes: The social structure of competition*. Cambridge, MA: Harvard University Press.

Campion, M., Medsker, G., and Higgs, A. (1993). Relations between work group characteristics and effectiveness: Implications for designing effective work groups. *Personnel Psychology*, 46, 823–47.

Cummings, T. G. (1978). Self-regulating work groups: A socio-technical synthesis. *Academy of Management Review*, 3, 624–34.

Gladstein, D. (1984). Groups in context: A model of task group effectiveness. *Administrative Science Quarterly*, 29, 499–517.

Glick, W., Miller, C., and Huber, G. (1993). The impact of upper echelon diversity on organizational performance. In G. Huber and W. Glick (eds.), *Organizational change and redesign*, (pp. 176–224). New York: Oxford University Press.

Granovetter, M. S. (1973). The strength of weak ties. *American Journal of Sociology*, 78, 1360–80.

Hackman, J. R., and Morris, C. G. (1975). Group tasks, group interaction process, and group performance effectiveness: A review and proposed integration. In L. Berkowitz (ed.), *Advances in experimental social psychology* (Vol. 8, pp. 47–100). New York: Academic Press.

Hansen, M. T. (1999). The search-transfer problem: The role of weak ties in sharing knowledge across organization subunits. *Administrative Science Quarterly*, 44, 82–111.

Homans, G. (1950). *The human group*. New York: Harcourt Brace Jovanovich.

Janis, I. (1982). *Victims of groupthink: A psychological study of foreign policy decisions and fiascos*. Boston: Houghton-Mifflin.

Jehn, K. A. (1995) A multimethod examination of the benefits and detriments of intragroup conflict. *Administrative Science Quarterly*, 29, 499–518.

Katz, D., and Kahn, R. (1978) *The social psychology of organizing*. New York: Wiley.

Katz, R., and Tushman, M. (1979). Communication patterns, project performance, and task characteristics: An empirical evaluation and integration in an R&D setting. *Organizational Behavior and Human Performance*, 23, 139–62.

Keck, S., and Tushman, M. (1993). Environmental and organizational context and executive team structure. *Academy of Management Journal*, 36, 1314–44.

Krackhardt, D. (1990). Assessing the political landscape: Structure, cognition, and power in organizations. *Administrative Science Quarterly*, 35, 342–69.

Krackhardt, D. (1992). The strength of strong ties: The importance of philos in organizations. In

N. Nohria and R. Eccles (eds.), *Networks and organizations*. Boston: Harvard Business School Press.

Lewin, K. (1951). *Field theory in social science: Selected theoretical papers*. Ed. D. Cartwright. New York: Harper & Brothers.

Louis, M. R., and Yan, A. (1999). The migration of organizational functions to work unit level: Buffering, spanning, and bringing up boundaries. *Human Relations*, 52, 25–47.

Moreland, R., Hogg, M., and Hains, S. (1994). Back to the future: Social psychological research on groups. *Journal of Experimental Social Psychology*, 30, 527–55.

Moreland, R., Levine, J., and Wingert, M. (1996). Creating the ideal group: Composition effects at work. In E. Witte and J. Davis (eds.), *Understanding group behavior: Small group processes and interpersonal relations* (Vol. 2, pp. 11–35). Hillsdale, NJ: Lawrence Erlbaum.

Roberts, K., and O'Reilly, C. (1979). Some correlates of communication roles in organizations. *Academy of Management Journal*, 22, 42–57.

Scott, S. (1997). Social identification effects in product and process development teams. *Journal of Engineering and Technology Management*, 14, 97–127.

Tushman, M. (1977). Special boundary roles in the innovation process. *Administrative Science Quarterly*, 22, 587–605.

Williams, K., and O'Reilly, C. (1998). Demography and diversity in organizations: A review of 40 years of research. In B. Staw and R. Sutton (eds.), *Research in Organizational Behavior* (Vol. 20, pp. 77–144). Stamford, CT: JAI Press.

15

Excel through Group Process

GERARDO A. OKHUYSEN AND KATHLEEN M. EISENHARDT

Does group process matter? Consider the following comparative cases from the administration of US president John F. Kennedy. One case is the Bay of Pigs Invasion. Shortly after coming into office in 1961, President Kennedy and his cabinet authorized the invasion of Cuba by an army of Cuban expatriates backed by the Central Intelligence Agency (CIA). The Bay of Pigs invasion was a devastating failure for the new administration. Most of the invading force was captured or killed within days of the landing. Yet less than two years later, the same group of decision-makers masterfully managed the Cuban missile crisis in which the two global superpowers, the United States and the Soviet Union, were on the verge of launching nuclear strikes against each other after the US discovered Soviet missile bases in Cuba. The danger of mutual destruction was imminent. Yet, through a series of decisions to combine military actions with the aggressive engagement of diplomatic alternatives, President Kennedy and his cabinet confronted the challenge posed by the Soviet missiles in Cuba and secured an agreement that removed them from the island peacefully.

Why were the two situations so strikingly different in their outcomes despite the almost identical composition of the groups involved? The answer is group process. In the case of the Bay of Pigs invasion, Kennedy and his cabinet engaged in a group process that was characterized by simplified thinking, lack of effective conflict, and ineffective patterns of participation (Janis, 1982). In contrast, in the Cuban missile crisis, Kennedy dramatically altered the group process. There was much greater use of conflict, more realistic thinking, and broader participation within the group (Janis, 1982). In other words, two decisions that were made by virtually the same group of people working less than two years apart exhibited substantially different group process and outcomes. So while group composition is clearly crucial for effective groups, group process is equally important.

In this chapter we explore how to build a great group process. We focus particularly on groups that demand active engagement and intense interaction among group members (Ashforth, 1988; Eisenhardt, Kahwajy, and Bourgeois, 1997a; Louis and Sutton, 1991). These groups include shopfloor teams that develop process improvements, cross-functional product development groups, ongoing task forces, and top management teams. By group process, we simply mean how group members go about interacting and making choices.

Our central argument is straightforward. Many people naively believe that group members must make difficult process trade-offs: conflict comes at the expense of speed, speed sacrifices getting along, and getting along cannot happen with conflict. Yet we think that the reality of effective group process is different. After all, conflict is absolutely essential for effective groups, especially ones facing difficult choices in high-velocity, hotly competitive industries. Speed matters too. A decision made too late can leave an organization hopelessly behind the competition. Group members also need to be able to work together to execute choices. In our view, superior group process involves solving the classic trade-offs of group process, not making them. That is, great group process is fast and conflictual, with group members who can disagree with one another and yet can walk away from meetings with mutual respect and the will to work together in the future.

In this chapter, we describe three antecedents that help groups to be fast, have high conflict, and still get along. These are: creating collective intuition, stimulating task-related conflict, and driving the pace of action. We argue that each of these antecedents consists of a cluster of tactics that shape group process. These tactics are interrelated such that they work with one another, supporting each other and offering synergies in group process. We also describe the pivotal role of the leader in shaping the group process that emerges.

BUILDING COLLECTIVE INTUITION

One of the myths of group process is that extensive information is unnecessary. The argument goes like this. The cost of gathering information is very high, and information is often ignored anyway due to the excessive demands on the time of group members (March and Simon, 1958; Simon, 1955). Therefore, it is not particularly useful to gather large amounts of information. Further, gathering extensive information is particularly fruitless in high-velocity situations where it becomes rapidly obsolete. As a consequence, group members should move ahead without spending too much time worrying about having lots of information.

In contrast, recent research takes a different view (Dean and Sharfman, 1996; Eisenhardt and Bourgeois, 1988; Wally and Baum, 1994). Groups with great process rely on more, not less, information than less effective groups. The difference is in the kind of information that they use. Ineffective groups rely on either historical information about past performance or speculative information about how the world might unfold. In contrast, groups with superior process center their attention on real-time and fact-based information about current operations.

A telling illustration comes from the Bay of Pigs invasion. During this debacle, the members of Kennedy's cabinet isolated themselves from key sources of information, and relied upon dated intelligence reports regarding the situation in Cuba. As a result, the cabinet did not have information regarding the preparedness of the Cuban armed forces and the related intelligence that indicated little support from the Cuban people for the invasion. They guessed about what Castro might do based on this limited and inaccurate information. They made choices based on what they hoped the situation would be, and not what it was. In striking contrast, many of these same members of Kennedy's cabinet relied on extensive data during the Cuban missile crisis. They received continual updates from a variety of sources on the movement of Soviet ships towards Cuba, the activities of civilians and the military on the island, and the progress of diplomatic contacts. This real-time information allowed cabinet members to maintain a constantly updated and accurate understanding of the situation.

Further, research suggests that real-time information about the current situation is particularly effective when different members of the group are responsible for specific pieces of it (Eisenhardt, 1989). In effect, members of groups with superior process adopt deliberately distinct information roles in the group. Often these roles are along the lines of functional expertise like engineering or marketing. This partitioning of responsibility for information cultivates a variety of different perspectives and provides depth of knowledge by focusing the attention of specific members on particular features of the situation. Not only is the information likely to be more accurate given that the group is leveraging the expertise of its members, but it is also likely to be obtained more quickly. For example, a group member from Human Resources can focus on turnover and hiring data as well as employment trends in the industry, providing critical staffing information to the group. In the same manner, the director of Research and Development can focus on technical trends in the industry, while the director of Marketing may focus on product introductions and product exits from the market. This focus is not only effective for internal data, but also for external information that can lead members to a more effective group process by focusing their attention on important stakeholders (Ancona, 1990).

Of course, simply having knowledgeable individuals in a group is of little use if their information is not available to be used collectively by the group. Indeed, one of the main challenges of group process is to ensure that information is effectively exchanged with all other members of the group (Stasser, 1992; Stasser and Stewart, 1992). In order to share and use information effectively, groups with great process engage in frequent interactions. In fact, they often set up "can't miss" meetings and in general have a greater number of regular interactions among members (Eisenhardt, Kahwajy, and Bourgeois, 1997a).

Again the Cuban missile crisis provides a positive exemplar. Kennedy's cabinet members took responsibility for gathering information about particular aspects of the situation for the group, including specific briefs from the state, defense, and justice departments, the intelligence agencies, and the branches of the military. Moreover, cabinet members met almost continuously, and were always available for meetings and information exchanges with the White House. Ultimately, these different perspectives were used to fashion the successful response to the Soviet missile threat within Cuba. In contrast, the Bay of Pigs invasion was characterized by much less clarity about information roles and much less dedication to frequent meetings. Unsurprisingly, the group process was ineffective.

While the comparison of the Bay of Pigs invasion with the Cuban missile crisis provides a particularly sharp comparison of process among groups with very similar composition, this same importance of real-time information, partitioned responsibility for that information, and frequent meetings appears in other kinds of groups as well. For example, Eisenhardt (1989) examined group process among top management teams in start-up ventures in the computing industry. In particular, she described how the members of one team, at a firm with the pseudonym Zap, operated. First of all, members of the management team at Zap claimed to "over-MBA it" and to "measure everything." They came close. They focused their attention on a wide variety of internal and external measures of current operations like bookings, backlog, revenue per employee, cash, and scrap in preference to refined, accounting-based indicators like profit. These group members also emphasized frequent operational meetings – sometimes two and even three times per week. The intensity at these meetings was high, with each being a "must attend" event on calendars. These meetings covered "what's happening" both inside and outside the company. Each member of the Zap top management team played an important role in gathering real-time information for these meetings. The VP Finance was responsible for much of the operating information. The VP Marketing was charged with tracking the moves of the competition. This meant constant travel and communication outside the firm for her. The VP R&D constantly worked his network of university, government, and industry ties to stay abreast of the latest in technology. One group member described the resulting group process as "we scream a lot, laugh, and resolve the issue." The typical outcome of this top management team was an effective decision that was made quickly (in two to three months, not the typical six to nine months).

Why does this combination of real-time information gathered by responsible group members and shared collectively lead to effective group process? One reason is that this combination of tactics is fast. In particular, continual tracking of information acts as an early warning system that allows group members to spot problems and opportunities sooner. This is especially true when group members meet often and so have developed a routine for working together. Therefore, when situations arise, members can go right to the problem, rather than groping about for relevant information. In addition, the development of distinct roles helps the information gathering process by ensuring that multiple perspectives are always represented (Eisenhardt, 1989), which in turn increases the potential range of action in the group (Schweiger, Sandberg, and Rechner, 1989).

A second reason that this combination of tactics builds effective group process is that the intense interaction creates groups whose members are more likely to disagree. Familiarity and friendship make such frank conversation easier because group members are less constrained by politeness and more willing to express diverse views. There is a more surprising effect as well. Intense interaction can lead to roles that go beyond functional or business ones. In effect, group members naturally organize into antipodal roles such as short vs. long term, or status quo vs. change (Guetzkow and Gyr, 1954) in response to their perceptions of balancing the natural tensions within a group. For example, while one or more members of a top management team may be concerned with the outlook for the firm five years into the future, others may focus instead on the present situation of the firm.

The familiarity that group members develop through their intense interactions is also one element that allows them to disagree in the short term, and yet still get along in the long term (Valley, Neale, and Mannix, 1995). Familiarity in a group develops as a consequence of the interactions among members and is constantly reinforced as members discover information regarding the expertise and preferences of their co-workers. The development of familiarity makes it easier for group members to separate task conflict from relationship or interpersonal conflict. Familiarity keeps task conflict from becoming relationship conflict through the trust that develops among group members (Simons and Peterson, in press). This trust comes from increased and intense interaction that allows the group to build common goals, ensuring the commitment and participation of all members. The familiarity that develops from intense and frequent interactions increases interpersonal knowledge regarding beliefs and norms, and makes work interactions easier (Jehn and Shah, 1997; Shah and Jehn, 1993). As individuals increase their knowledge about others and build trust in other members they are able to disagree on substantive issues without engaging in personal attacks or recriminations.

Similarly, the use of real-time information also helps group members to have conflict and yet still get along (Eisenhardt et al., 1997a). The argument is as follows. In groups, disagreement can be viewed as personal or as issue based (Amason, 1996; Jehn, 1995, 1997; Schweiger, Sandberg, and Rechner, 1989). Personal conflict tends to create a dysfunctional process in which members listen poorly, fail to engage, and are distracted from the problem-solving task for the group. In contrast, issue-based conflict is related to superior group process. By relying on facts, people tend to attribute disagreement simply to issue-based differences among reasonable people. This attribution helps group members to avoid becoming sidetracked by personal agendas and to move more quickly to the central challenges facing the group. It also helps them to avoid becoming bogged down in arguments about what might be. Facts depersonalize discussion because they are not some member's fantasies, guesses, or self-serving desires. An emphasis on factual data creates a culture of problem-solving, not personalities. The explicit anointing of individuals as experts adds to the effect. The designation of experts makes it easier for the group to call on them to share their perspective on a given issue (Stasser, Stewart, and Wittenbaum, 1995). By providing specific areas of the organization that members represent and are responsible for, the use of group roles for information-gathering helps to limit politicking by mitigating "turf" battles.

Overall, real-time information gathered by specific group members and shared together creates a kind of collective intuition regarding the challenges that they face. Through their experience individual members develop an ability to recognize and process information in blocks or patterns (Isenberg, 1988). Through repeated exposure to data, patterns become recognizable even when there is only a small amount of information available. This pattern processing (what we term "intuition") is faster and more accurate than processing single pieces of information. Through the development of a collective knowledge base, all group members can also tap into relevant experiences when new situations appear. The collective experience allows members to develop the ability to build linkages among seemingly disparate pieces of information (Isenberg, 1986, 1988). This "collective intuition" can help a group become faster and more effective in its work.

In contrast, groups with less effective group process rely more on projections of the future and refined data, particularly financial data. As a result, members of these groups have a less instinctive feel for what is going on. These groups rarely develop a systematic approach to their group process with roles and responsibilities clearly defined, and routines for the gathering and sharing of information. They meet infrequently and so operate as groups of strangers who have difficulty engaging productively with one another.

STIMULATING TASK CONFLICT

Consider the following story. On a hot and dusty August afternoon, a farming family was sitting on their front porch trying to get some relief from the heat of the midwest summer. One family member suggested an outing to Abilene, about a two-hour drive away, to get some lemonade. Another member agreed. Before long, the whole family was in the car, on the way to Abilene. With the sun beating down on the roof, the trip in the crowded car was even more unpleasantly hot than sitting on the family porch. The lemonade was not particularly memorable either. In frustration, one member finally expressed regret at ever leaving the porch. With that, everyone chimed in that they had never really wanted to go to Abilene in the first place. They had all simply assumed that everyone else did want to travel to Abilene, and so they agreed too.

The above story, dubbed the Abilene Paradox, has been told in a variety of ways and has become a classic parable in organizational behavior. In the Abilene Paradox, every group member disagrees with the group choice, but does not express that disagreement. No one voices objections because each assumes that the other group members agree with the stated position and its underlying assumptions. Because no one expresses disagreement, no one realizes that conflict exists. This, in turn, leads to increased internal pressures to self-censor opinions. In its extreme form, the Abilene Paradox leads to a poor group process in which group members engage in activities or adopt directions that no one in the group agrees with simply because no one is willing to be the first to voice objection.

Groupthink is an even more subtle manifestation of this inability to express disagreement. As described by Janis (1982) in his description of foreign policy debacles such as the Bay of Pigs invasion, the pressure of groupthink is insidious as group members fail to realize that they are engaging in simplified thinking, stereotyping of others, and related cognitive errors. Although groupthink can involve overt pressure to conform, very often people simply become so involved with the affiliative value of the group that they fail to think critically. In both the Abilene Paradox and groupthink, insufficient conflict creates a poor group process and related outcomes.

In contrast, groups with effective process have to exhibit extensive conflict. Group members recognize that conflict is a natural feature of many organizational situations in which reasonable group members should and often do disagree. Further, as research demonstrates, conflict stimulates innovative thinking, and creates better understanding of the options. This leads to better choices and implementation. Without sufficient conflict, group members have an impoverished process. They miss opportunities to question assumptions and overlook key elements of their situation. Given the value of conflict, groups with effective process make conflict part of that process.

One way that groups create conflict in their process is through team composition. Teams that are diverse in terms of age, gender, functional background, experience, and so forth are likely to see the world in different ways and so naturally create conflict. That is, the natural differences that exist across their areas of responsibility (e.g., marketing vs. logistics), focus of concern (e.g., labor unions vs. consumers), or other differences (e.g., gender) generate perspectives that are in conflict with one another. For example, it would not be unusual for a member representing manufacturing to be in disagreement with the opinions of the marketing or R&D department. In top management teams, one member who is particularly concerned with the current status of the organization may have major disagreements with someone whose focus is the future of the organization.

Another way in which conflict is introduced by members of a group is through the deliberate development of multiple alternatives for any given issue (Eisenhardt, 1989). As different alternatives are explored, disagreements over assumptions, outcomes, and objectives are clarified. This clarification, while conflictive, can lead to the development of greater confidence among group members that they have adequately explored the issues as well as a higher-quality process overall. Effective decision-making groups highlight this diversity and actively exploit it to uncover potential alternatives for the group (Schweiger and Finger, 1984; Schweiger, Sandberg, and Ragan, 1986). During the Cuban missile crisis, for example, military, legal, political, and diplomatic perspectives and options for action were always represented at the table and under active discussion.

Task conflict can also be generated by using "framebreaking" heuristics that lead to new perspectives and thinking. One such heuristic is "forecasting" (Eisenhardt et al., 1997a). Forecasting involves imagining future scenarios (i.e., assumptions about how the future will unfold) and then playing out various options in light of these scenarios. As a result, members can better grasp the range of possible futures and their options within them. A related heuristic is "backcasting." Using this technique, the group builds alternative future scenarios. Having developed these different future scenarios, group members choose the most desirable ones and then reason backwards to figure out how to achieve those futures.

Framebreaking heuristics can also involve members taking on particular roles within the group. Sometimes the role-playing simply means taking the perspective of a key competitor or some important internal constituent within the group's discussion. Group members may also take on a formal Devil's Advocacy role (Schweiger and Finger, 1984; Schweiger, Sandberg, and Rechner, 1989). The Devil's Advocate is a group member who is charged with questioning the assumptions and approaches of the group through critical evaluation. Since this role is formalized, it allows the Devil's Advocate to deeply explore issues and request clarification from other group members without the risk of censure that may come to an individual who pointedly disagrees with the group. Overall, role-playing heuristics allow members to argue and discuss alternatives with less risk of being reproached by other members of the group (Feldman, 1984; Murnighan and Conlon, 1991). For example, during the Cuban missile crisis, several cabinet members, including Attorney-General Robert Kennedy, explicitly took on the Devil's Advocate role. The formal adoption of this role by individuals allowed for a thorough discussion of the positive and negative implications of different alternatives, leading to a successful resolution of the Soviet threat.

Finally framebreaking heuristics can be relatively complex interventions into group process (Schweiger et al., 1989). For example, in Dialectical Inquiry, the group is divided into two sub-groups. One sub-group develops an alternative for a particular problem and presents it to the group. The second sub-group then critically analyzes the proposed solution and develops another iteration that keeps the best points, eliminates the worst, and adds new ones to improve the solution. The first sub-group then repeats this process, until the resulting synthesis is the distillation of the best ideas from members of both sub-groups within the group.

Why do conflict-creating devices such as diverse groups, framebreaking heuristics, and multiple alternatives lead to more effective group process? Obviously, they hasten the emergence of conflict and so accelerate the entire group process. Rather than waiting or hoping that conflict will emerge, group members simply create that conflict. Less obviously, especially in the case of multiple alternatives, these tactics often give group members confidence that they are not overlooking key information and perspective. Armed with such confidence, group members are likely to have a faster process. That confidence is especially crucial in high-velocity situations where the blocks to rapid group process are as much emotional (i.e., fear of the unknown) as they are cognitive.

More obviously, these tactics clearly improve group process by helping group members to come up with more varied viewpoints on their actions. They encourage group members to think over time, to reverse their usual path of thinking, and to assume new lenses for viewing the activities of the group. Through all of these tactics, group members are likely to develop a process that is more highly conflictual.

Finally, the combination of a diverse group, multiple alternatives, and especially framebreaking heuristics affects group process by legitimating conflict. This helps group members to get along even as they disagree. These tactics achieve this by encouraging group members to frame conflict as less centered on personal differences and more centered on problem-solving. That is, they put a cooperative, not competitive, perspective on the group process. For example, the use of a Devil's Advocate or of a Dialectical Inquiry procedure allows the group to formalize task conflict and use it as part of its work process. The artificial addition of such task conflict into the group allows members to capitalize on the group's problem-solving advantages, while at the same time providing legitimacy for the emergence of conflict within the group. The legitimacy of conflict that is afforded group members through the adoption of such tactics contributes to the prevention of premature and even false consensus.

In contrast, groups with members who fail to stimulate task conflict often miss opportunities to question key assumptions and to think more deeply about issues concerning the group. The contrast of the Bay of Pigs invasion with the Cuban missile crisis is telling here. In the former, group members failed to effectively develop alternative lenses on their data. The Cuban crisis was the reverse, with extensive use of Devil's Advocacy, outside experts, and creative thinking to build conflict into the group process.

Driving the Pace of the Process

One of the striking features of the literature on group process is the lack of attention to time. Of course, there are some exceptions (including those noted below), but very often authors ignore or misunderstand time. Yet, in the world of real groups, time is critical. In fact, with the emergence of the Internet, the convergence of consumer electronics with computing and telecommunications, globalization, and so forth, attention to time is becoming crucial for many groups. In places like Silicon Valley, quips like "snooze, you lose" or "the worst decision is no decision at all" underscore the importance of time. Pacing is a particularly significant aspect of time for group process because it keeps group members moving forward, even as it gives them opportunities to adjust to unforeseen problems and unexpected opportunities.

One way to drive the pace of the group is simply by developing a natural rhythm of action. For example, Eisenhardt (1999) describes how top management teams develop a sense of how long strategic decisions should take. Through the experience of decision-making and the perspective of self-reflection, they come to understand when a process is taking too long, which implies that the group is either tackling too large an issue or is simply slowing down. They also develop a sense of when the process is too fast. Similarly Brown and Eisenhardt (1997) studied product development groups and found that the more successful ones developed a rhythm for their process around consistent lengths of their projects. This rhythm accelerated and focused the project teams. Overall, pacing in a group reflects the collective experience of individuals, and yields more effective outcomes (Eisenhardt, 1999).

The use of deadlines is another way that group members set the pace of their process (Gersick, 1989). Deadlines influence the group process by providing an easy measure of the progress that the group has made. For example, if a group is one-third of the way to its deadline but has not completed one-third of the work, members can easily conclude that an increase in activity is necessary. In a particularly interesting study, Gersick (1989) found that groups with deadlines often paused at the midpoint of their schedule in order to assess their progress towards their goals in light of the deadline. As result of this pause, the groups often had an opportunity to assess their group process and to make major changes in that process in order to improve group performance.

More generally milestones and even simple process interventions such as "watch your time" or "ask others about their information" can effectively alter the process of groups. Such milestones and simple group interventions often trigger group members to stop and think, to evaluate their work, and to discuss potential changes in group process or direction. During these interruptions, group members have an opportunity to focus critically on their process and look for better ways to accomplish the task (Okhuysen and Eisenhardt, 1998). That is, the group members are able to address accumulated problems, discuss future directions, and take action. The result is a group process with alternating periods of both full engagement on the task and opportunities to change the direction and process of the group.

Group members also set the pace of their process through the use of consensus with qualification as the group decision rule (Eisenhardt, Kahwajy, and Bourgeois, 1997a). Consensus with qualification is a two-step process. First, group members try to reach consensus. But, if they cannot do so, then group members make the choice by some sort of decision rule such as the most involved member chooses, the group votes, or the leader decides. This type of decision rule was used in the Cuban missile crisis. In contrast, the Bay of Pigs invasion was characterized by the pursuit of forced consensus that led to an ineffective group process and a poor choice.

Why does the combination of rhythm, deadlines and milestones, simple interventions, and consensus with qualification lead to more effective group process? The obvious reason is that each of these tactics contributes to moving the group along more quickly. But more importantly, they can also drive a pace for the group that effectively creates an internal process metronome that keeps the group driving forward. So for example, milestones help group members to pace their activity (Okhuysen and Eisenhardt, 1998). Consensus with qualification provides a way for the group to stop an endless search for consensus that can waste time and energy as members pursue an objective that cannot realistically be achieved in a reasonable time frame. Similarly, deadlines set pace and close group discussion.

This combination of tactics also helps group members to oscillate their attention from task execution to improvement of their problem-solving strategy and/or group process. Such opportunities to stop and think create greater self-reflection. They center the group on going forward with the task, and yet they also stimulate thinking and perhaps conflict within the group by often providing opportunities to examine and change group process and task strategy.

Finally, setting the pace through internal rhythms, deadlines, and milestones, simple interventions, and consensus with qualification helps group members to get along. Such tactics signal the need for speed, even when group members disagree. They also provide a legitimate platform for group members to address issues of ineffective group process including personal (as opposed to task) conflict. Consensus with qualification is particularly useful for helping group members to avoid the frustration of endless consensus seeking. It helps them to take a realistic view of conflict as valuable and inevitable. At the same time, consensus with qualification lets group members resolve conflict (and maintain pace) in a way that is typically perceived as equitable (Eisenhardt, 1989). Most group members want a voice in their group's decisions, but rarely believe that they must always get their preferred choice.

Overall, tactics such as deadlines and milestones, rhythm, consensus with qualification, and simple interventions set a pace for group process that keeps groups on track in terms of time while still offering opportunities for reflection and change in their process. In contrast, groups whose members do not use these tactics are prone to ineffective use of time. They may make decisions so quickly that they forget important information. More likely, they will become bogged down in searches for consensus. These group members often stress the rarity of what they do, rather than recognizing its repetitive nature. They oscillate between letting critical issues languish and making "shotgun" moves with little thought.

LEADERSHIP

Thus far, we have argued that the tactics that are associated with creating collective intuition, stimulating quick task conflict, and setting the pace of the group all contribute to effective group process – that is, fast and high-conflict group process where members none the less get along. In this section, we focus briefly on the important role that the leader of the group plays in developing a great group process.

First of all, it is important to recognize that leaders have a disproportionate influence on group process. This influence is sometimes exerted in a negative, even if unintended, fashion. For example, during the Bay of Pigs invasion, President Kennedy took on an active role in the discussion of alternatives. This resulted in members of the group "going along" with the president's opinions rather than volunteering their true beliefs because they did not want to contradict the president with opposing evidence or alternative approaches. The active participation of President Kennedy in the discussions also hindered the development of multiple alternatives in the group. Both of these contributed to the failed policy decision. By contrast, during the Cuban missile crisis, the president purposefully stayed at arm's length from the cabinet deliberations. Instead, the cabinet met without the president, which allowed members to express disagreement with options and contributed to a better policy decision.

But leaders can also use their disproportionate influence on group process more positively. This is particularly the case when they provide legitimacy or "cover" to individuals who disagree or provide a critical perspective. The leader can adopt framebreaking heuristics such as Devil's Advocacy or Dialectical Inquiry more readily than can other members. By requesting multiple alternative approaches to a problem, the leader implicitly can legitimate differences of opinion. For example, when President Kennedy did not seek out alternatives during the Bay of Pigs decision, the group assumed that consensus was a very important value for him and acted accordingly. For the Cuban missile crisis, President Kennedy explicitly sought out alternative opinions, going as far as asking individuals from outside the administration to provide counsel to address the situation. By specifically requesting alternatives, President Kennedy provided cover for those members of the group that held differing opinions. By insisting that members be continually aware of the faults of each alternative, he ensured that the group respected differences of opinion. This approach signaled to the members of the cabinet that the president was less interested in a consensus opinion than in a well thought-out policy response to the Soviet threat. The legitimacy that a leader can bring to these differences of opinion can also help members prevent long-term negative effects from disagreement.

Leaders can also disproportionately influence the process of the group by stimulating explicit and even contrived attempts to have fun. Humor is effective within groups because it relieves tension and improves the cooperative outlook of team members as well as their listening skills (Eisenhardt, 1999). Humor bridges differences among group members as well (Kahn, 1989; Ziv and Gadish, 1990). Humor works as a defense mechanism to protect people from stressful situations that can arise in groups. Using humor, people can distance themselves from such situations by putting those situations into a broader life context, often through the use of irony. Humor, particularly given its ambiguity, can blunt the threatening edge of negative information. Group members can speak in jest about issues that might be threatening if said directly. Humor can convey serious messages in a less threatening way.

Two Mini-cases

This chapter has a continuing theme of comparing the group process of the Bay of Pigs invasion decision with that of the Cuban missile crisis. In this closing section, we wanted, however, to sharpen further the contrast between effective and ineffective group process by briefly comparing the top management teams of two entrepreneurial firms: Zap and Andromeda.

Earlier we described how the top management team of Zap achieved collective intuition. They had slavish dedication to a wide variety of real-time data, both quantitative and qualitative. They also met frequently as a group and e-mailed constantly. The CEO delegated responsibility for different types of information to specific managers. For example, the VP Marketing handled competitive intelligence while the

VP Finance was responsible for delivering information on key internal metrics. These tactics led to a deep intuition or "gut feel" about the industry among team members individually and collectively. But driving collective intuition was not the only significant piece of the group process puzzle at Zap. Zap managers explicitly stimulated task conflict within the team. They were a diverse group – executives whose ages ranged from twenties to fifties. They were gender mixed, with non-US members and with MBAs mixed with science Ph.D.s. The CEO of Zap explicitly further encouraged task conflict through framebreaking tactics, particularly scenario planning. He was fond of outlining scenarios for the future, and then challenging other Zap executives to think backwards to how the scenarios could have been achieved. He also believed in multiples alternatives. For example, the CEO encouraged his team to come up with a variety of ways to raise cash for the "war chest." As a result, the team developed four alternatives, including an innovative alliancing plan with a blue-chip customer that gave Zap both money and prestige. Finally, Zap managers maintained pace, primarily through consensus with qualification. So, for example in the cash-raising decision, the team could not agree on the best alternative among several alliancing options, an IPO, and a further venture round. After a reasonable amount of time was spent trying to find consensus, the CEO and his VP Finance made the choice. Some of the other group members disagreed with the final choice, but went along with it because they understood it and had been consulted. As a result of their effective group process, Zap managers made very rapid decisions (as in the cash decision, two-to-three month strategic choices), with high conflict, and yet camaraderie. Zap has become one of the superstars of the computing industry.

In contrast to the case of Zap is the top management team of a company that we called Andromeda. Managers at this venture emphasized planning. When faced with a major decision, they tried to predict what would happen. But they did not have an effective information system that let them stay in touch with their internal operations and external markets. Rather, their system focused on highly refined and dated accounting measures of performance. They also rarely met as a group. Therefore, they had difficulty developing an intuition about their business and they remained a group of strangers. The team at Andromeda also had difficulties with conflict. They did not use framebreaking heuristics to drive conflict. In fact, they tended to avoid conflict as being unpleasant and even unprofessional. However, this inability to express conflict made choices difficult. The team tended to delay decisions rather than to simply face the conflict. They also engaged in alternatives serially. For example, in one situation around sourcing technology for a new product, managers at Andromeda spent several months analyzing the option of in-house sourcing. When that proved infeasible, they then switched to an alliance relationship. Only after their first alliance negotiation failed did they move to a second potential partner. The whole process took almost a year, during which they lost an early product lead in the marketplace. Finally, Andromeda managers never developed a sense of pace. Every decision was a unique event. Ironically, the CEO strove for consensus, but then often made sudden and rash choices out of frustration and/or against deadlines. Decision-making at Andromeda often took over nine months for important strategic choices, while several members of the team were largely disengaged from the group. Andromeda has since failed, despite having excellent technology and strong venture financing.

CONCLUSION

This chapter discusses some of the factors by which groups achieve a great process. A great group process is one that is fast, that includes conflict, and where group members get along. The antecedent conditions that we discussed include sets of tactics around building collective intuition, stimulating quick conflict, and setting the pace of the group. We also indicated that the leader has a particularly powerful influence on the process of the group. Using research on groups and comparative examples from President Kennedy's cabinet during the Bay of Pigs invasion and the Cuban missile crisis as well as from two entrepreneurial companies, this chapter attempts to highlight some of the key ways that group members use to understand and improve their process. The result of such improvements can be high-quality and timely outcomes that improve the odds of the long-term survival of the group and its organization. These are the best possible products from the efforts of individuals in a group.

NOTE

We appreciate the helpful comments of Anita Bhappu and Tiffany Galvin on earlier drafts of this chapter.

REFERENCES

Amason, A. C., (1996). Distinguishing the effects of functional and dysfunctional conflict on strategic decision making: Resolving a paradox for top management teams. *Academy of Management Journal*, 39, 123–48.

Ancona, D. G. (1990). Outward bound: Strategies for team survival in an organization. *Academy of Management Journal*, 33, 334–65.

Ashforth, B. E. F., and Fried, Yitzhak (1988). The mindlessness of organizational behavior. *Human Relations*, 41, 305–29.

Brown, S. L., and Eisenhardt, K. M. (1997). The art of continuous change: Linking complexity theory and time-paced evolution in relentlessly shifting organizations. *Administrative Science Quarterly*, 42, 1–34.

Dean, J. W., and Sharfman, M. P. (1996). Does decision process matter? A study of strategic decision-making effectiveness. *Academy of Management Journal*, 39, 368–96.

Eisenhardt, K. M. (1989). Making fast strategic decisions in high-velocity environments. *Academy of Management Journal*, 32, 543–76.

Eisenhardt, K. M. (1999). Strategy as strategic decision making. *Sloan Management Review*, 40(3), 65–72.

Eisenhardt, K. M., and Bourgeois, L. J. III. (1988). Politics of strategic decision making in high-velocity environments: Toward a midrange theory. *Academy of Management Journal*, 31, 737–70.

Eisenhardt, K. M., Kahwajy, J. L., and Bourgeois, L. J. III. (1997a). Conflict and strategic choice: How top management teams disagree. *California Management Review*, 39, 42–62.

Eisenhardt, K. M., Kahwajy, J. L., and Bourgeois, L. J. III. (1997b). How management teams can have a good fight. *Harvard Business Review*, 75, 77–85.

Feldman, D. C. (1984). The development and enforcement of group norms. *Academy of Management*

Review, 9, 47–53.

Gersick, C. J. G. (1989). Marking time: predictable transitions in task groups. *Academy of Management Journal*, 32, 274–309.

Guetzkow, H., and Gyr, J. (1954). An analysis of conflict in decision-making groups. *Human Relations*, 7, 367–81.

Isenberg, D. J. (1986). Thinking and managing: A verbal protocol analysis of managerial problem solving. *Academy of Management Journal*, 29, 775–88.

Isenberg, D. J. (1988). How senior managers think. In D. E. Bell, H. Raiffa, and A. Tversky (eds.), *Decision making: Descriptive, normative, and prescriptive interactions*. New York: Cambridge University Press.

Janis, Irving (1982). Groupthink: Psychological Studies of Policy Decisions and Fiascoes. Boston: Houghton-Mifflin.

Jehn, K. A. (1995. A multimethod examination of the benefits and detriments of intragroup conflict. *Administrative Science Quarterly*, 40, 256–82.

Jehn, K. A. (1997). A qualitative analysis of conflict types and dimensions in organizational groups. *Administrative Science Quarterly*, 42, 530–57.

Jehn, K. A., and Shah, P. P. (1997). Interpersonal relationships and task performance: An examination of mediating processes in friendship and acquaintance groups. *Journal of Personality and Social Psychology*, 72, 775–90.

Kahn, W. A. (1989). Toward a sense of organizational humor: Implications for organizational design and change. *The Journal of Applied Behavioral Science*, 25, 45–63.

Louis, M. R., and Sutton, R. I. (1991). Switching cognitive gears: From habits of mind to active thinking. *Human Relations*, 44, 55–76.

March, J. G., and Simon, H. A. (1958). *Organizations*. New York: Wiley.

Murnighan, J. K., and Conlon, D. E. (1991). The dynamics of intense work groups: A study of British string quartets. *Administrative Science Quarterly*, 36, 165–86.

Okhuysen, G. (1998). Facilitating group processes: The role of social interaction in problem solving groups. Proceedings of Annual Academy of Management Meeting, San Diego, CA.

Okhuysen, G. A., and Eisenhardt, K. M. (1998). Creating opportunities for change: How formal problem solving interventions work. Proceedings of Academy of Management, San Diego, CA.

Schweiger, D. M., and Finger, P. A. (1984). The comparative effectiveness of dialectical inquiry and Devil's Advocacy: The impact of task biases on previous research findings. *Strategic Management Journal*, 5, 335–50.

Schweiger, D. M., Sandberg, W. R., and Ragan, J. W. (1986). Group approaches for improving strategic decision making: A comparative analysis of dialectical inquiry, Devil's Advocacy, and consensus. *Academy of Management Journal*, 29, 51–71.

Schweiger, D. M., Sandberg, W. R., and Rechner, P. L. (1989). Experiential effects of dialectical inquiry, Devil's Advocacy, and consensus approaches to strategic decision making. *Academy of Management Journal*, 32, 745–72.

Shah, P. P., and Jehn, K. A. (1993). Do friends perform better than acquaintances? The interaction of friendship, conflict, and task. *Group Decision and Negotiation*, 2, 149–65.

Simon, H. A. (1955). A behavioral model of rational choice. *Quarterly Journal of Economics*, 69, 99–118.

Simons, T. L., and Peterson, R. S. (in press). Task conflict and relationship conflict in top management teams: The pivotal role of intragroup trust. *Journal of Applied Psychology*.

Stasser, G. (1992). Information salience and the discovery of hidden profiles by decision-making groups: A "thought experiment". *Organizational Behavior & Human Decision Processes*, 52, 156–81.

Stasser, G., and Stewart, D. (1992). Discovery of hidden profiles by decision-making groups: Solving a problem versus making a judgement. *Journal of Personality and Social Psychology*, 63, 426–34.

Stasser, G., Stewart, D. D., and Wittenbaum, G. M. (1995). Expert roles and information exchange during discussion: The importance of knowing who knows what. *Journal of Experimental and Social Psychology*, 31.

Valley, K. L., Neale, M. A., and Mannix, E. A. (1995). Friends, lovers, colleagues, strangers: The effects of relationships on the process and outcome of dyadic negotiations. *Research on Negotiation in Organizations*, 5, 65–93.

Wally, S., and Baum, J. R. (1994). Personal and structural determinants of the pace of strategic decision making. *Academy of Management Journal*, 37, 932–56.

Ziv, A., and Gadish, O. (1990). The disinhibiting effects of humor: Aggressive and affective responses. *Humor*, 3, 247–57.

16

Manage Intra-team Conflict through Collaboration

LAURIE WEINGART AND KAREN A. JEHN

The basic principle we espouse in this chapter is that intra-team conflict should be managed using collaboration. Intra-team conflict occurs when team members hold discrepant views or have interpersonal incompatibilities. There has been a debate in organizational research regarding whether agreement or disagreement within teams is advantageous for overall performance. Conflict researchers (Amason, 1996; Jehn, 1995, 1997) have recently found that while *non-task* conflicts based on personality clashes and interpersonal antagonism are detrimental to team performance and morale, *task* conflicts can be beneficial if managed collaboratively. Our central argument is that collaboration can benefit both task and non-task conflict, but that task conflict should be actively managed (not necessarily eliminated) through collaboration in the work setting whereas non-task conflict should be collaboratively managed off-line, outside the work setting, (or avoided) to ensure high performance of teams.

Given that conflict is difficult to manage within teams and that teams are fairly unlikely to naturally possess an effective conflict approach, we present the key to managing intra-team conflict effectively – collaboration. Collaboration is a joint endeavor. It involves two or more people working together to complete a task, each bringing their own, potentially unique, perspective to the task. Collaboration includes teamwork – the coordination of the efforts of a group of people around a stated purpose. When embedded in the culture of an organization, it can be more than coordination and cooperation, but rather a continuous partnering of people based on shared values (Haskins, Liedtka, and Rosenblum, 1998). Collaboration can occur within the work setting or off-line, and developed through discussion and increased understanding.

In the past, it was assumed that all differences and conflicts within teams should be resolved or avoided. However, we assert that effective management of conflict includes collaboratively managing task conflict – maybe even using techniques to encourage task conflicts (De Dreu and Van de Vliert, 1997) – as well as resolving (or avoiding) non-task conflict. And while collaboration does not guarantee a high-quality solution (e.g., the necessary resources might not be available), it increases the likelihood that a jointly beneficial solution will be found.

There are three fundamental steps in managing team conflict through collaboration. The first step is to identify the type of intra-team conflict. We distinguish between two general types – task and non-task. The second is to identify appropriate collaboration strategies. These strategies are general approaches to resolving disputes. We argue that collaboration is a key strategy, but it needs to be applied differently, depending on the type of dispute. The third step is to identify useful collaborative techniques. These techniques are ubiquitous – they can be used to manage both task and non-task conflict. We address each step below.

Identifying the Type of Intra-team Conflict

The first major principle in dealing with intra-team conflict collaboratively is to determine the type of conflict. We differentiate between two general types of conflict that differ in terms of the content being disputed: task or non-task.

Task conflicts

These involve disagreements among team members on performance-related activities. Some of these performance-related activities have to do with the actual task and others have to do with the process of doing the task or delegating resources and duties. *Task content conflicts* are disagreements among group members' ideas and opinions about the task being performed, such as disagreement regarding an organization's current hiring strategies or determining the information to include in an annual report. Task content conflicts include debates over facts (driven by data, evidence) or opinions (De Dreu, Harinck, and Van Vianen, 1999). *Task process conflicts* are about logistical and delegation issues such as how task accomplishment should proceed in the work unit, who's responsible for what, and how things should be delegated (Jehn, 1997).

Non-task conflicts

These are disagreements and incompatibilities among group members about personal issues that are not task-related. Non-task conflicts frequently reported are about social events, gossip, clothing preferences, political views, and hobbies (Jehn, 1997). Non-task conflicts include relationship conflicts, conflicts that are characterized by more personal and interpersonal concerns, and are more likely to affect group maintenance functions, such as cohesiveness, but can also interfere with task performance. Take a research and development team: when the four researchers disagree about data interpretation and the meaning of the results, they are experiencing task content conflict. If they argue about who is responsible for writing up the final report and who will make the presentation, they are having a task process conflict. Disagreements about the fastest route to work, the best automobile on the road, and the intelligence level of anyone who would take the bus (which one member does) are non-task conflicts.

Collaboration Strategies and Intra-team Conflict

While non-task conflicts that arise within the team setting are consistently negatively associated with decreased performance and member morale, disagreement of ideas within a group can be beneficial. We assert that the detrimental effect of non-task conflict can be minimized if collaboratively managed *outside* of the task setting and the beneficial effect of task conflict can be maximized if collaboratively managed *within* the task setting. That is, task conflict is optimally addressed directly by team members in the work setting, whereas non-task conflict is better managed off-line. Thus, the appropriate collaborative strategy depends on the type of conflict experienced.

Task conflict

Perceived and observed task conflicts addressed directly by the team can improve team performance (Jehn, 1997). Disagreements related to the task can improve group decision-making, strategic planning, top management team and general task performance. The increased number of opinions and critical evaluation enhance effectiveness. Consistent with theories of groupthink and decision-making, when members agree with other group members about concepts or actions without presenting dissenting viewpoints, superior alternatives may be overlooked and thus performance may be suboptimal (Janis, 1982). Putting pressure on dissenters, self-censorship, and collective justifications all associated with groupthink increase defective decision-making.

Task conflict within teams can improve decision quality and strategic planning (Amason and Schweiger, 1994; Cosier and Rose, 1977). The cognitive, task-focused aspect of conflict enhances the assessment of shared information and deliberate, careful assessment of alternatives. The useful give and take among members, the consultative interaction and problem-solving, and the increased information exchanged enhances performance.

Non-task conflict

While *direct* collaboration is effective for task conflict, it is less so for non-task conflict. Collaboration (or contention) over non-task issues takes much time away from task performance, thus reducing functioning and effectiveness (Murnighan and Conlon, 1991). However, collaboration *can* be used effectively to resolve many non-task conflicts when engaged off-line. Off-line discussions give team members opportunities to discuss non-task conflicts in a more private and personal forum. Without an audience, disputants should be less likely to posture and more likely to be open to the other party's point of view. Off-line discussions can be engaged directly by the disputants or with the help of others. Sometimes facilitation might be necessary to bring the disputants together and dampen negative emotions.

However, some non-task conflicts are better avoided. Non-task conflicts that have their roots in deeply held values and assumptions are often impossible to resolve. For example, if two team members disagree over abortion rights, getting at underlying interests will not resolve this dispute if the fundamental difference is a definition of when life begins. Thus, trying to get at true underlying interests for non-task conflicts may result in even more intractable disputes. When non-task conflicts have a low potential for resolution they are sometimes better avoided (DeDreu and Van Vianen, 1999; Druckman, 1994).

COLLABORATIVE TECHNIQUES

Collaboration is effective in managing conflict, task or non-task, in that it sets a positive, team-oriented tone for the group (Mintzberg, Dougherty, Jorgensen, and Westley, 1996). Through collaboration disagreements can be transformed into opportunities for joint gain. Collaboration allows team members to avoid unnecessary compromise or domination, and to use integration and synthesis to invent creative solutions (Mary Parker Follett as cited in Mintzberg et al., 1996). Negotiated conflicts result in more mutually beneficial (or "integrative") outcomes when the participants engage in more collaborative communications (Brett, Shapiro, and Lytle, 1998; Weingart, Hyder, and Prietula, 1996). The presence (versus absence) of collaborative communications positively influences the effect of task disagreement on teams' innovativeness (Lovelace, Shapiro, and Weingart, 1999).

Collaboration within teams can be fostered by techniques that fall into three categories: group atmosphere, group member characteristics, and team member behavior. These categories are interrelated. For example, certain team member behaviors (e.g., information exchange) will influence the group atmosphere (e.g., more trusting) and vice versa.

Group atmosphere

For a team to be collaborative, its atmosphere must support interdependence, reliance, trust, open communication, and collective efficacy. While a positive group atmosphere can be considered a precondition for effective collaboration, it will also improve as the group experiences successful collaborative events. In this way, norms are developed which perpetuate interdependence, reliance on, and respect for one another.

Create a team orientation. Creating a team orientation refers to framing the group's activities as belonging to the team rather than solely as a set of individual accomplishments. With a team orientation, there is a sense that although we are *each* responsible for our individual contributions to the group, "we" are *jointly* responsible for the group's final product. Team-oriented members take personal pride in the team's performance and feel personally successful when the team is successful. When team goals and individual goals support one another, teams that focus on a meta-goal, or team-goal are more likely to have constructive conflict management (Thatcher and Jehn, 1998). This is in contrast to the case where individuals focus *only* on their own contribution, claiming (or denying) responsibility for the overall group's performance. Consider a sports team analogy. A sports team in which each member is solely concerned with their own performance statistics can result in uncoordinated activity that is suboptimal for the team as a whole (imagine two receivers trying to catch a football, rather than one blocking a defender for the other).

Develop collective efficacy. Supportive of a team orientation is the collective efficacy of team members. Collective efficacy refers to perceptions that the team is able to perform the task (in this case, resolve the conflict) (Bandura, 1986). Without collective efficacy, team members will see the conflict as having low resolution potential, and will be unlikely to try to manage the conflict. Often what is most important in predicting high performance is that team members feel they have the capabilities to resolve the task and non-task conflicts at hand (Jehn, 1997).

Develop trust. A key component in collaborative approaches to conflict resolution is trust in team members. As defined in chapter 19 in this volume, trust is defined as confidence in or reliance on another team member in terms of their morality (e.g., honesty) and competence. Collaboration is characterized by high levels of interdependence, information exchange, and therefore high reliance among team members. This high inter-reliance results in the need to trust one another. Trust influences the willingness to share information and receive information as accurate (Carnevale and Lawler, 1986; Kimmel, Pruitt, Magenau, Konar-Goldband, and Carnevale, 1980). Trust also decreases the likelihood that task conflicts will be perceived as attacking or personal in nature (Simons and Peterson, 2000). Trust in a team is influenced by the trustworthiness of team members as well as team members' willingness to be trusting. Both of these factors will be influenced by the composition of the team as well as the norms for honest and reliable behavior within the group.

Open conflict communication norms. Collaboration requires open norms for the expression of task-related conflict. Conflict communication norms can either be open to a free exchange of concerns and dissent or discouraging and avoidant of those exchanges. If group members feel that it is appropriate and acceptable to discuss their differing opinions, disagreements are more likely to have a positive effect on group process and performance than if these disagreements are discouraged or avoided (Lovelace et al., 1999). The ideal culture for a group is to have conflict norms that will allow constructive, open task-related debates but not critical, personal attacks detrimental to performance. In that non-task conflict can interfere with task performance, it should be addressed off-line, or avoided altogether.

When conflict norms result in avoidance, such that task conflict is suppressed, the lines of communication will need to be opened for collaboration to be successful. Openness and trust must be nurtured within these teams (Simons and Peterson, 2000). Trust must be allowed to develop over time – through positive experiences group members will grow more comfortable engaging in collaboration. The team leader can play an important role in setting the norms for conflict communication in the team (Lovelace et al., 1999). In addition, providing the team with the collaborative skills through training can aid in successful conflict management.

Group member behavior

Collaboration is enacted through group member behavior. Thus it is important to identify the behaviors that constitute collaboration. We look to the integrative negotiation literature, which has identified *integration of interests* as a collaborative strategic approach for managing conflict. Integration of interests includes increasing the availability of resources (thus, "expanding the pie") as well as sharing in the distribution of those resources. The literature on integrative negotiation has identified a host of tactics that aid in the identification of opportunities for joint gain. We focus on three that are central to the process: exchange information, use packaging and trade-offs, and work to break the chain of conflict escalation. While the list below is not exhaustive, it does reflect current thinking in integrative negotiation and conflict resolution.

Exchange information. A key mechanism for enacting an integrative strategic approach involves the exchange of truthful information. Exchanging information is believed to increase insight into the other party's motivational structure and the probability that negotiators will find integrative agreements, if a zone of agreement exists (Pruitt, 1981; Putnam and Jones, 1982). The benefit of sharing information varies depending on the type of information that is shared and how it is used. Sharing factual information, like constraints or costs, can be used to merely inform the other party (a collaborative application) or to substantiate one's position in an attempt to persuade the other party (a less collaborative approach). Sharing information about preferences for a given issue (i.e., what you want and why you should have it your way) can be more confrontational in nature and does not necessarily improve the quality of an agreement (Weingart et al., 1996). In contrast, exchanging information about priorities across issues (i.e., the relative importance of the issues to a negotiator and why) represents a collaborative type of information exchange as it involves multiple issues and can facilitate trade-offs across issues (Pruitt and Lewis, 1975; Thompson, 1991). Sharing information about priorities across issues is central to the development of integrative solutions through trade-offs (Weingart, Bennett, and Brett, 1993).

Use packaging and trade-offs. It is not uncommon for discussions of multi-issue conflicts to progress one issue at a time – with the group resolving one issue before moving to the next. The problem with this approach is that trade-offs cannot be made across issues. Trade-offs occur when both parties make concessions on less important issues (to themselves) to gain advantage on another (Pruitt, 1981). This tactic is effective at reconciling interests when parties have differing priorities on issues and when each party gains more than they lose in the trade-off.

In order to make an effective trade-off team members must have some understanding of others' preferences and priorities. Team members can discover trade-offs by exchanging information about priorities. This is a relatively direct approach in which team members know their own priorities (what issues are most and least important to them) and are willing to exchange this information. When team members are unwilling to share this information (because they fear the other party might not reciprocate, putting themselves at an information disadvantage), effective trade-offs can be identified by exchanging multi-issue offers (i.e., packaging). When issues are packaged together, instead of being considered independently and sequentially, it is easier to arrange trades or concessions as negotiators search for packages that are mutually beneficial (Thompson, Mannix, and Bazerman, 1988; Weingart et al., 1993). Discovering trade-offs through the exchange of packaged offers is a more indirect method in that team members must infer others' priorities by stated package preferences.

Work to break the chain of conflict escalation. One of the most difficult aspects of a successful negotiation is trying to balance the cooperative and competitive components of mixed-motive negotiations (Lax and Sebenius, 1986). Once a conflict takes on a competitive or personal tone, it is very difficult to shift it to a more cooperative interaction, as the conflict can escalate into a destructive cycle. One way to break the chain of contentious behavior is to respond with integrative, collaborative responses (Brett et al.,1998; Putnam and Jones, 1982). Collaboration is then more likely to continue when that collaborative behavior is reciprocated than when it is not (Weingart, Prietula, Hyder, and Genovese, 1999). Another method for breaking conflict spirals is explicitly labeling the contentious reciprocation as unproductive during the interaction. When a conflict is contentious and one party identifies the process as such, the other party would be hesitant to continue in a contentious manner without appearing intransigent. Directly responding to a threat by identifying it ("Are you threatening me?") demonstrates that the threat was not effective and may cause the party making the threat to shift tactics or refocus onto the process (Brett et al., 1998).

Team member characteristics

Two team member characteristics influence collaboration in negotiation and team conflict settings. The first is a cognition and the second a motive. These individual-level characteristics influence the behavior engaged, and ultimately the team's atmosphere.

Non zero-sum assumption.   Parties to a conflict often assume that the situation is win–lose (Thompson and Hastie, 1990). That is, they assume that one person's gain is another person's equal loss on any given issue. This assumption interferes with the discovery of mutually beneficial agreements because they do not effectively search for non process task information and they do not engage in behaviors (e.g., trading off across issues) necessary to improve joint gain (Pinkley, Griffith, and Northcraft, 1995). In contrast, collaboration involves group members who assume that the conflict can be resolved to group members' mutual satisfaction.

Social motives.   Social motives, whether derived from an individual's disposition (i.e., social value orientation) or situational cues (i.e., motivational orientation), influence the level of collaboration in a group. Of the many social motives that have been studied in the literature, cooperation – a high concern for self *and* high concern for other – has been most closely associated with collaborative approaches. Groups composed of cooperatively oriented members tend to achieve more mutually beneficial agreements than individual-istically oriented groups (i.e., groups comprised of members who are only concerned about their own outcomes) (Weingart et al., 1993). Groups that don't begin with all cooperative members, but include more cooperative members by the end of a meeting, are more likely to reach agreement (Weingart and Brett, 1999).

Social motives influence quality of agreements through their effect on group member behavior (Weingart et al., 1993). Cooperatively motivated team members tend to engage in more integrative tactics (see above) and fewer contentious tactics (e.g., threats, substantiation of position, power tactics) than do individualistically motivated team members. Team members who are solely self-interested often promote a feeling of competition and display more negative emotions. By perpetuating the conflict, individualistic team members can instill a lack of collective efficacy in others.

Social motives and a team orientation in the group's atmosphere are closely interrelated. Social value orientations (dispositional social motives) of individual team members should influence the ease with which a team orientation can be established. A team orientation will, in turn, send cues to team members, influencing their motivational orientation (i.e., situationally derived source of social motives).

THE ROLE OF NEGATIVE EMOTIONS

While many other emotions can be felt during a conflict episode (e.g., guilt, sadness, joy, delight; see Plutchik, 1962; Russell, 1978, for overviews), frustration and anger are those most often demonstrated in an organizational setting. Behavioral manifestations of emotion include yelling, crying, banging fists, slamming doors, and having an angry tone.

When negative emotions run high, collaboration between the disputants might not be possible. Collaboration requires a high level of interdependence. Team members that feel animosity, frustration, anger or distrust are not likely to be willing to rely on one another. Instead mediation by an outside party or co-team members might be necessary to sort through the negative emotions and ascribe more positive attributions to other team members' behavior. Team members who are not emotionally inflamed might take the disputants off-site, such as into a social setting for drinks, or a walk, where they can re-establish their interpersonal bonds and discuss their concerns. If the negative emotions are so inflamed among two members that they are not willing to talk, we recommend having two members who are closest to each of the adversaries talk, collaboratively, with each of the parties. Then the two facilitators (i.e., third and fourth parties) can talk and try to bring all four together. Finally, a trusted outsider to the team (e.g., manager or colleague) could help high negative emotion teams get to the point where they can engage in collaboration and constructive conflict without assuming the worst of others. It is also possible to restructure the group to separate the two opposing parties or factions, but we recommend this only as a last resort, as we assume that the specific team membership is critical to the specific task at hand.

CASE STUDIES

In order to illustrate the use of collaboration in teams, we present two case examples of team conflict: one managed ineffectively, the other effectively. The first provides an example of ineffective conflict management – the team lacks a common goal, team members are more concerned about satisfying their own concerns rather than finding solutions that are optimal for the team, and as a result get caught in conflict spirals. The second example shows how another team working on the same task is able to manage their conflicts using collaborative strategies and tactics.

These examples are compilations of conflicts we have observed in our research on teams in organizations. Both examples involve crossfunctional product development teams and focus on task conflict. These teams comprise many parties (including marketing representatives and suppliers), but here we will focus on two central parties – designers and engineers. The team's goal is to design a high-quality, low-cost automobile that will meet customers' preferences and desires. Each sub-group has its own concerns. The designers are responsible for the brand image and appearance of the car. The engineers are responsible for the functioning of the car and its components and have primary responsibility for keeping costs within budget. Unfortunately, these interests are not always in line with one another. A design change championed by the designers often necessitates a change in engineering design or increased costs. Or a product attribute desired by the customer (according to marketing) might not be feasible within design, cost, or function constraints. The use of teams in this context allows for representatives from each domain to jointly reach decisions that involve conflicting preferences.

In contrast to more typical product design approaches that treat the process in a more linear fashion (design, engineer, then market), *crossfunctional product development (CPD) teams* have the potential for input from the different sub-groups when making decisions. Joint decisions are more likely to reflect the interests and concerns of all parties involved. When crossfunctional teams are truly integrated – that is, they work as a collaborative team – they experience fewer design iterations and shortened product development cycles (Ulrich and Eppinger, 1995). *Integrated product development (IPD) teams* also produce higher-quality decisions – by reflecting the interests of all relevant parties, the decisions are less likely to require alteration or renegotiations (Cagan and Vogel, 1999).

While the potential for high-quality decisions increases, so does the potential for conflict. Differences must be tackled head on. Underlying assumptions must be surfaced, conflicting interests must be identified – "hidden agendas" brought out in the open. Whether these conflicts cripple the team or are leveraged into high-quality decisions depends on how the team manages this conflict.

Example 1: dysfunctional crossfunctional product development (CPD) team

Consider a crossfunctional product development team designing a subsystem of a new model of an automobile. This team is responsible for the design of the car's interior. They are at mid-stage in the design process. Many decisions have been made about the design and functionality of the interior. Models have been developed and general layouts for components (e.g., the console, instrument panel, etc.) have been determined. Engineering feels it has worked out most of the major functionality issues and was able to remain within budget, but just barely. Then design comes in with a change in styling. In order to maintain brand identity, the shape and flow from the instrument panel to the console needs to change. Engineering is furious. Implications for this change are large. The changes will require a redesign of the placement of internal components within the instrument panel and console. To make these changes will be costly – it will require money that is not there. Design is indifferent to these concerns – they believe that the aesthetic component is what sells the car – and their job is to make sure the automobile sends a coherent message to the customer.

Each group sees the problem from its own perspective and neither is willing to give ground. Engineering tells design, "it can't be done." Design is tired of engineering's "no can do" attitude and continues to put pressure on engineering until engineering is willing to "make it work." Several meetings occur in which engineering and design try to convince the other on the merits of their positions. Arguments get heated, tempers flare. Little progress is made. After many heated discussions, a compromise solution is reached which moves away from the design intent, compromises functionality, and increases cost.

This conflict can be characterized as a task conflict with low resolution potential (i.e., team members have low collective efficacy). It involved an important aspect of their task performance and needed to be resolved, but neither side believed they had the ability to resolve the conflict. There was no sense of a team orientation – rather than focus on developing the best product, each side focused on its own concerns. Conflict norms were more toward blaming and attacking than listening and building. Negative emotions were evidenced. What transpired was a contentious conflict, pitting "us" against "them," resulting in a solution that neither party was especially happy with. Was there another way out of this conflict? What could the team have done to find a better solution?

Example 2: collaborative integrated product development (IPD) team

Consider another design team working on the same component. This team faces the same change in styling. But this time, design presents the change in terms of a shared problem – they take responsibility for the change and are willing to consider its implications. Engineering is then willing to collaborate with design to try to make the change possible. The IPD team has a frank discussion about the implications of the change. Design tries to come up with less expensive and less disruptive ways to change the console and instrument panel while maintaining design intent. Engineering tries to develop innovative ways to fit the internal components in the new space. They also start looking for additional sources of funding for the change from the overall vehicle budget. Some discussions grow heated, but frustration is focused on the problem rather than one another, and is quickly dispersed. Several potential solutions are developed. A dominant option emerges which includes a slight design modification that provides adequate space for a key component and some additional funding is found.

This conflict situation differed in several ways from the previous example. While the conflict was as important to the IPD team as the first team, collective efficacy was high. Both engineers and designers believed a solution was possible. They viewed themselves as a team tackling a common problem. Conflict norms supported open information exchange and constructive discussions. Emotions remained under control. An integrative solution evolved because the entire IPD team "owned" the problem and worked together, collaboratively, to develop a solution. They trusted one another's expertise, motives, and information in a way that allowed them to reach a mutually satisfactory solution. A team orientation, trust in one another, and a belief that a jointly beneficial solution was possible motivated the team to search together for a solution. This search involved sharing information, creativity, some trade-offs, and an effort to avoid turning task frustration into personal attacks. In addition to a high-quality agreement, this successful conflict resolution process reinforced the team's belief in its ability to solve problems and will make the team more willing to tackle similar problems in the future.

SUMMARY

What differentiates these teams is the use of a collaborative approach to making decisions and resolving conflict. The first team's conflict was very contentious, plagued by *fixed-pie perceptions* and *individualistic orientations* – an "us versus them" framing of the problem. Much of the conflict revolved around ownership of the problem – engineering versus design. In contrast, the collaborative team *shared ownership* of the problem and developed solutions that recognized the concerns and interests of all parties involved. They *worked as a team* rather than a collection of individuals with their own concerns. The first team was not willing to openly *share information* nor did they *trust* the information that was received. The information exchange that did occur served the purpose of bolstering a priori positions. As a result, each side recognized the potential bias in information received. In contrast, the collaborative team used information to develop understanding and potential solutions. Because *motives were cooperative*, it was easier to *trust* the information provided. Finally, where the first team was very *positional* in making demands ("my way is the only way") resulting in a stalemate, the collaborative team used *creativity and trade-offs* to develop potential solutions. What resulted for the non-collaborative team was a time-consuming, contentious, and sometimes emotional and personal conflict and an unsatisfactory solution. The collaborative team was able to succeed because it managed the conflict by focusing on team goals, exchanging truthful information, developing trust, and using trade-offs and creativity to find integrative solutions that satisfied both engineering's and design's concerns. Collaboration proved to be an invaluable tool for managing conflict for this team – as it does for many others.

REFERENCES

Amason, A. (1996). Distinguishing effects of functional and dysfunctional conflict on strategic decision making: Resolving a paradox for top management teams. *Academy of Management Journal*, 39, 123–48.

Amason, A., and Schweiger, D. M. (1994). Resolving the paradox of conflict, strategic decision making, and organizational performance. *International Journal of Conflict Management*, 5, 239–53.

Bandura, A. (1986). *Social foundations of thought and action*. Englewood Cliffs, NJ: Prentice-Hall.

Brett, J., Shapiro, D., and Lytle, A. (1998). Breaking the bonds of reciprocity in negotiations. *Academy of Management Journal*, 41, 410–24.

Cagan, J., and Vogel C. (1999). Clarifying the fuzzy front end of new product development: Teaching engineering and industrial design students ethnographic methods to foster interdisciplinary inquiry into consumer needs. *Proceedings of 1999 ASME Design Engineering Technical Conferences: Design Theory and Methodology Conference* (DETC99/DTM–8786). Las Vegas, NV.

Carnevale, P., and Lawler, E. (1986). Time pressure and the development of integrative agreements in bilateral negotiations. *Journal of Conflict Resolution*, 30, 639–59.

Cosier, R., and Rose, G. (1977). Cognitive conflict and goal conflict effects on task performance. *Organizational Behavior and Human Performance*, 19, 378–91.

De Dreu, C. K. W., Harinck, F., and Van Vianen, A. E. M. (1999). Conflict and performance in groups and organizations. *International Review of Industrial and Organizational Psychology*, 14, 369–414.

De Dreu, C. K. W., and Van de Vliert (eds.) (1997). *Using conflict in organizations*. London: Sage.

De Dreu, C. K. W., and Van Vianen, A. E. M. (1999). Responses to relationship conflict and team effectiveness. Unpublished manuscript, University of Amsterdam.

Druckman, D. (1994). Determinants of compromising behavior in negotiation. *Journal of Conflict Resolution*, 38, 507–56.

Haskins, M. E., Liedtka, J., and Rosenblum, J. (1998). Beyond teams: Toward an ethic of collaboration. *Organizational Dynamics*, Spring, 34–50.

Janis, I. L. (1982). *Victims of groupthink*, 2nd edn. Boston: Houghton-Mifflin.

Jehn, K. (1995). A multimethod examination of the benefits and detriments of intragroup conflict. *Administrative Science Quarterly*, 40, 256–82.

Jehn, K. (1997). A qualitative analysis of conflict types and dimensions in organizational groups. *Administrative Science Quarterly*, 42, 530–57.

Kimmel, M. J., Pruitt, D. G., Magenau, J. M., Konar-Goldband, E., and Carnevale, P. J. D. (1980). Effects of trust, aspiration, and gender on negotiation tactics. *Journal of Personality and Social Psychology*, 38, 9–23.

Lax, D. A., and Sebenius, J. K. (1986). *The manager as negotiator: Bargaining for cooperation and competitive gain*. New York: Free Press.

Lovelace, K., Shapiro, D. L., and Weingart, L. R. (1999). Maximizing crossfunctional new product teams' innovativeness and constraint adherence: A conflict communications perspective. Submitted for publication.

Mintzberg, H., Dougherty, D., Jorgensen, J., and Westley F. (1996). Some surprising things about collaboration: Knowing how people connect makes it work better. *Organizational Dynamics*, Spring, 60–71.

Murnighan, J., and Conlon, D. (1991). The dynamics of intense work groups: A study of British string quartets. *Administrative Science Quarterly*, 36, 165–86.

Pinkley, R. L., Griffith, T. L., and Northcraft, G. B. (1995). "Fixed pie" à la mode: Information availability, information processing, and the negotiation of suboptimal agreements. *Organizational Behavior & Human Decision Processes*, 62, 101–12.

Plutchik, R. (1962). *Emotions: Facts, theories, and a new model*. New York: Random House.

Pruitt, D. (1981). *Negotiation behavior*. New York: Academic Press.

Pruitt, D., and Lewis, S. A. (1975). Development of integrative solutions in bilateral negotiation. *Journal of Personality & Social Psychology*, 31, 621–33.

Putnam, L. L., and Jones, T. S. (1982). Reciprocity in negotiations: An analysis of bargaining interaction. *Communication Monographs*, 49, 171–91.

Rempel, J. K., Holmes, J. G., and Zanna, M. P. (1985). Trust in close relationships. *Journal of Personality and Social Psychology*, 49, 95–112.

Russell, J. (1978). Evidence of convergent validity on the dimensions of affect. *Journal of Personality and Social Psychology*, 37, 345–56.

Simons, T. L., and Peterson, R. S. (2000). Task conflict and relationship conflict in top management teams: The pivotal role of intragroup trust. *Journal of Applied Psychology*, 85, 102–11.

Thatcher, S., and Jehn, K. (1998). A model of group diversity profiles and categorization processes in bicultural organizational teams. In Neale, M. A., Mannix, E. A., and Gruenfeld, D. H. (eds.), *Research on managing groups and teams, Vol. 1: Composition* (pp. 1–20). Stamford, CT: JAI Press.

Thompson, L. L. (1991). Information exchange in negotiation. *Journal of Experimental Social Psychology*, 27, 161–79.

Thompson, L., and Hastie, R. (1990). Social perception in negotiation. *Organizational Behavior and Human Decision Processes*, 47, 98–123.

Thompson, L. L., Mannix, E. A., and Bazerman, M. H. (1988). Group negotiation: Effects of decision rule, agenda, and aspiration. *Journal of Personality & Social Psychology*, 54, 86–95.

Ulrich, K. T., and Eppinger, S. D. (1995). *Product design and development*. New York: McGraw-Hill.

Weingart, L. R., Bennett, R. J., and Brett, J. M. (1993). The impact of consideration of issues and motivational orientation on group negotiation process and outcome. *Journal of Applied Psychology*, 78, 504–17.

Weingart, L. R. and Brett, J. M. (1999). Mixed motivational orientations in negotiating groups: Convergence and reaching agreement. Submitted for publication.

Weingart, L. R., Hyder, E. B., and Prietula, M. J. (1996). Knowledge matters: The effect of tactical descriptions on negotiation behavior and outcome. *Journal of Personality and Social Psychology*, 70, 1205–17.

Weingart, L. R., Prietula, M. J., Hyder, E., and Genovese, C. (1999). Knowledge and the sequential processes of negotiation: A Markov chain analysis of response-in-kind. *Journal of Experimental Social Psychology*, 35, 366–93.

Part VI

LEADERSHIP

17 Use Power Effectively
    GARY YUKL

18 Lead through Vision and Values
    MARKUS HAUSER AND ROBERT J. HOUSE

19 Foster Trust through Competence, Honesty, and Integrity
    SABRINA SALAM

17

Use Power Effectively

GARY YUKL

INTRODUCTION

One of the most important determinants of managerial effectiveness is success in influencing people. Effective managers influence subordinates to perform the work effectively, they influence peers to provide support and assistance, and they influence superiors to provide resources and approval of necessary changes. The concept of "power" has been very useful for understanding how people are able to influence each other in organizations (Mintzberg, 1983; Pfeffer, 1981, 1992). Power is usually defined as the capacity to influence people and events. It is a flexible concept that can be used in many different ways. For example, power has been used to explain the influence of groups on organization decisions, and the influence of one organization on another. In this chapter the focus is on the potential of one individual (called the "agent") to influence the behavior and attitudes of other individuals (called "target persons") in the same organization.

An agent will have more power over some people than over others and more influence for some types of issues than for others. Power is a dynamic variable that changes as conditions change. A person's power can increase or decrease dramatically over a relatively short period of time. Moreover, there are different types of power, and an agent may have more of some types than of others. This chapter will identify different types of individual power and describe effective ways to exercise each type.

The manner in which power is enacted usually involves influence behavior by the agent. Specific types of influence behavior are called influence tactics. This chapter will examine several influence tactics commonly used in organizations. The relative effectiveness of the various influence tactics will be described and the conditions for their successful use will be identified.

TYPES OF POWER

Behavioral scientists usually differentiate between position power and personal power. Position power is potential influence derived from one's position in the organization. This type of power is usually specified and limited by organizational policies, formal reward systems, legal constraints, and union contracts. Four specific types of position power are legitimate authority, reward power, coercive power, and information power (French and Raven, 1959; Yukl and Falbe, 1991). Personal power is potential influence derived from agent characteristics. Two specific types of personal power are expert power and referent power.

The research on power and influence is still too limited to provide clear and unequivocal guidelines on the best way to exercise each type of power (Yukl, 1998). Nevertheless, by drawing upon a diverse literature in the social sciences that includes research on power, leader behavior, motivation, communication, counseling, supervision, and conflict resolution, it is possible to develop some tentative guidelines. This section of the chapter will describe specific types of power and the conditions for exercising each type of power effectively.

Legitimate power

Legitimate power is derived from authority, which is the perceived right of the agent to influence specified aspects of the target person's behavior. The underlying basis for legitimate power is the agreement by members of an organization to comply with rules and legitimate requests in return for the benefits of membership (March and Simon, 1958). The conditions for continued membership may be set forth in a formal, legal contract, but the agreement to comply with legitimate authority is usually an implicit mutual understanding. Legitimate power is strengthened by an internalized value among people that it is proper to obey authority figures, show respect for the law, and follow tradition.

The amount of legitimate power reflects the chain of command and is usually much stronger in relation to subordinates than in relation to peers, superiors, or outsiders. However, even when the agent has no direct authority over a target person (e.g., a peer), the agent may have the legitimate right to make requests for necessary information, supplies, support services, technical advice, and assistance in carrying out interrelated tasks. The scope of authority for a position occupant is often specified in writing by documents (e.g., the job description, the employment contract, organization bylaws), but even when such documentation exists, there usually remains considerable ambiguity about an individual's scope of authority (Davis, 1968).

Authority is usually exercised by making a request or command orally or in writing. A polite request is more effective than an arrogant demand, because it does not emphasize a status gap or imply target dependence on the agent. Use of a polite request is especially important for people who are likely to be sensitive about status differentials and authority relationships, such as someone who is older than the agent or who is a peer rather than a direct subordinate.

Making a polite request does not imply that the agent should plead or appear apologetic about the request. To do so risks the impression that the request is not worthy or legitimate, and it may give the impression that compliance is not really expected (Sayles, 1979). A legitimate request should be made in a firm, confident manner. In an emergency situation, it is more important to be assertive than polite. A direct order by a leader in a command tone of voice is sometimes necessary to shock subordinates into immediate action in an emergency. In this type of situation, subordinates associate confident, firm direction with expertise as well as authority (Mulder, Ritsema van Eck, and de Jong, 1970). To express doubts or appear confused risks the loss of influence over subordinates.

Compliance with a request is more likely if it is perceived to be within the agent's scope of authority. A request that appears to be illegitimate is likely to be ignored or otherwise resisted, especially if the requested activity is also tedious, dangerous, or unpleasant. The issue of legitimacy is likely to be raised for unusual requests and for requests made to people over whom the agent has no direct authority. If there is any doubt about the right to make a request, its legitimacy should be verified by the agent.

Reward power

Reward power involves control over desirable resources and rewards. This type of power is greatest when the target is highly dependent on the agent for attaining the reward and cannot get it any other way. Reward power stems in part from formal authority. The authority to allocate rewards to others varies greatly across organizations and from one type of position to another within the same organization. The higher a person's position in the authority hierarchy of the organization, the more control over scarce resources the person is likely to have. Reward power over subordinates is usually much stronger than reward power over peers or superiors.

One form of reward power over subordinates is influence over their compensation, benefits, and career progress. Most managers are authorized to give pay increases, bonuses, or other economic incentives to deserving subordinates. Reward power is derived also from control over other tangible benefits such as a promotion, a better job, a better work schedule, a larger operating budget, a larger expense account, formal recognition (e.g., awards, commendations), and status symbols such as a larger office or a reserved parking space.

Reward power is also a source of influence over peers who depend on the agent for resources, funds, information, or assistance not otherwise provided by the formal authority system. Trading of favors needed to accomplish task objectives is a common form of influence among peers in organizations, and research indicates that it is important for the success of middle managers (Cohen and Bradford, 1991; Kaplan, 1984; Kotter, 1985). Access to a powerful person inside or outside the organization also provides an opportunity for an agent to seek favors for others who lack such access, thereby increasing the agent's reward power.

Upward reward power of subordinates is very limited in most organizations. Subordinates seldom have any direct influence over the reputation and career of their boss, unless the organization relies on ratings by subordinates to evaluate its managers. Nevertheless, subordinates usually have some indirect influence. If they perform well and speak favorably about the boss, his or her reputation will be enhanced (Mechanic,

1962). Occasionally subordinates also have reward power based on their ability to acquire resources outside of the formal authority system of the organization. For example, a department chairperson in a state university was able to obtain discretionary funds from grants and contracts, and these funds were used as a basis for influencing the decisions made by the college dean, whose own discretionary funds were very limited.

Reward power is most commonly exercised with an explicit or implicit promise to give the target person something under the agent's control for carrying out a request or performing a task. Compliance is most likely if the reward is something valued by the target person, and the agent is perceived as a credible source of the reward. Thus, it is essential to determine what rewards are valued by the people one wants to influence, and agent credibility should not be risked by making unrealistic promises or failing to deliver on a promise after compliance occurs.

Even when the conditions are favorable for using rewards, they are more likely to result in compliance rather than commitment. A promised reward is unlikely to motivate someone to put forth extra effort beyond what is required to complete the task. The target person may be tempted to neglect aspects of the task not included in the specification of performance criteria or aspects not easily monitored by the agent.

Rewards may result in resistance rather than compliance if used in a manipulative manner. The power to give or withhold rewards may cause resentment among people who dislike being dependent on the whims of a powerful authority figure, or who believe that the agent is manipulating them to his or her own advantage. Even when the reward is attractive, resistance may occur if the reward is seen as a bribe to get the target person to do something improper or unethical.

Coercive power

Another related source of power is control over punishments and the capacity to prevent someone from obtaining desired rewards. Compliance is motivated primarily by fear and is more likely if the agent is perceived as willing and able to punish the target person. The formal authority system of an organization usually specifies the legitimate use of punishment, which varies greatly across different types of organizations.

Coercive power is usually much greater in relation to subordinates than in relation to peers or superiors. Coercive power is derived from the authority of a manager to punish subordinates for violation of rules and policies, or failure to comply with legitimate orders and requests. Many different forms of punishment may be available, including dismissal, suspension, demotion, reassignment to a less desirable job, or a decrease in pay or benefits. However, the use of coercive power over subordinates is limited by the counterpower subordinates have over their leader. When leaders are tempted to use coercion on a large scale against followers, it undermines their authority and creates a hostile opposition seeking to restrict their power or remove them from office (Blau, 1956).

Opportunities for coercion of peers are usually very limited. A person can threaten to withhold future cooperation or complain to the superior of a peer who refuses to carry out legitimate requests. Sometimes a manager of one sub-unit has the authority to reject the products or plans of another sub-unit, and this authority also provides some coercive power. However, since mutual dependencies usually exist in lateral relations between managers of different sub-units, coercion is likely to elicit retaliation and escalate into a conflict that benefits neither party.

Upward coercive power is also very limited in most organizations, but subordinates often have more of this type of counterpower than they realize. It is possible for them to damage the reputation of the boss by restricting production, sabotaging operations, initiating grievances, holding demonstrations, or making complaints to higher management (Mechanic, 1962). In organizations with elected leaders, if enough subordinates want to remove a leader from office, they usually have sufficient power to do so.

Coercive power is invoked by a threat or warning that the target person will suffer undesirable consequences for noncompliance with a request, rule, or policy. The threat may be explicit, or it may be only a hint that the person will be sorry for failing to do what the agent wants. The likelihood of compliance is greatest when the threat is perceived to be credible, and the target person strongly desires to avoid the threatened punishment. Sometimes it is necessary to establish credibility by demonstrating the ability to cause unpleasant consequences for the target person. However, even a credible threat may be unsuccessful if the target person refuses to be intimidated or believes that a way can be found to avoid compliance without being detected by the agent.

It is best to avoid using coercion except when absolutely necessary, because it is difficult to use and likely to result in undesirable side effects. Coercion often arouses anger or resentment, and it may result in retaliation. In work organizations, the most appropriate use of coercion is to deter behavior detrimental to the organization, such as illegal activities, theft, violation of safety rules, reckless acts that endanger others, and direct disobedience of legitimate requests. Coercion is not likely to result in commitment, but when used skillfully in an appropriate situation, there is a reasonably good chance that it will result in compliance.

Control over information

Access to information and control over its distribution provide another source of power in organizations. Some positions are strategically located in the communication network of an organization, and such positions can provide exclusive access to vital information and control over its distribution (Pfeffer, 1981).

Control over information makes it easier to interpret events for people in a way that serves the agent's interests. It is easier to cover up mistakes and poor decisions, or to delay their discovery. The impression of agent expertise can be heightened by exaggerated reports of successful performance. People in leadership positions often have sufficient control over the distribution of information to keep subordinates dependent and make it difficult for them to challenge the leader's decisions.

Control over the upward flow of information can be used to influence decisions made by superiors (Mechanic, 1962; Pettigrew, 1972). The agent supplies information that biases the target's perception of the problem and evaluation of alternatives. For example, a manager was able to influence the selection of a computer by systematically providing the board of directors with information that favored one option and discredited others (Pettigrew, 1972).

Information power is also available in a boundary-role position in which a person has primary responsibility for dealing with outsiders who are important for the continued prosperity and survival of the organization. For example, when consumer preferences are changing rapidly, a person who has the contacts with key customers is likely to have considerable information power in the organization.

Expert power

Expert power is perceived expertise in solving problems and performing task activities (French and Raven, 1959). This type of power can be acquired by demonstrating competence, such as by making decisions or initiating changes that prove successful, or by giving advice or making predictions that prove to be correct. Expertise is a source of power only if others are dependent on the person for advice and assistance. The more important a problem is to the target person, the greater the power derived by the agent from possessing the necessary expertise to solve it. Dependency is increased when the target person cannot easily find another source of advice besides the agent (Hickson, Hinings, Lee, Schneck, and Pennings, 1971; Patchen, 1974).

Expert power depends to a large extent on the perception of others that the agent has unique expertise to solve important problems for them. Sometimes people over-estimate the agent's expertise, and the agent gains more power than is warranted. Sometimes expert power generalizes beyond the specific type of problem or task for which the person has special skills or knowledge. For example, a person who is skilled in conducting market surveys may also be considered an expert in designing new products, even though this person actually has little technical skill in product design. In the short run, perceived expertise is more important than real expertise, and some people are able to gain influence from pretending to have special expertise. However, over time, as the agent's knowledge is put to the test, target perceptions of the agent's expertise are likely to become more accurate.

When the agent has a lot of expert power and is trusted as a reliable source of information and advice, the target person may carry out a request without receiving any explanation for it. One example is a patient who takes medicine prescribed by a doctor without knowing much about the medicine. Another example is an investor who purchases stocks recommended by a financial consultant without knowing much about the companies that issued the stocks. It is rare to possess this much expert power. In most cases, the agent must support a proposal or request by making logical arguments and presenting evidence that appears credible. Successful influence depends on the leader's credibility and persuasive communication skills in addition to technical knowledge and analytical ability. Proposals or requests should be made in a clear, confident manner, and the agent should avoid making contradictory statements or vacillating between inconsistent positions.

Expert power is based on a knowledge differential between the agent and the target person, but the very existence of such a differential can cause problems if the agent is not careful about the way expert power is exercised. An agent who flaunts superior expertise may elicit resistance, especially if the target person is a peer or superior in the organization. In the process of presenting rational arguments, some people lecture in an arrogant, condescending manner, thereby conveying the impression that the listener is ignorant. In their efforts to sell a proposal, some people fire a steady stream of arguments, rudely interrupting any attempted replies and dismissing any objections or concerns without serious consideration. Even when the agent is acknowledged to have more expertise, the target person usually has some relevant information, ideas, and concerns that should be considered.

Referent power

Referent power is derived from the desire of others to please an agent toward whom they have strong feelings of affection, admiration, and loyalty (French and Raven, 1959). People are usually willing to do special favors for a friend, and they are more likely to carry out requests made by someone they greatly admire. The strongest form of referent power involves the influence process called personal identification. A person who identifies with an agent is usually willing to make great sacrifices to gain and maintain the agent's approval and acceptance. The target person is likely to do what the agent asks, imitate the agent's behavior, and develop attitudes similar to those expressed by the agent.

Referent power is usually greater for someone who is friendly, attractive, charming, and trustworthy. This type of power is increased by showing concern for the needs and feelings of others, demonstrating trust and respect, and treating people fairly. However, to achieve and maintain strong referent power usually requires more than just flattery, favors, and charm. Referent power ultimately depends on the agent's character and integrity. Over time, actions speak louder than words, and someone who tries to appear friendly but manipulates and exploits people will lose referent power. Integrity is demonstrated by being truthful, expressing a consistent set of values, acting in a way that is consistent with one's espoused values, taking personal risks to promote and defend important values, and carrying out promises and agreements.

Referent power is an important source of influence over subordinates, peers, and superiors, but it has limitations. A request based solely on referent power should be commensurate with the extent of the target person's loyalty and friendship toward the agent. Some things are simply too much to ask, given the nature of the relationship. When requests are extreme or made too frequently, the target person may feel exploited. The result of such behavior may be to undermine the relationship and reduce the agent's referent power.

Strong referent power will tend to increase the agent's influence over the target person even without any explicit effort by the agent to invoke this power. When there is a strong bond of love or friendship, it may be sufficient merely to ask the target person to do something. When referent power is not this strong, it may be necessary to invoke the salience of the relationship by making a personal appeal (an influence tactic described later in this chapter).

Another way to exercise referent power is through "role modeling." A person who is well liked and admired can have considerable influence over others by setting an example of proper and desirable behavior for them to imitate. When identification is strong, imitation is likely to occur even without any conscious intention by the agent. Because people also imitate undesirable behavior in someone they admire, it is important to be aware of the examples one sets.

How Much Power Is Needed?

Research shows that power is related to leadership effectiveness in complex ways. Effective leaders develop a considerable amount of expert and referent power, and they rely more on this personal power than on position power to influence people (Yukl, 1998). Nevertheless, some position power is usually necessary to accomplish the work. Without sufficient authority to reward competent subordinates, make necessary changes, and punish chronic troublemakers, it is difficult to develop a high-performing group or organization.

How much position and personal power is necessary will depend in part on what one seeks to accomplish. More power is needed to implement major changes in an organization, especially when there is strong opposition to change. In this difficult situation, a leader needs sufficient personal power to convince people that change is desirable, and sufficient position power to overcome the opposition and buy time to demonstrate that the proposed changes are feasible and effective.

Although some position power is needed by leaders to carry out their responsibilities, a person who has a great deal of position power may be tempted to rely on it too much instead of making an effort to develop and use expert and referent power. The notion that power corrupts is especially relevant for position power. Leaders with strong position power are more likely to perceive subordinates as objects of manipulation, devalue their worth, maintain more social distance from them, used rewards and punishments more often, and attribute the cause of subordinate achievements to the leader's power rather than to the intrinsic motivation and voluntary efforts of subordinates (Kipnis, 1974). Thus, a moderate amount of position power is probably optimal in most situations, rather than too much or too little (Yukl, 1998).

Extreme amounts of personal power can also corrupt a person. A leader with substantial expert and referent power may be tempted to act in ways that will eventually lead to failure (McClelland, 1975; Zaleznik, 1970). Surrounded by adoring supporters, a leader may begin to believe that he or she has a monopoly on wisdom and expertise. Thus, although it is desirable for a leader to develop strong personal power, it is also desirable for followers to retain some influence over key decisions. Effective leaders create relationships in which they have strong influence over subordinates but are also receptive to influence from them. These leaders consult with subordinates and encourage them to participate in making important decisions for the work unit.

Exercising Power

Up to now the discussion has involved the general use of power. However, when describing the exercise of power, it is usually more meaningful to focus on specific influence attempts. The success of an influence attempt is a matter of degree, but it is helpful to differentiate among three levels of success. Commitment means the person is enthusiastic about the request and makes a maximum effort to do it effectively. Compliance means that the person is indifferent about the request and makes only a minimum effort. Resistance means the person is opposed to carrying out the request and tries to avoid doing it. Commitment is desirable for requests that require the person to take initiative in dealing with problems and to be persistent in the face of setbacks and difficulties. Compliance is often sufficient for a simple, routine type of request.

As noted earlier, a common form of influence behavior in organizations is to make a "simple request" based on legitimate power. This form of influence is most likely to be successful if the request is reasonable, it is clearly relevant for the mission of the agent's work unit, it is something the target person knows how to do, and it does not jeopardize the target person's own job performance. However, even when a simple request is perceived to be legitimate, it often results in subordinate compliance rather than commitment. When the request involves actions perceived by the target to be unpleasant, unnecessary, or detrimental, the reaction to a simple request is likely to be resistance.

Specific influence tactics are usually necessary to gain commitment for requests not initially considered by the target person to be important and feasible. Over the past twenty years, several researchers have attempted to identify distinct types of influence tactics used by individuals in organizations (e.g., Kipnis, Schmidt, and Wilkinson, 1980; Schilit and Locke, 1982; Yukl and Tracey, 1992). This section of the chapter describes ten proactive influence tactics that are relevant for understanding effective influence in organizations. Each tactic will be explained briefly, and the conditions favoring its use will be described.

Legitimating tactics

When authority is ambiguous or legitimacy in doubt, an agent may use a legitimating tactic to establish the legitimacy of a request or command. Examples of legitimating tactics include providing evidence of prior precedent, showing consistency with organizational policies and rules, and showing consistency with professional role expectations. Another legitimating tactic is to indicate that the request was approved by higher management or someone else with proper authority. Sometimes the legitimacy of a request or command can be verified by documentation such as written rules, policies, charters, contracts, plans, job descriptions, or memos from authority figures.

Rational persuasion

With rational persuasion, the agent presents logical arguments and factual evidence that a proposal or request is important and feasible. In the most common form of rational persuasion, the agent emphasizes the potential benefits for the organization. This form of rational persuasion is appropriate when the target person shares the same task objectives as the agent but does not recognize that the agent's proposal is the best way to attain the objectives. On the other hand, if the agent and target person have incompatible objectives, this type of rational persuasion is unlikely to be successful for obtaining commitment or even compliance. Thus, it is usually advisable to check first for agreement on objectives before using this influence tactic.

Another form of rational persuasion is to emphasize the benefits of a request or proposal for the target person as an individual. The agent may explain how a request will further the target person's career, improve the person's skills, or make the person's job easier. Unlike exchange, the agent is not offering to give the target something, but is only pointing out that a proposed course of action will help get the target person something he or she wants.

An agent's technical knowledge is the source of facts and arguments used to build a persuasive case. However, in addition to facts and evidence, a persuasive case usually includes some opinions or inferences that the agent asks others to accept at face value because there is insufficient evidence to verify them. Thus, influence derived from rational persuasion is greater when the agent is perceived to be credible and trustworthy. Expert power, information power, and referent power can all enhance the effectiveness of rational persuasion. Finally, an agent needs considerable skill in persuasive speaking to present a case in a way that will have the maximum possible influence.

Inspirational appeals

An inspirational appeal is an attempt to develop enthusiasm and commitment by arousing strong emotions and linking a request or proposal to the target person's needs, values, hopes, and ideals. Some possible bases for appeal include the target person's desire to be important, to feel useful, to accomplish something worthwhile, to make an important contribution, to perform an exceptional feat, to be a member of the best team, or to participate in an exciting effort to make things better. Some ideals that may be the basis for an inspirational appeal include patriotism, loyalty, liberty, freedom, self-fulfillment, justice, fairness, equality, love, tolerance, excellence, humanitarianism, and progress. For example, employees are asked to work extra hours on a special project because it may save many lives.

Inspirational appeals vary in complexity, from a brief explanation of the ideological justification for a proposed project or change, to a major speech that articulates an appealing vision of what the organization could accomplish or become. The complexity of an inspirational appeal depends in part on the size of the task to be undertaken, the amount of effort and risk involved, and the extent to which people are asked to deviate from established, traditional ways of doing things. To formulate an appropriate appeal, the agent must have insight into the values, hopes, and fears of the person or group to be influenced. The effectiveness of an inspirational appeal also depends on the agent's communication skills, such as the ability to use vivid imagery and metaphors, manipulate symbols, and employ voice and gestures to generate enthusiasm and excitement.

Consultation

Consultation is an attempt to increase the target person's motivation to carry out a request or support a proposal by involving the person in determining how it will be done. Consultation can take a variety of forms when used as an influence tactic. For example, the agent may present a detailed policy, plan, or procedure to a target person who will be involved in implementing it to see if the person has any doubts, concerns, or suggestions for improvement. In the discussion that follows, which is really a form of negotiation and joint problem-solving, the agent tries to find ways to modify the details of the proposal to deal with the target person's major concerns. In another variation of consultation, the agent presents a general strategy or objective to the target person rather than a detailed proposal and asks the person to help plan how to attain the objective or to suggest specific action steps for implementing the strategy. The suggested action steps are discussed until there is agreement by both parties.

For consultation to be feasible, the target person must have at least moderate agreement with the objective that the agent wants to attain. The target person will not be very enthusiastic about suggesting ways to attain an objective that is unacceptable. Thus, it is important for the agent to understand the target person's attitudes towards the influence objective before selecting consultation as an influence tactic.

Exchange tactics

Exchange tactics involve an offer by the agent to reward the target person for doing what the agent requests. The essential condition for use of exchange tactics is control over rewards that are attractive to the person. In addition, the agent must be perceived as trustworthy enough to actually provide the promised rewards. Thus, exchange tactics are facilitated by the agent's reward power and credibility.

Use of an incentive is especially appropriate when the target person is indifferent or reluctant about complying with a request. In effect, the agent offers to make it worthwhile to comply by promising to provide a reward that is desired by the target person. The reward offered by the agent may take many forms, such as recommending a pay increase or promotion for the person, sharing scarce resources with the person, helping the person do another task, providing information, providing political support on some issue or proposal, putting in a good word to help advance the person's career, and offering to share the benefits obtained from a project or activity. Sometimes the promise may be implicit rather than explicit. That is, the agent may suggest returning the favor in some unspecified way at a future time.

Personal appeals

A personal appeal involves asking someone to do a favor based on friendship or loyalty to the agent. This tactic is one way to enact referent power, although when referent power is very strong, a personal appeal may not be necessary. If considerable effort is required to comply with a request, the target person should understand that the request is indeed important to the agent. If a request is not perceived to be important to the agent, it may be ignored or carried out with only a minimal effort. Thus, whenever appropriate, the importance of the request to the agent should be explained to the target person.

Personal appeals can take several forms. One form is to ask the target person to carry out a request or support a proposal as a personal favor. Another form is to emphasize the close relationship between agent and target before asking for something. A third form is to say that you need to ask for a favor before saying what it is. If the target person agrees, then it will be awkward to say no when the request is explained. The risk with this form of personal appeal is that the target person may feel resentment if manipulated into doing something unpleasant.

Ingratiation tactics

Ingratiation is behavior that makes the target person feel accepted and appreciated by the agent. Examples include giving compliments, showing respect, and acting especially friendly and helpful before making a request. When ingratiation tactics are sincere, they can strengthen a friendship, increase referent power, and make a target person more willing to consider a request. However, if the target person perceives that the agent is being insincere and manipulative, then ingratiation will not increase compliance.

An especially effective form of ingratiation is to explain how the target person is uniquely qualified to carry out a difficult request, and/or to express confidence that the target person is able to successfully carry out a difficult request. Ingratiation can be used not only for an immediate influence attempt, but also as a longer-term strategy to improve relationships with people and gain more referent power (Liden and Mitchell, 1988; Wayne and Ferris, 1990).

Pressure tactics

Pressure tactics include threats, warnings, repeated demands, and frequent checking to see if the person has complied with a request. Sometimes when a request has been ignored, an angry complaint to the person is sufficient to invoke the possibility of unpleasant consequences and induce compliance, particularly if the person is just lazy or apathetic rather than strongly opposed to the action. Sometimes explicit warnings or threats are necessary to get compliance with legitimate requests or rules that are unpopular.

Strong forms of pressure tactics such as threats of punishment are based on coercive power and depend on the target's perception that the agent is able and willing to carry out the threats. A limitation of most pressure tactics is that they may have serious side effects. Threats and intimidation are likely to undermine working relationships and may lead to avoidance by the target person or use of counterpower against the agent. For this reason, pressure tactics should not be used except as a last resort when other influence tactics have failed.

Coalition tactics

Coalitions are an indirect type of influence tactic wherein the agent gets assistance from other people to influence the target person. The coalition partners may include peers, subordinates, superiors, or outsiders (e.g., clients and suppliers). One form of coalition tactic is to have other people talk to the target person and express support for the agent's request or proposal. Another form of coalition tactic is for the agent to bring to a meeting someone who will help to present a proposal to the target person. A third form of coalition tactic is to use the prior endorsement of coalition partners as a basis for making a stronger appeal to the target person. The appropriate form of coalition depends on the nature of the request, the agent–target relationship, and the amount of resistance expected or encountered.

Coalition tactics are always used in combination with one or more of the direct influence tactics. For example, the agent and a coalition partner may both use rational persuasion to influence the target person. The tactics used by coalition partners are not always the same ones used by the agent. For example, in a version of the "good cop–bad cop" strategy, the agent uses ingratiation and rational persuasion, and the coalition partner uses pressure.

Upward appeals

Upward appeals occur when the agent seeks help from someone with authority over the target person. When the third party is asked to help influence the target person to do what the agent wants, then the upward appeal is also a coalition tactic. Upward appeals are used primarily as a last resort when repeated attempts to influence the target person with other tactics are unsuccessful. The target person for an upward appeal is usually a peer, but sometimes this tactic is used to influence a subordinate or the boss. It is risky to use an upward appeal to influence the boss, because it is likely to elicit resentment. Even when used with a peer, an upward appeal may cause resentment if it is viewed as an attempt to force the peer to do what the agent wants. The resentment may undermine agent–target relations, and it can lead to covert forms of resistance by the target person.

Another form of upward appeal is to ask someone with higher authority to mediate the disagreement and help find a mutually satisfactory solution. This form of upward appeal is especially useful for dealing with strong resistance by a peer. If skillfully handled by the third party, the intervention may improve rather than undermine relations between the agent and target. However, the need to ask a superior for help may reflect poorly on the interpersonal skills of the agent.

EFFECTIVENESS OF DIFFERENT INFLUENCE TACTICS

Research comparing influence tactics indicates that some are usually more effective than others (Falbe and Yukl, 1992; Yukl, Kim, and Falbe, 1996; Yukl and Tracey, 1992). Consultation and inspirational appeals are two of the most effective tactics for influencing target commitment to carry out a request or support a proposal. Rational persuasion can be very effective depending on how it is used. A strong form of rational persuasion (e.g., a detailed proposal, elaborate documentation, a convincing reply to concerns raised by the target person) is often effective, whereas a weak form of rational persuasion (e.g., a brief explanation, an assertion without supporting evidence) is much less likely to be effective.

Exchange and ingratiation are moderately effective for influencing subordinates and peers, but these tactics are difficult to use for influencing superiors. Subordinates do not have much to exchange with bosses, and offers of exchange are unlikely to be viewed as appropriate. Compliments made to the boss just before asking for something are likely to appear insincere and manipulative. Ingratiation is more effective when used as part of a long-term strategy for improving relations with superiors rather than as a tactic for an immediate influence attempt with a superior.

Personal appeals are moderately effective for influencing a peer with whom the agent has a friendly relationship. However, this tactic is only appropriate for a limited range of requests (e.g., get assistance, get a personal favor, change a scheduled meeting or deadline), and the outcome is likely to be compliance rather than commitment. Personal appeals are seldom necessary for influencing subordinates, and they are difficult to use with bosses.

The least effective tactics for influencing target commitment are pressure, legitimating tactics, and upward appeals. These tactics seldom result in target commitment, although they sometimes result in compliance. Nevertheless, compliance is all that is needed for some types of influence attempts (e.g., wear proper safety gear, provide requested information, turn in routine reports on time).

Coalition tactics can be effective for influencing a peer or superior to support a change or innovation. However, they are seldom effective for influencing someone to carry out an assignment or improve performance, especially when viewed as an attempt to "gang up" on the target person.

The effectiveness of an attempt can be increased by using more than one type of tactic at the same time or sequentially (Falbe and Yukl, 1992). When using tactics together in the same influence attempt, the agent should select tactics that are compatible with each other. In other words, it is best to select tactics that are easy to use together and that enhance each other's effectiveness. For example, rational persuasion is a very flexible tactic that is usually compatible with any of the other tactics. Strong pressure tactics are incompatible with personal appeals or ingratiation because they weaken target feelings of friendship and loyalty, which these other tactics are intended to strengthen. When tactics are used sequentially, some types (e.g., ingratiation, personal appeal) are more suitable for an initial influence attempt, whereas other types (e.g., legitimating, pressure, upward appeals) are usually reserved for a follow-up influence attempt (Yukl, Falbe, and Youn, 1993).

Even though some tactics are generally more useful than others, success is not guaranteed for any tactic or combination of tactics. The outcome of an influence attempt depends on other things in addition to the influence tactics that are used, including the agent's skill in using the tactics, the type of agent–target relationship, the type of the request (e.g., task-related, personal), and how the request is perceived by the target person (e.g., legitimate, important, enjoyable). A tactic is more likely to be successful if the target perceives it to be a socially acceptable form of influence behavior, if the agent has sufficient position and personal power to use the tactic, if the tactic can affect target attitudes about the desirability of the request, if it is used in a skillful way, if it is used for a request that is legitimate, and if it is consistent with the target person's values and needs (Yukl and Tracey, 1992).

Examples of Successful and Unsuccessful Influence Attempts

The following mini-case illustrates how important it is to develop an adequate power base and select an appropriate influence strategy. The provost in a large university asked each academic department with a graduate program to provide several masters students to participate in a new fundraising campaign. The masters students would telephone department alumni, describe the department's current activities and accomplishments, then ask for donations to help support the department. Assigning students to help with fundraising does not fall within the scope of legitimate authority for department chairs, so it is necessary to ask for volunteers. These students were overloaded with academic work, and they were reluctant to perform extra tasks not directly related to this work.

The chairperson of Department A had strong referent power with the masters students in his department. He was a supportive, considerate teacher who interacted with students outside of the classroom and showed strong concern for them as individuals. When he met with the students, he explained why the fundraising was important to the university and how it would benefit the masters program and future students. His strong rational appeals were supplemented with inspirational appeals based on student loyalty to the program. Most of the masters students in Department A volunteered to participate in the fundraising, and they were very effective in getting donations from program alumni who had not previously contributed funds to the university.

The chairperson of Department B had little referent power with students. He was arrogant and conceited in the classroom, he spent little time interacting with the masters students outside of class, and he did not develop close supportive relationships with them. At a meeting with the students to talk about the fundraising campaign, he said that the university needed more donations from alumni but did not explain how the department or the program would benefit. This weak rational persuasion was combined with pressure tactics. He demanded that the students participate and told them that they did not have any choice in the matter. The chairperson was able to pressure some of the students to agree to help with the fundraising. However, discussions among the students after the meeting revealed widespread resentment about the chairperson's coercion. Several students decided to complain to the provost. As a result, the provost did not use any masters students from Department B for the fundraising. Instead, she hired some undergraduate students and paid them an hourly wage to telephone department alumni. These undergraduate students were much less effective in getting donations from alumni.

CONCLUSION

Knowledge about power and influence tactics is useful for people who must gain cooperation and support from others to perform their job effectively. To influence people, it is essential to develop and maintain a substantial amount of expert and referent power. In addition, it is desirable to have sufficient position power to back up one's personal power. Position power should be exerted in a subtle, careful fashion that minimizes status differentials and avoids threats to the target person's self-esteem. People who exercise power in an arrogant and manipulative manner are likely to engender resentment and resistance.

The outcome of an influence attempt depends on what tactics are used, how skillfully they are used, and the context in which they are used. Combining tactics is usually more effective than using a single tactic. In general, the most useful tactics for eliciting commitment are consultation, inspirational appeals, and strong forms of rational persuasion. Before making an influence attempt that involves an important objective, it is essential to diagnose the situation carefully and select tactics that are mutually compatible and appropriate for the situation.

REFERENCES

Blau, P. K. (1956). *Bureaucracy in modern society*. New York: Random House.
Cohen, A. R., and Bradford, D. L. (1991). *Influence without authority*. New York: John Wiley & Sons.

Davis, K. (1968). Attitudes toward the legitimacy of management efforts to influence employees. *Academy of Management Journal*, 11, 153–62.

Falbe, C. M., and Yukl, G. (1992). Consequences for managers of using single influence tactics and combinations of tactics. *Academy of Management Journal*, 35, 638–53.

French, J. R. P., and Raven, B. H. (1959). The bases of social power. In D. Cartwright (ed.), *Studies of social power* (pp. 150–67). Ann Arbor, MI: Institute for Social Research.

Hickson, D. J., Hinings, C. R., Lee, C. A., Schneck, R. S., and Pennings, J. M. (1971). A strategic contingencies theory of intra-organizational power. *Administrative Science Quarterly*, 16, 216–29.

Kaplan, R. E. (1984). Trade routes: The manager's network of relationships. *Organizational Dynamics*, Spring, 37–52.

Kipnis, D. (1974). *The powerholders*. Chicago: University of Chicago Press.

Kipnis, D., Schmidt, S. M., and Wilkinson, I. (1980). Intra-organizational influence tactics: Explorations in getting one's way. *Journal of Applied Psychology*, 65, 440–52.

Kotter, J. P. (1985). *Power and influence: Beyond formal authority*. New York: Free Press.

Liden, R. C., and Mitchell, T. R. (1988). Ingratiatory behaviors in organizational settings. *Academy of Management Review*, 13, 572–87.

March, J. G., and Simon, H. A. (1958). *Organizations*. New York: Wiley.

Mechanic, D. (1962). Sources of power of lower participants in complex organizations. *Administrative Science Quarterly*, 7, 349–64.

McClelland, D. C. (1975). *Power: The inner experience*. New York: Irvington.

Mintzberg, H. (1983). *Power in and around organizations*. Englewood Cliffs, NJ: Prentice-Hall.

Mulder, M., Ritsema van Eck, J. R., and de Jong, R. D. (1970). An organization in crisis and noncrisis conditions. *Human Relations*, 24, 19–41.

Patchen, M. (1974). The locus and basis of influence on organizational decisions. *Organizational Behavior and Human Performance*, 11, 195–221.

Pettigrew, A. (1972). Information control as a power resource. *Sociology*, 6, 187–204.

Pfeffer, J. (1981). *Power in organizations*. Marshfield, MA: Pittman.

Pfeffer, J. (1992). *Managing with power: Politics and influence in organizations*. Boston, MA: Harvard Business School Press.

Sayles, L. R. (1979). *What effective managers really do and how they do it*. New York: McGraw-Hill.

Schilit, W. K., and Locke, E. A. (1982). A study of upward influence in organizations. *Administrative Science Quarterly*, 27, 304–16.

Wayne, S. J., and Ferris, G. R. (1990). Influence tactics, affect, and exchange quality in supervisor–subordinate interactions: A laboratory experiment and field study. *Journal of Applied Psychology*, 75, 487–99.

Yukl, G. (1998). *Leadership in organizations*. Englewood Cliffs, NJ: Prentice-Hall.

Yukl, G., and Falbe, C. M. (1991). The importance of different power sources in downward and lateral relations. *Journal of Applied Psychology*, 76, 416–23.

Yukl, G., Falbe, C. M., and Youn, J. Y. (1993). Patterns of influence behavior for managers. *Group and Organization Management*, 18, 5–28.

Yukl, G., Kim, , H., and Falbe, C. M. (1996). Antecedents of influence outcomes. *Journal of Applied Psychology*, 81, 309–17.

Yukl, G., and Tracey, B. (1992). Consequences of influence tactics when used with subordinates, peers, and the boss. *Journal of Applied Psychology*, 77, 525–35.

Zaleznik, A. (1970). Power and politics in organizational life. *Harvard Business Review*, 48, 47–60.

18

Lead through Vision and Values

MARKUS HAUSER AND ROBERT J. HOUSE

> ... the pretty thing that happens ... when you get a big noble purpose, is that it raises the whole aspiration of the corporation, of the people in the corporation, even the people who are least motivated by something like that. (Don Burr, *People Express*)

INTRODUCTION

Bill Gates, Jan Carlzon, Mother Theresa and Martin Luther King ... What do these people have in common? All these individuals share(d) an outstanding ability to attract, mobilize, and inspire people. Social, political, and management scientists studied these individuals for many years to distill the essence of their ability to capture the imagination and spirit of their followers. There is no lack of theories to explore their behaviors, leadership attributes, and effects on the followers. However, these theories lack integration and a shared understanding of the origins of effective leadership (Hauser, 1999b). Recent research sets out to disentangle and to integrate these existing, contradicting points of views. While the results of these efforts have been limited so far (House and Shamir, 1993; Hauser, 1999a), most authors agree on one principle: *Outstanding leaders lead through vision and values.*

Vision, according to *Webster's Dictionary*, means imaginative insight or foresight. More specifically, vision in the context of leadership and organizations is defined as a general, ideal, desirable state of the organization in the future (Kouzes and Posner 1987; Conger, 1989). It is argued here that a leader's vision "pulls together beliefs and images about ideal ways of doing things" (Thoms and Greenberger, 1995). How, then, is vision related to performance and change? Studies point to two levels on which vision has an effect: the organizational and the individual levels.

- ◆ *Vision on the organizational level.* Oswald, Stanwick, and LaTour (1997) found that strategic vision has a positive impact on organizational performance in highly competitive environments. Baum, Locke, and Kirkpartick (1998) report that the quality of vision had a positive effect on venture growth in entrepreneurial settings. The quality of vision is defined by its brevity, clarity, abstractness, challenge, future orientation, stability, desirability or ability to inspire, identification of intended products, markets, and strategy. These situation-specific results are backed by studies of top management by Hart and Quinn (1993) and middle managers by Howell and Higgins (1990). The former provide evidence that the leadership role of vision-setting is positively related to business performance and organizational/stakeholder effectiveness but not to short-term financial performance. The latter compared executives who were identified as successful innovation champions to non-champions. They found that champions articulated ideological goals (vision) whereas non-champions showed this behavior to a significantly lesser extent.

A different set of studies indicates that the content of the vision plays a critical role in the ability to change an organization (Doz and Prahalad, 1987; Coulson-Thomas, 1992; Larwood, Falbe, Kriger, and Miesing, 1995). The content of the visions studied by Larwood, Falbe, Kriger, and Miesling (1995) was related to the rapidity of firm change, and the amount of control the executives exercised.

While the research reported above indicates that vision has a positive effect on performance in for-profit organizations, there is some evidence that the content of the vision is related to the success of non-profit organizations as well. Roberts's (1985) case study of a visionary leader in a school district indicates that it is successful not only in changing economic, but also educational organizations. Trice and Beyer (1986) found similar evidence in two other social organizations.

◆ *Vision on the individual level.*   The articulation of a vision is a central concept in most charismatic leadership theories. The development and communication of a vision is one explanation for the success of charismatic/transformational leaders and their effect on the performance, attitudes, and values of their followers (Bass 1985; 1998; Hauser, 1999a; House, 1977). Howell and Frost (1989) found in laboratory experiments that charismatic leadership has a positive effect on the performance and attitudes of followers. Charismatic leadership, then, has been repeatedly related to higher performance of followers. In a meta-analysis by Lowe, Kroeck, and Shrivasubramaniam (1996) this relationship was supported for subjective and, to a lesser degree, for objective performance measures. In the book *Built to last* James Collins and Jerry Porras (1997) make it clear that visionary companies are not equivalent to organizations that are led by charismatic leaders. In that sense we want to stress that the principles we are proposing go above and beyond the literature on charismatic leadership. This literature, however, gives important insights on successful vision creation and implementation.

These studies provide strong evidence of the efficacy of visions as sources of direction for and motivation of organizational members. It is worth noting that, based on several hundred biographies that we have read, most outstanding leaders have one, and in rare cases two, successful visions in their entire life. While this vision might be adapted over time, its essence remains the same. Examples for great visions in the non-profit world and political arena are Martin Luther King's dream, Mother Theresa's focus on helping the poorest of the poor, and Mahatma Gandhi's vision of a free India. In the profit world visions play an important role as well. Visions that had a great impact on organizations and/or everyday life are Bill Gates's vision of the information age, Jan Carlzon's "moments of truth" that stresses the importance of each individual employee at SAS, and Don Burr's idea of a low-cost, employee-owned airline. These individuals had one great insight and passion in their lives and were totally committed to its implementation.

Despite the fact that this enumeration of leaders suggests that they are the origins of great visions there are other sources that should be mentioned. While it is generally true that most great visions are shaped by outstanding individuals there are cases in which the source of the vision lies in the imagination of the followers. The vision of the followers becomes accepted and articulated by the leader. Another source of vision is an outsider who brings new insights into an organization. For instance, USWeb, a leading Web design and implementation firm in the USA, acquired the crisis-stricken Mitchell Madison Consulting and provided them with a new attractive picture of its future. A great vision can also be conceived by a team of the above groups or inherited from prior members of the organization with the goal to implement it (House, 1995).

Outstanding leaders do not have to communicate a grandiose vision in order to be effective. They "embrace such ideologies as honesty, fairness, craftsmanship, high-quality services or products, a challenging and rewarding work environment, professional development for organizational members, freedom from highly controlling rules and supervision, a fair return to major constituencies, respect for the organizational members and customers, and regard for the environment in which the organization functions" (Berlew, 1974 cited in House, 1995).

While leadership through vision is related to performance of organizations, organizational units, and individuals, research indicates that the role defined as "vision setter" is the one least frequently pursued by top managers (Hart and Quinn, 1993). One of the reasons that executives infrequently take on this role is that they might not be aware of its impact on performance. Another cause for Hart and Quinn's (1993) findings might be that top managers do not possess the required skills to develop a successful vision. The first problem is solved by increasing the accessibility of the research results that relate visions to performance. The second problem requires more effort and asks for the development of top managers. Recent evidence indicates that some of the necessary skills to develop a successful vision can be trained (Thoms and Greensberger, 1995). Although this evidence is not sufficient to make a final statement on the trainability of the skills for "vision-setting" it is encouraging. Overall, managers are well advised to spend time on developing the necessary skills and/or people to become visionary leaders.

This short review of the literature provides us with the following three results:

1 Vision matters for the performance of organizations and individuals. Therefore, the development of a good understanding of the vision phenomenon and the adoption of its implications have the potential to increase the performance of organizations and individuals.

2 The role of "vision setter" is pursued less frequently than other executive roles. As "vision-setting" is strongly related to performance of organizations, there is potential to improve performance in many organizations by employing the power of vision.

3 Some of the skills necessary to develop a vision may be acquired through training. Therefore, leaders who are not able to develop a successful vision are likely to improve themselves by learning more about this phenomenon. However, there is still more research needed in order to provide more systematic knowledge with respect to the trainability of skills necessary to generate a vision.

Given these results, the question arises: how do managers become successful leaders through vision? This question taps into issues of the required personality and behaviors of the leader as well as some contingency factors. Personality characteristics that are discussed in the literature include the following: integrity, future orientation, and optimism. These characteristics are positively related to and explain 20 percent of the variance of visioning skills (Thoms and Greenberger 1995). Sashkin (1988) refers to motivational factors such as the need for power, power inhibition, and cognitive skills. The latter are a prerequisite in order to be able to explain the vision to others, and to expand the vision to a broader context and multiple situations. The literature on charismatic leadership refers to a wider set of personality characteristics that should be included here. In order to generate and implement a successful vision the leader has to be self-confident, oriented toward change and innovation, energetic, receptive to changes in the environment, and imaginative (Hauser, 1999b). There are many studies which refer to the importance of the personality of the leader in order to generate a successful vision and implement it in an organization. A study by Kirkpatrick and Locke (1996) denies this relationship and relates effectiveness to content of the vision only. However, the evidence for an impact of the personality of the leader on the effectiveness of a vision is still prevailing.

PRINCIPLES FOR LEADING THROUGH VISION AND VALUES

Aside from personality characteristics of the leader, we advance some principles for the content of successful visions as well as the process of generating and implementing a vision.

Principles for the content of the vision

1 ***The vision statement should meet the following criteria: brevity, clarity, abstractness, challenge, future orientation, stability, desirability or ability to inspire, identification of intended products, markets, and strategy (Baum, Locke, and Kirkpatrick, 1998)***

These criteria ensure that the vision can be communicated efficiently, that it induces motivation, gives general guidelines for behavior of the employees in ambiguous situations, and provides sufficient coordination of, and cohesion within, the organizations. The vision should also be broad enough to be stable over time even if the environment changes rapidly. This broad focus has to be translated into goals that give specific guidelines to the followers.

2 ***The vision should deal with issues of change, an idealized future for the followers, ideal goals, and people working together***

A vision of change and a positive future for the followers is required in order to inspire followers with the excitement of challenge and opportunity (Conger and Kanungo, 1987). Excitement, however, is not an automatic outcome of a vision of change. The vision has to be accompanied by a strong sense of ability to master the challenges of change. This sense can either be inspired through the leader or through high self-efficacy of followers (Bandura, 1986). The leader, for example, may show behaviors or possess characteristics that induce trust in his or her leadership and the ability to meet the challenges. The leader may also demonstrate a high degree of confidence in the followers and empower them to implement the required changes (House, 1977). The ideal vision and its values encourage the involvement of the self of the followers and consequently induce a strong motivation to achieve the vision (Shamir, House, and Arthur, 1993). The incorporation of the image of people working together leads to higher levels of cohesion, less conflict, more emotional attachment, and value congruence. Empirical results support this assertion. For instance, Shamir, Arthur, and House (1994) demonstrated that the use of inclusive terms such as "we" and "us" in the communication of the vision is related to followers' motivation and identification with the leader and the organization.

3 The vision should be situation-specific, appropriate, and yet unique in the industry

The vision has to relate to the domain and situation in which the organization functions. This means, for instance, that a leader of a hospital whose vision is only focused on cost-cutting will alienate many of the people who work there because they chose an occupation and an organization in order to help people instead of cutting costs. A study by Kirkpatrick, Wofford, and Baum (1999) indicates that the vision should arouse those motives in the followers that are appropriate for the situation in which the organization functions. More specifically, they pointed out that a vision that arouses the achievement and power motive has a positive effect on growth rates of manufacturing companies. No effect was found for the affiliation motive. Achievement and power are two motives that are essential to succeed in an organization that faces a competitive environment, whereas the same is not true for the affiliation motive. The affiliation motive, however, had a positive impact on group cohesiveness in service organizations. Therefore, this study indicates that the message in the vision should be aligned with the organizational situation in order to have a positive effect on performance.

Furthermore, a vision has to be unique in the industry, yet within the boundaries of acceptable values and propositions. A vision that cannot be distinguished from those of other organizations is unlikely to have an effect on employee motivation and identification. Without these effects the vision is unlikely to contribute to organizational performance. At the same time the vision has to be within the range of accepted norms of the followers and society in order to inspire and motivate (Shamir, House, and Arthur, 1993; Conger and Kanungo, 1987; Steyrer, 1995). In essence that means that there is a continuum of the content of a vision from ineffective imitation to successful, innovative differentiation to non-accepted oddness.

4 In articulating a challenging new vision, relate it to the past of the organization and align it with the values of the employees and the dominant society

Reference to the past ensures that the vision is more likely to be accepted than if it is unrelated to the experience and self-definition of the organization. A vision that incorporates the values of the members of the organization results in higher identification and ultimately higher levels of motivation (Shamir, Arthur, and House, 1994). To align the vision with the values of society at large helps to gain

social support beyond organizational members and translates into stable relationships with markets and stakeholders. There are some limitations to this assertion.
If an organization depends heavily on a minority within a country a deviation
from the predominant values in the society might be a source of competitive
advantage. Please also refer to the section below on Principle 4, in which we
discuss under which circumstances a deviation from societal values is in fact
beneficial for competitiveness. Mind, however, that those organizations which
deviate too much from the accepted norms will eventually face regulatory or
market reactions as a response to their behavior.

A good example for these four content-related criteria is the vision of Microsoft
given below:

> Microsoft's vision is to empower people through great software – any time, any
> place, and on any device. That means helping companies build friction-free knowl-
> edge-management systems, so information flows effortlessly through their businesses,
> and to implement flawless e-commerce operations. It means helping developers
> create great Web-enabled products for a wide range of devices. It means making PCs
> simpler and more reliable. It means helping consumers transform the Internet into
> their own "personal Internet" – a resource that learns from them over time and
> empowers them with all of the information they need, while protecting their privacy.
> Everything we do focuses on allowing people and organizations to create and
> manage their information. (Microsoft, 1999)

This statement relates very well to the past of the organization, the innovation-
oriented values of the followers, defines the market space, and envisions Microsoft
to help to empower the people in the information age. To compare the above with
a vision that does not meet the proposed characteristics, consider Acer's vision
statement: "Become a global company with NT$2.000 in revenue by the year
2000 with the help of a consortium of allied companies" (Acer, 1994). This
sentence is not related at all to the business and values in Acer. It does not have
the qualities to mobilize anybody except shareholders. The message is that Acer
wants to be big, but gives no indication why the vision is desirable. This vision
statement lacks any inspiration and actually resembles more a narrow goal instead
of a vision of the future of the company.

Principles for the process of generating and implementing the vision

5 Build cohesive understanding of the vision among the top management team

The consistent communication of the vision from the leader to the members of the
top management team is essential for the unambiguous understanding of the
vision at all levels of the organization. Time is well invested in making sure that
there exists a common understanding about the vision among the top management team. In one of the case studies presented below, the CEO of Tyrolit had to
lay off a senior manager in order to build a common vision among the management. In that specific situation it was better to lose a star than to lose the united
voice of the management toward the organization and the environment.

6 Encourage a high degree of participation in the implementation of the vision

The inclusion of followers in the process of the vision implementation ensures that the vision is based on information from all levels and functions in the organization. An organization that does not follow this principle is inclined to build its vision around filtered and/or obsolete information. Especially in hyper-competitive markets (D'Aveni 1994) the neglect of information provided by people who are closest to the rapidly changing markets may lead to visions that do not match current developments in the environment. Moreover, participation enhances the chances that the employees are able to incorporate their values in the vision. This is the basis for identification with the vision and the organization. For instance, organizational image theory (Dutton, Dukerich, and Harquail, 1994) argues that the identification of individuals with the organization depends on the degree to which the perceived enduring characteristics of the organization, such as the vision, preserve the continuity of its members' self-concept. If the vision is aligned with the values of the members of the organization, employees are prone to strongly identify themselves with the organization. A high level of identification is related to lower rates of voluntary turnover, higher involvement, more psychological ownership in the firm's destiny (Kouzes and Posner, 1987; Sims and Lorenzi 1992) and, ultimately, higher levels of motivation (Shamir, House, and Arthur 1993).

Jack Welch's Work Out program is a good example for implementing his vision of being number one or number two in each industry. The program is geared towards mobilizing all the individuals in the organization to introduce organizational change and implement all good ideas generated by all levels of the organization. The subordinates go on a retreat with their managers and collect ideas that have to be considered for implementation by their manager. The decisions about the implementation have to be made in front of the employees that contributed to the idea generation. If an idea is not implemented the manager needs to explain why not. The Work Out program ensures that all employees participate in the implementation process.

7 Articulate the vision in a dramatic way

Empirical studies indicate that the dramatic communication of the vision is essential in building excitement in the organization (Gardner and Avolio, 1998). Eye contact, vocal variety, and animated facial expressions are related to better identification with the leader and the organization and eventually to higher performance (Howell and Frost, 1989; Gardner and Avolio, 1998). Effective communication involves the use of dynamic language. Holladay and Coombs (1994) and Amwamleh and Gardner (1997) show that the same vision content causes more attribution of charisma if the communication is dynamic vs. non-dynamic. Dramatization of the vision leads to higher levels of identification of the follower with the vision, the leader, and the organization. Furthermore it increases organizational cohesion (Conger and Kanungo, 1998) and performance (Lowe, Kroeck, and Shrivasubramaniam, 1996).

Part of Jan Carlzon's success at Linjeflyg was that he got the employees to listen to him when he assembled all airline personnel in a hangar and climbed 15 feet up on a platform in order to make the following statement (Bartlett, Elderkin, and Feinberg, 1993): "As the new president, I don't know a thing about Linjeflyg. I can't save the company alone. The only chance for Linjeflyg to survive, is for you to help me – assume responsibility yourselves, share your ideas and experience so we have more to work with. I have some ideas of my own, and will probably be able to use them. But most important, you are the ones who must help me, not the other way round." While dramatic communication is not the only way to communicate the vision effectively, it is certainly one of the strongest tools in order to generate excitement for the implementation of the vision.

8 *Communicate the vision first to highly influential and cooperative individuals in the organization in order to guarantee its rapid adoption*

This principle suggests the use of opinion leaders in the organization in order to gain support for the implementation of the vision. Opinion leaders are not always individuals who are advanced in the hierarchy, but sometimes union leaders, supervisors or middle managers. Especially when the vision requires the organization to change radically, individuals high in the hierarchy are likely to oppose the changes more than individuals lower in the organization (Hauser, 1999b). While it is essential for the successful implementation of a vision to engage the top levels of the organization, it would be shortsighted to concentrate entirely on upper management. To include influential people at lower levels facilitates the successful implementation of the vision. An example to illustrate this is the case of Tyrolit, given later in this chapter.

9 *Link the vision to task cues and goals*

Vision strongly shapes the attitudes of members of an organization (Kirkpatrick and Locke, 1996). Attitudes, however, are not consistently related to behavior. The success of a vision, therefore, is ultimately related to the behavior of the members of the organization rather than to their attitudes. In order to guarantee that the behavior follows the vision, individual goals and incentives should be tied to the vision. People in the organization should be rewarded according to their contribution to the achievement of the vision. It is important, however, to understand that the incentive system should not reward specific individual behaviors. To do so would undermine the intrinsic motivation and cause the follower to focus only on the rewarded behaviors. Many other aspects that are necessary to achieve the vision will be ignored. Ideological visions, hence, should not be implemented with the help of strict, contingent incentive systems. In order to set the right guidelines the vision, which in itself is rather abstract, should be explained with the help of many examples. These examples should demonstrate how the vision and its inherent values are incorporated in the daily tasks and goals of the employees. Jan Carlzon provides a simple and effective example of how to link the vision to the tasks in the service industry. He called all customer contacts that people throughout the organization had "moments of truth" and spread this expression throughout the organization. The term "moments of truth" reminds every employee that she or he is responsible for the implementation of the vision of high-quality service that Jan Carlzon espoused for SAS.

10 ***Engage in behaviors that are consistent with the vision, highly visible, and involve personal sacrifice (House, 1977; Conger and Kanungo, 1998)***

Such behaviors demonstrate the commitment of the leaders to their vision. They induce trust in the vision and the integrity of the leader. In combination with a vision that includes the basic values of the followers these behaviors enhance followers' support for the vision and inspire them to engage in the personal sacrifices that are necessary to increase performance over and above the expected levels. Cardinal Kung, the head of the Catholic Church in China, was imprisoned for more than 30 years in solitary confinement for his loyalty to the Pope and his vision of a free Catholic Church of China. He had a choice. Several times he was offered the opportunity to leave the country with the help of Western firms. Instead he chose to stay with his people. His commitment gives hope to all individuals who suffer from religious persecution in China. Many others who followed him sacrificed their freedom, youth, and lives in order to achieve Cardinal Kung's vision. This example goes beyond what most business leaders would be willing to sacrifice. However, he is a good example of how personal sacrificing, persistent belief in the vision, and strong decisive actions inspire millions of people to live their lives according to their beliefs. In our opinion this example is also illustrative of leadership in for-profit organizations, as in many cases visionary leaders put heavy burdens on their personal life, family life, and health in order to implement their vision. Another example of personal sacrifices in the context of organizations is found in "whistle blowers." This expression describes employees who publicly expose non-ethical behaviors by their organization that conflict with their values and the vision of the firm. In doing so, they emerge as leaders who promote or form a new vision of the organization and, at the same time, face significant risks such as unemployment and being stigmatized in the labor market.

We want to express clearly that the engagement in personal sacrifice does not mean the forgoing of self-interest, but rather sacrifice in the interest of the values inherent in the vision. In the long run personal sacrifice and the pursuit of principled self-interest can be quite compatible. Especially in the for-profit world personal sacrifices for the achievement of the vision are often rewarded handsomely. From the perspective of the followers, however, personal sacrifices of the leader show commitment and a strong engagement. Given that the followers identify with the leader the outcome of this perception is stronger motivation and the willingness to sacrifice parts of their own life for the success of the vision. Although everyone might be rewarded in the end, it is not the anticipated reward that keeps people in the office until midnight. It is the example of the leader and the perspective of being able to contribute to the implementation of the vision and values of the leader.

11 ***Use symbols, metaphors, and images that are consistent with the vision (Benford and Hunt, 1992)***

Symbols, metaphors, and images are powerful messengers. They allow instant communication of the essence of the vision. They provoke more emotional reactions than written words because the non-verbal content of the vision bypasses conscious information-processing. Symbols, metaphors, and images help to anchor the vision deeply in the minds of the followers and ensure that the vision is passed on to the future generations of members of the organization. A new way to communicate a vision was chosen by Merix Corp., a $140 million electronic interconnect supplier based in Forest Grove, Oregon. It is one of the first corporations to try to capture the essence of its vision in an image.

These 11 principles should serve as a guideline to guarantee high-quality content and process of vision generation and implementation. In following these principles managers achieve several goals (see a review of empirical evidence by Fiol, Harris, and House, 1999). They give individuals direction, enable followers to identify themselves with the organization, and encourage high motivation and coordinated effort. The effects on the individual and organizational level include value congruence in the organization, a high level of implicit coordination, high cohesion, change, and adaptability, organizational growth, and a high level of organizational effectiveness.

Some caution concerning the generalizability of the principles

The above principles are of different significance and subject to adaptation depending on the situation. The importance of a vision and hence its impact on performance is directly related to its unique ability to generate orientation for the followers. In situations where traditional devices for guidance (plans, job descriptions, and the like) are not appropriate or do not yet exist, vision can function as a much stronger coordinating force than in situations that lend themselves to high formalization. An outstanding vision, therefore is especially important in times of rapidly changing environments, when specific rules might be dysfunctional due to their narrow focus and lack of adaptability, or in early stages of the organization when routines are not yet in place (Yukl, 1994).

Leaders who communicate a vision in multicultural settings, be these in a multinational firm or organizations with diverse workforces, need to consider that the values which are implicit in the vision might not be equally appealing to people from a different cultural background. In such instances the vision has to transcend cultural boundaries in order to be successful. This is accomplished by casting the vision in inclusive and abstract terms.

Aside from these general remarks, some of these principles are bound to specific assumptions and situations. Specifically sub-principles 1, 4, 6, and 7 need further discussion.

Principle 1.   Many authors indicate that an abstract vision is beneficial for its success. For instance, a study by Fiol, Harris, and House (1999) reports that an abstract vision is positively related to charismatic leadership, which in turn is related to higher performance of followers (Hauser, 1999b). The degree of abstractness, though, should also be related to the educational background of the followers and their ability to process abstract information. An abstract vision that is not understood by the followers will be unable to cause any positive effect. Therefore, we argue that the abstractness of the vision has to be seen in relation to the people to whom it is communicated or illustrated with specific examples, metaphors, and symbols.

Principle 4.   To relate the vision to the past of the organization in periods of radical organizational change is not recommended. The reference to the past is likely to encourage resistance to the new orientation and should be avoided. Likewise alignment of the vision with societal values that hinder the competitiveness of an organization is not recommended. For instance there are societies that have a low level of performance orientation (House, Hanges, Ruiz-Quintinilla, et al., 1999). To align the organization with this societal norm would be dysfunctional for the international competitiveness of the organization. Consequently, it is a critical task of the top management to decide which values should be included and where to risk an imbalance between the societal norms and the vision of the company. For instance, Vision, one of the largest investment funds in Switzerland, tries to take over large publicly traded organizations and force the management to maximize shareholder value. In the course of the shareholder value orientation the organizations shut down profitable but not value-maximizing businesses. In a society that, since the 1920s, has valued harmony between employers and employees, and in which the employer is supposed to act in a socially responsible way, this efficiency orientation is widely criticized.

Principle 6.   The need for a high degree of participation depends on the culture of the followers, on the degree of crisis/stress in the organization, and the ability of the leader to develop unique visions that are based on their own unique experiences. The attempt of a leader to be participative in the formation of the vision will result in disrespect in paternalistic countries (e.g. Saudi Arabia). Followers in these countries expect authoritative leadership, and perceive taking their opinions into consideration in forming the vision as a sign of incompetence and weakness. Similarly, followers who are confronted with an organizational crisis or stressful uncertainty have a strong tendency to look for a leader who tells them where to go rather than a leader who asks them in which direction they want to progress. In that sense participation should be applied with caution in paternalistic countries and in organizational crises. Finally, some of the greatest leaders in the world did not arrive at their vision through participation but through unique insights that were shared by the followers.

Principle 7.   The articulation of the vision in a dramatic way might lead to aversion in organizations and countries which have experienced charismatic leaders who led their organization or country into a disaster. In Germany, for instance, a leader who uses highly dramatic rhetoric is likely to be observed with suspicion due to the traumatic experience with Adolf Hitler, who communicated his vision in an extremely dramatic manner. Similarly, some cultures do not value dramatic behaviors. In the Nordic countries (Denmark, Sweden, Finland, and Norway) the dramatic communication of a vision lies outside the excepted social norms of conduct and is likely to lead to a rejection of the leader.

Contingencies that should be considered in the decision concerning the content of the vision, and the process by which it is developed and communicated, are the culture of the society, the values and experiences of followers, and the situation of the company.

When Leading through Vision Works: the Case of Tyrolit

Tyrolit is a firm situated in a small town in Austria with 2,900 employees and revenues of $320 million. It was founded by Swarovski Co. after World War II in order to take advantage of the knowledge that they had developed in cutting and polishing glass, metal, wood, and stone and to manufacture and sell products on the world market. Tyrolit is one of the leading manufacturer of precision grinding, cutting and dressing tools as well as drilling and sawing systems.

In the mid-1990s the company was faced with crumbling profitability, stronger competition, and more demanding customers. After some unsuccessful turnaround attempts, Mr. Andreas J. Ludwig and a new management team took over the operational and strategic leadership and began to fundamentally change the organization. In a joint effort they developed the vision for Tyrolit as an innovation-driven, high-quality, cost-effective organization able to set new standards for customer service and products.

While an innovative orientation has always been a part of the identity of Tyrolit, all the endeavors concerning the cost reduction and reorganization were faced with strong resistance from within the company. Some of the senior managers abroad simply ignored the new directions and guidelines for their business. Due to their strong relationships with the former top management the senior managers believed they were untouchable and therefore did not support the new structure and vision. It was not until Ludwig fired one of the oldest and most non-compliant country heads that the members of the organization realized how committed to the vision the new top management team was. Still resistance persisted at the lower levels. In order to change the attitudes of the workforce Ludwig took some of the most influential middle managers and foremen to negotiations with major customers. In these negotiations the employees experienced first-hand the difficulties facing the organization. Instead of price increases in line with inflation, which Tyrolit had been used to in the past, many of the large customers demanded a price cut! If these price reductions were not granted, the customers threatened, they would change suppliers. The experience of the demanding environment in which Tyrolit operated turned most the opponents of change into champions for the cost-reduction programs of Mr. Ludwig.

Not only through these hands-on experiences of the changing environment in the marketplace did Ludwig influence the perceptions of the people working in Tyrolit. He also demonstrated integrity and served as a role model in small things that concerned himself. For instance, when his personal telephone system was about to be modernized, he called it off, indicating that this was not a necessary investment and that his telephone worked just fine for him. He consciously chose to stick with his old telephone system as he was aware of the signal he was sending out to his employees: the cost-reduction program also applies to the top management. Further, Ludwig and his team worked day and night in order to communicate the new vision, to change the organizational structure and human resource system and lead Tyrolit again into the profit zone.

Due to a shared vision, role-modeling behavior, effective communication of the vision to the lower levels of the organization, and relation of the vision to the drivers of success of the company – innovation and quality – Tyrolit was again profitable two years after the new management took over and its growth rate exceeded the average for its sector. It has excelled in the task to provide customer service and innovative and reliable products for a reasonable price through involvement of the whole organization. Today Tyrolit is Europe's number one firm for bonded grinding tools and one of the world's two leading system suppliers. With 18 production and 12 sales companies and affiliates operating in over 60 countries throughout the world, the Tyrolit group is an integrated solution provider for technical problems in almost all industrial sectors and for all applications in that market. With its new organizational structure Tyrolit is well positioned to sustain the growth rates and lay the ground for its success in the future.

WHEN LEADING THROUGH VISION DOES NOT WORK: THE CASE OF PEOPLE EXPRESS

People Express (PE) was founded in 1980 as the first new airline to take advantage of the provision of the 1978 Airline Deregulation Act. The vision of the founder Don Burr was to provide fast-growing low-cost flights in the metropolitan areas of the eastern USA. Within two years PE grew into a company employing 1,200 people, with $62 million operating revenues, and profits of $3 million while only 20 percent of airlines showed positive results. Don Burr's start-up was not only exceptional in its growth but also in its philosophy of having all employees invest in the stock of the company at a discounted price. This procedure guaranteed that the interest of the employees and the company were aligned on a long-term basis.

Don Burr's leadership philosophy was to trust people's willingness and ability to work hard and to use their skill for the best of the company. He envisioned an exciting future for his employees, a fast-paced growth of the organization, life-long job security, interesting jobs through rotation programs, self-management, a culture of participation and collaboration in teams combined with compensation that was tied to the performance of the company. This vision and promise was very appealing to the people working in PE and should, in Burr's view, represent a new model of management.

While growth was perceived as a necessity for people's development, the extreme form it took in PE and the unusual corporate culture also resulted in problems of understaffing and consequently over-utilization of human resources. The constant strain led to a half-way-implemented job rotation program and other human resource policies, high stress, growing rates of sick-leave, disrupted family lives, and lower work morale. The fast pace of PE and the high levels of stress in the organization were beginning to affect the company's prospects and employee commitment. The service quality that PE offered to its customers suffered tremendously under these conditions and left many customers unsatisfied. Despite these signals the top management was committed to high growth rates and wanted to retain the challenging environment in PE. In 1982 the company started to undertake organizational changes. The president of PE, Gerald Gritner, resigned, as he was not comfortable with the pace of growth, and Don Burr took over that position. The job rotation program broke down because people remained in their positions in order to meet the challenges of work. In 1984 PE adopted a new structure and management philosophy in order to retain the spirit of an entrepreneurial firm. They formed organizational units around the planes, focused on leadership training programs, changed the recruiting, promotion and incentive system. For instance, PE started what they called an internship program. They hired college undergraduates and placed them into full-time positions based on their performance in the program. The incentive system changed toward rewarding immediate performance instead of the long-term-oriented incentive system PE previously had.

While PE was engaged in major activities to cope with its incredible growth, major developments happened in the marketplace. The low-cost strategy of PE was challenged by Continental, which started to serve the same market segment. The traditional, large, full-service airlines became aware of PE and its strategy to take on their traditional routes. For example, PE attacked American, Northwest, and Delta airlines on their most profitable routes with price discounts of as much as 70 percent. This triggered instant responses from the competitors. Prices were matched to the level of PE while the service was at a much higher level. Business customers and frequent travelers who had been attracted to PE due to their low prices returned to the traditional airlines. As a result the load factor of the planes, and with it the financial performance of PE, fell dramatically.

In the beginning of 1985 American Airlines (AA) introduced a yield management system that allowed differentiation of the price for each seat in a dynamic reservation system. PE did not have the information technology to introduce similar price discrimination strategies. The marketing campaign of AA attracted the traditional customers of PE. This left PE with two alternatives: match AA's price for all its available seats and accept huge losses, or keep prices above the lowest offered by AA and consequently risk losing its distinct market position as the low-cost airline.

PE reacted to the stiffening competitive environment by acquiring Frontier, a run-down airline in the midwest, and other small carriers with the goal of gaining critical mass in a consolidating industry. This move ended in substantial cash drains and introduced further internal problems as the cultures of the acquired airlines were very different from PEs.

Despite these efforts, PE's downfall was irreversible. Don Burr was forced to sell PE to Texas Air Corporation in September 1986. For many of the employees this was the end of the dream of a more humane workplace and a personal growth and success story. While this was the end of PE as a business entity, it still has an effect on the people who worked there. As a former employee expressed it: "I don't care what anybody says; it was the right way to do business. There was no fear, no barriers. It was the best education that I ever had; I am still learning from it. I'm still growing from it . . ." (Holland, 1993: 18).

CONCLUSION

A high-quality process of vision generation and implementation as well as a high quality of content of the vision are related to high organizational and follower performance. The 11 principles proposed here summarize the empirical knowledge concerning leading through vision and will help managers to provide a high-quality vision. Managers who follow these guidelines will be able to help their organizations to perform at a higher level.

Leading through vision, however, does not always lead to higher organizational performance. There are numerous examples showing that visionary leaders contribute as much to the downfall of organizations as to their success. When we analyze the causes for People Express's success and failure we recognize that having a great vision is not a substitute for good management.

Instead of consolidating the business after substantial growth, Don Burr continued to expand the organization despite the very clear signs of overstrained resources. The result was burn-out, an organizational structure that was not able to meet the challenges of a company of that size, and systems that could not support the number of clients and routes that PE had. Due to the continuous concentration on growth the internal alignment was not managed carefully enough and the steps to achieve the vision were not implemented consistently. A more careful integration of the insights of lower-level management would have led to the recognition that the resources were over-utilized and that this situation was jeopardizing the long-term achievement of the growth strategy. In addition to that the top management team was not on board concerning the implementation of the strategy, as can be seen by the recruiting process set up by the HR executive. This process was more geared towards selecting the best people rather than towards meeting the demand of people in order to achieve the growth strategy. Fatal strategic decisions such as the head-on attack of major players in the airline industry helped to accelerate the downturn of PE. Leading through vision may over-stretch the organization and create rigidity or misplaced efforts that does not allow achieving the vision through alternative strategies. Consequently, managers should carefully monitor signs of excessive workloads. They should also re-think their strategies on a continual basis. This requires top-managers to be committed to their vision but to be flexible in its implementation.

The lesson to be learned is quite simple: leading through vision is not a substitute for good management, but good management without a vision is like a blind man without a dog.

Note

We want to thank Ms. Terese Kung for her valuable comments on the substance of this chapter.

References

Awamleh, R., and Gardner, W. L. (1997). Perceptions of leader charisma and effectiveness: The effects of vision content, vision delivery, and organizational performance. Proceedings of the Southern Management Association Meetings, Atlanta, GA, 76–8.

Bandura, A. (1986). *Social foundation of thought and action: A social cognitive theory*. Englewood Cliffs, NJ: Prentice-Hall.

Bartlett, Ch. A., Elderkin, K., and Feinberg, B. (1993). *Jan Carlzon: CEO at SAS*. Harvard Business School Case Study 9-392-149.

Bass, B. M. (1985). *Transformational leadership*. San Francisco: Jossey-Bass.

Bass, B. M. (1998). *Transformational leadership: Industrial, military, and educational impact*. London/Mahwah: Lawrence Erlbaum Associates.

Baum, J. R., Locke, E. A., and Kirkpatrick, S. A. (1998). A longitudinal study of the relation of vision and vision communication to venture growth in entrepreneurial firms. *Journal of Applied Psychology*, 83(1), 43–54.

Benford, R. D., Hunt, S. A. (1992). Dramaturgy and social movements: The social construction and communication of power. *Sociological Inquiry*, 62(1), 36–55.

Berlew, D. E. (1974). Leadership and organizational excitement. *California Management Review*, 17(2), 21–30.

Collins, J. C., Porras, J. I. (1997). Built to last: Successful habits of visionary companies. London: HarperCollins.

Conger, J. A. (1989). *The charismatic leader: Behind the mystic of exceptional leadership*. San Francisco: Jossey-Bass.

Conger, J. A., and Kanungo, R. N. (1987). Toward a behavioral theory of charismatic leadership in organizational settings. *Academy of Management Review*, 12, 637–47.

Conger, J. A., and Kanungo, R. N. (1998). *Charismatic leadership in organizations*. Thousand Oaks, CA: Sage Publications.

Coulson-Thomas, C. (1992). Leadership and corporate transformation. *Leadership and Organizational Development Journal*, 13(4), IV–VII.

D'Aveni, R. (1994). *Hypercompetition*. San Francisco: The Free Press.

Doz, Y. L., and Prahalad, C. K. (1987), A process model of strategic redirection in large complex firms: The case of multinational corporations. In A. Pettigrew (ed.), *The management of strategic change* (pp. 63–83). Oxford: Basil Blackwell.

Dutton, J. E., Dukerich, J. M., and Harquail, C. V. (1994). Organizational images and member identification. *Administrative Science Quarterly*, 39(2), 239–63.

Fiol, C. M., Harris D., and House R. (1999). Charismatic leadership: Strategies for effecting social change. Working Paper, Wharton School, University of Pennsylvania.

Gardner, W. L., and Acolio, B. J. (1998). The charismatic relationship: A dramaturgical perspective. *Academy of Management Review*, 23(1), 32–58.

Hart, S. L., and Quinn, R. E. (1993). Roles executives play: CEOs, behavioral complexity and firm performance. *Human Relations*, 46(5), 543–74.

Hauser, M. (1999a). Theorien charismatische Führung: Kritischer Literaturürberblick und Forschungsanregungen. *Zeitschrift für Betriebswirtschaft*, 69(9), 1003–23.

Hauser, M. (1999b). *Charismatische Führung: Ein Schlüssel für radikalen Wandel in Unternehmenskrisen*. Wiesbaden: Gabler.

Holladay, S. J., and Coombs, W. T. (1993). Communicating visions: An exploration of the role of delivery in the creation of leader charisma. *Management Communication Quarterly*, 6, 405–27.

Holladay, S. J., and Coombs, W. T. (1994). Speaking of visions and visions being spoken: An exploration of the effects of content and delivery on perceptions of leader charisma. *Management Communication Quarterly*, 8, 165–89.

Holland, Ph. (1993). *People Express Airlines: Rise and decline*. Harvard Business School Case Study 9–490–012.

House, R. J. (1977). A 1976 theory of charismatic leadership. In J. G. Hunt and L. L. Larson (eds.), *Leadership: The cutting edge* (pp. 189–207). London: Cummings.

House, R. J. (1995). Leadership in the 21st century: A speculative inquiry. In A. Howard, *The Changing Nature of Work* (pp. 411–50). San Francisco: Jossey-Bass.

House, R. J., Hanges, P. J., Ruiz-Quintinilla, S. A., Dorfman, P. W., Javidan, M., Dickson, M., Gupta, V., et al. (1999): Cultural influences on leadership and organizations: Project GLOBE. In J. Mobley (ed.): *Advances in global leadership* (Vol. 1, pp. 171–233). Greenwich/London: JAI Press.

House, R. J., and Shamir, B. (1993). Toward the integration of transformational, charismatic and visionary theories of charismatic leadership. In M. Chemers and R. Ayman (eds.), *Leadership: perspectives and research directions* (pp. 81–107). New York: Academic Press.

House, R. J., and Spangler, Woycke (1991). Personality and charisma in the US presidency: A psychological theory of leader effectiveness. *Administrative Science Quarterly*, 36(3), 364–96.

Howell, J. M., and Frost, P. J. (1989). A laboratory study of charismatic leadership. *Organizational*

Behavior and Human Decision Processes, 43, 243–69.

Howell, J .M., and Higgins, C. A. (1990). Champions of change: Identifying, understanding, and supporting champions of technological innovations. *Organizational Dynamics*, 19(1), 40–55.

Kakabadse, A., McMahon, J. T., and Myers, A. (1995). Correlates of internal and external leadership of top management teams: An international comparative study. *Leadership and Organization Development Journal*, 16(7), 10–17.

Kirkpatrick, S. A., and Locke, E. A. (1996). Direct and indirect effects of three core charismatic leadership components on performance and attitudes. *Journal of Applied Psychology*, 81, 36–51.

Kirkpatrick, S. A., Wofford, J. C., and Baum, J. R. (1999). Leader motives and performance in service and manufacturing organizations. Washington, DC: unpublished manuscript.

Kouzes, J. M., and Posner, B. Z. (1987). *The leadership challenge: How to get extraordinary things done in organizations*. San Francisco: Jossey-Bass.

Larwood, L., Falbe, C. M., Kriger, M. P., and Miesing, P. (1995). Structure and meaning of organizational vision. *Academy of Management Journal*, 38, 740–69.

Lowe, K. B., Kroeck, K. G., and Shrivasubramaniam, N. (1996). Effectiveness correlates of transformational and transactional leadership: A meta-analytic review of the MLQ literature. *Leadership Quarterly*, 7, 385–425.

Oswald, S., Stanwick, P., and LaTour, M. (1997). The effect of vision strategic planning, and cultural relationships on organizational performance: A structural approach. *International Journal of Management*, 14(3/2), 521–9.

Roberts, N. C. (1985). Transforming leadership: A process of collective action. *Human Relations*, 38, 1023–46.

Sashkin, M. (1988). The visionary leader. In J. A. Conger and R. N. Kanungo (eds.), *Charismatic leadership* (pp. 120–60). San Francisco: Jossey-Bass.

Shamir, B., Arthur, M. B., and House, R. J. (1994). The rhetoric of charismatic leadership: A theoretical extension, a case study and implications for future research. *Leadership Quarterly*, 5, 25–42.

Shamir, B., House, R. J., and Arthur, M. B. (1993). The motivational effects of charismatic leadership: A self-concept-based theory. *Organization Science*, 4, 577–94.

Sims, H. P., and Lorenzi, P. (1992). *The new leadership paradigm: Social learning and cognition in organizations*. Newbury Park, CA: Sage.

Steyrer, J. (1995). *Charisma in Organisationen*. Frankfurt and New York: Campus.

Thoms, P., and Greenberger, D. B. (1993). A model of the relationship between leadership and time. Paper presented at the annual meeting of the Academy of Management, August, Atlanta, GA.

Thoms, P., and Greenberger, D. B. (1995). Training business leaders to create positive organizational visions of the future: Is it successful? *Academy of Management Journal* (Best Paper Proceedings), 212–16.

Trice, H. M., and Beyer, J. M. (1986). Charisma and its routinization in two social movement organizations. In L. L. Cummings and B. M. Staw (eds.), *Research in organizational behavior* (Vol. 8, pp. 113–64). Greenwich, CT, JAI Press.

Whitestone, D. (1983). *People express (A)*. Harvard Business School Case Study 9-483-103.

Yukl, G. (1994). *Leadership in organizations*. Englewood Cliffs: Prentice-Hall.

19

Foster Trust through Competence, Honesty, and Integrity

SABRINA SALAM

Trust is the foundation of any beneficial and successful relationship between individuals and between organizations (e.g., Mayer et al., 1995; McAllister, 1995). Interpersonal, or dyadic, trust is defined as the "extent to which a person is confident in, and willing to act on the basis of, the words, actions, and decisions of another" (McAllister, 1995: 25).

When discussing trust with managers in organizations, what they most want to know is how to increase trust within their organizations. Thus this chapter focuses specifically on how leaders can create trust with their followers. Trust is most real to them when described in terms of integrity, honesty, and competence. Creating the kind of environment and providing the kind of support that fosters high competence (Kouzes and Posner, 1993) and integrity (Kouzes and Posner, 1993; Yukl, 1994) fosters trust and thereby benefits the organization as a whole.

Integrity (loyalty to one's rational convictions in action) and honesty (the refusal to fake reality) are crucial because subordinates only act consistently and rationally on the basis of the words and decisions of another if they believe that these words and decisions are those of someone who can be believed.

Additionally, to create trust in subordinates, leaders must know what they are talking about. In other words, leaders must be competent. Only then will subordinates be confident that the leaders' ideas are relevant and useful. Trust may be partly domain specific (Zand, 1972). For example, actions that create trust in one's expertise in one area (e.g., running the advertisement campaign for a new product) do not automatically lead to a creation of trust in other areas (e.g., determining the overall strategy for the entire organization). However, this does not mean that domains can be totally isolated from each other. A leader who is ignorant with respect to task A, a critical part of his job, may not be trusted (correctly or not) to perform tasks B and C either.

THE BENEFITS OF TRUST

Leaders should foster trust in their organizations because it leads to many beneficial outcomes in organizational life.

Willingness to stay with the organization

The reasons employees leave an organization are very frequently related to their direct superiors and the trust these employees develop toward their superiors. For example, whether or not a supervisor follows up on promises made to the subordinate, whether or not a supervisor provides competent coaching for the subordinate, and whether or not a supervisor is fair in performance evaluations all affect the trust towards this superior which in turn is influential in a subordinate's decision to stay with an organization. When employees leave, their knowledge and expertise is lost, and it may be expensive to replace them.

Creativity, innovation, initiative

Subordinates with high trust in their leaders are likely to perceive lower risks in the relationship than subordinates with low trust in their leaders. Being innovative and creative usually entails a greater danger of making mistakes than following orders; but followers will perceive the risks to be lower if they trust their leader to know the job and treat them fairly. Creating this kind of trust is crucial if the leader does not want subordinates to be afraid to make mistakes. This is particularly the case because the power relationship between leader and subordinate is unequal. The amount of uncertainty, vulnerability, and hence risk an individual perceives is inherently higher for a lower-status member of a relationship (Kramer, 1996). The simple existence of vulnerability and uncertainty makes concerns about trust more salient for subordinates. Hence, the higher the vulnerability and uncertainty, the more likely a subordinate will be concerned about trust. Of course, this has limits. An effective leader cannot tolerate subordinates who are consistently ineffective.

It is particularly during times of organizational crisis and change that many employees feel a great amount of uncertainty and fear. They perceive a greater risk in being open, innovative, and creative, all of which are necessary for any implementation of a change process. If leaders are able to create trust, however, employees feel that they are "in good hands" even during uncertain times.

Communication

The amount of trust that exists between two individuals affects the efficiency and accuracy of communication between them. The greater the trust between, a leader and her/his employee, the more accurate their information exchange, the better performance goals are understood, and the higher the quality of communication that develops between them. It is especially important that subordinates feel free to bring up bad news and not feel that they, the messenger, will be shot. Once the leader is known to shoot the messenger, the messengers will be sure never to bring up negative information. Through its positive effects trust insures a free flow of information. Again, especially in times of organizational crisis, trust encourages undistorted communication and collaboration (Zand, 1972).

Commitment to decisions

When a leader is successful in creating trust in employees, these employees are likely to be more committed to both decisions developed jointly with the leader and to decisions made by the leader alone (Frost and Moussavi, 1992; Tyler and Degoey, 1996; Zand, 1972). Commitment to decisions is important in order to ensure their successful implementation. Many change programs in organizations, for example, fail because the majority of employees are not committed to them and do not implement the desired changes in their daily work. Employees revert to the "old way of doing things" with the only difference that they are now using, for example, more expensive tools and systems. Since trust encourages commitment to decisions, developing greater trust in the organization encourages the implementation of changes in the organization.

Performance

Trust affects employee performance. All the outcomes of trust described above positively influence the performance of subordinates, directly or indirectly. Furthermore, individuals and teams who trust their leaders demonstrate more vigilant and effective problem-solving (Deluga, 1994; Robinson, 1996; Zand, 1972). Therefore, given the same levels of competence, an employee who is in a relationship characterized by high trust will perform at higher levels than an employee who is in a relationship characterized by low trust.

Understanding the importance of trust in an organization is the first step in creating an effective organization. Equally important is understanding why competence and integrity (including honesty) are the fundamental components of trust.

DEVELOPMENT OF MORAL AND PRACTICAL TRUST

Competence and integrity directly foster two aspects of trust. The integrity and honesty of a leader increase *moral* trust of the subordinate in the leader. Competence increases *practical* trust which is the belief in the knowledge, skills, and abilities of the leader. Leaders creates the highest amount of trust if they are both competent and honest.

I will now describe what leaders of organizations can do to create trust in their subordinates. None of these actions will be a surprise to any leader. Most leaders are aware of what they should do to become better leaders. Nevertheless, many leaders fail to do so either because they are personally immoral or incompetent, or, more likely to be the case, they may get distracted by the extreme challenges they are faced with on a daily basis. Not only do they have to manage their subordinates but they also need to be aware and think about the latest moves of competitors in the market, newest product developments, government regulations, technical and process inefficiencies in their supply chain, etc. Therefore, it is necessary to remind leaders of what it takes to be an effective leader.

How to develop trust

Visibility of the leader's behavior.   Competence and integrity in the leader's behavior create trust in the subordinate. However, for a subordinate to be able to make an assessment of the leader's competence and integrity, the subordinate must be aware of and familiar with the leader's past actions and decisions. Hence, leaders can only create trust in subordinates if they ensure that the subordinates have knowledge and information about their behavior. Hence, ensuring the visibility of one's behavior is absolutely necessary for the creation of trust. There are several organizational procedures that ensure the visibility of behavior which I will discuss later. But the leader can ensure visibility through frequent contact and exchange of information with subordinates. This contact can be face to face or through other means (telephone, memos, e-mail, etc.). However, greater face-to-face contact leads to a richer and more high-quality exchange of information, which can only encourage the building of trust (Salam, 1998).

When leaders communicate face to face rather than through other means, they are able to convey information in greater detail, thereby preventing any misinterpretations by the subordinate. Also, face-to-face communication allows the subordinate to ask for immediate clarification. This in turn may trigger further explanations of a situation by the leader, which increases overall quality of communication, all of which is beneficial in the creation of trust. Face-to-face communication also allows the leader to physically demonstrate competence in a particular task, hence reinforcing any verbal advice the leader may give to a subordinate. In simple terms, in addition to allowing more detailed exchange of information, face-to-face contact provides the leader with the opportunity to not just "talk the talk" but also "walk the walk."

Creating trust through fairness.   Honesty and integrity imply fairness, i.e. looking at the facts objectively and acting accordingly. Fairness is a fundamental requirement for creating trust in subordinates. According to justice theory (which is described in greater detail in chapter 13 above), there are two aspects of fairness, procedural and distributive justice (e.g., Brockner and Siegel, 1996). Procedural justice refers to the fairness of procedures employed by an authority, while distributive justice refers to the fairness of outcomes. Research has demonstrated that procedural justice (i.e., fairness) affects attributions of trustworthiness to the party who determines the procedures, hence, leaders of an organization (Brockner and Siegel, 1996; Kim and Mauborgne, 1993). Brockner and Siegel (1996) argue that procedural justice affects two factors in the assessment of trustworthiness: ability and motivation. The former relates to the ability of a party to develop fair procedures or to engage in fair behavior (this is related to the practical aspect of trust). The latter refers to the intent or willingness of a party to engage in fair behavior (this is related to the moral aspect of trust). In other words, how fairly a leader behaves influences the development of both moral and practical trust of the subordinate in the leader (e.g., Brockner and Siegel, 1996). For example, a marketing manager who is unable to judge the quality of a market research report due to lack of competence in this area is unable to judge which of his employees has better capabilities in conducting market research and therefore is unable to appraise and reward performance fairly. Only if a leader is competent in a particular area is he at all capable of being fair. Whether this capability really translates into fair behavior depends on the integrity of the leader.

Fairness also requires consistent behavior. Behaving fairly in one kind of setting but not in others will cause doubts in the subordinates about the integrity of the leader.

Creating trust through integrity and honesty. The *sine qua non* of creating trust is always to tell the truth. While this may seem like a trivial statement, it is a principle that is difficult to follow. During times of crisis and change, business leaders often are faced with the challenge of either telling an uncomfortable truth or remaining silent. There are plenty of other situations in which, in the short term, it may be more comfortable not to tell the truth to subordinates; however, refraining from doing so will prevent the creation of trust.

It is often uncomfortable to tell the truth when one has been unable to keep promises or been unable to act on expressed convictions. In such situations, even telling the truth may not be enough to create trust. Behaving according to expressed promises and convictions is essential in creating trust. Therefore, leaders have to always bear the consequences of their actions and words. Leaders should only make those promises that they sincerely believe that they will be able to keep and then act accordingly. Allowable exceptions depend on the context. Not keeping promises can be forgiven if employees believe that the execution of the promise was prevented by something outside the leader's control that could not have been foreseen and if the broken promises do not occur often. This requires that leaders have knowledge of their own competencies and abilities, but also of their own power and knowledge of the company's capabilities and its environment as a whole.

Subordinates are limited in the information they can process and are sometimes subjective when it comes to interpreting events and outcomes. Furthermore, the same kind of leader behavior may appear for one group of stakeholders as consistent and for others as inconsistent with prior promises of a leader. Therefore, leaders need to ensure they explain the true reasons for any kind of behavior to those individuals affected by it. Explaining the reasons will help subordinates understand why the leader had to act in certain ways. This will leave less room for negative interpretations of leader behavior. Hence, leaders need to always act in a respectful, reliable, thorough, and responsible manner and encourage as well as support this behavior in their colleagues and subordinates.

Similarly, keeping subordinates informed of events within and outside the organization will also aid in a more objective and accurate interpretation of leader behavior. And sharing information about oneself that reveals knowledge about the competencies as well as personality of a leader will help subordinates to understand the leader's motives, facilitating an accurate interpretation of leader behavior. Hence, given that a leader acts in an honest and truthful manner, openness about oneself and events affecting the organization will support the creation of trust in subordinates.

Creating trust through competence. A leader needs to possess the competence, i.e. the knowledge, skills, and abilities, to perform certain actions and make certain decisions to create trust in subordinates. Remember that trust is partly domain specific. Therefore, leaders only need to possess high competence and self-efficacy in those areas where they have explicit responsibility. It is in these areas that leaders need to ensure that their skills and competencies are at a high level and continuously work on improving them. Leaders need to keep up to date with the most recent developments in their area of expertise. This is something that is increasingly difficult given the high frequency of innovations and changes in any business area.

Next to the technical skills, however, leaders need to maintain high levels of leadership competencies (e.g., how to manage people): being able to plan a career path together with subordinates, to set the right kinds of goals with subordinates, to fairly evaluate the performance of subordinates, to provide the right amount of coaching, and to effectively manage conflicts are all extremely crucial leadership skills. This also entails knowing and understanding your employees. Being able to empathize as well as correctly judge their competencies is essential to effective leadership. If successfully demonstrated, these attributes will create high degrees of trust in subordinates.

Another important leadership trait is self-awareness and a realistic judgment of one's abilities. Overestimating one's competencies will almost certainly lead to failure, and hence hamper the development of trust in subordinates. For leaders to demonstrate to subordinates that they know what they do and do not know is important in the creation of trust. It is a sign of objectivity to know when to ask for help and input in a particular task. Leaders will create high trust in subordinates if they approach the right subordinates who possess helpful knowledge and abilities to solve a particular problem, admitting that they would not be able to accomplish this task successfully alone. The leadership literature has had a long debate about the effectiveness of participative leadership. Research has demonstrated that it is not participative leadership as such that is effective. Rather, participation of subordinates will only be effective when the subordinates have valuable information or competencies to add that the leader does not have access to (see chapter 21 below). Leaders who are able to judge when they need input from subordinates will create higher trust than leaders who approach (or does not approach) subordinates when they have no valuable information available (or have no information available).

Organization-wide management practices to create trust. In the preceding sections of this chapter, I have explained what a leader can do in a one-on-one relationship with subordinates to create trust. A large part of being a leader, though, is to create the right kind of context and working environment in an organization in order to achieve organizational goals. In other words, for leaders to create the right kind of organizational culture through their actions is a powerful way of ensuring an environment characterized by trust.

Organizational culture is the shared values (what is important) and beliefs (how things work) that interact with an organization's processes, structures, and control systems to create behavioral norms (the *modus operandi*, or how we do things around here) (Uttal, 1983). It is a complex process to develop an organizational culture and many factors play into this. For leaders to ensure that the "right" kind of culture is developing in their organization, they need to exhibit consistent behavior that role-models the type of beliefs and values they want to create in their organization. Furthermore, the procedures and systems leaders employ also need to be in line with their desired culture. It is these kinds of actions of the leadership team that employees observe to understand what beliefs and values are rewarded in the organization they work in. If leaders can achieve the development of a high-trusting and high-performance oriented culture, they will clarify for their employees what kind of behaviors are expected from them, namely behavior characterized by trust and a motivation for high performance.

There are a number of organizational activities that leaders can undertake to create a high-trusting culture in their organization. Probably one of the most crucial measures to develop a high value for integrity is that all decision processes within the organization follow a set of fair and consistent rules and that adherence to these rules is transparent to every member of the organization. This can be assured through the involvement of at least some of the affected and involved employees whenever an organization makes particular company decisions, plans activities, or initiates changes. Furthermore, the decision processes that precede and accompany any organizational changes should be communicated widely as well as documented so that employees can review these processes whenever desirable.

Additionally, during the planning and implementation of any organizational changes, employees should always have the opportunity to have a dialogue with the decision-makers of the organization. This includes the opportunity to voice disagreements with organizational practices and the willingness of management to listen to disagreements. This will strongly increase the perceived fairness and integrity of the leadership team.

Organization-wide visibility of behaviors and decisions can be achieved through frequent two-way communication, transparent performance evaluation systems, interactive management style, physically open work setting or close physical proximity of offices, large company gatherings, etc. Organizational procedures such as awards for high performance, public recognition of praiseworthy behavior, joint celebration of success stories, experience-sharing sessions, and job rotations also encourage the exchange of information regarding the integrity and competence of colleagues' behaviors in organizations.

Leaders can also ensure through organizational practices that high levels of competence – an important cause for the development of trust – are maintained in an organization. In order to increase competence of individuals in organizations, even prior to effective training and development programs, specific and accurate job descriptions are necessary. Many organizations, however, suffer from unclear roles and responsibilities, which lead to an unclear definition of job functions. Several negative consequences result. Colleagues, supervisors or employees may "wrongfully" display low trust towards an individual only because they expect the individual to have competence in an area that is in the individual's mind not part of her/his job function. Another negative consequence is that individuals are trained and educated in the wrong kinds of skills and competencies. Every member of the organization needs to understand their own and their colleagues' roles and responsibilities in the entire business process. This ensures that people are only asked to perform those behaviors and make those decisions in which they are competent.

Encouraging a trusting and high-performance culture also entails that leadership identifies incompetent behaviors of employees and demonstrates that such performance is not tolerated, let alone rewarded, in their organization. As mentioned before, leaders can only detect incompetent behavior, though, if they are knowledgeable about what it means to "do a good job" in a particular area. This supports the importance of leader competence to create trust in subordinates. Similarly, leadership needs to visibly demonstrate that dishonest behavior of employees is also not accepted in their organization and sanction dishonest behavior whenever it occurs. Obviously, the company development program (training and education program) needs to be adequate in order to increase the right kinds of competencies of the employees. This development program needs to be comprehensive and long term. Furthermore, a process needs to be in place where the development program is continuously updated based on changes in the organization itself, the market of the company, technological changes in the industry, customer demands, etc. Hence, there are several organization-level measures leaders can undertake to create the right kind of organizational culture which facilitates the creation of trust in their subordinates.

Situations where integrity and competence will not be enough to increase trust

Given that the leader has competence and integrity, three factors affect the development of trust within the subordinate. One, the personal dispositions of the subordinate. Two, the knowledge of the subordinate about the leader's past actions. And three, the inferences, attributions, and processing of this knowledge. Each of these three aspects affects the development of both moral and practical trust.

Personal dispositions of the subordinate. Individuals differ in their tendency to trust others. The propensity to trust is a disposition that affects the amount of trust an individual experiences towards others (Mayer et al., 1995). The propensity to trust is a relatively stable trait of subordinates that "leads to a generalized expectation about the trustworthiness of others" (Mayer et al., 1995: 715). The propensity to trust is an important factor that affects the tendency of a subordinate to trust, particularly prior to having any other data on the leader available.

Negative personal experiences of individuals where they learned that trusting others is hurtful and has negative consequences can lead to the development of a low propensity to trust. Similarly, positive experiences where trust has been rewarded lead to a high propensity to trust. While this trait is difficult to change, experiences over a long period of time incompatible with existing propensity of trust levels can lead to a modification of this trait.

Given the same amount and kind of knowledge, the propensity to trust is likely to affect the level of trust an individual has. In other words, given the same levels of perceived leader competence and integrity, a subordinate with a weaker propensity to trust others is likely to have lower trust in the leader as compared to a subordinate with a stronger propensity to trust. It is interesting that individuals who tend to behave in trusting ways themselves also tend to project this trait and through that attribute higher trustworthiness to others (Deutsch, 1958).

Knowledge of the subordinate about the leader. While it is the leader's actions that do or do not create trust, it is the knowledge of these actions and the context of them that affect the creation of trust through their effect on assessments of trustworthiness by the subordinate (Mayer et al., 1995). While the leader might have an "objective" level of trustworthiness, perceived trust depends on the *personal* assessment of trustworthiness by the subordinate. The amount of information the subordinate has available and how the information is processed also affects this assessment of trustworthiness.

Subordinate information-processing. The development of trust depends on how the subordinates perceives their environment and what attributions they make based on these perceptions (Kramer, 1996; Meyerson, Weick, and Kramer, 1996). In other words, while objective data about the leader's past actions may be available, the development of trust depends on how the subordinate processes and interprets this information.

There is a large stream of research studying attribution theory (Weiner, 1974). A lesson learned from this research is that cognitions and mental frameworks affect what we perceive and how we perceive and interpret the vast amounts of information that impact on us in all social interactions. The field of decision-making (e.g., Kahneman and Tversky, 1984) also identifies how individuals differ in their "mental accounting" (Kramer, 1996). For example, how certain scenarios are framed is likely to affect the perceptions of trustworthiness in an individual. Therefore, next to influencing what the subordinate knows about the leader's actions, a leader can also influence how the subordinate processes this information by providing the appropriate framework in which a subordinate perceives a particular situation.

Through its effects on perceptions of the subordinate, trust also tends to reinforce itself. For example, employees with an initially high trust in leaders subsequently perceive fewer incidents of distrustful behavior from their leaders (Robinson, 1996). In the same way that initial trust affects subsequent perceptions of distrustful behavior, initial trust affects assessments of fairness, i.e., high initial trust leads to more positive assessments of fairness and low trust to more negative assessments of fairness (Tyler, 1988, 1994; Tyler and Lind, 1992).

EXAMPLES FROM PRACTICE

Below I will provide real-life examples from businesses where trust has been a major issue determining the success of various endeavors. These examples will illustrate how the principles explained in this chapter can be translated into real business situations. The first case illustrates factors that influence trust in interpersonal relationships while the second case illustrates factors that influence trust at an organizational level. The first case also points to the domain-specificity of trust. In this case, I will describe three leaders who are in a similar kind of situation, namely being for the first time in their career in the role of a team leader. However, these team leaders exhibit different degrees of integrity and competence and through that affect both the development of trust from their supervisor (the director) as well as from their subordinates (the team members) in different ways.

Moving from a functional to a product-oriented structure

The maintenance department of a large European logistics and transportation company, responsible for three products, used to be organized according to technical expertise. The department had one director (the supervisor of the leaders we are examining). Three functional managers reported to this director; their functions were mechanical, IT, and hydraulics. Several technicians and operators worked with each of the functional groups.

This operational structure, however, often functioned poorly in terms of cost and quality of service, so a new structure was put in place. In this new structure, teams were organized around products, rather than functions. Now the individuals reporting to the director were the expert technicians (the three leaders whose behavior we are examining). For the first time in their career, technicians were given responsibility for an entire product line and the management of a multi-functional team.

After six months of operation, the results varied and none of the teams were functioning according to the outlined principles. The director was surprised at the high degree of operating disparity between the teams, particularly because his trust in the different team leaders was inconsistent with the actual performance of the teams. Furthermore, within the teams, the atmospheres differed from being motivated and productive to dissatisfied and demoralized. The explanation for this confusing situation lies in the different types of behaviors the team leaders exhibited toward their supervisors and subordinates which in turn triggered differential perceptions of competence and integrity.

Product team 1 delivered the best results of all the teams. The director (supervisor of the team leader), however, was not happy at all with the leader of product team 1, hence did not trust the team leader's belief that these results were going to last in the long term. This unwillingness of the director to attribute the high performance of the team to the team leader's abilities stemmed from lack of communication between the director and the team leader which in turn triggered in the director's eyes a perception of low competence and integrity of the team leader. The team leader of product team 1 had no experience whatsoever in writing management reports, and therefore avoided his duties to the director, such as regular submission of management reports and communication with his director. This lack of competence in reporting to his boss as well as the lack of communication led to low trust of the director in the team leader. The lack of communication fostered the distrust of the director in the team leader because the director received no information that helped him attribute the positive results of the team to the team leader's competence. Furthermore, the director interpreted the lack of communication from the leader of team 1 as a sign of "bad conscience," hence attributing low integrity to the team leader.

Nevertheless, members of product team 1 (subordinates of the team leader) did develop high trust in their team leader which in turn led to their high performance. The team leader organized many occasions for communication and information exchange within the team. This fostered knowledge of one another, encouraged exchange of helpful information, and increased support the team members gave each other. Furthermore, the team leader did demonstrate high competence in the work content, but nevertheless allowed team members some decision-making power over their work, unless he saw a situation where intervention was necessary. This demonstrated not only high competence in both content as well as management but also demonstrated trust by the team leader in his team members. All of this fostered the development of both moral and practical trust within the team towards their leader. The development of moral trust was also fostered by the leader's fair and consistent evaluation of the team members' performances that resulted in a fair distribution of the bonuses.

The performance of product team 2 was lower than that of product team 1. Nevertheless, the director trusted the team leader of product team 2. In the director's opinion it was only because of the team leader that product team 2 achieved any good results at all. In other words, the director trusted the leader of product team 2. This situation, where the director trusted the team leader of product team 2 more than the leader of product team 1, despite its lower performance, can also be explained by the degree of perceived competence and integrity of the team leader. The team leader of product team 2 provided regular detailed management reports to the director. Furthermore, the team leader frequently met with the director formally as well as informally and told him about the work of the team. The team leader told the director that the poor results of the team were due to the low performance of the operators. Often, he, the team leader himself, had to jump in and get the operators' work done in order to compensate for their low performance. Hence, in the eyes of the director, the fulfillment of the team leader's responsibilities toward him demonstrated competence of the team leader regarding his management abilities. Furthermore, the director interpreted the team leader's willingness to jump in and help the team accomplish its task as demonstrating competence in his operational skills. In addition, the team leader demonstrated integrity toward the director by – in the eyes of the director – openly communicating to him the problems of the team and being willing to exceed his responsibilities by personally assisting in the team workload. All of this led to the development of both practical and moral trust by the director in the team leader.

Within product team 2, however, the atmosphere had gone sharply downhill. The operators in the team (subordinates of the team leader) did not appreciate the very direct style of management of the team leader. They felt like their leader was intruding into their work and not giving them enough space to accomplish their responsibilities. However, the mechanical technicians in the team (also subordinates of the team leader), who happen to be the former colleagues of the team leader under the old structure, did like the management style of the team leader. Hence, in terms of trust, there was a clear divide within the team. In the eyes of the operators, the team leader demonstrated very poor management behavior as well as low integrity. The operators felt that their team leader was micromanaging them, not letting them have enough room to perform their tasks well, not providing any coaching, and on top of all this, evaluating them unfairly. The operators felt that the team leader unfairly provided all the bonuses to his former colleagues, namely the mechanics in the team. This fostered conflicts between the operators and the mechanics in the team and triggered low trust between the operators and the team leader as well as between the operators and the mechanics within the team. The mechanics, on the other hand, felt that their team leader rightfully evaluated them as better than the operators and felt fairly treated. Furthermore, the team leader spent far more time coaching the mechanics than the operators; this led to a positive evaluation of the team leader from the mechanics' perspective, hence to high trust between the mechanics of the team and their team leader. However, the high trust between some of the subordinates and their team leader was not enough to create high performance for the team. This tense and conflict-filled atmosphere in the team led to the poor performance of the team as a whole.

Product team 3 also demonstrated poor results. The results of the team were worse than those of product team 1 and those of product team 2. Nevertheless, the director trusted the management capabilities of the team leader of product team 3, confusing the director even more about the mismatch between his judgment of the three team leaders and their teams' actual performance. Again, though, the director's perception of the competence and integrity of the team leader can explain this situation. The team leader of product team 3 had great skills in monitoring performance and in writing very detailed and informative management reports. The team leader was also very skilled in managing his budget, planning resources, and in setting performance goals based on this monitoring system. The director greatly appreciated this detailed information and demonstration of good management skills. Through that the director developed very high practical trust in the team leader.

Within product team 3, though, the atmosphere was very bad. All of the members of the team were unhappy with their team leader and had very low practical and moral trust in the leader. This was clearly due to the team leader's poor interpersonal, communication, and coaching skills. He avoided communication with his team members whenever he could. Furthermore, he was unable to provide valuable coaching, not only because he did not communicate with the team members, but also because he was assigned a product he had very little experience with. His team members complained that the team leader was a former member of the IT team, with little experience in producing this product. The team leader was always in his office doing paperwork, preparing detailed work schedules and charts to give to management, but never spent any time with his team members to help them accomplish their job. This led to extremely low practical trust between the team members and the team leader. There was never any basis to develop moral trust because the team members never received any information that helped them judge the integrity of their team leader.

This case illustrates the principles stated earlier in the chapter, namely that competence and integrity lead to the development of practical and moral trust, respectively. More importantly, though, it also demonstrates that information about the competence and integrity of a leader is required, otherwise there is no base to develop trust on. Furthermore, this case demonstrates that trust is *partly* domain specific. Trustworthiness is developed toward a specific characteristic of an individual; it is not a universal characteristic of an individual.

This case also points to another interesting aspect of trust in organizations. Should individuals use the same kind of criteria to evaluate the trustworthiness of a superior versus a subordinate? In the case illustrated above, the director clearly used different criteria than the team members to judge the performance of the three team leaders. This is due to the fact that particular behaviors of the team leader (such as writing accurate management reports, accurate forecasting, appropriate distribution of the budget, etc.) are salient for the director to do a good job in his position as a superior. Hence, a superior will tend to focus on these behaviors to make a judgment of their subordinates, even though a good superior should take a more holistic view to evaluate their subordinates' behaviors. The behaviors that are salient to a superior, though, are not the same behaviors that are salient for subordinates. For subordinates to do a good job, they depend on the coaching and team-management competencies of the leader (coaching, meeting management, conflict management). Since different behaviors are salient to superiors as opposed to subordinates, different behaviors are used to evaluate the trustworthiness of a leader. This means for leaders in organizations that they need to be aware of the different roles they play in organizations, namely being a superior as well as a follower at the same time. To be an effective leader means, therefore, managing all of those relationships in a way to create trust in the parties they get in contact with. Nevertheless, in the illustrated case, in order to make an accurate judgment of the team leaders' capability to manage their teams, the director should have attempted to find out more about the leaders' team-management competencies by talking to the team members directly.

Low trust through poor change management

An international chemicals company recently had gone through the implementation of an Enterprise Resource Planning (ERP) system. The purpose of implementing this tool was to optimize the supply-chain processes by having all of them based on the same kind of IT system. Through that, the company hoped for greater integration and a resulting increase in efficiency and productivity in its supply chain. A few months after the implementation of this tool, however, none of the hoped-for results were achieved. Processes were still ineffective and employees had to work with the new tools, but were applying their old ways of working. Overall, morale was low and employees developed greater and greater distrust in their management and doubted the success of the ERP system implementation.

Detailed interviews with employees provided insights into why this low level of trust developed. Employees did not understand why they had to go through this change and therefore perceived the necessity to make this painful change to a new system as something imposed on them by their leadership team. This lack of perceived control made employees feel treated unfairly, which in turn triggered low moral trust in the leadership. The perception that this new system was imposed on employees was due to the lack of communication from management explaining the need for a new IT system and discussing the reasons for this new system with their employees.

The management team also neglected to inform and educate employees in how and why their roles and responsibilities had changed with this new system being in place. Management never explained to employees how the entire business process had changed and what each employee's new part in the business process was and why all this was beneficial for the company. This in turn triggered perceptions in the employees that management itself did not know why it was making these changes, let alone being able to effectively implement this change. Hence, employees doubted the implementation capabilities of their leadership team which in turn triggered low practical trust in the leadership team.

All of this was topped by an extreme work overload. While the workload itself was not the biggest complaint, it was the lack of recognition from management that upset the employees the most. Due to this lack of recognition, stemming from the frequent absence of managers whenever they were needed, employees felt that management did not even know what the employees were working on. Hence, employees were unsure whether they were working on tasks for which there was no need. This in turn caused employees to believe that management did not even care about them and their work, all of which triggered low moral trust in the leadership team.

And lastly, employees felt that their management was demonstrating poor leadership qualities. There was very little communication, and what there was, was purely top-down, allowing no dialogue. There was a lack of an overall vision or strategy for employees, something desperately needed during hard and difficult times. Furthermore, employees felt that management was "talking the talk" but not "walking the walk." In other words, there was lots of discussion and complaining from management about the problems that needed to be fixed, but none of this talk was followed up by action. Probably most frustrating for the employees, they felt that not even management knew how to work with the new system. This lack of leadership competence in the employees' eyes also caused very low practical trust in their leadership team.

Hence, the employees clearly identified the causes of their low trust and disappointment with management. While open communication, mobilization through a clear vision, competent coaching from managers, fair processes, clear roles and responsibilities are important at any time, they are particularly important during times of change. Employees expect these kinds of behaviors from their management, and if they are missing, low trust, disappointment, bad performance, and resignation follow.

SUMMARY

Integrity and competence are the most critical characteristics of a leader in order to create trust in their subordinates. Integrity plus honesty leads to the development of moral trust, and competence leads to the development of practical trust. The development of trust, also, depends on the subordinate's personality (the propensity to trust), the knowledge of the leader's past actions, and the processing of that knowledge and information to assess the moral and practical aspects of trust. The moral and practical aspects of trust are related to each other, but nevertheless distinguishable.

In general, trust leads to many beneficial outcomes. For example, trust leads to greater willingness to stay with an organization, increased innovation and creativity, commitment to goals set by a leader, greater satisfaction with processes in interactive tasks with the leader, greater agreement with the leader's strategies and decisions, and higher performance.

In order to increase trust, leaders need to ensure integrity and honesty in all their words and actions as well as maintain high levels of competencies in their areas of responsibility. Furthermore, leaders should create an organizational culture characterized by high trust and high performance to encourage trusting and high-performing behavior in their employees.

REFERENCES

Brockner, J., and Siegel, P. (1996). Understanding the interaction between procedural and distributive justice: The role of trust. In R. M. Kramer and T. R. Tyler (eds.), *Trust in organizations: Frontiers of theory and research* (pp. 390–413). Thousand Oaks, CA: Sage Publications.

Deluga, Ronald J. (1994). Supervisor trust building, leader–member exchange and organizational citizenship behaviour. *Journal of Occupational and Organizational Psychology*, 67, 315–26.

Deutsch, Morton (1958). Trust and suspicion. *Conflict Resolution*, 2(4), 265–79.

Frost, Taggart F., and Moussavi, Farzad (1992). The relationship between leader power base and influence: The moderating role of trust. *Journal of Applied Business Research*, 8(4), 9–14.

Kahneman, D., and Tversky, A. (1984). Choices, values, and frames. *American Psychologist*, 39, 341–50.

Kim, W. Chan, and Mauborgne, Renee A. (1993). Procedural justice, attitudes, and subsidiary top management compliance with multinationals' corporate strategic decisions. *Academy of Management Journal*, 36(3), 502–26.

Kouzes, J. M., and Posner, B. Z. (1993). *Credibility*. San Francisco, CA: Jossey-Bass.

Kramer, R. M. (1996). Divergent realities and convergent disappointments in the hierarchic relation: Trust and the intuitive auditor at work. In R. M. Kramer and T. R. Tyler (eds.), *Trust in organizations: Frontiers of theory and research* (pp. 216–45). Thousand Oaks, CA: Sage Publications.

Mayer, Roger C., Davis, James H., and Schoorman, F. David (1995). An integrative model of organizational trust. *Academy of Management Review*, 20(3), 709–34.

McAllister, Daniel J. (1995). Affect- and cognition-based trust as foundations for interpersonal cooperation in organizations. *Academy of Management Journal*, 38(1), 24–59.

Meyerson, D., Weick, K. E., and Kramer, R. M. (1996). Swift trust and temporary groups. In R. M. Kramer and T. R. Tyler (eds.), *Trust in organizations: Frontiers of theory and research* (pp. 166–95). Thousand Oaks, CA: Sage Publications.

Robinson, Sandra. L. (1996). Trust and breach of the psychological contract. *Administrative Science Quarterly*, 41, 574–99.

Salam, Sabrina (1998). The effects of subordinate competence, leader competence, leader integrity, and technology on subordinate participation seeking, performance, satisfaction, and agreement. UMI Dissertation Information Service, Ann Arbor, Michigan.

Tyler, T. R. (1988). What is procedural justice? *Law and Society Review*, 22, 301–55.

Tyler, T. R. (1994). Psychological models of the justice motive. *Journal of Personality and Social Psychology*, 67, 850–63.

Tyler, Tom R., and Degoey, Peter (1996). Trust in organizational authorities: The influence of motive attributions on willingness to accept decisions. In R. D. Kramer and T. R. Tyler (eds.), *Trust in organizations: Frontiers of theory and research* (pp. 331–56). Thousand Oaks, CA: Sage Publications.

Tyler, T. R., and Lind, E. A. (1992). A relational model of authority in groups. In M. Snyder (ed.), *Advances in experimental social psychology* (25, pp. 115–92). New York: Academic Press.

Uttal, B. (1983). The corporate culture vultures. *Fortune*, Oct. 17.

Weiner, B. (1974). *Achievement motivation and attribution theory*. Morristown, NJ: General Learning Press.

Yukl, Gary (1994). *Leadership in Organizations*, 3rd edn. Englewood Cliffs, NJ: Prentice-Hall.

Zand, D. E. (1972). Trust and managerial problem-solving. *Administrative Science Quarterly*, 17, 229–39.

Part VII

ORGANIZATIONAL PROCESSES

20 Design Structure to Fit Strategy
    LEX DONALDSON

21 Use Participation to Share Information and Distribute
    Knowledge
    JOHN A. WAGNER III

22 Make Good Decisions by Effectively Managing the Decision-
    making Process
    GLEN WHYTE

23 Stimulate Creativity by Fueling Passion
    TERESA AMABILE

24 Manage Stress at Work through Preventive and Proactive
    Coping
    RALF SCHWARZER

25 Manage Conflict through Negotiation and Mediation
    M. SUSAN TAYLOR

26 Lead Organizational Change by Creating Dissatisfaction and
    Realigning the Organization with New Competitive Realities
    MICHAEL BEER

20

Design Structure to Fit Strategy

LEX DONALDSON

The organizational structure should be designed to fit the organizational strategy. This is the Principle of Designing Structure to Fit Strategy – the meta-principle of effective organizational structure.

This is a broad idea. However, there are sub-principles that follow from the meta-principle, which turn the broad idea into useful prescriptive guidance. The sub-principles make the principle of designing structure to fit strategy specific and actionable. By following these sub-principles, organizations can build structures that maximize their effectiveness.

The structure of an organization is the set of relationships between its members, such as who reports to whom on the organization chart or whether there is a "no smoking" rule. An organization coordinates the actions of its members in order to attain a goal (Scott, 1992). The strategy of an organization is its future intention of how it will attain its goals given its situation. The organization should adopt a structure that helps it to attain its goals and thereby promotes organizational effectiveness.

The structure that is most effective for an organization is one that fits its strategy (Chandler, 1962). Strategy determines the levels of four contingency factors: organizational size, innovation, diversification, and geographical diversity. These contingency factors, in turn, determine the nature of the tasks that confront members of the organization. Tasks can themselves vary on two dimensions: uncertainty and interdependence. Task uncertainty and task interdependence determine the mechanisms required to coordinate effectively the tasks. These coordination mechanisms underlie the different types of structure that are required to fit the strategy. The causal chain is: strategy, contingencies, task, coordination mechanisms, and structure. We will begin by outlining the coordination mechanisms and then discuss strategy, contingencies, and structures.

COORDINATION MECHANISMS

Task uncertainty and coordination mechanisms

Each organizational member needs to know what he or she should do in order to accomplish his or her task, so that their task dovetails with that of those being performed by other members. Coordination can be attained by either rule, plan, hierarchy or mutual agreement. Which of these coordinating mechanisms should be used depends upon the level of task uncertainty. Task uncertainty is the degree of predictability that working in a certain way will successfully accomplish the task. The coordination mechanism that is most effective is the one that fits the level of task uncertainty.

Rules state what should occur in each specified situation. A rule states that, if X occurs, then Y should be done, e.g., "If an employee is 15 minutes late then he or she will be fined for one hour's pay." Broadly understood, rules include standard operating procedures and written instructions for performing the task. They are also present in computerization and automation, and compose the software and hardware of these systems (Blau and Schoenherr, 1971). Thus rules are really part of the programming of decisions. Any particular case is decided by a framework that pre-exists that case. This allows the decision to be made quickly, without reflection or discussion. There is no necessity for involvement by a manager, so a member may simply follow the rule. A clerk can administer the rule. Thus rules economize on managers and allow delegation to lower-paid members (Blau and Schoenherr, 1971). A rule applies the same across all cases, so that rules foster consistency. This also means that rules treat every organizational member or client the same and so can be perceived as fair and equitable. However, a disadvantage of rules is that they are quite inflexible, in that whenever X occurs, then Y is prescribed – even though the situation may have changed so that Y is no longer useful. Therefore, rules are appropriate where the task is low on uncertainty, so that the when they were set they correctly anticipated future situations (Galbraith, 1973). Thus *rules fit low task uncertainty*.

Plans involve constructing a schedule of which member will do what and when. Plans can be flexible by being updated periodically as the situation changes. In this way, plans are appropriate where the task is less certain than for rules. Thus *plans fit quite low task uncertainty*.

Hierarchy uses managers to direct activities of their subordinates. By exercising judgment, managers achieve some flexibility in their decision-making, but managerial involvement is expensive because of their relatively high compensation and benefit costs. Where task uncertainty is medium then hierarchy should be used. Thus *hierarchy fits medium task uncertainty*.

Mutual agreement means that members agree among themselves who will do what and when. It relies upon the personal commitment of the members to the goals of the organization, or at least to the accomplishment of their tasks. By participating in decisions, members have increased understanding of what is required of them and tend to be more committed. Participation tends also to increase the quality of the decision by using the experience and initiative of members, and also saves the costs of supervision (Likert, 1961). However, mutual agreement has its own costs, in that it is a time-consuming process, because members have to resolve at the start of each time period who is going to do what. Mutual agreement should be used where task uncertainty is high. High task uncertainty makes it difficult for managers to know what is best, because of their limited expertise. This tends to lead organizations to hire educated people, such as professionals, who self-manage through mutual agreement (Hage and Aiken, 1970). Thus *mutual agreement fits high task uncertainty*.

The sub-principle of task uncertainty is:

- Tasks low on uncertainty should be governed by rules.
- Tasks somewhat low on uncertainty should be governed by plans.
- Tasks medium on uncertainty should be governed by hierarchy.
- Tasks high on uncertainty should be governed by mutual agreement.

Task interdependence and coordination mechanisms

Task interdependence refers to whether two tasks are connected and, if so, how intensively the tasks interact. The more intensive the connection between any two tasks, the greater the coordination that is needed. To facilitate coordination, organizational sub-units that are more interdependent should be placed closer together in the organizational hierarchy (Thompson, 1967). From the top of the hierarchy down, tasks are grouped according to their interdependence with one another, which defines organizational sub-units at each level. At the top of the hierarchy, reporting to top management are placed tasks that have no direct interdependence on each other, such as divisions whose products are unrelated to each other (this is termed pooled interdependence). At the next level down in the hierarchy are placed tasks that are moderately interdependent, such as where the product made by the manufacturing department becomes the input for the marketing department (this is termed sequential interdependence). At the bottom level in the hierarchy are placed tasks that are highly interdependent, such as milling and boring operations in a job shop, between which a product moves back and forth numerous times as it is fabricated (this is termed reciprocal interdependence).

The sub-principle of task interdependence is:

- The greater the interdependence between tasks, the greater their coordination needs to be and so the closer they should be located in the organizational hierarchy.

Thus the coordination mechanisms that should be used to structure an organization are set by task uncertainty and task interdependence. The tasks of an organization are set, in turn, by its strategy, as we shall now see. Thus strategy determines the tasks that determine the optimal structure.

STRATEGY

At least five different strategies may be distinguished: differentiation, innovation, low cost, market expansion, and risk reduction. Strategy affects the organization on four dimensions: size, innovation, diversification, and geographical diversity. These four dimensions are known as contingency factors because high organizational performance depends on fitting the organizational structure to each of them. Size is the number of people being organized; it relates to scale and is sought in a low-cost strategy. Innovation refers to materials, processes or outputs that are new to the organization and is sought in innovation or differentiation strategies. Diversification is producing services or products that are different from each other; the more different the services or products, the greater the diversification of the organization; it is sought in market expansion or risk reduction strategies. Geographical diversity is having different localities operate independently of each other; it is sought in market expansion or risk reduction strategies. Whenever an organization alters its strategy this tends to cause changes in one or other of the four contingency factors, i.e., in the levels of innovation sought or size or diversification or geographical diversity. Changes in one or other of these four contingency factors cause changes in task uncertainty or task interdependence. In this way, changes in strategy indirectly lead to changes in task uncertainty or task interdependence. Given that task uncertainty and task interdependence require particular structures, strategy ultimately drives the structural designs needed for effectiveness.

Specifically, increasing size decreases the uncertainty of many organizational tasks by making them more repetitive, leading to formalization. Increasing innovation increases task uncertainty, by requiring the solving of novel problems. Increasing innovation also increases task interdependence, because the various functional departments, such as research and manufacturing, have to interact to solve these novel problems. Increasing diversification and geographical diversity decreases task interdependence, because the different products or services or localities operate independently of each other. A consideration of each of these four contingency factors makes specific the organizational structures required to fulfill the meta-principle that structure must be designed to fit strategy.

Size

The volume of work performed by an organization, such as the numbers of products to be produced or customers to be served, affects the number of people required to perform it and thereby the size of the organization (i.e., the number of its members) (Blau and Schoenherr, 1971). In turn, organizational size determines the appropriate levels of specialization, formalization, hierarchy, and decentralization.

Size and specialization. Tasks need to be distributed among members so that each specializes in a certain task. This is to avoid the confusion of everybody trying to do the same thing at the same time, such as serving the same customer or operating the same equipment. Specialization also has the advantage that a member can become more expert in that task by repeatedly performing it. Also, for highly specialized tasks, their simplicity allows them to be performed by members who have little education, experience or training. This makes filling that role easier and allows lower pay. Thus the higher skill and lower cost advantages of specialization promote organizational efficiency.

The sub-principle of specialization is:

- ◆ The larger the organization, the more specialized should be the work of each member.

Size and formalization.   Increasing size means that some tasks, such as hiring employees or paying wages, are done repeatedly. Specialization also means that a member performs the same task repeatedly. Such repetition increases familiarity with the task and so reduces task uncertainty. This allows the task to be codified in rules, regulations, and standard operating procedures, which is referred to as formalization. Thus size increases formalization which promotes efficiency because of the increased programming of decisions (as discussed earlier). In contrast, an organization that fails to increase formalization as it grows in size is relying on more costly forms of coordination, such as the managerial hierarchy and so is being inefficient.

The sub-principle of formalization is:

♦ The larger the organization, the more formalized it should be.

Size and hierarchy.   The height of the hierarchy is affected by the span of control, that is, the number of members who are direct subordinates of each manager. As organizational size increases, the span of control increases for a manager until it becomes too wide. At this point a new intermediary level has to be introduced into the hierarchy between the manager and his or her erstwhile direct subordinates. In this way size leads to an increase in hierarchical levels, in order to avoid the breakdown in coordination that would occur if spans of control were too wide.

The sub-principle of hierarchical levels is:

♦ The larger the organization, the more hierarchical levels it should have.

Size and decentralization.   Larger size promotes decentralization. A larger number of members and customers increases the number of issues requiring managerial decision. Thus size increases organizational complexity. This complexity means that decisions cannot all be centralized, so that decentralization must increase as complexity increases. Decentralization means that some decisions are taken at levels down from the top of the hierarchy. The more decisions that are delegated and the further down the hierarchy that they are delegated, the greater is the decentralization. This means that some decisions are being taken by lower-level managers who have more knowledge of the local situation, avoiding delays and also the distortions that would occur if all information had to be fed up the hierarchy for centralized decision-making. Moreover, decentralization gives lower-level managers some degree of autonomy that helps involve and motivate them.

The sub-principle of decentralization is:

♦ The larger the organization becomes, the more it should decentralize decision-making.

In sum, as an organization grows larger so it should increase its specialization, formalization, hierarchical levels, and decentralization.

Innovation

A high rate of innovation means that, within a time period, there are a large number of outputs or processes that are new to the organization. The opposite of innovation is routine operation, which leads to low task uncertainty, which, as we have seen, is effectively organized by rules set by the hierarchy. Also, knowledge is centralized at the top of the organizational structure, so that decisions about other, medium uncertainty tasks can be taken centrally. This kind of organizational structure, which features high formalization, centralization, and psychological dependence of members on the hierarchy, is referred to as a mechanistic structure. Mechanistic structures are effective for routine tasks, especially low uncertainty tasks (Burns and Stalker, 1961).

In contrast, innovation requires that novel problems be solved. This often requires hiring technical experts or professionals and encouraging them to use their initiative, based upon a broad understanding of their task or the organizational mission. Such organizational members tend to coordinate through mutual agreement. Knowledge is diffused throughout the organizational structure, thus rendering ineffective a high degree of centralization. This kind of organizational structure, which features use of initiative by members, mutual agreement, decentralization, and also low formalization, is referred to as an organic structure (Burns and Stalker, 1961). Organic structures are effective for high uncertainty, innovatory tasks.

There is a continuum of organizational structures running from highly mechanistic through to highly organic, with many organizations lying at intermediary positions. Correspondingly, organizations vary in the level of their innovativeness. The more innovative the organization wants to be, the more organic its structure has to be.

The sub-principle of innovation is:

- ◆ The greater the innovation rate sought, the more organic the organizational structure should be.

Within an organization there can be variations in the level of organicness from department to department or section to section. These stem from variations in the uncertainty of the tasks being performed by each department. For example manufacturing is often mechanistic, because much of its work is repetitive, whereas research is usually organic, because its work is solving novel problems (Lawrence and Lorsch, 1967). Thus, far from a homogeneous organizational culture, the organization contains divergent sub-cultures.

The sub-sub-principle of innovation is:

- ◆ The greater the task uncertainty of any organizational sub-unit, the more organic it should be.

Nevertheless, despite such differences between departments in the same organization, where one department is interdependent on another they must achieve coordination.

Coordination mechanisms for innovation.   Innovation affects the mechanisms that should be used to coordinate the functional departments of an organization, through the effect of innovation on task uncertainty and task interdependence.

Where the organization does not wish to innovate, then there may be no research department. The task interdependence between functions may be of the low-intensity, simple, sequential kind: the sales department places an order upon the manufacturing department, which makes it and passes it on to the delivery department. The coordination mechanism that is required for sequential task interdependence is planning, because there is limited task uncertainty. The uncertainty that exists mainly arises from variations in throughput volume over time. Where plans cannot be used because of more uncertainty, coordination can be achieved through use of hierarchy.

In contrast, where the organization wishes to innovate, then there will usually be a research department. The task interdependence between functions will be of the highly intensive, reciprocal kind. The research department may have an idea for a new product, but the marketing department must examine the demand and price, and the manufacturing department must examine the feasibility and costs. Therefore a discussion needs to occur back and forth between the functional departments. Because the content and interactions involved in these discussions are uncertain, planning cannot be used and hierarchy does not suffice. Each department must adjust to the other and so their coordination is *ad hoc* and through mutual agreement (Thompson, 1967). The discussion is made more difficult by the sub-cultural differences of style, language, time frames, and values between the departments. The organization should create inter-functional teams to bring representatives of the functional departments together to facilitate cooperation. These teams may further be assisted by integrators who can act as facilitators. Inevitably, conflicts arise between the different perspectives of the functions and these should be resolved by open confrontation, that is problem-solving discussion, rather than by using power or being evasive (Lawrence and Lorsch, 1967).

The sub-principle of interdependence is:

◆ Where innovation is not required, interdependence between functional departments should be handled by planning through the hierarchy. Where innovation is required, interdependence between functional departments should be handled by cross-functional teams, facilitated by integrators and resolving conflict through confrontation.

Diversification

If the organization is undiversified (e.g., it produces a single product), then its tasks are interdependent – manufacturing makes what research designs – and so the main organizational sub-units are functions. Thus an undiversified organization should have a functional structure. Increasing diversification, by offering more diverse products or services, decreases the interdependence among the tasks of creating and selling each of these different outputs. If an organization is diversified, e.g., producing both automobiles and shoes, each of these two products is unrelated and so will have its own separate resources to design, make, and sell them. Such decreasing task interdependence reduces the amount of coordination of tasks and supervision required. Those tasks that are not interdependent become the primary building blocks of the organization and so are placed at the top of the hierarchy. Thus an undiversified organization should have a divisional structure. Hence diversification reduces task interdependence and so requires a shift from a functional to a divisional structure.

Divisionalization increases decentralization, so that the diversification that causes divisionalization also indirectly leads to more decentralization (in addition to that caused by size). Typically operational decisions are decentralized to the divisions, while strategic and major financial decisions remain centralized. A division has a complete set of operating resources and functions to design, make, and sell the product or service, so that the division can act autonomously from the rest of the organization. Therefore, information processing about the product and its environment can be mainly confined within the division. This reduces the need for most of the information about the product to flow to levels above the division, thus relieving the head office of work. In essence, where there are no synergies to be extracted from the operating divisions, then the corporate head office should play a minimal role. This role is confined to work such as supervising the managers in charge of the divisions, resource allocation across divisions, and managing corporate strategy (e.g., acquisitions and divestments). Thus the creation of autonomous divisions constitutes a significant increase in decentralization for the organization. Also, because the division operates independently of the other divisions, its performance can be assessed in terms of its profitability and the divisional manager rewarded on the basis of the profitability of his or her division.

However, the highly decentralized divisional structure only fits high diversification, that is, low task interdependence. In such a case, the products or services of the divisions are unrelated, i.e., they have nothing in common: materials, technologies, distribution or customers, etc. However, many companies are only moderately diversified, i.e., they have related products or services. The less diversified the company, that is, the more related its products or services, the greater their interdependence, i.e., through sharing materials or technologies, etc. This interdependence between divisions requires coordination, so such divisions are less autonomous than in the highly diversified case (just discussed). Consequently, the corporate head office is larger, contains more operating functions, and centralizes more decisions. For example, in a company making a related set of electronics products, some technology is in common across the product divisions, so research on it is conducted in a central laboratory, swelling the number of the staff in the corporate head office (Pitts, 1976). Another example is the vertically integrated forest products company, in which huge volumes of material pass from division to division down the value-added chain. These product flows need coordinating, so that divisional autonomy on production rates is curtailed and the corporate head office contains specialists in production planning and transportation (Lorsch and Allen, 1973). In essence, in related product or service organizations, there are operating synergies to be extracted from the divisions through their coordination and this entails a more "hands on" role for the corporate head office. Also, the managers in charge of the divisions are rewarded for their contribution to corporate profitability, not just the profitability of their division.

The sub-principle of diversification and divisionalization is:

- ◆ As the organization increases its diversification, it should divisionalize and use progressively more decentralization, a smaller head office with fewer operating functions, performance assessment of sub-units by profits rather than costs, and rewards for divisional managers based more on the performance of their division than of the corporation.

As seen, at low levels of diversification the organization should use a functional structure, whereas at high levels of diversification the organization should use a divisional structure. However at medium diversification there is a choice of either functional or divisional structures. Medium diversification is where there the products or services produced are related to each other in some way, for example having common materials, technology, skills, or customers. If the organization is structured functionally then the resources are managed in an integrated way, such as by a central manufacturing department that fosters economies of scale in purchasing and manufacturing. However, the focus on products or services and their markets is blurred, which impedes innovation and customer responsiveness. Hence a functional structure should be chosen where the medium diversification organization wishes to minimize costs, for example where it faces severe price competition.

Conversely, if the medium diversification organization is structured divisionally, then there is a strong focus by each division on each of its products or services and their markets. This fosters responsiveness to customers. Moreover, because each division has a complete set of functions, interaction among them is facilitated, thus boosting innovation. Responsiveness and innovation, in turn, enhance sales growth. However, the resources are scattered and duplicated across the divisions and not managed in an integrated way, so potential economies of scale in purchasing and manufacturing are sacrificed. Hence a divisional structure should be chosen where the organization wishes to maximize innovation and sales growth. Thus there is a trade-off, so that the medium diversification organization chooses to maximize either cost control or sales growth, while sacrificing the other.

The sub-principle of trade-off for medium diversifiers is:

◆ Medium diversified organizations should choose a functional structure where cost control is the main goal, and a divisional structure where sales growth is the main goal.

Some medium diversification organizations may wish to avoid the extremes of maximizing cost control or sales growth and instead may wish to compromise and have some cost control while attaining some innovation and customer responsiveness so as to attain moderate sales growth. They can retain both functional and product or service structures with equal emphasis by adopting a matrix structure of the functional-product, functional-project or functional-service types. Functional managers coordinate the common issues across the related products or services. A subordinate reports simultaneously to a functional manager and also to the manager in charge of a product or service. For example, the functional-project matrix of the Lockheed-Georgia Division of the Lockheed Aircraft Corporation features a manager for each function (e.g., engineering) and also a manager for each project, i.e., airplane type (e.g., C-5A), with subordinates reporting to both. The functional managers seek to control costs by optimizing the use of resources in an integrated way across projects, while the project managers facilitate interaction within their temporary teams (drawn from the functions), to speed innovation and to interface with their client (Corey and Star, 1971).

The sub-principle of compromise for medium diversification is:

◆ Medium diversified organizations should choose a functional-product matrix structure where both some cost control and some sales growth is the goal.

Geographical diversification

Geographical diversification is another way to reduce task interdependence. Each locality has its own complete set of resources and functions to design, make, and sell its product or service in its locality, so that it operates independently of other geographical areas of the organization. In this way, diversification along geographical lines can produce autonomous divisions, similar to product or service diversification, only the divisions are defined by locality.

The sub-principle of geographical diversity is:

◆ Where each locality operates independently of other localities then the structure should be geographical divisions.

In some organizations geographical diversity is at the medium level, so that there are significant differences between geographies, warranting a separate manager for each, while diversification is also medium, so that there also are significant differences between products, warranting a separate manager for each. Moreover, the activities of the products are distributed across the geographies in such a way that each product manager is coordinating his or her product across the geographies. Thus there will be both several geographical locality managers and several product managers. Each of their subordinates reports simultaneously to the managers of their geography and of their product. Hence the structure is a geography-product, or area-product, matrix (Davis and Lawrence, 1977). A frequently encountered example is the multinational corporation that has more than one distinct product or service, but which also produces and sells each of them in numerous different areas of the world (Galbraith and Kazanjian, 1988).

The sub-principle of medium geographical diversity and medium diversification is:

◆ Where there is a medium geographical diversity and medium diversification, then the organization should have a geography-product matrix structure.

CASE ILLUSTRATIONS

To more fully understand how these principles work in practice, we will discuss a positive example and then a negative example.

Product development at Toyota

Product development is sometimes supposed to be synonymous with an organic structure. However, this presumes that the products being developed are highly innovative, based on the creation of new science or technology, so that task uncertainty is high. In contrast, at Toyota Motor Corporation product development is evolution not revolution. Thus product development involves only moderate levels of task uncertainty, so that mechanistic elements are appropriate as well as organic elements.

Toyota mass produces high-quality, reliable automobiles, yet it is not a leading-edge innovator. As a high-volume automobile company, it faces tough cost pressures due to global competition. Hence new product development at Toyota seeks to create new models that are easily manufactured to tight costs and which share as much as possible across models in the range. This standardization has helped Toyota to introduce new models, and even some new products, thus "competing in time." Thus, while there is some degree of task uncertainty, it is moderate rather than high.

We will now describe product development at Toyota (Sobek, Liker, and Ward, 1998), coding each feature as to whether it is mechanistic or organic. Toyota features strong functions both for manufacturing and product development (mechanistic). Engineers remain in one or other function for most of their careers, so that, while they are rotated, it is within one of these functions (mechanistic), not between functions. There is a lengthy process of in-company training and on-the-job experience over many years before engineers rise to the higher levels where authority is vested (mechanistic). Younger engineers are closely supervised and mentored by their superiors (mechanistic), though the style is Socratic rather than directive (organic). Ongoing cross-functional coordination is provided by meetings (organic), but the extent of these is constrained in number and scope so that engineers can get on with their work.

There is considerable use of written documents (mechanistic). There are detailed, written standards for every part of the automobile (mechanistic). These are frequently updated by the engineers. Being written, they codify the knowledge, so that it is held by the company (mechanistic), not just by the individual. Meetings often work through detailed, written checklists. Requests for changes from one section to another are written and circulated prior to meetings. The decision of the meeting is then written up to record it formally (mechanistic). These documents conform to a standard format (mechanistic). Younger engineers are coached as to how exactly to write these documents and how to conduct the meetings (mechanistic).

There is cross-functional coordination provided by a chief engineer who leads the project and stands outside the functions (organic). However, the engineers working on the project remain in their functions, subject to the authority of their functional boss (mechanistic). Hence the project leader lacks line authority over the project and has to work by persuasion (organic). The credibility of the chief engineer rests in part on his engineering expertise and he is regarded not so much as the project manager as the lead designer (organic). There is a considerable amount of conflict involved, so that issues are thoroughly discussed (organic), rather than being settled forcibly or evaded.

Thus there are both mechanistic as well as organic elements in the organizational structure that is used for product development at Toyota, thereby fitting its strategy.

Product divisions at Nipont

Nipont (a pseudonym for a real Japanese corporation) had a functional structure. However, as it grew and diversified the range of its product offerings, Nipont replaced the functional with a divisional structure, following the pattern of most large corporations

(Rumelt 1974). It hoped that product divisions would offer greater flexibility and speedier response to each different product market, so as to boost innovation and attain faster sales growth. In the booming markets of the time this seemed appropriate. However, shortly after the adoption of the new divisional structure the environment changed in a way that made its divisional structure inappropriate.

International events led to a dramatic rise in the cost of oil, a major raw material, so placing pressure on Nipont's costs. This was compounded by increased competition from international competitors, who "dumped" their product into the Japanese home market at marginal cost, so placing pressure on prices. Squeezed by cost and price pressures, Nipont had to bring their costs under control. Unfortunately Nipont's divisional structure was unsuited to providing tight cost control.

The divisional structure at Nipont consisted of three product divisions: the Chemicals Division, Fibers Division, and Plastics Division. Each division operated autonomously, making its own decisions. However, in strategic terms, while Nipont was a diversified company, it was a company of only medium diversification, because its products were related. There were strong links between its three main products, i.e., substantial task interdependence. Fibers were the main product and were made by the Fibers Division. These are synthetic textiles that use materials made by the company, in common with the second main product, plastics, made by the Plastics Division. Much of the chemicals sold by the Chemicals Division were in fact by-products of the core processes used for the Fibers and Plastics Divisions.

Moreover, many of Nipont's production plants made more than one of these products. Two plants (Mishima and Nagoya) made products for all of the three product divisions. Other plants (Gifu and Shiga) made products for two of the product divisions. Therefore these plants were not under a unified command. The other plants each reported to their product division, so that control was split among the three product divisions. Therefore there was a lack of overall coordination of the company's production plants – despite their operations being interconnected. Thus there was no central control over manufacturing, sacrificing economies of scale. In a buoyant economy this had been a highly acceptable trade-off for the better flexibility and innovation potential offered by organization into separate product divisions. However, it became unacceptable as the environment forced an imperative towards reducing production costs. After a few years, Nipont reverted to a functional structure (Donaldson, 1979).

Given that the environments of organizations are frequently changing, this can lead them to alter their strategies, and they must then quickly change their structures in order to avoid misfit and ineffectiveness.

REFERENCES

Blau, Peter M., and Schoenherr, P. A. (1971). *The structure of organizations.* New York: Basic Books.

Burns, Tom, and Stalker, G. M. (1961). *The management of innovation.* London: Tavistock.

Chandler, Alfred D. Jr. (1962). *Strategy and structure: Chapters in the history of the industrial enterprise.* Cambridge, MA: MIT Press.

Corey, Raymond, and Star, Steven H. (1971). *Organization strategy: A marketing approach.* Boston: Division of Research, Graduate School of Business Administration, Harvard University.

Davis, Stanley M., and Lawrence, Paul R. (1977). *Matrix.* Reading, MA: Addison-Wesley.

Donaldson, Lex (1979). Regaining control at Nipont, *Journal of General Management*, 4(4), 14–30.

Galbraith, Jay R. (1973). *Designing complex organizations.* Reading, MA.: Addison-Wesley.

Galbraith, Jay R., and Kazanjian, Robert K. (1988). Strategy, technology and emerging organizational forms. In, Jerald Hage (ed.), *Futures of organization: Innovating to adapt strategy and human resources to rapid technological change.* Lexington, MA: Lexington Books.

Hage, Jerald, and Aiken, Michael (1970). *Social change in complex organizations.* New York: Random House.

Lawrence, Paul R., and Lorsch, Jay W. (1967). *Organization and environment: Managing differentiation and integration.* Boston: Division of Research, Graduate School of Business Administration, Harvard University.

Likert, Rensis (1961). *New patterns of management.* New York: McGraw-Hill.

Lorsch, Jay W., and Allen, Stephen A. (1973). *Managing diversity and inter-dependence: An organizational study of multidivisional firms.* Boston: Division of Research, Graduate School of Administration, Harvard University.

Pitts, Robert A. (1976). Diversification strategies and organizational policies of large diversified firms. *Journal of Economics and Business*, 28(3), 181–8.

Rumelt, Richard P. (1974). Strategy, structure and economic performance. Boston: Division of Research, Graduate School of Business Administration, Harvard University.

Scott, W. Richard (1992). *Organizations: Rational, natural and open systems*, 3rd edn. Englewood Cliffs, NJ: Prentice-Hall.

Sobek, Durward K., II, Liker, Jeffrey K. and Ward, Allen C. (1998). Another look at how Toyota integrates product development. *Harvard Business Review*, 76, 4, 36–49.

Thompson, James D. (1967). *Organizations in action.* New York: McGraw-Hill.

21

Use Participation to Share Information and Distribute Knowledge

John A. Wagner III

Participation is a process in which decision-making, problem-solving, action-planning, or similar activities are shared and performed jointly by hierarchical superiors and their subordinates. To participate, superiors and subordinates work together to identify alternatives, consider preferences, and finalize judgments. Defined in this manner, participation differs from direction, in which superiors follow autocratic procedures and act alone (Wagner, 1982). Participation also differs from consultation, in which superiors ask subordinates for their inputs and opinions but then weigh alternatives and make a final choice on their own (Vroom and Yetton, 1973). Less obviously, perhaps, participation differs from delegation, in which superiors remove themselves and cede complete authority to their subordinates. Whereas participation requires that outcomes reflect needs and interests shared across hierarchical levels, delegation is more likely to allow subordinates the autonomy to act in accordance with personal desires (Leana, 1987).

Social theorists have long suggested that participation influences human behavior by (1) involving participants directly in ongoing processes, thereby securing their commitment to participatory outcomes through the "sense of ownership" stimulated by their personal involvement, or by (2) providing participants the opportunity to exchange and collect information, and to become more fully informed and knowledgeable about ongoing activities and participatory results (e.g., Pateman, 1970). Organizational researchers have similarly speculated that participation might influence behavior in organizations through two distinct mechanisms, one termed *motivational* and the other *cognitive* (Barthlem and Locke, 1981; Locke and Schweiger, 1979; Miller and Monge, 1986; Schweiger and Leana, 1986; Wagner, Leana, Locke, and Schweiger 1997). Research on the two mechanisms sheds light on each mechanism's ability to predict and explain likely outcomes of participatory processes, and thus holds important implications for the management of organizational behavior.

Participation Does Not Always Motivate, and the Lack of It Does Not Always Demotivate

The motivational mechanism is thought to affect behavior in organizations through the heightened sense of personal commitment to or acceptance of participatory outcomes that comes from having a say in participatory processes and a part in shaping the outcomes of those processes. According to this explanation, participation stimulates a sense of commitment that motivates participants to support and implement participatory resolutions. Behavior is motivated and satisfaction is experienced as participants strive to see their resolutions through to completion.

Research on the motivational mechanism extends back to a series of studies conducted, during the 1920s and 1930s, at Western Electric's Hawthorne plant, located near Chicago, Illinois. In reviewing analyses of the effects of factors such as factory lighting, incentive payment, and supportive supervision on workforce satisfaction and performance, Hawthorne researchers noticed a pattern of results that seemed to indicate that workers were influenced by social conditions – specifically, by desires to satisfy needs for companionship and support at work – and that such conditions might have strong motivational effects. This led them to suggest that participatory involvement, in providing the opportunity to satisfy social needs, might motivate increased task performance and stimulate greater acceptance of organizational policies (Roethlisberger and Dickson, 1939).

Following up on this speculation, Coch and French (1948) performed a study of textile pieceworkers that appeared to indicate that workers would accept changes in job practices more readily if involved in the design and implementation of those practices. The authors identified participatory processes as effective in encouraging acceptance of and commitment to changed standards and procedures. They also characterized participation as a potentially powerful method of reducing personal frustration and aggression attributable to resistance to change.

Subsequent analyses of the motivational effects of participation focused increasing attention on *participation defined as a process of influence sharing*, and on the heightened personal commitment thought to accompany the redistribution and leveling of influence and authority in organizations. Theorists identified participatory processes as likely to have strong positive effects on workforce morale and satisfaction, feelings of involvement and commitment, and employee motivation and performance (e.g., Anderson, 1959; Dickson, 1981; McMahon, 1976; Patchen, 1964). Research first seemed to support this assertion (Fox, 1957; McCurdy and Eber, 1953; Pennington, Haravey, and Bass, 1958; Vroom, 1960), but as further evidence amassed, it became apparent that participation's motivational effects were neither as strong nor as generalizable as originally proposed. Some studies reported zero or near-zero relationships between participation and motivation, commitment, or performance (Alutto and Belasco, 1972; Castore and Murnighan, 1978; Ivancevich, 1977; Jenkins and Lawler, 1981; Rosenbaum and Rosenbaum, 1971), and others reported evidence of negative relationships between participation and the same outcome variables (Gibb, 1951; Green and Taber, 1980; Latham and Saari, 1979).

In the wake of these conflicting findings, Wagner and Gooding (1987) used a statistical technique called meta-analysis to aggregate the results of 70 published studies of participation, in order to estimate the strength of participation's general effects. After removing the effects of a troubling research artifact, percept-percept inflation (Crampton and Wagner, 1994), Wagner and Gooding discovered that participation correlated, on average, .11 with performance, .11 with satisfaction, and .10 with acceptance (i.e., commitment). Other analyses produced similar findings (e.g., Locke, Feren, McCaleb, Shaw, and Denny, 1980; Wagner, 1994; Wagner and LePine, 1999). After considering the available evidence, Locke, Alavi, and Wagner (1997) concluded that participation's likely correlations with performance and satisfaction are both on the order of .11. Changing levels of participation (i.e., from direction to participation) therefore explain only about 1 percent of the concurrent change in performance or satisfaction. This conclusion fails to support the use of participation as a motivational technique in the workplace.

When is participation most likely to motivate?

Despite documenting participation's general limitation as a motivational tool, Wagner and Gooding (1987) discovered situational conditions under which participation might have more substantial effects. In particular, their analysis suggested that participation is more likely to be related to employee satisfaction in instances where participation takes place in smaller groups – typically, groups of 12 or fewer members. Implied by this finding is the possibility that participants are unable to develop a sense of personal connection to or ownership of participatory outcomes in larger group settings, due perhaps to the fact that many people share in the creation of those outcomes, and thus each participant fails to derive satisfaction from participatory processes or results. In small groups, however, participation and satisfaction are correlated at the level of .25 on average, indicating that about 6 percent of the change in satisfaction can be attributed to participation's effects. The size of this relationship suggests that group size is an important situational condition and that participation in small groups has limited, but none the less noteworthy, utility as a practical means of stimulating workplace satisfaction.

Wagner and Gooding (1987) also reported that differences in task complexity have effects on the strength of relationships between participation and both satisfaction and acceptance. In each relationship, the effect is stronger when tasks are less complex, meaning more behaviorally routine and less cognitively demanding. Suggested is the possibility that participation can be used to enrich – make more challenging – otherwise oversimplified work. Participation's relationship with satisfaction is again somewhat modest, with an average correlation of .26 revealed in the presence of simple tasks, but its relationship with acceptance is more substantial, as evidenced by an average correlation of .32 under simple task conditions. Indicated by the latter finding is a fairly strong enrichment effect, in which increasing participation by individuals who otherwise perform simple tasks explains just over 10 percent of the corresponding increase in acceptance of the results of participatory processes.

PARTICIPATION DISSEMINATES INFORMATION

In contrast to the motivational mechanism's definition of participation as a process of influence sharing, within the framework of the cognitive mechanism the focus is on *participation defined as a process of information sharing.* From this perspective, participation's effects on organizational behavior are thought to be a function of the increased knowledge and deeper understanding afforded by participatory information sharing. Researchers have proposed that participatory information sharing might influence participant behaviors in several ways, for example: (1) knowing how to do a job increases the opportunity to do the job productively (Lawler and Hackman, 1969; Scheflen, Lawler, and Hackman, 1971); (2) understanding how a job fits into the larger picture of work group interdependence and organizational mission enables effective adjustment to changing work conditions (Ledford and Lawler, 1994; Williams, 1982); (3) sharing knowledge and insights encourages common understanding and greater cooperation (Dickson, 1981; Marrow and French, 1946); and (4) being able to access and make use of the collective information of an organization's membership increases the likelihood of successful organizational innovation and creativity (Stewart, 1997; Tannenbaum, 1968).

Research on the cognitive mechanism has sought to determine whether participation does, in fact, promote information sharing, and whether such sharing can have beneficial consequences for the performance of individuals, groups, or organizations. In one study, Latham, Winters, and Locke (1994) allowed some subjects in a laboratory experiment to share and discuss strategies for attaining assigned goals on a class-scheduling task, but prohibited other subjects from participating in similar discussions. Results of the experiment indicated that individuals who participated in strategy discussions formed better task strategies, felt more able to succeed in the task, and performed better on the task than did subjects barred from participation. Moreover, differences in strategy quality were found to explain much of the effect of participation on performance, indicating that participation improved performance by helping participants discover better performance strategies – a cognitive rather than motivational effect.

In another study, Scully, Kirkpatrick, and Locke (1995) manipulated the knowledge held by supervisors and subordinates in two-person laboratory groups. In one-third of the groups in the study, supervisors had the correct information needed to do their tasks, in one-third they had incorrect information, and in one-third they had no information whatsoever; subordinates were also split in thirds and assigned the same three levels of information; and half of the groups engaged in participatory information sharing while the other half did not. Results indicated that participation alone had no effect on subjects' performance, but that participation had beneficial effects on performance if the subordinate had correct information and the supervisor had none. In addition, performance suffered if the supervisor lacked correct information or if either or both members of a pair had incorrect information.

Suggested by these studies and others like them is the inference that participatory processes can be used to share or redistribute information, and that such redistribution can have positive effects on performance when it provides otherwise uninformed individuals with ready access to requisite knowledge and insights (Barthlem and Locke, 1981; Bass, Valenzi, Farrow, and Solomon, 1975; Lowin, 1968). Supported is the principle that participation will be beneficial when some individuals possess or can discover pertinent information and use participatory processes to disseminate it to others (Durham, Knight, and Locke, 1997).

When is participation most able to inform?

In addition to confirming participation's effectiveness in distributing information, Scully, Kirkpatrick, and Locke (1995) also provided evidence of an important situational condition – the degree of impactedness or "lumpiness" in the distribution of information, before participation – that appears able to determine whether participation will improve participant cognition and performance. Participation's effects appear to be strengthened by greater information impactedness, or conditions in which only a few individuals possess needed information and knowledge, since participatory information exchange allows participants to break down information disparities and increase the extent to which knowledge is shared and generally accessible. Conversely, participation's effects are typically weakened when information is already available to all, since additional information sharing is unnecessary and consumes resources more profitably devoted to other activities (Latham and Yukl, 1975; Bass and Valenzi, 1974; Williams, 1982).

Beyond the effects of information impactedness, speculation and the results of prior research suggest several additional situational conditions that might also affect the workings of the cognitive mechanism. One of these, interdependence, concerns the degree to which participants must work together to perform and succeed. Under conditions of low interdependence, individuals, groups, or organizations can perform successfully by working alone, while under conditions of high interdependence, individuals, groups, or organizations must work together to succeed. Differences in interdependence exert situational influence on participation's efficacy by affecting the amount of information required to coordinate ongoing relationships. While individuals performing independent tasks need not exchange much information to do their work, individuals performing interdependent tasks must share a great deal of information, including messages about what has been done, what must be done next, what adjustments need to be made in response to changing conditions, and so forth. To the extent that this information flow must be ongoing, that is, occurring as coordination problems emerge (as opposed to taking place on an occasional basis or through a supervisory intermediary), participatory "mutual adjustment" contributes to successful coordination and enhanced performance (Durham et al., 1997; Lawler, 1982; Sashkin, 1976).

Another situational condition, complexity, also appears likely to exert contingency effects on relationships between participation and performance. Complexity reflects the degree to which a task, objective, or situation is understandable, with low complexity referring to conditions that are simple and readily understood, and high complexity alluding to conditions that are complicated or intricate, and therefore difficult to interpret and comprehend. Successful performance in the presence of lower complexity is possible without additional information or insight. However, success under conditions of higher complexity requires access to the additional information needed to render the complex understandable. To the degree that participatory information exchange is able to provide such access, participation may produce little benefit when combined with low complexity but should provide appreciable benefit when paired with high complexity (e.g., Anderson, 1959; Singer, 1974). Note that this pattern is exactly opposite the configuration of effects revealed in research on the motivational mechanism, described earlier, wherein participatory enrichment improved performance on simple tasks.

Finally, the situational condition of change concerns the extent to which tasks, group conditions, and organizational contexts are stable, consistent, and predictable, under conditions of low change, versus dynamic, variable, and unpredictable, in situations of high change. In the presence of low change, success can be achieved by following familiar procedures, without modifying customary ways of doing things. In contrast, high amounts of change require that variability first be sensed, and that modifications then be made to existing plans and processes to match them to the demands of changing conditions. Such sensing and modification normally require information about the nature of change and the state of changed conditions. To the extent that such information is available to some but not necessarily all participants, participation can facilitate information dissemination and lead to successful adaptation and continued productivity (e.g., Abdel-Halim, 1983; Jermier and Berkes, 1979; Koch and Fox, 1978; Schuler, 1976).

Structuring Participation Can Make It More Effective

In thinking about participation, the first picture to come to mind is often that of a group of participants, seated casually around a table and engaged in spontaneous conversation. In fact, much research on participatory processes uses a physical arrangement that closely resembles this configuration. However, studies on group processes have indicated that grouping people together and asking them to suggest ideas and state opinions in front of others can stifle input into ongoing discussions. Especially when personal statements are readily attributable to individual participants, ideas and opinions that might be considered even the least bit controversial may remain unstated (e.g., Diehl and Stroebe, 1987).

To deal with this problem, researchers have suggested structuring group discussion sessions so that innovation or judgment is done individually and discussion occurs only to clarify the interpretation of information and brainstorm additional alternatives. Using the Nominal Group Technique (NGT), for instance, a group of individuals convenes around a table with a session coordinator and receives a description of the problem to be dealt with or issue to be addressed. Next, working alone, each participant writes down whatever ideas come to mind. The coordinator then asks each participant to share his or her ideas and writes them on a public display. Subsequently, participants discuss each other's ideas to clarify and expand on them, and then evaluate them as a group. Finally, participants rank the ideas privately, and the idea that ranks the highest among the participants is chosen as the group's final recommendation (Moore, 1987).

As an alternative to using discussion structuring such as the NGT, Locke, Alavi, and Wagner (1997) suggested that emerging information technologies – specifically groupware technologies – might be used to improve the effectiveness of participatory information exchange. For example, an electronic meeting support system can be used in a room of participants to display each individual's comments – typed in on personal computer terminals – anonymously on a projected screen. This manner of computer-mediated communication reduces the reluctance that participants might have to present unfavorable information or state controversial opinions. As a result, more information and information of higher quality can be exchanged among participants, and participants report more satisfaction with participatory processes and outcomes (Alavi, 1993).

In addition, videoconferencing can be used to bring together participants from several different sites. Although anonymity may be lost, participation is able nullify some of the negative effects of physical separation and encourage information sharing across great distance. Asynchronous approaches can also be used to structure participatory information exchange without the requirement of simultaneous presence. For instance, website bulletin boards and chat rooms can be set up for groups of participants, allowing them to share information and disseminate knowledge without requiring that everyone be available at the same time. Corporate e-mail systems can also be used to channel and catalog information exchanged among participants separated by both time and distance. Using such procedures, the prototypical face-to-face group is replaced by technological mediation (Locke, Alavi, and Wagner 1997).

CASE ILLUSTRATIONS

To illustrate some of the costs and benefits of encouraging participation in the workplace, consider the differing experiences of Volvo and Toyota. Well known as a Swedish producer of cars, trucks, and marine engines, Volvo's automotive operations were hailed, during the 1970s and 1980s, as among the foremost examples of progressive industrial participation (e. g., Jenkins, 1976). Assembly employees often worked in groups as direct participants in personnel decision-making (what group members to hire, reward, or fire), job design procedures (how to accomplish the group's work, how to divide and assign this work as individualized tasks, when to rotate among task assignments), and similar activities. Employees also elected worker representatives to serve on management committees charged with such tasks as insuring workplace health and safety, establishing corporate environmental policies, overseeing training programs, and assessing proposed product innovations. In addition, an employee representative sat on Volvo's corporate board of directors. Finally, newer plants at sites including Kalimar and Skovde were designed and built to support team-based manufacturing and, at the same time, reduce hierarchical distinctions between managers and workers by placing open management offices on the shop floor, providing central cafeterias to be used by all employees, and creating "small workshop" areas wherein individual teams could produce complete sub-assemblies without substantial outside intervention.

By the mid-1970s, Volvo's labor costs had grown to become among the highest in the automotive industry (Gyllenhammar, 1977). Although some of this expense could be attributed to the cost of complying with Sweden's social welfare regulations then in effect, as much as a 15 percent falloff in productivity appeared due to the redirection of workforce energy away from shopfloor production and toward participatory interaction (Swedish Employers' Confederation, 1975). As long as Volvo was able to command premium prices for its cars, due to the high perceived quality and durability of its products, the company was able to offset production costs and compete in the world marketplace. However, with the introduction of such Japanese lines as Lexus, Infiniti, and Acura, Volvo's position as a quality leader deteriorated and the company's ability to offset its high internal costs declined.

Initially, Volvo attempted to meet market challenges by implementing cost control measures that included shutting down most major operations at Kalimar, Skovde, and other newer plants, and cutting back on participatory programming in its older locations.

By 1994, however, rumors within the automotive industry suggested that Volvo was seeking a friendly merger to stave off bankruptcy or dissolution (Taylor, 1994). After considering several possible partners, in early 1999 Volvo sold its automotive business to Ford. Volvo's board of directors hoped to use the proceeds of this sale to shore up its truck operations, and ultimately, to merge these operations with the truck works of another Swedish firm, Saab Scania.

As Volvo's market position declined, during the late 1970s and 1980s, the position of Toyota, another automotive manufacturer, improved dramatically. Toyota typifies the approach used in Japanese-based companies of that era to organize shopfloor operations and structure managerial affairs. Its production facilities were set up as traditional assembly-line operations, and written, standardized instructions regulated most production processes (Shingo, 1981). Centralized, directive, and sometimes secretive management practices controlled company operations (Sethi, Namiki, and Swanson, 1984). In contrast to Volvo's attempts to involve workers in all phases of corporate management, Toyota's higher-level managers reserved the prerogative to lead the company without significant input from below.

Within this general structure, however, such practices as quality circles and *ringi* decision-making introduced a degree of participation into the shopfloor and lower managerial ranks. Quality circles consist of groups of operative employees that meet with their immediate supervisors on a regular basis, typically every week or two, for an hour or two at a time to discuss problems with production scheduling, product quality, shopfloor safety, and so forth. Circle participants work together to suggest solutions and improvements, which are then sent up the management hierarchy for further study and possible adoption (Ferris and Wagner, 1985). *Ringi* decision-making is a system in which proposed decisions are circulated among management subordinates and their hierarchical superiors for deliberation and approval. Often proposals are originated by senior managers and sent through the subordinate ranks for further refinement, although on occasion junior managers initiate the process with proposals of their own that are sent upward for approval (Cole, 1971).

In contrast to Volvo's experience, Toyota was able to control production costs and, at the same time, produce cars perceived by consumers to be of high quality and reasonable price. In an age of oil embargoes and environmental concerns, the company produced small, fuel-efficient cars that came to dominate the North American market. In the 1980s, Toyota introduced larger cars and later, the Lexus line of luxury automobiles. The company also expanded its production facilities worldwide. All the while, efforts to control costs and improve quality allowed Toyota to gain increasing market share at home and abroad.

In comparing Volvo's situation with Toyota's, there are obvious differences in the scope of participation implemented in the two companies, since at Volvo participatory processes were central to corporate governance while at Toyota they played an ancillary role. This difference alone seems to explain Toyota's greater relative efficiency as a producer of automobiles, since the same kinds of resources that were consumed in participation at Volvo were expended in production at Toyota. Yet, beneath this conspicuous difference lies a deeper explanation, originating in differences in the primary reasons why participation was enacted within the two firms to begin with.

At Volvo, participation was seen mainly as a way of restoring the ability of otherwise routinized manufacturing tasks to satisfy human needs, encourage commitment to the company and its products, and motivate attendance and successful performance (Aguren, Bredbacka, Hansson, Ihregren, and Karllson, 1985; Nicol, 1975). The fact that participation could encourage information exchange was acknowledged by Volvo's management, but this exchange was thought to be valuable more for the commitment and motivation that would be aroused than for the increased understanding or cognitive gain that might also occur (Gyllenhammar, 1977). Volvo's approach was clearly designed to activate participation's motivational mechanism.

At Toyota, in contrast, participation was used to redistribute information that would otherwise remain buried on the shopfloor or hidden among lower-level managers (Dore, 1973). Motivation at Toyota, as in other large firms in Japan, was presumed by management to come from a combination of religious deference to authority and cultural collectivism that tied each employee's welfare to the well-being of the employer. Such "Japanese management" practices as lifetime employment and seniority-based pay were used to remind employees of the permanence of their relationship with their employer and of the importance of working hard to bring honor to their company and its management (Wagner, 1982). The primary aim of participation was consistent – and at Toyota remains consistent to the present day – with the cognitive mechanism's focus on information sharing and improved understanding. As suggested by Toyota's experiences, participation can serve as an effective method of managing information and distributing knowledge.

CONCLUSION

Individual studies of participation's motivational effects have sometimes reported evidence of positive effects, leading researchers and practitioners alike to advocate the use of participation as a source of workplace motivation and employee satisfaction (e.g., Cotton, 1993; Gyllenhammar, 1977; Petersen and Hillkirk, 1991). However, more generalizable evidence suggests that participation's usefulness as a motivational tool is often quite limited. Only in small groups or in combination with simple tasks is participation likely to have appreciable effects, and even then only on the outcomes of satisfaction or acceptance. Managers facing problems with workforce motivation are better advised to look for solutions in such practices as goal-setting, job redesign, and incentive payment.

Although the collection of studies performed specifically to assess the cognitive mechanism is considerably smaller than the stream of research conducted on the motivational mechanism, a stronger case can be made for using participation to influence performance through its effects on the distribution of information among subordinates and their hierarchical superiors. Especially when information is unevenly distributed and the work being performed incorporates significant interdependence, complexity, or change, participation should yield substantial increases in participant knowledge and insight which, in turn, should enhance performance and effectiveness in the workplace. Structuring participatory sessions specifically to encourage the exchange of information should have additional positive effects. Managers seeking ways to improve the distribution of information and knowledge are well advised to consider participatory processes.

USE PARTICIPATION TO SHARE INFORMATION 313

REFERENCES

Abdel-Halim A. A. (1983). Effects of task and personality characteristics on subordinate responses to participative decision making. *Academy of Management Journal*, 26, 477–84.

Aguren, S., Bredbacka, C., Hansson, R., Ihregren, K., and Karlsson, K. G. (1985). *Volvo Kalimar revisited: Ten years of experience*. Stockholm: Efficiency and Participation Development Council.

Alavi, M. (1993). An assessment of electronic meeting systems in a corporation setting. *Information and Management*, 25, 175–82.

Alutto, J. A., and Belasco, J. (1972). A typology for participation in organizational decision making. *Administrative Science Quarterly*, 17, 117–25.

Anderson, R. C. (1959). Learning in discussions: A résumé of authoritarian-democratic studies. *Harvard Education Review*, 29, 210–15.

Barthlem, C. S., and Locke, E. A. (1981). The Coch and French study: A critique and reinterpretation. *Human Relations*, 34, 555–66.

Bass, B. M., and Valenzi, E. R. (1974). Contingent aspects of effective management styles. In J. G. Hunt and L. L. Larson (eds.), *Contingency approaches to leadership* (pp. 75–123). Carbondale, IL: Southern Illinois University Press.

Bass, B. M., Valenzi, E. R., Farrow, D. L., and Solomon, R. J. (1975). Managerial styles associated with organizational, task, personal, and interpersonal contingencies. *Journal of Applied Psychology*, 66, 720–9.

Castore, C. H., and Murnighan, J. K. (1978). Determinants of support for group decision. *Organizational Behavior and Human Performance*, 22, 75–92.

Coch, L., and French, J. R. P. Jr. (1948). Overcoming resistance to change. *Human Relations*, 1, 512–32.

Cole, R. E. (1971). *Japanese blue collar*. Berkeley, CA: University of California Press.

Cotton, J. L. (1993). *Employee involvement: Methods for improving performance and work attitudes*. Newbury Park, CA: Sage.

Crampton, S. M., and Wagner, J. A. III (1994). Percept-percept inflation in microorganizational research: An investigation of prevalence and effect. *Journal of Applied Psychology*, 79, 67–76.

Dickson, J. W. (1981). Participation as a means of organizational control. *Journal of Management Studies*, 18, 159–76.

Diehl, M., and Stroebe, W. (1987). Productivity loss in brainstorming groups: Toward the solution of a riddle. *Journal of Personality and Social Psychology*, 53, 497–509.

Dore, R. (1973). *British factory – Japanese factory*. Berkeley, CA: University of California Press.

Durham, C. C., Knight, D., and Locke, E. A. (1997). Effects of leader role, team-set goal difficulty, efficacy, and tactics on team effectiveness. *Organizational Behavior and Human Decision Processes*, 72, 203–31.

Ferris, G. R., and Wagner, J. A. III (1985). Quality circles in the United States: A conceptual reevaluation. *Journal of Applied Behavioral Science*, 21, 155–67.

Fox, W. M. (1957). Group reaction to two types of conference leadership. *Human Relations*, 10, 279–89.

Gibb, C. A. (1951). An experimental approach to the study of leadership. *Occupational Psychology*, 25, 233–48.

Green, S. G., and Taber, T. D. (1980). The effects of three social decision schemes on decision group processes. *Organizational Behavior and Human Performance*, 25, 97–106.

Gyllenhammar, P. G. (1977). *People at work*. Reading, MA: Addison-Wesley.

Ivancevich, J. M. (1977). Different goal setting treatments and their effects on performance and job satisfaction. *Academy of Management Journal*, 20, 406–19.

Jenkins, D. (1976). *Job power*. Garden City, NY: Doubleday.

Jenkins, G. D., and Lawler, E. E. III (1981). Impact of employee participation on pay plan development. *Organizational Behavior and Human Performance*, 28, 111–28.

Jermier, J. M., and Berkes, L. J. (1979). Leader behavior in a police command bureaucracy: A closer look at the quasi-military model. *Administrative Science Quarterly*, 24, 1–23.

Koch, J. L., and Fox, C. L. (1978). The industrial relations setting, organizational forces, and the form and content of worker participation. *Academy of Management Review*, 3, 572–83.

Latham, G. P., and Saari, L. M. (1979). Importance of supportive relationships in goal setting. *Journal of Applied Psychology*, 64, 151–6.

Latham, G. P., Winters, D., and Locke, E. A. (1994). Cognitive and motivational effects of participation: A mediator study. *Journal of Organizational Behavior*, 15, 49–63.

Latham, G. P., and Yukl, G. A. (1975). Assigned versus participative goal setting with educated and uneducated woods workers. *Journal of Applied Psychology*, 60, 299– 302.

Lawler, E. E. III (1982). Increasing worker involvement to enhance organizational effectiveness. In P. S. Goodman (ed.), *Change in organizations: New perspectives on theory, research, and practice* (pp. 33–70). San Francisco, CA: Jossey-Bass.

Lawler, E. E. III, and Hackman, J. R. (1969). Impact of employee participation in the development of pay incentive plans: A field experiment. *Journal of Applied Psychology*, 53, 467–71.

Leana, C. P. (1987). Power relinquishment versus power sharing: Theoretical clarification and empirical comparison of delegation and participation. *Journal of Applied Psychology*, 72, 228–33.

Ledford, G. E. Jr., and Lawler, E. E. III (1994). Research on employee participation: Beating a dead horse. *Academy of Management Review*, 19, 633–6.

Locke, E. A., Alavi, M., and Wagner, J. A. III (1997). Participation in decision making: An information exchange perspective. In G. R. Ferris (ed.), *Research in personnel and human resources management* (Vol. 15, pp. 293–331). Greenwich, CT: JAI Press.

Locke, E. A., Feren, D. B., McCaleb, V. M., Shaw, K. N., and Denny, A. T. (1980). The relative effectiveness of four methods of motivating employee performance. In K. D. Duncan, M. M. Gruneberg, and D. Wallis (eds.), *Changes in working life* (pp. 363–88). London, UK: John Wiley & Sons.

Locke, E. A. and Schweiger, D. M. (1979). Participation in decision making: One more look. In B. M. Staw (ed.), *New directions in organizational behavior* (Vol. 1, pp. 265–339). Greenwich, CT: JAI Press.

Lowin, A. (1968). Participative decision making: A model, literature critique, and prescription for research. *Organizational Behavior and Human Performance*, 3, 68–106.

Marrow, A. J., and French, J. R. P. Jr. (1946). A case of employee participation in a nonunion shop. *Journal of Social Issues*, 2, 29–34.

McCurdy, H. G., and Eber, H. W. (1953). Democratic vs. authoritarian: A further investigation of group problem-solving. *Journal of Personality*, 22, 258–69.

McMahon, J. T. (1976). Participative and power-equalized organizational systems: An empirical investigation and theoretical integration. *Human Relations*, 29, 203–14.

Miller, K. I., and Monge, P. R. (1986). Participation, satisfaction, and productivity: A meta-analytic review. *Academy of Management Journal*, 29, 727–53.

Moore, C. M. (1987). *Group techniques for idea building*. Beverly Hills, CA: Sage.

Nicol, G. (1975). *Volvo*. London, UK: William Luscombe.

Patchen, M. (1964). Participation in decision making and motivation: What is the relation? *Personnel Administrator*, 27, 24–31.

Pateman, C. (1970). *Participation and democratic theory*. London, UK: Cambridge University Press.

Pennington, D. F., Haravey, F., and Bass, B. M. (1958). Some effects of decision and discussion on coalescence, change, and effectiveness. *Journal of Applied Psychology*, 42, 404–8.

Petersen, D. E., and Hillkirk, J. (1991). *A better idea: Redefining the way Americans work*. Boston, MA: Houghton-Mifflin.

Roethlisberger, F. J., and Dickson, W. J. (1939). *Management and morale.* Cambridge, MA: Harvard University Press.

Rosenbaum, L. L., and Rosenbaum, W. (1971). Morale and productivity consequences of group leadership style, stress, and type of task. *Journal of Applied Psychology*, 55, 343–8.

Sashkin, M. (1976). Changing toward participative management approaches: A model and methods. *Academy of Management Review*, 1, 75–86.

Scheflen, K. C., Lawler, E. E. III, and Hackman, J. R. (1971). Long-term impact of employee participation in the development of pay incentive plans: A field experiment revisited. *Journal of Applied Psychology*, 55, 182–6.

Schuler, R. S. (1976). Participation with supervisor and subordinate authoritarianism: A path-goal theory reconciliation. *Administrative Science Quarterly*, 21, 320–5.

Schweiger, D. M., and Leana, C. R. (1986). Participation in decision making. In E. A. Locke (ed.), *Generalizing from laboratory to field settings* (pp. 147–66). Lexington, MA: Lexington Books.

Scully, J. A., Kirkpatrick, S. A., and Locke, E. A. (1995). Locus of knowledge as a determinant of the effects of participation on performance, affect, and perceptions. *Organizational Behavior and Human Decision Processes*, 61, 276–88.

Sethi, S. P., Namiki, N., and Swanson, C. L. (1984), *The false promise of the Japanese miracle.* Marshfield, MA: Pitman.

Shingo, Shigeo (1981). *Study of the Toyota production system from an industrial engineering viewpoint.* Tokyo: Japan Management Association.

Singer, J. N. (1974). Participative decision making about work: An overdue look at variables which mediate its effects. *Sociology of Work and Occupations*, 1, 347–71.

Stewart, T. A. (1997). *Intellectual capital: The new wealth of organizations.* New York: Currency Doubleday.

Swedish Employers' Confederation (1975). *Job Reform in Sweden.* Stockholm: Swedish Employers' Confederation.

Tannenbaum, A. S. (1968). *Control in organizations.* New York: McGraw-Hill.

Taylor, A. III (1994). New ideas from Europe's automakers: Managing the crisis at Volvo. *Fortune*, Dec. 12, 168.

Vroom, V. H. (1960). *Some personality determinants of the effects of participation.* Englewood Cliffs, NJ: Prentice-Hall.

Vroom, V. H., and Yetton, P. W. (1973). *Leadership and decision-making.* Pittsburgh, PA: University of Pittsburgh Press.

Wagner, J. A. III (1982). Individualism, collectivism, and the control of organization. Unpublished dissertation, University of Illinois, Department of Business Administration, Urbana-Champaign, IL.

Wagner, J. A. III (1994). Participation's effects on performance and satisfaction: A reconsideration of research evidence. *Academy of Management Review*, 19, 312–30.

Wagner, J. A. III, and Gooding, R. Z. (1987). Shared influence and organizational behavior: A meta-analysis of situational variables expected to moderate participation-outcome relationships. *Academy of Management Journal*, 30, 524–41.

Wagner, J. A. III, Leana, C. R., Locke, E. A., and Schweiger, D. A. (1997). Cognitive and motivational frameworks in research on participation: A meta-analysis of effects. *Journal of Organizational Behavior*, 18, 49–65.

Wagner, J. A. III, and LePine, J. A. (1999). Participation's effects on performance and satisfaction: Additional evidence from U.S. research. *Psychological Reports*, 84, 719–25.

Williams, T. A. (1982). A participative design for dispersed employees in turbulent environments. *Human Relations*, 35, 1043–58.

22

Make Good Decisions by Effectively Managing the Decision-making Process

GLEN WHYTE

THE SEVEN ESSENTIAL STEPS OF EFFECTIVE DECISION-MAKING

Making wise choices is the paramount and most challenging task of any executive. Successful managers meet this challenge by carefully managing the process by which hard decisions are made.

It is almost always true that well-made decisions are more likely to produce the desired results than decisions taken in a more haphazard way. Decision processes are a major determinant of the quality of decision outcomes. The principle that effective decision-making results in effective decisions, as well as the implications that flow from this principle, are the focus of this chapter.

This principle applies to a very broad category of decisions faced by individuals, groups, and organizations: decisions that have multiple objectives and important consequences for those who make them. For example, career decisions certainly fall into this category for individuals. The organizational analogue of the career decision, strategic decisions, also fall into this category. Strategic decisions have long-term implications. They establish new courses of action that have enduring consequences by setting the context for and possibly constraining subsequent decisions (Simon, 1976). Strategic decisions and those like them are non-routine and characterized typically by uncertainty, ambiguity, and conflict.

If good decision-making processes lead to good outcomes, then what precisely are effective processes? High-quality decision-making procedures are fairly easy to describe but hard to do because they require people to work to the limits of their abilities. These procedures consist of the following seven steps:

1 Identifying objectives to be achieved by the decision: important goals should be thoroughly considered and discussed at the outset and the major requirements of a successful choice should be specified.
2 Generating a comprehensive list of well-developed alternatives: a number of alternatives, not just one or two, should be thoroughly examined and seriously considered.

3 Searching widely for information with which to determine the quality of the alternatives: a comprehensive search should be conducted for all available and important bits of information relevant to the evaluation of the preferred course of action and other options.

4 Engaging in unbiased and accurate processing of all information relevant to the assessment of the alternatives: the information that has been gathered should be treated in such a way as to minimize the tendency to over-weight the significance of information supportive of the preferred alternative, and under-weight or ignore information that is not supportive.

5 Reconsidering and re-examining all the pros and cons of the alternatives: prior to making a final choice, previously considered alternatives, including those that were rejected, should be reappraised in light of any new information gathered and re-analyzed by fairly weighting information both favorable and unfavorable about their consequences.

6 Examining the costs, benefits, and risks of the preferred choice: the costs, benefits, and risks should be explicitly recognized, evaluated and, if feasible, adjusted to more desirable levels. Actively try to reduce the known risks before the choice is made.

7 Developing plans to implement the decision, monitor the results, and react in the event that known risks become a reality: in addition to determining how the decision will be implemented and tracking outcomes, also develop contingency plans in case problems in implementation occur and determine how other potential problems will be dealt with should they arise.

The basic principle underlying these seven steps is simple: complex, crucial, non-routine decisions which reflect these procedures are more likely than other methods to lead to satisfactory outcomes. These steps when taken in their entirety have been referred to as vigilant information-processing (Janis, 1982, 1989; Janis and Mann, 1977). Moreover, a decision-making process that leaves out even one of these seven procedural criteria when crucial decisions are being made is flawed. As the number of flaws increases, so do the chances for decision failure. The greater the number of steps that are omitted, the greater the chances that the ultimate consequences of the decision will be unsatisfactory. The more thoroughly that each of the criteria is engaged, up to some reasonable limit, the less likely it is that serious errors will contaminate the process and produce decision failure.

Decision-making can reflect all, none, or some of these procedures. Moreover, the criteria may be met to varying degrees. The distinguishing feature of an effective decision-making process is the accomplishment to a substantial degree of all seven steps of vigilant information-processing by the time decision makers have begun to commit themselves to a single option. Many people who study decision-making believe that when the process of decision-making approximates these seven steps, it becomes increasingly likely that the decision ultimately taken will prevail and attain the objectives of the decision maker. In short, vital decisions that manifest the seven steps of effective decision-making are likely to be both judicious and effective.

This is not to suggest that every major decision failure is the product of flawed decision-making, or that every time a fundamental decision is poorly made havoc will be wreaked. Errors in decision-making, however, are conducive to poor results. Such errors are likely to be reduced but not eliminated by effective decision-making practices. Unfortunately, even immaculately conceived decisions sometimes fail. Defective decisions based on ignorance and poor judgment sometimes succeed. Good luck can turn a sow's ear of a decision into a silk purse outcome, just as random events can transform a silk purse of a decision process into a sow's ear result. The basic premise remains, however, that decision-making processes that do not reflect to a substantial degree each of the seven steps of effective decision-making should not be expected to achieve results that will be satisfactory over the long term.

> For consequential decisions that implicate vital interests of the organization or nation, deliberate use of a problem solving approach, with judicious information search and analysis (within the constraints usually imposed by limited organizational resources), will generally result in fewer miscalculations and therefore better outcomes than any other approach. (Janis, 1989: 121)

The core steps of effective decision-making described here reflect in general the conclusion of many social scientists who have studied decision-making, among whom there exists some degree of consensus (e.g., Abelson and Levi, 1985; Baron, 1985; Donaldson and Lorsch, 1983; Einhorn and Hogarth, 1981; Eisenhardt, Kahwajy, and Bourgeois, 1997; Etzioni, 1968; George, 1980; Hammond, McClelland, and Mumpower, 1980; Kahneman, Slovic, and Tversky, 1982; Katz and Kahn, 1966; Lebow, 1987; Lindblom, 1980; Maier, 1967; Neustadt and May, 1986; Nutt, 1990; Simon, 1976; Stein and Tanter, 1980; Steiner, 1979; Taylor, 1965; Vroom and Jago, 1988; Zeleny, 1981). Not all authors referred to above agree on all the important details about effective decision-making procedures, but there is general agreement about the desirability of using a problem-solving approach and about the basic ingredients of such an approach.

ARE DECISION-MAKING PROCESSES AND DECISION OUTCOMES RELATED IN THE WAY DESCRIBED?

A growing body of evidence suggests that good processes lead to good outcomes in decision-making (e.g., Eisenhardt, 1990; Peterson et al., 1998). More specifically, a link appears to exist between the use of a problem-solving approach in making important decisions and the quality of outcomes attained. The most compelling evidence of this link is provided by Herek, Janis, and Huth (1987), who examined the relationship between the results of critical policy decisions and the quality of decision-making procedures used to arrive at those decisions. Decisions involving the management of 19 international crises by the US government were examined in terms of both the results achieved and the presence or absence of each of the seven procedural criteria that have been described as constituting the essential steps of an effective decision-making process. The 19 cases were chosen by independent experts who were unaware of the objectives of the study, based on the magnitude of threat they posed for war with the Soviet Union or China.

The quality of decision-making procedures used during each of the crises was evaluated by counting how many of the seven steps of effective decision-making originally described by Janis and Mann (1977) were taken. The decision-making processes observed across all crises were by no means standard, even when different decisions were made by the same group. In eight of the 19 crises, however, at least six of the seven steps were apparent, indicating both a capacity and willingness on the part of decision makers to employ an effective decision-making strategy in at least some circumstances.

Regarding the link between outcomes and process, the study revealed a strong relationship between a failure to engage in the steps of effective decision-making and poor outcomes. In contrast, decision makers who engaged in effective decision-making were more likely to attain their goals. The quality of process apparently influenced the quality of outcomes by minimizing the likelihood that decision makers would make preventable errors that would have increased the likelihood of decision failure. Good processes do not ensure good outcomes, but they do make them more probable.

Advice Regarding Process

Step 1

Effective decision-making begins with an understanding of the ends to be achieved and the problems to be solved. A decision made without awareness of its intended objectives is a solution in search of a problem. Establishing objectives provides an opportunity to create a common goal around which people can rally. Such goals should be stated in a way that it is mutually acceptable to participants in the decision-making process. In the absence of a shared goal, be prepared to waste a lot of time (Eisenhardt et al., 1997).

Objectives should be articulated in terms of specific, explicit, and clear goals. But care is required in formulating goals and objectives so that they reflect commitment to real needs, desires, fears, and concerns as opposed to commitment to the most obvious ways by which those issues might be addressed. Intended outcomes in decision-making of the sort under discussion should be formulated in terms of interests instead of potentially arbitrary positions. The distinction between interests and positions is one that has achieved prominence in the negotiations literature (e.g., Fisher, Ury, and Patton, 1991; Lax and Sebenius, 1986) and deserves equal attention in the field of crucial decision-making.

Interests may be implicit but they are what people truly care about; they refer to the ends that people would like to accomplish. Positions, in contrast, are public statements or demands and may be the means by which people advance their interests. Interests underlie and motivate positions. A position is often stated explicitly as a means by which to advance an underlying interest. A position, however, is another word for option in decision-making. Interests and positions should never be confused. Decision makers should be committed to their interests, but flexible about the positions they take to advance their interests.

Firms, for example, may decide to pursue strategies intended to increase market share when the underlying concern is profitability. If profitability is the real concern, however, there may be ways to address this concern other than by growing market share. The utility of the interests/position distinction has two components. First, satisfying basic interests is typically more important and valuable than the implementation of related positions. Second, often many different positions can satisfy an important interest.

One way to identify interests is to ask why a particular decision is being made in the first place. What is the logic and rationale, and what are the basic concerns, that are motivating the decision? Important questions with which to explore interests include asking what you want to achieve, why you want to achieve it, and why this objective is important to you (Lewicki, Saunders, and Minton, 1999). Without good answers to these questions, the likelihood that a decision will produce positive outcomes and enhance the satisfaction of those making or affected by it is small.

Determining priorities among the multiple interests that typically characterize the making of important decisions is also essential in the crafting of effective decisions. Rank-ordering interests before considering alternatives, to obtain clarity about what is truly important rather than merely desirable, is essential to the making of wise trade-offs among competing alternatives. Making rational trade-offs is critical to successful decision making, but this requires care particularly when multiple objectives that are hard to compare are being pursued simultaneously.

Framing.   An issue related to goals and objectives is decision-framing, a process that should be considered at the outset of decision-making. Decisions made in the absence of knowledge about how they will turn out are framed, consciously or otherwise, by the reference point or standard of comparison against which they are assessed. The potential consequences of choice can therefore be perceived as either a gain or a loss depending on where the reference point has been placed.

The literature contains many examples of preference reversals that have occurred through a shift in the reference level and the subsequent reframing of decisions, even though objectively the choices were unchanged. In one widely cited example (Tversky and Kahneman, 1981), subjects were asked to imagine that an outbreak of a rare disease was expected. Two programs were proposed in response to this event. Program A would save exactly 200 people with certainty. Program B would provide a one-third chance of saving 600 people and a two-third chance of saving nobody. When presented with these options, 72 percent preferred risk-averse option A. Other participants were presented with the objectively identical choice, but were told that with Program A, exactly 400 people would die with certainty. Program B, in contrast, would provide a one-third chance that nobody would die, and a two-third chance that 600 people would die. In this case, 78 percent preferred risky option B.

Different descriptions of otherwise identical choices suggest different neutral points of comparison, leading to different preferences. The neutral reference level implied by the characterization of the choice as saving lives is 600 dead; hence the choice is between a sure gain and potentially larger gains combined with the chance of no gains at all. In contrast, the neutral reference level implied by the characterization of the choice as people dying is 0 dead; hence the choice is between a sure loss and potentially greater losses combined with the chance of no losses at all. Individuals are often risk-averse in choices involving gains (i.e., positively framed choices) but risk-taking in choices involving losses (i.e., negatively framed choices). The dramatic reversals of preference produced by different descriptions of the same option in the lives saved/lost dilemma occur because of the conjunction of a framing effect with attitudes toward risk that differ for choices involving either losses or gains.

Decision makers should therefore attempt to be both conscious of and careful about how they frame their decisions. Decision makers should also be particularly chary about negatively framed choices. Decision makers who frame important choices negatively and as a result perceive themselves to be avoiding otherwise certain losses often make decisions that are excessively risky. Such decisions are likely to end badly. Much imprudent and even unethical behavior can be attributed to the adoption of a negative decision frame in the making of vital decisions (Whyte, 1989).

Decision makers who use phrases such as "The status quo is not an option" or "We have too much invested to quit" indicate more than a tendency to speak in cliches. They also indicate that they view the status quo as a negative deviation from a neutral point of reference, a sure sign that a negative decision frame has been adopted. Decisions about how to respond in the current situation therefore appear as choices between a sure loss on the one hand, and potentially greater losses combined with a chance to return to the reference point on the other. In such a case, most people are inclined to avoid sure losses by risking further losses in an attempt to return to the neutral reference point. In circumstances like these, caution is called for although seldom invoked. It would be helpful if decision makers in this case would also try to frame their decision positively, as a response to an opportunity, rather than negatively, as a response to a threat or impending loss. When decision makers frame important choices negatively, take cover. In part this is why the choice of frame is an act of both practical and ethical significance (Whyte, 1991).

Steps 2–7

Regarding the second and following phases in the process of effective decision-making, it is important to separate the act of identifying the goals to be achieved from the act of generating a comprehensive list of potential courses of action. Jumping to solutions before clarifying the issues to be addressed represents a defect in the decision-making process that can be fatal to the attainment of important objectives.

The task of generating a list of options can be done in a variety of ways. The nominal group technique, for example, may be used to create or identify ideas, options, or alternatives (Delbecq and Van de Ven, 1971). This technique requires that individuals put in writing as many ideas as possible in advance of meeting with the group. The group then evaluates the individually generated ideas. This approach takes advantage of the capacities of individuals to generate more and better ideas alone and the capacity of groups to more accurately evaluate the quality of the ideas generated.

Steps 3 and 4 refer generally to the tasks associated with evaluating options and selecting a specific course of action from those that are available. In this regard, not only is it important to select a course of action on the basis of how technically good it is, it is also important to judge a course of action on the basis of how acceptable it is to those who will be affected by it or who have the capacity to affect its success. Those judgments are facilitated by the development of criteria with which to evaluate the options in advance of the development of the alternatives.

Step 5 refers to the necessity for sober second thought to be applied prior to making any irrevocable moves. A story about Alfred P. Sloan, former chair of General Motors, describes him as acting in a way consistent with this advice in response to the easy consensus achieved by a group that he was leading. Almost immediately, he proposed that " . . . we postpone further discussion . . . to give ourselves some time to develop some disagreement and perhaps gain an understanding of what the decision is all about"

(Janis, 1982: 291).

Step 6 refers to the basic elements of risk management (MacCrimmon and Wehrung, 1986). Risk adjustment, perhaps by gaining more time, control, or information, can affect final outcomes through risk reduction as profoundly as can the act of choosing well from among the options. It is therefore as useful to actively try to reduce the known risks by adjusting them as it is to reduce the known risks by selecting wisely from the various alternatives.

Steps 1 through 6 refer broadly to the act of conception in decision-making, whereas step 7 refers to the less glamorous task of execution. It is a mundane fact of life that the quality of the option chosen is virtually irrelevant if the means by which the decision will be implemented goes unattended. A related issue is the extent to which people affected by or knowledgeable about the decision have been consulted prior to the making of the final choice.

People like to be consulted about important decisions, even when they understand that they will not make the final choice and regardless whether the input provided is reflected in the course of action ultimately pursued. People in particular like to be consulted about important decisions that affect them. In the absence of such consultation, do not expect individuals to enthusiastically cooperate in the implementation of the decision or to believe that the decision was fair. Consulting widely, and carefully considering the input received in advance of making the decision, is also advisable because doing so can increase the quality of the final choice. Soliciting input from experts, from those affected by the decision, and from those with the capacity to influence outcomes is one way to reduce errors, smooth and accelerate implementation, and enhance the quality of judgment (Vroom and Jago, 1988).

Effective decision-making sometimes requires that we consider the extent to which others will consider our decisions to be fair. Perceptions of unfairness or injustice produce intense negative reactions in people and induce motives to restore justice. People may become angry and attempt to punish those who perpetrate or benefit from the injustice. Decisions that induce widespread perceptions of unfairness may therefore be unsustainable, if not utterly incapable of implementation.

Social psychologists have identified three main sources of perceptions of fairness. Distributive justice refers to the outcomes of decisions. Procedural justice refers to processes used to make decisions. Interactional justice affects procedural justice judgments, and indicates the quality of interpersonal treatment that people have received during the decision-making process.

All three types of justice are relevant, but procedural justice has the most powerful effect on perceptions of fairness. Procedures that are consistent, bias-free, accurate, correctable, representative, and ethical have been found to induce fairness perceptions in a variety of contexts (Lind and Tyler, 1988). Decision makers should therefore be especially sensitive to these considerations, particularly if it is necessary to build commitment to the choice or when rapid implementation is required. Impression management may also be useful in building commitment to a decision whose virtues are not obvious at first blush.

Impediments to Effective Decision-making

Do people ever actually engage in the seven steps of effective decision-making as described here, or do these steps represent a standard that is seldom if ever attained? Some theorists have argued (e.g., Lindblom, 1980; Starbuck, 1983) that people consistently employ far more simplistic and non-analytical strategies such as selecting the first alternative that is satisfactory (satisficing) or muddling through to make crucial decisions. But a problem-solving approach does not imply an endless quest to optimize by searching for some mythical panacea. It does, however, imply a high degree of motivation to find a good solution and a commitment to work to the limits of one's capacities. Such motivation and commitment should be aroused by the high stakes associated with the sort of decisions under discussion.

Whether people will actually engage in effective decision-making, which might be costly and time-consuming, will depend on a number of factors. For example, do decision makers view the issue giving rise to the need for a decision as important and a priority? Do compelling reasons preclude the use of simple decision rules, such as satisficing, choosing the most socially acceptable option (Tetlock, 1985), or relying on a well-known analogy to make the choice? Do decision makers perceive an unambiguous threat or opportunity that has arisen suddenly?

Even when the answers to these questions are "yes," many factors can preclude the use of systematic decision-making procedures. These factors can include, among others, limited time and resources, past commitments, the need for social support or acceptance of the decision, emotions, stress, and perceptions of very high or very low self- or group-efficacy. When conditions such as these prevail, decision makers are not likely to adopt an effective decision-making strategy (Janis, 1989). The main objective of such a strategy is to select an alternative that will address as well as the situation permits the challenges posed by the threat or opportunity, while managing and minimizing the potential for catastrophic loss. Under many of the conditions just referred to, this goal is displaced by the need to deal with other perhaps less important but more pressing issues.

The obstacles to effective decision-making have to be removed before this type of process can be expected to occur. Decision-making when vital interests are at stake should always involve searching for a high-quality solution that takes into account all of the main requirements posed by the challenges to be addressed. There is no substitute for the critical thinking, careful analysis, searching for pertinent information, and planning that effective decision-making demands.

That is not to say, however, that intuition has no role to play in the process. Decision makers who track comprehensive real-time information in organizations concerning both operations and the environment can develop intuition, which provides people with the ability to process high volumes of information quickly. Fluency with the current situation accelerates decision-making by preparing people to cope with rapidly emerging developments, and places at their disposal the information they need to do so. With experienced and intuitive decision makers, effective decision-making processes that involve much information and many alternatives can be engaged quickly and well (Eisenhardt, 1990). Intuition refers to the capacity for analysis that has become second nature due to experience in similar or related situations. Chess grand masters, for example, often display a great capacity for fast and accurate judgment even if they cannot explain how they did so (Simon, 1983).

Regarding the implementation of effective decision-making techniques in organizations, two recommendations stand out. The consequences, both good and bad, of important decisions underscore the importance of solid decision-making practices. Knowledge of these practices should therefore facilitate improvements in the quality of decision outcomes. Training executives, even experienced ones, in how to effectively manage the process of decision-making is probably the most efficient way to disseminate this information.

But knowledge alone is not enough, in light of research indicating that even in groups of talented and experienced decision makers, effective decision-making practices are not always used. It would also be useful, therefore, in addition to evaluating executives on the outcomes of their choices, to evaluate them on the basis of the processes they used to make their choices. Reward systems can legitimize and encourage the effective making of decisions, particularly in light of the many and varied obstacles that may impede it.

Process is also affected by the composition of the group whose responsibility it is to make the decision. Ideally, decisions of the sort under discussion here should be made by groups composed of individuals who are moderately diverse in terms of skills, backgrounds, attitudes, experiences, and beliefs that are relevant to the issues under consideration. Such groups retain the capacity to eliminate clearly faulty reasoning while ensuring that a large amount of knowledge, information, and intellectual space will be available within the group to make the decision. Homogeneous groups are more likely to make a decision quickly and with less conflict, but at the cost of having explored fewer possibilities.

If the seven steps suggest that effective decision-making is a slow and cumbersome activity, recognize that it needn't be. Research suggests that speed is actually achieved in strategic choice by engaging in many of the practices described here. In short, working with common objectives, more rather than less information, and dealing with many alternatives both facilitate and accelerate the choice process while building the confidence necessary to make crucial decisions (Eisenhardt, 1990).

Developing and juggling multiple alternatives simultaneously saves time by facilitating comparative analysis, which helps in forming preferences and assessing alternatives. Multiple alternatives are fast, because analysis is facilitated by comparison. Considering many options all at once also instills confidence in the preferred option, because it diminishes the feeling that something better has been overlooked. Recognizing and developing options further ensures that contingency plans will be in place if the first choice begins to falter.

Conflict is inevitable and usually beneficial when groups engage effectively in the making of crucial decisions, providing that conflict is managed well. Fast decision makers employ and resolve conflict wisely. According to Eisenhardt (1990), "consensus with qualification" is a quick way to break an impasse while still maintaining group morale. This process is employed when individuals have discussed the issues but failed to obtain consensus. In that case, the senior manager and functional head most affected by the choice make the decision, with input provided by the rest of the group.

Consensus with qualification works, because it allows for dissent without obstructing the decision-making process. People also like it, probably because it provides them in general with a voice in decision-making and gives them real influence in decisions that directly affect them. Even when consensus is not forthcoming, everyone has a voice even if only a few make the choice.

Some Examples of the Process–Outcome Link

Lehman Brothers Kuhn Loeb

The principle that effective decision-making produces effective results will be illustrated with a couple of examples. The first example describes a situation in which effective decision-making was not practiced when the vital interests of a firm were at stake, with negative consequences for both the firm and its partners. The second example, in contrast, illustrates how effective processes can lead directly to positive outcomes.

Examples abound in the literature of situations in which leaders behaved incompetently during the process of decision-making and made crucial decisions that became, and deserved to become, fiascos. Many of these fiascos have been attributed to the groupthink phenomenon, symptoms of which induce defective decision-making (Janis, 1982). Members of this "hall of shame" include the space shuttle Challenger accident (Esser and Lindoerfer, 1989) and the Iran-Contra affair that plagued the second term of the Reagan administration ('t Hart, 1991). The example that will be referred to here is less well known, but equally illustrative of the link between decision process and outcome.

On July 26, 1983, board members of the Wall Street investment firm Lehman Brothers Kuhn Loeb voted on a plan to reorganize. The firm was enjoying its fifth successive year of record profits, was setting the industry standard in terms of return on equity, had more than tripled in size over the previous ten years, had stockpiled over $200 million in capital, and had done more mergers, acquisitions, and divestitures during the last three years than any other investment bank. In short, the firm was on the verge of achieving elite status among investment banking firms.

As described by Auletta (1986), the plan to reorganize was clearly not designed to solve a problem related to the performance of the firm, but it certainly created one. Six months after the vote, with the firm facing a cash crunch, it was sold to Shearson/American Express at a price that was negotiated from a position of weakness.

The board was asked to approve a plan proposed by Lewis Glucksman to install himself as leader with full responsibility for the firm's activities. The plan originated with Glucksman, who aspired to remove his co-chief executive officer, Peter G. Peterson, for reasons including envy of Peterson and a desire for increased prestige. To obtain Peterson's resignation and endorsement of the plan to the board, Glucksman had arranged for the firm to pay Peterson millions of dollars.

Glucksman had few of the qualifications and attributes that one would have hoped for in a replacement for Peterson. Moreover, the excessive termination payment to Peterson was to come directly from the board members as partners in the firm. Despite these issues, and despite the capacity of the board to amend or reject the proposal, the board immediately accepted the plan with nary a whimper from eight of the nine board members present. With one exception, the members showed no desire to critically assess the plan, let alone adopt an approach to the decision that even remotely resembled the seven steps of an effective decision-making process.

The solitary member who cast a critical eye on the plan, Peter Solomon, failed miserably in his attempts to persuade other board members to resist the plan and discuss the issues it raised, including whether the time was right for Peterson to leave and whether Glucksman had the right stuff to lead Lehman Brothers. "You guys are nuts to allow this to happen!" shouted Solomon. "We are allowing them [Glucksman and Peterson] to harm our investment" (Auletta, 1986: 107). Solomon's pleadings were greeted with silence. The board's only response was to request a minor change in the terms of Peterson's retirement package, which Peterson accepted.

None of the steps of an effective decision-making process were in evidence during this time. The board made no attempt to identify the problem for which Glucksman's plan was a solution. There was no attempt to identify other alternatives. There was no attempt even to evaluate the only alternative that was on the table. Questions about the impact of the proposal on the firm, and whether the proposal was in the best interests of the firm, remained unaddressed.

Consensus was prematurely obtained around an option that should have raised serious concerns among members of the board, yet except for Solomon's outburst they were mute. The momentous decision with which board members were faced was not treated as such. In acting as a rubberstamp, the board committed a serious error that it would not likely have committed had the decision been given due consideration.

The reaction of the partners to the news of the elevation of Glucksman to CEO was mixed, but not for long. Within weeks, the consequences of the board's approval of this transaction were becoming apparent. Glucksman's style and actions soon outraged many partners as he began to wreak havoc within the firm. At the same time, the market began to decline, profits started to shrink, and key partners began to jump ship. Within months and facing the possibility of bankruptcy, a for sale sign went up on the venerable House of Lehman (Aueletta, 1986).

Whatever the reasons, members of the board of Lehman Brothers Kuhn Loeb displayed an astounding unwillingness to engage in even the most rudimentary steps of effective decision-making. The demise shortly thereafter of Wall Street's oldest continuing investment banking partnership can be traced directly back to the way people in positions of authority made decisions and failed to engage in an effective decision-making process.

SmithKline Beecham

SmithKline Beecham PLC (SB) is a pharmaceutical company that recognized a need to engineer a process about how to make its most important decisions. These decisions concerned what research and development projects to support, and were crucial because only by deciding wisely in this regard would the company's future revenue stream be assured. Making good decisions about how much money and other resources a team or project should receive is a challenging judgment call at the best of times. At SB, this task was complicated by high uncertainty, technical complexity, and the fact that the bulk of information used to make these resource allocation decisions came from project advocates who were themselves in competition with one another for scarce resources. Decisions like these can easily become politicized and controversial, hardly a recipe for sound judgment. Fortunately, SB found a solution in a methodology that has both high credibility within the organization and the capacity to produce sound decisions about what drugs to invest in and how much to spend.

Decision-making at SB, as described by Sharpe and Keelin (1998), looks very much like the general problem-solving approach described earlier. An overarching goal was first established – in this case to increase shareholder value – and than a three-phase process was instituted to decide how this goal would be achieved.

During phase 1, project champions develop at least four alternatives involving varying levels of financial commitment to the project under consideration. Previously, only a single alternative involving full project funding would typically be put forward. Beyond simply increasing the range of options under examination, the process of generating multiple alternatives has a number of associated benefits, including fostering the development of new ideas and producing a better understanding of the critical issues.

Prior to submission for formal review and evaluation, the alternatives are put before a peer review panel. The panel is composed of managers from key functions and product groups who are given a mandate to ask tough questions and test major assumptions. The point of the mandate is to increase both the quality of the alternatives and the project team's confidence in them. After the managers do their work, the alternatives are modified to reflect the input received.

After revision, the alternatives are again submitted for review, this time to a group of senior managers. This group eventually decides the fate of all investment projects, but the purpose of the review at this point is simply to continue to discuss and further improve the alternatives, not evaluate them. SB follows a clear linear sequence in first trying to generate an array of attractive options before engaging in their evaluation. The act of developing alternatives is formally separated from the act of judging them, which occurs later.

In phase 2, the alternatives are assessed systematically. The criteria and methodology for evaluation are spelled out in advance, so the options are compared in a consistent, fair, and credible way. For example, similar information is provided for each project; the information must come from reputable sources that can be clearly documented; and the assessment itself must meet industry standards. Transparency and consistency of the process are also achieved by the use of a team of neutral analysts whose task is to ensure the integrity of the approach taken to evaluation.

Moreover, a peer review at this stage allows people the opportunity to challenge and perhaps revise the project evaluation process, followed by another opportunity at the senior management level to discuss and question the results. This phase ends only once people have reviewed the way in which the alternatives have been evaluated, and have agreed that the methodology used makes sense. The stage is thus set for choices to be made.

In phase 3, decisions are made regarding what projects have the highest value and are most worthy of support. A group composed of analysts who were not involved in either the process of generating alternatives or evaluating them is assigned the task of selecting from among the many options. Their objective is to identify the highest value portfolio of projects based on expected return on investment.

This three-phase process is built directly on a foundation of classical decision-making in which objectives are first defined, a comprehensive list of alternatives is developed and refined, and then evaluation of and selection from the alternatives occurs. At SB, this process has resulted in decisions about how much to invest, and where to invest it, that have taken the company in new directions. With no additional investment, these new directions have resulted in a portfolio of projects valued at 30 percent more than the old one. Moreover, a tripling of marginal return on investment has been realized, which in turn has led to a substantial increase in spending on development. As an added benefit, controversy surrounding the making of these complex resource allocation decisions has been reduced.

In a development related to the ongoing success of SB, in early 2000 a merger was announced between SB and Glaxo Wellcome PLC. The merger will create in terms of annual sales the world's number one drug maker, called Glaxo SmithKline PLC.

Decision-making at SmithKline Beecham illustrates the link between effective decision processes and positive results, and also provides guidance regarding the essential elements of effective decision-making. Decision-making at Lehman Brothers Kuhn Loeb, in contrast, is equally illustrative of the connection between low-quality decision-making practices and poor-quality results.

The eventual outcomes of crucial decisions are in many respects beyond our control. But the processes by which we make such decisions can be controlled, and should be controlled if the ultimate success of the decision is a concern. Strong evidence suggests that decision processes and outcomes are related, and that the seven steps of effective decision-making are associated with desirable outcomes. No claim is made, however, that effective decision-making as herein described is the only path to success. But over the short, medium, and long terms, effective decision-making practices provide substantial benefits. These benefits enable decision makers to make the most of whatever assets they happen to possess, and avoid pursuing courses of action that they will come to regret.

References

Abelson, R. P., and Levi, A. (1985). Decision-making and decision theory. In G. Lindzey and E. Aronson (eds.), *The handbook of social psychology*, 3rd edn., Vol. 1. New York: Random House.

Auletta, K. (1986). *Greed and glory on Wall Street: The fall of the House of Lehman*. New York: Random House.

Baron, J. (1985). *Rationality and intelligence*. New York: Cambridge University Press.

Delbecq, A. L., and Van de Ven, A. H. (1971). A group process model for problem identification and program planning. *Journal of Applied Behavioral Science*, 7, 466–92.

Donaldson, G., and Lorsch, J. W. (1983). *Decision making at the top: The shaping of strategic direction*. New York: Basic Books.

Einhorn, H. J., and Hogarth, R. M. (1981). Behavioral decision theory: Processes of judgment and choice. *Annual Review of Psychology*, 32, 53–88.

Eisenhardt, K. M. (1990). Speed and strategic choice: How managers accelerate decision making. *California Management Review*, Spring, 39–54.

Eisenhardt, K. M., Kahwajy, J. L., and Bourgeois III L. J. (1997). How management teams can have a good fight. *Harvard Business Review*, July–Aug., 77–85.

Esser, J. K., and Lindoerfer, J. L. (1989). Groupthink and the space shuttle Challenger accident. *Journal of Behavioral Decision Making*, 2, 167–77.

Etzioni, A. (1968). *The active society*. New York: Free Press.

Fisher, R., Ury, W., and Patton, B. (1991). *Getting to yes*, 2nd edn. New York: Penguin.

George, A. L. (1980). *Presidential decisionmaking in foreign policy: The effective use of information and advice*.

Boulder, Colo.: Westview.

Hammond, K. R., McClelland, G. H., and Mumpower, J. (1980). *Human judgment and decision making: Theories, methods, and procedures*. New York: Praeger.

Hart, P. 't. (1991). Irving L. Janis' victims of groupthink. *Political Psychology*, 12, 247–78.

Herek, G., Janis, I. L., and Huth, P. (1987). Decisionmaking during international crises: Is quality of process related to outcome? *Journal of Conflict Resolution*, 31, 203–26.

Janis, I. L. (1982). *Groupthink: Psychological studies of policy decisions and fiascos*, 2nd edn. Houghton Mifflin: Boston.

Janis, I. L. (1989). *Crucial decisions: Leadership in policymaking and crisis management*. New York: Free Press.

Janis, I. L. and Mann, L. (1977). *Decision making: A psychological analysis of conflict, choice, and commitment*. New York: Free Press.

Kahneman, D., Slovic, P., and Tversky, A. (eds.) (1982). *Judgment under uncertainty: Heuristics and biases*. New York: Cambridge University Press.

Katz, D., and Kahn, R. L. (1966). *The social psychology of organizations*. New York: Wiley.

Lax, D. A., and Sebenius, J. K. (1986). *The manager as negotiator*. New York: Free Press.

Lebow, F. N. (1987). *Nuclear crisis management: A dangerous illusion*. Ithaca, NY: Cornell University Press.

Lewicki, R. S., Saunders, D. N., and Minton, J. W. (1999). *Negotiation*, 3rd edn. New York: Irwin McGraw-Hill.

Lind, E. A., and Tyler, T. R. (1988). *The social psychology of procedural justice*. New York: Plenum Press.

Lindblom, C. E. (1980). *The policy making process*, 2nd edn. Englewood Cliffs, NJ: Prentice-Hall.

MacCrimmon, K. R., and Wehrung, D. A. (1986). *Taking risks: The management of uncertainty*. New York: Free Press.

Maier, N. (1967). Group problem solving. *Psychological Review*, 74, 239–49.

Neustadt, R. E., and May, E. R. (1986). *Thinking in time: The uses of history for decision makers*. New York: Free Press.

Nutt, P. C. (1990). *Making tough decisions: Tactics for improving managerial decision making*. San Francisco, CA: Jossey-Bass.

Peterson, R. S., Owens, P. D., Tetlock, P. E., Fan, E. T., and Matorana, P. (1998). Group dynamics in top management teams: Groupthink, vigilance, and alternative models of organizational failure and success. *Organizational Behavior and Human Decision Processes*, 73, 272–305.

Sharpe, P., and Keelin, T. (1998). SmithKline Beecham makes better resource allocation decisions. *Harvard Business Review*, March–April, 45–57.

Simon, H. A. (1976). *Administrative behavior: A study of decision-making processes in administrative organizations*, 3rd edn. New York: Free Press.

Simon, H. A. (1983). *Reason in human affairs*. Stanford, CA: Stanford University Press.

Starbuck, W. H. (1983). Organizations as action generators. *American Sociological Review*, 48, 91–102.

Stein, J. G., and Tanter, R. (1980). *Rational decision making: Israel's security choices*. Columbus, Ohio: Ohio State University Press.

Steiner, G. A. (1979). *Strategic planning*. New York: Free Press.

Taylor, D. W. (1965). Decision making and problem solving. In J. March (ed.), *Handbook of organizations*. Chicago: Rand McNally.

Tetlock, P. E. (1985). Accountability: The neglected social context of judgment and choice. In L. L. Cummings and B. M. Staw (eds.), *Research in organizational behavior* (Vol. 17, pp. 297–332). Greenwich, CT: JAI Press.

Tversky, A., and Kahneman, D. (1981). The framing of decisions and the psychology of choice. *Science*, 211, 453–8.

Vroom, V. H., and Jago, A. G. (1988). *The new leadership: Managing participation in organizations*.

Englewood Cliffs, NJ: Prentice-Hall.

Whyte, G. (1989). Groupthink reconsidered. *Academy of Management Review*, 14, 40–58.

Whyte, G. (1991). Decision failures: Why they occur and how to prevent them. *Academy of Management Executive*, 5, 23–31.

Zeleny, M. (1981). Descriptive decision-making and its applications. *Applications of Management Science*, 1, 327–88.

23

Stimulate Creativity by Fueling Passion

Teresa M. Amabile

People will be most creative when they feel motivated primarily by the interest, enjoyment, satisfaction, and challenge of the work itself – and not by external pressures. This is the "Intrinsic Motivation Principle of Creativity" (Amabile, 1996), and it suggests that the social environment, particularly the presence or absence of external pressures in that environment, can influence creativity by influencing people's passion for their work. Managers can influence the level of creativity in their organizations by establishing work environments that support passion for the work.

Intrinsic motivation is the motivation to do work because it is interesting, engaging, or positively challenging. In its highest form, it is called passion and can lead to complete absorption in the work (Csikszentmihalyi, 1990). The elements that make up intrinsic motivation include a sense of self-determination in doing the work (rather than a sense of being a pawn of someone else), a feeling that one's skills are being both fully utilized and further developed, and positive feelings about the work, which may be akin to positive affect or positive emotion (e.g., deCharms, 1968; Deci and Ryan, 1985; Lepper and Greene, 1978).

A considerable body of research over the past 25 years (conducted with both children and adults) has demonstrated that external pressures in the work environment, also called extrinsic motivators, can decrease intrinsic motivation and, as a result, can decrease creativity. Most of this research has been experimental, demonstrating that reduced intrinsic motivation and reduced creativity can be caused by each of several different extrinsic factors, including: expected external evaluation (Amabile, 1979; Amabile, Goldfarb, and Brackfield, 1990; Hennessey, 1989); surveillance (Amabile, Goldfarb, and Brackfield, 1990); contracted-for reward (Amabile, Hennessey, and Grossman, 1986; Hennessey, 1989; Kruglanski, Friedman, and Zeevi, 1971); competition with peers (Amabile, 1982, 1987); and constrained choice in how to do one's work (Amabile and Gitomer, 1984; Koestner, Ryan, Bernieri, and Holt, 1984). Each of these factors causes lower levels of intrinsic motivation and creativity. In fact, one experiment demonstrated that simply thinking about extrinsic motivators led to temporarily lower levels of creativity in adults (Amabile, 1985).

Non-experimental research in organizational settings has largely supported these findings, suggesting that these work environment factors operate as killers of intrinsic motivation and creativity at work. This research has also suggested, however, that certain other work environment factors operate as stimulants and supports of intrinsic motivation and creativity (e.g., Amabile, Conti, Coon, Lazenby, and Herron, 1996; Amabile and Gryskiewicz, 1987; Andrews and Farris, 1967; Pelz and Andrews, 1976; Stahl and Koser, 1978). Interestingly, although constraints on how to do one's work can undermine intrinsic motivation and creativity in organizations, clear ultimate goals for the work can support intrinsic motivation by providing a structure for focusing creative efforts.

Before effects of the work environment on the passion for creativity can be fully understood, it is important to define the basic concepts. Creativity within an organization is the production of novel, appropriate ideas by individuals or small groups. Those ideas can appear in any organizational activity, and are not limited to the domains usually considered to be "creative" (such as R&D, marketing, and strategy formulation). Innovation is the successful implementation of creative ideas by an organization. Notice that ideas cannot be merely new to be considered creative; they must be somehow appropriate to the problem or task at hand. Notice also that it is possible to have many creative contributions – that is, a great deal of creative behavior by individual employees or teams – without having any significant innovation within an organization. This outcome will arise if the new ideas are not communicated or developed effectively within the organization. However, it is not possible to have much innovation in an organization without considerable creativity.

Contrary to popular notions that creativity is the sole province of a few rare geniuses, creativity appears across most levels of human ability. Reviews of the literature suggest that, at low levels of intelligence, creativity is relatively low. However, at higher levels of intelligence (from slightly above average up to genius levels), all levels of creativity are found. In other words, the variability in creativity is much greater for higher levels of intelligence than for lower levels of intelligence (e.g., Stein, 1968; Wallach, 1971).

This suggests a continuum of creativity from the simplest "garden variety" ideas for small improvements to the highest levels of creative achievement in any field. Certainly, products at the highest levels of creativity appear to be qualitatively different from products at the lower levels; it seems odd to compare the invention of the microcomputer with an incrementally improved microcomputer processor. However, the underlying processes do appear to be the same. A useful analogy comes from work in dynamic systems, which has shown that the different gaits of a horse on a treadmill (walking, trotting, cantering, and galloping) do appear to be qualitatively different activities. Yet these qualitatively different outcomes arise from gradual quantitative increases in the underlying system: the speed of the treadmill and the energy output of the horse. Similarly, it is quite possible that the most astonishing human accomplishments come about by people doing more, and better, work than goes into the more ordinary instances of creativity in everyday life.

CONTEXTUAL FACTORS: FEATURES OF THE WORK ENVIRONMENT

Several specific features of the work environment can influence intrinsic motivation and creativity. *Challenge*, a sense of having to work hard on personally important, enriched, and meaningful tasks, appears to be crucial (see chapter 6 above). *Autonomy*, a sense of freedom in how to carry out one's work, also plays a significant role (see chapter 10 above). *Work group supports* include feelings of mutual support for ideas, constructive feedback on ideas, and shared commitment to the work within a team; they also include a broad diversity of skills and backgrounds within the team. *Supervisory encouragement* includes setting clear strategic goals for a project (while allowing the operational autonomy that is important for creativity), encouraging open communication and collaboration within the team, giving useful, positive feedback on ideas, and supporting the work group within the organization. *Organizational encouragement* is the sense that top management encourages, supports, and recognizes creative work (even when that work might not ultimately lead to a successful product), that there are mechanisms for fairly considering new ideas, and that the entire organization collaborates and cooperates to develop new ideas. *Organizational impediments* can have negative effects on intrinsic motivation and creativity; these include political problems within an organization, extremely negative criticism of new ideas, and an emphasis on maintaining the status quo.

All of these features have been identified through research within organizations (e.g., Amabile and Gryskiewicz, 1987; Andrews and Farris, 1967; Carson and Carson, 1993; Hatcher, Ross, and Collins, 1989; Oldham and Cummings, 1996; Pelz and Andrews, 1976; Stahl and Koser, 1978; Zhou, 1998). One study that used a validated instrument to assess the work environment (Amabile, 1995), and obtained outcome measures from independent expert assessments of creativity, demonstrated that these work environment factors distinguished organizational teams producing highly creative work from those whose work was disappointingly uncreative (Amabile, Conti, Coon, Lazenby, and Herron, 1996).

Note that two of the contextual features that relate to creativity stem from the nature of the work and how it is presented to an individual. A sense of positive challenge arises from the person's perception that the work uses and develops a set of important skills to accomplish an important goal. A sense of freedom arises from the extent to which the person has control over and discretion in carrying out the work. Because these features capture several aspects of the job characteristics model (Hackman and Oldham, 1980), job design must be considered an important part of the context for creativity.

DETERMINING FACTORS

The creative process is generally conceived as composed of four basic stages, which may occur in non-linear or repeating sequences: problem definition or problem finding, when people try to understand or articulate the specific problem to be solved; preparation, when they gather potentially relevant information from a number of sources; idea-generation, when they try to come up with interesting candidate ideas among which to select; and validation/communication, when the final idea is worked through and communicated to others (Amabile, 1996). Intrinsic motivation appears to have its strongest influence in the problem-definition and idea-generation stages. Both of these stages require particularly flexible thinking and deep involvement in the problem. It appears that intrinsic motivation fosters just this sort of thinking process. A recent study discovered that people who were more intrinsically motivated toward doing work in a particular domain (verbal activities or problem-solving) produced work that was independently judged as more creative (Ruscio, Whitney, and Amabile, 1998). Moreover, people who were intrinsically motivated were more likely to engage in exploratory, set-breaking behaviors while they were working on the task; that is, they were more likely to take novel, flexible approaches to the activity as they were trying to figure out how to tackle it. And intrinsically motivated people were more likely to concentrate on the activity, becoming deeply involved cognitively in it. Importantly, involvement mediated the effect of intrinsic motivation on creativity; in other words, intrinsic motivation appeared to influence creativity primarily because it influenced depth of involvement in the task.

Thus, the creative process can be thought of as a maze that the problem-solver has to navigate; getting out of the maze is analogous to finding a satisfactory solution to the problem. Following a familiar, straightforward path for solving problems of that type does indeed lead to an exit. However, such approaches to problems are unlikely to yield creative solutions. In order to discover those more creative solutions – those other ways out of the maze – it is necessary to deviate from the familiar, and to take the risk of running into a dead end. If people are primarily extrinsically motivated, they are motivated by something outside of the maze – by a reward or a deadline, for example. Under these work environment circumstances, they are unlikely to get very involved in the problem itself or do much exploration for a new solution. But if people are primarily intrinsically motivated – if they have a basic interest in the task and if their work environment allows them to retain that intrinsic focus – they enjoy the process of exploring for one of those more creative solutions.

Some research suggests a connection between positive affect, intrinsic motivation, and creativity. Experiments demonstrating a negative impact of extrinsic constraint on intrinsic motivation and creativity generally reveal that people not working under extrinsic constraint feel better about the experience and about the work that they have done (e.g., Amabile, 1979; Amabile, Hennessey, and Grossman, 1986). Moreover, people whose positive affect has been boosted by some pleasant experience (such as watching a comedy or being given a treat) become more flexible in their thinking (e.g., Isen, Daubman, and Nowicki, 1987). This suggests that positive work environments might influence intrinsic motivation in part by influencing how happy people feel about their work.

Certainly, the work environment's impact on motivation is not the only determinant of creativity. To stimulate creative productivity, managers should not only engineer supportive work environments; they should also select for employees who demonstrate high levels of each of the individual components of creativity (see Amabile, 1983, 1996), and they should help to develop those components. The first component is expertise, or skill in the domain where the person will be working. This expertise is a function of the person's talent in the domain, as well as of formal and informal education and experience. Not surprisingly, research has shown that, all else being equal, people are more creative if they have more education and experience in a field (McDermid, 1965; Scott and Bruce, 1994). The second component is a set of creativity-relevant processes stemming from the person's personality, cognitive style, and working style. In general, people produce more creative work if they are oriented toward risk-taking and independence, if they know how to take new perspectives on problems and question basic assumptions, if they have a high tolerance for ambiguity, and if they work hard by energetically and persistently pursuing the problems they are trying to solve (MacKinnon, 1965; Feist, 1999). The third component is intrinsic motivation. Although – as discussed above – intrinsic motivation can be influenced positively or negatively by extrinsic constraints in the work environment, people do differ from each other in their baseline levels of intrinsic and extrinsic motivation. Research has shown that there are stable individual differences in people's basic intrinsic motivation toward work (which can be broken down into challenge motivation and enjoyment motivation) and their basic extrinsic motivation toward work (which can be broken down into recognition motivation and compensation motivation) (Amabile, Hill, Hennessey, and Tighe, 1994). These basic intrinsic and extrinsic motivational orientations are more or less orthogonal, however; it is possible for people to be high on both intrinsic and extrinsic motives, high on neither, or high on only one.

A person's creativity skill (the second creativity component) can interact with features of the work context to influence the level of creative output. One study demonstrated that technical employees were most likely to produce patent disclosures and receive high ratings on creativity from their supervisors if they not only scored high on a test of individual creative personality, but also if they had complex jobs and non-controlling, supportive supervisors (Oldham and Cummings, 1996).

EXCEPTIONS TO THE BASIC PRINCIPLE

The research evidence overwhelmingly points to the importance of intrinsic motivation for creativity. However, under some circumstances, certain forms of extrinsic motivation may support intrinsic motivation and creativity – or at least not undermine it (Amabile, 1993). This "motivational synergy" is most likely to occur when people start out highly intrinsically motivated to do their work, and when the extrinsic motivators are limited primarily to the stages of the creative process that involve the preparation to generate ideas or the validation and communication of the final idea. Synergistic effects are unlikely when people feel that the extrinsic motivator – say, a reward – is being used to control their behavior. Synergistic effects are likely, however, when people feel that the reward confirms their competence and the value of their work, or enables them to do work that they were already interested in doing. There is considerable evidence that such "informational" and "enabling" rewards can have powerfully positive effects on intrinsic motivation (see Deci and Ryan, 1985).

In addition, three specific features of the social work environment require qualification: competition, time pressure, and resources. First, competition appears to have different effects on creativity depending on the locus of the competition (Amabile, 1982, 1987; Amabile and Gryskiewicz, 1987). When people are competing with peers (peers with whom they might ideally be sharing information), their creativity seems to be dampened. However, when they are competing with outside groups or organizations, creativity may be stimulated. Second, time pressure appears to have somewhat paradoxical effects although, overall, there appears to be a slightly negative impact of time pressure on organizational creativity (Amabile and Gryskiewicz, 1987; Amabile, Conti, Coon, Lazenby, and Herron, 1996). If people believe that there is a real urgency to solve the problem, because their unit, their organization, or the world has a clear need for a swift resolution, they may be spurred on to higher levels of creativity by that time pressure – as long as there is at least some time to explore alternative solutions and as long as the other work environment supports for creativity are in place. However, people who feel that arbitrary deadlines are being used to control them will likely produce lower levels of creativity. Third, the availability of tangible and intangible resources for projects has somewhat complex effects (Amabile and Gryskiewicz, 1987; Amabile, Conti, Coon, Lazenby, and Herron, 1996). Although, in general, an insufficiency of resources is associated with lower levels of creativity, there may be a threshold effect. That is, although it is rare to find high levels of creativity when resources are extremely scarce, adding resources above a sufficient level may not add to creativity.

Although the vast majority of studies on contextual effects on creativity have focused on the social work environment rather than the physical work environment, there is a small body of research suggesting that the physical environment may play a role. Specifically, it appears that people who work in densely crowded spaces that provide little protection from unwanted intrusions exhibit lower levels of creativity than those who work in more protected spaces (Aiello, DeRisi, Epstein, and Karlin, 1977; Alencar and Bruno-Faria, 1997). None the less, the weight of research evidence suggests that the social environment is a more powerful influence than the physical one.

Implementation

Managers can directly affect employees' intrinsic motivation and creativity by the ways in which they construct assignments, teams, and work environments. The research suggests that it is important to select people not only on the basis of their skills but also on the basis of their interests. People should be matched to projects that will effectively use their best skills and tap into their strongest passions. Teams should be formed so that, as long as they have some common language for discussing the problem at hand, the team members represent a diversity of backgrounds and perspectives. Team leaders and direct supervisors should clearly communicate overall strategic goals for a project, but allow the individuals working on the problem to make decisions about how to accomplish those goals. Supervisors and peers should be genuinely open to new ideas, but should also give constructively challenging feedback on those ideas. Top-level managers should clearly communicate their desire for creative ideas throughout the organization, recognizing such ideas when they occur, and rewarding creative work with additional resources that will enable people to do work that excites them. Moreover, there should be mechanisms to foster idea-sharing and general communication about work across the organization, as well as mechanisms for containing turf battles and political problems. Finally, sufficient resources should be provided for creative projects, and there should be a careful examination of time-frames and an avoidance of extremely tight or arbitrary deadlines where possible.

Some specific tools can be useful for fostering creativity in organizations. Techniques for creative thinking, such as brainstorming and the Creative Problem-Solving (CPS) Process that evolved from it, appear to increase the fluency, flexibility, and originality of people's thinking to some extent (e.g., Parnes, 1967). The paper-and-pencil instrument KEYS: Assessing the Climate for Creativity can diagnose an organization's work environment stimulants and obstacles to creativity (Amabile, 1995; Amabile, Burnside, and Gryskiewicz, 1999). And an "innovation office" within a company can serve as a mechanism for improving the care and attention given to new ideas. However, setting up an innovation office, or hiring consultants to "teach" creativity skills or conduct a work environment assessment, will most likely backfire unless such actions are accompanied by a deep management commitment to understanding and improving the context for creativity for the long term.

CASE STUDIES

A day-by-day study of project teams in several companies provides two clearly contrasting cases of support for intrinsic motivation and creativity within organizations (see Amabile, 1998). Each of the teams studied had been charged with carrying out a specific project that called for creativity. In many cases, the project involved developing a new product; in others, however, it involved solving a complex client problem or managing an entire product line. Two companies in the study stand in stark contrast. Chemical Central Research (a pseudonym) had teams of product developers who were highly intrinsically motivated, and who enjoyed considerable success in turning out creative work (as judged by experts). By contrast, National Houseware Products (also a pseudonym) had teams of product developers who were quite unmotivated in their work, and who exhibited a great deal of difficulty in doing work that even they themselves considered creative. Not surprisingly, Chemical Central Research and National Houseware Products scored significantly differently on each of the KEYS scales, with Chemical Central having higher levels of the creativity stimulants in the work environment, and lower levels of the creativity obstacles.

Managers at Chemical Central matched people with jobs that had them working at the top of their competency levels, continually developing new skills. Moreover, teams received support and coaching in teamwork skills, resulting in frequent examples of productive collaboration within the groups. As one Chemical Central scientist described such an incident:

> Individually, we have been doing all kinds of R&D work to come up with a product that has the required performance characteristics. Today the whole team met and agreed that it's time to consolidate and coordinate our efforts, so progress can be more readily measured.

By contrast, teams at National had difficulty functioning smoothly, perhaps because many people at National felt overwhelmed by their responsibilities:

> Just as we do every Monday, we had our team project review meeting. Today we reviewed 60 plus projects. It's more than any group of highly motivated, type A personalities can deal with. I worry that the entire team is reaching maximum overload and no one on the Operating Group seems to care.

Goal-setting was a clear process at Chemical Central, where top managers conferred with the product developers and then set a project's goals at the outset; the product development teams themselves were given real freedom around the implementation of those goals. At National, top managers maintained the fiction that their product development teams were "empowered" but, in reality, they equivocated on the setting of strategic goals for their teams and then periodically stepped in to micro-manage what the teams were doing. One National team member reported on a typical autonomy-limiting event:

> During our new product review meeting, the Operating Group basically told us what our top priorities were over the next 30 days for new product development; some of these priorities, we didn't necessarily agree with. It was discouraging that our "freedom" to choose our direction/priorities was taken away from us as a team and we were given our direction rather than being allowed to make more decisions on our own.

Moreover, project goals at National were continually shifted by management – usually without serious consideration of the team's views:

> A Quarterly Product Review was held with members of the Operating Group and the General Manager and President. The primary outcome from the meeting was a change in direction away from a new product to revitalization of a completely different type of product in the line. In fact, four priorities were defined for product development, none of which were identified as priorities at our last Quarterly update. The needle still points north, but we've turned the compass again.

Repeatedly, new ideas at Chemical Central were met with interest and collaborative efforts from management and other groups within the organization. By contrast, National's managers were routinely very critical of new suggestions. This behavior appeared to pervade the entire organization. One National team member described such an incident:

> Worked all day on the business plan for next year, trying to develop a plan that would continue to grow the business. I have some pretty radical ideas. I know they would grow the business and result in a stronger market position for our products. The problem is whether or not management will react favorably and allow me to implement them. Lately it is easier not to try to change things.

Chemical Central's General Manager had regular organization-wide update meetings, to share information on new product development projects and to give public recognition to good work that had been done since the last meeting. This often led to a positive sense of challenge among the Chemical Central teams:

> In the year end business meeting, our GM shared with us [the division's] top ten projects that he had recently presented to the very top management of the company. Our project was announced as the 7th priority project in [the entire division]. The team seemed excited and surprised, though a bit fearful of the high visibility.

Top management at National rarely even remarked on team successes, and lost several key players to other organizations where those employees felt they would be more highly valued. Moreover, National suffered from an excess of political behavior, where many top managers behaved in a way that served their own individual short-term interests or the interests of their allies – rather than the best interests of the company. By contrast,

managers at Chemical Central dealt with potential political problems in very straightforward ways:

> A team-mate and I, along with our Technical Director, brainstormed different ways of
> approaching and working with a scientist in another division who competes with a lot of
> [our division's] projects, including this one. We approached him to see if we could convince
> him to work with us to reduce our cycle time dramatically. He was intrigued by the
> challenge and our openness in coming to him, and he agreed. This will be a tremendous
> boon.

Contrasting behaviors could be seen at lower levels of management, too, including
project management. In general, Chemical Central team leaders supported the work of
team members:

> The team leader and I went over the next critical steps that we need to take, so we all agree
> on what information we need to have by the end of the project's next stage.

By contrast, some team leaders at National seemed to have difficulty even communicating effectively with their team members. For example, on one National team, the
leader unpredictably stopped talking periodically with one or more team members:

> I'm tired of being the team player. Ever since last week, the team leader hasn't been
> communicating with me. Others on the team keep asking me about things, assuming I
> know, and it is frustrating to be on a "team" when you have no idea what other team
> members are doing, especially if you are doing work for them.

Although the Chemical Central and National Housewares teams represent extremes in
the sample of project teams studied, other creative/successful and uncreative/unsuccess-
ful teams showed similar patterns of events, work environment perceptions, and motivation.

Is it possible to change work environments for the better, in terms of support for
intrinsic motivation and creativity? Another case study illustrates that it is indeed
possible. A few years ago, in an effort to dramatically increase the level of radical new-
product innovation, top managers at Procter & Gamble established a Corporate New
Ventures (CNV) team (see Amabile, 1997). Not only did this small cross-functional team
have top-level support and access to needed resources, but it was allowed considerable
autonomy in figuring out how to achieve its goal – to play an important role in
developing at least one major new P&G business each year. Moreover, the team was
composed of volunteers, all of whom had a high level of intrinsic motivation to take on
this challenge. The CNV team itself thought carefully, at its inception, about what sort
of work environment it wanted to establish for itself. This environment included constant
discussion of and feedback on new concepts, support for radically different approaches,
and development of clear mechanisms for articulating and testing new ideas. Work
environment assessments at the beginning of CNV and one year later revealed a
dramatic improvement on nearly all features of the work environment, as well as a
superiority of the CNV work environment in comparison to national norms. Moreover,
in the first three years of its existence, CNV had handed off 11 projects to the P&G
business sectors for execution.

Conclusion

People do their most creative work when they are passionate about what they are doing. Such high levels of intrinsic motivation are influenced both by a person's basic interest in a particular kind of work and by the work environment surrounding the person. Managers can support creative productivity by matching people to projects on the basis of interest as well as skill, by using rewards that recognize competence and support further involvement in the work, and by establishing a work environment across the organization – from the level of top management to the level of work groups – that removes the barriers and enhances the supports to active, collaborative, intrinsic involvement in the work.

Note

The author would like to thank Anne Cummings for her help in conceptualizing this chapter.

References

Aiello, J. R., DeRisi, D. T., Epstein, Y. M., and Karlin, R. A. (1977). Crowding and the role of interpersonal distance preference. *Sociometry*, 40, 271–82.

Alencar, E. M., and Bruno-Faria, M. F. (1997). Characteristics of an organizational environment which stimulate and inhibit creativity. *Journal of Creative Behavior*, 31, 271–81.

Amabile, T. M. (1979). Effects of external evaluation on artistic creativity. *Journal of Personality and Social Psychology*, 37, 221–33.

Amabile, T. M. (1982). Children's artistic creativity: Detrimental effects of competition in a field setting. *Personality and Social Psychology Bulletin*, 8, 573–8.

Amabile, T. M. (1983). Social psychology of creativity: A componential conceptualization. *Journal of Personality and Social Psychology*, 45, 357–77.

Amabile, T. M. (1985). Motivation and creativity: Effects of motivational orientation on creative writers. *Journal of Personality and Social Psychology*, 48, 393–9.

Amabile, T. M. (1987). The motivation to be creative. In S. Isaksen (ed.), *Frontiers of creativity research: Beyond the basics*. Buffalo, NY: Bearly Limited.

Amabile, T. M. (1993). Motivational synergy: Toward new conceptualizations of intrinsic and extrinsic motivation in the workplace. *Human Resource Management Review*, 3, 185–201.

Amabile, T. M. (1995). *KEYS: Assessing the climate for creativity*. Greensboro, NC: Center for Creative Leadership.

Amabile, T. M. (1996). *Creativity in context*. Boulder, CO: Westview Press.

Amabile, T. M. (1997). *Corporate New Ventures at Procter & Gamble*. Harvard Business School case no. 9–897–088. Boston, MA: Harvard Business School Publishing.

Amabile, T. M. (1998). How to kill creativity. *Harvard Business Review*, Sept.–Oct. 1998, 76–87.

Amabile, T. M., Burnside, R., and Gryskiewicz, S. S. (1999). *User's manual for KEYS: Assessing the climate for creativity*. Greensboro, NC: Center for Creative Leadership.

Amabile, T. M., Conti, R., Coon, H., Lazenby, J., and Herron, M. (1996). Assessing the work environment for creativity. *Academy of Management Journal*, 39, 1154–84.

Amabile, T. M., and Gitomer, J. (1984). Children's artistic creativity: Effects of choice in task materials. *Personality and Social Psychology Bulletin*, 10, 209–15.

Amabile, T. M., Goldfarb, P., and Brackfield, S. C. (1990). Social influences on creativity: Evaluation, coaction, and surveillance. *Creativity Research Journal*, 3, 6–21.

Amabile, T. M., and Gryskiewicz, S. S. (1987). *Creativity in the R&D laboratory*. Technical Report Number 30. Greensboro, NC: Center for Creative Leadership.

Amabile, T. M., Hennessey, B. A., and Grossman, B. S. (1986). Social influences on creativity: The effects of contracted-for reward. *Journal of Personality and Social Psychology*, 50, 14–23.

Amabile, T. M., Hill, K. G., Hennessey, B. A., and Tighe, E. M. (1994). The Work Preference Inventory: Assessing intrinsic and extrinsic motivational orientations. *Journal of Personality and Social Psychology*, 66, 950–67.

Andrews, F. M., and Farris, G. F. (1967). Supervisory practices and innovation in scientific teams. *Personnel Psychology*, 20, 497–515.

Carson, P. P., and Carson, K. D. (1993). Managing creativity enhancement through goal-setting and feedback. *Journal of Creative Behavior*, 27, 36–45.

Csikszentmihalyi, M. (1990). *Flow: The psychology of optimal experience*. New York: Harper Perennial.

deCharms, R. (1968). *Personal causation*. New York: Academic Press.

Deci, E. L., and Ryan, R. M. (1985). *Intrinsic motivation and self-determination in human behavior*. New York: Plenum.

Feist, G. J. (1999). The influence of personality on artistic and scientific creativity. In R. Sternberg (ed.), *Handbook of creativity* (pp. 273–96). Cambridge, UK: Cambridge University Press.

Hackman, J. R., and Oldham, G. R. (1980). *Work redesign*. Reading, MA: Addison-Wesley.

Hatcher, L., Ross, T., and Collins, D. (1989). Prosocial behavior, job complexity, and suggestion contribution under gainsharing plans. *Journal of Applied Behavioral Science*, 25, 231–48.

Hennessey, B. A. (1989). The effect of extrinsic constraints on children's creativity while using a computer. *Creativity Research Journal*, 2, 151–68.

Isen, A. M., Daubman, K. A., and Nowicki, G. P. (1987). Positive affect facilitates creative problem solving. *Journal of Personality and Social Psychology*, 52, 1122–31.

Koestner, R., Ryan, R., Bernieri, F., and Holt, K. (1984). Setting limits on children's behavior: The differential effects of controlling vs. informational styles on intrinsic motivation and creativity. *Journal of Personality*, 52, 233–48.

Kruglanski, A. W., Friedman, I., and Zeevi, G. (1971). The effects of extrinsic incentive on some qualitative aspects of task performance. *Journal of Personality*, 39, 606–17.

Lepper, M., and Greene, D. (1978). Overjustification research and beyond: Toward a means-end analysis of intrinsic and extrinsic motivation. In M. Lepper and D. Greene (eds.), *The hidden costs of reward*. New Jersey: Lawrence Erlbaum Associates.

MacKinnon, D. W. (1965). Personality and the realization of creative potential. *American Psychologist*, 20, 273–81.

McDermid, C. D. (1965). Some correlates of creativity in engineering personnel. *Journal of Applied Psychology*, 49, 14–19.

Oldham, G. R., and Cummings, A. (1996). Employee creativity: Personal and contextual factors at work. *Academy of Management Journal*, 39, 607–34.

Parnes, S. J. (1967). *Creative behavior guidebook*. New York: Scribner's.

Pelz, D. C., and Andrews, F. M. (1976). *Scientists in organizations*, 2nd edn. New York: Wiley.

Ruscio, J., Whitney, D. M., and Amabile, T. M. (1998). Looking inside the fishbowl of creativity: Verbal and behavioral predictors of creative performance. *Creativity Research Journal*, 11, 243–63.

Scott, S. G., and Bruce, R. A. (1994). Determinants of innovative behavior: A path model of individual innovation in the workplace. *Academy of Management Journal*, 37, 580–607.

Stahl, M. J., and Koser, M. C. (1978). Weighted productivity in R&D: Some associated individual and organizational variables. *IEEE Transactions on Engineering Management*, 25, 20–4.

Stein, M. I. (1968). Creativity. In E. F. Borgatta and W. W. Lambert (eds.), *Handbook of personality theory and research*. Chicago: Rand McNally.

Wallach, M. A. (1971). *The creativity–intelligence distinction*. New York: General Learning Press.

Zhou, J. (1998). Feedback valence, feedback style, task autonomy, and achievement orientation: Interactive effects on creative performance. *Journal of Applied Psychology*, 83, 261–76.

24

Manage Stress at Work through Preventive and Proactive Coping

RALF SCHWARZER

INTRODUCTION

Coping with stress at work can be defined as an effort by a person or an organization to manage and overcome demands and critical events that pose a challenge, threat, harm or loss to that person and that person's functioning or to the organization as a whole. Coping can occur as a response to an event or in anticipation of upcoming demands, but it can also involve a proactive approach to self-imposed goals and challenges.

Coping with stress is considered as one of the top skills inherent in effective managers. In samples recruited from business, educational, health care, and state government organizations, 402 highly effective managers were identified by peers and superiors. Interviews revealed that coping was second on a list of ten key skills attributed to managers. The management of time and stress was beneficial to the organization because the leaders were role models for employees. Moreover, the executives themselves benefited from successful coping in terms of performance and health (Whetton and Cameron, 1993). This underscores the importance of coping at the workplace. A host of research conducted during the last two decades has found that poor adjustment to demanding or adverse work environments can lead to illness, in particular to high blood pressure and cardiovascular disease (Kasl, 1996; Marmot, Bosma, Hemingway, Bruner, and Stansfeld, 1997; Siegrist, 1996; Theorell and Karasek, 1996; Weidner, Boughal, Conner, Pieper, and Mendell, 1997).

This chapter outlines a new theoretical approach to coping that makes a distinction between four perspectives, namely reactive coping, anticipatory coping, preventive coping, and proactive coping. This distinction is based on time-related stress appraisals and on the perceived certainty of critical events or demands. Reactive coping refers to harm or loss experienced in the past, whereas anticipatory coping pertains to inevitable threats in the near future. Preventive coping refers to uncertain threats in the distant future, and proactive coping involves future challenges that are seen as self-promoting.

In addition to this approach, numerous ways of coping are presented, and their use at the level of organizations and at the level of individuals is discussed. To begin with, the nature of stress at work will be described.

STRESS AT WORK

The experience of stress

The workplace provides numerous sources of stress. The job itself might involve difficult and demanding tasks that tax or exceed the coping resources of the employee. The role of an individual within the organization might be ambiguous or might even be the cause of frequent conflicts. Relationships at work could entail friction and impair function or motivation. Career development might be restricted or echo a constant struggle for acknowledgment. The organizational climate might reflect a battleground for competition. Further, it is possible that all of these examples are aggravated by non-work factors that interact with job stress. Adverse conditions are one of the factors that constitute or set the stage for experiencing stress, such as working shifts, long hours, place of work, overload, frequent travel, speed of change, and new technology. Often-cited stressors are job insecurity, friction with bosses, subordinates, or colleagues, and role conflict or ambiguity (Cartwright and Cooper, 1997; Quick, Quick, Nelson and Hurrell, 1997).

During the last two decades, surveys have found a "growing epidemic of stress" (Quick et al., 1997). This does not necessarily indicate that people experience more stress now than they did earlier in their lives, or more stress than earlier generations. Instead, it may signify greater public awareness of the stress phenomenon and the existence of a handy label for a common feeling. Research on the prevalence of stress is difficult because the term is not clearly defined. In the public health literature, and likewise in industrial and organizational psychology, a distinction is sometimes made between "objective stress," also called stressor, and "subjective stress," also called strain or distress. The former is used in research as an independent variable, and the latter as a dependent variable. However, in mainstream psychology, stimulus-based and response-based definitions are no longer preferred. Instead, transactional conceptions are widely accepted, in which stress is understood as a complex process, rather than as a descriptive variable or as an explanatory concept.

Cognitive-transactional theory of stress

Cognitive-transactional theory defines stress as a particular relationship between the person and the environment that is appraised by the person as taxing or exceeding his or her resources and endangering his or her well-being. Lazarus (1991) conceives stress as an active, unfolding process that is composed of causal antecedents, mediating processes, and effects. *Antecedents* are person variables, such as commitments or beliefs, and environmental variables, such as demands or situational constraints. *Mediating processes* refer to coping and appraisals of demands and resources. Experiencing stress and coping bring about both immediate *effects*, such as affect or physiological changes, and long-term effects concerning psychological, somatic health, and social functioning (see figure 24.1)

Cognitive appraisals comprise two simultaneous processes, namely primary (demand)

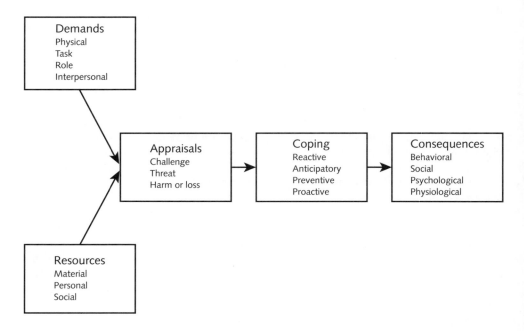

FIGURE 24.1 A process model of stress and coping

appraisals and secondary (resource) appraisals. Appraisal outcomes are divided into the categories challenge, threat, and harm/loss. First, *demand appraisal* refer to one's available coping options for dealing with the demands at hand. The individual evaluates his or her competence, social support, and material or other resources that can help to readapt to the circumstances and re-establish an equilibrium between the person and the environment. Hobfoll (1989) has expanded stress and coping theory with respect to the conservation of resources as the main human motive in the struggle with stressful encounters.

Three outcome categories occur as a result of demand and resource appraisals: a situation is appraised as challenging when it mobilizes physical and mental activity and involvement. In the evaluation of *challenge*, a person may see an opportunity to prove themselves, anticipating gain, mastery, or personal growth from the venture. The situation is experienced as pleasant, exciting, and interesting, and the person feels ardent and confident in being able to meet the demands. *Threat* occurs when the individual perceives danger, anticipating physical injuries or blows to their self-esteem. In the experience of *harm/loss*, some damage has already occurred. This can be the injury or loss of valued persons, important objects, self-worth, or social standing.

Assessment of stress

The main practical problem with transactional theories of stress is that there is no good way of measuring stress as a process. Therefore, all common procedures to assess stress are either stimulus based, pointing at critical events and demands, or response based, pointing at symptoms and feelings experienced. Some procedures measure the frequency or intensity of stressors, while others measure individual distress (strain). An example for a *stimulus-based* instrument is Spielberger's (1994) Job Stress Survey (JSS). It includes 30 items that describe stressors typically experienced by managerial, professional, and clerical employees. The respondents first rate the severity (intensity) of 30 job stressors (such as excessive paperwork, poorly motivated co-workers). Next, they rate the same list once more on a frequency scale. The two ratings result in scores that can be interpreted as state and trait job stress. Other instruments deal with critical events at the workplace, hassles and uplifts, and the work environment in general.

Response-based measures are available that entail symptoms, emotions, arousal, illness, burnout and behavioral changes. Job burnout, however, cannot be equated to stress, but has to be seen as a long-term consequence of stress (Burke, Greenglass, and Schwarzer, 1996; Maslach, 1999). The Maslach Burnout Inventory (MBI) is the standard measure in this field (Maslach, Jackson, and Leiter, 1966). Using measures for burnout, symptoms, mental disorder, or illness to tap the concept of "stress" is questionable and misleading because individual changes in these variables occur only at later stages of a stress episode. Thus, stress is confounded with its consequences. Any use of stress inventories involves a particular definition of stress that is not always made transparent and may even not reflect the researchers' theory.

In any case, no matter whether stimulus-based or response-based measures are used, individuals respond to them with their coping resources in mind. The transactional perspective entails the relationship between demands and resources, which is viewed as causing the resulting emotional response.

COPING WITH STRESS AT WORK

Consequences of poor adjustment to stress at work

Stress is inevitable, but the degree of stress can be modified in two ways: by changing the environment and by changing the individual. If coping attempts are unsuccessful, adverse consequences will result. Job performance may decline and job satisfaction fade, burnout symptoms emerge or accidents happen; further, social relationships at work may become tense, or mental and physical health could deteriorate, leading to sleep problems and substance abuse, etc. Poor adjustment to demanding or adverse work environments can lead to a number of health conditions, in particular high blood pressure and cardiovascular disease. The study of coping at the workplace has often been reduced to only a few variables, such as demands, control, decision latitude, social support, and opportunities for relaxation and exercise. The literature on occupational health has documented an array of findings where these variables were examined in relation to demand factors and population characteristics. Adverse health outcomes have been demonstrated most often (Kasl, 1996; Marmot et al., 1997; Siegrist, 1996; Theorell and Karasek, 1996; Weidner et al., 1997). Successful individual adjustment to stress at work depends partly on resources and partly on the nature of the stress episode.

In the following section, coping resources are described, then dimensions and perspectives of coping are examined that help to gain a better understanding of the psychological meaning of coping.

Antecedents of stress and coping: demands and resources

To characterize *demands* or situational stressors, Lazarus (1991) describes formal properties, such as novelty, event uncertainty, ambiguity, and temporal aspects of stressful conditions. For example, demands that are difficult, ambiguous, unexpected, unprepared, or are very time-consuming under time pressure, are more likely to induce threat than easy tasks that can be prepared for thoroughly and solved at a convenient pace without time constraints. The work environment can be evaluated with respect to the stakes inherent in a given situation. For example, demanding social situations imply interpersonal threat, the danger of physical injury is perceived as physical threat, and anticipated failures endangering self-worth indicate ego threat. Lazarus additionally distinguishes between task-specific stress, including cognitive demands and other formal task properties, and failure-induced stress, including evaluation aspects such as social feedback, valence of goal, possibilities of failure, or actual failure. By and large, unfavorable task conditions combined with failure-inducing situational cues are likely to provoke stress.

Personal resources refer to the internal coping options that are available in a particular stressful encounter. Competence and skills have to match the work demands. Individuals who are affluent, healthy, capable, and optimistic are resourceful and, thus, they are less vulnerable toward stress at work. Social competence, empathy, and assertiveness might be necessary to deal with specific interpersonal demands. It is crucial to feel competent to handle a stressful situation. But actual competence is not a sufficient prerequisite. If the individual underestimates his or her potential for action, no adaptive strategies will be developed. Therefore, perceived competence is crucial. This has been labeled "perceived self-efficacy" or "optimistic self-beliefs" by Bandura (see chapter 9 above). Perceived self-efficacy or optimism are seen as a prerequisite for coping with all kinds of stress, such as job loss, demotion, promotion, or work overload. Job-specific self-efficacy has been studied (for example, see measures of teacher self-efficacy by Schwarzer, Schmitz, and Daytner, 1999).

Social resources refer to the external coping options that are available to an individual in a certain stressful encounter. Social integration reflects the individual's embeddedness in a network of social interactions, mutual assistance, attachment, and obligations. Social support reflects the actual or perceived coping assistance in critical situations (see reviews in Pierce, Sarason, and Sarason, 1996; Veiel and Baumann, 1992). Social support has been defined in various ways, for example as a resource provided by others, coping assistance, or an exchange of resources "perceived by the provider or the recipient to be intended to enhance the well-being of the recipient" (Shumaker and Brownell, 1984: 13). Several types of social support have been investigated, for instance instrumental (e.g., assist with a problem), tangible (e.g., donate goods), informational (e.g., give advice), and emotional support (e.g., give reassurance), among others.

Dimensions of coping

Many attempts have been made to reduce the universe of possible coping responses to a parsimonious set of coping dimensions. Some researchers have come up with two basic distinctions, that is, instrumental, attentive, vigilant, or confrontative coping, as opposed to avoidant, palliative, and emotional coping (for an overview see Schwarzer and Schwarzer, 1996). A well-known approach has been put forward by Lazarus (1991), who separates *problem-focused* from *emotion-focused* coping. Another conceptual distinction has been suggested between *assimilative* and *accommodative* coping, whereby the former aims at modifying the environment and the latter at modifying oneself (Brandstädter, 1992). This pair has also been coined "*mastery* versus *meaning*" (Taylor, 1983) or "*primary control* versus *secondary control*" (Rothbaum, Weisz, and Snyder, 1982). These coping preferences may occur in a certain time order when, for example, individuals first try to alter the demands that are at stake, and, after failing, turn inward to reinterpret their plight and find subjective meaning in it.

Four coping perspectives in terms of timing and certainty

Work demands can be continuous or changing. They can reflect an ongoing harmful encounter, or they can exist in the near or distant future, creating a threat to someone who feels incapable of matching the upcoming demands with the coping resources at hand. Critical events at the workplace may have occurred in the past, leading to layoff, demotion or adverse restrictions. In light of the complexity of stressful episodes, coping cannot be reduced to either relaxation or fight-and-flight responses. Coping depends, among others, on the time perspective of the demands and the subjective certainty of the events. There are distinctions between reactive, anticipatory, preventive, and proactive coping. Reactive coping refers to harm or loss experienced in the past, whereas anticipa-

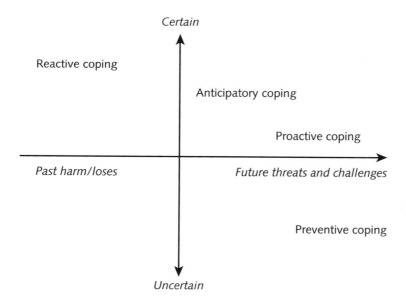

FIGURE 24.2 Four coping perspectives

tory coping pertains to inevitable threats in the near future. Preventive coping refers to uncertain threats in the distant future, whereas proactive coping involves future challenges that are seen as self-promoting (see figure 24.2).

Reactive coping.   Reactive coping can be defined as an effort to deal with a stressful encounter that is ongoing or has already happened, or with the aim to compensate for or to accept harm or loss. Examples of loss or harm are job loss, failing a job interview, having an accident at work, being criticized by the boss, or having been demoted. All of these events happened in the past with absolute certainty; thus, the individual who needs to cope has to either compensate for loss or alleviate harm. Another option is to readjust the goals or to search for meaning to reconcept one's life. Reactive coping may be problem focused, emotion focused, or social-relation focused. For coping with loss or harm, individuals have to be resilient. Since they aim at compensation or recovery, they need "recovery self-efficacy," a particular optimistic belief in their capability to overcome setbacks (Schwarzer, 1999).

Anticipatory coping.   Anticipatory coping can be defined as an effort to deal with imminent threat. In anticipatory coping, individuals face a critical event that is certain to occur in the near future. Examples are speaking in public, a confrontation at a business meeting, a job interview, adapting to a new job, increased workload, promotion, retirement, downsizing, etc. There is a risk that the upcoming event may cause harm or loss later on, and the person has to manage this perceived risk. The situation is appraised as an imminent threat. The function of coping may lie in solving the actual problem at hand, such as increasing effort, getting help or investing other resources. Another function may lie in feeling good in spite of the risk, for example by redefining the situation as less threatening, by distraction, or by gaining reassurance from others. Thus, anticipatory coping can also be understood as the management of known risks, which includes investing one's resources to prevent or combat the stressor. One of the resources is specific "coping self-efficacy." This is the optimistic belief in being able to cope successfully with the particular situation.

Preventive coping.   Preventive coping can be defined as an effort to build up general resistance resources that result in less strain in the future (minimizing severity of impact), less severe consequences of stress, should it occur, and less likely onset of stressful events in the first place. In preventive coping, individuals face a critical event that may or may not occur in the distant future. Examples are job loss, forced retirement, physical impairment, disaster or poverty. The individual plans for the occurrence of such non-normative life events that are appraised as threatening. Again, coping equals risk management, but here one has to manage various unknown risks in the distant future. The outlook creates anxiety sufficient to stimulate a broad range of coping behaviors. Since all kinds of harm or loss could materialize one day, the individual builds up general resistance resources, accumulating wealth, social bonds, and skills, "just in case." Skill development is a major coping process that helps to prevent disadvantages. General "coping self-efficacy" is a prerequisite to plan and initiate successfully multifarious preventive actions that help build up resistance against threatening non-normative life events in the distant future.

Proactive coping. Proactive coping can be defined as an effort to build up general resources that facilitate promotion toward challenging goals and personal growth. In proactive coping, people have a vision. They see risks, demands, and opportunities in the far future, but they do not appraise these as threats, harm, or loss. Rather, they perceive difficult situations as challenges. Coping becomes goal management instead of risk management. Individuals are not reactive, but proactive in the sense that they initiate a constructive path of action and create opportunities for growth. The proactive individual strives for improvement of life or work and builds up resources that assure progress and quality of functioning. Proactively creating better work conditions and higher perform-ance levels is experienced as an opportunity to render life meaningful or to find purpose in life. Stress is interpreted as "eustress," that is, productive arousal and vital energy.

Preventive and proactive coping are partly manifested in the same kinds of overt behaviors as skill development, resource accumulation, and long-term planning. How-ever, the motivation can emanate either from threat appraisal or from challenge ap-praisal, which makes a difference. Worry levels are high in the former and low in the latter. Proactive individuals are motivated to meet challenges and commit themselves to personal quality standards. Self-regulatory goal management includes an ambitious manner of goal-setting and tenacious goal pursuit. The latter requires "action self-efficacy," an optimistic belief that one is capable of initiating and maintaining difficult courses of action. The role of beliefs in self-regulatory goal attainment has been spelled out in more detail in the Health Action Process Approach (Schwarzer, 1992, 1999).

The distinction between these four perspectives of coping is highly useful because it moves the focus away from mere responses to negative events toward a broader range of risk and goal management that includes the active creation of opportunities and the positive experience of stress, in particular in the work domain. Aspinwall and Taylor (1997) have described a proactive coping theory that is similar, but not identical to the present one. Taubert (1999) has conducted a study to make psychometric discriminations between preventive and proactive coping. The Proactive Coping Scale is available for the public (Greenglass, Schwarzer, and Taubert, 1999).

Ways of Coping

Coping at the level of organizations: designing healthy workplaces

When an unexpected event happens, such as a strike or a takeover, an organization has to cope in a reactive manner. Reducing harm or compensating for loss are required, and the way this is done depends largely on the particular nature of the stress episode. When such events are imminent and certain, anticipatory coping is required. The adequate way of coping is highly idiosyncratic. Preventive coping is called for when no specific events are envisioned but a more general threat in the distant future comes into view. Such events could be the dangers of economic decline, potential mergers or downsizing, revised governmental employee health regulations, aging workforce, new technology, etc. When visions or challenges and a perceived potential for growth or mastery prevail, proactive coping is initiated. The latter two perspectives entail about the same set of innovations. In the literature, this is usually discussed as "primary prevention" or "organizational prevention" (Quick et al., 1997), which includes modifying work demands and improving relationships at work (see also Burke, 1993).

Physical settings can be redesigned to minimize distressful effects of the physical work environment, such as noise, heat, and crowding. The creation of pleasant and suitable offices or workshops, enriched by cafeterias and fitness centers, can elevate job satisfaction, job safety, and mental health, which indirectly may improve performance and loyalty. *Job redesign* is aimed at changing task demands, for example by partitioning the workload, job rotation, job enlargement, job enrichment, building teams, opening feedback channels, etc. (see chapter 6 above). *Flexible work schedules* can help to enhance the employee's control and discretion and allow for a better time management and integration of work and non-work demands. *Participative management* expands the amount of autonomy at work by disseminating information, decentralizing decision-making, and involving subordinates in a variety of work arrangements (see chapter 21 above). When a boss levels with the employees, tension and conflict is reduced, and awareness of partnership may arise. The empowerment approach has a similar focus (see chapter 10 above). *Career development* is another method of preventive or proactive coping to improve an estimable portfolio of skills and talents. A set of career paths must be made transparent, and various opportunities for promotion need to be created to motivate employees to set goals for themselves and strive for these goals. This needs to be enriched by an effective feedback and reward system. Self-assessment must be encouraged, and opportunities constantly need to be analyzed (Lawler, 1994).

Organizational prevention is also directed at interpersonal demands placed on individuals at the workplace (Quick et al., 1997). *Role analysis* is aimed at making the role transparent that someone holds within an organization. Clarifying one's role profile in comparison to the profiles of others may help to reduce tension, misperceptions, and conflict. Roles are defined as a set of expectations (by boss, peers, and subordinates) toward a particular position holder. If roles are misperceived, "role stress" will emerge. Thus, role analysis and correction of perceptions constitute a way of preventive coping. *Goal-setting* in itself can be regarded as a method of preventive coping in order to avoid miscomprehension about one's responsibilities and expected task performance. Negotiating proximal and distal work goals includes an agreement between supervisor and subordinate or team about the conditions under which they should be attained and the criteria that apply for their evaluation (see chapter 8 above). *Team-building* is a preventive coping method that aims at the establishment of cohesive and effective work groups that perform at a higher level than isolated individuals, partly because they resolve interpersonal conflicts and develop a cohesive spirit. *Social support* reflects broad-range prevention and intervention at all levels. The term denotes a coping resource as well as an interpersonal coping process, depending on the point in time within a defined stress episode. Social support is generally seen as a buffer against the impact of stress – although, empirically, main effects occur more frequently than statistical interactions (Schwarzer and Leppin, 1989). As a buffer, social support can be part of reactive coping after the event has struck. As a preventive and proactive coping strategy, social network-building equals the institution of a convoy that accompanies and protects the individual throughout the life course when times get rough.

Stress in organizations is related to their culture and leadership, organizational structures and developments. Proactive leaders have transformed stressed corporations into healthy ones, and restructuring has created relatively stress-free work environments, as has been documented for Southwest Airlines, Chaparral Steel Company, Xerox Corporation, Johnson & Johnson, or, as a negative example, Eastern Airlines (Quick et al., 1997).

Teacher stress and burnout can be prevented and mitigated at the level of schools by making them healthier workplaces. Based on his work in schools in Israel, Friedmann (1999) suggests tackling the sources of stress by reducing the degree of polarization in the classroom, reducing the number of pupils per class, and changing teachers' work schedules. To treat the symptoms of stress at the school level, he suggests creating a supportive atmosphere, opening channels of communication, involving teachers in decision-making, and developing an open and positive organizational climate.

Coping at the individual level within organizations

At the individual level, Friedmann (1999) suggests tackling the sources of stress by training teachers to cope with stressful situations, instructing them about the causes of burnout, and developing and improving their abilities in problem-solving, conflict resolution, and leadership. To treat the symptoms of stress, he suggests inservice training, holidays, support and assistance groups, and workshops.

Some general theoretical comments on individual coping have to be added here. If a person fails to meet a work goal, is rejected by colleagues, has a conflict with the boss, suffers from repetitive stress injury, or loses a contract or the job itself, *reactive coping* takes place because the demands or events are appraised as ongoing or as prior harm or loss. A range of mental and behavioral coping options are at the individual's disposal, depending on the available resources, preferences, and the nature of the stress episode. Relaxation is a commonplace recommendation to help alleviate negative emotions or arousal, although it does not contribute much to solving the underlying problem. Cognitive restructuring helps individuals to see the world with different eyes. Instrumental action may solve the problem at hand. Distinctions have been made between problem-focused and emotion-focused coping (Lazarus, 1991). Social relations coping (Hobfoll, 1998) or task avoidance (Parker and Endler, 1996) have been added as a third dimension. Talking with others, writing it down, and acting it out are other suggestions to help cope with adversity (Quick et al., 1997). The experience of harm or loss calls for compensatory efforts (mastery) or a search for meaning and flexible goal adjustment.

There is no basic rule or rank order of good and bad coping strategies that apply to harm or loss situations. It is also questionable whether one could come up with criteria for "successful coping" (Lazarus, 1991). The individual adapts in an idiosyncratic manner to the situation and evaluates the coping efforts retrospectively as having been more or less successful, which may not correspond with the evaluation of onlookers. If someone fails to adapt, social support needs to be mobilized from outside, and psychological counseling, therapy, traumatic event debriefing, or even medical care may become necessary.

If someone faces a critical event in the near future, such as a public presentation, job interview, medical procedure, or corporate decision about redundancy of jobs – in other words, situations that are appraised as threatening – this stress episode requires *anticipatory coping*. The range of coping options is the same as before. Increased effort to master the situation is adaptive only if the situation is under personal control (interview, presentation), whereas situations under external control (medical procedure, corporate decision) require mainly emotional and cognitive efforts (e.g., relaxation, reappraisal).

An individual who faces increasing work challenges or job volatility in the distant future, such as downsizing, mergers, demotion, promotion, entrepreneurship, is more apt to choose either *preventive coping* strategies (in the case of threat appraisal) or *proactive coping* strategies (in the case of challenge appraisal). The long-term accumulation of general resistance resources includes behavioral, social, and cognitive strategies. Coping with one's work demands, for example, comprises setting priorities, avoiding overload, delegating tasks, acquiring social support, planning, and having good time management (Quick et al., 1997). Managing one's lifestyle is directed at a healthy balance between work, family, and leisure. Workaholics do not maintain such a balance, and they hardly find refuge anywhere. Work stress can spill over into non-work settings, and vice versa, which places a particular burden on women and dual-career couples (Greenglass, 1995). Protecting life domains from daily hassles is an important aspect of self-regulation. Some companies grant their employees extra time for revitalization and personal growth, for example by funding sabbaticals. Healthy nutrition and physical exercise are other lifestyle ingredients that provide a protective shield against the experience of stress.

The cognitive way of coping has been labeled stress reappraisal, internal dialog, constructive self-talk, search for meaning, or optimistic explanatory style, among others. Individuals can develop a more positive view of stressful situations, which may facilitate all kinds of coping. Reinterpreting a threat as a challenge transforms preventive coping into proactive coping. Habitual mindsets that reflect a constructive approach to life are inherent in the concepts of perceived self-efficacy (see chapter 9 above), learned optimism (Seligman, 1991), and hardiness (Maddi, 1998).

The hardiness concept has been applied frequently to prevent and mitigate stress at work. It comprises the attitudes of commitment, control and challenge. The goal of interventions, conducted by the Hardiness Institute, lies in the promotion of these attitudes. Initially, participants respond to the HardiSurvey that assesses these three components and gauges how much work stress a person experiences. Clients then undergo the 16-hour HardiTraining course, consisting of exercises on how to cope with stress, relax, seek social support, eat right, and work out (Maddi, 1998). With a group of 54 managers, hardiness training was compared to relaxation training and to a social support control condition. The first group reported less strain and illness and higher job satisfaction. Thus, hardiness is seen as stimulating effective functioning and protecting wellness under stressful conditions.

Stress management programs are usually not implemented by corporations as stand-alone programs, but rather as part of more comprehensive *health promotion strategies* that also aim at preventive nutrition, physical exercise, smoking cessation, preventing the use of alcohol and drugs, and so on. IBM, Control Data Corporation, Illinois Bell, New York Telephone Company, B. F. Goodrich Tire, Citicorp, Johnson & Johnson, and Dupont are among the frequently cited companies that have established health promotion programs of high quality for their employees (see also Quick et al., 1997).

A good example of a program at the individual level within organizations is the "learned optimism training" that was conducted at Metropolitan Life Insurance Company (Seligman, 1991; Seligman and Schulman, 1986). Learned optimism is a proxy for a particular explanatory style that can be acquired to improve one's interpretation of stressful events in general or specifically at work. A diagnostic measure, the Attributional Style Questionnaire (ASQ), was developed, which ranks individuals on an optimism/pessimism scale. One prediction that this measure makes concerns job performance, for example successfully selling life-insurance. Insurance agents with high scores on the ASQ invest more effort and are more persistent in "cold calling" customers and attain better sales commissions than low scorers. By using this diagnostic instrument to select personnel, Metropolitan Life has saved millions of dollars. Many companies now use such scales in order to identify applicants who possess more than just drive and talent, namely the optimism necessary for success as well.

Based on Seligman's theory and his assessment procedure, a training program has been developed to teach employees cognitive coping with stress. Participants with chronic negative thoughts learn to talk to themselves in a constructive manner. If something goes wrong, pessimists tend to have hopeless thoughts ("I always screw up," "I'll never get it right"), that is, internal, stable, and global attributions of negative events. They learn to transform these thoughts into external, variable, or specific attributions, such as "Things didn't go well today, but I learned a lot from the experience." Workshop participants learn to listen to their own internal dialogue and to dispute their chronic negative thoughts and come up with a more balanced view of themselves, the world, and the future. The four-day course is administered by Foresight Inc., at Falls Church, Virginia. Unlike other courses for sales agents, which teach what to say to clients, this course teaches what to say to oneself when the client says no. Thus, it represents a cognitive coping training to reduce stress when facing interpersonal demands. The most typical exercise is to identify adverse events, the corresponding subjective belief, and the most likely subsequent emotions and behaviors. Then, after recognizing their explanatory style, the participants learn to dispute their thoughts. They are asked to make the revised explanatory style a new habit to supplant the automatic pessimistic explanations that they used to make all the time. In psychotherapy this is known as cognitive restructuring. This principle has turned out to be a powerful coping strategy that facilitates job performance, job satisfaction, and health.

CONCLUSION

Coping with stress is a normal and necessary experience in daily life. At the workplace, it gains particular importance because it is related not only to individual career goals, health, and satisfaction, but also to organizational success and social relations. To understand coping, a number of analytical dimensions, perspectives, theoretical models, and approaches have been suggested. In the present chapter, a new distinction between reactive, anticipatory, preventive, and proactive coping has been put forward because these coping perspectives have unique value for stress at the workplace, including the positive side of stress. Interventions have to be tailored to these perspectives. Events that are appraised as harmful or causing loss require different coping interventions than those that are appraised as threats or challenges. The current view connects coping theory with action theory and sets the stage for integrative programs at the organizational and individual level. It is in line with the contemporary trend toward a "positive psychology."

References

Aspinwall, J. G., and Taylor, S. E. (1997). A stitch in time: Self-regulation and proactive coping. *Psychological Bulletin*, 121, 417–36.

Brandtstädter, J. (1992). Personal control over development: Implications of self-efficacy. In R. Schwarzer (ed.), *Self-efficacy: Thought control of action* (pp. 127–45). Washington, DC: Hemisphere.

Burke, R. J. (1993). Organizational-level interventions to reduce occupational stressors. *Work and Stress*, 7(1), 77–87.

Burke, R. J., Greenglass, E. R., and Schwarzer, R. (1996). Predicting teacher burnout over time: Effects of work stress, social support, and self-doubts on burnout and its consequences. *Anxiety, Stress, and Coping: An International Journal*, 9, 261–75.

Cartwright, S., and Cooper, C. L. (1997). *Managing workplace stress*. Thousand Oaks, CA: Sage.

Friedman, I. A. (1999). Turning over schools into a healthier workplace: Bridging between professional self-efficacy and professional demands. In R. Vandenberghe and A. M. Huberman (eds.), *Understanding and preventing teacher burnout* (pp. 166–75). Cambridge, UK: Cambridge University Press.

Greenglass, E. R. (1995). Gender, work stress, and coping: Theoretical implications. *Journal of Social Behavior and Personality*. Special Issue: *Gender in the Workplace*, 10(6), 121–34.

Greenglass, E. R., Schwarzer, R., and Taubert, S. (1999). *The Proactive Coping Inventory (PCI): A multidimensional research instrument* [On-line publication]. Available at: http://userpage.fu-berlin.de/~health/greenpci. htm

Hobfoll, S. E. (1989). Conservation of resources: A new attempt at conceptualizing stress. *American Psychologist*, 44(3), 513–24.

Hobfoll, S. E. (1998). *Stress, culture, and community. The psychology and philosophy of stress*. New York: Plenum.

Kasl, S. V. (1996). The influence of the work environment on cardiovascular health: A historical, conceptual, and methodological perspective. *Journal of Occupational Health Psychology*, 1(1), 42–56.

Lawler, E. E. III. (1994). From job-based to competency-based organizations. *Journal of Organizational Behavior*, 15, 3–16.

Lazarus, R. S. (1991). *Emotion and adaptation*. London: Oxford University Press.

Maddi, S. R. (1998). Creating meaning through making decisions. In P. T. P. Wong, P. S. Fry, et al. (eds.), *The human quest for meaning: A handbook of psychological research and clinical applications* (pp. 3–26). Mahwah, NJ: Erlbaum.

Marmot, M. G., Bosma, H., Hemingway, H. Brunner, E., and Stansfeld, S. (1997). Contribution of job control and other risk factors to social variations in coronary heart disease incidence. *Lancet*, 350, 235–9.

Maslach, C. (1999). Progress in understanding teacher burnout. In R. Vandenberghe and A. M. Huberman (eds.), *Understanding and preventing teacher burnout* (pp. 211–22). Cambridge, UK: Cambridge University Press.

Maslach, C., Jackson, S. E., and Leiter, M. P. (1996). *Maslach Burnout Inventory manual*, 3rd edn. Palo Alto, CA: Consulting Psychologists Press.

Parker, J. D. A., and Endler, N. S. (eds.) (1996). Coping and defense: A historical overview. In M. Zeidner and N. S. Endler (eds.), *Handbook of coping: Theory, research, applications* (pp. 3–23). New York: Wiley.

Pierce, G. R., Sarason, I. G., and Sarason, B. R. (1996). Coping and social support. In M. Zeidner and N. S. Endler (eds.), *Handbook of coping: Theory, research, applications* (pp. 434–51). New York: Wiley.

Quick, J. C., Quick, J. D., Nelson, D. L., and Hurrell, J. J. Jr. (1997). *Preventive stress management in organizations*. Washington, DC: APA.

Rothbaum, F., Weisz, J. R., and Snyder, S. (1982). Changing the world and changing the self: A two-process model of perceived control. *Journal of Personality and Social Psychology*, 42, 5–37.

Schwarzer, R. (ed.) (1992). *Self-efficacy: Thought control of action*. Washington, DC: Hemisphere.

Schwarzer, R. (1999). Self-regulatory processes in the adoption and maintenance of health behaviors. The role of optimism, goals, and threats. *Journal of Health Psychology*, 4(2), 115–27.

Schwarzer, R., and Leppin, A. (1989). Social support and health: A meta-analysis. *Psychology and Health: An International Journal*, 3, 1–15.

Schwarzer, R., Schmitz, G. S., and Daytner, G. T. (1999). *The Teacher Self-Efficacy scale* [On-line publication]. Available at: http://www.fu-berlin.de/gesund/skalen/t_se.htm

Schwarzer, R., and Schwarzer, C. (1996). A critical survey of coping instruments. In M. Zeidner and N. S. Endler (eds.), *Handbook of coping: Theory, research and applications* (pp. 107–32). New York: Wiley.

Seligman, M. E. P. (1991). *Learned optimism*. New York: Knopf.

Seligman, M. E. P., and Schulman, P. (1986). Explanatory style as a predictor of productivity and quitting among life insurance sales agents. *Journal of Personality and Social Psychology*, 50(4), 832–8.

Shumaker, S. A., and Brownell, A. (1984). Toward a theory of social support: Closing conceptual gaps. *Journal of Social Issues*, 40, 11–36.

Siegrist, J. (1996). Adverse health effects of high-effort/low-reward conditions. *Journal of Occupational Health Psychology*, 1, 27–41.

Spielberger, C. D. (1994). *Professional manual for the job stress survey (JSSS)*. Odessa, FL: Psychological Assessment Resources.

Taubert, S. (1999). Development and validation of a psychometric instrument for the assessment of proactive coping. (Unpublished diploma thesis), Freie Universität Berlin, Germany.

Taylor, S. E. (1983). Adjustment to threatening events: A theory of cognitive adaptation. *American Psychologist*, 38, 1161–73.

Theorell, T., and Karasek, R. (1996). Current issues relating to psychosocial job strain and cardiovascular disease research. *Journal of Occupational Health Psychology*, 1(1), 9–26.

Veiel, H. O. F., and Baumann, U. (1992). The many meanings of social support. In H. O. F. Veiel and U. Baumann (eds.), *The meaning and measurement of social support* (pp. 1–9). Washington, DC: Hemisphere.

Weidner, G., Boughal, T., Connor, S. L., Pieper, C., and Mendell, N. R. (1997). Relationship of job strain to standard coronary risk factors and psychological characteristics in women and men of the Family Heart study. *Health Psychology*, 16(3), 239–47.

Whetton, D. A., and Cameron, K. S. (1993). *Developing management skills: Managing stress*. New York: HarperCollins.

25

Manage Conflict through Negotiation and Mediation

M. Susan Taylor

"Managers" often find that their formal authority falls far short of their responsibilities and their success is dependent on the actions of others outside the chain of command. Though people in this predicament may yearn for more control, there is often no practical way to follow the textbook advice to match authority with responsibility. "Indirect management" is the name we give this increasingly important phenomenon of concentrated responsibility but shared authority and resources. It calls for a very different approach from traditional line management. (Lax and Sebenius, 1986)

INTRODUCTION AND META-PRINCIPLE

Managers function in an increasingly complex world where competition is intense and global for virtually all product or service lines. Their revenue-generating initiatives require cross-unit cooperation and coordination, and the structural parameters or procedural precedents that might assist in the implementation of such initiatives are often absent or inconsistent. Even their work units are increasingly staffed by teams of employees who require and demand substantial self-determination in order to perform their jobs effectively. Together, these factors generate a perfect set of conditions for conflict in the managerial job – scarce resources, ambiguous lines of authority, conflicting goals, and high levels of interdependence. What exactly is meant by the term conflict? Essentially, I am speaking of the process that occurs when one party perceives that another has frustrated or is about to frustrate one or more of its concerns (Thomas, 1976). In which domains of a manager's job might we expect conflict to emerge? Both research and experience show us that conflict frequently occurs across many aspects of the manager's job, including in interactions with their own managers, dealings with peers or associates, discussions with the employees they manage, and in their need or desire to "shore up" their formal authority in the organization. Thus, conflict in the workplace is often a common occurrence that managers face and must attempt to resolve on virtually a daily basis.

This chapter focuses on the manager's role as conflict resolver. It is based on the meta-principle that negotiation and mediation processes, when used appropriately, enhance managers' effectiveness in resolving many of the conflicts that confront them. Although written from a normative perspective that is based on research findings, the chapter also explores descriptive information concerning what is known about the ways managers tend to deal with conflict.

How managers attempt to resolve conflicts

Some insight into the tactics managers used when directly involved in work disputes can be gained from examining their influence attempts with other parties. Past research has found that managers rely on different behaviors to influence the decisions of their bosses, peers, and employees (see table 25.1).

Still other research provides some assistance in identifying the underlying dimensions of conflict resolution present in managers' influence attempts. The work of Ury, Brett, and Goldberg (1988) on dispute resolution revealed three ways in which disputes may be resolved – interests, rights, and power. In the first case, parties may seek to reconcile conflicting interests by finding solutions that will appeal to a majority of the most important interests that underlie their dispute, i.e., the majority of the things that each most values. Alternatively, they may try to resolve conflicts based on whose "rights" are best supported or protected by some independent standard that has legitimacy in the eyes

TABLE 25.1 Differences in managers' attempts to influence the behavior of bosses, peers, and employees

Influence attempts with bosses
1   Providing rational explanations for the desired choice
2   Telling, arguing, or talking without supportive facts, data, or other individuals
3   Presenting a complete plan of the actions they want to implement
4   Using persistence or repetition in pressing for the preferred solution
5   Developing or cultivating the support of others, including employees and outsiders

Influence attempts with peers
1   Providing a rational explanation
2   Developing and showing the support of others
3   Presenting an example of a parallel situation
4   Making threats
5   Offering to trade favors or concessions with the peer

Influence attempts with employees
1   Showing confidence and support
2   Delegating guidelines or goals
3   Presenting rational explanations
4   Listening, counseling, and/or soliciting ideas
5   Presenting an example of a parallel situation

Influence attempts listed in order of frequency of use
Source: Taken from Keys and Case (1990)

of all those involved, e.g., a law or contract, or perhaps due to a socially accepted norm such as reciprocity or precedent. Finally, parties also may attempt to resolve conflicts according to who is more powerful, or who has the greater ability to get the other do to things he/she would not otherwise do. Unfortunately, however, as Ury et al. (1988) note, power differentials are generally difficult to determine without a costly "test of wills."

On inspection, there seem to be elements of all three methods – interests, rights, and power – in the descriptions of managers' influence attempts in table 25.1. For example, providing a rational explanation seems closely related to a reliance on interests, as does the provision of a complete plan; the showing of confidence and support; listening, counseling and/or soliciting of ideas; and offering to trade favors or concessions. Conversely, the presentation of a parallel situation seems to fall into the rights arena, where a manager is attempting to show that the current issue is similar to one previously handled in a particular way, perhaps due to rights or precedent. Finally, methods such as telling, arguing, or talking without support, using persistence or repetition, developing and showing the support of others, threats, and the delegation of guidelines or goals seem to illustrate the use of power in influence attempts. Nevertheless, descriptive information about the ways managers attempt to resolve conflict tells us very little about the effectiveness of their methods. Fortunately, the work of Ury et al. (1988) also provides some assistance in this arena.

The relative effectiveness of resolution methods

One method of assessing the effectiveness of different conflict resolution methods is to consider the "costs of disputing," including: (1) various transaction expenses, including those that are economic, psychological, and time-based; (2) the parties' satisfaction with the fairness of the outcomes and of the resolution process in general; (3) the effect of the resolution on the parties' relationship, particularly on their ability to work together on a day-to-day basis; and finally, (4) the likelihood of conflict recurrence, either between the two parties or between one of them and another party. Once assessing method effectiveness *vis-à-vis* these four criteria, Ury et al. (1988: 15) concluded that: "in general reconciling interests is less costly than determining who is right, which in turn is less costly than determining who is more powerful." Note, however, that rights and power may sometimes be used to enhance the effectiveness of interests reconciliation by setting boundaries around what will be determined through the reconciliation of interests. Thus, prior research seems to support the relative effectiveness of reconciling parties' interests as an appropriate conflict resolution method for managers. This, in turn, brings us to the topic of negotiation.

NEGOTIATION AS A MANAGERIAL TOOL FOR RECONCILING INTERESTS

Negotiation is a frequently applied technique for reconciling interests and may be extremely useful to managers when their interests are directly in conflict with those of others in the workplace, including those outside their chain of command, their employees, their bosses, and the support staff charged with the operations of various management systems in the organization, e.g., budget, human resources, etc. As Lax and Sebenius (1986: 2) have noted, "Negotiation is a useful skill for important occasions, but it also lies at the core of the manager's job. Managers negotiate not only to win contracts but also to guide enterprises in the face of change."

Essentially negotiation is defined as the "situation where parties, with some apparent conflict, seek to do better through jointly decided action than they could do otherwise" (Lax and Sebenius, 1986: 12). The body of research on the nature and effects of negotiation is now fairly substantial. It provides a number of principles regarding negotiation effects that subsequently generate several recommendations for enhancing managers' negotiation effectiveness.

Negotiation principles and recommendations

What has research revealed about negotiating behaviors that tend to enable managers to "do better through joint action"?

1 Following work by Fisher, Ury and their colleagues (Fisher and Ury, 1981) at the Harvard Negotiation School, higher joint gains frequently result from a *principled or collaborative* form of *negotiation* focused on achieving the interests of both parties' use of principled negotiation in situations where a long-term, rather than a short-term relationship exists or is envisioned between parties, where they share important values or principles that shape their goals in the negotiation, and where there are a number of different issues at stake such that the likelihood of creating a situation of joint gain is higher. This form of negotiation emphasizes:
   (a) the candid and open exchange of information about both parties' interests;
   (b) the intent to satisfy each party's interest to some degree, the focal party's (the manager's) to the greatest extent and the other party's at least to an acceptable degree;
   (c) creativity in identifying many options that might be used to satisfy interests;
   (d) the use of external standards, facts, or criteria (e.g., the use of the Blue Book to determine used-car values) to resolve disputes over the value of various options;
   (e) each party's identification of a "BATNA," the best alternative to a negotiated solution, in order to enhance their ability to "to do better through negotiating because they will not be forced to accept an undesirable offer simply to reach agreement;"
   (f) the enhancement of the relationship between parties by communicating in a manner that focuses on the issues, rather than on the people involved, and strives to improve the relationship, and at the least, does nothing to worsen it.
2 Begin the bargaining with a positive overture, perhaps by making a small concession, then reciprocate the other party's concessions.
3 Look beneath the other party's tactics and try to determine his or her strategy. Even threats and power plays can be attempts to guide you toward a mutually acceptable agreement. Be sensitive to this and follow it if it is beneficial to your interests.

4 Do not allow accountability to your constituents or surveillance by them spawn competitive bargaining which often spirals quickly out of control.

5 If you have power in a negotiation, use it − with specific demands, mild threats, and persuasion − to guide the other party toward an agreement.

6 Be open to accepting third-party assistance (more on this later in the chapter).

7 Attend to the negotiation environment. Be aware that your behavior and power and that of the other party are altered by it. Opponents who come from an environment of resource scarcity are often rewarded for competitive bargaining. Anticipate this and strive to protect your interests (Wall and Blum, 1991).

8 Negotiation tends to be more efficient (faster, more likely to reach agreement) and more likely to yield agreements in the interests of both parties (principled or collaborative negotiations) when parties have positive working relationships. Thus, strive to develop a positive working relationship with your negotiation partner by designing situations in which parties depend on one another for help across a number of separate issues and opportunities for action. When working relationships are already strained, suggest the use of problem-solving workshops to improve them before beginning the bargaining.

9 Teams of negotiators often respond more competitively than do individuals. Be alert to the possibility that contentious behavior will spiral and escalate the conflict when teams of negotiators are involved. Internal conflict within a team will greatly limit the likelihood of reaching agreement between the two parties. Thus, try to minimize within-team conflict before between-group negotiations start. Try to align the thinking on your own team by relying on pressure to obtain compliance from members who are less attached to the group (out-group members) and conciliation techniques for members who feel a greater sense of group commitment.

10 Early studies indicate that computer-mediated negotiations are less efficient, more hostile, and more likely to lead to poorer outcomes than are face-to-face negotiations, although considerable improvement results from repeated practice trials. Thus, consider e-negotiations to be in an experimental stage and apply them to conflicts of less importance and value, while working in a time frame that allows considerable practice in order to improve skills (Carnevale and Pruitt, 1992).

THIRD-PARTY ROLES: THE MANAGER AS MEDIATOR

In addition to being directly involved in conflicts with bosses, peers, outsiders, and employees, managers also must contend with conflict situations in which they are indirectly involved as third parties, such as the case where two employees from the manager's work group are engaged in a dispute. How do managers respond in these situations? Research by Sheppard (1984) indicates that they choose a third-party mode of conflict resolution based on four criteria: (1) *efficiency* pertains to whether the action taken will resolve the conflict with a minimal amount of resources, e.g., their time, employees' time, expense, etc.; (2) *effectiveness* deals with whether the action will insure the conflict is solved well and remains solved − for example, using a mode of resolution that involves listening to all parties' views, and then brainstorming an appropriate solution; (3) *participant satisfaction* refers to whether the action will insure that parties are satisfied with the outcome, possibly by letting them present their views and then inventing a solution that will satisfy both of them; and (4) *fairness* pertains to whether the action will solve the dispute in a way that the parties believe is fair according to some external standard. Research has shown that managers typically weight two of these criteria – efficiency and effectiveness – higher than the other two in choosing the set of actions they will take, and that this weighting encourages them to attempt to take control of the conflict situation.

Building on earlier work examining parties' satisfaction with conflict resolution as a function of their control over the outcome and resolution process, Sheppard (1984) proposed a fourfold classification system for the modes in which third parties, such as managers, may intervene in conflicts. His system was based on high and low levels of procedural and outcome control by the third party, and has been empirically tested in at least two studies. The classification system and study results are shown in table 25.2.

Effects of different intervention modes

Subsequent research on the effects of mode usage suggests that a greater reliance on the mediator mode might well enhance managers' effectiveness in resolving third-party

TABLE 25.2 Managers' third-party conflict resolution modes

1   *Inquisitorial intervention (high process control/high outcome control).* In this mode managers actively control the discussion between parties, frequently directing what is said, and they control the outcome by inventing and enforcing a solution that they believe will meet both parties' needs, much like an inquisitor or benevolent parent. Sheppard and his colleagues (Sheppard, 1983; Lewicki and Sheppard, 1984) found that the managers tend to use this method of intervention most frequently.

2   *Adversarial intervention/judge (low process control/high outcome control).* In this mode, a manager decides how the conflict will be resolved and enforces the resolution if needed. However, the manager does not try to actively control the process. Rather he or she allows the parties to determine how they wish to present information about the conflict, listens to the information presented, and then makes a decision. This style was the second most frequent used by managers.

3   *Providing impetus/motivating (low process control, low outcome control).* For this mode, a manager asks "What is going on here?" and then strongly signals the parties that strong punishment will be forthcoming if they don't solve their own dispute. This was the third most common mode of third-party intervention.

4   *Mediation (high process control/low outcome control).* In this mode a manager controls the process through which parties reveal information about their conflict but does not attempt to control the decision concerning how the conflict will be resolved. Mediation was virtually unused by the managers studied.

Source: Taken from Sheppard (1983)

conflicts. This research has shown that managers' use of a particular mode has important implications not only for the content of the resolution obtained but also for the
disputing parties' perceptions of the fairness of the outcome and to the procedure used.
Specifically, Karambayya and Brett (1989) found that managers who used the inquisitorial, adversarial or providing impetus/motivating modes tended to produce outcomes to
the conflict that favored one party over the other. Conversely, managers who used the
mediator mode tended to produce compromise outcomes that incorporated at least
some of each party's interests. Not surprisingly, employees were more satisfied when
their interests were either favored in the outcome, or when they experienced a compromise outcome. Further, those who experienced the mediator mode of third-party
resolution tended to perceive that the conflict outcome, resolution process, and mediator
were fairer than did those who experienced other modes. The importance of parties'
fairness perceptions should not be underestimated as they have been shown to impact
the effectiveness of conflict resolution, i.e., to strengthen the relationship between
parties, and aid in preventing a recurrence of the conflict (Karambayya, Brett, and
Lytle, 1992). Thus, although managers show a tendency to select modes of conflict
resolution that allow them greater control over the outcome implemented, in doing so
they run the risk of producing solutions that undermine the relationship between parties
making it difficult for them to maintain the conflict resolution achieved and to work
together in the future.

Why managers fail to use the mediation mode

Subsequent research has confirmed that intervention modes that provide managers with
greater control over the outcome of the conflict are more likely to be used in cases where
time pressures for settlement are severe and the settlement will have broad implications
for the resolution of other disputes in the work unit or organization. Other factors that
affect managers' tendency to take greater control of the mode of dispute resolution are
whether or not disputing parties will have to interact again in the future, whether the
manager possesses formal authority over the conflicting parties (i.e., their own employees
rather than peers), and whether the manager has limited experience supervising employees (Lewicki and Sheppard, 1985; Karambayya et al., 1992).

Consistent with these findings, other researchers have argued that managers often
attribute the causes of conflict to the personalities of the parties, rather than to differing
goals or interests, and that they often assume it is their job to intervene in conflicts
quickly and directly. Both of these factors would be expected to discourage their
assumption of a mediating style of conflict resolution (Kolb,1986; Kolb and Sheppard,
1987). Finally, it is also likely that managers don't rely on mediation to resolve third-
party conflicts, because they lack the basic skills set to do so. Consider what is known
about the types of behaviors that enhance the effectiveness of mediation.

Mediation behavior

Researching mediators across a variety of contexts, Kressel and Pruitt (1985) have
proposed and empirically confirmed three types of mediator behavior – reflexive, contextual, and substantive interventions. This research also has identified an active versus

passive dimension that underlies the three types of behavior (Kressel and Pruitt, 1985; Lim and Carnevale, 1990).

Reflexive interventions are mediators' attempts to make themselves into the most effective tools of conflict intervention by orienting themselves to the conflict between parties and by establishing ground rules on which their later behavior will be based. These behaviors occur early in the mediation process and involve gaining entry to the conflict, bonding with or gaining acceptance from both parties, and diagnosing the nature of the conflict and the types of tactics that are likely to result in agreement. Whereas it is commonly accepted that mediators must be neutral and disinterested in the conflicts of the parties they assist, this does not appear to be as important as believed. In fact, many times mediators are chosen because of their relationship with one party (e.g., labor mediation) and thus, the assumption that they can influence its behavior, or because their own interests are at stake in the conflict (e.g., international mediation) (Kressel and Pruitt, 1985).

Contextual interventions reflect mediators' attempts to impact the climate and conditions prevailing between parties and enable them to engage in problem-solving and to develop their own solution. It is also used to help parties deal with internal constituencies whose approval and support is critical to the success of their negotiation. Examples include communication facilitation, the diffusion of anger, the identification of important issues, the structuring of an agenda, and the establishment of a joint fact-finding process.

Substantive interventions concern how the mediator deals directly with the issues in conflict between the parties. They tend to occur later during the mediation process and include the exploration of potential compromises, the suggestion of possible agreements, and the assistance given to the parties in evaluating the pros and cons of various proposals.

Active versus passive approach refers to mediators' assertiveness or forcefulness in enacting any of the three types of interventions. Considerable evidence indicates that mediators often act assertively in disputes, particularly in the substantive domain. They frequently exert considerable pressure on the parties to agree to specific proposals. Such pressure is most likely to occur in cases where the mediator's own interests or values are involved, very high levels of tension or hostility exist, and there are institutional pressures on the mediator to avoid the high costs of litigation. Although the longer-term effects are not known (e.g., what happens after settlement), several studies have found that mediator assertiveness is positively associated with the incidence of settlement versus stalemate (Kressel and Pruitt, 1985).

Other research by Lim and Carnevale (1990) has indicated that mediators' use of various interventions were differentially effective across conflict situations. However, with one exception, tactics became more, rather than less, effective as the level of conflict intensified. In this case, when a party experienced high levels of internal conflict during a mediated conflict, both the use of contextual interventions intended to build trust between parties and the application of substantive interventions intended to suggest potential solutions were negatively related to the likelihood of settlement.

A summary of mediation principles and recommendations

To generalize several principles from managers' use of third-party conflict resolution modes at work:

1　There is considerable evidence that managers generally choose modes of third-party conflict resolution that allow them to control the conflict outcome or solution and/or to motivate the parties to reach resolution through fear of organizational sanctions.

2　Managers' tendency to rely on the inquisitorial, adversarial, and motivator modes seems to intensify in situations where time is short, the conflict outcome has implications for the rest of their unit or for the organization, and the disputing parties will not have to work together in the future.

3　The choice of a mediator mode of resolution has been found to yield many favorable results, including conflict outcomes that are less one-sided and more reflective of the interests of all parties, and greater perceptions of outcome, process and mediator fairness, conflict process fairness, and mediator fairness. These fairness perceptions, in turn, have favorable implications for the parties' acceptance of the agreed-upon outcome, the positive nature of their relationship, and the likelihood of conflict recurrence.

4　Managers interested in pursuing a mediation mode of conflict resolution should practice the enacting of:

(a) *reflexive interventions* that increase each party's trust of the manager's fairness, identify the underlying causes of the conflict, and select the types of behavior most likely to result in settlement;

(b) *contextual interventions* that facilitate communication between parties, help to diffuse anger and other intense emotions, assist in the identification of the most important issues of dispute, structure an agenda that provides for the systematic discussion of issues and incremental agreement, and develop unbiased processes for locating information needed to resolve the conflict; and

(c) *substantive interventions* that actively propose solutions to the conflict that may have escaped the attention of the parties while continually assuring the parties that the choice of solutions is left up to them.

5　When the conflict involves groups of employees who are experiencing internal conflict, managers acting in the mediator mode should attempt to resolve the internal dissension before directing contextual and substantive interventions at the between-group conflict.

EXCEPTIONS TO THESE GUIDELINES

There are definite exceptions to the recommendations provided within this chapter for enhancing the effectiveness of managers' negotiation and mediation skills. For negotiations, the recommendations provided earlier were developed for parties who rationally seek out solutions that will enhance and maintain their own interests. Where conflicting parties act irrationally, showing little concern for important interests, perhaps due to intense anger or latent hostility, drug or alcohol abuse, psychosis, or constraints placed on them by their constituents, the recommendations provided earlier are likely to prove much less effective. An example of this situation is provided in one of the case illustrations that follows this section. In a similar vein, when negotiators hold different principles, in particular those concerning what constitutes fairness in negotiation procedures and outcomes, agreement will often not result from the recommendations offered earlier. Instead parties often become hostile and rigid, unwilling to concede any option that is acceptable to the other, and thus are unable to reach agreement (Pruitt et al., 1991).

With respect to mediation, considerable research has found that mediation tends to be more effective under moderate levels of conflict. As the conflict intensifies, the probability that mediation will lead to an agreement diminishes rapidly (Kressel and Pruitt, 1985). Similarly, mediation is likely to result in cooperation and agreement by the involved parties only when they are motivated to bargain and resolve their conflict (Wall and Blum, 1991). Finally, employees' reactions to managers' attempts to mediate conflicts at work tend to be more positive when employees or peers are allowed some time to resolve the conflict on their own, without mediation. Swift intervention by a manager attempting to mediate a dispute between employees is likely to violate their sense of due process, and their perceptions of fairness, and subsequently, the longevity and effectiveness of any agreement reached (Conlon and Fasolo, 1990). Having examined some possible exceptions, it is time to further illustrate the application of the concepts themselves through the use of several case studies.

CASE STUDIES

Negotiating with irrational folks: the case of Jay Leno's agent

A splendid illustration of what happens when rational managers attempt to negotiate conflicts with irrational parties is provided in the book, *The Late Shift* (1994), which discusses the Letterman and Leno battle for late-night TV. According to the author, Bill Carter, this negotiation was highly influenced by the persona of Leno's long-time agent, Helen Kushnick. It was Helen who helped Jay, not initially liked or favored by NBC Tonight Show host Johnny Carson, obtain an edge over Carson's preferred choice, David Letterman. Realizing that NBC affiliate stations would have considerable influence in any decision about a new host for the Tonight Show, Kushnick convinced Jay to conduct several cross-country tours where he appeared live on many NBC affiliates and devoted considerable time to building rapport with their owners and managers. The support of the NBC affiliates, as well NBC executives' belief that Jay's personality and style of comedy were better suited to a long-term run on NBC's Tonight Show than were David Letterman's, ultimately clinched the deal for him. On May 16, 1991, Leno signed a lucrative agreement making him host of the Tonight Show on the departure of Johnny Carson. This contract also named Helen Kushnick as the executive producer on the show.

An understanding of the negotiations that unfold below requires some background on Helen Kushnick's negotiation style, personality, and relationship with Jay Leno. Helen's style was one of extreme contending. She had experienced much sadness during her adult life, including the death of her only son, who died while still an infant as the result of an AIDs-infected blood transfusion, the death of her husband from colon cancer, and her own illness from breast cancer for which she was undergoing chemotherapy at the time of the negotiations described here. On his deathbed, Jerry Kushnick, Helen's husband, asked Jay Leno to take care of his wife and his 11-year-old daughter, a promise

Jay made and then repeated publicly at the funeral. According to her close associates, Helen's style never faltered in the face of these overwhelming obstacles, it just became more intense. As Carter noted, "She didn't become beaten or bowed; she just became more determined, more driven, more ferociously focused than ever before" (Carter, 1994: 171). Angered by Johnny Carson's rejection of Jay, Helen secretly started a rumor that NBC was going to drop Carson for Jay, a rumor that caused incredible tension between the Network and Carson for a period of time before his retirement.

Once Jay Leno took over as Tonight Show host in 1991, NBC executives were surprised to find that he appeared stiff and uncomfortable in the host slot, without the spontaneity and humor that had consistently characterized him as a guest. Many attributed this change in style to Helen's influence on the show as executive producer. Angered by Carson's rejection of Jay and his refusal to invite Jay to appear on any of the final shows before his retirement, Helen repeatedly rejected NBC executives' request that Jay make a complimentary statement about Carson and his career on Jay's first show. The absence of such a statement was conspicuously noted in all the press given to Jay's opening and a source of embarrassment to him and to NBC. Helen went on to attempt to choreograph Jay's movements on the set, making them appear stiff and formal. She placed the blue-collar comic in expensive designer suits, and erupted in a tirade of name-calling and endless criticism of anyone who tried to question these changes. Soon her attacks extended to Jay himself; she publicly and privately belittled him and attacked his comedy and his intelligence. Jay never responded to the attacks or even appeared embarrassed by them, but many on the Tonight Show felt their effects were apparent in his shaky appearance on the set, particularly during the opening monologue. Further, Helen undertook a bloodletting campaign to protect Jay from the competition by blacklisting the signing of any guests who appeared on Arsenio Hall's show. Disliking Jerry Seinfeld, one of Jay's closest friends, she denied his request to use the Tonight Show set and to schedule a surprise guest appearance by Jay on Seinfeld's own show. For a time, she even blacklisted Seinfeld himself, the host of one of NBC's most popular shows, from the Tonight Show until NBC executive Warren Littlefield personally intervened.

Time and time again during this period, Helen ignored the pleas of NBC executives to tone down her "winner take all" approach, belittling their entreaties to protect the network's image and its long-term relationships with distinguished guests. Helen refused, and intensified her destructive activities, confident that her hold on Leno would prevent NBC from ever firing her, lest he leave the show as well. At first she was right. Ignoring NBC's multiple requests that Helen be fired, Jay instead asked that the network simply write out a list of what was acceptable for Helen to do and not do. Shortly afterward in the middle of a meeting, the executives and Jay watched as Helen changed from a cool, controlled rational person to a screaming, out-of-control rocking form, molded into a lotus position. Warren Littlefield then told Leno that she was totally out of control and had to go. Still Jay was reluctant to cut the 17-year bond between them and refused to assure Littlefield that he would show up for work if Helen were fired. Finally, Jay learned that Helen had started the rumor that NBC would replace Carson with Leno, a rumor he had personally denied starting to Johnny Carson himself. His support for Helen began to crumble and he signaled Littlefield that he would do the show, with or without Kushnick. On Monday morning when Helen arrived for work, the network handed her a letter of dismissal. Still Jay refused to support the action, issuing press releases that he supported Ms. Kushnick. He hoped to duck the conflict until after that day's show was taped, but Helen confronted him in his dressing room, raging and screaming so loud she could be heard throughout the set. When these tactics failed to work, she came at Leno with emotion, arguing that he had to quit the Tonight Show for Sarah, her daughter's sake. At this point, even Jay had had enough. He broke a glass cover on his desk to stop the tirade, refused to quit, and went on to display a dazzling performance on that night's show. Helen stormed off the studio lot shortly after the filming began, leaving Jay's direction in the hands of others. As soon as she left, NBC barred her from the set, posting little photos of her at all the studio gates.

Helen Kushnick's behavior provides a perfect illustration of the way in which irrational negotiators may use threats and intimidation to obtain their own way and ignore even courteous entreaties from the other party to maintain a long and valued relationship. Clearly unable to see the impact of her behavior on the interests that network held supreme, Helen simply grew more and more confident that she could do whatever she pleased, no matter how negatively it impacted her long-term interests or those of the network, because of her power over Jay, the network's star. Time and time again, she chose to satisfy short-term emotional needs, rather than to preserve the long-term interests and relationship at stake. As shown here, neither principled nor contending approaches tend to work with irrational negotiators. Instead a party caught up in this kind of exchange is generally better off to find a strong BATNA, or satisfying alternative, and exit the relationship without agreement.

The importance of ferreting out the other party's interests

Richard Shell, a negotiation professor at the Wharton School, tells the following story about identifying the other party's interest in his book, *Bargaining for Advantage* (Shell, 1999). Shell quotes Ed Crutchfield, CEO of First Union Corporation, one of America's fastest-growing banks. A negotiator who has conducted more than 80 acquisitions, Crutchfield is credited with the following statement about how to prepare for a negotiation: "You have to get outside your own wants and needs and learn all you can about what is meaningful to the other person. And it is not always another billion dollars" (Shell, 1999: 78). Crutchfield has a right to offer some advice, having recently made one of the largest banking acquisitions, that of CoreStates Financial Corporation, for more than $16 billion. Toward the end of a very long negotiation, he was struck with the realization that CoreStates' CEO, Terry Larsen, seemed more and more hesitant to recommend the deal to his board. Larsen's growing hesitation was surprising, since Crutchfield knew he had met most of Larsen's financial demands. He wondered what could account for the holdup.

Remembering Larsen's reputation for initiating many investments in the Pennsylvania, New Jersey, and Delaware areas of CoreStates' operations, Crutchfield finally put it together. The issue had nothing to do with price. Rather Larsen was concerned that First Union would abandon the community commitments that he had made. Such an action would not only hurt the community but would also subject Larsen to the criticism that he had sold out his community to make big bucks. Realizing the problem, Crutchfield was aided in solving it by the fact that both banks shared a common value for providing corporate support to worthwhile causes. He offered Larsen the opportunity to establish a $100 million independent community foundation that would offer grants in the CoreStates area after the acquisition. Although only one half of 1 percent of the full purchase price, the foundation offer addressed Larsen's unsatisfied interest. He became an advocate for the merger, recommending its approval to the board, which subsequently accepted it.

The First Union–CoreStates negotiation illustrates a number of important principles of negotiation. First, don't assume you know the other party's interests or that they will be negatively correlated with your own. Instead, work very hard to ferret them out. As the old negotiation mantra states, "the other party is much more likely to give you what you want in the negotiation when you give them what they want." Of course your chances of being able to satisfy deep-seated interests and forge a long-term relationship are higher when the parties share common values, such as the importance of community service for each of the two banks. Finally, never underestimate the power of intangible needs, such as saving face, being treated fairly, or protecting one's principles. These needs, often the easiest to satisfy if recognized, frequently derail many negotiations because parties simply under-estimate their importance.

References

Carter, B. (1994). *The late shift*. New York: Hyperion Press.

Carnevale, P. J., and Pruitt, D. G. (1992). Negotiation and mediation. *Annual Review of Psychology*, 43, 531–82.

Conlon, D. E., and Fasolo, P. M. (1990). Influence of speed of third-party intervention and outcome on negotiator and constituencies fairness judgments. *Academy of Management Journal*, 33, 833–46.

Fisher, R., and Ury, W. (1981). *Getting to yes*. New York: Penguin.

Karambayya, R., and Brett, J. M. (1989). Managers handling disputes. *Academy of Management Journal*, 32, 687–704.

Karambayya, R., Brett, J. M., and Lytle, A. (1992). Effects of formal authority and experience on third party roles, outcomes and perceptions of fairness. *Academy of Management Journal*, 35, 426–38.

Keys, B., and Case, T. (1990). How to become an influential manager. *Academy of Management Executive*, 38–49.

Kolb, D. (1987). Who are organizational third parties and what do they do? In M. A. Bazerman, R. A. Lewicki, and B. H. Sheppard (eds.), *Research on negotiations in organizations* (Vol. 1, pp. 207–28). Greenwich, CT: JAI Press.

Kolb, D., and Sheppard, B. (1985). Do managers mediate or even arbitrate? *Negotiation Journal*, 1, 379–88.

Kressel, K., and Pruitt, D. G. (1985). Themes in the mediation of social conflict. *Journal of Social Issues*, 41, 179–98.

Lax, D. A., and Sebenius, J. K. (1986). *The manager as negotiator*, New York: Free Press.

Lewicki, R. J., and Sheppard, B. H. (1985). Choosing how to intervene. *Journal of Occupational Behaviour*, 6, 49–64.

Lim, R. G., and Carnevale, P. J. (1990). Contingencies in the mediation of disputes. *Journal of Personality and Social Psychology*, 58, 259–72.

Pruit, D. G., Pierce, R. S., Zubeck, J. M., McGillicuddy, N. B., and Welton, G. L. (1991). Determinants of short-term and long-term success in mediation. In S. Sorchel and J. A. Simpson (eds.), *Conflict between people and peoples*. Chicago: Nelson Hall.

Shell, G. R. (1999). *Bargaining for advantage*. New York: Viking Press.

Sheppard, B. H. (1983). Third party conflict intervention: A procedural framework. In *Research in organizational behavior* (Vol. 6, pp. 141–90). Greenwich, CT: JAI Press.

Thomas, K. (1976). Conflict and conflict management. In M. D. Dunnette (ed.), *Handbook of industrial/organizational psychology* (pp. 889–935). Chicago: Rand McNally.

Ury, W. L., Brett, J. M. and Goldberg, S. J. (1988). *Getting disputes resolved*. San Francisco: Jossey-Bass.

Wall, J. A., and Blum, M. W. (1991). Negotiations. *Journal of Management*, 17, 273–303.

26

Lead Organizational Change by Creating Dissatisfaction and Realigning the Organization with New Competitive Realities

Michael Beer

We are living in a world in which the only constant is change. Companies must respond to rapid changes in markets and technology if they are to survive and prosper. Senior executives must, in turn, lead a process of change that develops employee dissatisfaction with the status quo and realigns the organization as a total system with new business realities.

Consider the case of Apple Computer (Beer and Gibbs, 1990). Founded by Steve Jobs and Steve Wozniak in a garage in Silicon Valley in 1977, the company was the first to develop and produce a personal computer. The Apple II and its successor the Macintosh led the industry in technology, design, and user-friendliness. In 1980 the company had virtually 100 percent of the market. It had grown 100 percent a year and was among the fastest-growing companies in the world. In 1990 its revenues reached $5.5 billion and employment reached 14,500. By 1997, however, the company's market share was down to 3 percent and its revenues and number of employees were shrinking. It was also losing money and had lost the race to dominate the personal computer market to Dell, Compaq, and IBM.

Apple's dominance in the computer market declined despite the fact that in 1983 John Scully, at the time president of PepsiCo, was brought in as Apple's new CEO to enable the company to cope with new competitive realities. As we shall see throughout this chapter, Scully failed to lead organizational change. His task was to mobilize energy for change by creating dissatisfaction with the status quo and then to realign the organization with new competitive realities. This meant developing organizational behaviors Apple did not possess. Though the company had talented and creative technical people it lacked several other critical organizational behaviors which have been shown to be essential for success in uncertain and rapidly changing environments (Lawrence and Lorsch, 1967; see also Kotter and Heskett, 1992; Lawler, 1997).

Business performance has been shown to be associated with the following organizational behaviors:[1]

- *Coordination* between functions, businesses, and geographic regions around businesses and/or customers is essential for speed of response to customer needs and a cost-effective operation. Apple's individualistic culture and lack of cross-functional teams made coordination between Marketing, Sales, and Research & Development difficult. Consequently, the company failed to recognize and respond to a rapidly growing business market that demanded new and lower-cost products.
- *Commitment* to customer needs and an economically successful business is essential for any enterprise. Without that commitment employees' interests are not aligned with the purpose of the business. Apple's people were committed to technical innovation not to meeting customer needs in a changing market. This blinded them to the possibility that a less elegant and lower-cost technical solution being introduced by competitors (low-cost PCs with a DOS operating system) might succeed.
- *Competence* in the function most critical to success, and in management and leadership are both essential. Some companies rely on selling or distribution for success. Others rely on merchandizing. Still others may rely on technical skills in research and development. Apple's historic success was based on technical innovation and it needed to sustain this capability. The company lacked, however, managerial and leadership capability at every level. As a result of its rapid growth technically excellent people without managerial and leadership skills that take time to develop were promoted to key positions.
- *Communication* that engages people and groups in honest dialogue is essential in an uncertain and rapidly changing environment. It enables an airing of differences and leads to a resolution of conflicting views. This in turn ensures good decisions. For this trust and skills in dialogue are needed. Top management must communicate to lower levels its intended direction and lower levels must feel free to communicate to top management if they believe the direction is flawed or organizational barriers exist to successful implementation. At Apple lower-level managers that saw the need for lower-cost computers were ignored. Similarly differences between key functions – at Apple Research & Development (R&D) and Marketing – were never discussed in a way that would enable R&D to understand threats Marketing perceived.
- *Creativity* and innovation in both technical and administrative matters is essential for a business to retain its competitive edge. Apple succeeded largely on the basis of its creativity and innovation in technology. But it lacked the capacity to innovate and change its approaches to organizing and managing people, something that was essential if it was going to succeed in a changing marketplace.

Leading organizational change is about defining a new strategic direction for the business and then developing those organizational behaviors required to implement the new direction. Of course, implementing the new direction typically also leads to redefinition of direction as the organization learns through the process of implementation what works and what doesn't work. That is why the behaviors above, particularly open communication and creativity, are also essential to the capacity of the organization to adapt and renew itself. The effectiveness of an effort to lead change should be judged by the extent to which it develops the behaviors needed to implement the new direction, *and* the extent to which it develops the capacity of the organization to renew itself in the future.

The story of Apple illustrates the tendency of all organizations to develop inertia in the face of success. Why does this happen to organizations? What are the essential principles of organizational change that leaders in John Scully's position must follow if, unlike Scully, they are to overcome the natural tendency of organizations to maintain the status quo?

BASIC FACTS ABOUT ORGANIZATIONAL BEHAVIOR AND CHANGE

This section presents basic facts managers must understand about organizational behavior and change if they are to succeed in the difficult task of leading change. They explain why organizations resist change and what is needed to change them. (Beer Eisenstat, and Spector, 1990; Katz and Kahn, 1978; Pfeffer, 1997; Schein, 1990).

Organizations are complex open systems

A variety of organizational facets – structure, human resource policies, management processes, values and skills of people, and the leadership behavior of top management – conspire to produce an organization's distinctive pattern of behavior. These facets are interdependent and are continuously engaged in a process of mutual adaptation to achieve "fit" or congruence with the organization's chosen strategy (Lawrence and Lorsch, 1967). By an open system we mean that the organization is subject to influence by the external environment, largely through the influence of markets, society and/or the larger corporate organization (if the organization is a sub-unit of a larger corporation).

Figure 26.1 illustrates the key dimensions that must fit together for an organization to be effective. It suggests that organizational behavior is shaped by four forces – the organization's environment and the emergent strategic task the organization must manage to succeed, the organization's design, the people selected and promoted and the behavior of leaders and their top team. Organizations naturally evolve toward an equilibrium state in which these elements fit tightly. In the short term fit leads to organizational effectiveness. The organization has developed certain behaviors required for its success and has developed leadership behavior, structures and systems to cause these behaviors consistently. When the environment changes and places new demands on the organization realignment and change is required, however.

Implicit in this formulation is a contingency perspective. It holds that the best way to organize and manage people depends on the nature of the situation (Lawrence and Lorsch, 1967). We know for example that the optimal structure of an organization depends on the nature of the environment and strategy (Nadler and Tushman, 1988). At the same time there is growing evidence that sustainable advantage depends on organizing and managing people around a set of values and principles including the use of teams, collaboration, egalitarianism, training and development for employees, and open communication (Pfeffer, 1998). The five Cs listed above reflect these findings.

Organizational alignment develops a distinctive and persistent culture

Culture is defined as the assumptions, beliefs, and resultant behavior leaders invent or discover to solve problems in the external and internal environment. It is what these leaders teach new members as the correct way of perceiving, thinking, and acting to solve

FIGURE 26.1 Organizational alignment model

problems (Schein, 1990). The tendency of managers to attract, select, and promote people based on how similar they are to those already in the organization increases the strength of the culture (Schneider, 1994). Under the leadership of its founder Steve Jobs Apple Computer attracted, selected, and promoted employees who were individualistic and committed to elegant technology. This created a strong culture that demanded conformity to these values and eschewed more pragmatic business considerations.

That companies develop a persistent culture and have difficulty in adapting is evident in the survival rate of companies. A substantial number of the Fortune 500 companies 20 years ago – Gulf Oil, Digital Equipment, International Harvester, Scott Paper, US Steel, and Westinghouse – no longer exist.

Organizations vary in the strength of their culture, however. Moreover, sub-cultures typically exist in various parts and sub-units of the organization. Organization change involves confronting the persistent pattern of behavior that is blocking the organization from higher performance, diagnosing its consequences, and identifying the underlying assumptions and values that have created it.

Organizational behavior is resistant to change

Fundamental organizational change calls into question existing patterns of management – the authority, decision rights, and values of existing managers and departments. When a changing environment threatens an organization's capacity to survive, top management is challenged to redefine how it will compete. It must define new objectives and a new strategic task. It should not be surprising that making these changes is painful. Key members of the organization will experience psychological losses (Beer, 1991). Their power and status may diminish. Past relationships may be disrupted. New skills may be required threatening employees' sense of competence and self-esteem as well as their careers and job security. The perception of these potential losses leads to resistance. For example, Research & Development – the technical function at Apple Computer – stood to lose some of its influence in designing products if Apple were to compete more aggressively in selling personal computers to the business market. Consequently careers, self-esteem, and the very sense of identity and meaning technical people derived from work were also threatened.

All human beings employ emotional and cognitive processes to defend themselves against threat (Argyris and Schon, 1996; Lawrence, 1998). Moreover, people make sense of past behaviors by forming beliefs that rationalize them and by escalating commitment to them. These human characteristics prevent managers from learning that their actual behavior – their theory in action – is inconsistent with their stated aspiration – their espoused theory. These human characteristics cause organizational policies, management practices, and leadership behavior and style to persist in the face of new realities unless skills and norms of inquiry and constructive conflict resolution are developed (Argyris and Schon, 1996; Lawrence and Lorsch, 1967). All attempts to change organizations must overcome defensiveness of individuals and groups, cause learning to occur, or result in the replacement of individuals not capable of learning. Effective change efforts attempt to maximize the amount of learning and minimize the need for replacement. This enables the organization to retain the wealth of company-specific knowledge about customers, products, and technology that is lost when key people are replaced.

Substantial evidence exists that many efforts to change organizations do not succeed in making a fundamental transformation in organizational culture (Beer et al., 1990; Schaffer, 1988; Hall, Rosenthal and Wade, 1993). They produce only superficial change due to the fact that underlying assumptions and beliefs about the business and how it should be managed are not confronted. These change efforts are characterized by wave after wave of programs – education and training initiatives for all employees, continuous changes in structure, the development of mission and value statements, or initiatives such re-engineering and total quality management.

Consider a large industrial enterprise whose financial performance lagged the industry. Management felt that the cause was the ineffectiveness of its managers. With the help of a new senior human resource executive hired from a company known for its best human resource practices a four-week management education program was launched in an effort to change the company. The program's faculty was world class and the content highly relevant, including a module on competition and strategy, organizational effective-ness, leadership, and interpersonal skills. The last module of the program involved participants working on analyzing and making recommendations to top management about an important corporate problem. Participants were so enthusiastic about the potential of the program for changing the company that they asked top management to go through the program. They were certain that if the company were to adopt the ways of thinking and doing embedded in the program the corporation would regain its competitive edge. Top management agreed to go through the program. Despite the enthusiasm of all parties involved in the program (faculty, students, and top management) three years later top management and managers who went through the program indicated in interviews and surveys that very little change had occurred in the company's pattern of management.

John Scully's efforts to change Apple Computer also suffered from programmatic change, thereby delaying a dialogue about the real underlying problems. During a five-year period Scully changed the organization's structure four times. Apple's strategy did not change, however. Neither did organizational behaviors such as coordination between Marketing, Sales, and R&D and communication between top management and lower levels.

Programs fail because the top management team has delegated the task of change to a staff group or consultants. In this way they avoid the difficult task of confronting the underlying causes of the problems faced by the firm. These are often connected to their own assumptions and beliefs about the nature of the business and the best means for organizing and managing people. It is far easier for a CEO to obtain agreement from key people to a program or initiative than it is to breach defenses that block learning about deeper underlying problems. This requires leadership – the hard work of developing commitment to change and making difficult decisions about people who will not or cannot change.

Forces for organizational change: dissatisfaction and leadership

Given the natural tendency of all management to defend the past and resist change, it has been observed that change does not seem to occur unless a sense of urgency exists among the organization's leaders (Kotter, 1997). This does not typically occur unless they become highly dissatisfied with the status quo (Beer, 1991). Dissatisfaction with the status quo arises naturally as a result of a variety of problems that threaten the firm's capacity to sustain its performance. Financial losses, a long and protracted decline in stock price, shrinking market share, loss of a major customer, high employee turnover or a union strike are all forces that can bring management to a realization that change is needed. The more severe the crisis the higher the dissatisfaction with the status quo and the more energy will be released to take action. And it takes enormous amounts of human energy to confront entrenched assumptions and practices.

Severe problems may not be enough, however. As we saw in the case of Apple Computer, management was able to ignore dramatic changes in their markets and a shrinking market share. The missing ingredient was leadership (Kotter, 1997). John Scully was unable to mobilize the commitment to change of key people, particularly his top team. He lacked the courage to engage people in a dialogue about historic assumptions, practices, and norms of behavior. Change leaders, it has been found, possess the capacity to confront difficult issues. Indeed, companies that succeed in transforming themselves appear to do so as a result of changes in their top team (Virany et al., 1992). Leaders, typically new leaders, develop a top management team that is like-minded about the need for and the direction of change (Beer and Eisenstat, 1996a). A united and effective top team results in consistent action across all parts of the organization. Without this, lower-level employees perceive an inconsistency between the new direction espoused by top management and their actual behavior. This raises doubts about top management's commitment and makes it unlikely that commitment to change at lower levels will develop.

Consistency between means and ends

There is great variation in the consistency between ends and means chosen by leaders. To the extent that the means contradict the values and practices leaders intend to embed in the future organizational state, people question management's true commitment to the values and practices they espouse. Trust between leaders and lower-level people declines. Lowered trust makes it more difficult for leaders to engage people and mobilize commitment to change.

Leaders who intend to develop high-performance organizations characterized by the behavior and practices discussed above (good coordination and teamwork, high creativity, open communication, high commitment, and good interpersonal and leadership skills) are not successful unless they involve people in the change process (Beer et al., 1990). Contradictions between words and deeds are inevitable, of course, in any complex organizational change process. But a strong bias towards involvement appears to be necessary. Just as importantly, management's willingness and skills in encouraging lower levels to raise issues of inconsistency between their (management's) words and their actions builds the trust and partnership with lower levels high-performance organizations typically embody.

HOW TO LEAD CHANGE: SEVEN SUB-PRINCIPLES FOR SUCCESSFUL CHANGE

The dynamics of organizational behavior and change discussed above translate into *seven* steps a general manager must take to lead change in his or her organization. These steps assume that the leader is dissatisfied with the status quo and feels that change is needed to cope with new competitive realities. Effective leaders are always on the look-out for discontinuities in the organization's environment says Andrew Grove, CEO of Intel. His book *Only the paranoid survive* (Grove, 1996) captures well the need for constant vigilance.

Unfortunately incumbent top managers are often slow to recognize the need for change and/or are too timid in confronting managers and workers below them with the need for change. Under these circumstances change cannot take place until the leader is replaced. The price of not being vigilant can be seen in statistics for CEO tenure. Average CEO tenure in 1999 is just about half of what it was in 1990, 5.5 versus 10.5 years. Leaders who are not dissatisfied with the status quo are removed so significant organizational change can occur. Even new managers, however, can fail to manage change if they do not understand and/or are unskillful in leading change. As a new CEO John Scully had nine years to change Apple Computer. He failed because he did not take the steps outlined below.

1 Mobilize energy for change

Energy for change must be mobilized in the top management team. It is mobilized by creating dissatisfaction with the status quo as was noted above. The following three actions can mobilize energy for change.

- ◆ *Demanding improved performance and behavior.* Leaders can energize organizational members by articulating demanding goals and standards for behavior. When Jack Welch took over General Electric in the early 1980s he told all business unit managers that they had to get their business units to be number 1 or 2 in their industries or the business would be sold. Stan Mahalik, Executive Vice-President for Manufacturing at Goodyear Tire and Rubber, energized his 100 plant managers around the world to change their operations by telling them that unless their tires met certain quality standards they would become scrap. This energized them to search for new technology and management approaches. Percy Barnevik, CEO of ABB, articulated new performance goals and behavioral standards at a world-wide meeting of the top 500 executives in the company within weeks of a merger that formed the company. With regard to behavior, taking action even if it is wrong, he said, is better then not taking action at all.

♦ *Exposing the top team and employees to feedback.* A general manager who is dissatisfied with the status quo has come by this view through awareness of low quality, high cost, poor profits, dissatisfied customers or unhappy shareholders. Exposing managers and workers to this information through presentations as well as direct experience is a powerful way to unleash energy for change. When Louis Gerstner took over IBM after it had fallen on hard times in the early 1990s he asked all top executives to visit at least one customer a month. These visits gave them new insights into what was happening in the industry and how IBM needed to respond. Staff groups in corporations have been energized to become more effective when they have been exposed to feedback from line organizations they serve. Manufacturing plant managers faced with a resistant workforce and union have taken workers and union leaders on trips to see customers, displayed competitive products in the lobby of the building, and informed employees about the plant's financial performance through presentations and display of information on bulletin boards.

♦ *Exposing employees to model organizations.* Exposing managers and lower levels to radically different practices in other companies or within the same company can unleash energy. This has been referred to as benchmarking best practice. A visit to an innovative team-based manufacturing plant unleashed energy in managers, workers, and union leaders to transform Navigation Products, their business unit, to a similar model of management, one that promised to improve coordination across functions, build trust, and improve communication (Beer et al., 1990). In the early 1980s the automobile companies sent managers by the hundreds to Japan to learn about manufacturing methods that gave Japanese manufacturers a significant edge in quality.

2 Develop a new compelling direction

Feedback and information is not enough. A new direction must be developed. To develop this direction, change leaders orchestrate a series of discussions in their management team to develop an understanding of what this information means for change in the company's direction. Exactly how successful is the organization being in its product or service offering? Why is it not successful? What is the implication for the future survival and success of our organization? What should be the new objective and strategy and what are the implied priorities? Discussing these questions in the light of the feedback and data to which managers have been exposed can lead to a new understanding and sense of urgency.

Jerry Simpson, general manager of Navigation Products, held a series of meetings with his top team that led them to defining new and ambitious goals for the business and a new direction (Beer et al., 1990). A study of 25 business units undergoing change found that units that had changed the most were more likely than lagging units to have established a clear and broadly understood link between business problems and the need for change (Beer et al., 1990). Making the link is what makes the new direction compelling to members of the organization. It is quite important that the whole top team be involved in the formulation of the new objectives and strategy. This builds the commitment needed to implement the new direction.

Moreover, the general manager or CEO can use the work of developing a new direction to develop their top team's effectiveness. Research shows that effective strategy formulation and implementation depends on top team effectiveness (Eisenhardt, 1989; Beer and Eisenstat, 1996a). Team effectiveness is developed through encouraging new behavior, coaching and if needed replacement of those key executives who do not play a constructive role in the team and/or do not become committed to the new direction.

3 Identify organizational barriers to implementing the new direction

Often the resistance to change is at the highest levels of the company. Hierarchy insulates top management teams from the effects of their behavior and policies. Exposing top management to feedback about what employees perceive as barriers to implementing a new strategy further creates dissatisfaction and identifies what changes in organization and behavior are needed to implement the new strategy. John Scully began his belated and therefore unsuccessful effort to change Apple Computer after an attitude survey showed strong negative sentiments in the company about the lack of strategic clarity and problems with top management's leadership.

Beer and Eisenstat (1996a) asked top teams, as part of a planned effort to develop an organization capable of strategy implementation, to appoint tasks forces of eight of their best employees. Task force members interviewed organizational members one or two levels below the top about barriers to strategy implementation. Task forces then fed back their findings to top teams using a carefully crafted process that enabled the task force to be honest and management to be non-defensive. Six barriers were consistently identified across many organizations. They were:

- ◆ unclear strategy and conflicting priorities
- ◆ an ineffective top team
- ◆ a general manager who was either too autocratic or too laissez-faire (not confronting problems)
- ◆ poor coordination
- ◆ poor vertical communication
- ◆ inadequate leadership and management and its development at lower levels.

Because these barriers were known to everyone but were not discussable Beer and Eisenstat called them the "silent killers." Like hypertension, they can cause an organizational heart attack – organizational failures in implementing strategy. Until a commitment is developed by top teams to overcome the fundamental management problems represented by the silent killers it is unlikely that a new strategic direction can be implemented. Many change initiatives fail because underlying management problems are not confronted and overcome. Change leaders should, therefore, make an effort to collect data about barriers perceived by lower levels so plans for change can incorporate their voice about leadership and management problems. Efforts to change organizations without this step lead to cynicism and low commitment. Of course, this requires top managers to be open to learning about their own role in the organization's performance problems. If this does not happen, as it often does not, a new general manager or CEO is appointed when these problems begin to affect performance in a significant way.

4 Develop a task-aligned vision

Having heard the voice of lower-level employees regarding barriers to achieving the new strategic direction, the top team must work together to fashion a vision of the organization's future state. They will have to envision how the elements in the organizational model presented in figure 26.1 will need to change to enable a change in organizational behavior. The following questions will have to be answered.

- ◆ How should the organization be redesigned to ensure the appropriate coordination between functions that must work together to implement the strategic task defined in step 2 above? Redesign of the organization will include changes in structure and business systems. These changes are intended to change roles, responsibilities, and relationships so that the new strategy can be implemented. For example, business, customer or product and project teams may be created.
- ◆ How will the top team's own leadership behavior change to enable the new organization to function effectively? These changes may include modification in the CEO's style or changes in the frequency and focus of top management meetings and work. For example, Ray Gilmartin, CEO of Becton Dickinson, received feedback from an employee task force that he too closely supervised the corporate strategic planning process and that there were too many meetings. He responded by delegating more responsibility to his sector presidents and changing the focus and content of his top team's management work (Beer and Williamson, 1991).
- ◆ What changes in people's skills will be needed to make the new organization work? Changes in human resource policies and practices will be needed to ensure that the right people with the right skills occupy the new roles designated by the reorganization.

5 Communicate and involve people in implementation

The new organizational vision has to be communicated to the whole organization. People in the organization should be told why a new strategy is needed and how the new organizational arrangements will help shape new behavior and better performance. Articulating the links between new competitive realities and the new organization will enable people to commit to the changes.

Consider what Don Rogers, the general manager of the Electronic Products A Division at Allentown Materials Corporation did in this regard (Beer, 1998). Rogers's top team had just decided to implement cross-functional new product development teams to enhance product development success, a strategic imperative for them to compete in their industry. Rogers and his whole top team visited 13 locations over a two-month period to communicate with every salaried employee how the new organization would work and why they were adopting it. The why included telling all employees about competitive problems that led to change and organizational barriers that had been uncovered through a survey and diagnosis of the division. Communication was two-way. After Rogers and his team presented their change plan employees met in small groups to discuss what they heard. They then assembled to raise questions and challenge management. A *dialogue* between top and bottom is essential for top management to learn about potential problems they will encounter in implementation so that they can make changes in their action plans accordingly. And that dialogue must be continuous and ongoing for change to succeed.

6 Support behavior change

After the new organization is implemented employees, particularly those whose roles and responsibilities have been most impacted by the organizational changes, will need support to develop needed skills and attitudes. This is often done through consultants who coach individuals and teams. It can also be done through training and education programs. In the Electronic Products Division mentioned above, consultants sat in on all team meetings for the first six months and coached the teams and their leaders in how to work in these new, unfamiliar arrangements. Moreover, consultants brought together key managers in pairs of departments whose relationships were blocking coordination, and facilitated a discussion that led to improvements. The purpose was to change the climate within which teams were operating, thereby increasing the probability of their success.

7 Monitor progress and make further changes

Organizational change is an action learning process. As the new organizational arrangements are enacted much is learned about how to modify structure, systems, policies and practices, and behavior to achieve intended results. Top and lower-level managers discover how to carry out their new roles and responsibilities and gain insights into how their own styles and skills need to be changed. Those who cannot adapt decide to leave on their own or are asked to leave. As time goes on the organization begins to function more effectively and this is translated into better performance. Should performance not improve the change cycle must begin again with steps 1 to 7.

ORCHESTRATING CORPORATE-WIDE STRATEGIC CHANGE

A large organization is typically made up of many interdependent units. Leading change is the responsibility of unit leaders at every level. Corporate-wide change requires top management to play two roles (Beer et al., 1990; Ghoshal and Bartlett, in press). They must lead a change process within the top management unit. This process would define how the corporate whole will coordinate the activities of the corporation's many independent sub-units to achieve the wider purpose of the corporation. Corporate leaders also orchestrate a process which encourages leaders in each of the corporation's sub-units to lead their own task alignment process. It is their role to orchestrate the diffusion of managerial innovations in leading units through conferences, visits to leading-edge units, and, most importantly, through the transfer of successful leaders from leading-edge to lagging units (Beer et al., 1990).

Where should corporate-wide change start? Sometimes unit change comes about naturally at the periphery, in businesses and manufacturing facilities far from headquarters and/or in business units offering quite different products or services from the parent. It is in these units that managers are faced with different competitive demands and/or have the freedom to innovate and lead change. Under these circumstances changes are only adopted by other organizational sub-units if top management actively works to move the innovations and the managers who led them to other parts of the large company (Beer et al., 1990; Walton, 1987).

Clearly, corporate-wide change will occur much more quickly if top management has conviction that change is needed. Top management's role is to encourage, even demand, that managers of independent business units, manufacturing plants, retail stores, or country organizations (in global companies), lead change in their units (Beer et al., 1990; Ghoshal and Bartlett, in press). It is not to drive change through corporate staff and consultant led programs. As discussed earlier these will fail to mobilize energy and leadership at the unit level needed for change to succeed. Moreover, corporate programs prevent top management from discovering who of their unit managers are effective leaders.

Examples of Organizational Change

We will first summarize briefly the case of Apple Computer used throughout this chapter to illustrate an unsuccessful effort to lead change. We then review two successful change efforts.

Apple Computer: a case of failure

John Scully did not restore Apple to its former dominant market position. He was unable to develop sufficient dissatisfaction with the status quo to produce the energy needed for change. He never created a top team capable of agreeing on Apple's new strategic direction. As late as 1988 he appointed to a key top management position an executive whose strategic vision was diametrically opposite to one that Apple had to take to cope with new competitive realities. His inclination to avoid conflict prevented him from confronting key strategic issues. And he never led a change process that enabled his top team to discover and discuss the silent killers that blocked them from defining a new compelling direction, redesigning Apple's organization and selecting new managers suited to the new direction. Consequently shareholders, customers, and employees failed to derive the value (stock price, lower-cost products, and career opportunities respectively) that a successful enterprise would otherwise have yielded.

Hewlett Packard's Santa Rosa Systems Division (HP/SRSD): successful unit-level change

The Hewlett Packard Santa Rosa Systems Division is a case of successful change at the unit level but failure by top management to spread innovation to other units (Beer and Rogers, 1997). In 1992 HP/SRSD was formed to manage and grow a new measurement systems business for HP. By 1994 the division was experiencing many problems and its performance did not meet HP's top management's expectations. There were numerous reasons for this. The division had organized itself and was being managed in a manner similar to HP's traditional test and measurement business. Yet the systems business was significantly different, particularly with respect to the need to customize systems. The mismatch between the traditional approach to organizing and managing and the demands of a very different business environment and strategy created many tensions between functions and between the top team and the remainder of the organization.

Data collected by a task force of the division's best employees revealed that the six silent killers described above were blocking organizational effectiveness. Employees perceived the general manager's style was laissez-faire. He was not engaging his top team in a discussion of conflicting strategies and priorities perceived by lower levels. Consequently coordination between several functions essential for successful execution of two interdependent strategies was not occurring. Section managers in R&D who had been assigned to lead cross-functional teams were ineffective in gaining consensus in their teams. And, while everyone in the division knew of these problems and complained about them to each other in private conversations, they could not feed back their perceptions to the division manager and his staff. The division manager and his staff were also aware of tensions and knew the division was failing, but never openly discussed these problems.

With the encouragement of his human resource executive, the division manager hired an external consultant, who, using a process called Organizational Fitness Profiling (Beer and Eisenstat, 1996b), helped the top team go through a task alignment process that surfaced these issues for discussion and diagnosis. The top team identified their own ineffectiveness as a team, the general manager's style, and the structure and the roles and responsibilities assigned to functions and cross-functional teams as the root of poor coordination and performance. In that same meeting they agreed on a change in structure, defined new roles for key people and teams in the structure, and created new ground rules for how the top team would operate and how decisions would be made.

Data collected a year later by the same task force and an employee survey showed significant improvement though some issues persisted. Sales had tripled and profits went up 250 percent. While the division's management attributed some of the improvements in the division's performance to an upturn in the market they served, they felt that they would not have been able to take advantage of market demand without the changes in organizing and managing they had made. The division manager and his team also decided to lead a task alignment process once a year as a way of fostering continuous change. Four years later HP's top management felt that SRSD, which had lagged its sister divisions in performance and effectiveness, was now a model to which other divisions could look. Division management had successfully led change.

Unfortunately, however, top management failed in its role of orchestrating strategic change throughout the larger organization. They did not do anything to actively spread to other divisions innovations in organizing and managing or the unique task alignment process used by HP/SRSD to improve its performance.

ASDA: successful corporate-wide strategic change

In contrast, ASDA, a UK grocery chain, offers an example of excellent top man- -agement leadership of strategic change (Beer and Weber, 1998). With the company £1.5 billion in debt and near bankruptcy, Archie Norman was appointed as CEO to turn it around. Upon arriving in December 1991, he met with his top team and quickly resolved to make changes in some people at the top. He also announced that while he did not have any preconceived ideas about what the problems were or how to solve them, he would insist on debate and transparency. He also announced that a "renewal store" would be identified where managers would be given license to innovate in the retail proposition, the physical space, and in the way people were organized and managed. He promptly began an assessment of the company's situation by making unannounced visits to many of the company's 200 stores. There he talked to lower-level workers and store management asking them to tell him about barriers to store performance. They quickly informed him that for years headquarters, particularly the Trading (purchasing) Department, had not been listening to stores about what products the stores thought would sell.

Within months he began to reshape the way the top team worked together and in the way the Trading Department at corporate headquarters communicated with and treated the stores. He told everyone that stores were to be "loved" and listened to. He established multiple mechanisms for communication between headquarters and the stores, and between store management and customers and employees. Within nine months a totally new approach to retailing and organizing and managing a store was created in the "renewal store" by the store manager and his top team working with a corporate cross-functional team. Sales increased immediately, as did morale. Over a five-year period virtually every store in the company had gone through the renewal process. Sales and profits not only improved, but also improved at a faster rate than its competitors. By 1998 the stock price had multiplied eightfold.

The success of the renewal program – the heart of the change effort – rested on top management's recognition that it had to spread innovation in the first renewal store to all 200 stores. What enabled this to happen was top management's decision to withhold financial resources for a given store's renewal until its management had exhibited the behavior and values of teamwork, delegation, and communication top management thought were critical to store performance. In effect they were assessing the extent to which each store's management had turned "silent killers" into organizational and managerial strengths. In stores where this did not happen quickly enough they replaced the store manager. Six years after the change effort began over 50 percent of store managers had been replaced with leaders who would and could lead store renewal.

How Universal are these Change Guidelines?

So long as the objectives of organizational change are the development of organizational capabilities for sustained competitive advantage over time, the principles and guidelines offered in this chapter hold. If, however, the objective is to enhance shareholder value without regard to developing organizational capability for the long term, management is not advised to follow these guidelines. They are much more likely to succeed with these short-term objectives by drastic restructuring, cost reductions, and layoffs. Considerable evidence exists that such steps enhance the stock price of companies in the short term. This is precisely what Al Dunlap did in just a few years as CEO of Scott Paper. What was not downsized was sold. The company no longer exists today.

There are, of course, many instances where top management wants to build organizational capability for the long term but the company's performance is so poor that drastic steps have to be taken to reduce costs in the short run. Under these circumstances there are two options (Beer and Nohria, in press). The first option is to phase the change process so that cost reduction and layoffs come first, followed by the action steps outlined in this chapter. That is what Jack Welch did at General Electric with great success. The second option is to press forward with both cost reduction and layoffs while also following the guidelines in this chapter for a change process that builds organizational capability. There is evidence that such a dual strategy, cost reduction and investment in building organizational capability, can lead to successful change (Beer et al., 1990). Companies that emphasized cost reduction at the expense of the steps described here did not successfully change their culture. The case of ASDA, discussed above, is another example.

Embedded in the change process recommended here is an assumption that leaders value excellence, people, involvement, teamwork, and learning, including learning about themselves. Autocratic, controlling, and defensive leaders are unlikely to be able to implement the action steps described above. These steps require a commitment to building organizational capability, organizational learning, and to empowering leaders throughout the organization to lead change in their sub-units. The somewhat slower pace of capability-building change demands that leaders buy time by managing expectations of capital markets. Again, the case of ASDA described above is an excellent example of what can be done in this regard. Archie Norman told financial analysts and stockholders that they could not expect to see improvements in financial performance for three years.

Conclusion

Organizations are complex systems normally resistant to change. Multiple facets of the organization – its design, its leadership, and its people – become tightly aligned with the historic strategy of the organization. This tight alignment leads to a distinctive and persistent pattern of behavior resistant to change. Resistance is caused by fear that change will result in losses of power, status, esteem, and position. Fear leads to defensiveness and the inability to consider new alternatives and to learn about what has to change.

Organizations change when leaders use environmental pressures, poor performance or the prospect of poor performance, to develop dissatisfaction with the status
quo. When people realize that the organization's future is endangered, energy for
change is released. Successful change managers lead a process that approximates
the seven steps described in this chapter. They mobilize energy for change, develop
a new compelling direction, identify organizational barriers to implementing the
new strategy, develop a task-aligned vision of how the organization will operate in
the future, communicate the vision and involve people, support behavior change
through coaching, and continuously monitor change.

In large multi-unit corporations the responsibility for change lies with leaders at
every level, not just with corporate top management. Top management's responsibility is to demand that unit managers lead change consistent with the competitive
task faced by their unit. They then spread change to all parts of the larger
organization through transfer of managers from leading-edge to lagging units.
They also lead change in the top management unit. Change can start anywhere,
but will be slow to spread unless top management creates a context that encourages
change in sub-units.

The capacity to lead an organization through change is increasingly important
as the pace of competition and change increases. Effective change management
enhances organizational performance, economic value, and organizational effectiveness needed in the long run. Managers who do not recognize the need for
change or lack skills to lead it will ultimately be replaced as the performance of
their organization lags expectations.

NOTE

1 The term behavior incoporates the description of actual behaviors as well as the description of
attitudes and skills that are proxies for behavior.

REFERENCES

Argyris, C., and Schon, D. A. (1996). *Organizational learning II: Theory, method and practice*. Reading,
MA: Addison-Wesley.
Beer, M. (1980). *Organization change and development: A systems view*. Santa Monica, CA: Goodyear.
Beer, M. (1991). *Leading change*. Boston, MA: Harvard Business School Note, Harvard Business
School Press.
Beer, M. (1998). *Allentown Materials Corporation: The Electronic Products Division (B)*. Boston, MA:
Harvard Business School Case, Harvard Business School Press.
Beer, M., and Eisenstat, R. A. (1996a). *The silent killers: Overcoming hidden barriers to organizational fitness*.
Boston, MA: Harvard Business School Working Paper 97–004.
Beer, M., and Eisenstat, R. (1996b). Developing an organization capable of strategy implementa-
tion and learning. *Human Relations*, 49, 597–619.
Beer, M., Eisenstat, R., and Spector, B. (1990). *The critical path to corporate renewal*, Boston, MA:
Harvard Business School Press.
Beer, M., and Gibbs, M. (1990). *Apple Computer (abridged): Corporate strategy and culture*, Boston, MA:

Harvard Business School Case, Harvard Business School Press.

Beer, M., and Nohria, N. (eds.) (in press). *Breaking the code of change*. Boston, MA: Harvard Business School Press.

Beer, M., and Rogers, G. A. (1997). *Hewlett Packard's Santa Rosa Systems Division*. Boston, MA: Harvard Business School Case, Harvard Business School Press.

Beer, M. and Weber, J. (1998). *ASDA (A) (A1) (B) (C)*. Boston, MA: Harvard Business School Case, Harvard Business School Press.

Beer, M., and Williamson, A. (1991). *Becton Dickinson: Corporate strategy and culture*. Boston, MA: Harvard Business School Case, Harvard Business School Press.

Eisenhardt, K. M. (1989). Making fast strategic decisions in high velocity environments, *Academy of Management Journal*, 32, 543–76.

Ghoshal, S., and Bartlett, C. A. (in press). Building behavioral context: A blueprint for corporate renewal. In M. Beer and N. Nohria (eds.), *Breaking the code of change*. Boston, MA: Harvard Business School Press.

Grove, Andrew (1996). *Only the paranoid survive*. New York: Doubleday.

Hall, G., Rosenthal, J., and Wade, J. (1993). How to make re-engineering really work. *Harvard Business Review*, Nov.–Dec.

Katz, D., and Kahn, R. L. (1978). *The social psychology of organizations*. New York: Wiley.

Kotter, J. (1997) *Leading change*. Boston, MA: Harvard Business School Press.

Kotter, J., and Heskett, J. (1992). *Corporate culture and organizational performance*. New York: The Free Press.

Lawler, Edward III (1997). *The new logic of organizations*. San Francisco, CA: Jossey-Bass.

Lawrence, P. (1998). *A four factor theory of human needs*. Boston, MA: Harvard Business School Working Paper.

Lawrence, P. R., and Lorsch, J. W. (1967). *Organization and environment*. Boston, MA: Division of Research, Graduate School of Business Administration, Harvard University.

Nadler, D., and Tushman, M. L. (1988). *Strategic organizational design*. Homewood, IL: Scott Foresman.

Pfeffer, J. (1997). *New directions for organization theory*. New York: Oxford University Press.

Pfeffer, J. (1998). *The human equation*. Boston, MA: Harvard Business School Press.

Schaffer, R. H. (1988). *The breakthrough strategy: Using short term successes to build the high performance organization*. Cambridge, MA: Ballinger.

Schein, E. H. (1990). Organizational culture. *American Psychologist*, 45, 109–19.

Schneider, B. (1994). The people make the place. *Personnel Psychology*, 40, 437–54.

Virany, B., Tushman, M., and Romanelli, E. (1992). Executive succession and organization outcomes in turbulent environments: An organization learning approach. *Organizational Science*, 3, 72–91.

Walton, R. E. (1987). *Innovating to compete: Lessons for diffusing and managing change in the workplace*. San Francisco: Jossey-Bass.

Part VIII

WORK, FAMILY, TECHNOLOGY, AND CULTURE

27 Promote Equal Opportunity by Recognizing Gender
Differences in the Experience of Work and Family
NANCY P. ROTHBARD AND JEANNE M. BRETT

28 Use Information Technology as a Catalyst for Organizational
Change
MARYAM ALAVI AND JONATHAN PALMER

29 Make Management Practice Fit the National Culture
MIRIAM EREZ

27

Promote Equal Opportunuity by Recognizing Gender Differences in the Experience of Work and Family

NANCY P. ROTHBARD AND JEANNE M. BRETT

Our meta-principle has two parts. First, men and women experience work and family roles differently, specifically with respect to career advancement, behavioral and psychological involvement in roles, role stress, and coping with the work–family interface. Second, in order to promote equal opportunity for men and women, people need to recognize that these differences exist.

We develop this meta-principle first by defining terms and presenting a model. We argue that gender differences in the experience of work and family stem from different opportunity structures for men and women that are manifest in work structures, sex typing of jobs, family structures, and gender role socialization. Our model of opportunity structures provides an explanation for why gender differences exist in men and women's experience of work and family and identifies levers for change, which over time may contribute to equal opportunities for men and women in work and family. We should point out however that some of these levers (for example, work structures) may be easier to change than others (for example, gender role socialization).

Our principle is directed to young men and women entering the workforce who seek to shape their own work and family opportunities. It is directed to managers who have the opportunity to make policy that affects work structures and sex-typing of jobs and to make decisions that affect individual employees. It is directed to representatives of government, social, and religious institutions that have the opportunity to make social policy that affects work structures, sex-typing of jobs, family structures, and gender role socialization. And it is directed to the men and women currently in the workforce who have the ambition to push the boundaries of societal expectations about the experience of work and family roles.

DEFINITIONS

Work is instrumental activity intended to provide material support for non-work pursuits (Piotrkowski, Rapoport, and Rapoport, 1987). Work generally involves a person contributing to the mission of an organization that in turn compensates the contributor financially (Burke and Greenglass, 1987; Kabanoff, 1980). Family is a group of people who are related by biological ties, marriage, social custom, or adoption (Burke and Greenglass, 1987; Piotrkowski et al., 1987). Both work and family roles are enacted in the context of a social organization (Zedeck, 1992). Work roles are all the parts played by an individual associated with gainful employment as defined above. Family roles are all the parts played by an individual associated with that individual's immediate or extended household. Experience refers to how roles are perceived, understood, remembered, and enacted. Gender refers to the biological sex of the individual. In using the term gender we recognize that biological sex differences that exist between men and women may account in part for the gender differences discussed here. However, following Rossi (1985) we suggest that biological, evolutionary arguments may explain the origins of certain gender role expectations. For example, the expectation that women are caregivers and nurturers may arise from the fact that biologically women are able to give birth and physically feed their infants. These biological differences may then be inputs to the evolving societal expectations and socialization about women's roles as caregivers, nurturers, and skillful purveyors of relational expertise. However, it is the societal expectations and socialization processes that men and women internalize and which are more proximal antecedents of experienced gender differences that we discuss here.

Model

We argue that gender differences in the experience of work and family roles stem from differential opportunity structures for men and women and are manifest in career success, role involvement, and coping with the stresses of work and family. Figure 27.1 presents our model. Opportunity structures are environments that provide men and women with chances for success, advancement, and progress. The term, "opportunity structure" is widely used in the employment literature. Here we extend the usage to include opportunities for involvement and identity development, and for a stress-free existence. Opportunity structures are determined by the confluence of many factors. Our analysis of the causes of our meta-principle focuses on four structural factors. The structure of work refers to the real or imagined skill requirements of the job and the position of the job within the organization. Sex-typing of jobs means the ascription of characteristics stereotypical of males or females to particular jobs. Family structure refers to the individual's status with respect to marriage, parenting, and dual employment. Gender role socialization refers to the expectations held by society about the appropriate roles of men and women. These four factors are conceptually distinct; however, they interrelate to provide opportunities for career advancement, behavioral and psychological involvement in roles, and to determine stress and coping at the interface of work and family roles.

Our perspective is distinctively structural. We recognize that not all people with a common structural profile are the same. Individual-level factors such as motivation and talent will contribute to individual differences in career advancement, behavioral and psychological involvement in roles, and stress. Yet the large gender differences in the experience of work and family roles lead us to focus on the structural barriers that despite motivation and talent are difficult to overcome for both men and women.

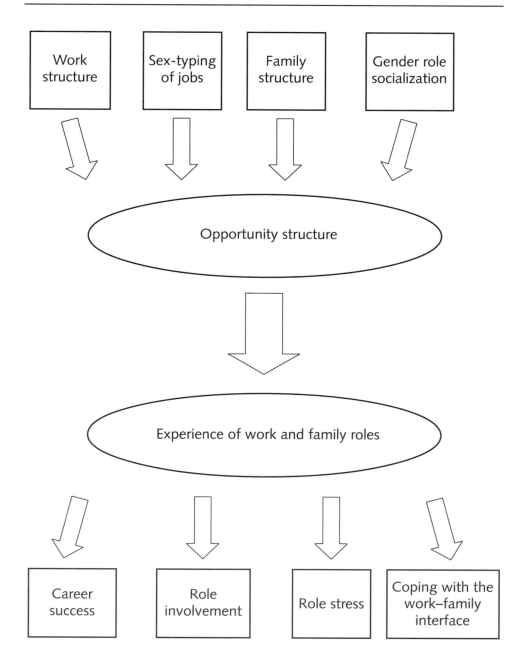

FIGURE 27.1 Model of opportunity structure and gender differences in the experience of work and family roles

Gender and Career Success

Men and women experience work differently because they do not realize the same degree of career success. In order to promote equal opportunities, it is important to first recognize that women lag men in career advancement, compensation, and networking opportunities.

Gender and career advancement

Men and women differ in their level of career advancement. According to 1998 US Labor Department statistics, women have become equally represented in the executive, managerial, and professional labor force, holding 49 percent of these positions. However, within this segment of the workforce, women overwhelmingly hold lower-level positions. The proportion of women who have attained elite positions in corporate offices and boardrooms is low. Women comprise 3.8 percent of corporate officers (i.e., those holding the title of chairman, vice chairman, CEO, president, COO, SEVP, or EVP) and 11 percent of directors in Fortune 500 companies (1998 Catalyst Census of Women Corporate Officers and Top Earners). As of 1999, only three women head Fortune 500 companies.

The differences between men and women in managerial rank do not seem to be due to differences in number of promotions, rather, the differences appear with respect to level (Melamed, 1995; Haberfeld, 1992; Landau, 1995; Judge et al., 1995; Cox and Harquail, 1991; Stroh, Brett, and Reilly, 1992). Men's promotions apparently offer bigger career leaps than women's and the opportunity structure of employment explains why. Differences in opportunity structure start with sex-typing of jobs (Blau and Ferber, 1992). Some jobs have historically been staffed by women, others by men. Recruiters anticipate women will apply for some jobs and not for others, and women themselves self-select into gendered occupations. Persistent role stereotypes of men, of women, and of the managerial role result in a perceived lack of fit between the ascribed characteristics of women and assumed requirements of managerial jobs (Heilman, 1983; Davies-Netzley, 1998) and reduce opportunities for women.

Although human capital, such as education, also affects opportunity structures, when human capital is controlled there are still fewer women at higher ranks than would be expected given their strong presence within the category of managerial and professional workers. So there must be other factors beyond human capital that affect women's opportunity structures. Differential development opportunities, for example training or international experience, leave women with a real skill deficit. Behaviors, like career interruptions for family reasons (Lyness and Thompson, 1997), a history of changing employers (Stroh, Brett, and Reilly, 1996), and the desire to work part-time (Schneer and Reitman, 1995) are all more characteristic of managerial women than men and may affect future career opportunities. These behaviors may be interpreted as evidence that women are less psychologically committed to their careers than men are. However, as we explain in the section on exceptions, while there are clear-cut behavioral differences between men and women in job involvement, there are few documented differences in work commitment between male and female employees (see 'Exceptions' below).

Gender and compensation

Paid compensation is a second indicator of career success. The gender gap in wages is substantial and persistent. "For more than four decades, comparisons between the wages of men and women employed full time, year-round have shown an earnings differential of approximately 40 percent" (Wellington, 1994: 839). Women earn about three-quarters as much as men (Jacobs, 1995). At career entry women earn 84 cents for every dollar men earn (Marini and Fan, 1997). Among managers, women's compensation growth lags that of men by 11 percent (Stroh, Brett, and Reilly, 1992).

Researchers have offered a number of different explanations for the gap. Differences in occupational aspirations due to gender role socialization have several effects on opportunity structures that could contribute to the gender gap in wages (Marini and Fan, 1997). One effect is that women invest in less education and training than men, leaving them with less human capital than men have (Becker, 1975). Another effect is that women prefer jobs with different characteristics than men (Thacker, 1995). The theory of compensating differentials argues that job autonomy, or friendly co-workers, compensate for high wages. Presumably women are more willing and able to make this trade-off than men.

Family structure also appears to affect men and women's earnings differently. For example, the later women enter the workforce the lower their earnings, while the later men enter the workforce the higher their earnings (Marini and Fan, 1997). Being married and having children is negatively associated with women's earnings, but positively associated with men's earnings. For women these effects may be due to human capital, but the effect of marriage on men's earnings is direct, after other factors have been controlled (Stroh and Brett, 1996; Schneer and Reitman, 1993).

Sex-typing of jobs lowers pay for both men and women holding those jobs, because certain occupations and types of skills typically held by women are devalued (England, Herbert, Kilbourne, Reid, and Megdal, 1994). Based on 1990 census data, more than one-half of employed women would have to change occupations before women would be distributed in occupations in the same proportions as men (Jacobs, 1995). Furthermore, the status of an occupation is often beginning to decline before women are permitted to enter in large numbers (Jacobs, 1995).

Women and men's opportunity structures provide differential access to and benefit from influential decision makers (Dreher and Cox, 1996). These differential opportunity structures reflect differences in the nature of men and women's network and mentoring relationships. Mentors provide challenging assignments, exposure and upper-level visibility, protection and direct forms of coaching, and sponsorship. The average annual compensation advantage of MBA graduates who established mentoring relationships with white males was $16,840 (Dreher and Cox, 1996). Female graduates, however, were less likely to form such relationships than male graduates were.

Researchers can account for between 30 percent (Marini and Fan, 1997) and 50 percent (Jacobs, 1995) of the gender gap in wages and compensation growth with factors such as education and work experience. The gap that is left is usually attributed to discrimination. Of course, it is arguable that discrimination contributes to the gap itself, for example by causing differences in aspirations, differential meaning associated with family structure, the sex-typing of jobs, and differential opportunity structures for men and women.

Gender and networks

A third indicator of career success is network composition and networking strategies. Men and women's network relationships differ both within organizations and in broader social networks (Burt, 1992; Ibarra, 1992, 1993, 1997; Munch, McPherson, and Smith-Lovin, 1997). Within organizations, women's networks include both men and women and tend to be broader than men's networks that tend to be dominated by other men. Women's network ties linking them to others tend to be weak, that is, a tie tends to be either a friendship tie with another woman or an instrumental tie, typically with a man (Ibarra, 1992). Men's ties tend to be strong, that is, a tie tends to be both friendship and instrumental. Men's ties are also more likely than women's to link them to powerful coalitions in organizations (Brass, 1985).

These differences in network characteristics are related to differential career success for men and women. Women's career success is hampered by their lack of centrality in male networks and dominant coalitions (Brass, 1985). Moreover, differences in men and women's communication patterns as suggested by Deborah Tannen's (1990) work may further complicate this issue in that if women and men don't communicate in the same way, important advice conferred on women by men may be misconstrued. In addition, women's weak network ties do not confer the same promotion benefits as those accorded to men who have similarly weak ties (Burt, 1992; Granovetter, 1982). One explanation is that weak ties may be less useful for people, like women, who are in "insecure positions" or lack credibility than for people like men who are secure and credible without strong ties (Granovetter, 1982; Burt, 1992; Ibarra, 1992). Women who lack legitimacy within the inner circles of the organization may need strong ties to strategic players to signal their legitimacy and advance (Burt, 1992; Ibarra, 1992).

One powerful driver of gender differences in the nature of network relationships may be the opportunity structures provided by the organization (Ibarra, 1993). Women are often numerical minorities within organizational power elites, and consequently, they typically have a smaller set of "similar others" to draw on in developing professional relationships (Ibarra, 1993; Kanter, 1977). A second cause of these differing network patterns may be gender role expectations. Men and women who have equivalent positions in organizations may operate in different social contexts because of different gender role expectations regarding appropriate work behavior. These different social contexts may require different network strategies to achieve similar career outcomes (Ibarra, 1997).

GENDER AND ROLE INVOLVEMENT

There are gender differences in behavioral and psychological involvement in work and family roles. Behavioral involvement is the amount of time spent in work and family roles; psychological involvement is the degree of psychological identification with a role (Lobel, 1991).

Gender and time

Men and women spend different amounts of time in work and family roles (Leete and Schor, 1994). In 1989, fully employed men's work hours (all hours spent working as well as paid leave from work) were 42.3 hours per week. Fully employed women's work hours were 36.1 hours per week. In 1989, fully employed men's family maintenance hours averaged 13.8; fully employed women's were on average 22.5. Research from the late 1990s confirms that this pattern continues to persist (Rothbard and Edwards, 1999).

For women, the factors predicting family maintenance hours include being married (increases by 200 hours per year), working in the paid labor market (reduces by 22 hours per year), having a child under the age of 3 (increases by 550 hours per year), having a child over the age of 3 (increases by 200 hours per year). For men, the factors predicting family maintenance hours include being married (increases by 100 hours per year), having a child under the age of 3 (increases by 161 hours per year), or child between 3 and 18 years (increases by 100 hours per year), and actual work hours (decreases by 20 hours per year). The variation in the household labor explained by these factors is substantially less for men than for women (Leete and Schor, 1994).

The reasons why women spend less time in the paid labor market and more time in family maintenance are social and structural. Women are continuing to enact their gendered role socialization by doing the majority of the work associated with maintaining home and family (Hochschild, 1989). At the same time the nature of work is changing toward a greater emphasis on knowledge work and hours at work are being used as indicators of both productivity and commitment (Perlow, 1998). Work structures, practices, and expectations associated with knowledge work assume that employees are willing and able to make work a priority over family (Perlow, 1998). Women who wish to compete with men in the world of knowledge work are expected to meet the same standards as the men. However, even as the norms for men and women in the workplace are the same, the norms for men and women in the family are not. Women cannot ignore the time demands of family maintenance, and given fixed resources of time and energy, the distribution of their time is balanced away from paid labor market work toward family maintenance activities.

Gender and identity

Men and women have different levels of work and family identity. Men tend to be more identified with work than women (see Rabinowitz and Hall, 1977 for a review). Conversely, women are generally more identified with family than men (Aryee and Luk, 1996; Bielby and Bielby, 1989; Parker and Aldwin, 1994). There are several explanations for gender differences in work identity, including labor market status and gender role socialization. When researchers control labor market status, work identity differences disappear (Mannheim, 1993; Mannheim, Baruch, and Tal, 1997; Rabinowitz and Hall, 1977), suggesting that when women have similar work status, opportunities, and experiences as men they identify similarly with work (Bielby, 1992; Mannheim, 1993; Mannheim et al., 1997). Gender role socialization that causes men and women to treat a woman's function in the paid labor market as secondary to her function as a wife and mother may also cause gender differences in work identity (Bielby, 1992; Mannheim, 1993).

Both structural and gender role socialization explanations account for differences in family identity. Men and women face different family-related opportunities and constraints (Bielby, 1992). When men and women's household responsibilities are similar, they are equally identified with and committed to family (Bielby and Bielby, 1989).

Moreover, gender role socialization suggests that women should view family as more central to their identities than men, because norms about the division of labor regarding household and child-rearing activities place the bulk of these responsibilities on women (Bielby and Bielby, 1989; Bielby, 1992).

GENDER AND ROLE STRESS

The evidence of differences between men and women in the experience of role stress and work–family conflict is mixed. First, women generally spend more cumulative time in work and family roles than men (Berk and Berk, 1979; Hochschild, 1989; Pleck, 1985). In some studies, accumulated role time (often called role overload) leads to greater stress and work–family conflict for women (e.g., Greenhaus, Bedeian, and Mossholder, 1987; Gutek, Searle, and Klepa, 1991). In other studies, the time spent in work and family roles, separately or combined has inconsistent effects on women's family stress and well-being (e.g., Pleck, 1985). Furthermore, women may experience greater family stress than men, and men may experience greater work stress than women (Gutek et al., 1991).

There are several explanations for these mixed findings. The rational explanation is that actual structural determinants such as time spent in a role are associated with increased stress and conflict in that role. The logic is that because women tend to spend more time on family and household activities than men do (Berk and Berk, 1979; Gutek et al., 1991; Pleck, 1985), women experience greater conflict and stress from the family than men. Likewise, because men tend to spend more time in work activities than women do (Pleck, 1985), they should experience greater conflict and stress from work than women. Although some support exists for the rational explanation, the findings are not consistent.

Although women do spend longer hours in family-related activities than men, they often report no greater conflict and stress, perhaps because of gender role expectations (Gutek et al., 1991). This explanation rests on the persistence of traditional gender role norms depicting work as the proper domain for men and family as the proper domain for women. It proposes that additional time spent in one's appropriate gendered domain will be less of an imposition and generate less role stress and conflict than additional time spent in one's opposite gender domain (Gutek et al., 1991).

A third explanation for gender differences in role stress and conflict relates to work and family structures and people's opportunities for control. Karasek's (1979) demands and control model explains that the degree of stress and conflict people perceive depends jointly on their role demands and the degree of control they have over those role demands. Work–family research reports that women's work and family role demands are higher than men's and that men have more control over their time than women (e.g., Duxbury, Higgins, and Lee, 1994; Pleck, 1985). That dual-earner women are less able to manage work and family than dual-career women is also evidence supporting Karasek's demands and control model (Duxbury and Higgins, 1994). Dual-career women spend more time in paid employment than dual-earner women, yet report less stress and conflict. Likewise, they spend the same amount of time in family activities as dual-earner women, but report less family stress and conflict. Consistent with the predictions of the demands and control model, dual-career women have more control over their work and family demands.

Gender and the Work–Family Interface

Men and women often use different strategies to manage the work–family interface. Men tend to compartmentalize and segment roles more than women do (Andrews and Bailyn, 1993; Crosby, 1991). More men use a segmented approach to dealing with work and family whereas more women use a synergistic mental model (Andrews and Bailyn, 1993). A segmented model is one where work and family roles are kept mentally separate, in contrast to a synergistic mental model where they are integrated. Women are more likely than men to manage multiple roles simultaneously, whether because of preference, need or both (Andrews and Bailyn, 1993). Women may be more facile with the interplay between multiple roles than men because women both have a greater need for and get more practice at juggling (Crosby, 1991). Women may find it easier to generate synergies between work and family, whereas men may view the two roles as separate and distinct.

A segmented versus synergistic mental model may reflect differences in the way men and women cope with the work–family interface. Coping by separating work and family roles may appear appropriate and natural to a person with a segmented mental model (Lambert, 1990; Piotrkowski, 1979). Because men generally have more segmented mental models of work and family than women do, they may naturally cope by segmenting work and family roles.

Differences in gender role expectations for men and women may explain why men and women have different mental models of work and family (Andrews and Bailyn, 1993; Eagly, 1987). Mental models are akin to the idea of gender schemas (Valian, 1998). Gender schemas are cognitive repositories of internalized societal expectations. Gender schemas affect attitudes and behaviors. Often what is imaginable (although subject to important limitations) for a female professional in terms of parental leave, reduced schedule, or flex time, is unthinkable for a male professional. Both men and women believe that it is more difficult for a male professional to maintain a positive impression in the organization while negotiating a reduced schedule than it is for a female professional (Andrews and Bailyn, 1993). As a result, societal expectations residing in our gender schemas may make it more difficult for men than women to think synergistically about work and family roles.

Exceptions

Exceptions to the first part of our meta-principle that men and women experience work and family differently may include affective responses to work and family roles, such as satisfaction and commitment. First, gender differences that occasionally appear in job attitudes such as job satisfaction disappear when researchers control for job characteristics, and other demographic factors such as tenure, age, education, income, and occupational level (Lefkowitz, 1994). Although men and women may achieve marital satisfaction in different ways (Wilkie, Ferree, and Ratcliff, 1998), no gender differences are evident in the marital satisfaction research. Second, although there are differences in men and women's role involvement in terms of psychological identification and time devoted to a role, there is no consistent relationship between the affective commitment that men and women display towards their organizations or families (Mathieu and Zajac, 1990).

Social comparison processes may explain the lack of differences in satisfaction. Men may refer to other men and women to other women in making the social comparisons on which satisfaction is based. For example, women comparing themselves to other employed women in their acquaintance may evaluate their working conditions more positively than if they compared themselves to similarly employed men. The structural demands of work and family roles and people's opportunities for exit may explain why there are no differences in commitment for men and women. Role demands may require similar levels of commitment from men and women because role behaviors are often prescribed and limited. Likewise, the opportunities that men and women have for exiting a particular work or family situation may be similar. For example, in a relatively tight labor market and a society where exiting family situations is commonplace, men and women may both have opportunities to leave a job and find a new one, or to divorce and remarry.

There are also exceptions to the second part of our meta-principle that recognizing gender differences will help promote equal opportunity. Recognizing these differences is the first step in promoting equal opportunity. But recognition is not sufficient to promote equal opportunity, if people do not implement changes to work and family structures.

LEVERS FOR CHANGE AND CASE STUDIES

The differences that men and women experience in work and family roles are likely to continue if the factors affecting the opportunity structure of men and women remain the same. In short, recognizing differences is not sufficient to equalize opportunities for men and women. In order to effect change, contribution must replace face time in the way work is evaluated. Moreover, while progress in socializing boys and girls to take non sex-role dictated family responsibilities has been made since the onset of the feminist revolution in the 1970s, acceptance of non-traditional role behaviors, especially for men, is holding back further progress that can be spurred by highlighting more non-traditional role models. So too has progress been made in the sex-typing of jobs, and so too is more progress necessary. Where will the pressure for continued progress come from? External factors, such as the tight labor market, are one source of pressure. The tight labor market may cause employers to re-evaluate work structures and redesign jobs to be more flexible and appealing to women, or to search more broadly and identify women who otherwise would not have been considered. As more and more women take jobs that were traditionally male, the sex-typing of those jobs will disappear, unless the job becomes seen as a feminine job. More dual-career families and more single-parent families will ultimately affect gender role socialization because these changes will produce more alternative models of family structure. Change is likely to be slow and occur in pockets where social environmental factors stimulate and reinforce men and women who are willing to push the boundaries of work and family structures.

Case study: change at Hewlett Packard

One pocket where change is evident is at Hewlett Packard (Abelson, 1999). Hewlett Packard's newly appointed CEO, Carleton Fiorina, is a woman, one of three female

CEOs among the Fortune 500. The groundwork for this appointment has been years in the making. Over the past seven years, Hewlett Packard has made work–life issues a priority. Nearly all employees determine their own work hours to some extent; a large number opt to work at home at least some of the time; about 12 percent have a formal telecommuting arrangement. Why did this happen? Talent in the electronics industry is a scarce commodity. Turnover of seasoned female managers in the early 1990s was significant and the chief executive in 1992, Lewis E. Platt, knew what managing work and family meant.

In 1981 when Platt was a rising general manager at HP, his wife Susan handled the child-rearing and housekeeping chores. When Susan died, all of her roles and responsibilities fell to Platt. He recalls that HP was a white male haven, and says, "here I was a white male, doing really well at HP and I was suddenly thrust into a different role." According to Platt, the sudden change in his family structure shattered his old assumptions that any difficulties women had in the workplace were of their own making. "I couldn't cope any better than they did," says Platt, comparing himself to female managers with families. Platt says he came to understand the ebb and flow of careers. He admits that in 1981 he was probably a marginal employee juggling grief over his wife's death, his responsibilities to his children, and his job, but he realized that one day he would be able to come back and give HP the time and energy to be a senior manager.

The opportunity structures depicted here at HP are rare. They came about because of labor market demands and the family experience of one key male manager who was willing to cut back at work for family, and then able to ramp back up his involvement at work when relieved of some family responsibilities. There are so few other examples of change in opportunity structure that it is impossible to know whether all four factors affecting opportunity structure must change for men and women to experience work and family roles similarly, or whether change in one factor is sufficient to bring about change to the system.

Case study: barriers to women in corporate leadership

The HP case described above is a positive example of how changing the opportunity structures for men and women can promote equal opportunity and pave the way for talented, motivated professionals to change their experiences of work and family. Such cases are few and far between. Catalyst's 1996 study of women in corporate leadership identifies many barriers to changing women's opportunity structures that still exist. Change has been slow. Catalyst's study reveals that only 23 percent of women executives believe that opportunities for women have improved greatly during the last five years. When asked to identify the three factors holding women back, 52 percent cite stereotyping and preconceptions about women, 49 percent cite exclusion from informal networks of communications, and 47 percent cite the lack of significant general management or line experience. These factors correspond closely to gender role socialization, sex-typing of jobs, and work structures, respectively. Regarding work–family balance, women executives reported that they employed several strategies including purchasing domestic and child-care services. Women executives also cited a supportive partner as critical for managing personal and professional commitments. These strategies for managing work and family balance entail changing family structures where women are typically in charge of home maintenance activities, freeing up their time to take advantage of work-related opportunities. These strategies also reveal the importance of financial resources and personal support for changing family structures and overcoming barriers to opportunity.

Although women executives still face barriers to opportunity as shown by the Catalyst study, several levers for change do exist. In particular, senior women in the Catalyst study identified several company-initiated strategies that could help change existing opportunity structures, such as changing the structure of work and minimizing the sex-typing of jobs. In particular, 55 percent suggested the identification and development of high-potential employees, 50 percent cited giving women high-visibility assignments, and 33 percent argued that cross-functional job rotations would increase women's opportunities for career advancement. CEOs surveyed in the same study agreed that giving women high-visibility assignments was important (74 percent) and endorsed several other effectiveness strategies: 54 percent believed that succession planning should incorporate gender diversity, 44 percent believed in instituting formal mentoring programs, and 41 percent thought individual managers should be held accountable for women's advancement. Despite the promise of these strategies many are in the early stages or have not yet been initiated. Only time will tell how effective they will prove to be.

These two case studies illustrate the ways that gender differences can affect men and women's work and family experiences via different opportunity structures. In particular, with these cases we have illustrated how one element of men and women's work and family experiences, career success, is affected by both barriers and changes to opportunity structures as shown in our model.

CONCLUSION

In conclusion, our meta-principle – promote equal opportunity by recognizing that men and women face differing experiences of work and family – is critical for understanding how work and family issues play out in our organizations and our lives. Moreover, our model of opportunity structures and gender differences allows us to pinpoint several levers for change that may promote equal opportunity by helping us to recognize gender differences and change opportunity structures in the ways men and women experience work and family.

REFERENCES

Abelson, R. (1999). A push from the top shatters a glass ceiling. *New York Times*, Aug. 21, 1999.

Andrews, A., and Bailyn, L. (1993). Segmentation and synergy: Two models linking work and family. In J. C. Hood (ed.), *Men, work, and family*. Newbury Park, CA: Sage.

Aryee, S., and V. Luk (1996). Balancing two major parts of adult life experience: Work and family identity among dual-earner couples. *Human Relations*, 49, 465–87.

Becker, G. S. (1975). *Human capital*. Chicago: University of Chicago Press.

Berk, R., and Berk, S. F. (1979). *Labor and leisure at home*. Beverly Hills, CA: Sage.

Bielby, D. D. (1992). Commitment to work and family. *Annual Review of Sociology*, 18, 281–302.

Bielby, W. T., and Bielby, D. D. (1989). Family ties: Balancing commitments to work and family in dual earner households. *American Sociological Review*, 54, 776–89.

Blau, F. D., and Ferber, M. A. (1992). *The economics of women, men and work*, 2nd edn. Englewood Cliffs, NJ: Prentice-Hall.

Brass, D. (1985). Men's and women's networks: A study of interaction patterns and influence in an organization. *Academy of Management Journal*, 28, 327–43.

Burke, R. J., and Greenglass, E. (1987) Work and family. In C. L. Cooper and I. T. Robertson (eds.), *International review of industrial and organizational psychology* (pp. 273–320). New York: Wiley.

Burt, R. (1992). *Structural holes: The social structure of competition*. Cambridge, MA: Harvard University Press.

Cox, T. H., and Harquail, C. V. (1991). Career paths and career success in the early career stages of male and female MBAs. *Journal of Vocational Behavior*, 39, 54–75.

Crosby, F. (1991). *Juggling: The unexpected advantages of balancing career and home for women and their families*. New York: Free Press.

Davies-Netzley, S. A. (1998). Women above the glass ceiling: Perceptions on corporate mobility and strategies for success. *Gender & Society*, 12, 339–55.

Dreher, G. F., and Cox, T. H. (1996). Gender, and opportunity: A study of compensation attainment and the establishment of mentoring relationships. *Journal of Applied Psychology*, 81, 297–308.

Duxbury, L., and Higgins, C. (1994). Interference between work and family: A status report on dual-career and dual-earner mothers and fathers. *Employee Assistance Quarterly*, 9, 55–80.

Duxbury, L., Higgins, C., and Lee, C. (1994). Work–family conflict: A comparison by gender, family type, and perceived control. *Journal of Family Issues*, 15, 449–66.

Eagly, A. H. (1987). *Sex differences in social behavior: A social-role interpretation*. Hillsdale, NJ: L. Erlbaum Associates.

England, P., Herbert, M., Kilbourne, B., Reid, L., and Megdal, L. (1994). The gendered valuation of occupations and skills: Earnings in 1980 census occupations. *Social Forces*, 73, 65–99.

Granovetter, M. (1982). The strength of weak ties: A network theory revisited. In P. V. Marsden and N. Lin (eds.), *Social structure and network analysis* (pp. 105–30). Beverly Hills, CA: Sage.

Greenhaus, J. H., Bedeian, A. G., and Mossholder, K. W. (1987). Work experiences, job performance, and feelings of personal and family well-being. *Journal of Vocational Behavior*, 31, 200–15.

Gutek, B. A., Searle, S., and Klepa, L. (1991). Rational versus gender role explanations for work–family conflict. *Journal of Applied Psychology*, 76, 560–8.

Haberfeld, Y. (1992). Employment discrimination: An organizational model. *Academy of Management Journal*, 35, 161–80.

Heilman, M. (1983). Sex bias in work settings: The lack of fit model. In B. M. Staw and L. L. Cummings (eds.), *Research in organizational behavior* (Vol. 5, pp. 269–98). Greenwich, CT: JAI Press.

Hochschild, A. R. (1989). *The second shift : Working parents and the revolution at home*. New York: Viking.

Ibarra, H. (1992). Homophily and differential returns: Sex differences in network structure and access in an advertising firm. *Administrative Science Quarterly*, 37, 422–47.

Ibarra, H. (1993). Personal networks of women and minorities in management: A conceptual framework. *Academy of Management Review*, 18, 56–87.

Ibarra, H. (1997). Paving an alternative route: Gender differences in managerial networks. *Social Psychology Quarterly*, 60, 91–102.

Jacobs, J. (1995). *Gender inequality at work*. Thousand Oaks: Sage Publications.

Judge, T. A., Cable, S., Boudreau, J. W., and Bretz, R. D. (1995). An empirical investigation of the predictors of executive career success. *Personnel Psychology*, 40, 485–518.

Kabanoff, B. (1980). Work and nonwork: A review of models, methods, and findings. *Psychological Bulletin*, 88, 60–77.

Kanter, R. M. (1977). *Men and women of the corporation*. New York: Basic Books.

Karasek, R. A. (1979). Job demands, job decision latitude, and mental strain: Implications for job redesign. *Administrative Science Quarterly*, 24, 285–308.

Lambert, S. J. (1990). Processes linking work and family: A critical review and research agenda. *Human Relations*, 43, 239–57.

Landau, J. (1995). The relationship of race and gender to managers' ratings of promotion potential. *Journal of Organizational Behavior*, 16, 391–400.

Leete, L., and Schor, J. B. (1994). Assessing the time-squeeze hypothesis: Hours worked in the United States, 1969–89. *Industrial Relations*, 33, 225–43.

Lefkowitz, J. (1994). Sex-related differences in job attitudes and dispositional variables: Now you see them. *Academy of Management Journal*, 37, 323–49.

Lobel, S. A. (1991). Allocation of investment in work and family roles: Alternative theories and implications for research. *Academy of Management Review*, 16, 507–21.

Lyness, K. S., and Thompson, D. E. (1997). Above the glass ceiling? A comparison of matched samples of female and male executive. *Journal of Applied Psychology*, 82, 359–75.

Mannheim, B. (1993). Gender and the effects of demographics, status, and work values on work centrality. *Work & Occupations*, 20, 3–22.

Mannheim, B., Baruch, Y., and Tal, J. (1997). Alternative models for antecedents and outcomes of work centrality and job satisfaction of high-tech personnel. *Human Relations*, 50, 1537–62.

Marini, M. M., and Fan, F. (1997). The gender gap in earnings at career entry. *American Sociological Review*, 62, 588–604.

Mathieu, J. E., and Zajac, D. M. (1990). A review and meta-analysis of the antecedents, correlates, and consequences of organizational commitment. *Psychological Bulletin,* 108, 171–94.

Melamed, T. (1995). Barriers to women's career success: Human capital, career choices, structural determinants, or simply sex discrimination. *Applied Psychology and International Review*, 44, 295–314.

Munch, A., McPherson, J. M., and Smith-Lovin, L. (1997). Gender, children, and social contact: The effects of childrearing for men and women. *American Sociological Review*, 62, 509–20.

Parker, R., and Aldwin, C. (1994). Desiring careers but loving families: Period, cohort, and gender effects in career and family orientations. In G. P. Keita and J. J. Hurrell Jr. (eds), *Job stress in a changing workforce: Investigating gender, diversity, and family issues* (pp. 23–38). Washington, DC: American Psychological Association.

Perlow, L. A. (1998). Boundary control: The social ordering of work and family time in a high-tech corporation. *Administrative Science Quarterly*, 43, 328–57.

Piotrkowski, C. S. (1979). *Work and the family system.* New York: Free Press.

Piotrkowski, C. S., Rapoport, R. N., and Rapoport, R. (1987). Families and work. In M. Sussman and S. Steinmetz (eds.), *Handbook of marriage and the family* (pp. 251–83). New York: Plenum.

Pleck, J. H. (1985). *Working wives, working husbands.* Beverly Hills, CA: Published in cooperation with the National Council on Family Relations [by] Sage Publications.

Rabinowitz, S., and Hall, D. T. (1977). Organizational research on job involvement. *Psychological Bulletin*, 84, 265–88.

Rossi, A. S. (1985). Gender and Parenthood. In A. S. Rossi (ed.), *Gender and the life course.* New York: Aldine Publishing Company.

Rothbard, N., and Edwards, J. (1999). Investment in work and family roles: A test of identity and utilitarian motives. Working Paper, Northwestern University.

Schneer, J. A., and Reitman, F. (1993). Effects of alternative family structures on managerial career paths. *Academy of Management Journal*, 36, 830–43.

Schneer, J. A., and Reitman, F. (1995). The impact of gender as managerial careers unfold. *Journal of Vocational Behavior*, 47, 290–315.

Stroh, L. K., and Brett, J. M. (1996). The dual-earner dad penalty in salary progression. *Human Resources Management*, 35, 181–201.

Stroh, L. K., Brett, J. M., and Reilly, A. H. (1992). All the right stuff: A comparison of female and male managers' career progression. *Journal of Applied Psychology*, 77, 251–60.

Stroh, L. K., Brett, J. M., and Reilly, A. H. (1996). Family structure, glass ceiling, and traditional explanations for the differential rate of turnover of female and male managers. *Journal of Vocational Behavior*, 49, 99–118.

Tannen, D. (1990). *You just don't understand: Women and men in conversation*. New York: Morrow.

Thacker, R. A. (1995). Gender, influence tactics, and job characteristics preferences: New insights into salary determination. *Sex Roles*, 32, 617–38.

Valian, V. (1998). *Why so slow? The advancement of women*. Cambridge: MIT Press.

Wellington, A. J. (1994). Accounting for the male/female wage gap among whites: 1976 and 1985. *American Sociological Review*, 59, 839–48.

Wilkie, J. R., Ferree, M. M., and Ratcliff, K. S. (1998). Gender and fairness: Marital satisfaction in two-earner couples. *Journal of Marriage and the Family*, 60, 577–94.

Zedeck, S. (ed.) (1992). *Work, families, and organizations*. San Francisco: Jossey-Bass.

28

Use Information Technology as a Catalyst for Organizational Change

Maryam Alavi and Jonathan Palmer

The information age is upon us. A few clicks of a mouse button provide instant access to everything from current stock prices to video clips of current movies, with millions of bytes of information in between. Like the steam engine helped the transition into the industrial age, information technology is fueling the transition into the information age.

The phrase information technology (IT) refers to a range of computer and communication capabilities (both hardware and software) used to process, store, retrieve, and transmit information in digital form. Today, information technology is highly pervasive in industrialized nations and is changing society, business, and the nature of work in these nations. Consider the following statistics: in 1995 over one-third of US households possessed at least one personal computer (Turban, McLean, and Wetherbe, 1996). A decade ago, the Gartner Group reported that 76 percent of all desk workers in the US were using computers, and in large organizations that figure rose to 84 percent. Overall, according to Gartner's estimate, 26 percent of the 113 million US employees used computers in their jobs in 1990 (Post and Anderson, 1998). One can infer additional major growth in these statistics over the past decade. Furthermore, sizeable investment in information technology is being made across different industries.

Why do firms invest so heavily in IT? What are the organizational impact and outcomes of IT? What positive changes can be expected and realized from IT applications in organizational settings? These questions have been of great interest to both researchers and practitioners in the field of information systems (IS) over the last 40 years. It is expected that the study of the organizational impact and benefits of IT will increase in popularity and importance due to the increasing dependence of global commerce on IT as well as the steady introduction of new information technology with new capabilities. Studies of various forms of IT systems and applications in organizational settings (Harris and Katz, 1991; Keen, 1991; Markus, 1994; Orlikowski and Hofman, 1997; Soe and Markus, 1993) have established that IT use in organizations can lead to four major categories of changes. These categories consist of: (1) gaining large-scale efficiencies in business processes and transactions (e.g., Davenport, 1993; Speier, Harvey and Palmer, 1998; Tapscott and Caston, 1993); (2) enhancing communication, information access, and decision-making (e.g., Alavi, in press; Alavi and Joachimsthaler, 1992; Leidner and Elam, 1995); (3) changing the basis of competition and industry structure to a firm's advantage (e.g., Benjamin and Wigand, 1995; Clemons and Row, 1991; Porter and Millar, 1995); and (4) exploiting new business models (e.g., Drucker, 1988; Palmer and Griffith, 1998; Rayport and Sviokla, 1995). These categories are not mutually exclusive and a particular firm can realize various changes simultaneously through the effective use of various IT capabilities. A classic example of a company that has used information technology as a catalyst for organizational change and profitability is Federal Express (FedEx). The company started using information technology aggressively in the 1980s to gain large-scale efficiencies in package delivery operations. Next, FedEx used IT to enhance customer service through effective information management (e.g., self-service package tracking via the World Wide Web), and to dominate its industry through the provision of innovative information services (e.g., supporting the e-commerce activities of its clients). The Federal Express case will be described in more detail in the latter part of the chapter.

GAIN LARGE-SCALE OPERATIONAL EFFICIENCIES

The use of information technology for transaction-processing systems and enterprise resource-planning systems can greatly enhance the operational efficiency of organizational processes. Transaction-processing systems (TPS) constitute the earliest form of IT applications in most organizations. TPS, by drawing on the rapid data-processing and transmission capabilities of computers and communications networks, expedite the execution, tracking, storing, and transmission of basic business transactions. Every business, regardless of its size and independent of the specific products and/or services that it offers, faces routine and repetitive tasks that support mission-central operations. Examples include receiving customer orders, fulfilling orders, billing customers, and paying employees. Needless to say, the manual execution of these tasks is slow, error prone, and expensive and is thus infeasible in medium and large organizations. The application of advanced information technology (e.g., client/server architecture, on-line processing) to business transaction-processing can greatly enhance organizational efficiency and cost savings. Consider the case of Ford Motor Company, which improved the efficiency of its accounts payable process by 75 percent by installing a new computer system and instituting an "invoiceless processing" system (described in Turban, McLean, and Wetherbe, 1996). Under the old system configuration, when the purchasing department created a purchase order, it sent a copy to the accounts payable department. Later, once the goods were received, the materials control department sent a copy of the receiving document to the accounts payable department. In the meantime, the accounts payable department received an invoice from the vendor. The invoice was compared with the purchase order and the receiving document. If the three documents matched, the vendor's invoice was paid. Otherwise, an accounts payable clerk would investigate the discrepancy. Once the discrepancy was resolved, new documentation was generated to issue the vendor's payment. The investigation of the mismatches was a labor-intensive and time-consuming process. Ford therefore decided to reduce and possibly eliminate these investigations. Under the new system configuration, Ford has asked its suppliers to stop sending invoices. Instead, the purchasing department initiates an order by logging it onto an on-line database. Once the goods arrive at the receiving docks, the new system automatically matches the receipt record and the purchase order. If the two records match, the delivered goods are accepted and the computer issues payment. In case of a mismatch, the order is simply returned. The new system increased the efficiency of operations of the accounts payable department by 75 percent while enhancing the accuracy of the financial information and simplifying the material control process at Ford.

New forms of transaction-processing systems referred to as enterprise resource planning (ERP) systems are likely to have a major impact on business processes across different industries. An ERP system is a highly integrated set of software modules designed to handle the most common business function transactions including general ledger accounting, accounts payable, accounts receivable, inventory management, order management, and human resources. At the heart of an ERP system is a single common database that collects data from and feeds data into all the software modules comprising the system. When an information item is changed in one of the software modules, related information is automatically updated in all other modules. By integrating information, streamlining data flow, and updating information across an entire business in a real-time mode, ERP systems can lead to dramatic productivity and efficiency gains in operations. Consider the efficiency gains at IBM's storage systems division after the deployment of an ERP system. The division reduced the time required for repricing its products from five days to five minutes and the time required to complete a credit check from 20 minutes to three seconds (Davenport, 1998). Once Fujitsu Microelectronics implemented an ERP system, it was able to close its financial books in four days (compared to eight days prior to the ERP system) and reduce order-filling time from 18 days to two days.

ENHANCE DECISION-MAKING AND COMMUNICATION

Decision-making and communication constitute two core organizational processes. Complex and challenging demands are placed on these two core processes in the current and emergent business environments, particularly due to globalization and the increased volatility of business and competitive environments.

Globalization has dispersed the operation of large firms across time and geography, increasing the need for effective and efficient ways to communicate across distance. Change in business and competitive environments in and of itself is not new. After all, it has been said that change is the only constant. However, the *rate* of change in today's economy has greatly increased, making it a major force to contend with. The rapid rate of change increases decision-making complexity in several ways. An increase in fluctuations and uncertainty in the decision environment requires more sophisticated analysis for developing, evaluating, and selecting alternatives. An increase in the uncertainty and complexity of decision tasks further increases the information-processing requirements of the decision maker. Larger volumes of information from various sources need to be assembled and organized more frequently. And finally, the rapid rate of change combined with the increased complexity in analysis and information requirements in decision environments increases the time-pressure on decision makers. It is simple to see that the traditional approaches to organizational decision-making and communication (manual information analysis and management, and the face-to-face mode of interactions) are becoming impractical. Information technology in the form of decision support systems and group support systems provides powerful capabilities in meeting the decision-making and communication demands of modern organizations.

The decision support system (DSS) concept was first articulated by Gorry and Scott Morton (1971) as an interactive computer-based system that enables decision makers to use data and analytical models to solve unstructured problems. The objective of decision support systems is not to replace the decision maker but to support and augment his/her judgment and experience in order to improve decision-making effectiveness. DSS draws on a variety of hardware and software tools to provide a range of information management and analytical capabilities, including sensitivity analysis, goal-seeking, and immediate access to information items at different levels of detail (the drill-down capability). Sensitivity analysis refers to the study of the impact of changes in decision variables on the decision outcomes. A popular form of sensitivity analysis is "what if" analysis. Decision models incorporated in DSS deal with uncertain decision variables and make estimates of and assumptions about these variables. To check the sensitivity of the proposed solutions to these estimates and assumptions, the decision maker can use "what if" analysis to reset the value of the decision variables of interest to investigate the level of change in the model solution. For example, using a DSS, a marketing manager can ask and answer this question: *what* will the market share be *if* the advertising increases by 5 percent?

In information systems literature, several researchers have articulated and investigated the relationship between DSS and organizational decision-making processes and outcomes. For example Huber (1990) set forth a rigorous theoretical argument that the use of decision support systems could lead to improved organizational intelligence and decision-making. Leidner and Elam (1995) in their study involving 91 users of decision support systems in 22 organizations found that the use of DSS led to better decision-making outcomes as well as enhancing user mental models. Research conducted by Robey (1974, 1976) demonstrated the positive impacts of computers on decision-making outcomes and user satisfaction. Thus, the information access and analytical capabilities offered by DSS can bring about changes and improvements in decision-making processes and outcomes.

Information technology, with its vast capacity for creating, transmitting, and storing messages, can also play a key role in the support of communication and collaboration processes in organizations. Information technology applied to the support of organizational communication and collaboration processes is referred to as group support systems (GSS). More specifically, GSS refers to a range of computer- and communication-based capabilities designed to support work group interaction processes in order to enhance the performance of groups in organizational settings (Alavi, in press). Dominant forms of GSS tools include electronic mail and computer conferencing systems, videoconferencing, and electronic meeting systems.

There has been a major growth in the application of group support systems in organizations over the past decade. Consider the following examples and changes resulting from the applications of group support systems. Anderson Consulting uses the Lotus Notes software system as a corporate backbone for the support of organizational communication. Notes is deployed to over 10,000 people worldwide (Ryan, 1995) and is used for a variety of group functions, including e-mail, project management, and information exchange and capture. E-mail has greatly increased the efficiency of communication processes at Anderson with a large number of mobile workers and consultants who work at the client sites. In fact, the ability of rapid communication among employees and information capture via Notes throughout the global firm is becoming a major competitive advantage (Magnet, 1994).

In another company, the engineering and marketing departments were located in two different states. Yet the departments needed to work together on a regular basis. Videoconferencing was used to support communication and collaboration between the two departments. The company believed that the introduction of videoconferencing had led to a six-month reduction in the product development cycle. Prior to videoconferencing, once every month, a representative from engineering and a representative from the marketing departments would travel to meet face to face to resolve the marketing and production issues and problems. After adopting videoconferencing, the monthly face-to-face meetings were supplemented with weekly and *ad hoc* videoconferencing meetings. This facilitated follow-ups on the face-to-face meetings as well as the timely resolution of issues as they would arise (instead of waiting for the next monthly face-to-face meeting). In this company, videoconferencing increased the frequency of communication and enabled the inclusion of staff in the discussions who would not otherwise participate in the monthly face-to-face meetings. Thus, in turn, product quality was enhanced and product cycle time was reduced.

These exemplars and the GSS research literature (e.g., Benbasat and Lim, 1993; DeSanctis and Poole, 1995; George et al., 1991) point out that, in general, three types of value-added organizational change can be expected from group support system applications. These include: (1) reducing the effects of time and distance barriers that constrain face-to-face interactions and communication; (2) enhancing the timeliness, range, depth, and format of the information available to organizational members; and (3) improving performance and effectiveness by reducing group process losses (e.g., evaluation apprehension) through more efficient and structured group interaction processes.

In summary, information technology in the form of decision support systems and group support systems can play a major transformational role in organizations through their impact on the key organizational processes of decision-making and communication. Future developments in this area will depend not only on technological advances but also on our understanding of and open-mindedness toward their applications and the resulting changes.

CHANGE THE COMPETITION AND INDUSTRY STRUCTURE TO YOUR FIRM'S ADVANTAGE

Information technology offers organizations opportunities to change the competitive landscape by more effectively defining the dimensions of competition. The information intensity (Porter and Millar, 1985; Palmer and Griffith, 1998) of products and services has become an important element in defining competitive advantage. Information intensity includes the amount of information that goes into the development of the product or the service, the amount of information required by consumers to utilize the product, and the amount of information required across the value chain to develop and deliver the product or service. Firms have redefined the basis of competition by providing additional information regarding their products or in extending the information content. For instance, Merrill Lynch developed the cash management account, which for the first time allowed customers to see all of their financial portfolio and transactions in a single account. This additional information provided a distinct competitive advantage over the other financial services firms. American Airlines's use of the Sabre system provided significant advantages in the booking and capacity management functions for the airline *vis-à-vis* its competitors. This was accomplished by providing enhanced information for planning purposes and a pre-eminent position on travel agent screens for American Airlines flight information. Numerous electronic goods manufacturers, including Sony and Motorola, provide substantial additional information in product use and servicing through enhanced user manuals and updated information and after-sale technical support via Web sites.

Industry structure has also been changed through the implementation of information technology. Information-intensive industries such as retail banking and insurance have seen a steady shift from reliance on face-to-face, bricks-and-mortar-based interactions with customers to increasingly automated ones. This shift has come through the use of automated teller machines (ATMs), phone, and the Internet to conduct various types of transactions from withdrawal of funds to application for loans.

Highly fragmented industries have also been restructured through the use of information technology. Two recent examples are the travel industry and the office products delivery industry. Traditionally, the travel industry involved numerous independent travel agents presenting travel options of providers such as airlines, hotels, and rental cars to business and leisure travelers. The advent of the Internet has significantly changed the industry structure, with providers providing services direct to customers via Internet sites. This disintermediation of the travel agent represents a major structural change for the industry.

Office product delivery has also traditionally been a fragmented industry, with local delivery companies operating within specific geographic areas. Corporate Express saw the opportunity to pull together this fragmented market through the use of information technology. Through a series of over 200 acquisitions of local carriers and the implementation of a comprehensive inventory management system, the firm has grown to over $8 billion in annual turnover and substantially changed the industry structure by using information systems to merge previously fragmented operations.

Supply-chain management has been a critical area for the use of information technology to change the competitive dimensions. Retailing and wholesaling relationships have been significantly influenced through the spread of electronic data interchange (EDI) in which supply-chain partners exchange data on sales trends, inventory replenishment, and in-store space allocation and management. Improvements in supply-chain efficiencies have led to several significant competitive advantages for firms such as WalMart and JC Penney, including improved bargaining power over suppliers, reduced inventory costs, and enhanced in-store space management.

The use of IT to change competitive dynamics often involves identifying opportunities for greater use of information in: (1) the supply chain; (2) the description of the product or its use; or (3) the after-sale support or service dimension. Industry structures can be changed when the use of information technology can: (1) aggregate previously fragmented markets; (2) replace existing channels at lower cost or improved convenience; or (3) more effectively bundle products and services.

Competitive advantages achieved through information technology can also come from the influence IT has on the nature of product and service offerings. For example, the personal computer and software industry has used IT to change its product by providing enhanced services including the packaging of Internet service, technology support, and product updates for a specified period of time as a part of the initial product purchase. Many firms have created new products by utilizing information on customer responses or shopping patterns. Retailers, like Nordstrom, have used customer feedback to design new apparel and accessory products. Banks have provided enhanced ATM services to incorporate account verification and loan applications at specific high-traffic sites. IT can also provide access to new markets and reduce locational constraints as Internet retailers now can serve truly global audiences. The Slovenian wine industry association offers an example, as the launching of their website generated sales that absorbed all of their annual inventory over a six-month period.

Exploit New Business Models

The speed, scope, and ubiquity of information technology offer the opportunity to exploit entirely new business models in a variety of industries. The opportunity for firms to enhance customer relationships by offering 24/7 (24 hours a day, 7 days a week) access to purchasing, product information, and service offers an enhanced model for customer convenience and connection. This capability has influenced both Internet-based retailers as well as traditional retailers in the provision of customer convenience (Palmer, 1997).

The Internet has dramatically increased the range of marketing approaches available to many organizations. The specific impact of this new technology on organizations depends on the underlying market position and product or service offerings of the firm. Designing World Wide Web sites to take advantage of the new marketing opportunities is a challenge for most companies.

The shift in underlying marketing fundamentals may be the driving force luring many organizations, such as General Motors, Exxon, JC Penney, WalMart, and others onto the Web. The Web represents a fundamental paradigm shift in the way business operates (Clark, 1997; Palmer and Griffith, 1998). It moves organizations beyond the physical constraints of their traditional realm and creates a virtual community in which businesses compete. From a strategic standpoint, the Internet provides for "frictionless" commerce in which transaction value enhancement provides rapid transaction coordination with little time or transaction cost and an active global marketspace (Gates, Myhrvold, and Rinearson, 1995; Rayport and Sviokla, 1995). The Internet also drives new competitive paradigms based on information flows, online delivered content, and new commercial scenarios (Berthon, Pitt, and Watson, 1996; Clark, 1997; Hoffman and Novak, 1996).

These market situations suggest differing opportunities for product and service branding, interactivity, and information manipulation in website design (Forrester Reports, 1997; Schubert and Selz, 1997). The Internet capabilities of information storage and retrieval also offer sellers a wide range of opportunities to provide consumers with comparative products and services.

Those firms whose product's core benefits are derived from information are able to bypass middlemen, putting them in direct contact with their buyer. Alternatively, organizations whose core product benefit is tangible can utilize the technology to improve efficiency in inventory management, logistics, and marketing while retaining the core offering (Shanklin and Griffith, 1996; Palmer and Griffith, 1998). Thus, information-intensive organizations, such as Aetna, Allstate, and the like will utilize the new technology differently than hard-good manufacturers such as Goodyear, Exxon, and others.

The Web provides organizations an opportunity to present information regarding their products and services to both customers and suppliers. The potential of reaching global markets with product and service information as well as the ability to provide user interaction with the website provides significant marketing opportunities.

The Internet has almost unlimited "potential" in the markets of the future. As a direct marketing and advertising mechanism it provides product manufacturers or service providers access to a vast and ever-expanding market. Internet technology continues to improve and the audience continues to grow. The potential exists for consumers to interact with companies via the Internet. This interaction can support critical marketing capabilities including: (1) direct sales via a friction-free environment; (2) reproducing descriptive and experiential product information; (3) extensive array of potential product offerings; and (4) the ability to search for and select products based on consumer-defined attributes (Palmer and Griffith, 1998).

Auction, dealer, and broker markets offer the potential for multiple business models on the Internet. The potential for new efficiencies in cost structure and allocation of resources is significant (Bakos, 1998). Information technology can change the industry structure by providing an electronic marketplace and significantly changing the bargaining power of market participants by changing the control of price, availability, delivery, and quality. Other influences include the capability of rapid product development and mass customization.

In general, the flexibility in product and service features, the rapid transfer of information, and the declining transaction costs have changed customer expectations regarding delivery times, quality, and convenience.

Beware of IT Implementation Issues

Considering the prevalence of IT applications and the large and growing investments in them in modern organizations, one might expect a consistently positive set of outcomes associated with IT initiatives. This, however, is not always the case. Both research and practice have shown that due to implementation failures, IT may not lead to the planned or expected organizational changes described above. One form of implementation failure involves the cancellation of an IT project before the completion and installation of the system. For example, in 1995, 31 percent of large IT projects were cancelled in US companies prior to their completion for an estimated total cost of $81 billion (Robey and Boudreau, in press). Research studies of IT implementation failures are uncommon. Nevertheless two examples of case studies of large-scale IT project cancellations can be provided: (1) the Taurus Project of the London Stock Exchange (Drummond, 1996); and (2) the centralized payroll processing system of the New Zealand Department of Education (Myers, 1994). Another form of IT implementation failure involves situations in which the IT system is completed and installed, but the targeted organizational users resist the system, or do not use it in the intended way. For example, the use of French Railway's computerized reservation systems was strongly resisted by both the railway employees and its customers (Mitev, 1996). Another interesting example is provided by Robey and Boudreau (in press) and involves a system originally described by Kraut, Dumais, and Koch (1989). One of the goals of the system, a computerized record-keeping system, was to enhance the operational efficiency of the organization by reducing the opportunities for social interactions among employees during working hours. After the system installation, although the employees were more isolated, they "invented" a new and unintended way of using the system for social interactions. They used a memo field designed for capturing customer comments for passing messages back and forth among themselves, undermining the expected organizational efficiency gains from the IT system.

Thus, the successful implementation of IT systems is a prerequisite for realizing the planned and expected changes associated with these systems. The researchers in the information systems field have identified several factors that seem to contribute to the implementation success of IT systems. These factors include top management support and commitment, user involvement in the planning and design of the IT system, and user training in the use of IT (Alavi and Joachimsthaler, 1992; Lucas, Ginzberg, and Shultz, 1991). Top management support and IT commitment are prerequisites for the success of all forms of organizational change initiatives, including IT-centered change. This is partly due to the need for top management support and commitment for garnering organizational resources required for IT implementation. Furthermore, top management support is shown to influence the level of individual users' personal stake in the IT implementation success (Lucas, Ginzberg, and Shultz, 1991). The strength of the relationships between user involvement and training and IT implementation success was established through the meta-analysis study of Alavi and Joachimsthaler (1992). This finding is consistent with the views presented in normative models of organizational change (e.g., Kolb and Frohman, 1970) and the diffusion of the innovation model (Cooper and Zmud, 1990) of IT implementation. These models highlight the importance of involvement and training as the means to create a favorable and accepting environment in which to bring about the IT-centered change.

Other researchers investigating IT implementation issues have suggested that the above-mentioned factors seem to be necessary, but not sufficient, conditions for the success of large-scale IT implementations (Markus and Robey, 1988; Robey and Boudreau, in press). According to these researchers, organizational change associated with large-scale IT applications is complex and should be addressed at different levels of analysis including individual, group, and departmental as well as the organizational and strategic levels. Consider the enterprise resource planning (ERP) systems described earlier in this chapter. At the operational level, these systems can lead to highly integrated, coordinated, and efficient core operational processes. These benefits are achieved by imposing generic and streamlined workflow logic encoded in the software on the organization. This impact at the operational level may restrict the latitude of authority at the individual worker level. On the other hand, the standardization of workflow and information items across departments may empower cross-functional teamwork in the organization. At the same time, the company's move toward generic and standardized processes may have a negative impact on the competitive positioning of the firm, if customized processes are a source of competitive advantage for the firm. For example, Dell Computer found that its ERP implementation would not fit its new, decentralized management model (Davenport, 1998).

In summary, to enhance the success of IT implementation and to realize the desired organizational changes, IT impacts should be considered and planned for at multiple levels of analysis *simultaneously*. Failure to do so may lead to negative and unexpected consequences.

CASE STUDIES

Implementation failure at Compusys

Difficulties in implementing information technology successfully can influence efficiency, communication, and competitiveness. Compusys (a pseudonym) was one of the largest computer manufacturers and system integrators throughout the 1980s and early 1990s. Their experience with implementing CONFIG shows that even the best in technology when poorly implemented can have negative results. CONFIG was a decision-support system designed to improve the efficiency of configurations of the company's products to improve the installation at client sites. CONFIG enabled sales staff to quickly identify key components, wiring, and other installation requirements in response to a specific client need. The system could improve the communication between sales and technical staff and provide an opportunity for competitive advantage in the high-end computer market by providing quicker, more specific, and more accurate responses to customers, and lower costs and reconfiguration expenses of internal processes.

The system was designed by the technical configuration experts and aimed at supporting sales staff in the field. Reconfigurations were costing the company money and the technical experts bore the brunt of the extra work. In its early implementation, 75 percent of the sales staff had tried CONFIG, but only 25 percent were actually using it. By the third year, fewer than 10 percent of the sales staff were using the system.

A redeployment of the systems was undertaken after the third year. The upgraded system had a better user interface and was technically superior. Yet, usage remained low. Two key issues emerged: users had no motivation to do what the system enabled them to do and using the system made it harder for sales staff to do what they were motivated to do. The organizational reward systems did not provide an incentive for sales staff to reduce configuration errors, but rather to sell more systems. There were no metrics or incentives for quote accuracy. In addition, working through CONFIG to generate more accurate quotes took longer and took the sales staff away from making additional sales calls.

This experience is an example of the negative impacts of the organizational structure and incentives on the successful implementation of information technology. This lack of alignment resulted in a loss of potential benefits in efficiencies as well as losses in organizational communication and market competitiveness. This example is explored in more detail in Markus and Keil (1994).

Large-scale IT-enabled organizational change at Federal Express

Federal Express (FedEx) has utilized information technology to gain large-scale efficiencies in business processes, enhance its communication and decision-making processes, and change the industry structure to its advantage.

Credited with changing the package delivery industry by guaranteeing overnight delivery (Hammer and Champy, 1993: 156), FedEx has continued to be an industry leader in the use of information technology to support increased product differentiation by allowing customers and FedEx employees to select delivery timing. The logistics capability supported by US, European, and Asian transportation hubs and an extensive package-tracking information system has resulted in substantial cost savings, and these efficiencies have generated significant growth in FedEx market share throughout the world. These sophisticated logistics and tracking systems have, as a result, become a competitive necessity in the package-delivery industry. Information systems are critical to business simplification and efficient processes and are highly integrated into the core activities of FedEx (Treacy and Wiersema, 1995).

FedEx uses an internal intranet for enhanced communication throughout the firm. This intranet provides employees access to information, policies, customer details, and new product or service announcements throughout the company's global operations. The immediacy of the information transfer and access has allowed decision-making to be made at the local level, another competitive advantage enabling FedEx to respond to local market conditions more effectively. In addition, an internal business TV network keeps employees up to date on company activities. For example, when the company acquired Flying Tiger, the news was provided to employees via this in-house network, so they did not have to learn about it from outside sources first (Keen, 1991). The effective intra-organizational information-sharing has led to enhanced employee trust, teamwork, and loyalty.

The advent of the Internet provided an opportunity for FedEx to enhance the logistics chain as well as its customer relationships, changing the nature of competition within the industry. Using the Internet, FedEx allowed its customers to track the delivery of their packages online. Allowing customers to track packages reduced internal costs to FedEx. Furthermore, by linking to the FedEx databases, the company's corporate customers were able to better serve their own clients, increasing their loyalty to FedEx and reducing the likelihood of switching to another provider (Goldman, Nagel, and Preiss, 1995). This use of the Internet resulted in improved customer satisfaction and involvement, while reducing costs through the reduction of call centers. In addition, FedEx information technology capabilities include a knowledge base of expertise in shipping, customs brokerage, and governmental regulations, which supports the globalization of their business and is value-added information for FedEx customers.

FedEx has extended its expertise in information technology applications to position itself as a logistics integrator. This new business model goes beyond that of package delivery to develop warehousing, notification, tracking, and packaging technology for its customers. This enhanced business model also includes multiple new revenue streams from each of the value-adding activities. This model is particularly attractive given the development of Internet-based selling of physical products requiring full logistics support. An example is the FedEx alliance with Laura Ashley. Under this agreement, FedEx took over the warehouse and distribution activities. This provided a global distribution network for Laura Ashley and firmly established FedEx as a logistics provider.

Conclusions

Information technology can serve as a significant catalyst for organizational change. The impact of information technology can improve operating efficiencies across the organization and improve the communication processes and decision-making of employees. Other impacts include the opportunity for information technology to change the basis of competition, by increasing the role of information in key business activities and enhancing products and services and the dimensions on which they compete. New business models also become possible through information technology, allowing firms to change their approach to the market, management of the organization, and competitors.

Implementation of technology continues to be a challenge for all companies. The tremendous potential for improvements through information technology is only fully realized when existing organizational processes, incentives, and culture are reflected in the implementation process. Successful use of information technology involves strong organizational commitment and a clear identification of the role information technology will play.

References

Alavi, M. (in press). Group support systems: Tools and applications. *Encyclopedia of microcomputers.*

Alavi, M., and Joachimsthaler, E. (1992). Revisiting DSS implementation research: A meta-analysis of the literature and suggestions for researchers. *MIS Quarterly*, 95–116.

Bakos, Y. (1998). The emerging role of electronic marketplaces on the Internet. *Communications of the ACM*, 41(8), 35–42.

Benbasat, I., and Lim, L. H. (1993). The effects of group task, context, and technology variables on the usefulness of group support systems: A meta-analysis of experimental systems. *Small Group Research*, 24(4), 430–62.

Benjamin, R., and Wigand, R. (1995). Electronic markets and virtual value chains on the information superhighway. *Sloan Management Review*, Winter, 62–72.

Berthon, P., Pitt, L., and Watson, R. (1996). Marketing communication and the World Wide Web. *Business Horizons*, 39(5), 24–32.

Clark, B. (1997). Welcome to my parlor. *Marketing Management*, Winter, 11–25.

Clemons, E., and Row, M. (1991). Sustaining IT advantage: The role of structural differences. *MIS Quarterly*, 15(3), 275–92.

Cooper, R. B., and Zmud, R. W. (1990). Information technology implementation research: A technological diffusion approach. *Management Science*, 36(2), 123–39.

Davenport, H. (1998). Putting the enterprise into the enterprise systems. *Harvard Business Review*, 121–31.

Davenport, T. (1993). *Process innovation: Reengineering work through information technology.* Boston, MA:

Harvard Business School Press.

DeSanctis, G., and Scott Poole, M. (1996). Transitions in teamwork in new organizational forms. *Advances in Group Processes*, 14, 156–76.

Drucker, P. (1988). The coming of the new organization. *Harvard Business Review*, 66(1), 45–53.

Drummond, H. (1996). The politics of risk: Trials and tribulations of the Taurus project. *Journal of Information Technology*, 11, 347–57.

Forrester Reports (1997). Interactive technology strategies (J. M. Robb, J. C. McCarthy, and H. D. Sheridan), Feb. 1, 1–17.

Gates, B., Myhrvold, N., and Rinearson, P. (1995). *The road ahead*. New York: Viking Penguin.

George, J., Easton, G. K., Nunamaker, J. F. Jr., and Northcraft, G. B. (1991). A study of collaborative group work with and without computer based support. *Information Systems Research*, 1(4), 394–415.

Goldman, S., Nagel, R., and Preiss, K. (1995). *Agile competitors and virtual organizations: Strategies for enriching the customer*. New York: Van Nostrand Reinhold.

Gorry, A., and Scott Morton, M. (1971). A framework for management information systems. *Sloan Management Review*, 13.

Hammer, M., and Champy, J. (1993). *Reengineering the corporation: A manifesto for business revolution*. New York: Harper Business.

Harris, S., and Katz, J. (1991). Organizational performance and information technology investment intensity in the insurance industry. *Organization Science*, 2(3), 263–95.

Hoffman, D., and Novak, T. (1996). Marketing in hypermedia computer-mediated environments: Conceptual foundations. *Journal of Marketing*, 60(3), 50–68.

Huber, G. (1990). A theory of the effects of advanced information technologies on organizational design, intelligence, and decision-making. *Academy of Management Review*, 15(1), 47–71.

Keen, P. (1991). *Shaping the future: Business design through information technology*. Boston: Harvard Business School Press.

Kolb, D. A., and Frohman, A. L. (1970). An organizational development approach to consulting. *Sloan Management Review*, 12(1), 51–66.

Kraut, R. S., Dumais, R. S., and Koch, S. (1989). Computerisation, productivity, and quality of work-life. *Communication of the ACM*, 32, 220–38.

Leidner, D., and. Elam, J. J. (1995). The impact of executive information systems on organizational design, intelligence, and decision making. *Information Systems Research*, 6, 645–64.

Lucas, H. C. Jr., Ginzberg, M. J., and Schultz, R. L (1991). *Information systems implementation: Testing a structural model*. Norwood, NJ: Ablex Publishing.

Magnet, M. (1994). *Fortune Magazine*, June 27, 79.

Markus, M. L. (1994). Electronic mail as the medium of managerial choice. *Organization Science*, 5(4), 502–25.

Markus, M. L., and Keil, M. (1994). If we build it they will come: Designing systems that users want to use. *Sloan Management Review*, Summer, 11–25.

Markus, M. L., and Robey, D. (1988). Information technology and organizational change: Causal structure in theory and research. *Management Science*, 34, 583–98.

Miter, N. N. (1996). More than a failure? The computerized reservation systems at French Railway. *Information Technology and People*, 9(4), 8–19.

Myers, M. D. (1994). A disaster for everyone to see: An interactive analysis of a failed IS project. *Accounting, Management and Information Technologies*, 4(4), 185–201.

Orlikowski, W., and Hofman, J. (1997). An improvisational model for change management: The case of groupware technologies. *Sloan Management Review*, 38(2), 11–21.

Palmer, J. W. (1997). Electronic commerce in retailing: Differences across retailing formats. *The Information Society*, 13(1), 97–108.

Palmer, J. W., and Griffith, D. (1998). An emerging web site design model for marketing.

Communications of the ACM, 41(3), 44–51.

Porter, M., and Millar, V. (1985). How information gives you competitive advantage. *Harvard Business Review*, July–Aug., 149–60.

Post, G. V., and Anderson, D. (1998). *Management information systems: Solving business problems with information technology*, Chicago: Irwin.

Premier 100, *Computerworld*, Sept. 13, 1993.

Rayport, J., and Sviokla, J. (1995). Exploiting the virtual value chain. *Harvard Business Review*, Nov.–Dec., 75–85.

Robey, D. (1974). Task design, work values, and worker response: An experimental test. *Organizational Behavior and Human Performance*, 12(2), 264–73.

Robey, D. (1976). The impact of alternative decision technologies on user behavior. *Decision Sciences*, 7(1), 93–105.

Robey, D., and Boudreau, M. (in press). Accounting for the contradictory organizational consequences of information technology: Theoretical directions and methodological implications. *Information Systems Research*, 10.

Ryan, H. W. (1995). *Groupware: Technology and applications*. Englewood Cliffs, NJ: Prentice-Hall.

Schubert, P., and Selz, D. (1997). Web assessment: A model for the evaluation and the assessment of successful electronic commerce applications. *Proceedings of the 31st Hawaii international conference on systems sciences*.

Shanklin, W., and Griffith, D. (1996). Crafting strategies for global marketing in the new millennium. *Business Horizons*, 39(5), 11–16.

Soe, L., and Markus, M. L. (1993). Technological or social utility? Unraveling explanations of email, vmail and fax use. *Information Society*, 9(3), 213–36.

Speier, C., Harvey, M., and Palmer, J. W. (1998). Implementing intra-organizational learning: An infrastructure to support business process re-engineering. *Knowledge and Process Management*, 5(2), 76–86.

Tapscott, D., and Caston, C. (1993). *Paradigm shift: The new promise of information technology*. New York: McGraw-Hill.

Treacy, M., and Wiersema, F. (1995). *The discipline of market leaders*, New York: HarperCollins.

Turban, E., Mclean, E., and Wetherbe, J. (1996). *Information technology for management: improving quality and productivity*. New York: John Wiley & Sons.

29

Make Management Practice Fit the National Culture

Miriam Erez

The process of globalization has created new challenges for today's managers. Many of them work for multinational companies, and for international joint ventures. Others have gone through international mergers and acquisitions, or formed alliances with firms in other countries.

In the late 1980s, the fierce competition between Japan and the USA called attention to the cultural factor. At that time, articles in the business papers reflected fear and loathing of Japan, trying to understand how Japan was growing, why it was dangerous, and what to do about it (*Fortune*, 26 Feb. 1990). Over the years, an increasing number of American managers found themselves negotiating with the Japanese, marketing their products in Japan, offering services to foreign customers, and managing operations outside their home countries. As a result, the popularity of guidebooks on how to do business with the Japanese and other foreign countries grew. The need for such books testifies to the fact that managers have recognized their lack of knowledge and competence in managing across cultural borders.

In the late 1990s, the competition between companies in different cultures turned from conflict to cooperation in the form of mergers, joint ventures, and business alliances. In the last year, the business news headlines captured large-scale international mergers such as the ones between Ford–USA and Volvo–Sweden; Chrysler–USA and Mercedes-Benz–Germany; Deutsche Bank–Germany and Bankers Trust–USA; and between Renault–France and Nissan–Japan. A wedding ceremony has become a common metaphor for international mergers, with a question mark concerning whether these mergers will last, or disintegrate.

The mode of cooperation rather than competition requires a better understanding of the international partner than merely knowing the competitor. It seems that the need for understanding cross-cultural differences and similarities is becoming increasingly crucial for effective international partnerships and their managers.

The objective of this chapter is to propose principles which could serve as guidelines for managers in selecting and implementing effective management practices outside their home country.

The Main Principle: Effective Managerial Practices Should Best Fit the National Cultures Represented in the Workplace

Managers and employees in different cultures bring to their workplace the codes of behavior and norms of their own cultures. These norms and cultural values shape the organizational processes and managerial practices in the organizations. Therefore, different managerial practices are implemented in organizations in different parts of the world. For example, in individualistic cultures, such as that of the USA, the selection procedure of new employees is based on their personal records. In collectivistic cultures, such as that of Mexico, recommendations by family members, who already work for the company, serve as an important criterion for selecting new employees. In the USA, promotion to higher managerial levels is based on personal achievements, as they appear in the performance appraisal records. However, in collectivistic and hierarchical cultures such as that of Japan, seniority plays a major role in promotion decisions. Payment based on results constitutes a greater part of Americans' compensation packages compared to those in Europe. In European countries, flat salaries are more common than in the US. The compensation package of American managers consists of a large portion of stock options, whereas this is less common for managers in European countries.

There are so many different codes of behavior and variations of management practices that they cannot all be described in the "how to" books. Managers, therefore, should use a small number of principles that will guide their choice of practices, and their behavioral norms.

The principle of fit between cultures and management practices can further be divided into the following sub-principles.

The first sub-principle: identify the cultural characteristics of the country you have business with

Employees evaluate management practices as enhancing or threatening their well-being and self-worth. Managerial approaches that are at odds with prevailing cultural values are unlikely to be effective because the employees won't like to adopt them. Since cultures differ in the values they endorse, people from these cultures often interpret the same managerial practices quite differently.

Culture is best defined as a shared meaning system (Hofstede, 1980; Kluckhohn, 1954; Schwartz, 1992; Shweder and LeVine, 1984). In metaphorical terms, culture is the software of the mind (Hofstede, 1991). Culture shapes the core values and norms of its members. These values are shared and transmitted from one generation to another through social learning processes of modeling and observation, as well as through the effects of individual actions (Bandura, 1986). Homogeneous societies form tight cultures, and their norms and values are closely shared by most members of the society. Societies consisting of sub-groups with dissimilar norms and values form loose cultures (Triandis, 1989).

Cultures differ in their content components. The two values that depict most of the variance among cultures are: collectivism versus individualism, and power distance.

Individualism–collectivism portrays the level of interrelatedness among members of one culture (Hofstede, 1980; Triandis, Bontempo, Vilareal, Masaaki, and Lucca, 1988). Collectivism means preference to work in teams, subordination of personal goals to group goals, concern for the integrity of the group, and intense emotional attachment to the in-group. In contrast, individualism emphasizes personal autonomy and independence, adherence to personal goals, and less concern and emotional attachment to the in-group (Triandis et al., 1988). The United States, Australia, and England are highly individualistic cultures, whereas South America, Pakistan, Korea, Japan, and Taiwan are highly collectivistic.

Power distance reflects the level of equality in the society. High power distance means low equality in the society and a clear power structure in organizations. Employees in such cultures know their place in the organizational hierarchy, and there are clear status symbols that differentiate between employees at different organizational levels. On the other hand, in low power distance cultures, employees feel free to disagree with their boss and to express their ideas openly. Malaysia, the Philippines, Arab countries, and India are known for their high level of power distance. In contrast, Israel, Scandinavia, and New Zealand are known for their low levels of power distance.

Recently, a group of more than 80 researchers, headed by Robert House from the Wharton School, has joined efforts to conduct the *Globe Study* in sixty different countries. This study assesses differences and similarities in cultural and organizational values, as well as in preferences for leadership characteristics. Figures 29.1 and 29.2 portray the cultural values of collectivism and power distance in a sample of eight countries, including the USA, England, West Germany, East Germany, Russia, Finland, Japan, and Israel.

The results demonstrate that in this sample, Japan appeared as the country with the highest level of power distance, and Israel as the most egalitarian country. Similarly, the USA is the most individualistic culture, and Japan and Russia are the most collectivistic cultures in this sample.

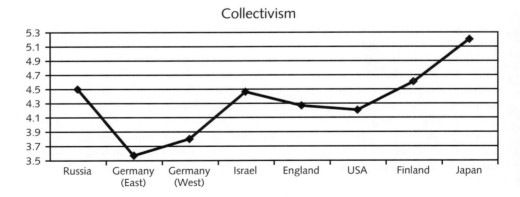

FIGURE 29.1 The cultural value of collectivism in eight different countries

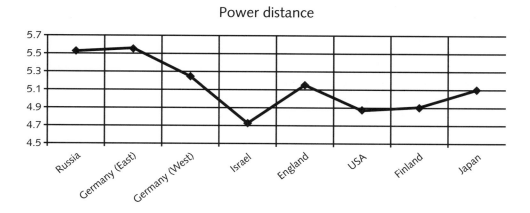

FIGURE 29.2 The cultural value of power distance in eight different countries

Three additional values that help differentiate among cultures are: Uncertainty avoidance, masculinity/femininity, and future time orientation.

Uncertainty avoidance reflects the extent to which members of the society feel threatened by uncertain or unknown situations. High levels of uncertainty lead to anxiety. Organizations that seek to avoid uncertainty have formal rules and regulations, clear task definitions, and low tolerance for deviation from the rules and norms. On the other hand, organizations with high tolerance for uncertainty are less formal, more flexible, and allow for higher levels of heterogeneity in norms and behavior. Cultures with high levels of uncertainty avoidance are: France, Belgium, Greece, and Portugal. Cultures with low levels of uncertainty avoidance are Denmark, Sweden, and Singapore.

Masculine versus feminine cultures. The former pertains to societies in which social gender roles are clearly distinct (i.e., men are supposed to be assertive, tough, and focused on material success, whereas women are supposed to be more modest, tender, and concerned with the quality of life). Femininity pertains to societies in which social gender roles overlap (i.e., both men and women are concerned with the quality of life) (Hofstede, 1991). Japan is classified as the most masculine country, followed by Austria, Venezuela, and Italy. The most feminine cultures are Sweden, Norway, the Netherlands, and Denmark.

Future time orientation reflects the extent to which the culture focuses on long-term planning and outcomes, and on the delay of gratification. The Dragon countries, including Japan, Hong Kong, and Korea, are high on this scale.

Employees internalize the cultural values and use them to evaluate the meaning of different managerial and motivational approaches as either opportunities or threats. For example, differential reward systems would be positively viewed by employees in individualistic cultures, and team-based incentives would be appreciated by employees in collectivistic cultures.

People in different cultures internalize the prevalent cultural values of their society. Therefore, they differ in the meaning they ascribe to a particular managerial approach. To further understand what motivates employees in other cultures, and how they interpret the meaning of various managerial practices, managers should first develop self-awareness and understanding of their own motives and values.

The second sub-principle: understand yourself and the cultural values you represent

The self is shaped by the shared understanding within a particular culture of what it means to be human (Cahoone, 1988; Cushman, 1990). The enduring attachments and commitments to the social environment help define the individual (Sandel, 1982). People develop self-knowledge through direct experience and evaluations adopted from significant others.

People strive to have positive self-perceptions and to experience self-worth and well-being. They strive to fulfill the motives of enhancement, efficacy, and consistency. Self-enhancement reflects the motive of maintaining a positive cognitive and affective state about the self; the motive of self-efficacy is the desire to perceive oneself as competent and efficacious; self-consistency is the desire to sense and experience coherence and continuity.

People monitor and evaluate the extent to which their behavior leads toward the fulfillment of the three motives and the degree to which the work setting offers opportunities for such behaviors (Bandura, 1986; Markus and Wurf, 1987).

The self and the self-motives are shaped by the cultural values and they set the standards and criteria for self-evaluation. These criteria vary across cultures and, consequently, they shape different selves. Individualistic cultures shape the *independent self*, who attends to personal criteria and standards for evaluating the meaning of certain management practices as enhancing or inhibiting opportunities for self-worth and well-being (Triandis, 1989; Markus and Kitayama, 1991). On the other hand, collectivistic cultures shape the *interdependent self*, who internalizes the criteria and standards advocated by his/her reference groups.

One common measure of the independent and interdependent self is the Twenty-statement Test, asking a person to write 20 statements starting with the words "I am." People with a strong independent self use individual characteristics, such as "I am smart," "I am tall," more frequently than those who rank high on the interdependent self scale. The latter use attributes that reflect their relationships with others, such as "I am a father," "I am a member of the golf club," etc.

Managerial and motivational practices that satisfy the self-motives of the independent self would be different than those satisfying the interdependent self. For example, self-enhancement driven by the independent self motivates individuals toward personal accomplishment. The independent self evaluates positively managerial practices that provide opportunities for individual success. People driven by the interdependent self, on the other hand, experience enhancement when they contribute to the success of the group. Similarly, self-efficacy becomes salient in the case of the independent self, whereas collective efficacy, or the perceptions of the group as competent, is important for the interdependent self. Finally, self-consistency of the independent self is interpreted in reference to the individual's personal history. On the other hand, the interdependent self evaluates the level of collective consistency in line with the collective history of the group to which the person belongs.

The self constitutes the link between the macro-level of culture and managerial

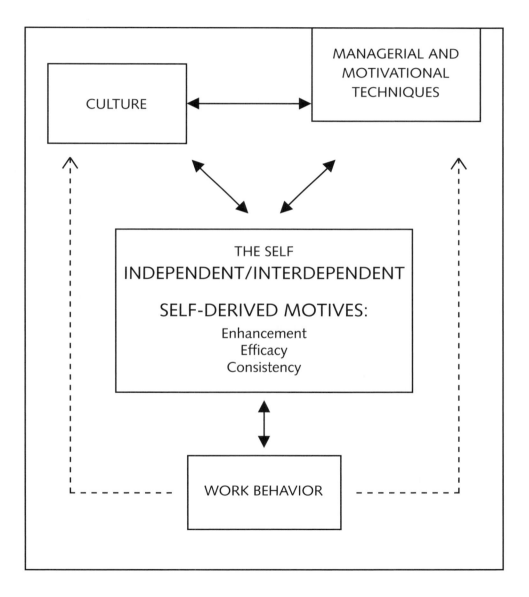

FIGURE 29.3 The model of cultural self-representation

practices, and the micro-level of employee behavior. Employees use their cultural values as criteria for evaluating the potential contribution of various management practices to the fulfillment of their self-derived motives. Erez and Earley's model of cultural self-representation (1993) portrays the above relationships between culture, self, management practices, and employee behavior (see figure 29.3).

Managers who are aware of their own cultural values and motives can transfer this knowledge and develop understanding of other people's values and motives. Once they identify the cultural characteristics of people from other cultures, they can develop a better understanding as to how employees in foreign cultures would react to various managerial approaches.

The third sub-principle: understand the cultural meaning of various managerial practices

Managerial practices represent certain ideological or philosophical frameworks. For example, differential reward systems and flat salary systems reflect different value systems. The former represents cultural values of individualism and inequality, whereas the latter represents cultural values of collectivism, where productivity is measured on the team level and compensation is based on team performance. Top-down communication systems represent high power distance, whereas two-way communication systems represent low power distance. Formal rules and regulations and extensive written documentation represent high uncertainty avoidance, whereas flexibility, risk-taking, and low levels of formality represent low uncertainty avoidance. Long-term investment in R&D represents future time orientation, whereas short-term goals and balance-sheet reports every quartile represent short-term orientation. Finally, the high percentage of women in socially oriented professions rather than in engineering and the sciences, and their low representation in the top managerial levels, represent masculine rather than feminine cultures.

Very often, consultants and practitioners serve as agents of certain managerial techniques. They advise management how to implement these techniques, following success stories in other places, while overlooking the cultural and ideological meaning of such techniques. For example, the CEO of one steel company in Israel, who came to the company after many years of military service, was known for his authoritarian leadership style. He visited the steel industry in Japan and was very impressed with the participative management approach and the quality control circles in Japan. Upon returning to Israel he called all his senior managers, told them about his visit, and commanded them that "from now on, you are going to implement participative management in the organization." Obviously, his "tell" style was not a good model for participative management.

The three sub-principles – understanding the cultural values, knowing your self-motives and values, and understanding the values reflected by various managerial approaches – should serve managers for selecting and implementing managerial practices that best fit the cultural values. These three sub-principles constitute the general principle that proposes that successful implementation of managerial practices depends on their congruence with the cultural values embedded in the organization where they are being implemented.

Group focus

Rewards	The rule of equity or needs
	Group-based rewards
	Unequally distributed organization-
	   based rewards
	Unequally distributed employee
	   stock ownership plans
		Rewards	The rule of equality or needs
			Equally distributed
			   organization- based rewards
			Equally distributed
			   employee stock ownership
			   plans

Decision- making/ goal-setting **Job design**	Centralized Autocratic Group-based programs Team work controlled by top management teams	**Decision- making/ goal-setting** **Job design**	Delegation of authority Group decision-making Group goal-setting Socio-technical systems Autonomous work groups Self-managed teams Quality circles

High power distance ———————————————— **Low power distance**

Rewards	The rule of equity
	Individually based rewards
	Individually based profit sharing
	Individually based stock options
		Rewards	The rule of needs or equality
			Welfare and fringe benefits
			   based on demographics
			   (e.g., family size, disability,
			   etc.)

Decision- making/ goal-setting	Autocratic Centralized individual Assigned, individual goals	**Decision- making/ goal-setting**	Delegation of authority decision-making Personal involvement in goal
Job design	Individual jobs in a hierarchy of control	**Job design**	Enrichment of individual jobs

Self-focus

FIGURE 29.4 Management practices according to cultural dimensions of group versus individual focus, and power distance

Matching management practices to cultural variations

Management practices represent the way managers do things in their organizations: the way they delegate authority, allocate rewards, make decisions, design jobs, and implement programs such as quality improvement.

Figure 29.4 portrays the differences between cultures with group versus individual focus, and with high versus low power distance, in the implementation of management practices.

The following section elaborates on the implementation of rewards, participation in decision-making, and quality improvement systems in different cultures.

Reward allocation. One of the key questions is how to allocate rewards in order to enhance motivation. If you are an American manager, you are most likely implement the principle of "rewards for performance." However, in the global world there are three principles for reward allocation: the principle of equity, i.e., according to each individual's contribution; the principle of equality, i.e., equal shares to all individuals; and the principle of need, i.e., according to each individual's needs.

In most individualistic cultures, the rule of equity serves as the criterion for reward allocation. Employees receive rewards based on their individual contribution to goal attainment. For this purpose managers use individual performance appraisal to evaluate the individual's contribution.

On the other hand, the rule of equality fits in with group-oriented, collectivistic values. Chinese managers, who have collectivistic values, used the equality rule in allocating rewards to in-group members more than did Americans (Leung and Bond, 1984; Bond, Leung, and Wan, 1982). In fact, Chinese people used the rule of equality more than Americans did for allocation to both in-group and out-group members. However, for out-group allocation, the rule of equality was used when the allocation was public, but the rule of equity was used when allocation was done privately. Similarly, Koreans perceived more favorably allocators who used the equality rule than those using the equity rule, compared to Americans. In Europe, the Swedish people used the rule of equality more frequently than the Americans did (Tornblom, Jonssons, and Foa, 1985). The Swedish education system discourages competition in favor of cooperation and teamwork. In addition, the Swedish viewed the need rule more positively than did the Americans. The need rule was most highly preferred in India (Berman and Singh, 1985). Allocation on the basis of need predominates in collectivistic cultures, and particularly when needs become visible, as is the case in India (Murphy-Berman, Berman, Singh, Pachauri, and Kumar, 1984).

The above findings lead to the conclusion that the application of an inappropriate distribution rule may cause feelings of injustice, and demotivate employees. Therefore, knowledge about cross-cultural differences with regard to preferences of allocation rules is vital for implementing motivational techniques.

Employee participation, and teamwork. Participation in goal setting and decision-making is not value-free. From a political perspective, it increases workers' control over the means of production, and it conveys the belief that participatory democracy is a social value in and of itself. Ideological differences between the US and Europe led the pro-participation voice in the US to advocate voluntary adoption of participative practices, whereas, in many European countries, government legislation mandates compulsory participation. In general, European countries, including England, Scandinavia, and West Germany, when compared to the US, are known to be more socially oriented, and to display lower levels of power distance between different organizational levels (Hofstede, 1980).

It is, therefore, reasonable to propose that cultural background can influence the level of employees' participation in decision-making in organizations. Moreover, employees in highly egalitarian and group-oriented cultures, such as that of Israel, reacted negatively to goals that were assigned to them, as compared to employees who were allowed to participate in goal-setting. This negative response to assigned goals was not observed among employees in more individualistic and less egalitarian cultures, such as the US (Erez and Earley, 1987). In individualistic cultures, group goals often result in social loafing and free-riding because group members do not share responsibility to the same extent as group members in collectivistic cultures. On the other hand, social loafing was not observed in group-oriented cultures, such as China and Israel (Earley, 1989; Erez and Somech, 1996). In individualistic cultures, social loafing disappears when individual group members are held personally accountable and responsible for the group outcomes (Weldon and Gargano, 1988). This means that in individualistic cultures, effective teams should be designed with low levels of interdependence among group members, to allow individual group members to feel personally accountable for group performance, and to be able to identify their individual contributions.

Quality improvement in Japan versus the US. The quality of products and services becomes a major factor in the competitive advantage of companies. Therefore, programs of quality improvement are implemented all over the world. However, these programs take different forms in different cultures. Let's look at the differences between the quality improvement programs in Japan and those in the US.

Japan. In Japan, the prevalent method of quality improvement is the quality control circle. These "circles" are small groups in the same work unit that voluntarily and continuously undertake quality control activities in the workplace.

In line with their group-focus culture, Japanese quality improvement (QI) programs are designed for teams. From the employee's perspective, this system allows everyone to participate and have the opportunity to experience enhancement and efficacy as part of the group. Quality circles (QCs) encompass all the organizational levels, from top to bottom, and they are both hierarchical and lateral. Through participation in QCs, employees successfully identify significant problems and create solutions to these problems. In accordance with Japan's high power distance, a group leader is appointed to each QC. This person receives extensive training in quality and team management, and runs the meetings.

Quality improvement activities on the company level are supported by the nationwide organization of the QC Headquarters at JUSE (Japanese Union of Scientists and Engineers). This organization provides information about how to start quality control circles' activities, how to operate them, and how to maintain and assure their continuation. The organization established the national Deming prize, which is awarded to companies that have attained remarkable results in quality improvement.

USA. In contrast to Japan, quality control circles are less popular in the United States.

The following section elaborates on the implementation of rewards, participation in decision-making, and quality improvement systems in different cultures.

A survey conducted on the Fortune 1000 companies (Lawler, Mohrman, and Ledford, 1992) revealed that 70 percent of companies reported that almost none of their employees were involved in QC-type programs, and only 2 percent of companies reported that 80 percent of their workforce was involved in quality circles. Quality control circles are not a natural outcome of an individualistic society such as that of the USA. In general, American workers place a stronger focus on personal evaluation and personal standards. Therefore, they are more highly motivated when they feel personally responsible and accountable for the level of quality, than when they work within other frameworks. To encourage teamwork, individual contribution to team-level activities should be acknowledged and rewarded.

Although personal responsibility for quality is necessary, it is not enough to effectively implement a company-wide program in a complex organization. At this level, a system approach, including strategies at the organizational, team, as well as individual level, is necessary to make QI effective. The US national initiative to reward quality improvement programs of systems, rather than those of an individual or team, was led by the creation of the Malcolm Baldridge National Quality Award, established in 1987. The award recognizes firms that have achieved excellence through adherence to the quality improvement process. Among the winners since 1987 are Motorola Inc., Federal Express, Xerox Business Products and System Group, General Motors Cadillac Division, IBM Rochester, and the Wallace Company.

Japan versus the US. The most notable characteristic common to Japanese companies that won the Deming Award and American companies that won the Baldridge Award is the thorough involvement of their top management teams in setting the vision of quality improvement, communicating it to employees throughout the entire organization, and becoming personally involved in the implementation process.

Second, Japanese companies and all Baldridge Award winners encourage employees to voice their concerns and show involvement. Yet in the US a greater emphasis has been placed on the individual employee: attitude surveys monitored employee satisfaction and identified problem areas. The results were fed back to the managerial levels, and managers were asked to address employee concerns. In Japan, the emphasis is mainly at the team level, and most of the activities of quality improvement are processed via the quality control circles.

Third, in both countries quality improvement programs grant employees more authority, and responsibility for quality improvement. However, in Japan employee involvement is exhibited mainly through team participation in identifying quality problems and in generating and implementing solutions to the problems. In contrast, in the US the emphasis on employee involvement is manifested by delegating responsibility to individual employees. For example, customer service is improved by allowing employees to have more discretion in making decisions while serving their customers, thus eliminating the need for time-consuming approvals of a definite set of decisions. Japanese managers show support through group participation, whereas American managers use empowerment to delegate authority to individual employees.

Fourth, in both countries training was found to be crucial for the acquisition of knowledge and skills and for the internalization of values and behavioral norms of quality improvement. The Quality Award winners in the US invest more in training than other companies do. Training programs help develop skills and abilities necessary to perform well not only as individuals but also as teams. In many work situations, effective performance depends on the coordination among team members and on their collaborative efforts. In such cases, training programs that educate employees to become effective team players facilitate a cultural change from individualistic to group-oriented values.

Fifth, an employee appraisal system is crucial to quality improvement because it measures the employee's accomplishments. Although Deming himself objected to individual-level performance appraisal, it is still used by most of the American winners of the Baldridge Award. This is consistent with the individualistic culture in the US, where workers look for personal evaluations. Westinghouse uses a management-by-objectives (MBO) performance review system, with quality improvement as a major criterion for evaluation. Deming objected to MBO as well, because it is outcome rather than process driven, and it emphasizes quantitative rather than qualitative results. Yet MBO can be modified to emphasize processes and to set quality rather than quantity goals. For example, Motorola, which had already cut defects from 6,000 per million to only 40 per million in just five years, had a goal of further cutting defects by 90 percent every two years throughout the 1990s. Quality criteria are often included in employee performance evaluations. Federal Express, for example, rates employees on both quality of work and customer service. Xerox evaluates employees on an individual basis, but contribution to the team is one important criterion for evaluation. Thus, the American way of managing employees for quality improvement differs from that of the Japanese, as it is geared toward the individual employee rather than toward the team.

Sixth, similar to the appraisal system, the reward system and recognition programs in the US integrate rewards based on individual and team levels. At Xerox, individuals are nominated for the President's Award, or the Xerox Achievement Award. Teams compete for the Excellence Award and the Excellence in Customer Satisfaction Award. Westinghouse has implemented peer review for determining their quality achievement winners.

In addition to individually based pay systems, there are also organizationally based pay systems, such as employee stock ownership plans, profit-sharing, and gain-sharing. While it is the individual incentive pay system that is prevalent in the most successful Fortune 1000 companies, over 50 percent of these companies use, in addition, reward practices that include non-monetary recognition, team incentives, knowledge/skill-based pay, and cafeteria-style benefits.

Individually based recognition and rewards are inconsistent with Deming's approach, which advocates cooperation rather than competition. Unlike American companies, Japanese companies offer recognition and rewards to their quality improvement teams.

To summarize, programs of quality improvement have common characteristics that are universal, such as: shifting authority and responsibility down to the employees themselves, training employees to improve their knowledge and give them the skills necessary for quality improvement, evaluating employees' contribution to quality improvement, and rewarding their achievements. However, in the US and Japan these general principles take different forms that are congruent with the different cultural values. Successful QI programs in the US include a strong focus on the individual in terms of delegation, evaluation, and rewards. Employees are empowered to be personally accountable for quality. While team-level components are present, companies work to facilitate their effectiveness through training and measuring individual contribution to team efforts. These strategies fit well with the tenets of US culture. In Japan, on the other hand, quality control circles regulate the quality improvement activities. Employees become part of the quality improvement program by participating in the QC circles. The hierarchical structure of the Japanese culture can be observed in the hierarchical organization of the QI activities. From the national level to the organizational level, and down to the organizational units and quality improvement teams, these differences in the form of implementation of quality improvement programs reflect the cultural differences between the US and Japan. Global managers should be sensitive to such cultural differences and implement managerial practices that are congruent with the cultural values.

INTERNATIONAL MERGERS AND ACQUISITIONS: RECONCILING CULTURAL DIFFERENCES

International mergers and acquisitions (M&A) have become a major phenomenon in today's business world. They create an excellent opportunity for examining the process of cultural change when companies from two different cultures merge into one company. An acquisition means that one organization acquires ownership over the other, whereas merger is the joining or blending of two previously discrete companies.

The objective of mergers is to strengthen the financial health of the company, such that the combined organization will be financially stronger than the sum of the two separate companies. Mergers and acquisitions create a competitive advantage in terms of knowledge-sharing, market-sharing, and attracting shareholders. However, in the long run, between 50 and 80 percent of mergers fail. Human problems seem to explain half of these failures (Cartwright and Cooper, 1996). One of the key problems in mergers and acquisitions stems from underestimating the difficulty of merging two cultures. In the case of international M&A, the cultural differences are reflected at both the organizational and the national level. Mergers and acquisitions are stressful to the employees. They often mean loss of identity, non-use of their knowledge and skills, increased ambiguity, inability to focus on the work itself, and loss of key people who leave the organization.

National cultures and organizational cultures can be described on similar dimensions (House et al., 1998). Cultures can differ on five dimensions: (1) their power structure (national level – egalitarian/non-egalitarian, organizational level – centralized/decentralized); (2) in the way people relate to each other (national – collectivism/individualism, organizational – team/individual focus); (3) in their tolerance for risk and ambiguity (national – high /low uncertainty avoidance, organizational bureaucratic/non-bureaucratic); (4) in their values of masculinity/femininity (high/low differentiation between male and female roles at both the societal and organizational levels); (5) in their time orientation (long/short orientation at both the national and organizational level).

What happens when organizations from two different cultures merge together? First, the two organizations have to agree on the form of acculturation. Acculturation involves two factors: the desire to maintain one's own cultural identity, and the desire to develop a relationship with the other culture (Berry, 1980; Nehavandi and Malekzadeh, 1988). These two dimensions lead to four different types of acculturation: (1) maintaining one's own values combined with a strong desire for relationships leads to *integration*; (2) maintaining one's own values without a desire for a relationship with other cultures leads to *separation*; (3) low maintenance of one's own values combined with a strong desire for a relationship leads to *assimilation*; (4) low maintenance of one's own values combined with a low desire for a relationship leads to *marginalization*. The two organizations should agree on whether they both prefer integration, assimilation, or separation. Problems occur when there is no agreement and one organization attempts to impose its preferred mode of acculturation on the other organization.

When the two organizations reach a consensus on the form of acculturation, the scope of the differences in their cultural values affects the successful implementation of the acculturation process. The merger will be successful when there is a cultural fit or when the acquiring organization allows the other organization to maintain its independence. According to Cartwright and Cooper (1996), when the acquiring organization is characterized by high power distance and the acquired organization by low power distance, there will be a cultural clash and merger failure. Furthermore, if one accepts the thesis that capitalism has a competitive advantage in world economics over other institutional forms, then one may predict that acculturation will be easier when the acquiring organization is also more individualistic, less bureaucratic, and with low levels of gender role differentiation.

Cultures differ from each other in their resistance to change. The strongest resistance to change characterizes cultures of high power distance, low individualism, and high uncertainty avoidance. Among these cultures are most Latin-American countries, Portugal and Korea, followed by Japan, France, Spain, Greece, Turkey, and Arab countries. Cultures with low levels of resistance to change are low on power distance, high on individualism, and low on uncertainty avoidance. This category includes the Anglo countries, Nordic countries, and the Netherlands, followed by Singapore, Hong Kong, and South Africa (Harzig and Hofstede, 1996).

Managers should, therefore, take into consideration the cultural characteristics of both the acquiring company and the acquired company. For example, when an American company acquires a Mexican company, it is not enough to know that the characteristics of the American company facilitate the acculturation process. One should also take into consideration that the cultural gap between the two companies is quite high, and that it is not easy to change the Mexican company's culture. Suppose that a Japanese company acquires an American company. On one hand, the American company typically should be more amenable to change; nevertheless, the cultural gap between the two organizations is quite high, and the adjustment to a culture of high power distance, high collectivism, and high uncertainty avoidance, such as the Japanese culture, is not easy.

The procedures adopted for acculturation play an important role in determining its effective implementation. The initiation of any cultural change should start from the top. The top management team should articulate the combined company's vision, clarifying the added value to the two companies and their employees. They should be able to effectively communicate their vision and prevail on employees to endorse it as well. To overcome resistance to change, integration teams should be formed, consisting of representatives of both organizations. These teams should first study the cultural characteristics of the two companies. They should offer realistic merger previews that minimize the ambiguity and stress, and help develop realistic expectations. Extensive involvement of members of both organizations helps overcome resistance to change, by increasing the commitment to the merger process, sharing knowledge and information necessary for successful adaptation to change, and establishing group norms that facilitate the change.

The integration teams should stimulate a two-way process of communication, encouraging employees to share their concerns, identifying problems before they escalate, and developing mechanisms to respond to and take into consideration employees' concerns. The two companies should assure the well-being of their individual employees by dealing with aspects related to pay, pensions, and job security. The importance of integration teams becomes even more evident in the case of international mergers, where more learning and understanding is required to narrow the cultural gap between the two companies.

SUMMARY AND CONCLUSIONS

Managers in the third millennium are global managers. They have to learn about cultural differences, and how these differences shape the most effective managerial practices. The development of sensitivity to others begins with self-knowledge. Managers who learn about their own motives and cultural values can understand what motivates employees in other cultures. Managers who are sensitive to the variation in cultural values understand how such values shape the motives for coming to work, getting results, and innovating and initiating new developments. This knowledge enables them to modify and implement managerial practices that will be motivational and contribute to a person's sense of self-worth and well-being. The main principle that should direct managers of the global world proposes the adoption of those effective managerial practices that best fit the cultural values of the organizations where they are implemented. This principle is supported by three sub-principles: self-knowledge; the identification of cultural values of different countries; and understanding of the meaning ascribed to various managerial practices by people with distinct cultural backgrounds. Successful global leaders are those who adopt these principles and use them as guidelines for implementing managerial approaches around the globe.

REFERENCES

Bandura, A. (1986). *Social foundations of thoughts and action: A social cognitive theory*. Englewood Cliffs, NJ: Prentice-Hall.

Berman, J. J., and Singh, P. (1985). Cross-cultural similarities and differences in perceptions of fairness. *Journal of Cross-Cultural Psychology*, 16, 55–67.

Berry J. W. (1980). Acculturation as varieties of adaptation. In A. Padilla (ed.), *Acculturation: Theory, models, and some new findings* (pp. 9–25). Boulder, CO: Westview.

Blackburn, R., and Rosen, B. (1993). Total Quality and HRM: Lessons learned from the Baldridge Award-winning companies. *The Academy of Management Executive*, 7, 49–67.

Cahoone, L. E. (1988). *The dilemma of modernity: Philosophy, culture, and anti-culture.* Albany: State University of New York Press.

Cartwright, S., and Cooper, C. L. (1996). *Managing mergers, acquisitions, and strategic alliances: Integrating people and cultures.* Oxford: Butterworth Heinemann.

Cushman, P. (1990). Why the self is empty: Towards a historically situated psychology. *American Psychologist*, 45, 599–611.

Earley, P. C. (1989). Social loafing and collectivism: A comparison of United States and the People's Republic of China. *Administrative Science Quarterly*, 34, 565–81.

Earley, P. C. (1993). East meets West meets Middle East. Further explorations of collectivistic and individualistic work groups. *Academy of Management Journal*, 36, 319–48.

Erez, M., and Earley, P. C. (1987). Comparative analysis of goal-setting strategies across cultures. *Journal of Applied Psychology*, 72, 658–65.

Erez, M., and Earley, P. C. (1993). *Culture, self-identity, and work.* New York: Oxford University Press.

Erez, M., and Somech, A. (1996). Group performance loss: The rule of the exception. *Academy of Management Journal*, 39, 1513–37.

Harzig, A.-W., and Hofstede, G. (1996). Planned change in organizations: The influence of national cultures. In P. A. Bamberger, M. Erez, and S. B. Bacharach (eds.), *Research in the sociology and organizations: Cross-cultural analysis of organizations* (Vol. 14, pp. 297–340). Greenwich, CT: JAI Press.

Hofstede, G. (1980). *Culture's consequences: International differences in work related values.* Newbury Park, CA: Sage.

Hofstede, G. (1991). *Cultures and organizations: Software of the mind.* New York: McGraw-Hill.

House, R. J., Hanges, P. J., Ruiz-Quintanilla, S. A., Dorfman, P. W., Javidan, M., Dickson, M., Gupta, V., et al. (1999). Cultural influences on leadership and organizations: Project Globe. In M. J. Gessner and V. Arnold (eds.), *Advances in global leadership* (Vol. 1, pp. 171–233). Stanford, CA: JAI Press.

Kluckhohn, C. (1954). *Culture and behavior.* New York: Free Press.

Lawler, E. E. III, Mohrman, S. A., and Ledford, G. E. Jr. (1992). *Employee involvement and total quality management: Practices and results in Fortune 1000 companies.* San Francisco: Jossey-Bass.

Leung, K., and Bond, M. (1984). The impact of cultural collectivism on reward allocation. *Journal of Personality and Social Psychology*, 47, 793–804.

Leung, K., and Park, H. J. (1986). Effects of interactional goal on choice of allocation rule: A cross-national study. *Organizational Behavior and Human Decision Processes*, 37, 11–120.

Markus, H. R., and Kitayama, S. (1991). Culture and the self: Implications for cognition, emotion, and motivation. *Psychological Review*, 98, 224–53.

Markus, H. R., and Wurf, E. (1987). The dynamic self-concept: A social psychological perspective. *Annual Review of Psychology*, 38, 299–337.

Murphy-Berman, V., Berman, J., Singh, P., Pachuri, A., and Kumar, P. (1984). Factors affecting allocation to needy and meritorious recipients: A cross-cultural comparison. *Journal of Personality and Social Psychology*, 46, 1267–72.

Nehavandi, A., and Malekzadeh, A. R. (1988). Acculturation in mergers and acquisitions. *Academy of Management Review*, 13, 79–90.

Sandel, M. J. (1982). *Liberalism, and the limits of justice.* Cambridge: Cambridge University Press.

Schwartz, S. H. (1992). Universals in the content and structure of values: Theoretical advances and empirical tests in 20 countries. In M. Zanna (ed.), *Advances in experimental social psychology* (Vol. 25, pp. 1–65). Orlando, FL: Academic Press.

Shweder, R., and LeVine, R. (1984). *Culture theory.* New York: Cambridge University Press.

Thierry, H. (1987). Payment by results systems: A review of research 1945–1985. *Applied Psychology: An International Review*, 36, 91–108.

Tornblom, K. Y., Jonsson, D., and Foa, U. G. (1985). Nationality, resource, class, and preferences among three allocation rules: Sweden vs. USA. *International Journal of Intercultural Relations*, 9, 51–77.

Triandis, H. C. (1989). The self and social behavior differing cultural contexts. *Psychological Review*, 96, 506–20.

Triandis, H. C., Bontempo, R., Vilareal, M. J., Masaaki, A., and Lucca, N. (1988). Individualism and collectivism: Cross-cultural perspectives on self–ingroup relationships. *Journal of Personality and Social Psychology*, 54, 328–38.

Weldon, E., and Gargano, G. M. (1988). Cognitive loafing: The effects of accountability and shared responsibility on cognitive effort. *Personality and Social Psychology Bulletin*, 14, 159–71.

Index

360-degree appraisals 68–9

ABB 377
Abilene Paradox 216
absenteeism
  conscientiousness and emotional stability,
    selection on 17
  goal-setting 116–17
  job satisfaction 76, 92
  self-efficacy 133
Acer 262
Aetna Life & Casualty 82, 411
agreeableness 16, 17, 21–2
Allentown Materials Corporation 380, 411
American Airlines (AA) 270, 409
American Express 167, 325
American Federation of Government
    Employees 161
American Pulpwood Association 109, 112
America Online 101
America West 81
Anderson Consulting 407–8
Andromeda 222
Apple Computer 370–5, 376, 378, 381
Arnam, William Van 12
ASDA 383, 384
Attributional Style Questionnaire (ASQ)
    353
attribution theory 282
autonomy
  and creativity 333

Job Characteristics Model 77, 78, 82, 83
  stress management 350

Barnevik, Percy 377
Barry, Marion 10
Bay of Pigs invasion 211, 212–13, 218,
    219, 220–1
Becton Dickinson 379
Behaviorally Anchored Rating Scales
    (BARS) 67
benchmarking 111–12, 377
Bettis, Jerome 190
B. F. Goodrich Tire 352
Big Five personality dimensions 16, 21–2,
    23–4
Booze, Allen & Hamilton 102
Borman, Frank 146–7
brainstorming 337, 339
Branson, Richard 144–5
Bruce, Earle 191
burnout 123, 345, 351
Burr, Don 257, 258, 269, 270

career development programs 102, 350
career success and gender 392–4
Carlzon, Jan 258, 263–4
Carson, Johnny 365, 366
Cash, Tom 166–7
Castro, Fidel 212–13
Challenger space shuttle accident 325
Chaparral Steel Company 351

Chemical Central Research 337–9
China 426, 427
Cisco Systems 161–2
Citicorp 352
Citigroup 102
Civil Rights Act (1991) 9
cognitive restructuring 353
commitment
  to decisions: change management 375,
    378–9; participation 304, 305; trust
    276
  to information technology 412
  organizational: and performance 371;
    procedural justice 185–6; profit-
    sharing 153; turnover 91–2, 94,
    99, 102
  to goals 107, 109–13, 115, 116
  to visions 265
  to work 392, 397–8
communication
  boundary activity 200, 201, 205–6
  change management 379–80
  collaboration 230
  expert power 246–7
  gender differences 394
  information technology 406–8, 414
  inspirational appeals 250
  leadership through vision and values
    263–4, 265–6, 267
  national culture 424
  and performance 371
  self-efficacy 122
  training 48
  trust 275–6, 277, 280, 283, 284–5,
    286–7
Compaq 370
competence
  fostering trust through 274–87
  pay for performance 154
  and performance 371
  stress 346
competition 335, 408–10
Compusys 413–14
computers see information technology
conflict
  decision-making 324
  escalation 231–2
  gender factors 396
  group process 212, 214–15, 216–18,
    220, 222

management: through collaboration
    226–36; impetus provision 361,
    362, 364; inquisitorial intervention
    361, 362, 364; through negotiation
    and mediation 356–68; rights
    357–8
  non-task 226, 227, 228–9
  open conflict communication norms 230
  resolution 206
  stress 343
conscientiousness 5–6, 15–26
consensus with qualification 219–20, 222,
    324–5
consistency 278, 376
consultation
  decision-making 322
  and participation, difference between
    304
  power, effective use of 250–1, 253
Continental 147, 270
Control Data Corporation 352
Conway, Mike 81
cooperation 232
  see also collaboration
coordination
  mechanisms 291, 292–3, 296–7
  and performance 371
CoreStates Financial Corporation 367–8
Corporate Express 409
Creative Problem-Solving (CPS) Process
    337
creativity
  and encouragement 333
  and performance 371
  positive effect 334
  stimulation by fueling passion 331–40
  trust 275
  turnover 101
Crew Resource Management (CRM)
  training 56
Crutchfield, Ed 367–8
Cuban missile crisis 211, 213, 217, 218,
    219, 220–1
culture, national 418–32
  assimilation 431
  mergers and acquisitions (M&As) 418,
    430–2
  paternalistic 267
  self-awareness 422–4
  separation 431

Dailey, James L.   192
decentralization   295, 298
decision-making
    appraisal systems   60
    contextual factors   31
    decision support systems (DSS)   407, 408
    effective management   316–28
    framing decisions   320–1
    groupthink   216, 228, 325
    information technology   406–8
    in interviews   31–6
    objectives   319
    positions   319
    problem-solving approach   318, 323, 327
    research   30–1
    rhythm   219
    ringi   311
    satisficing   323
    trust   282
delegation   304, 428
Dell Computer   370, 413
Delta Airlines   270
Deming prize   427, 428, 429
Denmark   267
depression
    empowerment   140, 142
    learned helplessness theory   20
Devil's Advocacy role   217, 218, 221
Dialectical Inquiry   217, 218, 221
Digital Equipment   373
Duncan Hines   82
Dunlap, Al   384
Dupont   352

Eastern Airlines   146–7, 351
emotional factors
    creativity   334
    emotional stability, selection on   15–26
    empowerment   142
Employee of the Month programs   173
empowerment
    motivation   137–47
    national culture   428
    stress management   350
enterprise resource planning (ERP) systems
    406, 412–13
entrepreneurship
    pay for performance   156
    self-efficacy   122, 124
    Virgin Group   144

environmental factors
    change   372–3
    creativity   332–3, 336
    goal-setting   114–15
    national culture   418–32
    stress management   349–51
    training, systematic design   51–3
Equal Employment Opportunity
    Commission   8
equity theory   181
expectations   109, 110, 112–13
extraversion   16, 21–2
extrinsic motivation   331, 334, 335
Exxon   410, 411

fairness
    conflict management   361, 362, 364–5
    decision-making   322
    trust   277–8, 282
    see also procedural justice
Federal Express (FedEx)   405, 414–15, 429
feedback
    appraisal systems   60, 64, 67, 68–9
    change management   377, 378
    goal-setting   109, 116
    Job Characteristics Model   77, 78, 83
    self-efficacy   127
    training   50, 52
    turnover   98
feminine cultures   421
Finland   267
Fiorina, Carleton   398–9
First Union Corporation   367–8
Five Factor Model (FFM) of personality
    16, 21–2, 23–4
Ford Motor Company   311, 405–6
Foresight Inc.   353
French Railway   412
Frontier   270
Fujitsu Microelectronics   406

Gandhi, Mahatma   258
Gates, Bill   258
General Aptitude Test Battery (GATB)
    11–12
general cognitive ability *see* intelligence
General Electric Company
    change management   377, 384
    empowerment   145–6
    goal-setting   115

General Electric Company (*cont.*)
  leadership through vision and values   263
general mental ability (GMA) *see* intelligence
General Motors   321, 410
Germany   267
Gerstner, Louis   377
Gilmartin, Raymond V.   102, 379
Giuliani, Rudolph W.   191
Glaxo SmithKline PLC   328
Glaxo Wellcome PLC   328
Glucksman, Lewis   325–6
goals
  by interviews   32
  coaches   110, 111–13
  conscientiousness   19–20
  creativity   332, 338
  distal   114, 115
  for motivation   107–17, 332
  in training   50
  proximal   114–15
  self-efficacy   132–3
  self-regulation   116–17
  specificity   108–9
  stress management   350
Goodyear Tire & Rubber   377, 411
Gritner, Gerald   269
group
  atmosphere   229–30
  humor   221
  process: excel through   211–23;
    framebreaking heuristics   217, 221,
    222
  support systems (GSS)   407–8
Grove, Andrew   376
Growth Need Strength (GNS)   83–4
Guha, Ramanathan   101
Gulf Oil   373

Haire, Mason   109
Hall, Arsenio   366
Health Action Process Approach   349
Hewlett Packard (HP)   173, 382–3, 398–9
Hitler, Adolf   267
Hogan personality inventory (*HPI*)   23
Home Depot   173
Hope, Bob   167

IBM
  change management   370, 377
  information technology   406

stress management   352
Illinois Bell   352
incentives
  gainsharing   152, 156, 160, 161
  global pay   161–2
  independent self   422–3
  leadership through vision and values
    264, 269–70
  lump-sum bonuses   151, 160–1
  merit pay   151
  pay for performance   150–62: bonuses
    151, 160–1; values   154
  piece-rates   150–1, 160–1
  profit-sharing   152, 153, 156, 160
  stock options   152, 161–2
  training, transfer of   52
  variable pay   151
India   426
individualism   420, 422, 426, 427
information
  exchange   231
  group process   212–14, 215
  power   242, 245–6
  sharing by participation   304–12
information technology (IT)   52
  appraisal systems   65, 69–70
  as change catalyst   404–15
  conflict management   360
  efficiency   405–6
  electronic data interchange (EDI)   409
  participation   309–10
  "what if" analysis   407
innovation   332
  and performance   371
  self-efficacy   122–3
  structure designed to fit strategy   291,
    296–7
  trust   275
  turnover   101
integrity
  conscientiousness and emotional stability,
    selection on   5, 17
  fostering trust through   274–87
  intelligence, selection on   8
  referent power   247
Intel   376
intelligence
  creativity   332
  selection on   3–12
interests

conflict management 357, 358, 367–8
decision-making 319–20
International Harvester 373
International Paper (IP) 102
Internet *see* information technology
interviews, employment 6, 8, 29–39
intrinsic motivation 155
creativity 331–4, 335, 337
intuition
collective 212–15, 222
decision-making 323–4
Iran-Contra affair 325
Israel 424, 427

Japan 418, 419, 424–30, 431
JC Penney 409, 410
Jennings, Edward 191
Job Characteristics Model (JCM) 76–83
job design
creativity 333
empowerment 140, 141
stress 350
Job Diagnostic Survey (JDS) 77, 78–9
job enlargement 81, 82
job enrichment 81–2, 122, 306
job rotation 79–81, 82, 102
job satisfaction
conscientiousness and emotional stability,
selection on 18
gender factors 397–8
goal-setting 108
mental challenges 75–88
participation 305, 306
pay for performance 153
promotion through mental challenge
75–88
task identity 76, 78, 82, 83
task significance 76, 78, 83
teachers 85–6, 87
turnover 76, 90, 91–4, 97, 99–100
value-percept theory 85
values 84–5
Job Stress Survey (JSS) 345
Jobs, Steve 370, 373
John Deere 82
Johnson & Johnson 351, 352, 418
justice
distributive 277, 322
interactional 322
procedural *see* procedural justice

Kane's Performance Distribution Assessment
67
keiretsus 144
Kennedy, John F. 211, 212–13, 220–1
Kennedy, Robert 217
KEYS 337
KFC 179
King, Martin Luther 258
knowledge
conscientiousness 19
distribution by participation 304–12
intelligence 4–5
training, systematic design 46, 54
Korea 426
Kung, Cardinal 265
Kushnick, Helen 365–7
Kushnick, Jerry 365

Larsen, Terry 367–8
Laura Ashley 415
leadership
change management 375–9
charismatic 258, 266, 267
group process 220–1
power, effective use of 241–55
trust 274–87
through vision and values 257–71
learning
goal-setting 113–14
intelligence as key to 3–4, 5
motivation 47–8
pay for performance 158
psychological theory of 5
theories 48–9
see also training
legal issues
conscientiousness and emotional stability,
selection on 17, 18
intelligence, selection on 8
personality assessment 23
procedural justice 184
Lehman Brothers Kuhn Loeb 325–6, 328
Leno, Jay 365–7
Letterman, David 365
life satisfaction 18, 76, 397
Lincoln Electric Company 160–1
Linjeflyg 263–4
Littlefield, Walter 366
Lockheed Aircraft Corporation 299
London Stock Exchange 412

Lorenzo, Frank   147
Luckett, Phil   190
Ludwig, Andreas J.   268

Mahalik, Stan   377
Malcolm Baldridge National Quality Award
    428, 429
management-by-objectives (MBO)   429
management by wandering about (MBWA)
    99–100
marginalization of cultures   431
Mary Kay Cosmetics   174
masculine cultures   421
Maslach Burnout Inventory (MBI)   345
mediation   233, 356, 360–4, 365
    active   363
    contextual   363, 364
    passive   363
    reflexive   363, 364
    substantive   363, 364
    upward appeals   253
mentors   393
Merck & Co.   102
Merix Corporation   266
Merrill Lynch   409
Metropolitan Life Insurance Company
    352–3
Mexico   419, 431
Microsoft   101, 262
Mitchell Madison Consulting   259
Mixed Standards Rating Scale   67
modeling
    corrective   127
    mastery   128, 130–2
    role   247, 279
    self-efficacy, increasing   111–12, 126,
        127, 128–9
monitoring   158, 380
Motivating Potential Score (MPS)   83
motivation
    appraisal systems   60
    conflict management   361, 362, 364
    conscientiousness and emotional stability
        15, 16, 19, 20–1
    consultation   250
    empowerment   137–47
    extrinsic   331, 334, 335
    through goal-setting   107–17
    intrinsic *see* intrinsic motivation
    job satisfaction   92

to learn   47–8
participation   304–6, 312
pay for performance   150–62
procedural justice   181–93
recognition for performance improvement
    166–79
reward power   244
self-efficacy   120–33
transfer of training   53
trustworthiness   277
Motorola
    information technology   409
    pay for performance   157, 160
    quality improvement   429
multinational corporations   161–2, 266, 300

national culture   418–32
National Education Association (NEA)   86
National Football League (NFL)   190–1
National Homeware Products   337–9
Navigation Products   377, 378
NBC   365–7
NEO personality inventory   23
network relationships   393, 394
neuroticism   16, 18, 20
New York City, taxi drivers' strike   191
New York Telephone Company   352
New Zealand Education Department   412
Nipont   301–2
Nominal Group Technique (NGT)   309,
    321
Nordstrom   410
Norman, Archie   383, 384
Northwest Airlines   270
Norway   267
Novak, David   179

Office of Personnel Management (OPM)
    10
Ohio State University (OSU)   191–2
Organizational Alignment Model   372–3
organizational behavior modification (OB
    Mod.) approach   167–8, 170–1, 175
organizational change
    dissatisfaction, managing change through
        370–85
    information technology as catalyst
        404–15
    management through dissatisfaction and
        realignment   370–85

national culture 431–2
realignment, managing change through 370–85
organizational citizenship behaviors
conscientiousness and emotional stability 5–6, 16–17, 19
and job performance, difference between 5–6
procedural justice 189
organizational factors
conflict management through negotiation and mediation 356–68
creativity, stimulation by fueling passion 331–40
decision-making 316–28
empowerment 140, 141
participation to share information and knowledge 304–12
pay for performance 156
realignment, change through 370–85
recognition for performance improvement 171
stress management 342–54
structure designed to fit strategy 291–303
trust, development 279–81
vision 257–8
Organizational Fitness Profiling 382
outcome expectancies 109, 110, 113

participation
change management 376, 379–80
in decision-making 322, 324–5
and direction, difference between 304
in goal-setting 115–17
for information sharing and knowledge distribution 304–12
leadership through vision and values 263, 267
mutual agreement 292
national culture 426–7, 428
procedural justice 182–3, 186–7, 191
ringi decision-making 311
stress management 350
task interdependence 308
in training 52
trust, development 279, 280
People Express (PE) 147, 257, 269–70
PepsiCo 179
perfectionists 140

performance appraisal
accuracy 62–6, 67, 68, 69, 70
behavioral accuracy 64, 66
classification accuracy 63–4, 66
design to improve performance 60–71
multi-source 68–9
national culture 429
procedural justice 182–3
Performance Distribution Assessment 67
personality
assessment 23–4
dimensions of 15–16, 21–2
job satisfaction 85
leaders 260
see also conscientiousness; emotional stability
Peterson, Peter G. 325–6
Philip Morris 11–12
Pizza Hut 179
Platt, Lewis E. 399
power
coalition tactics 252, 254
coercive 242, 244–5, 252
conflict management 358, 360
corruption 248
effective use of 241–55
exchange tactics 251, 253
exercising 248–53
expert 242, 246–7
influence tactics 241, 249–55
ingratiation tactics 251–2, 253, 254
legitimate 242–3, 249
legitimating tactics 249, 253–4
personal 242, 246–7, 248: appeals 251, 253, 254
persuasion, rational 249–50, 252, 253, 254, 255
position 242–6, 248
pressure tactics 252, 253–4, 255
punishment systems 244–5, 252
rational persuasion 249–50, 252, 253, 254, 255
referent 242, 247, 254–5: ingratiation tactics 252; personal appeals 251
reward 242, 243–4
types 242–7
upward appeals 253–4
power distance 420–1, 425, 426, 431
Proactive Coping Scale 349
procedural justice

procedural justice (*cont.*)
  decision-making 322
  group-value model 183, 184–5
  instrumental model, procedural justice
    183
  interactional justice 322
  interpersonal determinants 183–5
  motivation 181–93
  relational model 183, 184–5
  self-interest model 183
  sincerity 186–7, 251–2
  structural determinants 182–3
  trust, development 277
Procter & Gamble (P&G) 339
Project A 25–6

quality
  conscientiousness 19
  improvement 427–30
Quality Circles (QCs) 427–8, 430
  Toyota 311

recognition for performance improvement
  166–79
resiliency 127, 128, 131
resources
  creativity 336
  for goal attainment 113
  and stress 346
retaining employees *see* turnover
reward system
  creativity 335
  decision-making 324
  empowerment 140, 141
  national culture 424, 425, 426, 429
  see also wages and salaries
risk
  decision-making 320–1, 322
  pay for performance 157–8
Rogers, Don 379–80
role modeling *see* modeling

Saab Scania 311
salaries *see* wages and salaries
SAS 258, 264
Saudi Arabia 267
Scott Paper 383, 384
Scully, John 370, 372, 375, 376, 378, 381
Sears, Roebuck and Company 159
Seinfeld, Jerry 366

selection
  adverse impact 8
  appraisal systems 61
  on conscientiousness and emotional
    stability 15–26
  on intelligence 3–12
  interviews 29–39
  national culture 419
Selection and Classification Project (Project
  A) 25–6
self-efficacy 120–1
  collective 229–30, 235
  conscientiousness 19
  corrective modeling 127
  emotional stability 20–1
  empowerment 138–9, 142
  enactive mastery 111, 115
  goal-setting 109, 110–13, 117
  mastery: cognitive 130–2; guided
    126–30; modeling 128, 130–2
  organizational impact 122–4
  pay for performance 157
  role rehearsal 127, 128–9
  self-regulatory competencies, cultivation
    of 132–3
  social recognition 171–2
  sources 124–33
  stress 346, 348, 349, 352
  training evaluation 54
self-esteem 110–11
self-handicapping paradox 20
self-regard 85
self-regulation 116–17
sensitivity, social 184, 186–7
sex-typing of jobs 392, 393, 398
Shearson 325
Simpson, Jerry 378
size, organizational 291, 294–5
skills
  change management 379
  pay based on 81
  perfecting 127–8
  stress 346
  training, systematic design 46, 54
  variety 77, 78, 82, 83
Sloan, Alfred P. 321
Slovenian wine industry 410
SMART goals 115
SmithKline Beecham PLC (SB) 326–8
social cognitive theory

recognition for performance improvement 168–70, 174
self-efficacy 124, 125
Solectron Corporation 159–60
Solomon, Peter 326
Sony 409
South Korea 426
Southwest Airlines 351
space shuttle Challenger accident 325
stability
emotional 15–26
workforce 100–1
stereotypes 31, 392
Stonesifer, Patty 101–2
strategic alliances 418
stress
antecedents 346
anticipatory coping 342, 347–8, 349, 351–2
assessment 344–5
cognitive-transactional theory 343–4
consequences 345
coping mechanisms 342–54
demands 346
experience 343
health promotion strategies 352
management 342–54
objective 343
preventive coping 342, 347, 348, 349, 352: organization level 349–50
proactive coping 342, 347, 348, 349, 352: organization level 349–51
reactive coping with stress 342, 347, 348, 351
role 396
self-efficacy 123
subjective 343
structure
designed to fit strategy 291–302
divisional 298–9, 301–2
functional 297, 298, 299–300, 301, 302
hierarchy: as coordination mechanism 292; and organizational size 295
industry 408–10
interviews 32–9
matrix 299, 300
mechanistic 296, 301
mutual agreement as coordination mechanism 292–3, 296
organic 296, 301
organizational size 291, 294–5
reciprocal intrdependence 293
rules as coordination mechanism 292
sequential interdependence 293
specialization 294
strategy, designed to fit 291–302
structured interviews 32–9
supervisors
empowerment 140, 141, 145
encouragement and creativity 333
goal-setting 112
training, transfer of 52–3
support
for change 380
creativity 333, 334
for information technology 412
stress management 346, 350
Swarovski Co. 267
Sweden 267, 426

Taco Bell 179
tardiness 17
teams
agreeableness 22
atmosphere 229–30
behavior of members 229, 230–2
boundary activity, successful 199–208
characteristics of members 229, 232–3
cohesiveness 205
collective efficacy of members 229–30, 235
configuration 202–3, 205
conflict management through collaboration 226–36
creativity 339
crossfunctional product development (CPD) 234–5
decision-making 324
emotional stability 20
group process 211–23
integrated product development (IPD) 234, 235
national culture 426–7, 428
orientation 229
pay for performance 151, 156–7, 159–60
self-efficacy 122
stress management 350
task conflicts 226, 227, 228
training, systematic design 55–6

telecommuting 399
Texas Air Corporation 147, 270
theft by employees 183–4, 189
time factors
   creativity 335–6
   decision-making 324
   gender differences 394–5
   group process 212, 218–20, 222
   information technology 406
Tolia, Nirav 101
Toyota Motor Corporation 300–1, 311,
   312
trade-offs 231
trade unions 158–9
training
   analyzing needs 44, 46–8
   appraisal systems 61, 66
   change management 380
   decision-making 324
   designing and developing instructions
      44–5, 48–51
   evaluating 45, 53–5
   extraversion 22
   frame-of-reference 66
   goal-setting 113, 116–17
   implementing 45, 51–3
   information technology 412
   instructional principles 50–1
   intelligence, selection on 4, 10
   of interviewers 32, 33–4, 37
   leadership through vision and values 259
   national culture 428–9
   openness to experience 22
   procedural justice 188–9
   self-efficacy 122, 127–30
   systematic design 43–57
   transfer 50, 51, 52–3: self-efficacy
      128–30
   and turnover 100–1
Tricon 179
trust
   collaboration 230
   exchange tactics 251
   fostering through competence, honesty,
      and integrity 274–8
   group process 215
   and honesty 274–87
turnover
   conscientiousness and emotional stability,
      selection on 17

control through understanding 90–103
dysfunctional 96–7, 100, 101
functional 96–8, 100, 101
intelligence, selection on 6
job satisfaction 76, 90, 91–4, 97, 99–100
pay for performance 153
shocks 93, 94–6, 98–9, 101
trust 275
unfolding model of voluntary turnover
   90, 93–6, 98–9
workforce stability 100–1
Twenty-Statement Test 422
Tyrolit 262, 264, 267–9

uncertainty
   avoidance 421
   environmental 114–15, 406
   task 291, 292–3, 296, 297, 301
   see also risk
unions 158–9
United Steelworkers Union 10
United Way 99
University of Washington 116–17
US Steel 9–10, 373
USWeb 259

Van Arnam, William 12
videoconferencing 309–10, 408
videotapes 127, 128, 131
Virgin Group 144–5
Vision 267
vision 257–71, 379
   abstract 266
   appeals: inspirational 250, 253, 255;
      personal 251, 253, 254; upward
      253–4
   imagery to communication 265–6
   inspirational appeals 250, 253, 255
   metaphors to communicate 265–6
   symbolism to communicate 265–6
voice see participation
Volvo 310–12

wages and salaries
   Eastern Airlines 146–7
   equal opportunity 393
   intelligence, selection on 9
   job rotation 81
   job satisfaction 77, 83–4, 86, 87
   national culture 419, 429

pay for performance   150–62
WalMart   409, 410
Warmke, Dennis   12
Warner, Tom   86–7
Washington, DC police force   10–11
Welch, Jack
  change management   376–7, 384
  empowerment   145–6
  vision and values   263
Western Electric   305
Westinghouse   373, 429
Weyerhaeuser Company   109, 114
withdrawal cognitions   92, 99

see also absenteeism; turnover
Wonderlic Personnel Test   6
work–family interface
  segmented model   397
  synergistic model   397
World Wide Web see information technology
Wozniak, Steve   370

Xerox Corporation   351, 429

Yahoo!   101

Zap   214, 221–2